# BELONGING AND ISOLATION IN
# THE HELLENISTIC WORLD

PHOENIX

Journal of the Classical Association of Canada
Revue de la Société canadienne des études classiques
Supplementary Volume LI

EDITED BY SHEILA L. AGER
AND RIEMER A. FABER

# Belonging and Isolation in the Hellenistic World

UNIVERSITY OF TORONTO PRESS
Toronto Buffalo London

© University of Toronto Press 2013
Toronto Buffalo London
www.utppublishing.com
Printed in Canada

ISBN 978-1-4426-4422-9

**Library and Archives Canada Cataloguing in Publication**

Belonging and isolation in the Hellenistic world / edited
by Sheila L. Ager and Riemer A. Faber.

(Phoenix. Supplementary volume ; 51)
Includes bibliographical references and index.
ISBN 978-1-4426-4422-9

1. Hellenism.   2. Greece – Civilization – To 146 B.C.   3. Mediterranean
Region – Civilization.   4. Belonging (Social psychology) – Mediterranean
Region.   5. Social isolation – Mediterranean Region.   I. Ager, Sheila Louise,
1956–   II. Faber, Riemer   III. Series: Phoenix. Supplementary volume
(Toronto, Ont.) ; 51

DF77.B44 2012     938′.08     C2012-904621-3

This book has been published with the help of a grant from the Canadian
Federation for the Humanities and Social Sciences, through the Awards to
Scholarly Publications Program, using funds provided by the Social Sciences and
Humanities Research Council of Canada.

University of Toronto Press acknowledges the financial assistance to its publishing
program of the Canada Council for the Arts and the Ontario Arts Council.

University of Toronto Press acknowledges the financial support of the Government
of Canada through the Canada Book Fund for its publishing activities.

# CONTENTS

*List of Illustrations*   ix

*Acknowledgments*   xi

Introduction: Belonging and Isolation in the Hellenistic
World: Themes and Questions   3
SHEILA AGER AND RIEMER FABER

**Part One: Intercultural Poetics and Identity   17**

1 'If I Am from Syria – So What?': Meleager's Cosmopoetics   19
REGINA HÖSCHELE

2 Invective from the Cultural Periphery: The Case
of Hermeias of Kourion   33
PETER BING

3 Genre and Ethnicity in the Epigrams of Meleager   47
KATHRYN GUTZWILLER

**Part Two: On the Margins? Ethnicity and Hellenicity   71**

4 Belonging and Isolation in Central Anatolia: The
Galatians in the Graeco-Roman World   73
ALTAY COŞKUN

5 The Importance of Being Aitolian   96
JOSEPH SCHOLTEN

6 Democracy in the Hellenistic World   111
GLENN BUGH

**Part Three: *Symploke*: Mediterranean Systems and Networks   129**

7 Polybios and International Systems Theory   131
ARTHUR ECKSTEIN

8 Networks in the Hellenistic Economy   143
GARY REGER

9 Diplomacy and the Integration of the
Hasmonean State   155
CLAUDE EILERS

**Part Four: Alexandria: The Invention of a City   167**

10 Founding Alexandria in the Alexandrian Imagination   169
ANDREW ERSKINE

11 The Birth Myths of Ptolemy Soter   184
DANIEL OGDEN

12 'Alexandrianism' Again: Regionalism,
Alexandria, and Aesthetics   199
CRAIG I. HARDIMAN

**Part Five: Integration: Social In-Groups and Out-Groups   223**

13 Staging the *Oikos*: Character and Belonging
in Menander's *Samia*   225
CHRISTINA VESTER

14 Making Yourself at Home in the Hellenistic World   245
RUTH WESTGATE

15 Mère-patrie et patrie d'adoption à l'époque hellénistique:
Réflexions à partir du cas des mercenaires
crétois de Milet   268
PATRICK BAKER

**Part Six: *Insulae*: Geopolitics and Geopoetics   293**

16 'Entirely Ignorant of the Agora' (Alkiphron 1.14.3): Fishing
and the Economy of Hellenistic Delos   295
EPHRAIM LYTLE

17 De l'ouverture au repli: Les prêts du sanctuaire de Délos   316
LÉOPOLD MIGEOTTE

Contents  vii

18  Connections, Origins, and the Construction of Belonging
    in the Poetry of Kallimachos  325
    MARY DEPEW

    *References*  341
    *Contributors*  387
    *General Index*  391

# ILLUSTRATIONS

12.1  Bust of a Ptolemy (II? III?)   204

12.2  Head of Ptolemy VI   204

12.3  Statue inscribed for Arsinoë II   207

12.4  Head of Ptolemy I   207

12.5  Head of Ptolemy VI   208

12.6  Head of a Ptolemaic Queen (Arisnoë III?)   208

12.7  Head of a Ptolemaic Queen   209

12.8  Head of Ptolemy VIII   209

12.9  Tazza Farnese   210

14.1  Delos, Maison du trident   247

14.2  Masonry Style wall painting in room N of the Maison des comédiens, with frieze of comic scenes   247

14.3  Vestibule mosaic in the Maison des dauphins, with the 'sign of Tanit'   248

14.4  Panathenaic amphora mosaic in the *exedra* (I) of the Maison du trident   248

14.5  Lato, houses above the Prytaneion   257

14.6  Trypetos, House B1-3, viewed from the entrance   257

14.7  Delos, Ilot de la Maison des comédiens   259

# ACKNOWLEDGMENTS

The editors would like to express their sincere gratitude to a number of individuals and organizations for their support in this project. We were able to host the 2008 Waterloo gathering that gave rise to this collection through the generous financial support of the Social Sciences and Humanities Research Council of Canada, which awarded us a workshop grant. Financial assistance for the workshop was also forthcoming from the University of Waterloo, specifically from the Vice-President Academic, Dr Amit Chakma, and the Dean of Arts, Dr Ken Coates. The present volume has been published with the help of a grant from the Canadian Federation for the Humanities and Social Sciences, through the Awards to Scholarly Publications Program, using funds provided by the Social Sciences and Humanities Research Council of Canada. We would also like to thank the University of Toronto Press and its anonymous reviewers, whose comments were very helpful to us.

We also wish to extend warm thanks to those local individuals who helped in making the workshop a success and in facilitating the production of this volume. Several of our graduate students – Mike Moloney, Laura Roncone, †Justin Stricker, and Andrea Barrales-Hall – looked after workshop logistics and assisted in the preparation of the index. Our colleagues Dr Craig Hardiman and Dr Christina Vester gave their assistance as members of the local organizing committee, and our administrative assistant, Brigitte Schneebeli, provided invaluable support behind the scenes.

Finally, we would like to thank all the contributors and participants. Among these individuals are a few who, while they did not give a paper, added substantially to the discussions. We would therefore like to recognize Dr Andrew Faulkner (University of Waterloo), Dr Maria Liston (University of Waterloo), Dr Eriko Ogden (University of Exeter), and †Dr Jeanne Rutenburg (University of Maryland) for their thoughtful contributions. It was a stimulating and rewarding gathering in no small part because of these lively discussions. It is to Jeannie's memory that we dedicate this volume: for us her participation in the workshop symbolized what 'belonging' means.

BELONGING AND ISOLATION IN
THE HELLENISTIC WORLD

# INTRODUCTION

# Belonging and Isolation in the Hellenistic World: Themes and Questions

## SHEILA AGER AND RIEMER FABER

For much of the history of classical scholarship, the time from Alexander's death in 323 BC until Rome's mastery of the Mediterranean in the first century AD was regarded as a period of slow cultural decline following the glorious achievements of fifth-century Athens. Greek civilization and culture, though spreading far and wide across the empire Alexander had carved out, seemed fragmented, decadent, and individualized. In recent decades, however, scholars have reassessed this view and applied the more positive criteria of differentiation, change, and renewal.

The current view holds that the Hellenistic period was a time of innovation, resurgence, and transition. In particular, it was a time of unprecedented cultural interchange, as Greeks and Macedonians encountered new peoples, new ways of life, and new ideas in the wake of Alexander's conquests. These changes ushered in what has conventionally been designated as the unexampled cosmopolitanism of the Hellenistic world. But a broad characterization of the Hellenistic world as 'cosmopolitan' may obscure the reality of individual experience(s) during these centuries between the death of Alexander and the rise of Rome. Not all people, communities, or states would have responded in the same fashion to the pressures of change. Tensions between the individual and his or her community, and between the small, local community and the 'global' community of the Hellenistic *oikoumene* would have been evident. For many, the broadening horizons in the Hellenistic period would have brought with them a crisis of identity, and a sense of being adrift in a world that had undergone a radical structural change.

To address these and related issues, a conference was held in August 2008 at the University of Waterloo to explore the theme 'Belonging and Isolation in the Hellenistic World.' The theme is not a new one, having been treated in both general surveys and specialized studies in recent decades. For an introduction to several aspects of this theme, the reader may wish to consult part 4 of Blackwell's *Companion to the Hellenistic World* (Erskine 2005), entitled 'Greeks and Others'; it includes several chapters with suggestions for further reading and rich, up-to-date bibliographies. Convinced that the complexities of the era require that this theme be examined throughout the entire range of disciplines, the conference organizers encouraged participants to use a variety of perspectives: social, artistic, economic, literary, political, and historical. Whereas the program was not all-inclusive, and some developments distinctive of the Hellenistic era were not covered (e.g., philosophy, science), the presentations addressed the central issue from a variety of viewpoints. And as the concepts of 'belonging' and 'isolation' may be subject to a range of meaning and application, it was proposed to consider certain polarities in particular. One of them is the relationship between individual and community, as this was a time when different groups within increasingly multicultural cities competed or collaborated with each other in the context of an overtly Greek cultural framework. At the level of the polis, notions of belonging or isolation underscored the relations between male and female, slave and free, in-group and out-group. On the regional level, issues of commerce, politics, and trade were marked by polarities of alliance or rivalry. In other spheres, the strength of the bond between polis and kingdom was crucial to the prosperity of entire communities. And on an even larger scale, the dynamics of the relation between centre and periphery was shifting constantly, so that expressions of belonging were adapted frequently. Throughout the conference, the discussions that followed each presentation, and which culminated in a final round-table session, demonstrated that Hellenistic notions of belonging and isolation presumed the interconnectivity of polis, region, and *oikoumene*.

The resultant, present publication offers a broad assessment of the nature of belonging and isolation in the Hellenistic era. The eighteen contributions have been arranged into six parts, each of which highlights an aspect of the theme: I. Intercultural Poetics and Identity (Bing, Gutzwiller, Höschele); II. On the Margins? Ethnicity and Hellenicity (Bugh, Coşkun, Scholten); III. *Symploke*: Mediterranean Systems and Networks (Eckstein, Eilers, Reger); IV. Alexandria: The Invention of a City (Erskine, Hardiman, Ogden); V. Integration: Social In-Groups and Out-Groups (Baker, Vester, Westgate); and VI. *Insulae*: Geopolitics and Geopoetics (Depew, Lytle, Migeotte). As each part includes an introduction explaining the thematic coherence of the three chapters it comprises, the purpose of the following paragraphs is to identify the major themes that permeate the entire collection, and to pose some questions for further study.

The cataclysmic changes brought about by Alexander's campaigns and the construction of the new kingdoms created a whole new layer of potential belonging. Yet for most Greeks, daily life and identity were still centred on the traditional institutions of the *oikos* and the polis. Nevertheless, the upheaval, the new opportunities, and the questioning spirit ushered in by the Hellenistic period all had their impact on conventional notions of identity and belonging.

The *oikos*, the household in its broadest sense, was in Aristotle's view the fundamental building block of the polis.[1] Membership in a polis – citizenship – was therefore rooted in membership in an *oikos*. Christina Vester (chapter 13) presents a reading of the *Samia* that challenges conventional notions of civic belonging, suggesting that in Menander's Athens, virtuous behaviour in the *oikos* might have a higher claim to membership in the body politic than mere right of birth. Nevertheless, a strict devotion to civic traditions – including the prize of citizenship – was for Greeks in the Hellenistic age a means not only of asserting the continuity of their own *poleis*, but also of demonstrating their very 'Greekness.' In spite of the dominance of the new kingdoms, the polis was still a quintessential sign of Hellenicity, and Glenn Bugh (chapter 6) argues that polis identity and traditions of citizen-rule became more important than ever in the face of non-Greek populations.[2]

Although the rapid expansion of frontiers, the mobility of populations, and the creation of new cities led to a necessary relaxing of barriers to citizenship in many cases, we can still see the habitual reluctance to share the precious trophy of belonging. The foundation of Alexandria-by-Egypt necessitated, at least initially, something of an open-door policy to new citizens, but even here the complexity of the population's organization highlights the special quality of actual citizenship.[3] Meanwhile, older *poleis* continued to guard their prerogatives jealously. Patrick Baker (chapter 15) explores the peculiar status of mercenaries, vital to civic defence, yet outsiders in the community they served. In the case of the Cretan mercenaries who lived for so many years in Miletos, we see the dual barriers to their status: offered citizenship by the Milesians, but barred from membership in the regular military and from the post of *phrourarch* for twenty years from their arrival; and damned by their Cretan homeland if they took the Milesians up on their offer.

A new centre such as Alexandria had less invested in a historical sense of the identity of its citizens, and was so situated, both geographically and politically, as to become an exemplar of multiculturalism.[4] Yet Andrew Erskine (chapter 10) shows us that traditional affiliations and ties of belonging still fell along ethnic and cultural lines. Alexandria was not one city, but many cities: a Greek polis (but one lacking the rich traditions of self-government of the older *poleis* of the Greek world); a Macedonian royal capital; and an Egyptian city. Its foundation stories and the birth myths of the ruling Ptolemies, discussed by both Erskine and Daniel Ogden (chapter 11), featured distinct elements intended to appeal to the variegated population of the city. Although Alexandria's population may never have been fully integrated, its rulers had created something entirely new in their quest to find modes of belonging for its residents.[5]

Whether viewed as membership in a community or affiliation with one, belonging requires mechanisms whereby it may be conveyed and advertised. If it is true that the criteria for inclusion were constantly shifting throughout the Hellenistic world, how did political rulers, ethnic communities, or individuals assert their right to belong? One important means of legitimizing membership in a constituency is to create the perception of membership. Membership may be forged or invented. As Regina Höschele (chapter 1) demonstrates from Meleager's epigrams, admission to the coterie of literary elites could be obtained by rejecting traditional, culturally specific values of aesthetics and replacing them with new, cosmopolitan ones. Another strategy, as Mary Depew demonstrates for Kallimachos in the geographical setting of Alexandria (chapter 18), was to create a series of connections between Alexandria and Athens that brought with them cultural and social links which authorized the poet's own claim upon the Greek literary past.

The manipulation of myth to forge connections that endorse the right to belong is not restricted to literary strategies; it also serves political and social goals. Thus, as Erskine in chapter 10 demonstrates for the features of Hellenism in Alexandria's foundation legends, the promotion of links between Alexander and the Ptolemies, however strained these may have been, advances the royals' claim to legitimate power. The more or less official but clearly forged genealogies of Ptolemy Soter support the dynasty's unusual position vis-à-vis the Macedonian dynasty on the one hand, and the local culture of Alexandria on the other, as Daniel Ogden illustrates in chapter 11.

This representation of legitimate membership in the new world order extended throughout the Mediterranean world, and it was avidly pursued by communities that had been portrayed previously as marginal. The Greek *poleis* of West Pontos made an effort to appear Hellenized (Bugh, chapter 6), and the Aitolians differentiated themselves from the Gauls in order to validate their own Hellenicity (Joseph Scholten, chapter 5). Some communities employed their domestic architecture to express the extent to which they participated in, or withdrew from, increasing Hellenic cosmopolitanism. Ruth Westgate (chapter 14) argues that while the diverse population of Delos employed house design to convey the city's self-portrayal as a cosmopolitan melting pot, the uncomfortable position of Crete in the midst of competing political and economic forces caused it to opt for a more cautious and conservative strategy of architecture. It thus becomes clear that examination of the mechanisms whereby communities exhibited and asserted their right to belong leads to discoveries about the underlying social, political, and economic motivations for their self-representation.

Examining the variegated examples of belonging and isolation in the Hellenistic world may lead one into the trap of imagining a tidy matrix, a pigeonholing of cases based on a rigid set of parameters. The parameters are of course anything but rigid: they are multifaceted, fluctuating, and highly subjective. Like yin and yang, the concepts of belonging and isolation cannot be imagined one without the other. In-groups cannot exist apart from out-groups, and what is inclusion from one angle is exclusion from another. Furthermore, as Gary Reger demonstrates (chapter 8), one may simultaneously be part of several different groups or networks (and, by the same token, *not* be part of still other groups or networks).

Several papers in this collection explore the liminal places where isolation and belonging meet and mingle, or even where such concepts cease to have meaning. The Greek world had always been made up of Greeks and 'others,' *barbaroi*, but the careers of Alexander and his Successors and the creation of a Hellenistic *oikoumene* broke down many barriers, while maintaining or raising others. Greeks might still see non-Greeks as 'other,' but the demands of dealing with a Graeco-Macedonian royal bureaucracy compelled many non-Greeks to gain a fluency in Hellenic language and culture. Greeks and Egyptians in Ptolemaic Egypt might have separate court systems, and Greeks might still contemn those who did not know how to *hellenizein*, as an Arab (?) camel-driver complains,[6] but non-Greeks could have a stab at Greek belonging if they learned the rules.

The political domination of Greek polities (the great and small kingdoms, the leagues, and even now the *poleis*) in the Hellenistic age meant that intercultural 'belonging' was, in general, unidirectional: it meant the adoption of a Greek identity by non-Greeks. It is true, as Erskine and Ogden (chapters 10 and 11) point out, that the Ptolemies of Egypt were careful to put on a Pharaonic face for their Egyptian subjects, but for the most part things went the other way. Many Egyptians in Ptolemaic Egypt found it profitable to learn at least some Greek and to take Greek names,[7] and the native kingdoms of northern and eastern Asia Minor Hellenized their courts when freed from Persian domination.

Belonging to the Greek club, however, as Jonathan Hall points out in his work *Hellenicity*, was perhaps more about behaviour – or at least perceptions of behaviour – than about ethnic identity or linguistic ability.[8] The courtesan Chrysis's behaviour in Menander's *Samia* fits her to be a proper Athenian *politis*, and not simply a foreign sex worker; conversely, the young Athenian Moschion undermines his own citizenship, at least in moral terms, by his reprehensible actions.[9] As with early Hellenistic Athens, so with the Hellenistic *oikoumene* in general: norms and expectations of behaviour supersede ethnic origins. Hellenism and Hellenicity (at least from the point of view of those who professed such an identity) were to be associated with culture, with civilization, with learning, with letters, with political sophistication and diplomatic finesse. Hence, as Claude Eilers shows us in chapter 9, the Jews of the Hasmonean kingdom, a highly cultured people with a long history of literacy, were able to fit with ease into an international society with recognized patterns of diplomatic behaviour. Claiming a purely fictitious kinship with the Spartans, the Jewish kingdom was also able to negotiate a complex web of diplomatic networks that involved Rome, Pergamon, and the ancient polis of Athens. We must assume that in spite of the Jews' own injunctions on graven images and intrusions into their sacred space, it was not distasteful to Hyrkanos I to have his own statue raised in a pagan Athenian *temenos* of the Demos and the Graces (Joseph. *AJ* 14.153). It was all part of belonging to the club.

Civilized standards of behaviour – or at least the rhetoric surrounding such standards – could be expected to apply to ethnic Greeks themselves. The Aitolians who saved Delphi from the marauding Celts in the early third century were not the same Aitolians who in the fifth century spoke an impossible dialect and ate their meat raw (Thuc. 3.94). The latter were brutish and bestial, their inability to speak intelligible Greek a sign of their essentially un-Hellenic character; the former were heroic warriors, defending the Greeks against the ultimate barbarian. As saviours of Delphi – the heart and centre of the Hellenic world[10] – the Aitolians of the early Hellenistic age were able to lay claim to their own Hellenicity. Yet what can be given can also be taken away. If (at least some) Aitolians could not forbear from traditions of piratical behaviour, and if their claim to be the protectors of Delphi was lost, as it was in the early second century, then the Aitolians, as Scholten demonstrates in chapter 5, were on the road to isolation once more.

In a world marked by dislocation, intercultural encounters, and the rough abrasions of contact between peoples of different languages and customs – all of it often in the context of ongoing military conflicts – one response to the dilemma of 'fitting in' could be to embrace one's own parochialism, to reject consciously the opportunities of the brave new world. The inhabitants of Delos chose a path of minimal risk (and minimal gains) in their economic policies in the Hellenistic period: Léopold Migeotte (chapter 17) shows that the Delians, despite their island's situation as a crossroads of trade, chose to look inward and isolate themselves from the greater financial opportunities and challenges presented by the world around them. On the island of Crete – often, like the Aitolians, associated with piracy and generally un-Hellenic behaviour[11] – domestic architecture from the Hellenistic period may suggest a proud embracing of a purely local culture. Westgate (chapter 14) argues that the marked absence of domestic decoration attested elsewhere in the Hellenistic world may have been a way to identify oneself with the local community. Isolation becomes belonging, and belonging implies isolation.

Another response could simply be to supersede any notions of belonging altogether, by adopting a stance of intercultural insouciance. The poet Meleager, born in Syria in a Hellenic or Hellenized household, living in Phoenician Tyre as a young man, and in his later years becoming a citizen of Kos, was perhaps the epitome of Hellenistic worldliness. He is discussed by two of our contributors, Höschele (chapter 1) and Kathryn Gutzwiller (chapter 3), who point to the deliberate cosmopolitanism of Meleager's poetics and his shrugging off of any attempts to impose definitive categories on him. 'If I'm from Syria,' he says, 'so what?' Making the bold claim that Gadara is Syria's Athens, Meleager declares that he has no need to seek admission to any kind of club, Hellenic or otherwise. His stance may be compared with that of Kallimachos, who reverses Hellenic ethnocentricity and proudly declares that he has never left Egypt and has no desire to do so. As Depew (chapter 18) shows us, Kallimachos's Alexandria is the destination of all good things; the poet's isolation from the world around him loses all meaning if the good things of the world come to him.

If there were many ways of defining 'belonging' in the Hellenistic era, there were just as many ways of experiencing isolation. While it is often pointed out that the colonization movements of the archaic period entailed considerable displacements of people, during the Hellenistic age there was a general increase in mobility and in dislocations of a less formal nature. Perhaps the more fluid social and political structures of the Hellenistic era also drew greater attention to the sense of isolation that was experienced by individuals, families, communities, and federations.

Throughout the Hellenistic era entire groups of people continued to be identified by Greeks as 'the other' on either ethnic or cultural grounds. The Aitolians, who despite their Greek pedigree had not been granted membership in the Greek *oikoumene* during the Classical era, struggled to rid themselves of the stigma of isolation. As Scholten demontrates in chapter 5, the Aitolian-led repulsion of the Gauls in 279/278 BC seemed like a ticket to belonging, but it would not take long before old prejudices would rise again and the Aitolians would experience alienation. Not unlike the Aitolians, the

Galatians themselves were symbolic of barbarism for generations (a characterisation that has endured until very recently), as Altay Coşkun shows in chapter 4. In fact, even the imprecise and sweeping term 'Galatians' may have functioned as a handy stereotype that reinforced the perception of these tribes as excluded from the civilized Greek *oikoumene*.

Interestingly, while some groups strove for entry into the Greek fold, others derived advantages from being perceived as isolated. As was noted already, by means of their unadorned and conservative domestic architecture, the communities on Crete exhibited intentional isolation in the context of their politically sensitive region. For the purposes of economic advantage, the island of Delos imposed on itself a carefully controlled insularity (thus Migeotte, chapter 17). The fishermen of Delos, as Ephraim Lytle shows (chapter 16), did not aspire to the membership within the polis, but focused their attention towards the sea. City states that did not possess sufficient martial power of their own hired mercenary soldiers. These men, as Baker observes (chapter 15), represented an isolated group within the community – accepted but not embraced. And then there are the isolated groups and individuals who had no opportunity to voice concerns about their status, and whose stories were never told.

Within the Greek polis, in which foreigners were isolated from the citizen class, the concepts of isolation and belonging received renewed attention. Vester, in her reading of Menander's *Samia* (chapter 13), treats the crucial role that is granted to the Samian Chrysis, a foreign hetaira and thus an outsider. Posing as a citizen-class mother, Chrysis preserves an entire *oikos* to which she does not belong. The irony is that one who has been isolated acts to preserve the political and social standards of the polis. By demonstrating that an outsider is equally worthy of belonging as formal members are, the play develops the tension between the political and the moral criteria for belonging to the polis.

It may be true that the fragmentation of the empire upon the death of Alexander fostered the isolation of regions that were centred on their own courts. However, we ought not to look for isolation where it does not exist. A good example of this inclination is evidenced by the modern tendency, until recently, of isolating artistic aesthetics into styles associated with particular regions such as Antioch, Rhodes, or Alexandria, and of raising these purportedly isolated styles into norms for artistic interpretation. In chapter 12 Craig Hardiman reminds us to be wary of facile applications of terms such as 'regionalism' and 'Alexandrianism.'

The term 'Hellenistic,' as discussed above, references a concept that is in constant need of revisitation and revision. The participants in the Waterloo conference wrestled with this concept in the course of defining the parameters of our discussion. What are the temporal limits of 'Hellenisticity'? What are its geographic limits? Is the term primarily linguistic, cultural, ethnic, or political? This is not the place to engage in the search for a definition that is certain to prove elusive and that moreover should probably remain elusive. Nevertheless, the issue of just what we mean when we talk about a 'Hellenistic' world did arise repeatedly in our attempts to identify characteristics that we might attach to this world.

Temporally, our discussion tended to favour the conventional limits set on the Hellenistic period, i.e., the career of Alexander the Great and the death of Cleopatra. But several of the papers pushed this temporal limit, in both directions. Astounding as the career of Alexander was, and profound as the changes that ensued as a result of it were, these events should not be allowed to obscure the continuity of life and culture in the Greek world. Bugh (chapter 6) explores the dedication that Hellenistic *poleis* – including Athens – had to their traditional notions of Classical democracy. Arthur Eckstein's essay (chapter 7) moves us from internal to external politics, specifically the fraught relations between security-conscious states in an anarchic international system. Eckstein's exploration of Polybios's international systems theory relates it back to Thucydides, generally regarded as the first political theorist of a Realist stamp; he shows us how little the concerns and actions of states change over time.

Pushing the temporal limit in the other direction is Coşkun's contribution (chapter 4). The Galatians – those bogeymen of the Hellenistic world – were long considered the epitome of barbarism, and played a valuable role in the self-presentation of powers such as Pergamon and the Aitolians.[12] But as Coşkun points out, the Galatians ultimately established themselves as members of the international club, and Themistios's declaration in the fourth century AD that they were 'genuine Romans' underlines both the shifting nature of Galatian identity and the continuity of the Hellenistic world into the Roman period.

The nature of Rome's 'belonging' in a Hellenistic context was addressed in other papers as well. By 200 BC the Romans had become indisputably part of the Hellenistic world, although monarchs like Philip V and Antiochos III still cherished hopes of confining Roman interests to the western half of the Mediterranean. Other powers, such as Pergamon and Rhodes, actively sought to engage Rome and draw it into the nexus of Hellenistic relationships. In military terms, Rome's engagement with the Hellenistic east may seem to be a slow but relatively steady progress of Roman armies marching eastward and converting the Hellenistic world into a Roman empire. And yet Eckstein shows us that the Romans were by no means more militaristic than the Hellenistic monarchies.[13] In political terms, Roman engagement with the east was more complex. The Roman intrusion into the Hellenistic Mediterranean was in large part the result of Greek diplomacy, not Roman aggression.[14] Moreover, the Romans expended considerable diplomatic energy in the Hellenized east themselves, as Eilers (chapter 9) demonstrates, though certain apparently ruthless examples of Roman 'diplomacy' have tended to colour the overall picture.[15]

The intricacy of cultural and political interaction that took place between Rome and the Greek east in the Hellenistic period was well captured by a Roman poet: 'Graecia capta ferum victorem cepit et artes intulit agresti Latio.'[16] The military victor was itself captivated by the culture of the Greeks. It was not assimilation, it was not Hellenization – it was something unique. The relevance of Horace's remark to the topic at hand is that the comments made above with respect to 'belonging' in a Hellenistic context tended to presume a political/military dominance, direct or indirect, by a Greek (or Graeco-Macedonian) power. But Roman belonging was measured differently. Just as many native Egyptians saw fit to adopt Greek names under Ptolemaic rule, so many Greeks, as the Hellenistic world was absorbed into the Roman Empire, assumed a Roman name: the Kleitosthenes family of Thera featured members named Flavius and Claudianus and Claudia.[17] In cultural terms, however, the Romans recognized the richness of Hellenic accomplishments.

If the term 'Hellenistic' is a complex and evasive one, it becomes more so when it is accompanied by 'world.' The phrase 'Hellenistic world' traditionally suggested a phenomenon that saw the 'world' going through a process of *hellenizein*. Modern scholarship has shown this scenario to be overly simplistic and grounded in a colonialist viewpoint. But it remains true that the Hellenistic period was the first time in Western history when the concept of an encompassing 'world' civilization came into being. The affairs of the western and eastern Mediterranean became inextricably bound together in these years through Polybios's process of *symploke*. The geographic limits of the Hellenistic world, by virtue of the very meaning of *hellenizein*, were far more vast than those of the purely 'Greek world.' Defining 'belonging' and 'isolation' becomes that much more challenging when dealing with an *oikoumene* of such breadth and complexity.

Several of our contributors examined the microcosm of belonging in an *oikos* or a polis, as we saw above; others approached the question from a macrocosmic level. Reger, for example, applies contemporary social network theory to the Hellenistic Mediterranean in the context of an exploration of the Hellenistic economy and ways of comprehending and structuring it (chapter 8). The layers of belonging – of *homophily* for various characteristics, as Reger points out – are vividly rendered through prosaic examples of ordinary people: traders, fishermen, mercenaries, and so on. Roman generals and Hellenistic kings might dominate the literary traditions of Hellenistic history, but the core and infrastructure of society rested on the doings of the commonplace. The contributions of Baker, Vester, Westgate, and Lytle underline this fact.[18] Conversely, the doings of the commonplace add up to the social and political movements that attract the interest of those wishing to document the larger actions of history. Eckstein's essay emphasizes the anarchic political system that continues to dominate the world of interstate relations today. We all belong to this system, but the system itself is based on multiple isolations: fear, security consciousness, distrust, lack of knowledge, and so on.

The geography of the Mediterranean basin being what it is, the sea necessarily played a large role in the connectedness of the Hellenistic *oikoumene*. Several of the papers reference the convergent nature of islands such as Delos and Cyprus, hubs where cultures met and mingled.[19] Yet the sea divides as much as it connects and islands by definition are isolated. Crete in particular stands out in this respect. It was often thought of as a cultural backwater, a home of mercenaries and pirates already in the Classical age. In the Hellenistic period, Crete still exported both; its *poleis*, moreover, tore themselves apart with repeated conflict.[20] Westgate (chapter 14) examines a more positive side to Cretan isolation, an isolation that involved a statement of local belonging rather than belonging in the *oikoumene*.

Within the larger Hellenistic *oikoumene* existed nodes of cultural production that modern scholarship has chosen to view as regional schools. While such putative nodes fit neatly into a tidy picture of orderly webs of connectedness, the reality is of course much less systematic. Scholarship in general has a tendency to look for patterns, to minimize inconsistencies, to seek solutions. Hardiman (chapter 12) challenges the notion of tidy regional schools of artistry, in particular the idea that an aesthetic of 'quality' somehow typifies Alexandrian art.

Thus far this introduction has sought to identify certain themes that arose out of the several papers and that were pursued in our discussions. It still remains to comment on the methodologies employed by the participants, and to anticipate future directions for scholarship in this area. As may be expected from a collection of essays that treat several subjects from the perspectives of different disciplines, a variety of theoretical and methodological approaches are employed in this book, and a diversity of sources are adduced as evidence. Two essays, for example, explicitly apply a modern theory of investigation. In his examination of Polybios's account of the patterns of political integration, Eckstein employs the contemporary international systems theory of the school of Realism (chapter 7). Reger, on the other hand, pursues social network analysis in a study of Hellenistic networks of economy (chapter 8). Other essays follow theoretical approaches that are seen as meeting the current needs; for instance, in her study of citizenship and morality in the comedy of Menander, Vester (chapter 13) privileges cultural poetic analysis, in which society is deemed a primary agent of literary production.

Several contributors found that comparative analysis was a fruitful approach to the polarized concepts of belonging and isolation. Comparisons of communities from disparate geographical regions in particular produced telling results. In addressing the question of the continuation of democratic institutions and practices of classical Greece into the Hellenistic era, Bugh (chapter 6) draws comparisons and contrasts between 'central' Athens and 'peripheral' Black Sea communities. Gutzwiller (chapter 3) illustrates how Meleager's epigrams foreground the differing socio-cultural values of Tyre, Kos, and Rome. Westgate (chapter 14) demonstrates how comparison of the strategies in domestic architecture at Delos and Crete reveal significant differences in the social, political, and economic aspirations of these dissimilar communities.

The examination of the theme 'belonging and isolation' from the different perspective offered by each discipline generated results that may be particular to that discipline; this in turn leads to the realization that issues of belonging and isolation did not develop in a homogeneous fashion throughout the Mediterranean world. The picture that emerges is one of *layers* of tension regarding membership and association, or exclusion and segregation, throughout Hellenistic civilizations and cultures.

One of the challenges in applying concepts of belonging and isolation to a study of the Hellenistic era is that there was no 'voice' for those individuals in society or for those communities in the larger *oikoumene* who were marginalized or altogether excluded. Such outcast parties may have had no access to the means of self-representation. The importance of recognizing the lack of evidence in support of minority groups is critical to the argument of two essays in particular. In surveying the changing fortunes of the Galatians in the history of the Graeco-Roman world, Coşkun (chapter 4) demonstrates the biased portrayal of these people in the one-sided writings of those who were entrenched members in the Greek club. Not dissimilar was the experience of the Aitolians, who, as Scholten (chapter 5) shows, struggled to break free of the stereotype of borderline barbarism through their appropriation of cultural Hellenicity. Moreover, this lack of a counterbalancing voice in defence of the marginalized must make one wary of uncritical acceptance of the extant evidence, whether it is epigraphic, literary, artistic, etc.

In conclusion, we wish to observe that the discussions at the conference, and the essays in the present volume, have identified several aspects of the theme, 'belonging and isolation,' that are broached but not treated exhaustively in this collection. Of the several questions that arose repeatedly, the following appeared to be of greatest consequence to Hellenistic scholarship generally. We suggest that this weighty and well-known question is worthy of further exploration: what precisely are the boundaries of 'the Hellenistic period,' in time and space? To what extent did the ideals, norms, and practices of Greek and non-Greek societies of the classical period continue in *poleis* through-out the Mediterranean basin in the era following the death of Alexander? And, at the other end of the continuum, when does Rome's involvement in the political, economic, and social activities of the Hellenistic Mediterranean become so prominent that the very fabric of Hellenistic societies was altered irrevocably? On what grounds is it warranted even to impose geographical or historical *termini* upon a complexity of multicultural societies that are experiencing vastly different developments at various speeds?

At the risk of making facile comparisons, and of appearing to reduce complex historical phenomena to clichés, we note that several contributors to this volume expressed the sentiment that similarities appear to exist between contemporary geopolitical movements and those of the Hellenistic era. It certainly does seem that the traditional dynamics of belonging and isolation have reached an end, that the world is 'opening up,' and that opportunities for new political and social alignments are emerging.

## Notes

1 Arist. *Pol.* 1.1253b; see Nagle 2006.

2 On the polis in the Hellenistic world, see, e.g., Gauthier 1993; Giovannini 1993; Gruen 1993.

3 See Fraser 1972: 1.38–92.

4 See, most recently, the contributions in Hinge and Krasilnikoff 2010.

5 On the duality of Alexandria and the cultural impact of that duality, see, e.g. Stanwick 2002; Stephens 2003.

6 *P. Col. Zen.* II 66 (trans. Bagnall and Derow 2004: no. 137). The identity of this individual is not known for certain.

7 Although in general it was the Egyptians who would have had to learn some Greek for the sake of economic or political advancement, there were at least a few Greeks who saw value in learning Egyptian (see Bagnall and Derow 2004: nos. 136, 139).

8  See Hall 2002, esp. 220–6.

9  See Vester, chapter 13.

10  For the myth of Zeus's eagles meeting at Delphi after being released from the opposite ends of the earth, see Strabo 9.3.6 C420.

11  For an assessment of the Cretans that rivals his negative take on the Aitolians, see Polybios 2.4.3; 4.8.11; 11.46–7.

12  For a discussion of the role of the Galatians in Pergamon's and Aitolia's self-presentation as saviours of Greeks and the Greek way of life, see Koehn 2007.

13  See chapter 7 and Eckstein 2006 and 2008.

14  The most detailed study remains Gruen 1984. For a more bleak interpretation of Roman actions, see Harris 1975–91.

15  The classic example is perhaps C. Popillius Laenas's harsh ultimatum to Antiochos IV in 168 BC, the so-called Day of Eleusis (Polyb. 29.27; Livy 45.12; Diod. 31.2). There is also the example of M. Acilius Glabrio and the Aitolian *deditio* in 191 BC (Polyb. 20.9–10); for a different reading of the latter incident, see Eckstein 1995b.

16  Hor. *Epist.* 2.1.156–7.

17  *IG* XII.3 325–6.

18  Chapters 13, 14, 15, and 16.

19  See Bing, Westgate, Lytle, Migeotte, and Depew (chapters 2, 14, 16, 17, and 18).

20  See Baker (chapter 15) and the remarks of Polybios cited above.

# PART ONE

# Intercultural Poetics and Identity

One distinguishing feature of the literary production of the Hellenistic era is the wide range of authors' geographical origins. Kallimachos was a native of Cyrene, west of Egypt; Theokritos hailed from Syracuse, in Sicily; and Poseidippos was born in Macedonian Pella. The writings of the Graeco-Syrian epigrammatist Meleager, whose poetry is the subject of two contributions in this section, reveal sensitivity to the cross-cultural social, religious, and linguistic forces that were in play at the time. Born in Gadara (modern-day Umm Qais in Jordan) on the margins of the Greek *oikoumene*, Meleager lived for some time in Phoenician Tyre, and died on the island of Kos.

In her contribution, Regina Höschele illustrates the nature of Meleager's cultural apologetics from five autobiographical epigrams. His Hellenocentric cosmopolitanism capitalizes on an expanding Hellenization whereby peripheral communities are drawn into the Greek orbit. While Homer, the paragon of Greek literary culture, may be portrayed as Syrian, Gadara is represented as Attic. This confluence of Hellenic and liminal cultures is expressed also by the common association of the poet Meleager and the ruler Ptolemy Philadelphos with the island of Kos. Such cosmopolitan discourse accords with the larger poetic strategy of the *Garland*, which forges a new construct out of heterogeneous subjects, styles, and metrics. Thus for Meleager cultural refinement is not bound to national identity but affiliation with the Muses.

Peter Bing's essay demonstrates the value in considering also those obscure writers whose works survive only in brief fragments. Although nothing is known of Hermeias other than that he came from Kourion on the southern shores of Cyprus, the extant few lines of his choliambic verse inveighing against Stoics and their founder Zeno do provide evidence for our understanding of the cultural and literary milieu of the island in the

Hellenistic era. Establishing his artistic credentials through literary allusion, metrical precision, and thematic emulation, Hermeias employs regional ethnic identities to disparage Zeno. Associations between Zeno and the conventionally untrustworthy Phoenicians, who may have founded his hometown of Kition, illustrate how notions of identity and belonging may have operated on a regional level.

In her paper, Kathryn Gutzwiller broaches the topic of mutual intercultural influences and evidence for them in literature. Increasing dominance had empowered Rome to arbitrate political disputes in the Mediterranean world, but it does not yet figure prominently in Greek literature. Indeed, the evidence for the Roman cultural elements in the collection of epigrams is restricted to one poignant phrase: 'Roman platter of boys.' Discussing the generic, social, and political factors that may have functioned in this expression, Gutzwiller illustrates how especially the sexual mores that varied between Tyre and Rome are reflected in this trifold metaphor of sexual, culinary, and literary elements.

# 1

# 'If I Am from Syria – So What?': Meleager's Cosmopoetics[1]

## REGINA HÖSCHELE

Νᾶσος ἐμὰ θρέπτειρα Τύρος· πάτρα δέ με τεκνοῖ
  Ἀτθὶς ἐν Ἀσσυρίοις ναιομένα Γαδάροις·
Εὐκράτεω δ' ἔβλαστον ὁ σὺν Μούσαις Μελέαγρος
  πρῶτα Μενιππείοις συντροχάσας Χάρισιν.
εἰ δὲ Σύρος, τί τὸ θαῦμα; μίαν, ξένε, πατρίδα κόσμον
  ναίομεν, ἓν θνατοὺς πάντας ἔτικτε Χάος.
πουλυετὴς δ' ἐχάραξα τάδ' ἐν δέλτοισι πρὸ τύμβου·
  γήρως γὰρ γείτων ἐγγύθεν Ἀίδεω.
ἀλλά με τὸν λαλιὸν καὶ πρεσβύτην σὺ προσειπὼν
  χαίρειν εἰς γῆρας καὐτὸς ἴκοιο λάλον.    (*Anth. Pal.* 7.417 = Gow-Page *HE* 2)

(The isle of Tyre raised me; my true hometown, however, was Gadara, Syria's Athens. From Eukrates I sprouted, I Meleager, who first by the help of the Muses raced against Menippos's Graces. If I am from Syria, so what? We all, stranger, inhabit ONE country: the world; it was ONE chaos that gave birth to all mortals. In old age I carved these lines into a tablet before [entering] the tomb, for age is a close neighbour to Hades. But if you greet me, the chatty old man, may you, too, reach chatty old age.)[2]

This text is one in a series of four, possibly five, self-epitaphs by the Hellenistic poet Meleager, which were once included in his *Stephanos*, a four-book anthology of epigrams edited around 100 BC.[3] It has long been noted that the *Anthologia Palatina* contains several large sequences of the *Garland* that more or less preserve the poems' original arrangement.[4] The collection's remnants thus permit us to gain a fairly good picture of its intricate design, as has been brilliantly demonstrated by Kathryn Gutzwiller.[5] Based on her structural analysis, we may observe that Meleager's self-epitaphs formed part of the first section in the book of sepulchral epigrams, which was primarily dedicated to literary figures of the past.[6] By adding to this sequence multiple epigrams composed for his own tombstone (a marvellous act of self-memoralization!), Meleager stakes his claim to be counted among the members of Hellas's Dead Poets Society. Coming from the margins of the Greek *oikoumene,* the Gadarene poet is well aware of the temporal, spatial, and cultural gulf that separates him from the revered exponents of Hellenic culture, who are commemorated in the preceding epitaphs. He is therefore at pains to assert his own Greekness, that is, his sophistication and refinement, by playing down the differences between the various ethnicities. As this paper will show, Meleager utilizes the cosmopolitan Weltanschauung advocated in *Anth. Pal.* 7.417 to affiliate himself with the intellectual elite of the Greek world, while representing his life's journey as a gradual movement toward its cultural centre. In what follows I will investigate how the epigrammatist strategically elevates his Syrian roots and fashions for himself a mixed identity that is, I argue, consistent with the poetological discourse of his anthology.

While emphasizing the equality of each and everyone – we are all inhabitants of the same world and descendants from the same Chaos – Meleager's cosmopolitanism seems to be borne by a firm belief in the cultural supremacy of Hellas. The statement εἰ δὲ Σύρος, τί τὸ θαῦμα (5, 'If I am from Syria, so what?') betrays a certain feeling of inferiority, coupled with the manifest need to apologize for his background: it anticipates and answers potential objections on the part of biased Greeks, who might look down upon a Syrian-born poet writing in their language. What Meleager affirms, then, is not so much the parity of Greeks and barbarians as the possibility of being Greek notwithstanding one's origins. He may consider himself a citizen of the world, but he does so hardly in the sense of the Cynic philosopher Diogenes, who is said to have coined the term κοσμοπολίτης (cf. Diog. Laert. 6.63);[7] for his is a distinctly *Greek* world. Here is someone who wholeheartedly embraces the expansion of Hellenism in the wake of Alexander's conquests, since it allows him to have a share in what formerly belonged to a single people. Significantly, Homer is pictured as having accompanied Alexander on his military campaign (Plut. *Alex.* 26 αὐτῷ συστρατεύειν ἔοικεν Ὅμηρος), and thanks to the Macedonian ruler the children of Persians, Susinians, and Gedrosians learned to chant the tragedies of Sophokles and Euripides, or so Plutarch claims[8] – anecdotes that nicely convey how Alexander's invasion of the East could be reinterpreted as a primarily cultural enterprise. In this context, national identities do not matter any more, since Greekness has, so to speak, become transnational.[9] Far from advocating the equality of all civilizations, Meleager adheres – let me emphasize this once more – to a completely Hellenocentric cosmopolitanism.

Thus his hometown of Gadara distinguishes itself not through its indigenous culture, but through its Hellenism. By characterizing the Syrian city as Attic, the poet not only symbolically shifts the geographical centre of the Greek world to its periphery, but also pays homage to a by-gone era, that of classical Athens, which, though the polis itself had long since lost its political significance, was still seen as the pinnacle of Hellenic culture. In a similar vein, Meleager seems to have turned the greatest poet of all time into his compatriot: as Athenaios reports (4.157b), he claimed, in one of his Menippean satires, that Homer had the Achaians abstain from fish (despite the rich supplies of seafood in the Hellespont), because he was Syrian by birth and simply followed the practice of his fatherland.[10] This observation should have settled, once and for all, the hotly debated question of where the illustrious bard had been born.[11] In any case, it provided Meleager with a poetic forefather – he could not have chosen a more venerable one – and made Syria the very cradle of Greek poetry! No more need, then, to justify why Meleager's native country could be considered a part of Hellas and its culture – for was it not here that it all began? Does not the *Iliad* itself attest to its author's Syrian heritage?[12]

Interestingly, the Stoic Zenodotos, in his sepulchral epigram on Zeno, followed a comparable strategy in order to ennoble the philosopher's place of birth, Phoenician Kition. Associating it with the introduction of the Greek alphabet, Zenodotos seems to imply that Hellenic culture actually originated from Phoenicia (*Anth. Pal.* 7.117.5–6 = Gow-Page *HE* 1.5–6):[13] εἰ δὲ πάτρα Φοίνισσα, τίς ὁ φθόνος; ἦν καὶ ὁ Κάδμος / κεῖνος, ἀφ' οὗ γραπτὰν Ἑλλὰς ἔχει σελίδα (And if your native land is Phoenician, what reproach is there in that? Kadmos, too, was from there, from whom Greece acquired the written word).

Like Syria, Phoenicia is a sort of proto-Hellas, which can be taken as a second guarantee for Meleager's innate Greekness. For it is very likely that the epigrammatist alludes to Zenodotos's lines[14] in his self-epitaph (εἰ δὲ Σύρος ~ εἰ δὲ πάτρα Φοίνισσα, τί τὸ θαῦμα ~ τίς ὁ φθόνος), and thus subtly affirms the Hellenicity of the land he lived in as a young man – as it happens, Tyre is the very city Kadmos came from.

A latter-day Homer, Meleager also was a kind of wandering singer. At least he represents his own life as a gradual movement away from the fringes of the *oikoumene* toward its centre: born in Gadara and raised in Phoenician

Tyre,[15] he spent his later years on Kos. By locating his second abode on an island (note the emphatic position of νᾶσος at the beginning of our poem, *Anth. Pal.* 7.417), Meleager underlines his early detachment from the Asian continent.[16] Although the city of Tyre was connected with the mainland, ever since Alexander the Great had built a causeway from the shore to the sea fortress – thus precipitating its conquest in 332 BC – Meleager treats the place as though it was still entirely surrounded by water. From there, it seems, he just had to hop on to the next island, which was to become the final destination of his life's journey, as we learn from the following poem (and let us not forget that Homer, too, though 'born in Syria,' ended his life on a Greek island of the Aegean, allegedly on Ios).

As Irmgard Männlein-Robert has observed, Meleager's epitaphs are conceived as companion pieces and mutually supplement each other – a technique applied by many Hellenistic epigrammatists, who not only delighted in rewriting poems by other authors, but were also experts in the art of self-variation.[17] While the general matrix remains the same, with almost stereotypical repetition of certain key phrases, each epigram contains a unique bit of autobiographical and poetological information not provided elsewhere in the series.[18] Thus, while talking at length about his old age in the second half of *Anth. Pal.* 7.417, Meleager waits until the following text to reveal where he spent his final years:

> Πρώτα μοι Γαδάρων κλεινὰ πόλις ἔπλετο πάτρα,
>    ἤνδρωσεν δ᾽ ἱερὰ δεξαμένα με Τύρος·
> εἰς γῆρας δ᾽ ὅτ᾽ ἔβην, ἁ καὶ Δία θρεψαμένα Κῶς
>    κἀμὲ θετὸν Μερόπων ἀστὸν ἐγηροτρόφει.
> Μοῦσαι δ᾽ εἰν ὀλίγοις με, τὸν Εὐκράτεω Μελέαγρον
>    παῖδα, Μενιππείοις ἠγλάισαν Χάρισιν.　(*Anth. Pal.* 7.418 = Gow-Page *HE* 3)

(My first hometown was the famous city of Gadara, the next to welcome me was holy Tyre, who turned me into a man. When I had grown old, she who also nurtured Zeus, Kos, fed me – now a citizen of Merope – in old age. And the Muses adorned me, Meleager, son of Eukrates, more than most with the Graces of Menippos.)[19]

The 'Zeus' whom Kos is said to have nurtured is none other than Ptolemy Philadelphos, who was born on the island in 308 BC. This creates an interesting link between Meleager and the Hellenistic ruler, who had done so much for the promotion of Greek culture in Egyptian Alexandria. Remarkable too is the way in which Meleager plays with our readerly expectations: only at the end of the hexameter (3) do we realize that he is talking about Kos, not

Crete, the legendary birthplace of Zeus (the *aprosdoketon* is highlighted not least by the verse's monosyllabic ending). At first we might wonder whether Meleager is offering us yet another alternative version of the god's genesis – the location of Zeus's birth was, after all, disputed, at least in Hellenistic poetry (cf. Kallim. *Hymn* 1.5: γένος ἀμφήριστον)[20] – but in retrospect it should become clear that he is referring to another divinity, the Alexandrian monarch, whom contemporary panegyrists closely associated with the Olympian god[21] – no doubt, a deliberate ambiguity. Such associations must have been encouraged by the king himself, who, in a highly symbolic manner, made the celebrations of his birthday coincide each year with the Basileia, an annual festival in honour of Zeus Basileus.[22]

Meleager, for his part, humorously inscribes himself in the literary tradition concerning Ptolemy's birth, which was, for instance, commemorated by Kallimachos and Theokritos. Prenatal Apollo, in the *Hymn to Delos*, famously tells his pregnant mother Leto not to bear him on Kos, since the island is reserved for the advent of another deity:

οὔτ' οὖν ἐπιμέμφομαι οὐδὲ μεγαίρω
νῆσον, ἐπεὶ λιπαρή τε καὶ εὔβοτος, εἴ νύ τις ἄλλη·
ἀλλά οἱ ἐκ Μοιρέων τις ὀφειλόμενος θεὸς ἄλλος
ἐστί, Σαωτήρων ὕπατον γένος·           (Kallim. *Hymn* 4.163–6)

(I do not blame the island nor do I begrudge her anything, since she is brilliant and rich in pasture as any other. But by will of the Fates another god is owed to her, from the outstanding race of the Saviours.)

This memorable scene might, I submit, have inspired the characterization of Ptolemy as Zeus in Meleager's poem (after all, it only makes sense that little Apollo would have given way to the equivalent of the mightiest god). Significantly, it is up to the reader of Kallimachos's hymn to infer the identity of that ominous θεὸς ἄλλος (just as Meleager's reader has to guess whom exactly he means with Δία in line 3): for over twenty lines Kallimachos does not indicate Ptolemy's name, until Apollo, the prophet-to-be, addresses the yet-to-be-born king as ἐσσόμενε Πτολεμαῖε (Kallim. *Hymn* 4.188). However, by describing him right away as belonging to the 'outstanding race of the Saviours' (166), Kallimachos simultaneously evokes the title of Ptolemy's father and that of Zeus Soter – there can be no doubt that the figures of king and god were strongly intertwined, and Meleager's brief reference reflects precisely this conflation.

Theokritos *Idyll* 17, in turn, relates the story of Ptolemy's birth in the style of a mythic narrative, which features, as one of its actors, personified Kos: after Berenike had borne the child, Kos received him in her arms from his mother (δεξαμένα παρὰ ματρὸς, *Id.* 17.59); upon seeing the baby, she rejoiced (Κόως δ' ὀλόλυξεν ἰδοῖσα, 17.64) and delivered a short speech, wishing that Ptolemy might honour her as much as Apollo had honoured Delos (17.66–70).[23] Meleager, too, has Kos personified, though in his case the island is rather cast in the role of a geriatric nurse (ἐγηροτρόφει, 4). While being largely metaphorical and evocative of inscriptional formulae à la *Mantua me genuit*,[24] the idea of Kos as a nurse playfully connects Meleager's epigram with the full-fledged personification in Theokritos's encomium (note, too, how the participle δεξαμένα that refers to Kos in Theokritos *Id.* 17.59 is used in reference with Tyre at *Anth. Pal.* 7.418.2, the city which *received* Meleager from his hometown Gadara – could this suggest a conscious allusion to Theokritos's account?).

We do not know which biographical circumstances led Meleager to Kos, but in the context of his poetic autobiography the place seems well chosen indeed: through its link with Philadelphos, to which the poet subtly draws our attention, the island appears associated with one of Hellas's new cultural centres, functioning, so to speak, as an intersection between the two worlds, traditional Greece and the broader Hellenistic *oikoumene*. It is noteworthy that Meleager's physical journey towards Greece, which on a metaphorical level symbolizes his intellectual pursuit of true Hellenicity, should end in a sort of liminal space that simultaneously points in both directions and makes Meleager a compatriot of the Alexandrian patron of arts. Though separated by two centuries, the poet and the prince partake in the same cultural-political discourse, the spread of Hellenism outside the geographic boundaries of Greece. Clearly, Meleager wants us to perceive parallels between himself and Ptolemy (the analogy is underlined not least by several verbal correspondences: καὶ Δία (3) ~ κἀμὲ (4), θρεψαμένα (3) ~ ἐγηροτρόφει (4), Κῶς (3) ~ Μερόπων ἀστὸν (4). The two might move in opposite directions (while the king began life in a venerably Greek place and then moved to the periphery, Meleager started out on the margins and moved towards the centre), but the crucial point is that, figuratively speaking, they both travel between the worlds.

Turning to the next epitaph, we may observe that Meleager's three-step 'Hellenization' – from Syria via Phoenicia to Greece – is wittily reflected in the trilingual greeting that he addresses to passers-by at the end of the poem (*Anth. Pal.* 7.419.7–8 = Gow-Page *HE* 4.7–8): ἀλλ' εἰ μὲν Σύρος ἐσσί, «Σαλάμ», εἰ δ' οὖν σύ γε Φοῖνιξ, / «Αὐδονίς», εἰ δ' Ἕλλην, «Χαῖρε», τὸ δ' αὐτὸ φράσον (If you are Syrian, I wish you: 'Salaam'; if you are Phoenician:

'Audonis'; if you are Greek: 'Chaire' – do wish me the same!). True to his cosmopolitan ideology, Meleager imagines here an audience that consists of Greeks and non-Greeks alike and yet is bound together by its common knowledge of the Greek language. For, though saluted in their native tongues, Syrians and Phoenicians are implicitly portrayed as Hellenophone – at least within the fiction of the epigram, which presupposes that they can read the primary language it is written in. The combination of those three 'hellos,' in any case, marvellously iconizes both Meleager's multinational personality and the multicultural (if Hellenophone) character of his imagined readership.[25]

Significantly, while the fiction underlying the epitaph implies that Syrian, Phoenician, and Greek travellers actually pass by Meleager's tomb on Kos, the poet also envisions a dissemination of his texts beyond the tombstone. In *Anth. Pal.* 7.417.7 he says that he wrote the epigram's words on tablets (ἐν δέλτοισι) before his burial, which allows us to picture their 'after-tablet life' in two parallel media: inscribed upon his grave, and written on papyrus. Commonly the δέλτος served as a medium for poetic sketches, before the text's final version was transferred to the papyrus scroll in which it would then circulate (recall, for instance, the scene in Kallimachos's *Aitia* where the young author puts writing tablets on his knees, as he is about to start composing poetry, *Ait.* 1.21–2 Pf.). By characterizing his act of writing upon such tablets as χαράττειν – a verb that is often used with reference to writing upon a hard surface such as stone (cf. LSJ III) – Meleager simultaneously evokes the medium of the tombstone. The expression ἐχάραξα . . . ἐν δέλτοισι thus subtly points to both modes of reception (the one in front of the tomb and the one on the written page),[26] and we are invited to imagine the poems not only fixed at the burial site, but also travelling throughout the *oikoumene* – even back to Gadara and Tyre, where they might greet readers in their native language.

Let us pause here for a brief moment to summarize. Evoking the conventional diction of epigraphic poetry, Meleager's self-epitaphs offer us the kind of information that can be found in countless tombstone inscriptions, both authentic and literary (Who was the deceased? Who were his parents? Where did he come from? What was his profession? Where did he spend his life?); all those seemingly matter-of-fact details, however, are invested with a deeper meaning. On a figurative level, the poet reconfigures the Greek *oikoumene* as an intellectual landscape, in which he moves, in the course of a lifetime, away from the margins towards the centre. At the same time he emphasizes his innate Greekness by relocating Attika at the cultural periphery from where he originated. Meleager thus combines a centripetal with a centrifugal movement (reflected too in Ptolemy's migration from Kos to

Egypt), both of which serve to bridge, if not eliminate, the gulf between the two worlds.

As we have seen, Meleager advocates a cosmopolitan Weltanschauung in order to affiliate himself with the cultural elite. In what follows, I would like to argue that his cosmopolitanism is also in harmony with the *Garland's* overall poetological discourse, which is based on the ideas of blending and entwining, of bringing distinct elements together in a heterogeneous, yet coherent, whole. Meleager has, I suggest, very consciously fashioned for himself a mixed identity that corresponds with the mixed nature of his work. As its title indicates, the anthology is conceived as a στέφανος, a textual wreath in which the poems of numerous authors are woven into one another. The image of the garland, developed at length in the collection's preface (to which we shall return later), is self-reflexively evoked throughout the anthology: again and again Meleager refers to garlands or garland-like objects and has inserted a high number of concrete and figurative *stephanoi* into his *Stephanos*.[27]

What is more, Meleager's self-epitaphs present his entire literary oeuvre – not only the *Garland* – as a sort of mixture. *Anth. Pal.* 7.419 (= Gow-Page *HE* 4), for instance, praises him for having joined 'sweet-crying Eros and the Muses with the cheerful Graces' (ὁ τὸν γλυκύδακρυν Ἔρωτα /καὶ Μούσας ἱλαραῖς συστολίσας Χάρισιν, 3–4). At the end of *Anth. Pal.* 7.421 (= Gow-Page *HE* 5), which contains the description and interpretation of an enigmatic tombstone relief (the epic hero Meleager and his attributes are shown to stand for the homonymous poet and his work), the dead author is addressed as follows: 'greetings to you even among the deceased, since you who have combined Eros's Muse and the Graces into a single learned work' (χαῖρε καὶ ἐν φθιμένοισιν, ἐπεὶ καὶ Μοῦσαν Ἔρωτος[28] / καὶ Χάριτας σοφίαν εἰς μίαν ἡρμόσαο, 13–14). Last but not least, the epitaph series starts with an anonymous epigram, *Anth. Pal.* 7.416, which may or may not be by Meleager himself, but which is doubtlessly in the spirit of the other poems and makes use of the same imagery: Εὐκράτεω Μελέαγρον ἔχω, ξένε, τὸν σὺν Ἔρωτι / καὶ Μούσαις κεράσανθ' ἡδυλόγους Χάριτας (I hold Meleager, the son of Eukrates, stranger, he who has mixed the sweet-speaking Graces with Eros and the Muses). The Graces mentioned in these poems (cf. also *Anth. Pal.* 7.417.4 and 418.6) refer to Meleager's collection of Menippean satires, which bore the title *Charites* (cf. Ath. 4.157b), while Eros and the Muses signify his erotic poetry. As Kathryn Gutzwiller has demonstrated, they furthermore evoke the stylistic quality of χάρις, which can be said to characterize both Meleager's satiric and his epigrammatic oeuvre.[29] Of particular significance in our context is, however, that Meleager's Menippean satires, a prosimetric genre uniting serious and comic elements (*spoudogeloion*), themselves constitute a mixture. Their double nature is, as the speaker of *Anth. Pal.* 7.421 points out, emblematized by the double-edged spear, the ἄμφηκες γέρας (9), of Artemis, which the hero Meleager holds in his hands. But that is not all: according to the exegete of the tombstone relief, the warrior's spear may also refer to the elegiac distich of Meleager's erotic poetry, with its alternation of hexameters and pentameters (Λατῴας δ' ἄμφηκες ἔχεις γέρας ἔς τε γέλωτα / καὶ σπουδὰν καί που μέτρον ἐρωτογράφον; you are holding Artemis's double-edged gift, which stands for laughter and seriousness, and perhaps also for love-poetry's metre, 9–10). Symbolizing the dual nature of both satires and epigrams, the double-edged spear thus turns out to be double-natured itself, that is, interpretable in two different ways.

In view of Meleager's poetological imagery, his self-representation as Graeco-Syrian gains a special meaning. Like his oeuvre, the poet is, it seems, a sort of mixture – and so was his father, whose name can be derived from the adjective εὔκρατος ('well-tempered, well-mixed'). It almost makes you wonder whether Meleager's dad was really called Eukrates (cf. *Anth. Pal.* 7.416.1, 417.3, 418.5, 419.3) – does it not somehow appear too good to be true?[30] In any case, one of the epigrams in book 12 of the *Palatine Anthology* contains an etymological pun on Meleager's own name, which again highlights the composite nature of his personality. In *Anth. Pal.* 12.165 (= Gow-Page *HE* 98) the poet talks of his simultaneous passion for a dark boy and a fair-skinned lad, explaining it as follows:

Λευκανθὴς Κλεόβουλος, ὁ δ' ἀντία τοῦδε μελίχρους
    Σώπολις, οἱ δισσοὶ Κύπριδος ἀνθοφόροι.
τοὔνεκά μοι παίδων ἕπεται πόθος· οἱ γὰρ Ἔρωτες
    πλέξαι κἀκ λευκοῦ φασί με καὶ μέλανος.[31]

(White as a blossom Kleoboulos, and, opposite him, dark-coloured Sopolis – the two flower bearers of Kypris. Here's why I am haunted by a longing for the boys: the Erotes, you see, say they have woven me of black [μέλανος] and of white [λευκοῦ]).

Self-ironically, Meleager claims that he is compelled by his very name to desire boys of light and dark complexion, since it combines in itself the two colours, black (μέλας) and white (ἀργός = λευκός).

Provided we take the personal pronoun με in line 4 as direct object, not as subject of the accusative-with-infinitive construction, Meleager strikingly represents his own self as a wreath woven from black and white flowers. One might object that it would be more natural to see the poet here, as elsewhere, in the role of a garland weaver, not in that of a garland,[32] but, as odd as the image may seem at first sight, I think this is precisely the point of the epigram (though of course we cannot exclude a certain ambiguity). For the idea that the creator of the *Stephanos* is himself a *stephanos* recalls the widespread ancient topos *talis oratio, qualis vita,* which held that an author's very nature was reflected in his works.[33] Could it not be that Meleager playfully suggests such a close correspondence between his psyche and his poetry? If so, it is all the more remarkable that πόθος, the word used to describe the poet-lover's desire in line 3, also denotes a particular kind of garland (Ath. 15.679c–d), which was made from flowers called πόθοι; according to Theophrastos (*Hist. Pl.* 6.8.3), these flowers came in two variants: dark like hyacinths and pale white. What could be more fitting?[34]

Meleager, the 'black-and-white' lover of boys, whose composite name accounts for his dual passion, also, I would like to suggest, associates himself with those two colours in the preface to his anthology. After listing numerous epigrammatists whose poems the reader is about to encounter in the *Garland* – each is identified with a flower or another kind of plant – Meleager characterizes his own writings as πρώιμα λευκόια or 'early growing white violets' (*Anth. Pal.* 4.1.56). At first glance the λευκόιον seems to evoke only one of the two colours: white (λευκός). However, the flower's name might incorporate a hidden reference to its dark counterpart. Ancient authors commonly describe violets as 'black,'[35] and without further qualification ἴον almost exclusively refers to the dark violet.[36] Is the term λευκόιον, then, not a sort of oxymoron that combines black and white in the same manner as *Mele-agros* (though in reverse order)?

Be that as it may, Meleager doubtlessly draws our attention to the composite nature of his name in order to underline the composite nature of his personality (Syrian by birth, Greek in spirit), which, in turn, is reflected in the composite nature of his anthology. By putting together this collection of epigrams, the cosmopolitan poet, who so emphatically declares that we all inhabit *one* world, has, in a way, created a cosmos of his own, one that spans both time and space. The *Garland* is an ideal community of poets brought together into a *single* work (cf. εἰς ἕνα μόχθον, *Anth. Pal.* 12.257.3) by Meleager's editorial activity. Significantly, the inhabitants of this poetic *oikoumene* are not only of the most diverse provenance, but also stem from different ages. However, this too is a cosmos of exclusive inclusivity. At the beginning of the *Garland*'s preface the Muse is asked: Μοῦσα φίλα, τίνι τάνδε φέρεις πάγκαρπον ἀοιδὰν / ἢ τίς ὁ καὶ τεύξας ὑμνοθετᾶν στέφανον (*Anth. Pal.* 4.1.1–2) (Dear Muse, to whom do you bring this song full of fruit? Or who was it that plaited this garland of singers?). She first answers the second question: ἄνυσε μὲν Μελέαγρος· ἀριζάλῳ δὲ Διοκλεῖ /

μναμόσυνον ταύταν ἐξεπόνησε χάριν· (*Anth. Pal.* 4.1.3–4) (Meleager made it: with much effort he created this delightful present as a souvenir for much-admired Diokles). Then she goes on to name the various poetic flowers that were woven into the garland (5–56), and at the very end she provides an answer to the first question:[37] ἀλλὰ φίλοις μὲν ἐμοῖσι φέρω χάριν· ἔστι δὲ μύσταις / κοινὸς ὁ τῶν Μουσέων ἡδυεπὴς στέφανος. (*Anth. Pal.* 4.1.57–8) (I offer this as a gift to my friends – the Muses' sweet-speaking garland is common to all initiates). So it is the literary elite who are granted access to Meleager's universe, not all and sundry (note the emphatic enjambment between μύσταις and κοινός, which underlines the importance of being initiated in the Muses' mysteries).

Though coming from the periphery of the Hellenistic *oikoumene*, Meleager successfully made himself a central figure of Hellas's epigrammatic tradition, thereby proving that cultural refinement is not tied to a specific national identity: one can be Greek without being Greek. By gathering together the poems of numerous authors from different times and combining his own epigrams with theirs, Meleager eliminated the spatial and temporal boundaries that separate him from his poetic predecessors. What unites the members of his community is not their ethnicity, but their affiliation with the Muses. In this sense we too, as readers, are invited to enter the universe constituted by Meleager's sweet-speaking *Garland*. And if we are from Canada – so what?

## Notes

1 My heartful thanks to Peter Bing, Niklas Holzberg, and David Konstan, who have read this essay in various drafts and from whose comments I have benefited a lot.

2 Translations are my own.

3 For the division of Meleager's *Garland* into four books, see Cameron 1993: 19–33 and 49–56 for its date.

4 See Weisshäupl 1889; Radinger 1895; and Wifstrand 1926.

5 See Gutzwiller 1997, and 1998b: 276–322.

6 The section originally contained *Anth. Pal.* 7.406–20, 707–19 (on famous persons; except 711, 717) and 421–9 (enigmatic epitaphs); further poems might have been removed by Kephalas and included in his opening section at the beginning of *Anth. Pal.* 7. See Gutzwiller 1998b: 307–9.

7 For cosmopolitanism in ancient thought, see Baldry 1965; Moles 1996; Long 2008; and Konstan 2009.

8  Plut. *Mor.* 328d5: ἀλλ' Ἀλεξάνδρου τὴν Ἀσίαν ἐξημεροῦντος Ὅμηρος ἦν
ἀνάγνωσμα, Περσῶν καὶ Σουσιανῶν καὶ Γεδρωσίων παῖδες τὰς Εὐριπίδου
καὶ Σοφοκλέους τραγῳδίας ᾖδον. On Alexander's passionate engagement with
Homer (Strabo *Geog.* 13.1.27 fittingly characterizes him as φιλόμηρος), see
Zeitlin 2001: 201–3 and 206.

9  The idea that being Greek is more a matter of the mind than of ethnicity is
already to be found in Isokrates *Paneg.* 50: 'Our city [Athens] has surpassed all
other human beings in thought and speech to such an extent that her disciples
have become teachers of the rest, and she has brought about that the name
"Hellenes" no longer seemed to be tied to race, but to *dianoia* [intelligence,
understanding].' The dissociation of Greek identity from ethnic origin becomes
especially important in the Second Sophistic, where *paideia* is considered one
of the most significant criteria for Greekness; see, e.g., Whitmarsh 2001, esp.
294–303 on Favorinus. For *paideia* in the Second Sophistic, see also Schmitz
1997; and Borg 2004.

10  I am grateful to Peter Bing for calling this passage to my attention.

11  An intriguing artistic representation of this dispute could be seen in the
Homereion at Alexandria, where a statue of Homer was surrounded by figures
of the cities that laid claim on him (cf. Ael. *VH* 13.22). For a list of the places, see
Raddatz 1913: 2190–9; for the various theories regarding Homer's ethnicity, see
Heath 1998.

12  Similarly, the narrator of Lucian's *True Stories* reports that Homer (according to his own testimony) came from Babylon, his real name being Tigranes
(*VH* 2.20) – 'a close neighbor, it now seems, to Lucian's own place of origin in
Syria' (Zeitlin 2001: 246; see now also Kim 2010: 164–8). Kalasiris, the internal narrator of Heliodoros's *Aithiopika*, likewise constructs Homer in his own
image by representing him as Egyptian (3.14.2–4), while the external narrator
Heliodoros emphasizes his non-Greek origin and indicates Phoenician Emesa as
his hometown (10.41.4); see Whitmarsh 1999: 96–7 and 104–6. I am grateful to
Tim Whitmarsh for pointing this parallel out to me.

13  On the epigram, see Bing, chapter 2 in this volume.

14  As Gow-Page observe ad loc., Stadtmüller supposed that Zenodotos borrowed
from Meleager, 'but the imitation, if it exists, may be the other way.'

15  Tyre also features in Meleager's erotic epigrams as home to beautiful boys (see
*Anth. Pal.* 12.59 and 12.114); see Gutzwiller, chapter 3 in this volume.

16  I owe this observation to Peter Bing.

17  Cf. Männlein-Robert 2007b: 372–9. On *variatio* in Hellenistic epigram, see
Tarán 1979; on epigrammatic companion pieces, see Kirstein 2002.

18  Männlein-Robert 2007b: 376: 'im Sinne einer gegenseitigen Ergänzung
geben erst alle Selbstepitaphien Meleagers *zusammen* dem Rezipienten die

autobiographischen und poetologischen Hinweise, die der Autor vermitteln möchte.' She rightly points out that the repetition in vocabulary 'erinnert an den formelhaften Tenor inschriftlicher Selbstepitaphien.'

19 The information on Kos is given in a single line at *Anth. Pal.* 7.419.6: Κῶς δ' ἐρατὴ Μερόπων πρέσβυν ἐγηροτρόφει (note the repetition of Μερόπων and ἐγηροτρόφει in the same *sedes* as in *Anth. Pal.* 7.418.4). Similarly, the bit about Gadara and Tyre is condensed from two lines at *Anth. Pal.* 7.417.1–2 and 418.1–2 into one at *Anth. Pal.* 7.419.5 ὃν θεόπαις ἤνδρωσε Τύρος Γαδάρων θ' ἱερὰ χθών.

20 On Kallimachos's uncertainty about Zeus's birthplace (Crete or Arkadia?) (ἐν δοιῇ μάλα θυμός, Kall. *Hymn* 1.5), see Stephens 2003: 79–96; for the various traditions concerning the god's birth, see Schwabl 1978: 1206–14.

21 For Zeus's association with Ptolemaic rulers (as reflected in Hellenistic poetry and contemporary inscriptions), see Schwabl 1978: 1404–5. On the association of Ptolemy Philadelphos and Zeus in Kallimachos's *Hymn to Zeus* and Theokritos *Idyll* 17, see Stephens 2003: 148–51. In the case of Kallimachos's first hymn, scholars debate, inter alia, whether the real subject of the poem is Zeus, Ptolemy, or both; for a summary of the discussion, see Clauss 1986: 156–7. Stephens 2003: 79 argues that 'the poet himself seems to have induced the reader's aporia by setting up an imaginative field in which fiction, Zeus, Ptolemy, and kingship are effectively intertwined.'

22 See Koenen 1977: 4–7, 29–32, 47–9.

23 For the temporal relation of Kall. *Hymn* 4 and Theokr. *Id.* 17, see Hunter 2003: 5–6.

24 An astonishing parallel to Vergil's epitaph is provided by a Greek inscription from the fifth century BC (*CEG* 77): Σπάρτα μὲν πατρίς ἐστιν, ἐν εὐρυχόροισι <δ'> Ἀθάναις / ἐθράφθε, θανάτο δὲ ἐνθάδε μοῖρ' ἔχιχε. For this analogy and the reception of Vergil's epitaph in Latin sepulchral epigram (both literary and inscriptional), see Frings 1998.

25 According to Aulius Gellius, the Roman poet Ennius also envisioned himself as trilingual and thus standing at the crossroads of three cultures: *Quintus Ennius tria cordia habere sese dicebat, quod loqui Graece et Osce et Latine sciret* (Quintus Ennius used to say that he had three hearts, because he could speak Greek, Oscan and Latin, *NA* 17.17.1). Remarkably, the Roman world is almost completely excluded from Meleager's poetic universe, except for one reference to a Ῥωμαϊκὴ λοπάς in *Anth. Pal.* 12.95.10, for which see Gutzwiller, chapter 3 in this volume.

26 See Männlein-Robert 2007b: 374.

27 See Höschele 2010: 172–94. See also Bing (1988: 33–4) on the coronis poem (*Anth. Pal.* 12.257); and Guichard 2000.

28 I am following the text of Page (1975), who reads Ἔρωτος instead of the transmitted Ἔρωτι.

29  See Gutzwiller 1998a: 87; and Männlein-Robert 2007a: 245.
30  Could there be an additional pun relating Eukrates and Oineus, the father of the mythological hero Meleager (*Anth. Pal.* 7.421.11), whose name suggests the Greek word for wine (οἶνος)?
31  For the reading of line 4, cf. Gow-Page ad loc.
32  Thus, e.g., Gutzwiller 1997: 194n48.
33  On this topos, see Möller 2004. For Meleager's metamorphosis into a garland, see Höschele 2010: 176–84.
34  This was first observed by Pedzopoulos 1931: 172–3. Gutzwiller 1997: 195, taking Meleager as subject, states: 'A garland called πόθος made from the flowers called πόθος would, one assumes, consist of blossoms both light and dark, Meleager's πόθος is not only, then, his desire for boys, whether light or dark, but also the variegated garland he is compelled by his own name to weave from them – meaning of course the epigrammatic poetry he writes about them.'
35  See, e.g., Theok. *Id.* 10.28 (καὶ τὸ ἴον μέλαν ἐντὶ) and *Anth. Pal.* 4.1.21 (ἴον μέλαν).
36  According to LSJ, the only exception is Theophr. *Hist. Pl.* 6.8.1.
37  For the two lines as part of the Muse's speech, see Bornmann 1973 and 1975.

# 2

# Invective from the Cultural Periphery: The Case of Hermeias of Kourion[1]

## PETER BING

The reputation of Hermeias of Kourion hangs on a slender thread: his work survives in only a single fragment, a mere five choliambic lines preserved by Athenaios from a work entitled *Iambi*. Perhaps we can attribute to him a further single line in cretic-paeonics (*Suppl. Hell.* 484), which is cited by Hephaistion as being by a certain Hermeias. As there is no indication of ethnicity, however, we cannot be sure. No one else breathes a word about Hermeias. We know nothing of his life, such as his parentage, dates, education, career, titles of other works.[2] Still, amongst the vestiges of ancient Cypriot poetry, a five-line fragment is no small thing. Indeed, it counts as an important remnant, and we must mine it for whatever it can tell us about Hellenistic literary culture on this island – an island damned by P.M. Fraser as 'conspicuous' for its 'poverty . . . in intellectual matters' (1972: I.307, cf. also 620). Was Cyprus, then, an isolated cultural backwater? That is the question we should keep in mind as we look at this poet's remains.

In fact, the five choliambic lines tell us a good deal about Hermeias's qualities as a poet, and they certainly contain clues about the time in which he lived, his education, and awareness of the iambographic tradition. The fragment is a fierce attack on Stoics and, in all likelihood, also on their founder, his fellow Cypriot Zeno of Kition. Its *terminus post quem* is thus the foundation of the Stoic school by Zeno around 300 BC. How long thereafter should we date it? Only detailed analysis of the fragment will help us approximate the answer. I cite it here along with its context in Athenaios:[3]

ὁ Μυρτίλος κᾆτα ἀποβλέψας εἰς τοὺς τὰ τῆς στος αἱρουμένους
τὰ Ἑρμείου τοῦ Κουριέως ἐκ τῶν Ἰάμβων προειπών·

Ἀκούσατ', ὦ Στύακες, ἔμποροι λήρου,
λόγων ὑποκριτῆρες, οἳ μόνοι πάντα
τὰν τοῖς πίναξι, πρίν τι τῷ σοφῷ δοῦναι,
αὐτοὶ καταρροφεῖτε, κᾆθ' ἁλίσκεσθε
ἐναντία πρήσσοντες οἷς τραγῳδεῖτε.          5

παιδοπῖπαι ὄντες καὶ τοῦτο μόνον ἐζηλωκότες τὸν ἀρχηγὸν ὑμῶν τῆς σοφίας
Ζήνωνα τὸν Φοίνικα, ὃς οὐδέποτε γυναικὶ ἐχρήσατο, παιδικοῖς δ' αἰεί, ὡς
Ἀντίγονος ὁ Καρύστιος ἱστορεῖ ἐν τῷ περὶ τοῦ βίου αὐτοῦ. (13.563d–e)

(p. 117 Wilamowitz)

1 στόακες A ; στοίακες E: τοὺς στωικοὺς στύακας λέγει CE Epitomes
2 ὑποκρητῆρες A, corr. Mus.
3 πρινὴ A, corr. Pors.

Myrtilos then looked towards those who hold to the principles of the Stoa and recited lines from the *Iambi* of Hermeias of Kourion:

Listen, you bulging Stoic pricks [or: Screwics],[4] merchants of drivel,
hypocritical windbags, who all by yourselves
snatch whatever's on the platters, before giving a crumb to the wise man,
and gulp it down; and after that you're caught in the act,
doing just the opposite of what you pompously proclaim

since you are oglers of boys, and in this alone you ape your wisdom's founding father, Zeno the Phoenician, who never resorted to women, but always boys, as Antigonos of Karystos states in his Life of him.

First let us look at the poem's metre. It is the choliamb (or skazon) – that is, the 'limping iamb' – a type of verse especially associated with the mid-sixth-century iambographer Hipponax. The metre varies the traditional iambic trimeter by having each line drag to a close usually with three long syllables. Martin West (1982: 41) called this a 'deliberate metrical ribaldry, in keeping with the studied vulgarity' of the iambographer. As Arnd Kerkhecker (1999: 7) notes: 'Early in the third century . . . after a period of almost complete obscurity, there is a sudden burst of Hipponactean verse, a choliambic craze.' Third-century practitioners include Kallimachos, Phoinix of Kolophon, Parmeno of Byzantion, Herodas, and Kerkidas of Megalopolis.

It is, of course, dangerous to draw far-reaching conclusions from only five lines, but Hermeias's metrical style appears most closely to resemble that of Kallimachos's choliambs. Like most Hipponactean, and *all* Kallimachean, choliambs, Hermeias has short third anceps throughout. This means that there are no ischiorrhogic endings – – – – –‖, that is, lines ending with five longs in a row. Further, it does away with the need to observe Porson's Bridge, as there is never a long third anceps requiring a word end. Beyond this, Hermeias's five lines contain no resolution. This is something with which Kallimachos is likewise very sparing (West 1974: 116 and 1982: 161). Archilochos and Hipponax, by contrast, exhibit one instance per eleven lines. Turning to another criterion, syllables preceding *muta cum liquida*, the two instances in Hermeias (ὑποκριτῆρες, line 2, and πίναξι, line 3) are equivocal but do not contradict the metrical habits of Hipponax and Kallimachos. The long omicron in ὑποκριτῆρες tells us nothing, since lengthening the vowel within a word is normal in *iambos* (West 1974: 114). However, the final iota of πίναξι (line 3) may be read as short,[5] and thus may point towards specifically Hipponactean practice. For while Archilochos and Semonides consistently make the final syllable preceding *muta cum liquida* long, Hipponax can go either way (West 1974: 113–14). The same holds true for Kallimachos (West 1982: 161).

In all, then, from what we can see of his technique, Hermeias is no dilettant. He is rather an exponent of that meticulous and strictly regular Hellenistic choliamb found also in Kallimachos – one that turns a recognizable tendency in its archaic model into a steadfast rule. From this metrical standpoint, at least, he fits perfectly into that third-century BC revival of Hipponax mentioned before. The second possible fragment of Hermeias (*Suppl. Hell.* 484), a single line composed in apparently stichic cretic-paeonics, likewise allows us to locate him comfortably in the context of early Hellenistic metrical exploration. For it is comparable to verses written by Simias of Rhodes (frs. 13–15 Powell, *Coll. Alex.*), a well-known metrical experimenter in stichic forms, who flourished around 300 BC.[6]

Hermeias's painstaking metrical artistry is consistent with what we can glean from his subject matter and diction as well. This is a poet who knows his archaic exemplar, and is well versed in conventions of the genre. In denouncing the Stoics he makes use of the iambographer's typical stock in trade: food, sex, money – these are the main lines of attack.

To be sure, these traditional vehicles of attack were not deployed in archaic *iambos* to insult *philosophers*, who did not even exist then as a meaningful category. It was Comedy, above all, that adopted the conventions of earlier *iambos* (Rosen 1988) and turned them against philosophers (among many others). These remained a favoured comic target well into the Hellenistic era, and were attacked on traditional thematic lines, like those set out before.[7] G.E.L. Owen (1983: 15–19) has shown, further, how the conventions of verbal assault were absorbed from Comedy, in turn, by the orators of the fourth century BC, and thence made their way into 'philosophical invective,' the ruthless slander of philosophers by other philosophers (or by their pamphleteering students). By Hellenistic times, philosophers are targeted in a variety of poetic genres beside Comedy – in Timon of Phlios's hexametric *Silloi*, for instance, or in the *Chreiai* of Machon. By adopting the choliambic pose of Hipponax, Hermeias of Kourion returns the traditional modes of attack to their ur-genre, and commandeers the philosopher as a new butt of specifically iambic scorn. New era, new target – the vehicle, however, remains the same.[8]

Before turning to his themes of food, sex, and money, Hermeias begins with the attention-grabbing imperative 'listen!' (Ἀκούσατ'). This lands us at once within the well-known territory of iambic invective. The directive to 'listen' is found already in Archilochos (ὦ λιπερνῆτες πολῖται, τἀμὰ δὴ συνίετε / ῥήματα, fr. 109 W). Sousarion of Megara in the sixth century BC begins an *iambos* (1 W) with the words: 'Listen up, O people! Sousarion is telling you these things' (Ἀκούετε λεῴ· Σουσαρίων λέγει τάδε). Ἀκούετε λεῴ was a standard way of beginning proclamations (cf. at Athens Ar. *Ach.* 1000, *Pax* 551, *Av.* 448). The parallel is instructive, as it reveals an important aspect of the iambic poet's persona. His manner commands attention; his voice carries moral authority and a message – like a herald's.

Hellenistic poets of *iambos* adopt that same pose. Phoenix of Kolophon, for instance, has his dead but feisty iambic character Ninus announce to all who pass that they must 'listen . . . for really I am making a proclamation as a herald' (ἄκουσον . . . / . . . οὐ γὰρ ἀλλὰ κηρύσσω, fr. 1.13–15). Kallimachos's *Iambi* are full of commands to 'listen.'[9] The most striking comes at the start of the first *Iambos* (fr. 191.1), which begins: 'Listen to Hipponax' (Ἀκούσατ' Ἱππώνακτος). Placed in the mouth of the original choliambic poet, the command has particular authority. It is striking that Hermeias shares with Kallimachos the aorist plural (coupled with elision, moreover). We find it only in these two iambographers, and I suspect the one inspired the other. But who influenced whom?[10] There may be a clue in Hermeias's use of the name Στοίαξ or Στύαξ (rather than the later frequent Στωικός), a comic-slangy coinage in the morphologically uncommon -αξ suffix, expressing contempt.[11] This derisory name may provide a clue: could it be that, coming just after their shared initial Ἀκούσατ', it might recall at some level Kallimachos's Ἱππών-αξ'? If so, that might argue for Kallimachos's priority, since Hipponax is essential to the overall conception of his first *Iambos*, while Hermeias could just as well have called his Stoics something else.[12]

Following the command to 'listen,' Hermeias turns to the three themes I mentioned before: money, food, and sex. With regard to the first, he sets his sights on a common target of abuse in Hellenistic *iambos*: avarice.[13] He mocks the Stoics in line one as ἔμποροι, 'traffickers' or 'merchants' playing on the long-standing Greek 'equation of trade with deceit' (Kurke 1999: 74). Merchants always arouse suspicion. The fact that what these merchants traffic in is λῆρος, 'drivel,' only proves their dishonesty: they seek profit by purveying a worthless commodity.[14] The stench of fraud grows stronger with the following appositive phrase, λόγων ὑποκριτῆρες (2). For these merchants are not just ὑποκριτῆρες in the sense of 'declaimers'; they are (with a different nuance) 'dissemblers' of *logoi*. This makes their trafficking the more outrageous.[15] Framed thus as deceptive mountebanks,[16] driven by greed, and dishonestly bent on merchandising drivel (dressed up though it is as knowledge), they naturally provoke the indignation of the iambographer – a post-Platonic iambographer, we should add, who clearly builds here on Plato's scathing dissection of the particular type of acquisitive art (κτητικὴ τέχνη) practiced by the Sophist: ψυχεμπορική and μαθηματοπωλική (*Soph.* 224, et passim).

Next comes food: in lines 2–4 Hermeias attacks their gluttony – another traditional theme. Already in archaic poetry Hesiod's bantering Muses insulted herdsmen as 'mere bellies' (*Theog.* 26). Hipponax, too (fr. 128 W), derides an enemy for eating οὐ κατὰ κόσμον, sucking down food like Charybdis, without even bothering to cut it (τὴν ποντοχάρυβδιν, /τὴν ἐγγαστριμάχαιραν, line 1–2). And similarly, Archilochos (fr. 124b.4–5 W) rebukes an addressee by saying 'your belly led astray your mind and wits to shamelessness' (ἀλλά σεο γαστὴρ νόον τε καὶ φρένας παρήγαγεν / εἰς ἀναιδείην.). Not surprisingly, the verb 'to gulp down' in line 4 of Hermeias (καταρροφέω) appears already in Hipponax, in the simplex form ῥυφεῖν (fr. 165 W = 175 Degani, cited in Photios' *Lexikon* 2. 137 ῥυφεῖν· τὸ ῥοφεῖν Ἴωνες· οὕτως Ἱππῶναξ). Hermeias knows his source.

The accusation in lines 2–4 that Stoics by themselves gobble down everything on the platters before the wise man can get his portion recalls a similar insult in Kallimachos's first *Iambos* (fr. 191.27). There, Hipponax compares himself to a sacrificer, and the crowd of Alexandrian scholars to Delphians coming from the sacrifice; the latter make off with all the meat, leaving nothing at all for him. The *Scholia Florentina* explain this verse by referring to the story of another master of invective, Aesop. He is said to have criticized the Delphians for their greed in snatching all the sacrificial meat, and for his pains was chased over a cliff and to his death (cf. Schol. Flor. *ad* Kall. fr. 191.27, and *POxy* 1800, fr. 2, col.2, 32ff. = Testimonium 25 Perry p.221).[17] Did Hermeias deliberately evoke this situation here? If so, we must wonder about the force of the definite article in the phrase πρίν τι τῷ σοφῷ δοῦναι (v.3). It may be 'generic,' referring to any *sophos* such as the iambic speaker/poet. It may, on the other hand, be 'particular' and refer to a definite individual (Smyth 1956: nos. 1119–21). In that case, does 'that well-known wise man' specifically recall Aesop?

The final theme is sex: As Benjamin Acosta-Hughes (2002: 248) has put it, attacking sexual misconduct is a 'traditional iambic strategy,' and its use 'in the Hellenistic period is pre-figured by the censure of Bupalus and Arete, and Neoboule and Lycambes in the poetry of Hipponax and Archilochus.'[18] The theme appears already in line 1 if we read Στύακες, as epitomes C and E suggest (τοὺς στωικοὺς στύακας λέγει), rather than Στοίακες of E, or the unmetrical στόακες of A, which Dindorf corrected to Στώακες.[19] I believe that Στύακες is correct, first of all because it is clearly *lectio difficilior*. A witty coinage based on στύω, to stiffen or get an erection,[20] Στύακες is a pointedly obscene pun on Στωικοί or Στοίακες that exploits the derogatory tone of its -αξ suffix (cf. note 11 above). Moreover, it humorously anticipates the allegation that they are παιδοπῖπαι. Hermeias was of course not the only iambographer to attack pederastic misconduct among the Stoics. In the last quarter of the third century BC, Kerkidas of Megalopolis was clear in his condemnation (fr. 6 Livrea).[21] But Hermeias here cleverly turns the very *name* of the Stoics into a rebuke.[22]

Sex returns as a theme at the end of the fragment. After their filling meal, what better pastime than to gratify another appetite? That is the point of κᾆθ' (4) – it lays bare the conventional sequence (first food, then sex), followed even by the Stoics, who hypocritically proclaim their temperance even as they indulge their lusts. To be sure, the surviving lines 4 and 5 do not mention sex explicitly. But the word immediately following in Athenaios's text almost certainly came from the poem. It is the hapax παιδοπίπης. This pointedly and learnedly varies a Homeric hapax, παρθενοπίπης (*Il.* 11.385), with which Diomedes insults Paris in good iambic fashion, after the latter has struck him in the foot with an arrow.[23] For Hermeias, παιδοπίπης thus specifies the particular transgression in which the Stoics have been caught: they are seducers of boys.

The learned coinage highlights another stylistic trait that links Hermeias with Hipponax: his striking use of neologism.[24] In addition to παιδοπίπης, there is Στύαξ or Στοίαξ in verse 1 (rather than Στωικός), and ὑποκριτήρ in line 2 (replacing the common ὑποκριτής). Here again – as with considerations of metre, style, and subject matter – we find that Hermeias fits well with what we otherwise know of the early Hellenistic choliambic revival. A date in the third century BC, such as has been proposed by most scholars (though without real argument), appears justified.[25]

Given that παιδοπῖπαι plausibly comes from our poem, may we see in the remainder of Athenaios's sentence a paraphrase of its further content, and find traces of its diction? A.D. Knox (1929: 274–5) certainly thought so, ingeniously reconstructing 3+ additional choliambic lines:[26]

ὡς παιδοπῖπαί τ' ἐστὲ καὶ μόνον τοῦτο
Ζήνωνα τὸν Φοίνικα ἐοίκατε ζηλοῦν
ὃς οὐδ' ὄναρ γυναικί, παιδικοῖς δ' αἰεί
ἐχρήσατ'.

I would not go so far as Knox. But I do consider it likely that Athenaios provides some inkling of how Hermeias's poem went on, particularly in its mention of biographical details from the life of Zeno. Some part of this information was, as Athenaios reports, available in Antigonos of Karystus's *Life of Zeno*. But which part is unclear – perhaps just the detail about Zeno's exclusive interest in boys, that is, the content of the relative clause, ὃς οὐδέποτε γυναικὶ ἐχρήσατο, παιδικοῖς δ' ἀεί. In view, however, of Antigonos's date in the latter part of the third century BC, I wonder whether this *Life* might not have been a source of Hermeias's information. Hermeias was a learned poet, as we have seen, and it would not be out of character for him to have mined a prose source for material (on this topic see Bing 1993).

Hellenistic tradition about Zeno's teaching on sexual matters falls into two opposing strands. On the one hand, Zeno's conception of Eros is presented as a model of temperance and restraint: it prepares the way for friendship, concord, and even liberty (Ath. 13.561c–d = *SVF* 1.61). On the other, Zeno adopted in his early writings many doctrines of the Cynics, which later Stoics, among others, found shocking and tried to purge from the master's writings. These included a blithe rejection of traditional sexual morality: marriage, for instance, was to be abandoned in favour of purely carnal relations between the sexes (Diog. Laert. 7. 131); incest might be permissible; men should take male lovers who are willing, but use force on those who are not.[27]

As far as our passage from Athenaios is concerned, biographical anecdote supplants doxography in the manner typical of early Hellenistic antiquarian scholarship.[28] That is, Zeno's *teachings* about sex are presented in terms of *who he was* and *how he lived his life*. One biographical strand stressed his sober indifference to physical pleasure or pain. It became proverbial to call someone 'more temperate than Zeno the philosopher' (Diog. Laert. 7. 27).[29] Interestingly, this more hagiographic view of Zeno tends to displace any questionable behaviour onto his sidekick (or low-born doppelgänger), his pupil/slave Persaios, also from Kition (cf. Ath. 13. 607a–e, Diog. Laert. 7.36, Ath. 4. 162b–e). The other biographical approach was more disparaging, and I believe we see it at work in two features of our passage: 1) the reference to Zeno's sexual inclinations and 2) the mention of his ethnicity.

To be sure, the passage from Athenaios distinguishes Zeno's behaviour from that of his outrageous Stoic followers denounced by Hermeias. But the compliment is backhanded, for it still shines a harsh light on his carnal predilections. The euphemistic verb in the clause οὐδέποτε γυναικὶ ἐχρήσατο, παιδικοῖς δ'ἀεί makes it clear that what's at issue here is sex, not ennobling friendship. Such a sentiment seems to me entirely at home in the context of iambic attack, and I think it plausible to see it as reflecting something present in Hermeias's poem.

The second biographical feature is Zeno's Phoenician ethnicity. On a purely factual level this has some basis. As Diogenes Laertios points out, and as has been abundantly confirmed by archaeology, Zeno's hometown of Kition was settled by Phoenicians (Κιτιεὺς ἀπὸ Κύπρου, πολίσματος Ἑλληνικοῦ Φοίνικας ἐποίκους ἐσχηκότος, 7.1). To be called a Phoenician, however, was not considered praise. The biographical tradition about Zeno makes that very clear.

Right from the start, Zeno is assigned stereotypically Phoenician traits. According to Diogenes Laertios, he came to Athens from Phoenicia transporting a shipload of dye (7.2). That is, he is assimilated to the conventional view of Phoenicians as they already appear in Homer's *Odyssey* as skilled sailors and shrewd merchants. They are also, of course, deceitful and rapacious adventurers, against whom one must guard one's wife and children.[30] Significantly, in Diogenes Laertios it is usually *others* who refer to Zeno as Phoenician, and they do so in a derogatory manner. Polemo, for instance, charges him with slipping into his lectures, stealing arguments and dressing them up in Phoenician fashion to conceal them, (οὐ λανθάνεις, ὦ Ζήνων, ταῖς κηπαίαις παρεισρέων θύραις καὶ τὰ δόγματα κλέπτων Φοινικικῶς μεταμφιεννύς, 7. 25). In other words, he accuses Zeno of thievish Phoenician guile. In another anecdote, his teacher, Krates, makes him walk about with a pot of lentils so as to cure his excessive fastidiousness. When Krates smashes the pot, and sees how Zeno flees in humiliation as its contents drip all over him, he calls after him: 'Why run away, my little Phoenician (Φοινικίδιον, 7.)? Nothing terrible has befallen you.' The belittling diminutive combined with the ethnic slur evidently mocks Zeno's fussy Phoenician refinement. Most tellingly, Diogenes Laertios cites a sepulchral epigram on Zeno, by Zenodotos the Stoic, which ends with the couplet, 'and if your native land is Phoenicia, who can begrudge it? Wasn't Kadmos from there too, from whom Greece acquired the written word?' (εἰ δὲ πάτρα Φοίνισσα, τίς ὁ φθόνος; οὐ καὶ ὁ Κάδμος /κεῖνος, ἀφ' οὗ γραπτὰν Ἑλλὰς ἔχει σελίδα; 7. 30 = *Anth. Pal.* 7. 117.5–6 = 1. 5–6 Gow-Page *GP*). We find the same derogatory connotation already in a third-century BC poet: Timon of Phlios in his *Silloi* portrayed Zeno as 'an old Phoenician woman . . . greedy for everything' (καὶ Φοίνισσαν ἴδον λιχνόγραυν, fr. 38.1 Di Marco = Diog. Laert. 7. 15). As Massimo Di Marco comments on this passage, the mention of his origin is intended to denigrate Zeno as a non-Greek.[31] Similarly, in a fragment from the *Galatai* by Hermeias's fellow Cypriot, the early third-century BC comic poet Sopater of Paphos,[32] a speaker mocks Stoic hypocrisy by asserting that he will put to the test their claims of self-control by roasting them: 'then, if I see one of you during the roasting so much as twitch his leg, he shall be sold to a Zenonian master for export, as being ignorant of wisdom' (εἶτ' ἐὰν ὀπτωμένων / ἴδω τιν' ὑμῶν συσπάσαντα τὸ σκέλος, / Ζηνωνικῷ πραθήσεθ' οὗτος κυρίῳ /ἐπ' ἐξαγωγῇ, τὴν φρόνησιν ἀγνοῶν, lines 10–13). Though the word 'Phoenician' does not appear here, the reference to Zeno evidently plays on the stereotype of his Phoenician ethnicity, for he is pictured as a ruthless merchant engaged in the slave trade. Those who fail to meet the Stoic standard will be sold abroad as slaves by someone like Zeno.[33]

By contrast, Antigonos of Karystos (in Diog. Laert. 7.12) relates that Zeno himself insisted on his identity as Kitian, which is what he called himself; *others* call him Phoenician: 'for when he was one of those who contributed to the restoration of the baths and his name was inscribed upon the pillar as "Zeno the philosopher," he requested that the words "of Kition" should be added' (τῶν γὰρ εἰς τὴν ἐπισκευὴν τοῦ λουτρῶνος συμβαλλομένων εἰς ὢν καὶ ἀναγραφόμενος ἐν τῇ στήλῃ, 'Ζήνωνος τοῦ φιλοσόφου,' ἠξίωσε καὶ τὸ Κιτιεὺς προστεθῆναι).

In all, then, calling Zeno a 'Phoenician' is an insult, and thus fitting for an iambic poem. I think it likely that Hermeias used it. If so, it would have been more pointed coming from a fellow Cypriot.[34] Perhaps it was a Cypriot audience as well that would best have appreciated the slight.

This brings us to a final, and particularly pressing, question in any discussion of Cypriot poetry. Did it develop in a Cypriot milieu, or not? And to what extent was it intended for local consumption? In looking at Hermeias, for instance, and recalling his cosmopolitan awareness of literary models and metrical nicety, should we consider him a home-grown phenomenon, whose training occurred locally, and whose audience was largely indigenous? Or was he, like so many eminent figures of Cypriot origin in the early Hellenistic period (including Zeno), one of those who sought a more conducive setting abroad in which both to learn and ply his trade? In pre-Hellenistic times, Cypriot ambition in the domain of literary culture is certainly evident in Nikokles's patronage of Isokrates (n.b. how the orator highlights the choral and musical performances, as well as athletic competitions that Nikokles staged in honour of his dead father Evagoras, *Evag.* 9.1), or the notice that Aristotle addressed his *Protreptikos* to 'Themison, king of the Cypriots' (Stob. 4.32.21). But both these works are ultimately aimed at a non-Cypriot readership, for Cypriot kings took pains to project their power, and nurture their prestige, on the Greek mainland. Nikokreon, king of Salamis between 332/331 and 311/310, for instance, pursues such a cultural policy in making repeated donations of Cypriot bronze for forging the shield that served as prize at the Argive Heraia. In return the Argives erected a statue of the king at Argos, whose epigram (*CEG* 812), spoken in the voice of the monarch himself, stresses both Nikokreon's Argive descent from Aiakos and his Cypriot upbringing.[35] Thus, in the form of this statue, a representative of Cyprus would forever after be present at one of the most venerable Greek festivals.[36] Yet despite such attempts at cultural promotion, signs of an indigenous literary scene in Cyprus are remarkably few. That is particularly so in the early Ptolemaic period on Cyprus, following the island's conquest by Ptolemy I in 295/294 and on into the first half of the second century BC.[37] The question remains thus with regard to Hermeias as well as others: should we speak of Hellenism in Cyprus, or rather of the Hellenism of those *from* Cyprus? Or was there some mixture of the two?

## Notes

1  I am grateful to Profs Marco Fantuzzi, Maria Noussia, Jon Bruss, Charles Fuqua, and Martyn Smith for their comments and criticism on earlier drafts of this paper. Above all, I wish to thank Prof. Ioannis Taifakos for drawing my attention to Hermeias of Kourion in the first place.

2  Given the near total lack of data, it is perhaps not surprising that the one scholarly article listed in *L'Année Philologique* as devoted to our fragment describes its author as 'the Cretan Hermeias'; see Redondo 1993: 167.

3  The quotation comes in a section (starting at 561a) in which philosophers present at the party debate the usefulness of Eros as well as its dangers. It opens with Pontianos's statement that Zeno of Kition considered Eros a positive force, a god of friendship, concord, and liberty, as well as one who contributed to the safety of the state. The discussion moves on, however, by acknowledging that Eros can be either good or bad (562 a ff.).

4  'Screwics' is my attempt to render Hermeias's obscene play on 'Stoics,' Στύακες, from στύω, to stiffen or get an erection. For the implications of the name in this poem, and within the iambographic context, cf. p. 38 and below.

5  While there is no certainty of this, I would argue that the syntactic break at the caesura before the πρίν-clause makes it unlikely that the final syllable of πίναξι would have run into the following word. Note that in Hipponax fr. 176, the only

instance in this poet of *muta cum liquida* following caesura, the preceding final syllable is scanned short.

6 Cf. West (1982: 145), who makes the interesting observation that Simias 'kept his metra distinct by word division. This really belongs under the heading book lyric. But the poem of Hermeias (of Kourion? *Suppl. Hell.* 484) in which the metra were not grouped together in regular systems might have been sung on a public occasion.'

7 Weiher 1913; Webster 1970: 110–12; Gallo 1981: ch. 1, 'Filosofi e Filosofia nella Commedia Ellenistica: Batone,' esp. 64–7.

8 Cf. Kallimachos in *Iambos* 1, where Hipponax similarly deploys traditional *iambos* against new and different targets: φέρων ἴαμβον οὐ μάχην ἀείδοντα /τὴν Βουπάλειον (fr. 191.3–4). For Kallimachos as largely maintaining the conventions of archaic *iambos* in the context of his new era, see Rosen 2007: 172–206.

9 Cf. fr. 194.6 (ἄκουε δὴ τὸν αἶνον) fr. 195.1–2 (᾿Ω ξεῖνε – συμβουλὴ | ι γὰρ ἔν τι τῶν ἱρων – / ἄκουε τἀπὸ καρῳ δ|[ίης), and possibly fr. 203.25.

10 On the great uncertainty regarding the date of Kallimachos's *Iambi*, see Kerkhecker 1999: 283n72.

11 See Buck and Petersen (1945: 614–15): 'the suffix in Attic slang, almost always with a deteriorative shade ... its development in this direction clearly belongs to popular speech as represented in comedy.'

12 If this line of argumentation is correct, it would confirm in a more direct manner the Kallimachean influence we previously detected in the metre.

13 See Kall. fr. 222, and fr. 202.58–67.

14 Already Solon condemns the pursuit of unjust profit in his elegy to the Muses (13.7–8, 11–13 W): χρήματα δ' ἱμείρω μὲν ἔχειν, ἀδίκως δὲ πεπᾶσθαι / οὐκ ἐθέλω· πάντως ὕστερον ἦλθε δίκη. / ... ὃν δ' [scil. πλοῦτον] ἄνδρες τιμῶσιν ὑφ' ὕβριος, οὐ κατὰ κόσμον / ἔρχεται, ἀλλ' ἀδίκοις ἔργμασι πειθόμενος / οὐκ ἐθέλων ἔπεται, ταχέως δ' ἀναμίσγεται ἄτηι. See also his description of the merchant in lines 43–6.

15 The rare form ὑποκριτήρ instead of ὑποκριτής (cf. LSJ s.v.) adds a humorously pompous tone, since the suffix in-τήρ is normally 'restricted to cult or solemn words,' thus Redondo (1993: 168), citing Chantraine 1933: 325. Redondo tries to defend the transmitted text, ὑποκρητῆρες, but leaves his readers in the dark as to what he thinks it means.

16 In using this term, I am thinking not just of the medicine-show connotations of ὑποκριτῆρες, but of τραγῳδεῖτε in line 5.

17 More generically, the situation resembles that in *Odyssey* 1.132–45, where Telemachos brings the disguised Athena apart from the ravenous suitors, and serves her alone.

18 For the theme in Kallimachos, cf. esp. *Iambos* 5.

19 Among modern editors, Kaibel and Knox print στοίακες; Powell Dindorf's correction of στόακες to στώακες, and Gulick στύακες.

20 Henderson (1975: 112) notes that Comedy plays on στύειν precisely in names, as here, e.g., in Euboulos's Ἄστυτοι, 'the limp ones,'or Ἀστυάναξ γέγονα CA 744.

21 See Livrea (1986: 140–58), according to whom the poem is a critique of *some* Stoics who lead boys astray, but contrasts these with the good example of Zeno (cf. 6b.8–9 τ[οῦτ'][ἐ]στὶ ποτ' ἄρσενας ἄρσ[ην,/ τοῦτ' ἔ[ρ]ως Ζανωνικός.). For third-century attacks on Stoic pederasty in a related poetic genre, see Timon of Phlios, *Silloi* frs. 65–6, with commentary in Di Marco 1989: 263–8.

22 Whether we read Στοίακες or Στύακες, the word has important implications for the history of Stoicism. If, as style and versification suggest, we should date Hermeias to the third century BC, then this would be a *very* early use of the term 'Stoic'to describe members of the philosophical school. That is even more the case if we read Στύακες since, as a play on words, it assumes familiarity with the concept of a 'Stoic.' So far as I can see, the earliest occurrence of the word Στωικός meaning a 'Stoic' apart from Hermeias is in Kerkidas (fr. 6a.4 Livrea). Philodemos is the earliest cited in LSJ for ἡ στοά in the sense of the philosophical school. It is possible, then, that Hermeias is our earliest surviving reference to the term 'Stoic.'

23 Note also that at *Od.* 19.67 Penelope's serving woman, Melantho, scolds the disguised Odysseus, asking him if he will still wander around the house and 'spy on the women' (ὀπιπεύσεις δὲ γυναῖκας).

24 For such neologisms as typical of iambographers, cf. Williams (2006: 351), who sees 'extravagant coinages' in 'the iambic tradition generally.'

25 Thus Maas 1912; Kerkhecker 1999: 7; Canfora 2001: 1423n4. More cautiously, Gerhard 1909: 212: 'Sein Leben fällt frühestens ins dritte Jahrhundert: ob erst gleichzeitig mit Chrysippos (Bernhardy, Grundr. II 1² 1856 S.476), bleibt ungewiss'; see also Di Marco 1998.

26 This may be found in the Loeb edition of *Theophrastus Characters, Herodes, Cercidas and the Choliambic Poets*. It was retained in the 1993 revision, but Kerkidas and the Choliambic poets are now being segregated into a separate volume.

27 These last elements of Stoic behaviour come from Philodemos's polemical tract *de Stoicis* 7 (Dorandi), in which he describes without distinction the views of Diogenes and Zeno in their respective *Politeiai*: παραχρῆσθαι τοῖς ἄρ | [ρεσιν οἳ] κἂν ἐρῶνται, κἄμ μὴ καὶ | [οἷοί] τε [ὦσι] ἀσμένως ἐπιδιδό | [ναι τοῖς πρ] οσαιτουμένοις, συν | [βιάζεσ]θαι, see Dorandi 1982: 102 with commentary p. 124–5, and cf. col.XX 17–23. On Zeno's views about sexual morality, see generally Rist 1969: 54–80, esp. 63–8.

28 Like that of Antigonos of Karystos, mentioned above. See Bollansée 1999: 186: 'Modern historians of philosophy have had a hard time trying to hide their disappointment, their frustration and their exasperation over the fact that . . . the major part of ancient *testimonia* pertaining to philosophers relate some bizarre, manifestly invented anecdote, while the doxographical aspect is virtually absent from the evidence.'

29 Ἤδη δὲ καὶ εἰς παροιμίαν σχεδὸν ἐχώρησεν. ἐλέγετο γοῦν ἐπ᾽ αὐτοῦ· τοῦ φιλοσόφου Ζήνωνος ἐγκρατέστερος (Diog. Laert. 7. 27). In an epigram, the poet Poseidippos rejects Zeno's moderation as *antithetical* to the poetry of sympotic Eros; cf. Poseidippos 123.3–4 AB = 1 Gow-Page *GP*: σιγάσθω Ζήνων ὁ σοφὸς κύκνος, ἅ τε Κλεάνθους / μοῦσα, μέλοι δ᾽ ἡμῖν ὁ γλυκύπικρος Ἔρως. See Gutzwiller 1998b: 159.

30 See Winter 1995: esp.248–9. This aspect of the Phoenicians in the Greek view is summed up as follows by Ribichini (1983: 445): 'l'immagine dei fenici . . . "abili tessitori d'inganni", pirati ed avventurieri, rapitori di donne e di bambini, sempre pronte a tradire l'amico per venderlo schiavo.'Among various stories of Phoenician treachery, see especially that of Eumaios at *Od.* 15. 403–84, who tells how he was abducted as a child by Phoenician traders, who with subtle guile (πολυπαίπαλοι, 15.419) seduced his Phoenician nurse (ἠπερόπευον, 419). Note the sexual rapaciousness here, and how they lead a child astray (cf. παιδοπῖπαι).

That this view of Phoenicians was long-standing is clear from Herodotos 1.1 and 5, who tells how according to the Persians the conflict between East and West began when the Phoenicians abducted Io from Argos. Similarly, at 2. 54–6 he relates that the Egyptians say that the original priestesses of Zeus Ammon in Libya and at Dodona were sisters carried off by Phoenicians and sold as slaves in these two countries. Thuc. 1.8 refers to the Phoenicians as pirates. According to the *Certamen Homeri et Hesiodi* 25f., some say that Homer's mother was an Ithakan woman sold as a slave by the Phoenicians.

31 Di Marco 1989: 196–7: 'la menzione delle origini fenicie serve . . . a deprezzare il filosofo in quanto non greco.'

32 Nesselrath 2005: 423–53 has a useful discussion this fragment.

33 Cf. the many stories about Phoenicians as hard-hearted slavers, beginning already in Homer (n. 30 above). I wonder whether there is also an indirect swipe here at Zeno's blundering sidekick, Persaios of Kition, who in the biographical tradition is sometimes seen as Zeno's slave, is repeatedly exposed as failing to live up to his master's standard, and is packed off by Zeno – ἐπ᾽ ἐξαγωγῆι as here – as his proxy to the court of Antigonos Gonatas (Diog. Laert. 7. 36).

34 The same holds true for Sopater of Paphos's depiction of Zeno as a ruthless Phoenician slave trader (above).

35  ματρ[όπο]λίς μοι χθὼν Πέλοπος τὸ Πελαζγικὸν Ἄργος,
    Πνυταγόρας δὲ πατὴρ Αἰακοῦ ἐκ γενεᾶς·
    εἰμὶ δὲ Νικοκρέων, θρέψεν δέ με γᾶ περίκλυστος
    Κύπρος θειοτάτων ἐκ προγόνων βασιλῆ.
    στᾶσαν δ’ Ἀργεῖοί με χάριν χαλκοῖο τίοντες
    Ἥραι ὃν εἰς ἔροτιν πέμπον [ἄε]θλα νέοις.

(My mother city is the land of Pelops, Pelasgian Argos,
   and Pnytagoras my father sprang from the race of Aiakos.
I am Nikokreon, raised in the wave-beaten land
   of Cyprus, king from the most divine ancestors.
The Argives set me up to render thanks for the bronze
   for Hera, which I would send to the festival as prizes for the youths.)

36  His speech, moreover, might even contain a dash of Cypriot colouring: Note
    the use of ἔροτις (= ἑορτή) in the last line (6), a possibly Cypriot form (cf. LSJ
    s.v. ἐροτή and Hansen's note. ad line 6.

37  See S. Aneziri who notes (1994: 180) that guilds of Dionysiac *technitai* were
    only established on Cyprus in the second half of the second century BC,
    and that 'dabei können wir uns auch nicht auf andere Zeugnisse stützen, da
    auf der Insel keinerlei inschriftliche Belege für musische und dramatische
    Veranstaltungen gefunden worden sind (Siegerlisten, Choregieinschriften,
    Dekrete für die Agonen-organization u.a.).' See also Aneziri 2003: 242–3.

    Recently S. Barbantani (2005: 152–61) has argued that Ptolemaic domina-
    tion of Cyprus in the second and first centuries BC may ultimately have intro-
    duced to the island itinerant poets who were commissioned to write poems for
    local (Ptolemaic) festivals. One such, she suggests, was the hymn to Arsinoë-
    Aphrodite (P. Lit. Goodsp. 2, I–IV), of uncertain date, but probably Hellenistic
    of the second or first centuries BC, which could have belonged to a Cypriot
    milieu, and might have been 'composed by a wandering poet, or by a foreign
    erudite interested in local traditions' (161).

# 3

# Genre and Ethnicity in the Epigrams of Meleager[1]

## KATHRYN GUTZWILLER

The biography of Meleager, the erotic epigrammatist and anthologist of the *Garland* (ca 100 BC), is known from four self-epitaphs.[2] Born in Syrian Gadara to a father with the Greek name Eukrates, he spent his young manhood in Phoenician Tyre and his declining years as a citizen of Kos. His life thus illustrates the experience of moving from a Syrian town where Greeks and Hebrews intermingled with the indigenous population to a once-powerful Phoenician city, now largely Hellenized, and then to a Greek city with a proud literary and cultural tradition, and this during a period of increasing Roman domination in political, financial, and social arenas. It is easy to imagine that he continually experienced the correlative phenomena of belonging and isolation as he moved from one ethnic centre to another. His homeland of 'Syrian Gadara' he calls 'Attic' (*Anth. Pal.* 7.417.1–2),[3] suggesting the inherent conflict of receiving a Hellenized education while inhabiting a town with radically different local traditions.[4] In Tyre, which 'received' (δεξαμένα, *Anth. Pal.* 7.418.2) him and 'nourished' (θρέπτειρα, *Anth. Pal.* 7.417.1) him to manhood, he surely socialized with Tyrians interested in Greek literature and art, and yet would have been a foreigner, ethnically different. It was Greek Kos that offered him, in old age, the public and legal mark of acceptance through citizenship, a gift perhaps earned by his lifelong struggle to compete with the best of the earlier Greek epigrammatists.

Meleager lived in all three cities during a period of relative political and intellectual freedom. At the time of Meleager's birth, perhaps about 140 BC, Seleukid power was collapsing and Roman dominance was not yet fully in place. As a result, local control reasserted itself. Gadara enjoyed a period of independence until the Hasmonean takeover in 103 BC, presumably after the young Meleager had migrated to Tyre.[5] The conquest of Tyre by Alexander the Great, who linked the island city to the mainland with a permanent mole, was followed by about two centuries of Ptolemaic and Seleukid political dominance. After becoming a free city in 126 BC, Tyre seems then to have enjoyed a period of pride in its Phoenician heritage, coloured by long-standing Hellenizing influences. Famed for their sought-after crimson dye made from the murex, the merchants of Tyre carried on a flourishing shipping business throughout the eastern Aegean.[6] When Meleager refers to ships sailing to Rhodes (*Anth. Pal.* 12.52 = *HE* 81) or sailing from the Bosporos to Kos (*Anth. Pal.* 12.53 = *HE* 66), he is likely thinking of such Phoenician vessels. Given the ease with which inhabitants of Hellenistic Tyre might have travelled, his final move to the bustling trading centre of Kos seems a natural one. As the birthplace of Ptolemy Philadelphos, Kos early became a Ptolemaic protectorate and was associated with some of the famous scholars and poets working in Alexandria in the third century (Philitas, Herodas, Theokritos). Because of its loyalty to Rome, Kos remained a free city until the end of the Republic, flourishing as a port of call for travellers from many parts of the Mediterranean world.

Rome looms large in the background for all these Hellenistic cities. Long before Pompey's conquest of Syria in 64/63 BC, from the earlier part of the second century, Rome had been the de facto arbiter of political disputes among the major players in the East. Throughout that century Roman traders had a visible presence at the Aegean ports frequented by the Tyrians, and their commercial interests brought them into Syria as well.[7] Politically and militarily, Romans were an inescapable presence in the Greek East. Yet Meleager mentions Rome only once in his epigrams, and not at all in the biographical poems. The experience of other Greek epigrammatists from Syria suggests, however, that this single reference may belie the importance of Rome in his literary career.

Meleager anthologized a large number of epigrams by Antipater of Sidon, an older contemporary who was likely known to him personally. According to Cicero (*De or.* 3.194), Antipater was admired in elite circles in Rome for his ability to produce Greek epigrams extemporaneously.[8] Rome is mentioned in several of his epigrams – an inscription for a portico dedicated by a wealthy banker to Rome and Athens as the dual protectors of Delos (*IDélos* 2549 = *HE* 42), two epigrams on the destruction of Corinth (*Anth. Pal.* 9.151 = *HE* 59, *Anth. Pal.* 7.493 = *HE* 68), and another on a Greek dancer who could tame Roman aggression with her soft charms (*Anth. Pal.* 9.567 = *HE* 61). A somewhat younger epigrammatist, Archias of Antioch, is well known as the cultured poet admired and defended by Cicero; he too produced extemporaneous verse at Rome (Cic. *Arch.* 18). Both poets were acquainted in Rome with Quintus Lutatius Catulus, who with Valerius Aedituus and Porcius Licinus wrote Latin erotic epigrams based on poems anthologized by Meleager. Scholars have long recognized, though often inadequately, the importance of the *Garland* as a model for the Latin poetry of the late Republic and Augustan periods,[9] but the possible influence of Rome upon Meleager has remained unremarked. My project in this essay is to tease out the interaction of genre with ethnicity in Meleager, that is, to ask how his epigrams reflect the realities of the places in which he resided and particularly to consider the literary implications of his one allusion to Rome.

The phrase παίδων Ῥωμαϊκὴν λοπάδα, 'Roman platter of boys,' occurs at the conclusion of a pair of epigrams, in which Meleager wishes his friend Philokles erotic success with a series of boys:

τερπνὸς μὲν Διόδωρος, ἐν ὄμμασι δ᾽ Ἡράκλειτος,
   ἡδυεπὴς δὲ Δίων, ὀσφύϊ δ᾽ Οὐλιάδης.
ἀλλὰ σὺ μὲν ψαύοις ἁπαλόχροος, ᾧ δέ, Φιλόκλεις,
   ἔμβλεπε, τῷ δὲ λάλει, τὸν δὲ ... τὸ λειπόμενον·
ὡς γνῷς οἷος ἐμὸς νόος ἄφθονος· ἢν δὲ Μυΐσκῳ
   λίχνος ἐπιβλέψῃς, μηκέτ᾽ ἴδοις τὸ καλόν.    (*Anth. Pal.* 12.94 = *HE* 76)
**1** τερπνὸς P: στέρνοις Graefe **2** Οὐλιάδης Dübner: Οὐδ-P

(Delightful is Diodoros, and all eyes are on Herakleitos,
   Dion is sweet in speech, and Ouliades in his loins.
So go ahead, caress the delicate-skinned one, Philokles, gaze upon
   the next, chat with the third, and with the fourth ... the rest –
so that you know how my mind lacks jealousy. But if you look
   lustfully on Myiskos, may you never again see beauty.)

Εἴ σε Πόθοι στέργουσι, Φιλοκλέες, ἥ τε μυρόπνους
   Πειθὼ καὶ κάλλευς ἀνθολόγοι Χάριτες,
ἀγκὰς ἔχοις Διόδωρον, ὁ δὲ γλυκὺς ἀντίος ἤσθω
   Δωρόθεος, κείσθω δ᾽ εἰς γόνυ Καλλικράτης,
ἰαίνοι δὲ Δίων τόδ᾽ εὔστοχον ἐν χερὶ τείνων
   σὸν κέρας, Οὐλιάδης δ᾽ αὐτὸ περισκυθίσαι,
δοίη δ᾽ ἡδὺ φίλημα Φίλων, Θήρων δὲ λαλῆσαι,
   θλίβοις δ᾽ Εὐδήμου τιτθὸν ὑπὸ χλαμύδι·
εἰ γάρ σοι τάδε τερπνὰ πόροι θεός, ὦμάκαρ, οἵαν
   ἀρτύσεις παίδων Ῥωμαϊκὴν λοπάδα.    (*Anth. Pal.* 12.95 = *HE* 77)
**3** ἤσθω *scripsi*: ἤδη P: ἴζοι Jacobs **10** λοπάδα Saumaise: λωπ-P

(If the Desires cherish you, Philokles, as well as perfume-scented
  Persuasion and the Graces who gather the flowers of beauty,
May you hold Diodoros in your arms, and let sweet Dorotheos
  sit opposite you, and Kallikrates lie against your knee;
May Dion warm up this straight-shooting horn of yours, hardening it
  With his hand, and may Ouliades peel back its skin, Scythian style;
May Philon give you a sweet kiss, may Theron chat with you,
  and may you squeeze Eudemos's tit under his cloak.
If some god should give you these delightful gifts, O blessed one,
  what a Roman stew of boys you will prepare!)

In the first poem, Meleager encourages his friend to enjoy the special charms of each of four boys, including intercourse with one, while he will refrain from jealousy as long as Philokles keeps away from his favourite, Myiskos. In the second, the poet wishes his friend success with an even greater number of boys and a wider array of activities until his blessed good fortune culminates in the culinary metaphor of seasoning a 'Roman platter of boys.' These two epigrams are unusual, practically unique in the Meleagrian corpus, for their sexual explicitness, and they are arranged in such a way within the erotic book of the *Garland* that the Roman reference occupies a marked position. As Albert Wifstrand first pointed out, within the epigrams for male and female love objects originally drawn from the *Garland* but later separated by a Byzantine editor into books 5 and 12 of the *Anthology*, there can be identified a long sequence of strictly pederastic poems (*Anth. Pal.* 12.54–97).[10] In my further analysis of Meleager's arrangement, I have noted that epigrams devoted to single boys are succeeded by epigrams about multiple boy-loves, first two or three (*Anth. Pal.* 12.88–91) followed by an 'inescapable labyrinth' of boys in Rhianos *Anth. Pal.* 12.93 = *HE* 3 and then the lists for first five and then eight boys in the two Philokles epigrams. The 'Roman platter' marks the culmination of this escalation of pederastic desire, as the following epigrams turn to single boys, now overripe or greedy ones, to conclude the long pederastic sequence.[11] Our phrase also has links with other epigrams in the sequence. The food metaphor in *Anth. Pal.* 12.95 looks back to Meleager *Anth. Pal.* 12.92 = *HE* 116 where the lover's eyes are roasted in beauty, smoked in fire, because Eros is the 'consummate cook of the soul.' It also echoes in Glaukos *Anth. Pal.* 12.44 = *HE* 1 where the epigrammatist warns pederasts to seek other passions because boys now refuse traditional gifts and demand cash and rich food dishes (λοπὰς καὶ κέρμα); this is the only other occurrence of the word λοπάς in the *Anthology*. If I am right in my analysis of the original order here, Glaukos's warning to παιδοφίλαι once ended the long pederastic sequence, as a transition to heterosexual poems. As we can see, then, the 'Roman platter' occupied a position of some significance in Meleager's erotic book, marking the turn from this crescendo of satisfied desire with boys to poems about the disappointments that accompany boy love.

What, then, is this Ῥωμαϊκὴ λοπάς? To take the second word first, λοπάς refers, like our term *casserole*, to a cooking and serving dish and also to the food prepared in it, typically mixed dishes such as stews.[12] The verb ἀρτύω, with the basic meaning *arrange, prepare*, was the term of art for preparing or seasoning such dishes.[13] Meleager's use of this metaphor draws on a long tradition of associating the pleasures of dining with the pleasures of sex. The word is frequent in comedy, as in Aristophanes's *Ekklesiazousai* 1169–75, where an enormous comic compound describing a dish of multiple dainty ingredients begins λοπαδο-. Jeffrey Henderson points out that bowls and dishes, including λοπάδες, 'tend to appear in descriptions of cunnilingus, probably because one commonly licks them clean after preparing sauces.'[14] In a parodic poem entitled 'Attic Dinner' by Matron of Pitane, a series of λοπάδες (*SH* 534.86) contain tempting fare after which the diners lust according to their preferences for male or female sexual partners. The ancient reader would, then, naturally read Philokles's λοπάς as an image for sexual enjoyment, as its mixture of ingredients tropes Philokles's multiple partners. Philokles is presented as both cook and consumer of a tasty λοπάς, the various acts granted him by some god resulting in an orgy of sexual satisfaction with multiple boys.[15] This association of a λοπάς with sexual pleasure does not, however, explain why it is *Roman*. But before considering that question, I wish to demonstrate that its contents – its boys – are in fact Tyrian.

*Anth. Pal.* 12.94 and 12.95 are linked as a pair not only by the presence of Philokles as *erastes* but also by the reappearance of three of the boys in 12.94 – Diodoros, Dion, and Ouliades – among the eight boys in 12.95. And importantly, six of the ten boys named in 12.94 and 12.95 appear also in 12.256, where Meleager lists flower-like boys who have been plaited by Eros into an 'all-fruited' garland for Aphrodite; of these seven, only one – Asklepiades – does not appear in the paired epigrams:

πάγκαρπόν σοι, Κύπρι, καθήρμοσε χειρὶ τρυγήσας
    παίδων ἄνθος Ἔρως ψυχαπάτην στέφανον.
ἐν μὲν γὰρ κρίνον ἡδὺ κατέπλεξεν Διόδωρον,
    ἐν δ’ Ἀσκληπιάδην τὸ γλυκὺ λευκόιον.
ναὶ μὴν Ἡράκλειτον ἐπέπλεκεν ὡς ἀπ’ ἀκάνθης
    †εἰς† ῥόδον, οἰνάνθη δ’ ὥς τις ἔθαλλε Δίων.
χρυσανθῆ δὲ κόμαισι κρόκον Θήρωνα συνῆψεν,
    ἐν δ’ ἔβαλ’ ἑρπύλλου κλωνίον Οὐλιάδην.

ἀβροκόμην δὲ Μυῖσκον ἀειθαλὲς ἔρνος ἐλαίης,
  ἱμερτοὺς ἀρετῆς κλῶνας, ἀπεδρέπετο.
ὀλβίστη νήσων ἱερὰ Τύρος, ἦ τὸ μυρόπνουν
  ἄλσος ἔχει παίδων Κύπριδος ἀνθοφόρον.         Mel. *Anth. Pal.* 12.256 = *HE* 78
5 ἐπέπλεκεν P: ἐνέπλεκεν Brunck    εἰς P: ἐν *Parisinus suppl. gr.* 557: ὡς Scaliger: εἰς
Lumb: θεὶς Graefe

(As an offering of all fruits for you, Cyprian, Eros has culled by hand
  boy-blossoms to fashion a garland that deceives the soul.
In it he has plaited the lovely lily that is Diodoros,
  and that sweet white violet Asklepiades.
So too he interwove Herakleitos, like a rose from a thorn,
  and Dion blossoms there, like a vine's bloom.
He has attached Theron, a golden-haired crocus,
  and added a shoot of thyme, Ouliades.
And delicate-haired Myiskos, an ever-blooming olive sprig,
  desirable plant of excellence, he has harvested.
Most blessed of islands is holy Tyre, which has a grove,
  perfume-scented, bearing Cypris's boy-flowers.)

This epigram seems to refer to a ritual involving flowers and boys that took place in the sacred grove of Aphrodite at Tyre, that is, the sanctuary of the Phoenician Astarte known to have existed in this city.[16] The boys in 12.256 are, therefore, undoubtedly Tyrians, and by extension the boys in 12.94 and 12.95 should be as well. In one of his self-epitaphs (7.419), Meleager refers to Tyre as θεόπαις, which can be translated 'with godlike boys,' perhaps both a sexual and ritual reference. It is natural to assume that Philokles was also either a Tyrian citizen or a resident there and that Meleager's acquaintance with him stemmed from his years in that city.

Interestingly, seven of the ten boys appearing in 12.94 and 12.95 – all except Kallikrates, Philon, and Eudemos – appear in other epigrams in the *Garland's* erotic section, and these are all epigrams either labelled ἄδηλον, 'anonymous,'[17] or attributed to Meleager, but not to any of other anthologized poets.[18] Diodoros, who appears in 12.94, 12.95, and 12.256, is celebrated by Meleager in 12.63 (with Herakleitos) and in 12.109, and also by an anonymous poet in 12.156. Herakleitos, appearing in 12.94 (next to Diodoros) and in 12.256, is mentioned in 12.63 (with Diodoros) and 12.72, both by Meleager, and in 12.152, which is attached without a heading to a poem labelled as anonymous.[19] Dion, appearing in the big three (12.94, 12.95, and 12.256), reoccurs in Meleager's 12.128. The favourite Myiskos, mentioned in 12.94 and 12.256, appears in eleven other epigrams by Meleager (12.23,

12.59, 12.65, 12.70, 12.101, 12.106, 12.110, 12.144, 12.154, 12.159, 12.167).
Dorotheos, from 12.95, is named as well in anonymous 12.66. Theron, found
in 12.95 and 12.256, is mentioned by Meleager in 12.41, 12.60, and 12.141.
In addition, we may note, concerning two boys not in the Philokles poems,
that Apollodotos, mentioned by Meleager with Theron in 12.41, appears also
in anonymous 12.151, and Dionysios, celebrated by Meleager in 12.81, appears in three anonymous epigrams (5.142, 12.67, and 12.107).[20] There are
clearly, then, strong connections between boys known to Meleager and boys
in the anonymous epigrams.

What are we to make of these connections? Andrew Gow pointed out
that the frequency of anonyma in Meleagrian sequences was much higher
than anonyma in epigrams from the later anthologies of Philip or Agathias
and that this was due to the large number of anonyma from book 12.[21] He
concluded that 'Meleager has incorporated epigrams from an erotic, and at
least largely paederastic, collection which did not name their authors.'[22] He
did not notice, however, the meaningful overlap in boys' names between
Meleager and the anonyma, with the concentration of names in 12.256 on
the Tyrian grove and in the Philokles pair. This overlap makes it difficult
to assume that Meleager anthologized a collection of epigrams whose authors were unknown to him, since he evidently knew a good number of the
*eromenoi* celebrated in the anonymous poems. It seems more likely that
Meleager suppressed any indication of authorship, and it is possible that the
epigrams had not been previously published at all but were known to him
through personal relationships in Tyre. Possibly the anonyma in books 5
and 12 represent epigrams by multiple hands, but I think that the circumstances of their arrangement in the *Garland* and their general similarity
of tone and style suggest a single or perhaps primary author. While other
Hellenistic poets have no qualms about authoring pederastic epigrams, it
is not difficult to imagine circumstances under which a particular individual might not wish to acknowledge publicly composition of παιδικά. A socially or politically prominent person could fit into this category, or even
someone resident in Tyre but from an ethnic group that disparaged such
'Hellenizing' practices. I propose that Meleager stealthily acknowledges this
poet in his epigrams on Philokles, by providing the pederastic author with
a pseudonym.

This theory of the anonyma in the erotic book of the *Garland*, with the
marked reference to the 'Roman platter of boys,' is supported by the arrangement Meleager gives the anonymous epigrams in relation to epigrams
by named poets. In the surviving long sequences (*Anth. Pal.* 5.134–215,
12.37–168), Meleager presents short related groups of two to five poems in
which the earliest epigram is typically placed first, followed by poems that

vary its theme, motifs, or wording. We may note that, based on this principle, none of the anonymous poems are varied or imitated by third-century epigrammatists, which suggests that all the anonyma are later. On the other hand, third-century epigrammatists are imitated or varied in anonyma; for instance, Poseidippos *Anth. Pal.* 5.134 = *HE* 1 is imitated by anon. 5.135, Kallimachos *Anth. Pal.* 12.102 = *HE* 1 by the pair of anon. 12.103 and 104, Asklepiades 5.167 = *HE* 14 by anon. 5.168, Aratos 12.129 = *HE* 1 by anon. 12.130, and Hedylos 5.199 = *HE* 2 by anon. 5.200 and 201. The anonyma themselves are commonly imitated or varied by Meleager, who was perhaps more influenced by the anonymous pederastic poems than by third-century erotic epigrammatists. The anonyma were composed, we may conclude, after the innovative period of epigrammatic development in the third century and before Meleager wrote most or all of his epigrams.

It is worthwhile pausing to notice the close relationship between these anonyma and Meleager's own epigrams. To give one example, an anonymous epigram on Dionysios as the garland's rose offers a model for Meleager's epigram on Heliodora as the garland's garland:

Τίς, – ῥόδον ὁ στέφανος Διονυσίου ἢ ῥόδον αὐτός
  τοῦ στεφάνου; δοκέω, λείπεται ὁ στέφανος.        (anon. 5.142 = *HE* 23)

(Which is it? Is the garland Dionysius's rose, or is he
  the garland's rose? For me, the garland loses.)

Ὁ στέφανος περὶ κρατὶ μαραίνεται Ἡλιοδώρας·
  αὐτὴ δ᾽ ἐκλάμπει τοῦ στεφάνου στέφανος.        (Mel. 5.143 = *HE* 45)

(The garland withers on the head of Heliodora,
  but she gleams forth, the garland's garland.)

In a number of instances, two anonymous epigrams are placed just before a poem in which Meleager varies both anonyma. For example, two anonymous couplets which favourably compare first Eubios and then Arkesilaos with Eros are offered as a dual model for Meleager's couplet on Timarion:

πτανὸς Ἔρως, σὺ δὲ ποσσὶ ταχύς· τὸ δὲ κάλλος ὁμοῖον
  ἀμφοτέρων· τόξοις, Εὔβιε, λειπόμεθα.        (anon. *Anth. Pal.* 12.111 = *HE* 28)

(Eros is winged, and you are swift of foot. You both have
  equal beauty. It's his bow that conquers us, Eubios.)[23]

εὐφαμεῖτε, νέοι· τὸν Ἔρωτ' ἄγει Ἀρκεσίλαος
πορφυρέῃ δήσας Κύπριδος ἁρπεδόνῃ.          (anon. *Anth. Pal.* 12.112 = *HE* 15)


(Keep respectful silence, youths. Arkesilaos leads Eros
bound by Cypris's purple bowstring.)[24]

καὐτὸς Ἔρως ὁ πτανὸς ἐν αἰθέρι δέσμιος ἥλω,
ἀγρευθεὶς τοῖς σοῖς ὄμμασι, Τιμάριον.          (Mel. *Anth. Pal.* 12.113 = *HE* 62)

(Even Eros himself, the winged one, was caught and bound
in the air, hunted down by your eyes, Timarion.)

The verbal aspect of Meleager's imitation is obvious, since πτανὸς Ἔρως in
12.111 is transformed into Ἔρως ὁ πτανός in 12.113, while δήσας in 12.112
becomes δέσμιος in 12.113. In addition, while the two anonymous epigrams
vary the theme of erotic conquest by referring to Eros's power over Eubios's
lover in 12.111 and the boy Arkesilaos's capture of Eros in 12.112, Meleager
repeats the theme of the latter poem but varies it by attributing the conquest
of Eros to a woman named Timarion.[25] Numerous other examples could be
similarly analysed, with Meleager varying sometimes a single anonymous
epigram and sometimes a set of two:

anon. 12.61–2 and Mel. 12.63[26]
anon. 12.66–7 and Mel. 12.68
anon. 12.69 and Mel. 12.70
anon. 12.79 and Mel. 12.80[27]
anon. 12.39–40 and Mel. 12.41
anon. 12.99–100 and Mel. 12.101
anon. 12.115–16 and Mel. 12.117
anon. 12.136 and Mel. 12.137
anon. 12.140 and Mel. 12.141
anon. 12.143 and Mel. 12.144 (both on statues)
anon. 12.156 and Mel. 12.157

The influence of the anonymous pederastic epigrams on Meleager's own
erotica extends beyond these pairings, since Meleager sometimes takes
over phraseology from anonyma that do not immediately precede his
epigram. For instance, ὡς ἐπ' ἀκάνθαις . . . ῥοδέαν φυομένην κάλυκα in

anon. 12.40.3–4 = *HE* 12.3–4 becomes ὡς ἀπ᾽ ἀκάνθης †εἰς† ῥόδον in Mel. 12.256.5–6, τὸν τρυφερῇ παιδὸς σαρκὶ χλιαινόμενον in anon. 12.136.2 = *HE* 10.2 is adapted almost formulaically in Mel. 5.151.6, 5.165.4, and 12.63.4, and ἐκεραυνοβόλει in anon. 12.140.4 = *HE* 16.4 inspired κεραυνοβόλον in Mel. 12.63.2, κεραυνομάχαν in Mel. 12.110.2, and κεραυνοβολεῖν in Mel. 12.122.6 (all on boys in the Zeus role). It is clear, then, that the anonyma function as an intermediary between the early third-century erotic epigrammatists and Meleager's own erotic verse; they demonstrate the principles of variation that Meleager follows, and they provide important thematic and linguistic models for him to emulate. And importantly, as we have seen, the anonyma and Meleager's epigrams draw upon the same Tyrian social circle to depict relationships between adult males and their objects of desire, both adolescent males and women.

To fill out this picture, I draw attention to another epigrammatist from the *Garland* who varies or imitates anonymous epigrams. We have already observed that the *eromenos* Dionysios appears in one epigram by Meleager (12.81) and three anonymous ones (5.142 quoted above, 12.67, and 12.107). Amazingly, it has been unnoticed that he also appears as an author, who writes a response to one of the anonymous poems:

τὸν καλόν, ὦ Χάριτες, Διονύσιον, **εἰ μὲν** ἕλοιτο
  **τἀμά**, καὶ εἰς ὥρας αὖθις ἄγοιτε καλόν·
**εἰ δ᾽ ἕτερον στέρξειε** παρεὶς ἐμέ, μύρτον ἕωλον
  ἐρρίφθω ξηροῖς φυρόμενον σκυβάλοις.          (anon. *Anth. Pal.* 12.107 = *HE* 24)

(O Charites, if that beautiful Dionysios should choose me,
  then please preserve his beauty from season to season,
But if he love another and reject me, let that stale myrtle berry
  be tossed out, swept up with the dry rubbish.)

**Εἰ μὲν ἐμὲ στέρξεις**, εἴης ἰσόμοιρος, Ἄκρατε,
  Χίῳ καὶ Χίου πουλὺ μελιχρότερος·
**εἰ δ᾽ ἕτερον** κρίναις ἐμέθεν πλέον, ἀμφὶ σὲ βαίη
  κώνωψ ὀξηρῷ φυόμενος κεράμῳ.          (Dionysios *Anth. Pal.* 12.108 = *HE* 3)

(If you love me, Akratos, may you be the equivalent
  of Chian wine, and much sweeter than Chian.
But if you judge another better than me, may a mosquito
  fly around you – one born in a vinegar jar.)

Here the anonymous poet prays that Dionysios will love him faithfully, but if the boy prefers another, anonymous curses him as symposium rubbish worthy of being swept away. Dionysios replies, amoebean-style, praising the *erastes* as sweeter than sweet wine if he loves truly but cursing him with a mosquito's torment if he should prefer another boy. Though the first poem is labeled ἄδηλον, Dionysios addresses his lover as Akratos, meaning *Unmixed*, assuredly a pseudonym playing on the wine reference and symposium imagery.[28] Another epigram ascribed to a Dionysios,[29] a two-line epitaph for a woman from Tyre buried at Sidon (7.462), occurs in a long *Garland* sequence from the epitaphic book (*Anth. Pal.* 7.406–507) where it follows a two-line epitaph by Meleager (7.461); the order here, I submit, may indicate that Dionysios's poem is chronologically later than Meleager's.[30] These Dionysios epigrams help fill out our evidence for the Tyrian circle of individuals involved in both erotic and literary pursuits, by supporting the chronology that I have suggested.

As a last piece of evidence for this Tyrian literary group, we need to glance at Antipater. While he is often referred to in the lemmata as a Sidonian (to distinguish him from the Philippan Antipater from Thessalonike), Meleager in an enigmatic epitaph for him (imitating one of Antipater's characteristic epitaphic types) names his fatherland as 'the proud mother of the Phoenicians, Tyre of many boys' (7.428.13–14 = *HE* 122.13–14). This suggests that Antipater was resident at Tyre at some point in his life, whether or not it was his birthplace,[31] and Meleager likely knew him there. Although the great majority of Antipater's epigrams are epitaphic or dedicatory, Meleager speaks of him in this epitaph as an erotic poet – 'perhaps foremost in matters of the Cyprian and through the Muses a versatile composer' (15–16). It is worth noting that this picture is supported by what we know about Antipater in Rome, where he associated with Catulus and others who composed erotic, sometimes pederastic, epigrams in Latin. There survives only one erotic epigram by Antipater from a secure Meleagrian sequence, *Anth. Pal.* 12.97 = *HE* 65, and this poem follows an ἄδηλον epigram on a similar theme of a boy's physical imperfection, *Anth. Pal.* 12.96 = *HE* 33; the order here may indicate, given Meleager's usual practice, that the Antipater epigram was inspired by the anonymous poem.[32] It seems likely, then, that Antipater of Sidon was at some point in his life part of the Tyrian group of lovers and poets.

To summarize up to this point. All this evidence indicates that the anonymous pederastic epigrams anthologized by Meleager were composed by an influential poet, or less likely set of poets, living at Tyre in the late second century, who imitated the same third-century erotic epigrammatists imitated by Meleager and who was/were in turn imitated by Meleager, as well as by the young Dionysios, and possibly by Antipater. The idea that Meleager anthologized 'an earlier book of anonymous poems by various hands is hard to reconcile with the evidence that he knew a significant number of the Tyrian boys celebrated in the *anonyma*: he must also have known their lovers. It seems most plausible that the need for anonymity was not something general to a group of pederastic epigrammatists but specific to one individual. As Dionysios refers to his *erastes* – the anonymous author of 12.107 – with the pseudonym Akratos, so I suggest that Meleager likewise uses the name Philokles as a pseudonym for the *erastes* of 12.94–5.[33] In Phoenicia this Greek name, meaning 'lover of fame,' would have had an exalted ring, since the king of Sidon and viceroy of the navy under Ptolemy I was named Philokles, son of Apollodoros.[34]

This brings us back to the Ῥωμαϊκὴ λοπάς and its metaphorical implications. We have observed how Meleager uses the food image to trope Philokles's sexual proclivities. I further suggest that it may function as a metaphor for an existing or projected collection of erotic epigrammatic poetry by 'Philokles,' a nom de plume for the anonymous epigrammatist. Complex metaphors for literary genres and collections came into use during the second and early first centuries BC. The bucolic poet Bion, for instance, openly identifies himself as a cowherd (fr. 10.4–5), and Artemidoros attached to his compilation of bucolic poetry an epigram in which the 'bucolic Muses' are troped as herd animals now gathered into one fold. Perhaps the best example comes from Meleager's proem (*Anth. Pal.* 4.1), where the garland is set out as the image for his anthology, an intertwining of poets as flowers in a massive festoon of epigrammatic verse.[35] In *Anth. Pal.* 12.256, composed during Meleager's younger days in Tyre, the same image had been used, for a set of flower-like boys gathered by Eros into a garland. This wreath of boys suits well Meleager's sentimental approach to erotic verse, celebrating boys' beauty or desirability and focusing on the lover's pathetic condition of longing. The spicier pederastic relationships that he wishes for Philokles called for a different kind of image, that of the boy stew 'seasoned up' or 'arranged' in a λοπάς. The most difficult question remains, however: why is this λοπάς Roman?

Was it just that the Tyrians enjoyed a tasty dish called 'Roman stew'? This possibility, as far as I know, cannot be proven or unproven but offers a meagre point, and a weak climax for such a marked position in the *Garland* sequence. Another possible explanation, perhaps not too far-fetched, is that Philokles was a Roman resident at Tyre. Romans were certainly travelling in the Greek East for commercial and political purposes throughout the second century, and elite Romans were well educated in Greek language and literature. We should note as well that variation of earlier epigrams would have been an excellent starting place for a non-native speaker to develop skills in Greek poetic composition. If such a philhellenic Roman were present in the Tyrian literary circle, he just might have provided a conduit for Antipater's migration to Rome. Romanness would also explain the need for anonymity, since in this period a Roman of stature would have good reason to avoid projecting himself publicly as a pederastic poet of Greek epigrams. A few years later Roman gentlemen such as Catulus could get by with composing Latin adaptations of such epigrams as forms of *lusus*, but much changes in Roman acceptance of Greek ways during the second half of the second century.[36] It makes perfect sense to speak of a Roman λοπάς if the one who creates it was in fact a Roman. There is another, not incompatible, explanation for the Ῥωμαϊκὴ λοπάς, however, which brings us back to its use as a literary metaphor.

From at least as early as Rudolf Hirzel,[37] Meleager's Ῥωμαϊκὴ λοπάς has been interpreted as a translation of *lanx satura*, a phrase attested only with reference to the etymology of satire. The *locus classicus* is a passage from Diomedes's *Ars grammatica*, in which four possible origins for the term *satura* are offered: from Satyrs because this sort of poetry contains *ridiculae res pudendaeque*; from a *lanx satura* because of the *copia et saturitas* of the many and varied food offerings presented to the gods on such a platter; from a kind of stuffing made with several ingredients; or from an omnibus law.[38] Scholars have generally concluded that the 'correct' etymology involves derivation from *satur* through a stage in which *satura* was an adjective with *lanx* before becoming nominal with the meaning 'medley, miscellany,'[39] but the other etymologies undoubtedly reflect perceptions of the genre as it developed over time. According to Diomedes, Ennius's *Saturae*, a poetic miscellany eventually known in four books, was significantly different from the carping character of later satire as composed by Lucilius, Horace, and Persius, and he adds that the poetry of Ennius and Pacuvius was called satire merely because it was a mixture of poems (*ex variis poematibus*). Scholars have pointed out that Ennius may have used this designation in imitation of early Hellenistic poetic collections with such generic titles as σύμμεικτα ἐπιγράμματα or ἄτακτα, or the slightly more creative σωρός, 'heap,' of epigrams by Poseidippos.[40] Although it is often claimed that the few fragments of Ennius's *Saturae* (we know nothing of Pacuvius's) have already the satiric tone that defines the genre in its later manifestations,[41] it remains unclear how the etymology from *lanx satura* leads in that direction. Meleager's Ῥωμαϊκὴ λοπάς, when mentioned at all in discussions of the development of satire, is cited to vouch for the etymology from *lanx*,[42] and to my knowledge no scholar has taken account of the relevant fact that Meleager also wrote prose in the style of Menippos, his countryman from Gadara. He tells us this in his self-epitaphs, and Athenaios mentions two of his prose works, the *Charites* (4.157b) and *Symposion* (11.502c). Since Menippos was from at least the time of Varro the primary Greek model for the prosimetric form of satire, there is clearly a link here that warrants exploration. I turn then to teasing out how Meleager's 'Roman platter/stew' may shed some light on the puzzling development of this genre, claimed by Quintilian to be *tota nostra* (*Inst.* 10.1.93) but clearly somehow resulting from a combination of Greek and Roman forces.

To do this, we must look once again at culinary metaphors for literary forms. Food and dining are constant themes in extant satire, often with mockery of extravagant consumption.[43] Juvenal, who devotes practically an entire poem to a turbot (*Sat.* 4), likely alludes on some level to the *lanx satura* as satire's origin when he programmatically calls the varied human behaviour that is his subject matter the *farrago*, 'mixed fodder,' of his little book (1.86).[44] Certain Greek metaphors lie in the background of satire's programmatic association with mixed foodstuffs. The λοπάς, mentioned in Aristophanes and fragments of later comedy, was the main course at a banquet, a savoury stew often made of choice and expensive fish, traditionally seasoned with caraway, vinegar, silphium, cheese, and coriander (Anaxipp. fr. 1.7–8 K-A). It was typically contrasted with lentil soup, or φακῆ, often seasoned only with vinegar, and consumed as a first course or as a simple meal for the poor. As early as the fifth century lentil soup was associated metaphorically with critical or pedestrian types of literary production. Hegemon of Thasos, an early parodist, gave himself the nickname Φακῆ; in a preserved fragment of his poetry, Athena calls him 'foul Lentil Soup' as she chides him on to perform his parodies (Ath. 9.406e–407a, 15.698c–699a; cf. Arist. *Poet.* 1448a12–13).[45] The idea that lentil soup fostered the exercise of reason, in opposition to a life of luxury driven by carnal desires, appears particularly in Cynic writings, where biting wit was employed to criticize the profligate and exalt asceticism. Demetrius (*Eloc.* 170), asserting that even the 'rational' (φρόνιμοι) use laughter on the right occasions as at symposia, cites as an example the criticism of luxurious living in the poetry of the Cynic Krates of Thebes, apparently including an 'encomium of lentil soup directed against the sexually unrestrained.

Our best source for the significance of lentil soup is a passage in Athenaios that begins with a lengthy quotation from *The Cynics' Symposion* by Parmeniskos (4.156c–157d). At a banquet in Athens, a half-dozen Cynics first debate the best kind of water (a parody of praise of wine) and then enjoy a meal consisting solely of large bowls of lentil soup or lentils soaked in vinegar. When courtesans enter, they laugh at the Cynics who dine on lentils rather than fish (with double entendres about flatulence). One hetaira asks if they eat no fish in accordance with the principles of their 'ancestor' Meleager, who argues in his *Charites* that Homer, being a Syrian by birth, depicted the Achaians abstaining from fish according to the practice of his own homeland.[46] Or perhaps the Cynic diners, she suggests, have read only Meleager's comparison of porridge and lentil soup (likely his *Symposion*). The implication is that, from the Cynic or Menippean perspective, Meleager associates his Syrian heritage with a simple manner of life, dependent on commonplace vegetable products and lacking the sea's gastronomic bounty. Karneios then defends the Cynics' choice of food on the basis that heavy nourishment inhibits the authoritative part of the soul and blocks reason (φρόνησις). Athenaios appends to the Parmeniskos section a number of quotations that further connect reason with lentil soup. He mentions the Stoic doctrine that the sage will do everything well, including 'seasoning thoughtfully lentil soup' (φακῆν φρονίμως ἀρτύσει, 4.158a), and Timon of Phlios's criticism of a philosopher who had not 'learned how to boil Zenonian lentil soup thoughtfully' (Ζηνώνειόν γε φακῆν ἕψειν ὃς μὴ φρονίμως μεμάθηκεν, 4.158a–b = *SH* 787). The contrasting use that philosophers made of φακῆ and λοπάς underlies an instruction from Krates not to 'exalt a stew above lentil soup' (4.158b = *SH* 353), taken by Plutarch (*Mor.* 125f) as advice to avoid the ills of a luxurious life. A line from the comic poet Strattis (Ath. 4.160b = 47 K-A), in parody of Euripides (*Phoen.* 460), warns against mixing perfume with lentil soup – a proverbial saying that was known to both Klearchos and Varro 'the Menippean' (Ath. 4.160c; cf. frs. 549–51 Astbury from the τὸ ἐπὶ τῇ φακῇ μύρον section of Varro's *Saturae Menippeae*).

I argue, then, that when Meleager wishes for Philokles a 'Roman stew of boys,' he is implicitly contrasting this extravagant sexual meal of his friend with a more austere and critical 'Menippean' manner, which he himself practised during his youthful years in Gadara. As the contrasting food images of λοπάς and φακῆ signify differing styles of life, so too they connect to differing literary modes of expression. The metaphor of lentil soup, which is associated with wit, rationality, simplicity, and criticism of extravagance, is suited to parodic genres of the Cynic type, particularly the pedestrian blend of prose and poetry that is found in Menippean discourse.[47] Meleager's continuing self-identification with this strand is shown by his epitaphs in which he expresses pride in both his erotic poetry and his earlier Menippean works (one of which included a comparison of lentil soup and porridge). At first glance, Meleager's epigrammatic poetry, troped with the garland,[48] seems a departure from his Menippean phase, and in several erotic epigrams Meleager makes it clear that the choice of the 'garland' life of love and poetry involves repudiation of his earlier philosophical restraint. In one (*Anth. Pal.* 12.23 = *HE* 99), the poet who once laughed at the *komoi* of lovers has been caught by Eros and placed on Myiskos's doorway with the inscription 'spoils from Sophrosyne' (σκῦλ' ἀπὸ Σωφροσύνης). In another (*Anth. Pal.* 12.101 = *HE* 103), Myiskos exalts over the wounded poet, proclaiming that he tramples on the 'arrogance of his sceptre-bearing wisdom' (κεῖνο φρύαγμα σκηπτροφόρου σοφίας), a reference to Meleager's former life of Cynic haughtiness. Since Myiskos is one of the Tyrian boys, this new life dominated by passion is evidently a product of Meleager's years in the Phoenician city. As I have shown elsewhere, however, Meleager provides in his self-epitaphs an association of his Menippean writings with his epigrammatic verse under the rubric of the Charites, as emblems of literary charm;[49] support for this association comes from Demetrius's *On Style*, where in his discussion of the polished style, the critic claims two types of literary *charis*, one associated with poetic charm, such as found in Sappho, and one with wit, such as found in the Cynic style. Meleager's transition from a Menippean persona in his prose writings to the pathetic lover of his epigrams was not, then, a complete abandonment of his earlier literary manner but an adaptation to a poetic genre more suited to his adult style of living and loving.

It is from this dual perspective as former Menippean and sentimental lover that Meleager comments on his hedonistic friend's 'Roman platter' of boys. Through denial of Myiskos to Philokles because of Meleager's devotion to him, Philokles's λοπάς is carefully distinguished from Meleager's own erotic collection; Philokles is compelled by a lust-driven orgy of desire for multiple boys, in contrast to Meleager's sustained passion for a single love object. This fits of course with the cultural associations of the λοπάς, which include gluttony, sexual licence, and indulgence in a luxurious life without rational restraint. Within the *Garland*, as I have argued, the Roman platter is perhaps an emblem of an existing or projected poetic assemblage reflecting Philokles's erotic experiences;[50] elsewhere, however, the literary equivalent of the Ῥωμαϊκὴ λοπάς, or *lanx satura*, is satire. Is a poetic collection on erotic themes compatible with the Roman genre of satire, or, to ask the question differently, what version of satire might Meleager have known? Chronologically, he could have known of Ennius, but also perhaps Pacuvius, and maybe even Lucilius, who began publishing in the late 120s. From any or all of these Meleager might have come to interpret *satura* as a mixture of poems. Diomedes defines *lanx satura*, as it was used by Ennius and Pacuvius, as *varia poemata*, apparently a medley of poems composed by a single poet, and Lucilius speaks of *nostra poemata* (1013 Marx = 1084 Krenkel) perhaps with the same sense of shorter poems gathered into a collection. That concept would fit nicely an epigram book by Meleager's anonymous poet, who is possibly to be equated with Philokles, whether a real name or a pseudonym. The additional associations of λοπάς with symposiastic excess, in contrast to Cynic simplicity, may also fit with Ennius's *Saturae*, as a few of the meagre fragments suggest. When Ennius says, 'it's not my way, even if a dog has bitten me' (*Sat.* 63 Vahlen), he seems to be rejecting doggish carping, and in another fragment he associates his own poetry with sumptuous dining by proclaiming, 'I never poeticize unless I have the gout' (64). It was Varro, it seems, who gave satire its Cynic flavour as metaphorical 'lentil soup'; he brought the Menippean prose element into his *Saturae*, which, as mentioned above, included a section titled 'perfume in lentil soup.' Meleager's earlier Menippean writings and the 'satiric' Roman-style λοπάς that he attributes to Philokles, while presented as quite distinct, may, then, eventually come to stand behind two strands of the one genre that the Romans called satire.

Lastly, we should explore the possibility that the sexual excess troped as a 'Roman platter of boys' points also to an early connection between *satura* and Satyr. While the etymology is linguistically incorrect because the Latin adjective should then be *satyrica*, the ancients made their etymologies on looser grounds, and spelling with a *y* was dominant in the later tradition. An association between Tyre and the word *Satyros* in the anecdotal history about Alexander's siege of the city may come into play here as well.[51] According to Artemidoros (4.24), during the siege Alexander dreamed that he saw a Satyr playing on a shield, and the diviner Aristander explained the dream by etymologizing Satyrus as σὰ Τύρος, 'your Tyre,' an omen of the city's conquest. Plutarch (*Alex.* 24.8–9) has a slightly different version in which the Satyr teases Alexander by running around and keeping out of reach until at last coming into his hands. This story was undoubtedly well known in the Hellenistic age, as an emblematic account of how Tyre came to combine Greek and Phoenician culture. In his playful, sexually suggestive capitulation to Alexander,[52] the Satyr can be read as a symbol of Tyrian receptivity to foreign influences and dominance. Meleager hints that the city had a special reputation for pederasty, by calling it θεόπαις in one epigram (7.419.5) and πολύπαις in another (7.428.14). In the fluid world of Graeco-Roman etymology, the term *lanx satura* might then be heard, in multi-ethnic Tyre, as meaning a 'satiric platter,' a 'Satyr's platter,' or a 'platter of your Tyre.' This polyvalence suggests that Philokles is presented not only as a 'satyric' satirist, the first such known, but also as someone who lays claim to Tyre, whether as a Phoenician citizen or, as the translation of *satura* by Ῥωμαϊκή in the equation Ῥωμαϊκὴ λοπάς = *lanx satura* suggests, even as a Roman destined to dominate Tyre in the manner of Alexander. This lends some support to the possibility that Philokles was a Roman, though clearly a thoroughly Hellenized one capable of understanding these playful, complex etymologies. As erotic epigrammatist Meleager, however, finds his experience of Tyrian licence coloured and tempered by his education in 'Attic' Gadara, the hometown of Menippos.

At the intersection of Syrian, Phoenician, Greek, and Roman worlds, Meleager shows us that literary influence was not always from east to west, Greek to Roman, but that Roman literature had a claim of its own. A careful examination of the named individuals in the epigrams of Meleager and in the anonymous epigrams he anthologized demonstrates a circle of acquaintances in Tyre with erotic and literary interests. The reference to the Ῥωμαϊκὴ λοπάς in *AP* 12.95 indicates that the Roman genre of *satura* was familiar to members of this group. How they came to know of satire is uncertain, but it is indeed possible that Roman philhellenes brought this knowledge to Tyre, shared in the epigram production going on there, and carried back to Rome information about the Greek epigram. Antipater of Sidon surely had some such guide to Rome, someone who introduced him to the higher echelons of Roman intellectual society. Though Meleager was never to our knowledge in Rome, he too seems to have known something of early Latin literature. In one of his self-epitaphs (*Anth. Pal.* 7.419.7–8 = *HE* 4.7–8), his triple ethnic heritage is famously enshrined in the request that a passerby greet him in Syrian, Phoenician, or Greek. Should we think here of Ennius's three hearts, or three tongues – Oscan, Greek, and Roman (Gell. *NA* 17.17.1)? Is Meleager's declaration of mixed ethnicity an echo of Ennius's experience as the creator of Roman literature from a mixture of Italic and Greek elements?

## Notes

1  For useful suggestions I thank the audience at the Waterloo conference and later audiences at Cambridge, Bryn Mawr College, and CUNY.

2  *Anth. Pal.* 7.417 = *HE* 2; *Anth. Pal.* 7.418 = *HE* 3; *Anth. Pal.* 7.419 = *HE* 4; *Anth. Pal.* 7.421 = *HE* 5. For discussion, see Gutzwiller 1998a; Männlein-Robert 2007b: 372–9; Höschele, chapter 1 in this volume. Also, the following abbreviations occur in this chapter:

Astbury: Astbury, R., ed. 2002. *M. Terentius Varro, Saturarum Menippearum Fragmenta*. 2nd ed. Leipzig.

Cappelletto: Cappelletto, P., ed. 2003. *I frammenti di Mnasea*. Milan.

*GKL*: Keil, H. 1857–70. *Grammatici latini*. 8 vols. Leipzig.

*HE*: Gow, A.S.F., and D.L. Page., eds. 1965. *The Greek Anthology: Hellenistic Epigrams*, 2 vols. Cambridge.

*IDélos*: *Inscriptions de Délos*. 1926: Paris.

K-A: Kassel, R., and C. Austin, eds. 1983–2001. *Poetae Comici Graeci*. 8 vols. Berlin.

Krenkel: Krenkel, Werner, ed. 1970. *Lucilius Satiren*. 2 vols. Leiden.

Marx: Marx, F. 1904. *C. Lucilii carminum reliquiae*. Leipzig.

*SH*: Lloyd-Jones, H. and P. Parsons, eds., 1983. *Supplementum Hellenisticum*, Berlin.

Vahlen: Vahlen, J., ed. 1928. *Ennianae poesis reliquiae*. 3rd ed. Leipzig.
Voigt: Voigt, E.-M. 1971. *Sappho et Alcaeus*. Amsterdam.

3 When Meleager was growing up in the second century BC, Gadara's primary claim to fame as a producer of Hellenic intellectuals was Menippos, an important but unconventional thinker of the Cynic cast. A generation or two after Meleager, the Epicurean philosopher Philodemos, also from Gadara, demonstrates the accuracy of the claim that 'Attic' culture was available in his hometown. On the Hellenization of Phoenician cities generally, see Millar 1983; on Hellenistic Gadara, see Fitzgerald 2004; for other Syrian intellectuals and their influence on Rome, see Rey-Coquais 1994: 47–90.

4 Evidence in Meleager for local Gadaran traditions is sparse. It has been suggested that the reference in Mel. *Anth. Pal.* 12.165 = *HE* 98 to two *eromenoi*, one blonde and one brunette, refers to hot springs near Gadara, named Eros and Anteros, and known to the miracle worker Iamblichos, as reported in Eunap. 459; when Iamblichos spoke a magic incantation, the springs displayed two boys, one with light hair and one with dark (Geiger 1986). It has also been suggested that *Anth. Pal.* 7.535 = *HE* 126 on Pan refers to a statue of that god in the Panion near Gadara (Robert 1948: 10–11; Rey-Coquais 1994: 49n9). A casual reference to Jewish sexual practices on the Sabbath in *Anth. Pal.* 5.160 = *HE* 26 indicates acquaintance with Hebrew culture, probably obtained during his early years in his native city (Jacobson 1977).

5 Fitzgerald 2004: 365. Grainger 1991 offers an overview of the history of Hellenistic Phoenicia.

6 On Phoenician overseas activity, see Grainger 1991: 187–219. Tyrian presence in the islands is exemplified by a *koinon* of Herakleistai formed on Delos by 154/153 BC, an association of merchants and shippers from Tyre, who dedicated a *temenos* to their native Melqart in the Hellenized form of Herakles (*IDélos* 1519, ll. 35–54).

7 For instance, the Poseidonastai of Berytos set up a statue of the goddess Roma in their *temenos* on Delos (*IDélos*1778) and granted multiple honours to a Roman banker, M. Minatius, who must have engaged with them in joint commercial ventures (*IDélos* 1520). Romans commonly made dedications there to Phoenicians deities assimilated to Greek gods (*IDélos* 1751–55); see Picard 1920; Bruneau 1970: 622–30. For the political and commercial conditions under which Syrians and Phoenicians migrated to Delos, the centre of the Roman slave trade, in the second half of the second century, see Rauh 1993: 44–6.

8 Argentieri (2003: 29–33) dates Antipater's birth ca 180/170 and his death ca 100 BC.

9 For the influence of the *Garland* on the contents and structure of Catullus's *liber*, see Gutzwiller 2012.

10 Wifstrand 1926: 14–17. The original unity of heterosexual and pederastic
epigrams in one book is shown by *BKT* 5.1.75; see Wifstrand 1926: 10–13;
Cameron 1993: 11; Gutzwiller 1998b: 32–3, 35; Argentieri 1998: 16–17.

11 Gutzwiller 1998b: 287–91.

12 For an illustration of such a dish, see Sparkes and Talcott 1958: fig. 44.

13 As in Soph. (?) *TrGF* 1122, Pherek. fr. 113.23 K-A, Eup. fr. 365 K-A, Anaxipp. fr.
1.41 K–A; Galen, 6.653, λοπάδας . . . ἠρτυμένας ποικίλως; cf. ἄρτυμα, *condiment, seasoning*. For the primary and secondary meanings, see LSJ s.v. ἀρτύω.

14 Henderson 1991: 143–4, citing Ar. *.Eq.* 1034, of Kleon, νύκτωρ τὰς λοπάδας καὶ
τὰς νήσους διαλείχων, and Eup. fr. 60.2 K-A, πῶς ὦ πολλῶν ἤδη λοπάδων τοὺς
ἄμβωνας περιλείξας. Of course, cunnilingus is not one of the actions mentioned
in our epigrams, but the reader might hear a pun on λοπάς and λοπᾶν, a by-
form of λέπειν, 'peel,' 'husk,' a common obscenity for retracting the foreskin,
the action expressed by περισκυθίσαι in v. 6.

15 The future ἀρτύσεις implies the projected enjoyment of the various sexual
acts that the speaker wishes a god to grant Philokles. Meleager uses this type
of mixed condition, with a potential optative in the protasis and future in the
apodosis, elsewhere as well (*Anth. Pal.* 5.214.3–4 = *HE* 53.3–4, 5.215.5–6 =
54.5–6, and 12.53.7–8 = 66.7–8).

16 Such sacred groves were common in Aphrodite sanctuaries. Sappho fr. 2 Voigt
implies one, the epithet of the Aphrodite under the Athenian Acropolis was
ἐν Κήποις, 'in the Garden' (*IG* I[3] 369.80), and Strabo 14.6.3 mentions a
Hierokepis near the sanctuary of Aphrodite at Old Paphos. The worship of
Aphrodite Ourania, though first attested at Tyre in 380 AD (Rey-Coquais 2006:
23–4 no 9), is known at other Phoenician cities much earlier (Hdt. 1.105, on an
ancient sanctuary at Askalon), where she was assimilated to the Oriental goddess known to the Phoenicians as Astarte. Achilles Tatius (2.15.2) later describes
a sacrifice at Tyre to Herakles (that is, Melqart, who may have shared Astarte's
sanctuary), which involved the mingling of odours from burnt perfumes and
bouquets of mixed flowers.

17 Gow (1958: 26–9) argues that, generally, Meleager as editor used ἄδηλον for
epigrams whose authorship was in dispute and ἀδέσποτον for hackneyed verses
known to all and for inscriptions.

18 The only possible exception is *Anth. Pal.* 12.60 = Mel. *HE* 95, which is ascribed
to Meleager in P but to Dionysios Sophistes in *Laurentianus* XXXII – 50
and in a feminized version to Noumenios in the Appendix Barberino-Vaticana.
The Numenios version is undoubtedly secondary, but see below for a Dionysios
among the Tyrian epigrammatists in the *Garland* (cf. Luck 1967: 45–6).

19 Gow-Page print it as anonymous (*HE* 29), as does Aubreton, but both suggest
that Meleager is a possible author (Gow-Page 1965: II 574; Aubreton, Irigoin,
and Buffière 1994: 55n1).

20 Ypsilanti (2005: 92–4) discusses Meleager's epigrams on boys as thematic groups.

21 Since books 5 and 12 were separated by a later editor, we should include the smaller number of anonyma labelled ἄδηλον from book 5: 5.98, 5.100, 5.135, 5.168, 5.303 (all gender-neutral); 5.99 (gender-uncertain); 5.142 (on Dionysios and so misplaced in book 5); 5.200, 5.201, and 5.205 (on women who are not presented as objects of the speaker's desire); I omit 5.305, more likely by Agathias than Meleager's anonymous poet. Not surprisingly, the two ἄδηλα outside of the long Meleagrian sequence in book 12 – 12.17, 12.19 – are both pederastic (and probably reordered). It is significant that when gender is specified, only boys, never women, are objects of desire in all the ἄδηλα poems from books 5 and 12.

22 As stated by Page (Gow-Page 1965: II 560), citing Gow 1958: 20ff.

23 Reitzenstein (1893: 173) understood the epigram differently: Eubios and Eros are equally beautiful, but because Eubios lacks a bow, he is defeated in the competition. In my view, it is the lover who succumbs to love because Eros overpowers him with his bow. The first-person verb shows that the lover (or the lover together with his beloved) is the defeated, not Eubios alone.

24 Alternately, ἁρπεδόνη may mean a cord for hunting game.

25 Timarion, who appears in Mel. *Anth. Pal.* 5.96, 5.204, and (as Timo) in 5.197–8, also belongs to the Tyrian circle, since the *eromenos* Diodoros, known from six epigrams by anonymous or Meleager, is captured by her eyes in *Anth. Pal.* 12.109.

26 This example is vexed by uncertainty of attribution. Editors normally print anon. *Anth. Pal.* 12.61 = *HE* 17 and 12.62 = *HE* 18 as separate poems, but they are joined in P and could be read as a single quatrain on the Persian boy Aribazos. If, however, it is right to view the lines as two epigrams, then the second one has lost its attribution. Gow-Page (1965: II 568) propose the possibility of Meleager as author, but for stylistic reasons I think this unlikely.

27 *Anth. Pal.* 12.79 = *HE* 11 is labelled ἄδηλον in P but attributed, unpersuasively, to Meleager in the Appendix Barberino-Vaticana.

28 Gow-Page discuss the two poems under their respective authors, without acknowledging any association between them. Aubreton et al. (1994: 39n1) suggests that the 'inconnu' Dionysios is a copyist's mistake, apparently meaning that the name is drawn from the previous epigram. Tarán (1979: 45–50) observes that the two poems are connected but misses the importance of the order, by assuming that the anonymous poet may be either earlier or later than Dionysios. In fact, Kallim. *Anth. Pal.* 12.230 = *HE* 6, which Tarán takes as Dionysios's model, is much closer in form and language to the anonymous epigram, which was surely the direct model for the *eromenos* Dionysios.

29 The epigram is ascribed to Dionysios in the Palatine ms. Planudes has ἀδέσποτον, which is not a label used by Meleager and so carries less authority.

30 In his list of anthologized poets in the proem, *Anth. Pal.* 4.1, Meleager mentions just before his own 'white violets' the 'many newly written shoots of

others' (ἄλλων τ' ἔρνεα πολλὰ νεόγραφα, 55). This unnamed group of recent epigrammatists may have included not only our anonymous poet but also young writers like Dionysios who had not yet earned a place of honour in the list of recognized poets.

31  Argentieri 2003: 32.

32  A few epigrams earlier, in *Anth. Pal.* 12.79, either the anonymous poet (or less likely Meleager, see note 27) writes about an Antipater who reignites a dying flame of love with a single kiss. Since it is such a common name, we need not assume this *eromenos* is the Sidonian.

33  The immediately preceding epigram in the *Garland* sequence may signal that the name Philokles is a disguise. Of the three boys celebrated in 12.93 by the third-century poet Rhianos, one is named Philokles, and in accordance with Meleager's technique of arrangement the juxtaposition should be purposeful. In Rhianos, Philokles is a beautiful *eromenos* (cf. *kalos* Philokles in Aratos *Anth. Pal.* 12.129 = *HE* 1), whereas in Meleager's following epigrams he has become a lustful *erastes*. Rhianos's third-century date rules out the possibility that this Philokles is a single historical person. The allusion must rather be a literary game, suggesting, I surmise, that Philokles as an *erastes* is heir to the tradition of third-century pederastic epigram, likely represented by a poetic collection by Rhianos from which several epigrams are found in the *Garland* (*Anth. Pal.* 12.38 = *HE* 1, 12.58 = 2, 12.93 = 3, 12.121 = 4, 12.146 = 5, and with a doubtful ascription, 12.143 = 10).

34  Full discussion in Hauben 1987. It is usually assumed that Philokles is a translation of a Phoenician name and that Philokles was somehow related to the Sidonian royal family, but Grainger (1991: 62–4) entertains the possibility he was a Greek.

35  See Höschele 2010: 171–229 for the garland metaphor within Melelager's anthology.

36  For an account, see Gruen 1990.

37  Hirzel 1895: 440n4.

38  *GLK* I 485–6: 'Satura dicitur carmen apud Romanos nunc quidem maledicum et ad carpenda hominum vitia archaeae comoediae charactere compositum, quale scripserunt Lucilius et Horatius et Persius. et olim carmen quod ex variis poematibus constabat satura vocabatur, quale scripserunt Pacuvius et Ennius. satura autem dicta sive a Satyris, quod similiter in hoc carmine ridiculae res pudendaeque dicuntur, quae velut a Satyris proferuntur et fiunt; sive satura a lance quae referta variis multisque primitiis in sacro apud priscos dis infere-batur et a copia ac saturitate rei satura vocabatur . . .; sive a quodam genere farciminis, quod multis rebus refertum saturam dicit Varro vocitatum . . . alii autem dictam putant a lege satura, quae uno rogatu multa simul comprehendat, quod scilicet et satura carmine multa simul poemata comprehenduntur.'

39  See Ernout-Meillet 1959: *s. satur*; Walde-Hofmann 1939: *s. satura*; Van Rooy 1965: 18–19.

40  E.g., Waszink 1972: 105; Gratwick 1982: 160; Coffey 1989: 16–17; Freudenburg 2005: 3. The first title is found on P. Petrie II 49a (ca 250 BC), apparently a collection of elegiac verse by Poseidippos; see Gutzwiller 1998b: 25, 156. The second, ἄτακτα, is found as a title of works by Philitas; for interpretation, see Bing 2003. The 'Heap' is mentioned in schol. A *ad Il.* 11.101 and has been the subject of much speculation; see Gutzwiller 1998b: 18–19.

41  E.g., Van Rooy 1965: 32–3; Waszink 1972: 111–12; Coffey 1989: 24 (cautiously); Hooley 2007: 16–19.

42  Van.Rooy 1965: 26n59; Coffey 1989: 16.

43  See Hudson 1989: 69–87; Gowers (1993: 109–219) traces the metaphor of *lanx satura* through Roman satire ('food is the guts of Roman satire,' 109).

44  Gowers (1993: 192) suggests an allusion to Kallimachos's description of Antimachos's *Lyde* as a 'fat writing' (fr. 398 Pf.), and this is of course in contrast to his own 'thin Muse' (*Aet.* fr. 1.24).

45  See Olson and Sens (2000: xxxi–xxxv) on Hegemon and other epic parodists. Sopater, a parodist of the late fourth/early third century, composed a play entitled Φακῆ, in which a Spartan mercenary commander was parodied for his elegantly fashioned vinegar cruet (Ath. 6.230e = fr. 18 K-A; cf. 15.702b = fr. 19), the point being the simplicity of the condiment in contrast with the extravagance of the vessel.

46  For Atargatis as a goddess who forbade her people to eat fish, see Mnasea, fr. 48 Cappelletto.

47  On parody as an important ingredient in Menippean satire, see Relihan 1993: 25–8.

48  On the symposium images of the garland, wine, love, and song in the opening sequence of the Meleager's erotic book, see Gutzwiller 1997: 171–90.

49  Gutzwiller 1998a: 86–91.

50  It might be objected that the anonymous (Philoklean?) pederastic epigrams from the *Garland* are not any more sexually explicit than Meleager's poems. *Anth. Pal.* 5.99, ascribed to ἄδηλον in P, offers one explicit example, though problematized by the less likely ascription to Meleager in Appendix Barbarino-Vaticana. It should be remembered, however, that all these epigrams were selected by Meleager for inclusion in his anthology, and so they represent his preferences and not necessarily the full range of anonymous compositions.

51  I thank Arthur Eckstein for suggesting a connection to this anecdote and Regina Höschele for reminding me of it.

52  In book 2 of Achilles Tatius's novel, set in Tyre, a slave named Satyros facilitates the love affair between Klitophon and Leukippe.

# PART TWO

# On the Margins? Ethnicity and Hellenicity

The papers in this section all deal with populations that were in some way isolated – whether geographically, ethnically, or culturally – from the *koine* of the Hellenistic world. If 'Hellenicity' is to be defined primarily in cultural terms, rather than ethnic ones, the diffusion of Greek language and culture throughout the Mediterranean and the Near East in the Hellenistic period provided multiple opportunities for the adoption of Hellenic identity. As Altay Coşkun's paper demonstrates, the Galatians – once the terror of Asia Minor – eventually assimilated to such a point that they could even be addressed as 'genuine Romans.' Yet this assimilation took centuries to achieve, and the very fact that their Hellenizing and Romanizing was worthy of mention is an indication that the Celts had long been considered the 'other,' the quintessential barbarian.

The emphasis on culture over ethnicity as a marker of identity allowed for the marginalization even of native Greeks who, like the Aitolians, failed to live up to general expectations of Hellenic behaviour. Such a characterization is of course tendentious, intended to portray those frequent enemies of Polybios's native Achaia as barbarian outsiders among their fellow Greeks. And yet Polybios was not the only contemporary to call into question the Aitolians' Hellenicity: Thucydides had already remarked that the majority of Aitolians were almost unintelligible in their speech and ate their meat raw (3.94). Joseph Scholten's paper explores the issue of Aitolian marginalization and their bid for acceptance into the Greek club in the Hellenistic period. Such acceptance as they received was in large part the result of their successful defence of Greece (and Hellenism) against the invading Celts; juxtaposed against a blackly barbaric nation, the Aitolians took on a rosy Hellenic hue.

In addition to commenting on their peculiar language and diet, Thucydides also states that the Aitolians of his day lived in widely scattered villages – in other words, that they were not familiar with the politically and culturally advanced institution of the polis. Political sophistication was particularly associated with Hellenism, and even in the Hellenistic period, when the international impact of the individual polis had largely disappeared, *poleis* still clung to their principles of internal citizen-rule. Glenn Bugh shows us that the democratic ideal did not disappear in the Hellenistic age, and that it was in fact another measure of Hellenicity, particularly for the *poleis* of the Black Sea, distanced from other Hellenes and facing pressures from surrounding 'barbarians': Celts, Scythians, and others.

Belonging to the Greek club in the Hellenistic period was thus marked by the achievement and expression of certain cultural and political norms, rather than by any particular ethnicity. Galatians might join, if they were prepared to play by the rules – and Aitolians might be blackballed, if they behaved like the flesh-eating Cyclopes.

# 4

# Belonging and Isolation in Central Anatolia: The Galatians in the Graeco-Roman World

## ALTAY COŞKUN

## I. The Celts' Intrusion into the Hellenistic World: A First Overview[1]

When Lysimachos had to confront Seleukos I near Koroupedion in western Asia Minor in 281 BC, Celtic tribes from the Balkan region seized the opportunity to attack Macedon. The death of both kings encouraged further invasions. In his attempt to stop them, Ptolemy Keraunos, the new ruler of Macedon, was killed in 279 BC. Immediately thereafter, the warlord Brennos gathered more than two hundred thousand warriors to intrude into central Greece. Their bloody traces can be followed all the way up to the sanctuary of Apollo at Delphi, where, under the lead of the Aitoloi, the Greeks inflicted a terrible defeat upon them. Just before this clash, a splinter group of around twenty thousand warriors had defected from the Celtic throng. They plundered their way through Thrace, and ended up besieging the walls of Byzantion. When they failed to take the city and were likewise prohibited from crossing over to Asia, they split up again. Soon afterwards, the smaller part under Loutarios stole a few ships and crossed the Hellespont. The main corps led by Leonnorios was finally hired by Nikomedes I of Bithynia, and their transport over the Bosporos was provided for by Byzantion in 278 BC.

Shortly thereafter, Leonnorios and Loutarios joined forces again, in order to secure the throne to Nikomedes against his brother and rival Zipoëtes. While the latter enjoyed the support of King Antiochos I, the son of Seleukos I, the former was allied with the Northern League, which was headed by Herakleia Pontika. As soon as the Seleukid influence was banned from the Bithynian coast, the Galatians turned south and west, and oppressed the rich coastal cities. Around the same time, they took possession of their new dwelling places somewhere in south-eastern Bithynia, southern Paphlagonia, and north-eastern Phrygia. From these bases, they gained control over adjacent areas in eastern Phrygia and western Kappadokia.[2]

For the third and early second centuries BC, a confusing variety of allegiances and conflicts is reported, including some victories by the Seleukids, the Attalids, and the Mithridatids over 'the Galatians' and some successes of the latter over the former. No single battle seems to have imposed a longer-term foreign rule on the invaders or on their descendants. The most serious defeat was inflicted on them by the Roman general Manlius Vulso in 189 BC, but from 188 on they managed to outplay the competing powers to their own benefit. In 166 BC, they were even accepted into the friendship of the Romans and thus received valuable diplomatic protection against the ambitions of the Pergamene kings.[3]

By this time, the most powerful Galatian tribe were the Tolistobogioi, who lived in the west around Bloukion and Gordion. Their eastern neighbours, the Tektosages, dwelt somewhere between Ankyra and the Great Salt Lake. The Trokmoi seem to have occupied the territory east of the Halys around Tavium much later than hitherto acknowledged, probably not before the end of the second century BC.[4] Even after the Tolistobogian king Deiotaros gained control over the whole of Galatia in the mid-first century and after Augustus transformed central Anatolia into the province of Galatia in 25 BC, these three tribes maintained their distinctiveness and inner autonomy. Over the next centuries, the tribal centres developed into Hellenistic cities. Greek and Roman personal names also gradually spread to the rural areas. This tendency culminated in AD 212, when the Galatians were included in the offer of Roman franchise to all the free inhabitants of the empire. But traces of their tribal distinctiveness survived for another two or three generations.[5]

## II. Preliminary Reflections on 'Belonging and Isolation' in Asia Minor, followed by Some 'Isolationist' Views on the Galatians

Whether the Galatians 'belonged' to the 'Graeco-Roman world' or were 'isolated' in (or from) it is not as easy a question as it might seem at first glance.

An adequate answer requires some preliminary reflection on the underlying notions of the terms at issue. While the boundaries of 'Roman-ness' can be circumscribed in a comparatively clear-cut way (though not without pitfalls),[6] 'Hellenicity' is a much more evasive entity. Of course, it is not the aim of this article to discuss the competing criteria that are usually applied to define 'Hellenic' or 'Hellenistic,' such as how one ponders the weight of linguistic, cultural, political, geographical, and chronological aspects.[7] I would only like to point out that the degree of a particular town's or tribe's 'belonging' to or 'isolation' in the Graeco-Roman world very much depends on the set of criteria one applies, whether deliberately or subconsciously.

. With respect to the polities of inland Asia Minor in the Hellenistic period, the scarcity of primary evidence poses an additional problem. We can approach their 'ethnic identities' (if this handy but contested term is admitted) only tentatively by describing how they communicated with their closer or farther neighbours, trafficked goods and shared tastes, styles, and values with them. But even if positive testimony is available, it is still hard to tell whether their inhabitants actually felt some sort of belonging to a larger Phrygian, Anatolian, Greek, or Graeco-Roman community.

And in particular respect to 'the Galatians,' we are facing two further problems. First, modern usage of this ethnic is inconsistent, while ancient authorities apply it widely and vaguely. Secondly, our sources predominantly mirror out-group views, and these tend to be rather unfavourable or at least tendentious for the most part. Thus the impact of prejudice, sweeping generalization, and distortion is pervasive in ancient as well as in modern accounts.

Both conditions have nurtured the prevailing narrative of the so-called 'Elephant Victory.' Namely, according to most modern accounts, we are to believe that King Antiochos I crushed the Galatians and settled them in the remote and arid hinterland of Phrygia. They are said to have remained 'uncultivated barbarians' for the next two and a half centuries, being little affected by the spread of Hellenic language or urban culture among their direct neighbours. Admittedly, they were hired time and again as mercenaries, but even as such they acted in their exclusive tribal units, for they would do so most efficiently by displaying their fear-inspiring wildness rather than by trying to fight in a disciplined phalanx.[8]

A vivid impression of their distinctive appearance and manners is conveyed by the first-century BC historian Diodoros: 'Certain of them despise death to such a degree that they enter the perils of battle without protective armour and with no more than a girdle about their loins . . . And when any man accepts the challenge to battle, they then break forth into a song in praise of the valiant deeds of their ancestors and in boast of their own high achievements, reviling all the while and belittling their opponent, and trying ... to strip him of his bold spirit before the combat. When their enemies fall, they cut off their heads and fasten them about the necks of their horses' (5.29.2–3; Loeb trans.).

According to Sir William Ramsay, for long the most influential scholar on the Galatians, they were still earning their living as cattle breeders, slave traders, and mercenaries when Augustus decided to transform central Anatolia into a Roman province. The emperor's noble aim allegedly was to civilize these barbarians, or, in Ramsay's terminology, to 'de-Gallicize' them. Ramsay had experienced the British Empire at its height, and, for him, a cultural mission of the Romans was so apparent that he thought his claim did not require confirmation by sources.[9] Although serious scholars nowadays tend to refrain from outspokenly racist statements, the ancient commonplace of 'the Barbarian' has continued to flourish in Galatian historiography. Thus as recently as 1975, Ronald Mellor called the inhabitants of the *provincia Galatia* 'little more than savages' (Mellor 1975: 89).

Stephen Mitchell, however, to whom we owe the most thorough and complete account of Galatian history, has yielded much less to widespread bias and paid more respect to the multifarious sources. Avoiding moralistic judgments, he describes instead the conditions of migration and settlement as well as the development of social and political relations. Nevertheless, where ancient and modern authorities remain united in their opinion, Mitchell tends to support the traditional view. In this, the approach of Karl Strobel differs radically.

### III. *Terror Gallicus*, the Ideology of *Keltensieg*, and Karl Strobel's 'Inclusive' Counter-Design of the Galatians

Strobel claims that most ancient sources and modern accounts are seriously distorted by anti-Celtic bias. Notwithstanding a general Hellenic disposition to denigrate non-Greeks, the conception of Celts as barbarians *par excellence* has its roots in the propaganda of those who defeated them: the victors instrumentalized their victories to enhance the legitimacy of their rule. After the triumph of the Aitolian League at Delphi in 279 BC, Hellenistic kings likewise styled themselves as 'saviours' of the civilized world, regardless of how glorious their fight against the Celts had been. Their *Keltensieg* was then immortalized on coin imagery, in panegyric poetry, through sculptures exhibited in the most distinguished sanctuaries of the Greek world, and by means of cult rituals for the saviour-kings. These ancient 'mass media' not only brought the divine achievements to public awareness, but also shaped the contemporary and future imagination of the evil and mad nature of the Celts.[10]

Most prominent are the monuments that the Attalids erected in Pergamon and sponsored in Delphi, Athens, and Delos between the later third and the mid-second centuries BC.[11] After refusing to pay tribute to the Tolistobogioi and defeating them repeatedly from 240 BC on, Attalos I sought every opportunity to have his deeds assimilated to the mythical victory over the Titans and Giants. Perhaps the most famous sculpture is that of the 'Dying Galatian,' which is known to us thanks to a Roman marble copy.[12] Characteristic features are the golden torc, the moustache, and the shaggy hair, all of which elements are also mentioned in Diodoros's digression on the Celts. Some art historians would also call attention to the pointed physiognomy of the face. But beyond these ethnic markers, the Galatian appears with an athletic body in heroic nakedness.

Probably to the same iconographic program belonged the 'Galatian Killing His Wife and Himself,' again preserved only as a Roman marble copy.[13] The very first – romantic – impression one may have is certainly misleading: the warrior is not killing himself because he has found his wife dead; rather, it is he himself who has killed her by stabbing her in the armpit – one can see the blood spilling out of her right sleeve. Two alternative interpretations have been offered: either the battle against Attalos was lost and the Galatian wanted to save himself and his wife from slavery, or we have before us another variation on the topic of Galatian lethal madness. The most impressive version is told by Justin. It appears in the context of a battle with Antigonos Gonatas: 'And when also the Gauls prepared themselves for the battle, they slaughtered cattle for the auspices; since their entrails predicted heavy defeat and destruction, they were not seized by fear, but by madness, and hoping to expiate the threats of the gods by the slaughter of their kin, they butchered their wives and children, thus initiating the war with the murder of their kin' (*Epit.* 26.2.2).

At any rate, these 'Attalid Galatians' were understood as despisers of death and masters of cruelty, though this was accomplished without vilifying them: in their heroic postures, they inspire fear and veneration at the same time. Their conqueror, in turn, deserved the highest praise. How importantly the Galatian victories figured in Pergamene propaganda is also made clear in Polybios's tribute to Attalos I: 'It is therefore appropriate to admire the magnanimity of the aforesaid, for he invested his means for nothing else than to achieve kingship; there is nothing greater or more beautiful which could be mentioned. In the beginning, he not only strived for the above-mentioned aim by benefits and favours towards friends, but also through deeds in war. Namely, after defeating the Galatians, who then were the most cruel and belligerent people in Asia, he then declared himself king for the first time' (18.41.5–7).

This way, the ideology of *Keltensieg* fused the Galatian and the barbarian into one savage nature, thereby imprinting the imagination of generations to come. Such stereotypes were absorbed by the Romans, while they were fighting fiercely against the Gauls in Cisalpina in the later third and early second centuries. At the same time, the memory of the sack of Rome in 387 BC was revived. The Gallic chieftain was allegedly called *Brennos*, just as the leader of the attack on Delphi: coincidence or fabrication? Later on, Caesar repeated anti-Celtic prejudice in his *Commentarii de bello Gallico* to enhance his own achievements.

In the face of such a powerful *Keltensieg* tradition, Strobel claims that the whole of Galatian history has been distorted and needs to be rewritten. In his counter-design, the Galatians were welcome within the Hellenistic world and struggled under the same conditions as other major players. Instead of booty, they primarily longed for new arable land; instead of driving off the indigenous people from their soil, they included them socially and cultur- ally; after the 'Galatization' of the Phrygians, the Galatians even became the promotors of Hellenization in Central Anatolia. And while Livy reports that the *poleis* and kings paid taxes to the Galatians, Strobel speaks of remunera- tion of services or gift exchange.[14]

This fresh (though perhaps overly idealizing) approach is combined with a painstaking description of the Galatian landscape, archaeological fieldwork in eastern Galatia, as well as Celtic and anthropological studies. All of this has indeed highly stimulated my own research. But it is apparent that Strobel's contentions are repeatedly too sweeping, and they themselves finally add up to a tendentious image of the Galatians. Hence, a critical re-examination not only of ancient and modern explicit statements, but also of their underlying premises, is highly promising. Consequences pertain to nearly every pe- riod and aspect of Galatian history, sometimes not even foreseen by Strobel himself. A good example is the above-mentioned 'Elephant Victory.' For the tradition of a glorious victory on the battlefield is mainly based on a panegy- rical version initiated at the Seleukid court: it was designed to cover up the king's incapability to expel or subdue the Galatians, who were only pacified by a costly diplomacy.[15]

### IV. Ethnic Labels as Indicators of 'Belonging'? A Discussion of Celtic Unity versus Diversity in Central Anatolia

Further important insights can be gained by reflection on the use of ethnics. Greek and Roman authors chiefly limit the label *Celti/Keltoi* in its strict sense to the Gauls living in or near the boundaries of modern France. But they also use it more generally as a collective term for northern barbarians, including Germanic and even Scythian peoples. Closer to the modern usage of 'Celts' were the Greek *Galatai* and the Latin *Galli* respectively: thus were called not only the Celts of western and central Europe, but also the ones in southern and eastern Europe, who produced the invaders of Asia Minor.[16]

Many modern accounts, however, tend to limit the term 'Galatians' to 'Celts of Asia Minor.' Myself, I even go one step further. As an analytical term, I apply 'Galatians' solely to the Celts that occupied the region on both sides of the Sangarios bow and the middle Halys, as well as to their descendants. Accordingly, beyond the Tolistobogioi, Tektosages, and Trokmoi, I also include other Celtic tribes that were over time absorbed by one of the former three, unless they were extinguished. But I am more hesitant with Celts attested elsewhere in Hellenistic Anatolia, as long as no direct links to the core of Galatia can be established.[17] This distinction is not only due to the later arrival of further Celts in Asia Minor, but also arises from different patterns in onomastic habits, material culture, and political allegiances.[18]

Be this as it may, ancient writers predominantly employ the generic terms *Galli/Galatai* instead of the individual tribal names. Frequently, this usage was – or still is – due to ignorance of the appropriate names in the contexts at issue. But ideological motivations will also have played their roles in distorting the representation of Celts. For to enhance the prestige of one's victory, claiming the defeat of '(the) Galatians' was more likely to inspire admiration among contemporaries than, e.g., that of '(the) Trokmoi,' since most individual tribal names would simply have meant little or nothing to a Hellenized or Roman audience.

The impact of such terminological imprecision is significant. For the lack of distinction – combined with the persistent cultivation of barbarian stereotypes – has repeatedly induced non-Celts to assume a cultural homogeneity or a social connection among these 'barbarians.' A telling example is a short story told by Parthenios in the mid-first century BC about a Milesian woman who was captured by a Galatian, when they raided Ionia (i.e., around 277/276 BC), and was taken to his home in Gaul in the hinterland of Marseilles. The location has certainly been induced by the name of the Celt, *Kavaros*, which resembles the Gaulish tribal name *Cavari*.[19]

The same diffuse notion of the Celts seems to be at work when ancient authors (frequently followed by modern) draw close connections between the Volcae, Volcae Tectosages, and Tektosages in southern Gaul, central Germany, Pannonia, and Anatolia. Particularly revealing is the widespread but fanciful story of the 'Tolosan Gold,' i.e., the gold that Servilius Caepio discovered in Tolosa during the Cimbric War (105 BC). Many writers believed that it was the booty of those Celts who had returned home after attacking Delphi in 279 BC, although Poseidonios rightly claimed it to be of local, i.e., Gaulish, origin.[20]

Another consequence of this terminological indifference is the widespread assumption that neighbouring Galatian tribes formed a political union or at least used to concert their military and diplomatic actions. While frequent cooperation among some Galatian tribes cannot be denied, there is actually no unquestionable evidence for any action uniting all Galatians politically before the days of King Deiotaros in the first century BC. And even for this later period, the evidence of a fragmentation of Galatian interests is much stronger. However, my 'analytical' approach to 'the Galatians' has still to be confronted with the clear-cut description in Strabo's *Geography*, which forms the basis for nearly all modern views on the subject.

## V. The Unitarian Picture of the Galatians in Strabo's *Geography*

In Strabo's *Geography*, we learn, among other things, about the close locations of the territories of the Galatian tribes, the identity of their language and customs, and their common origin: allegedly the Gaulish tribe of the (Volcae) Tectosages. Their political unity is illustrated more precisely by their subdivision into twelve identical subtribes plus a common assembly in the so-called Oak-Wood (*Drynemeton*).[21]

Some of these assertions, however, appear to result from speculations on the onomastic material rather than being source-based facts. A closer analysis of Strabo's presentation will demonstrate the deliberate schematism that he imposes on Galatian society and history. Inconsistencies arise not only by adducing independent authorities such as Memnon of Herakleia, who speaks of seventeen tribal units and two supreme commanders for the year 278 BC, and Livy, who names four *reguli* for 189 BC and construes a geographical landscape different from Strabo's.[22] Discrepancies also occur within the *Geography* itself.

For example, in his earlier treatment of southern Gaul, Strabo does not mention the theory that all of the eastern Galatians had derived from the Tektosages; instead, he supposes that the Tolistobogioi and Trokmoi stemmed from homonymous Gaulish tribes, which at the time of writing were extinct. While neither of the explanations is likely to be true,[23] it is noteworthy that, in his Galatian chapter, the author has opted for a version that implies a higher degree of uniformity. This observation is closely linked with another deliberate choice: for the sake of insinuating homogeneity, Strabo only mentions the name of Leonnorios and suppresses the independent actions of Loutarios. But he must have known the latter from the same sources as the former. Instead, the reader is misled to deduce *Tolistobogios* and *Trokmos* as the names of Leonnorios's subordinate companions.

Most important for the assumption of a federal state with a common foreign policy is the geographer's description of the threefold tetrarchical constitution:

> The three tribes spoke the same language and differed from each other in no respect; and each was divided into four portions which were called tetrarchies, each tetrarchy having its own tetrarch, and also one judge and one military commander, both subject to the tetrarch, and two subordinate commanders. The council of the twelve tetrarchs consisted of three hundred men, who assembled at Drynemetum, as it was called. Now the Council passed judgment upon murder cases, but the tetrarchs and the judges upon all others. Such, then, was the organisation of Galatia long ago, but in my time the power has passed to three rulers, then to two, and then to one, Deiotaros. (12.5.1 C567; Loeb trans.)

This description of a Galatian constitution is for the most part accepted today (with the exception of the present author),[24] even though the constitution itself is said to go back to the times prior to the migration. Even if we disregard the complete isolation of this allegation among the ancient sources, and likewise suppress general concerns about the stability of the posited system,[25] it is, again, Strabo himself who causes suspicion; for, in a previous chapter, he seemed to presuppose that, at the turn from the second to the first century, only a single ruler of all the Tolistobogioi existed. And only the latter view finds support in the epigraphic documents.[26] Moreover, the entire body of evidence outside the *Geography* suggests that the tribes were ruled monarchically throughout the Hellenistic period. Accordingly, the elite is designated as *basileis* in Greek or *reguli* in Latin texts related to the third and second centuries BC, thus coming close to the Celtic *riges* (i.e., 'chieftains') well known from the European context but indirectly attested in Galatian onomastics as well.[27]

In contrast, the title of *tetrarches* lacks any relevant parallel in the Celtic world, despite repeated claims to the opposite.[28] In Anatolia, it appears no earlier than around 100 BC, but even then it does not imply a limitation of the ruler's power by any other Galatian official or institution. Most probably, it was Mithridates VI Eupator of Pontos who bestowed this label on four (not twelve) rulers of four (not three or twelve) hitherto autonomous Galatian tribal units. Designed as a means to control central Anatolia, the title outlived its creator after the downfall of Pontos. Its survival was owing to its confirmation by the Romans. And only in the 40s BC did it emancipate itself from its etymological reference to four territories, when the Romans also declared non-Galatian eastern petty dynasts to be 'tetrarchs.'[29]

## VI.  Three Intermediate Conclusions

Whether or not one is prepared to follow my alternative view of Galatian constitutional history, three conclusions impose themselves so far:

1) Strabo's sketch may at best have been close to reality for a very limited period. It can no longer be regarded as the institutional background to assumed common activities of the Galatians throughout the third and second centuries BC – even less so, since the geographer himself attributes only juridical powers to the council of the Drynemeton.
2) We should allow for much more autonomy and diversity of diplomatic affiliations among the eastern Celts in general, and the Galatians in particular. If, over time, the latter did develop a sort of common identity, that was surely less the result of their common language and the similarity of other cultural features than it was of massive military and political pressures.
3) Thus, whenever we read '(the) Galatians' in ancient and (most) modern accounts on Anatolia, we are well advised to translate this into '(members of) one or more of the Celtic or Galatian peoples living in Asia Minor.'

Up until now, we have prepared the ground to address several other historical problems. I shall now choose three further examples – relevant not only to current Galatian disputes, but also to more complex issues of the Graeco-Roman World.

## VII.  Warriors, Nomads, or Farmers? Galatian Lifestyle(s) and the Incentive(s) for Their Migration(s)

Travellers to central Turkey nowadays experience a mainly arid and infertile region. This impression seemed to support the view that Antiochos relegated the Galatians to the inhospitable hinterland of Anatolia after his 'Elephant Victory.' Others assume that, as cattle-breeding nomads or robbers, the invaders were quite happy with their rough and remote environment.[30] But Strobel has demonstrated that the quality of the soil and the microclimate worsened significantly only during the later Byzantine period.[31] In fact, many parts of Galatia, such as the river valleys, were highly productive in cereals, as we know for the high and late Roman Empire, while other strips were covered with forests. On this basis, Strobel contradicts the traditional opinions and claims that the migrants had longed for arable land from the beginning on. He therefore rejects all the references to their nomadic or brigand lifestyles as distortions or exaggerations.[32]

Strobel may be right to claim that much of the Galatian territories constituted prizes for their military service (unanimously attested by Strabo, Memnon, and Justin).[33] But one could likewise claim with Livy that they conquered the land in their own right.[34] However this may be, as long as archaeological indications for a society of predominantly settled farmers are lacking, it is difficult to dismiss Strabo's testimony to the immense livestock of King Amyntas or Livy's description of the desert-like Axylon ('tree-less steppe').[35] Not to mention the widespread attestation of Galatian mercenaries in the service of Hellenistic kings or cities. Hence, there is no necessity to posit a single favourite form of subsistence for the whole of Galatia.[36]

Given the scarcity of the evidence, tribal names deserve to be considered as additional sources for the early Hellenistic period. As indicated above in section 4, most scholars regard all Volcae, Volcae Tectosages, and Tektosages attested between Gaul and Anatolia as ethnically related.[37] Strobel even feels encouraged to construe an itinerary of migrants who left their homes in the German *Mittelgebirge*, moved through the Balkans, and finally settled in Asia Minor to resume their work as farmers.[38] The strength of the argument rests, on the one hand, on the partial homonymy of the ethnics. On the other hand, in order to follow Strobel, one has to deny those who raided Macedonia, Greece, or the Ionian cities a serious interest in booty, and further ignore that the experience of enriching raids and extortions or of serving as highly paid mercenaries may well have changed previous habits or aims. Hence there is little to commend this ingenious construction.

Likewise, an etymological analysis speaks against the assumption of direct connections between the aforementioned groups. It is now mostly accepted that 'Volcae' stems from the Gaulish *volca*, which originally meant 'falcon,' but later also became a synonym for 'warrior.'[39] The martial motif would of course be attractive as a tribal name, and it cannot be excluded that in one case or another it may have been chosen as such. But it is no less plausible that some tribes called their military body *volca*, and that this became the name of a levy sent out to found a colony at times of overpopulation. Alternatively, a whole tribe could have been called after its army – initially perhaps by foreigners, but the designation may have been appealing enough to be accepted by the members of the tribe themselves.[40] For the latter onomastic process, we can draw on strong analogies: think only of the Germanic *Alle-Mannen*.[41]

But the most striking parallels are the following: at the time when the Tolistobogioi, the Trokmoi, and the Tektosages entered the Anatolian stage, their new neighbours called them neither *Celti* nor by their individual tribal names, but addressed them as *Galatai*. This means 'brave fighters' in Gaulish and goes well with their military occupation. It was accordingly that the Romans denoted their Celtic oppressors *Galli* and not after their individual ethnics.[42] Later on, the term 'Volcae' became the general denomination of the Celts in the Germanic languages. German *welsch*, French 'Wallon,' and English 'Wales' are direct descendants.[43] In the face of such evidence, the concept of a genetic or ethnic uniformity of all Volcae (Tectosages) cannot reasonably be upheld.

However this may be, not 'Volcae,' but 'Tektosages' is attested for some Celts of Asia Minor. This designation can be translated as 'Seekers of a Roof/House.' It certainly fits well a group of men, women, and children who had to emigrate, in order to ease the strain on the alimentary supply of their home community.[44] And in fact high fertility, overpopulation, and hunger are repeatedly spelt out as motivations for the Celtic movements to the east in the early third century BC.[45] There were then plenty of such colonizing missions, and in some cases the generic term 'Tektosages' may have developed into an individual ethnic, without necessarily implying a relation between all namesakes – or a desire for cultivating cereals.

At any rate, the Anatolian Tektosages appear to have been at some distance from the two groupings that Livy and Memnon attest as the allies of Nikomedes I of Bithynia and as masters of the Aegean coast, groupings that were in all likelihood the forefathers of the Tolistobogioi and the Trokmoi. An inimical relationship is even implied in a fragment of Apollonios of Aphrodisias: according to him, the tribe that later settled around Ankyra had been hired by Mithridates I of Pontos.[46] Another difference pertains to the question of the demographic make-up of these bands. For the hordes led by Leonnorios and Loutarios are said to have comprised twenty thousand men, only half of whom were unarmed. This is not the armed/unarmed proportion of a whole tribe (men, women, children) on the move, as commonly claimed (and quite plausibly so for the Tektosages),[47] but rather that of Celtic warriors accompanied only by their clients and servants.[48]

The obvious conclusion of this section must be a plea for taking more seriously the diversity of the origins, environments, lifestyles, and policies of the Galatians. Such an analytical (as opposed to synthetic) approach will automatically lead up to several further insights or questions as to settlement patterns, demography, intercultural processes, and political affiliations, most of them highly relevant to the theme of 'belonging and isolation in central Anatolia.' For the time being, I confine myself to questioning the assumption that there was an intrinsic feeling of 'belonging to a Galatian society' in the third and second centuries BC.

### VIII. *Amicitia populi Romani*: Rhetorical Façade or Reality? The Example of King Deiotaros Philorhomaios

The next spotlight takes us down to the first century BC, and it provides me with an opportunity to mention the actual starting point of my Galatian studies: a Trier-based research project on Roman foreign relations, in particular on the notion of friendship within Roman diplomacy.[49]

Classical scholarship has traditionally viewed *amicitia populi Romani* either in terms of *Völkerrecht* as a.type of interstate contract, or as a euphemistic label for crude hegemony. On the one hand, however, the Romans did not generally shrink from openly naming hierarchies; and, on the other, they insisted in calling their diplomatic partners – whether kings, cities, or other distinguished persons – 'friends.' This observation leads us to hypothesize that the choice of words would have had some impact on those relations. Of course, we were not ignoring the asymmetric nature of such 'friendships' or the several reported instances in which Roman behaviour towards some 'friends' fell short of *amicitia*. But we still suppose that such a relation would normally imply mutual benefits and allow for affection between individuals, unless such interpersonal links had rather been the stimulus for establishing interstate friendship.[50]

The Tolistobogian tetrarch Deiotaros has been a rewarding test case. Already in the 90s BC, he supported Sulla's war against Kappadokia, and in the subsequent decades, he was Rome's staunchest ally in the wars against Mithridates Eupator of Pontos. Nearly all of the Roman generals who fought in the East made friends with him, many lauded him before the Roman senate or in public assemblies. In 64 BC, Pompey raised him to kingship and presented him with large parts of the former Pontic realm. These resources enabled him to run a standing army and to defend Asia Minor against further attacks from the Black Sea region or the Parthians. Inevitably, he got involved in the Roman Civil War, in which he sided with his most important benefactor, Pompey. After the latter's death, he had to make peace with Caesar, who renewed his older friendship bonds with the king, but nevertheless stripped him of half of his realm. Their relationship remained difficult. In 45 BC, Tectosagen rivals of the king hoped to get rid of him by accusing him of having plotted against Caesar.[51]

To a modern audience, Deiotaros is mainly known thanks to the apologetic speech that Cicero then held in his defence. It is not only full of praise for the ally, but also expresses the latter's deep affection for the Roman people and Pompey in particular. Among other things, Cicero points out his deep concerns at the outbreak of the Civil War in 49 BC: 'vir huic imperio amicissimus de salute populi Romani extimescebat, in qua etiam suam esse inclusam videbat' (As the closest friend of this empire he was deeply worried about the safety of the Roman people, in which he saw included even his own) (*Deiot.* 11).

Most modern judgments differ significantly from that of Cicero. Marcel Lob, a French editor of the apology, characterizes Deiotaros as 'sultan mi-grec, mi-barbare, intelligent sans doute, actif, courageux au combat, mais cupide, ambitieux, rusé, sans dignité, toujours aux côtés du plus fort, cruel jusqu'à la férocité et vindicatif au bord même de la tombe.' And further: 'de ce sultan mi-grec . . . Cicéron a fait un vieillard doux et grave, noble, généreux, fidèle à l'amitié, même dans le malheur, et dévoué de toute son âme – on se demande pourquoi – aux seuls intérêts de Rome. César . . . dut écouter sans rire ce panégyrique d'une outrance toute professionnelle.' Arnold Jones comments: 'The history of Galatia for the twenty years which succeeded Pompey's settlement consists largely in the intrigues and murders of Deiotaros, who had set his heart upon ruling the whole country.' H. Willrich claims 'dass . . . unter dem hellenistischen Firnis unverfälschtes, rohes Barbarentum lag.' Denis Saddington finds Deiotaros 'certainly not a sympathetic character, nor could he be plausibly credited with laudable qualities.'[52]

Up until now, the king has not been deemed worthy of a monograph, although Wolfgang Hoben and Sir Ronald Syme at least assigned him a biographic chapter in their books on Asia Minor. In the face of Deiotaros's deeds, both cannot but acknowledge some of his achievements. Syme especially stresses his loyalty to Pompey, but on the whole, the view of a violent and unpredictable tyrant shines through repeatedly in his account. His German colleague even explicitly denies Deiotaros's capability of cherishing interpersonal relations.[53]

Such judgments are, again, based on diffuse anti-Celtic resentments rather than on relevant sources. For even if one discards the above-quoted apology as tendentious, one can adduce many other testimonies. For example, Cicero, as proconsul of Cilicia in 51 BC, was happy to send his son and nephew to the king's court for summer holidays.[54] And in a letter to the Roman senate, he praised the Tolistobogian as the single reliable ally of the Romans at the critical time of the Parthian War.[55] Brutus is reported to have made a surprisingly emotional speech on behalf of his friend in 47 BC. A century later, Lucan, in his epic *Pharsalia*, styles Deiotaros as the personification of friendship and loyalty, contrasting him with many others who had left Pompey after Caesar's victory in 48 BC. Interestingly, Plutarch, in the later first and early second centuries AD, understands 'Galatian' as synonymous with 'barbarian,' but whenever he speaks of Deiotaros, one has the impression that he regarded him as a wise and honourable man.[56]

But gradually the memory of the king's achievements for Rome vanished. Deiotaros somehow became the personification of pre-Roman Galatia, whereas the name of the country 'naturally' implied a hostile attitude towards the civilized world. Anti-Celtic resentments thus returned to the narrative. In the sixth century AD, for example, the Byzantine chronicler John Malalas describes the provincialization of Galatia as the result of a war that Augustus fought against Deiotaros. And in the twelfth century, John Tzetzes writes: 'This Ankyra that I am speaking of was, as I have discovered, founded by the Roman Octavius Caesar after killing Deitarus [sic], the tetrarch of Galatia.'[57] These quotations nicely link up to our next spotlight.

## IX. The 'Soft' Provincialization of Galatia

Amyntas, the last king of Galatia, died in 25 BC. Instead of appointing a successor, Augustus imposed his rule on the whole realm, which extended as far southwards as the Pamphylian coast. In the next decades, other smaller territories that had been ruled by independent Galatian princes were attached to the province. My research in the latter's history has been motivated by the question of why the first emperor did not continue the successful tradition of *reges amici populi Romani*. When I did not find a clear answer, I at least wanted to understand better what it actually meant in this specific case: to be transformed into a province.[58]

Recent scholarship has abandoned euphemistic ideas of civilizing missions. But they continue to assume an active policy of urbanization, if only to facilitate the political control and the economic exploitation of a country. In the case of central Galatia, most historians see the particular need to foster urban development, since (with the distinct exception of Strobel) they mostly consider the inhabitants to have conducted a nomadic lifestyle still in the late first century BC, if not well into the Christian era. Accordingly, common opinion holds that the Tolistobogioi received the formerly independent temple state of Pessinous as their urban centre, the Trokmoi Tavium, and the Tektosages Ankyra. The latter is also believed to have been raised to metropolitan status, hosting the residence of the *legatus Augusti pro praetore*. Further 'essentials' of provincial rule such as the imposition of Roman tax or jurisdiction have likewise been taken for granted.[59]

In addition, several historians favour the view that, from Augustus onwards, the establishment of a central cult for the Goddess Roma and the God Sebastos (i.e., Augustus) coincided. In fact, the Ankyran temple for these two divine powers appears to be the most impressive of all inland Anatolia.[60] And the devotion of the Galatians to these is not only attested by a flow of inscriptions and coin imagery down until the third century AD, but also by the honorific title of the three tribes: with (or soon after) the inauguration of the cult, they obtained the privilege to call themselves *Sebastenoi Tolistobogioi*, *Sebastenoi Tektosages*, and *Sebastenoi Trokmoi*, the apposition meaning 'Devoted to the God Augustus.'[61]

Unfortunately, a closer look at the evidence once more drives me into 'heresy.' A new analysis of the famous priest list inscribed on the north-west *anta* of the temple seems to enable us to date the inauguration of the cult exactly to 5 BC, the beginning of the construction of the temple to 2 BC, and the inauguration of the temple to AD 14.[62] For the time being, I am happy to draw on the authority of Stephen Mitchell: he formerly argued for the initiation of the cult under the first Roman governor and for the inauguration of the temple in 19 BC, but he now considers accepting my suggestions with only minor changes.[63] At any rate, this new chronology separates the inauguration of the cult from the provincialization by some twenty years and thus clearly speaks against any functional connection between the divinization of the emperor and the establishment of Roman rule.

I was even more surprised to see that there is no trace of a noticeable urban development before the mid-first century AD, when civic architecture and epigraphy came into broader use. Likewise missing is any reference to a governor's acting or even residing in Ankyra before the reign of Hadrian, when the city's title *metropolis* is attested for the first time. Moreover, the evidence for the merging of the Phrygian temple state of Pessinous and the Tolistobogian tribe stretches from the late Augustan until the Trajanic periods, thus mirroring a slow development rather than a clear-cut Roman policy.[64]

As it seems, urbanization mostly resulted from the practical needs of the Parthian War, which was constantly fought or at least feared since the era of Nero: the movement of the legions to the eastern frontiers encouraged road engineering through central Galatia and intensified agricultural production. This way, the growth of the focal point Ankyra, as well as the foundation of several smaller towns throughout central Anatolia, was fostered. And it was during the Parthian War of Trajan when the provincial boundaries were deeply reshaped and perhaps other reforms – such as the imposition of a regular tax – were put into practice. Beforehand, the Galatians contributed to the empire by serving as a rich reservoir of soldiers.[65]

As it seems, Augustus did not pursue a master plan to 'civilize' the Galatians or to interfere seriously with their traditional lifestyles, which had in fact been beneficial to the empire. I thus tentatively suggest that we speak of it as an example of 'soft' provincialization, though only for core Galatia. But other parts of Amyntas's realm, especially Pisidia, had to accept thousands of Roman veteran colonists and thus underwent strong changes at the outset.

## X. Instead of a Summary: Reconstructing the Galatian Past in the Fourth Century AD

This paper concludes with another late antique retrospective on the Galatians: in AD 383, the philosopher Themistios had to address the emperor Theodosius on behalf of the Senate of Constantinople. The main difficulty of the speech was to gloss over the weakness the emperor had shown by paying a high price to pacify the Goths. The orator therefore praises the mildness and prudence of Theodosius for finishing a deleterious war. Instead of replenishing Thrace with even more dead bodies, he had won new colonists to cultivate the soil.[66] Next, Themistios continues with a historical example:

Just look at the Galatians at the Pontos! They crossed over to Asia under the law of war and, having driven away everything west of the Halys, they stayed in this land which they now inhabit. And neither Pompey nor Lucullus annihilated them, although this would easily have been possible, nor Augustus or any of the Emperors after him, but, instead, they dispensed with their atrocities and made them a part of their empire. And no one still addresses the Galatians as barbarians nowadays, but even as genuine Romans. Although their old name remained with them, their way of life already is akin (to ours). Like us they pay taxes and like us they serve in the army, like all the others they receive magistrates and obey the same laws. Thus we shall soon see also the Scythians. (*Or.* 16.19 211c–d)

To draw on Lucullus, Pompey, or Augustus as examples of mercy is ahistorical, since they had not fought against the Galatians but rather owed their own military success to a significant extent to the Galatians. Moreover, it is anachronistic to purport sweepingly that provincial rule was welcomed as a benefit already in the days of Augustus. Apparently, the previous misdeeds of the eastern Celts had occupied a more prominent position in the collective memory of the Hellenized world than the later services of the Galatians as friends and allies of the Roman people and as loyal subjects of the emperor respectively.

This retrospective not only marks the beginning and the end of my studies on the Galatians, i.e., their violent intrusion into Asia Minor, their inclusion in Hellenistic power games, their incorporation into the Roman Empire, and the final normalization of their provincial status. The same passage also nicely exemplifies the long persistence of anti-Celtic resentments, their flexible instrumentalization in political propaganda, and their negative effects on modern perspectives on ancient Galatia. The testimony of Themistios further hints at the possibility that political, social, and cultural terms of 'belonging' or 'isolation' need not necessarily coincide. And last, though not least, this late antique version of the Galatian past once more illustrates how useful Galatian histories may be to teach students a basic but never trivial lesson: that all history is construction.

## Notes

1  On early Galatian history, see Stähelin 1907–73; Moraux 1957; Nachtergael 1977; Szabó 1991; Mitchell 1993: 1.13–20; Strobel 1996 and 2002; Tomaschitz 2002; Strootman 2005: 104–15; Coşkun 2011. Historical maps of the Celtic migrations or of Galatia are to be found, e.g., in Belke 1984; Mitchell 1993; Strobel 1999; Koch 2007; Coşkun 2008a and 2008b.
2  The main sources are Livy 38.16; Memnon *FGrH* 434 F 11; Just. *Epit.* 24.7–8 ; 25.2; Paus. 1.4.5 ; 10.18.7 ; 10.19.4–12; Strabo 12.5.1 C566. Cf. Tomaschitz 2002.
3  For the history of Galatia, see the references above in n.1. For the Romans, see below, sect. VIII.
4  The occupation of this land by the Trokmoi is traditionally dated to the 270s/260s BC. But see Coşkun 2011.
5  For the history of imperial Galatia, see below, sect. IX.
6  See, e.g., Woolf 1994; Dench 2005; Coşkun 2009b.
7  See, e.g., Gerber 1998; Shipley 2000: 302–12; Hall 2002; Weber 2007.
8  See especially Stähelin 1907–73; Moraux 1957; Wörrle 1975; Mitchell 1993: 1.13–20; Tomaschitz 2002; Strootman 2005: 104–15. Strobel 1996, 1999, 2002 offers many nuances, see below, sects. III and VI. Completely different is Segre 1930: 503–6, who also minimizes the effect of the war, but his date of 278 or early 277 BC is completely untenable.
9  Ramsay 1939: 202 and 1922: 176: 'It was a means of unifying Galatia by hellenizing the province, and de-gallicizing the three tribes.' Also Ramsay 1900: 79–85 on barbarism, nomadism, and demography. Cf. further Stähelin 1907–73: 71 and 103, according to whom the Galatians 'nach alter grausamer Barbarensitte . . . gemeuchelt hatten'; thus their defeat by Attalos I soon after 240 BC was a 'Triumph der hellenistischen Kultur über die Barbaren.'
10 Strobel 1994 and 1996. Cf. also Schalles 1987: 53–127 and Schmidt-Dounas 2000: 232–44, 293–319 (on the archaeological remains); Barbantani 2001 (focus on poetry); Strootman 2005 (who presents most of the evidence of royal propaganda in chronological order); Koehn 2007, esp. 89–127 (intriguing

analysis of the distinct functions of *Keltensieg* propaganda: the Aitolians and Attalids illustrated the altruistic nature of their rule, the Antigonids and the Seleukids their military might, and Ptolemy II his divinity); most recently, Kistler 2010.

11 On their identification and interpretation, see now Schmidt-Dounas 2000, esp. 232–42 and 293–312 and Koehn 2007: 110–27. There is no reason to claim – with Shipley 2000: 53 and 312–13 – monuments of a *Keltensieg* erected by Philhetairos of Pergamon.

12 Museo Capitolino inv. no. 747. To my knowledge, the best photo is in Andreae 2001: pl. 47.

13 The so-called Ludovisi Group. Museo Nazionale Romano, Palazzo Altemps inv. no. 8608. To my knowledge, the best photo is in Andreae 2001, pl. 46.

14 Strobel 1994, 1996: 10, 55–115, 263–4; Livy 38.16.10–12, with Coşkun 2011.

15 For more detail, see Coşkun ca 2012a.

16 I follow Strobel 1996: 139–61 in disclaiming that linguistic criteria are still the safest means to decide on a tribe's Celticity. Conspicuously, the term *Celti* was not applied to the peoples of Britannia and Scotia (i.e., modern Ireland), whereas the Celtic-speaking inhabitants of the Iberian peninsula were called *Keltiberoi*. See, e.g., Strobel 1996: 123–35; Freeman 2001: 5–7; Koch 2007: 2–4. The scope of this paper does not allow me to enter into the debates of 'Celtoscepticists' and 'Celtomaniacs.' For a summary, see Koch 2007: 1–17.

17 I thus include the Ambitouti, Tosiopi, Toutobodiaci, and Voturi, but exclude the Aegosages, whom Attalos I had recruited as mercenaries in eastern Europe, and likewise the Rhigosages, who served Antiochos III. See Freeman 2001: 65–77 for references; and Coşkun ca 2012a.

18 See Coşkun ca 2012b (onomastics); Bittel 1976, Müller-Karpe 1988, Koch 2007 §19 (LaTène finds in Anatolia); Mitchell 1993 1 and Coşkun 2011, opposing Strobel 1996 (politics).

19 Parth. *Amat. Narr.* 8 = *Peri Herippes*, ed. Lightfoot 1999: 320–5 with commentary at 412–18; also Macro 2007: 169–71. The editorial notice to the piece identifies Aristodemos of Nysa's *Historiae* as Parthenios's source; the name of the Galatian is only attested for Aristodemos's version. *Kavaros* is also the name of the last king of Thylis in eastern Thrace in the last third of the third century BC (Polyb. 4.46; 4.52; 8.22 [24]). Another namesake is attested in an inscription of Phrygia (Islam Köyi): Ramsay 1897: 614 no. 524 = Freeman 2001: 37.

20 See esp. Strabo 4.1.13 (C188), quoting his contemporary Timagenes (*FGrH* 88 F 11) for the mainstream view (cf. Just. *Epit.* 32.3.6–11), but also the objections raised by Poseidonios (*FGrH* 87 F 33); the latter reasonably argues for a local source of the gold, though notably without contradicting the Gaulish origin of the invaders of Greece. On the Volcae Tectosages in the *Hercyniae silvae*, see Caes. *B Gall.* 6.24.1–4; Just. *Epit.* 32.3.12 (*Tectosagi* [*sic*] in Illyricum

and Pannonia), but also 20.5.7–9; 24.4.1–5; 24.4.6–24.5.14; 24.6–8; 25.1–2 (Asia Minor) on *Galli* moving eastwards. For further references on Tolosa, see Nachtergael 1977: 95–6, 105–6; and Tomaschitz 2002: T 43 with pp. 132–4. See also below, sect. VII with n.38.

21 Strabo 12.5.1–3 C566–8. They are named *Volcae* Tectosages only in 4.1.13 (C188). The notion of their unity seems also to be the explanation for the belief that the Galatians 'split up' into three tribes after their settlement in Asia Minor; cf., e.g., the Loeb translation of Livy 38.16.4 (despite the original *cum tres essent gentes*); also Maier 2000: 101: 'zerfielen die Kelten Kleinasiens in die drei Stämme.'

22 Memnon *FGrH* 434 F 11.3 = Tomaschitz 2002: T 50.3. Livy 38.18.3 on the Tektosages (conflicting with 38.15.15 and Polyb. 21.37.2 on the Tolistobogioi); 38.19–23 on the Trokmoi. On the history of the Trokmoi, see Coşkun 2011.

23 The ethnogenesis of the Galatian tribes will probably always remain controversial. For different approaches, cf. Strobel 1996, 2002, and 2007; Darbyshire, Mitchell, and Vardar 2000; Coşkun 2012b, 2006b, 2011.

24 See, e.g., Maier 2000: 101; Bringmann 2002; Meid 2007: 52. For further references, see below, n.25.

25 See Coşkun 2004, although I withdraw my previous view that the Galatian tetrarchy was introduced only by Pompey. Note, however, that Zwintscher 1892: 10–11 was the first to posit a purely Hellenistic background. Others (such as Stähelin 1907–73: 43–5; Jones 1971: 114–15; Mitchell 1993: 1.27; Darbyshire, Mitchell, and Vardar 2000: 81–2) think rather of a blend of Hellenistic and Celtic roots.

26 See in particular *IDidyma* 475 = Bringmann and Steuben 1995: 329–31 no. 276.35–41 (ca 90 BC) and *RECAM* II 188 (ca 42 BC). Beyond this, note that Strabo assigns his constitutional sketch only to a vague past (*palai*).

27 For names like *Aioiorix, Gaizatorix, Sinorix*, see Freeman 2001.

28 Scholars such as Mommsen 1884: 316, 319–20; Birkhan 1997: 141; and Strobel 1999: 335–6 and 2002: 273–8 refer to a few Celtic polities structured in four units. But these examples are purely coincidental, since examples of a two-, three-, or fivefold structure could easily be adduced as well. What is more, there is no evidence that the rulers of such subunits bore titles explicitly referring to the fourth part of any whole. As appears from his longish rejection of my ideas (Coşkun 2004), Strobel 2007: 391–6 (followed by Radt 2008: 415 without discussion) has not understood the point of this – and of most other – arguments.

29 He was in the position to do so upon occupying their territories in 107–102 BC. Cf. Just. *Epit.* 37.4.6: *nec territus minis Galatiam quoque occupat.* – The fourth tribe seems to have been that of the Tosiopoi, see Coşkun 2010 s.vv.

Eposognatos, Eporedorix, Domnekleios. On non-Galatian tetrarchies, see Coşkun 2013a.

30 See, e.g., Stähelin 1907–73: 14, 40–1; Moraux 1957: 71–4; Belke 1984: 49; Szabó 1991: 304; Birkhan 1997: 140; also Otto 1931: 408–9n17.

31 Strobel 1996: 58–66; 80–105; also Strobel and Gerber 2000: 225–7. Strobel is followed by Darbyshire, Mitchell, and Vardar 2000: 164–5.

32 Nomadism is taken for granted, among others, by Wörrle 1975: 62; Mitchell 1993: 1.51, 96.

33 Strabo 12.5.1 C566; Just. *Epit.* 25.2.11. The land is qualified as prize (and not punishment) also by Bittel 1976: 242–3. Tomaschitz 2002: 158 points out that it sufficed the Galatians' needs appropriately.

34 Livy 38.16.9–13; Memnon *FGrH* 434 F 11.4 = Tomaschitz 2002: T 50.4. This view goes along with my demystification of the 'Elephant Victory' (above, n. 15).

35 Strabo 12.5.4–6.1 (C568); Livy 38.18.4. Unconvincing: Strobel 1996: 93–6.

36 I shall argue below in section IX that only Roman imperial policy in the second half of the first century AD meant strong incentives to enhance the agricultural production.

37 For the claim of close ethnic connections, see, e.g., Szabó 1991: 305, 307, 314; Birkhan 1997: 87; Tomaschitz 2002: esp. 163 (despite his criticism of Strabo at 160–1). But *contra* already Niese 1898: 139: 'man sieht aus Strabo mit aller deutlichkeit, dass man darüber nicht etwa nachrichten hatte, sondern dass es sich nur um meinungen und vermutungen handelte, die sich vor allem auf die namensähnlichkeit stützten'; similarly Nachtergael 1977: 105–6. On the sources, see above, n.20.

38 Strobel 1996: 172–82; cf. Strobel 2002: 244–5.

39 Cf. *DLG*²: 327. But cf. also Rübekeil 1992: 61, who explains that the meaning 'warrior' directly goes back to the lexeme 'to tear, to rob, to kill.'

40 Such a view is however rejected by Strobel 1996: 173–82. Slightly inconsistent is Rübekeil 1992: 60–1: he does not exclude the possibility that 'Volcae' initially might have been a generic term (*Sammelbegriff*), but prefers the assumption of a 'singulären Entstehung des Namens *Volcae* . . ., da die Namensträger nach Ausweis der Quellen durchweg der keltischen Sprachgemeinschaft angehörten und sich wohl auch in ihrer ethnischen Tradition auf einen Punkt zurückführen lassen.' He considers the combination with *Tectosages* as a later development brought along by a 'kriegerische Überschichtung anderer Stämme,' 'so dass *Volcae* die Herrschaft, *Tectosages, Arecomici* usw. dagegen das Substratethnos bezeichnete . . . jedenfalls deutet die Verteilung der Belege darauf hin, dass der Name *Volcae* zur Zeit seiner literarischen Überlieferung Sammelbegriff für verschiedene keltische Stämme war.' A seeming connection with German *Volk* is to be excluded, for the latter stems from Indo-European *plH*-meaning 'to

fill,' just as Lat. *vulgus* (cf. Greek *plēthos*), as Jürgen Zeidler (Trier) has kindly explained to me.

41 See Strobel 1996: 131–5, also on *Franci*.

42 See, e.g., Strobel 1996: 131–7; Darbyshire, Mitchell, and Vardar 2000: 77.

43 On the afterlife of Gallo-Roman *Volcae*, see Rübekeil 1992: 59–72 (though without following my own explanation).

44 See also Loman 2005 on mercenaries who served Hellenistic kings and were accompanied by their families. I am only reluctant to generalize this circumstance of familial accompaniment.

45 Thus Livy 38.16.1 (*Galli magna hominum vis seu inopia agri seu praedae spe . . . pervenerunt*); 38.16.13 (*multitudine etiam magna subole aucta* [until 189 BC]); 38.17.17 (*extorres inopia agrorum profecti domo*); Memnon *FGrH* 434 F 8.8; Just. *Epit.* 24.4.1; 25.2.1. Besides, lust for booty is mentioned by Livy 38.16.1 and Just. *Epit.* 25.2.1. High fertility is also attested for the Gauls: see Strabo 4.1.2 (C178); 4.4.3 (C196).

46 Apollon., *Karika* B.17, in Steph. Byz. *s.v. Ankyra* = *FGrH* 740 F 14 = Bosch 1967: no. 1 = Tomaschitz 2002: T 55. In contrast to Nikomedes I of Bithynia, Mithridates had broken away from the Northern League by 278 BC. Cf. Coşkun 2011; differently Mitchell 1993: 1.16n38, 19–20. On the context, see also Otto 1931: 408–9.

47 Livy 38.16.9. For the traditional interpretation, see Stähelin 1907–73: 7–8; Bengtson 1977: 402–3; Heinen 1984: 423; Mitchell 1993: 1.15; Birkhan 1997: 139. Differently, Tomaschitz 2002: 148–50: half of the men were armed poorly, if at all, and thus received weapons from Nikomedes I; cf. Memnon *FGrH* 434 F 11.4 = Tomaschitz 2002: T 50: τούς βαρβάρους ἐξοπλίσας.

48 Note the *trimarkisia* ('three horses') attested by Paus. 10.19.11: a fighting unit consisted of one knight, two slaves and three horses, so that the knight could be supplied or even substituted during a battle. Likewise, Diod. Sic. 5.29.2 attests to the service of clients as chariot steerers or shield bearers. But cf., on the other hand, the report of the Celtic mercenaries of Antigonos Gonatas by Polyaenus, *Strat.* 4.6.17 = Tomaschitz 2002: T 44: in 276 BC, the ratio of combatants to non-combatants (including women and children) was three to seven.

49 See http://www.sfb600.uni-trier.de – link: 'Teilprojekte' – link 'A 2.'

50 See, e.g., Coşkun 2005, 2008a, 2010a; also Braund 1984; Burton 2003.

51 The evidence is collected by Syme 1995: 127–36 and Coşkun 2005: 127–54.

52 Lob 1967: 95; Jones 1971: 118; Willrich 1944: 224; Saddington 1993: 92.

53 Hoben 1969: 64–126, esp. 112–14: 'Persönliche Bindungen waren ihm weitgehend fremd,' also 169–73; and Syme 1995: 127–43.

54 Cic. *Att.* 5.17.3 (110 SB): *Cicerones nostros Deiotarus filius* (i.e., the homonymous son of Deiotaros Philorhomaios), *qui rex a senatu appellatus est, secum*

*in regnum; dum in aestivis nos essemus, illum pueris locum esse bellissimum duximus;* also Cic. *Att.* 5.18.4 (111 SB) and 5.20.9 (113 SB).

55 Cic. *Fam.* 15.2.2 (105 SB): . . . *ut Artavasdes, rex Armenius, quocumque animo esset, sciret non procul a suis finibus exercitum populi Romani esse, et Deiotarum, fidelissimum regem atque amicissimum rei publicae nostrae, maxime coniunctum haberem, cuius et consilio et opibus adiuvari posset res publica;* 15.4.5 (110 SB): *interea in hoc tanto motu tantaque exspectatione maximi belli rex Deiotarus, cui non sine causa plurimum semper et meo et tuo et senatus iudicio tributum est, vir cum benevolentia et fide erga populum Romanum singulari, tum praestanti magnitudine et animi et consili, legatos ad me misit se cum omnibus suis copiis in mea castra esse venturum.* Also Cic. *Fam.* 15.1.5–6 (104 SB); Cic. *Att.* 5.18.2 (111 SB). On the crisis, also Cic. *Fam.* 3.3.1; 8.5.1; 8.10.1; 15.1–2 (66, 83, 87, 104–105 SB); Cic. *Att.* 5.15.1; 5.18.1 (108, 111 SB).

56 Plut. *Brut.* 4.3–4; Luc. 8.202–843; Plut., esp. *Mor.* 257e–258f and *Crass.* 17.2. Plut. *Mor.* 1049c refers to a different Deiotaros.

57 Malal. *Chron.* 9.13 (ed. Dindorf: 221–222 = ed. Thurn: 168 = Bosch 1967: no. 47); Tzetz. *Chiliades* 1.139 = Bosch 1967: no. 48.

58 See Coşkun 2008a: 133–64 with map 4. On the development of imperial Galatia, cf. also Coşkun 2008b, 2009a, 2009c.

59 On the province of Galatia, see, e.g., Ramsay 1900 and 1939; Magie 1950; Bosch 1967; Halfmann 1986; Rémy 1986 and 1989; Mitchell 1986, 1993, 2007, and 2008; French 2003; Strubbe 2005; Strobel 2007.

60 Among the references in the previous note, see esp. Mitchell 2007. The best documentation of the temple is now Kadıoğlu et al. 2011; cf. besides Krencker and Schede 1936 and Mitchell 2008b.

61 The numismatic evidence starts in or soon after AD 68: *RPC* I 3568–70; II 1620–2, 1624–6. For the earliest epigraphic evidence under Claudius, see now Mitchell 2008a: 472.

62 See Coşkun 2009a, 2009c, 2013b.

63 See Mitchell and French 2012 = I. Ankara I no. 2.

64 See (in addition to the references in nn. 58–62 and 65) esp. Devreker 1984; Belke 1984; Bennett 2003; Weber-Hiden 2003; Arslan 2004; Strubbe 2005; Kadıoğlu/Görkay 2007; Claerhout and Devreker 2008 for the evidence.

65 Beside the references quoted above (nn. 58–9, 64), see also Coşkun 2008c on Galatian recruits and Coşkun 2008a on city foundations.

66 For Themistios and the historical context, see Vanderspoel 1995: esp. 204–8.

# 5

# The Importance of Being Aitolian

## JOSEPH SCHOLTEN

### 'The Importance of Being Aitolian'

The political community of the north-central Greek mainland known as 'the Aitolians' (οἱ Αἰτωλοί) occupies a middle ground in regard to the overarching theme of this collection and to the specific experiences of the other two communities featured in this section. While Athenians of the Hellenistic era experienced a progressive contraction in their military power, reach, and political independence, they never relinquished their claim to the normative cultural status they had established during the fifth and fourth centuries BC. The *koine* culture of the Hellenistic *oikoumene* was at its core Athenian culture, albeit spread – ironically – through the agency of the Athenians' would-be political masters, the Macedonian *basileis*. The Galatian Celts, by contrast, began the Hellenistic era at the opposite edge of the cultural continuum, and were used as touchstones of the exotic and dangerous throughout the period by regimes seeking to bolster their status in the Hellenic pecking order.

The trajectory of Aitolian identity[1] in the Hellenistic period falls between the extremes of the Athenians and the Galatians. Marginal to, and marginalized by, the Aegean Greek mainstream during the Classical era, Aitolians and their state – whether termed an *ethnos* or *koinon*[2] – deployed a standard repertoire of cultural symbols and behaviours during the Hellenistic age to assert their belonging within the Greek club. The success of these efforts may be measured in the reactions of Greek neighbours, many of whom now found 'Aitolian' a desirable new political identity to overlay onto their existing local and ethnic associations. Yet a tension arose between the older, marginal definition of being Aitolian, and the identity forged during the

Hellenistic era. As a consequence, during this period 'Aitolian' could be employed as a term of inclusion and of exclusion, of belonging and isolation, reflecting an identity that was both embraced and rejected situationally across the era. By its conclusion, however, the dissonance between what 'Aitolian' had meant, and what it came to mean, helped to re-isolate Aitolians from the world around them.

## From Marginal to Mainstream

Prior to the Hellenistic era, the place of Aitolians in the Aegean Greek cultural and political world was ambiguous. If the arbiter for belonging within the broad tent of Hellenic was Homer,[3] then Aitolians could claim charter membership. Not only do 'Aitolians' show up in the catalogue of the forces arrayed against Troy presented in the second book of the *Iliad* (under the leadership of Thoas: *Il.* 2.638–44, 15.281–4); the Homeric poems also display a familiarity with a cycle of mythic material revolving around the Aitolians' main settlement, Kalydon (*Il.* 9.529–99). The popularity of this Kalydonian/Aitolian cycle only grew as the boundaries of Hellas expanded. During the Hellenistic era, the main character in the Kalydonian cycle of stories, the hero Meleagros, could serve as a namesake for our Gadaran garland maker, and a wall decoration for Oscan aristocrats in Pompeii.[4]

A major obstacle to determining Aitolian self-perceptions and representation is the lack of *voces Aetolicae* in the surviving ancient literary tradition. Extensive physical evidence does exist, but most Aitolian settlements, for example, remain underexplored.[5] Given the widely recognized interpretive pitfalls and limitations associated with such material, perhaps this is a disguised blessing. Theoretical approaches to human community formation, however, such as the peer polity interaction model, do provide some basis for conjectures drawn from this physical material, for example, by establishing that the adoption and adaptation of cultural products – including material culture – between groups can provide general measures of belonging or isolation (Renfrew and Cherry 1986).

Greek political communities that emerged across the Archaic and Classical eras found focal points for the creation of local or regional identity in common sanctuaries and cults (Snodgrass 1980). By this measure, too, Aitolians could claim to belong in the Greek mainstream. The sanctuary/cult of Apollo at Thermon – located at a regional communication node on the east end of the Lake Trichonis basin of the mid-Acheloös river valley – early on reflected communal significance in the form of a shrine that itself marked an important stage in the development of Greek sacred architecture.[6]

The sanctuary of Apollo Thermios, however, also suggests an arrested adolescence in Aitolians' early cultural development. Whereas other early-bloomer cult centres in the central and southern mainland – such as the Apollo sanctuaries at Corinth or Delphi, or those of Hera and Zeus at Olympia – continually remade themselves across the Archaic and Classical eras, reshaping the visual aesthetics of Hellenic monumental art and architecture both in style and material, the Apollo temple at Thermon maintained its early archaic form: mudbrick and wood on stone foundations, seemingly frozen in time.[7]

Thucydides certainly stresses this characteristic of Aitolians in his history. Far from being mainstream Greeks, Aitolians are portrayed by Thucydides, and by the characters and events he describes, as a backward, isolated *ethnos* whose behaviour is, at points, arguably barely human. At some points Thucydides lumps Aitolians together with neighbouring regional populations in the north-west mainland in his exclusionary rhetoric – for example, their penchant for going about armed in public.[8] At other times, however, his comments are directed solely at Aitolians, and push them beyond the bounds of the human, let alone Hellenic. While numerous and warlike, Aitolians dwell in small, scattered, unfortified villages, and those living in more remote locations are said, like some sort of latter-day Cyclopes, to be barely intelligible, and to eat raw meat.[9] Thucydides's contemporary, the playwright Euripides, while less extreme, nonetheless reiterated this questioning of Aitolians' membership in the Hellenic fold. The central character in the Aitolian/Kalydonian cycle – the hero Meleagros – was the eponymous subject of one of his lost dramas. In another work, however, Meleagros also makes an appearance. (Eur. *Phoen.* 134) When introducing that character, Euripides pointedly describes the hero's attire as *mixobarbaros*.

Scholars have long recognized, of course, that such characterizations of Classical-era Aitolians have their problems.[10] Most obviously, the writers and speakers are exclusively oppositional. Thucydides's specific stigmatization of Aitolians precedes an account of an Athenian-led incursion into Aitolian lands (427 BC) that ended in disaster – and a disaster in which Thucydides apparently had a personal stake.[11] The shadow of this Aitolian expedition could well also account for Euripides's comments.[12] As for Thucydides's initial remarks, they come in the 'Archaeology' of his first book, one of whose functions is to set up Athens as the pinnacle of the Hellenic (Saïd 2001). An Aitolian might respond to these generic charges, 'And if I am old-fashioned, so what?'

It is nonetheless striking, when we try to judge where Aitolians fit within the continuum from belonging to/isolation from normative Hellenicity, that more than a century after Thucydides and Euripides, we again find a Greek writer pushing Aitolians beyond the human and into the monstrous. Douris of Samos,[13] in his account of the generation of chaos that followed the death of Alexander, records a hymn sung by an Athenian chorus to mark the return to their fair polis of the Macedonian dynast, Demetrios Poliorketes. The Athenian chorus describes Aitolians as a new sphinx menacing Greece from a rocky perch, and beseeches its Real and Present god to make peace by putting an end to its predation, for to plunder their neighbours was 'an Aitolian *thing*' (line 29). An inscription at Delphi suggests that Demetrios deployed this same isolating, exclusionary rhetoric against Aitolians' behaviour with audiences far beyond Athens (Lefèvre 1998b: lines 21–3).

As with the Athenians generations before, however, so Demetrios and his minions were stigmatizing Aitolians against the background of a conflict with them. Indeed, as they wended their way into the Hellenistic era, Aitolians could hang their *petasoi* of Hellenicity on this very conflict. In the struggles that followed Alexander's death, the Aitolian polity emerged as a core player in central and southern Greece's collective defence of Hellenism's most cherished value, *eleutheria* (freedom) against whoever held the throne of Macedonia (and, by extension, the reins of power in Thessaly).[14] It was, most likely, this larger struggle that led Aitolians in the early years of the third century BC to push their frontier eastward across the Parnassos massif to the edge of the Kephissos river valley, in the process establishing control over the panhellenic sanctuary at Delphi.[15] Thus, where Demetrios Poliorketes in the late 290s saw bandits and monsters (terrorists?), Aitolians could style themselves defenders of Greek Freedom – symbolized by one of its holiest shrines.

Aitolians could also point to collective monumental and institutional creations in the interval as indices of their belonging within the Greek tent. Aristotle (or one of his collaborators: fr. 473 [Rose]) thought that the Aitolians of his day had a *politeia* of sufficient significance to include it in his collection of constitutions. Since that collection also embraced non-Greek communities, such as the Carthaginians, however, the Aitolians' inclusion does not necessarily prove that Aristotle's circle included them within its parameters of the Hellenic. By Aristotle's day, however, Aitolians had certainly begun to provide Thermon with the sorts of elaborations typical of Greek politico-cultic centres. Such cultural imitation is seen at other times and places throughout human history, and has gained the designation 'symbolic entrainment' in scholarly literature (Renfrew and Cherry 1986). A new mythic pedigree, centred on an eponymous hero, Aitolos, was given sculptural form there.[16] A likeness of this icon probably graces the reverse of one of the coinages later issued by 'The Aitolians' (Tsangari 2002). Whatever the dangers of interpreting images on coins, there can be little doubt that the style of the original statue was fully in the mainstream of late Classical Greek art. So too was the monumentalization provided for the natural spring at Thermon, perhaps the font of the cult's existence (Antonetti 1990a). In the third century, three stoas – prototypical Hellenistic civic edifices, of unusual length – were added, along with other sacred and secular structures, a multitude of statuary, and an encircling *temenos* wall. Numerous other Aitolian sites gained state-of-the-art fortifications in the fourth and third centuries, as well as some added accoutrements found widely in Greek urban centres, such as theatres.[17]

## Ultimate Insiders

Any argument about whether Aitolians belonged within the Greek fold was, seemingly, obviated by the events of 279/278 BC. In those months, a Celtic war band that had already helped reduce Macedonia to chaos descended upon the central and southern mainland.[18] Aitolians both organized and anchored the Greek defence against the incursion, primarily in and around the strategic choke point at Thermopylai. The Gauls – including a flying column that went straight for Delphi – were repulsed. For Aitolians, the price was steep: a second Gallic flying column took advantage of the absence of Aitolia's warriors to descend on and horribly sack the largest settlement in eastern Aitolia, Kallion.[19]

Whatever the presentation and reception of their hegemony over Delphi prior to these events, in their aftermath Aitolians (collectively and individually) moved quickly and aggressively to claim a leading place among the defenders of the Hellenic.[20] In bald imitation of Athens and her peers after the Persian wars (more symbolic entrainment?), Aitolians quickly surrounded the temple of Apollo with Gallic *spolia* – quite literally, in the case of shields hung on its western and southern faces.[21] Strolling through the site centuries later, Pausanias could still note, as well, a statuary group honouring the Aitolians' commanders (10.15.2), and a statue of a female figure seated atop a pile of Gallic shields: she is identified as Aitolia personified (10.18.7). This statue, Pausanias explains, commemorates the eventual destruction of the Gallic flying column that had sacked Kallion (Reinach 1911). Further, if the Aitolian polity did not itself construct the stoa located just outside Delphi's west *temenos* wall, on an extension of the temple terrace, as a display case for additional Gallic *spolia*, they certainly appropriated it for that purpose and filled the terrace that fronted it with additional monuments.[22]

Collectively, these monuments served to create a visual garland that placed one of the most symbolically important centres of the Hellenic world in the protective embrace of Aitolians (Scholten 2000: 40–1). The location of these monuments assured that the visitors from throughout the Greek-speaking world who thronged the sanctuary during the Panhellenic Pythia festival would, as they moved between the stadium, theatre, and temple, constantly be reminded that the Aitolians belonged within their ranks.[23]

Not all the nods after 279/278 BC to the Aitolians' newly burnished Hellenicity were so blatantly self-congratulatory. The council of the Delphic-Anthelic Amphiktyony that governed the sanctuary of Apollo now for the first time admitted 'the Aitolians' to its ranks, seating Aitolian representatives alongside those from *ethne* whose membership in the club of the Greeks was secure: Boiotians, Dorians, Thessalians et al.[24] And *poleis* and sanctuaries near and far joined in the thanksgiving for the second delivery of Delphi from the barbarian.[25]

Aitolians continued to exploit their *aristeia* in the years that followed. Indeed, it is arguable that Aitolians set in train the well-known Hellenistic use of the Gallic to symbolize all that threatened the Greek (Koehn 2007). Their new claim to leadership in the Hellenic world was not uncontested. The Athenians, in fact, challenged the Aitolian narrative about the defeat of the Gauls, claiming the leading role for the small contingent they had sent to Thermopylai.[26] Across the third century, the Hellenistic Great Powers – Seleukids, Antigonids, Ptolemies – all followed the Aitolian lead, acting to contain – to isolate – Gauls (in particular the branch in Anatolia that acquired the appellation Galatians) as a means to assert their leadership among Hellenes. A generation later, the Attalids joined the game, and played it to its artistic apotheoses in the early second century: the dying Gauls they commissioned to rim the acropolis at Athens, and the great altar at Pergamon.

While commemoration of their anti-Gallic exploits was the chief medium through which Aitolians of the third century expressed their belonging within the larger Hellenic community, they also did so by other means. One particularly striking example of additional Aitolian symbolic entrainment to the Greek was their creation of a coinage in gold. For coin type and obverse die-style they chose to use the standard set for the Hellenistic world by Alexander: Attic staters, featuring a bust of Athena wearing a helmet. And Aitolians secured the services of leading craftsmen to execute this program, perhaps even hiring them away from rival states.[27]

Silver coinage followed, albeit on two separate weight standards. The more plentiful issues were in three denominations – staters, drachmas, and triobols – and within a weight standard common to Greek states around the Gulf of Corinth and Ionic Sea. Their obverse and reverse programs, likewise, followed the Hellenic mainstream in featuring deities, demigods, and mythic allusions: Apollo(?)/Aitolos(?); Artemis/Aitolia (seated atop her stack of Gallic shields); Meleagros(?)/the Kalydonian boar.[28] The 'Aitolos'

figure, however, may offer an example of 'symbolic *disdainment*' in its noticeable resemblance to the reverse issues of the Aitolians' Macedonian rival,
Demetrios Poliorketes.

A limited issue of Attic standard silver tetradrachms minted by the
Aitolians, probably in the 230s BC in connection with their war with
Demetrios's grandson, Demetrios II, is more direct in its deployment of imagery to include and exclude. As with the earlier gold issues, so these coins
also adopt a weight and obverse program popularized by Alexander. Also
like the gold issues, the silver tetradrachms feature on their reverse a ren-
dering of Aitolia atop her pile of Gallic shields. Prominently displayed amid
that pile, however, is a round shield of a design featured by the Antigonids
on their coinage (Scholten 2000: 143–4). In these few strokes of the die en-
graver's tool, Aitolians recalled their earlier defence of the Greek against
the barbarian, their subsequent and ongoing defence of mainland *eleutheria*
against the Macedonian (Scholten 2005), and also the Macedonians' employment of barbarians – who had laid waste Macedonia itself, before descending on Delphi – as mercenaries in their struggles against the heartland
of Hellenism. Belonging and isolation, claimed and imposed on the same
side of the coin.

The height of the Aitolians' Hellenism offensive was their reorganization
in the mid-240s BC of a local Delphic festival, the Soteria, into a penteteric,
Panhellenic event to rival (or overshadow?) the Pythia.[29] Greek communities
around the Aegean and beyond recognized the festival and, by implication,
the Hellenicity of its sponsors. Indeed, this Aitolian action was itself part of
a larger trend among Greek states – large and small – during these years
towards producing new and/or more elaborate festivals. Greek athletes and
performers came from impressive distances, following in the footsteps of
their sculpture- (Pliny *HN* 36.4.9–10) and coin-producing precursors – part
of a notable shift of talent from traditional centres such as Athens. Literary
types, including Nikandros of Kolophon, Aristodama of Smyrna, and the
epigrammatist Poseidippos, gravitated to the Aitolian cultural orbit.[30]

All the while that Aitolians were in these ways pushing past any obstacles to full membership in the Hellenic club, they were also opening up the
ranks of the Aitolian. Across the course of the middle and later third century
BC, inscriptions whose prescripts record the composition of the council of
the Delphic-Anthelic Amphiktyony document a slow but steady growth in
the size of its Aitolian delegation, and a corresponding decrease/disappear-
ance of delegations from smaller *ethne* such as Ozolian Lokrians, Dolopians,
Opountian Lokrians, and Dorians of the Metropolis.[31] Inscriptions from
Thermon (now a proper epigraphical archive, in best Greek fashion) contextualize the Amphiktyonic documents by recording the holding of high

office within the Aitolian polity in this same period by a growing number of individuals from towns outside the confines of what Thucydides would have recognized as 'Aitolia.'[32] Another document from Thermon records an explicit offer of membership within the Aitolian polity to a neighbouring population: the Akarnanians.[33] The formulation οἱ ἐν Αἰτωλίαι πολιτεύοντες ('those exercising citizenship in Aitolia'), found in so many decrees concerning all Aitolians,[34] when contrasted with another formulation such as τό ἔθνος /τὸ κοινόν τῶν Αἰτωλῶν,[35] or simply, οἱ Αἰτωλοί,[36] indicates that such *isopoliteia* offers were accepted.

The sum effect of all these documents is to suggest that, across the early Hellenistic era, not only had 'Aitolian' become an acceptable identity within the larger Hellenic world, it had even become a desirable one. Against the background of ongoing pressure from (now Antigonid) Macedonia (Scholten 2005), more and more of the various communities of central Greece became part of a 'Greater Aitolia.'

The inscription *SEG* 38 (1988) 1476, found in the excavations of the Letoön sanctuary at Xanthos in Lykia, provides one example of a community from central Greece claiming and asserting 'Aitolian-ness' at the height of its utility. The inscription commemorates an embassy to Xanthos from the polis Kytenion, in the region Metropolitan Doris. The delegation is on a tour, seeking aid in the refortification of their town, and appeals to the Xanthians on the grounds of common ancestry. On first reading, this document seems a familiar example of the penchant of Greek polities – particularly in the Hellenistic period – to engage genealogy in the service of diplomacy.[37] It has also elicited scholarly attention for its confirmation of a Macedonian military campaign in central Greece in the early 220s BC – an invasion that previously had only been dimly attested in the lacunose literary tradition for this area and era.[38]

For the purposes of this paper, however, what is most striking about this document is its demonstration of the flexibility and contingency of regional *ethnos* identity in the Hellenistic era. The decree duly identifies the ambassadors by their traditional *ethnos* identity, Dorians 'of the Metropolis' (line 8). Surprisingly, however, the ambassadors are also described as coming 'from the *koinon* of the Aitolians.' The desire of these Kyteniote Dorians to be identified with Aitolians stands in stark contrast to attitudes about Aitolia/Aitolians in the literary sources mentioned above.

Yet the regional interactions implicit in these events are fully in keeping with the conclusions of recent work on the nature of Greek *ethnos* identity. Drawing heavily on comparative work in the field of modern ethnic studies, these scholars have highlighted the malleability and permeability of boundaries, both physical and conceptual, between Greek regional groupings, and the artificiality of *ethnos* identity. They also foreground the highly contingent nature of an individual's or group's expression of *ethnos* affiliation.[39] All of these characteristics are evident in the Kyteniotes' actions.

A series of inscriptions found at Karthea on Keos offers a further illustration. This dossier records efforts by an even more remote community to become 'Aitolian,' in this instance, through a complex interaction between the residents of that community, 'the Aitolians,' and the residents of the Aitolian polis Naupaktos.[40] Several aspects of this exchange are of interest in the current context. Behind these decrees, it seems, lay a Kean mission to the *demos* of Naupaktos, through whose agency Keans hoped to obtain their 'Aitolianicity.'

Naupaktos might seem an unobjectionable port of entry to Aitolia; after all, it was the home of a quintessential Aitolian figure, Agelaos, who delivered the prophetic 'Clouds gathering in the West' speech of 217 BC in Polybios's *History* (5.104). Yet Thucydides would certainly have found Naupaktos a bizarre choice as intermediary between Aitolians and anyone. In his day, Naupaktos was the staging point of the Athenian attack *against* what was then 'Aitolia.' Indeed, Thucydides presents the Naupaktians as the *agents provocateurs* for that expedition.[41] Xenophon, writing a generation later, notes a change in Naupaktian affiliation – but to the Achaian *ethnos*, across the Corinthian Gulf.[42] Only in the early third century, it seems, did the Naupaktians 'become Aitolians.' Did this twisting history of the Naupaktians' *ethnos* affiliation play a role in their interactions with Keans over the possibility of the latter becoming Aitolians?

## The Limits of Belonging

If the fact that Aitolians were willing to allow Keans (and others) to belong to their community is significant for the theme of this collection, the corollary fact that the Keans found that identity desirable is doubly so. What prompted the Keans to *desire* to become Aitolian? The likeliest answer – fear – signals that, for all the evidence of Aitolians' desire to be accepted within the Greek fold, and of the Hellenistic world's acceptance of them, a major anomaly persisted in Aitolian attitudes and behaviour. That anomaly made it possible for opposing Hellenistic states to resurrect the old rhetoric of isolation against Aitolians. The effectiveness of the tactic can be measured in the internal debate it seems to have sparked among Aitolians, a dispute that led a large body of its adult males to abandon the belonging of their homeland in favour of the isolation of mercenary service.

The Aitolians' fatal deviance from Hellenic norms is most clearly articulated by the leading voice in the extant Hellenistic historiographic record:

Polybios. Those passages from the preserved section of his *History* in which Aitolians appear, whether individually or collectively, regularly include an authorial interjection whose drift is – once again – to push Aitolian behaviour outside the bounds of normative Hellenism and/or humanity. The core of Polybios's complaint is that Aitolians have a lifestyle of excessive extravagance. The homes around Thermon, for example, are crammed with luxurious trappings despite only being used during the festival of Apollo each autumn (5.8.4–8), and the Aitolian Alexandros Isios's personal fortune of two hundred talents made him the richest man in Greece (21.26.7–19). This hyperopulence leads Aitolians to prey upon their neighbours in order to feed their greed (4.3.1–3). Obnoxious self-display (*alazoneia*), says Polybios, was an inbred Aitolian trait, covetousness (*pleonexia*) an 'Aitolian thing' (4.3.5) alongside unbridled desire (*horme*). Nothing non-Aitolian was off-limits to them: seizures of the sacred were as honourable as of the profane, and no distinction was drawn between friend and foe (45.62.3–4). In his account of the abortive peace negotiations between Philip v and Flamininus at Nikaia (198) during the Second Macedonian War, Polybios has Philip v deliver a brilliant summation of this portrait of Aitolians as avaricious, unprincipled, unreasoning freebooters, outside the community of Hellenes. Polybios also has the Aitolian delegate to those talks reject Philip's demand that Aitolians give up their custom of plundering any party to any conflict, anywhere: to do so would be to take the Aitolian out of Aitolia (18.4.7–5.8).

Polybios's limitations as a source on Aitolians (individually and collectively) are sufficiently familiar (especially to scholars of the Hellenistic era) as to require little elaboration here.[43] It is enough for our purposes to note that the initial Polybian passages noted above are from his narrative of the opening of the so-called Symmachikos Polemos ('Allied War,' commonly referred to via the Latinate as the Social War [220–217 BC]), which pitted the Aitolian community against a Macedonian-led 'Hellenic Alliance.' Among the latter were Polybios's Achaians, under the leadership of Polybios's great avatar, Aratos of Sikyon. Moreover, a major bone of contention leading to this conflict was Messenia, near and dear to Polybios's Arkadian hometown, Megalopolis (Scholten 2000: 275–94). As for the complaints of Philip V, these occur against the background of the third conflict with the Aitolian polity during his reign. In the intervals, Philip's actions were, arguably, hardly different – a hypocrisy not lost on Polybios. Indeed, when Rhodes and Crete went to war, Philip sent a squadron of ships to prey on the contestants – and entrusted command of this operation to a soldier of fortune named Dikaiarchos, who was originally from . . . Aitolia.[44]

The case of the Keans, however, suggests that we should not entirely dismiss Polybios's allegations against the Aitolians. For, in response to the

Kean interactions with the Naupaktians, the Aitolian community issued a decree that specifically protected Keans from the very sorts of predations denounced by Philip V. These protections were extended to Keans 'because they were Aitolians' (*IG* IX.1$^2$ 1, 169a.4–5). Nor is this document unusual – many other communities in and around the Aegean sought and obtained such dispensations from the Aitolian community in the later years of the third century BC.[45] Measured against all the various examples noted above of Aitolians adhering to (and, indeed, helping to define) the standard Hellenic practices of their day, in this one custom Aitolians seem to opt for isolation, as if saying, 'And if we are Aitolians, so what?'

That attitude may have been at the heart of an internal dispute among Aitolians that led a critical mass of them to emigrate in the years just before and after 200 BC. The Polybian-Livian tradition indicates that during that short time span the Ptolemaic court sent agents to Greece in search of new mercenaries for their army, as yet another confrontation loomed with the Seleukids. Altogether, these efforts enticed sixty-five hundred recruits to take ship for Alexandria. Two considerations make it likely that a large portion of this draft came from Aitolia. First, and more generically, mercenary service had a long and venerable history among Aitolians (Scholten 2000: 182–3). Second, and more specifically, the agent sent to lead the recruitment was a former chief executive (*strategos*) of the Aitolians' polity, Skopas (Scholten 2000: 337). Polybios specifically connects Skopas's decision to leave Aitolia for service with the Ptolemies to his loss of an intense internal struggle for control over the direction of his homeland. At the heart of this Aitolian schism, according to Polybios, was a mountain of debt that the Aitolians had piled up as a consequence of their outrageous (to Polybios, at least) lifestyle and the constant warfare that it engendered. Skopas, along with his long-time sidekick (and fellow former *strategos*) Dorimachos, was elected *nomographos* by his fellow Aitolians in order to relieve this debt. When his efforts failed – thwarted by Alexandros Isios – Skopas left Aitolia in pursuit of more golden pastures.[46]

## A Return to Isolation

As Skopas and his associates departed their homeland at the outset of the second century, the era of Aitolian acceptance within the Hellenic fold, and especially in the area of Aegean Greece, was beginning to draw to a close. Polybios, in his accounts of their further adventures, continues to describe Skopas and friends as Aitolians, and claims that Skopas, at least, left Aitolia in order to recoup his fortunes in preparation for a return to power in his homeland. Nonetheless, in entering the Ptolemaic service he and other Aitolians were isolating themselves from their homeland and traditional identity. At the same time, another internal rift opened within the remaining Aitolian community, over how to react to the increasing involvement of Romans in the affairs of mainland Greece. Initially friends and allies of the Romans, after two joint wars that did not accomplish their anti-Macedonian, pro-freedom agenda, Aitolians transferred their attentions to the Seleukid monarch Antiochos III – and proceeded to blunder their way into a disastrous war with their erstwhile ally. In its aftermath, Aitolians lost their protectorate over Delphi, and also some of the new communities that had come within their association through the course of the preceding century (Derow 2005: 58–65). In subsequent years, Aitolian isolation accelerated, fed by growing internal dysfunction within its leadership. That struggle reached its nadir in the aftermath of the Third Macedonian War, when one body of Aitolian leaders connived with Roman commanders in the massacre of their rivals (Livy 45.28.6–8).

This massacre seemingly marks the death knell of 'Aitolian' as a unifying identity within the larger Greek community. Through the remainder of the second century traces of the Aitolian polity persist, in the form of a declining coinage, and sling bullets from Numantia in Spain bearing the inscription *Aitolon*.[47] Evidently, at least some among the forces that besieged that site in the 130s BC self-identified as 'Aitolian.' Nonetheless, the arc of Aitolian identity was distinctly downward.

Athenians, by comparison, at this point continued to claim an important space in the Hellenistic imagination. As indicated in Glenn Bugh's contribution to this collection, Athenian political institutions continued to function, a model to their world regardless of the decline of Athenian military and diplomatic power. Moreover, by the late second century BC Athens was firmly established as the epicentre of Greek philosophy, and was well on its way to becoming the quasi-university town it remained for the course of antiquity. To the Attalid adornments of Athens' Acropolis mentioned above could be added a pair of stoas built at its foot. And these gifts were matched by donations from other dynasts, a rivalry that underscores the continuing centrality of Athens within the Greek world.

If the Galatian communities of central Anatolia would never attain that status, as the second century came to a close their politico-cultural vector was at least beginning to point away from the isolation of bogeymen and whipping posts. The transition to acceptance would take another century, not to mention the searing ordeal of the Roman civil wars. Yet, at the far end, Galatia and its peoples were sufficiently integrated with their Hellenistic colleagues that the followers of Jesus included them in their missionary destinations. By that point Aitolia and its people had come full circle, once again isolated from the world around them.[48]

## Notes

1 Researchers who study issues of human identity distinguish between an *emic* perspective – i.e., what the individual or group at issue thinks and presents and how peers receive that presentation – and an *etic* one – i.e., what a dispassionate, objective analysis says about an individual's or group's 'true' identity. There is no need here for an extended course of such emics/etics; it suffices to note that our concern is with the emic – that is, what Aitolians thought and presented, and how other Greeks received (or refuted) that presentation. See Malkin 2001a: 17.

2 On the significance of these terms, cf. Beck 1997 and Morgan 2003.

3 Konstan 2001: 31–2.

4 The popularity of the Meleagros story could, of course, also reflect the success of the Classical Athenian campaign of marginalization mentioned below. Perhaps Hellenotropic populations such as those at Pompeii and Gadara found Meleagros appealing because he occupied a 'middle ground' between the Greek and the barbaric. On the space between Hellenic and native in the Hellenistic era, see Thompson 2001; Gutzwiller, chapter 3, and Höschele, chapter 1, both in this collection.

5 Bakhuizen 1993–4; Bommeljé et al. 1987; Dietz et al. 1998; Lefèvre 2002; Papapostolou 1983–93; Pritchett 1991: 47–82; Reger and Risser 1991; Tsangari 2002; Weissl 1999.

6 Funke 1985: 16 and n. 39; Antonetti 1990b: 167–99, 1991a.

7 Biers 1996: 110, 132, and figs. 6.7 and 6.8; Stucky 1988. This assessment of the history of the Apollo sanctuary at Thermon is based on work done there through summer 2000. For more recent discoveries and reactions, see the annual reports issued by the excavator, I.A. Papapostolou, in *Praktika* and *Ergon*.

8 Thuc. 1.5.1–3; cf. Malkin 2001b.

9 Thuc. 3.94.3–5; cf. Konstan 2001: 32.

10 See, e.g., Antonetti, 1987, 1990b: 69–110.

11 Funke 1985: 11; Pritchett 1997: 47–82.

12 Cf., however, the significance of male costume in the construction of fifth-century BC Athenian democratic identity (Cohen 2001).

13 *FGrH* 76 F13 (preserved by Athenaios [6 253b–f]).

14 Mendels 1984; cf. Bosworth 1976.

15 Flacelière 1937; Scholten 2000: 16–25.

16 Strabo 10.3.2; see also Arist. *fr.* 560 [Rose]; Funke 1985: 17–19.

17 Antonetti 1990a; Dietz et al. 1998; Weissl 1999; Scholten 2000: 25–6, 65.

18 Walbank 1988: 252–8; Billows 1995: 210–12.

19 Paus. 1.3.5–4.6; 10.19.5–23.14; Just. *Epit.* 24.4.1–8.16; Diod. Sic. 22.9; Nachtergael 1977: 15–125; Scholten 2000: 31–7.

20 See Koehn 2007.

21 Paus. 10.19.4; Amandry 1978.

22 Amandry 1978; Bousquet 1985.

23 Cf. Champion 1996.

24 Scholten 2000: 38–9; Lefèvre 2002 [= *CID* IV]: no. 12; cf. Paus. 10.8.3. See Lefèvre 1998a; Sánchez 2001.

25 Erythrai: *FdeD* III.1 514; Kos: *Syll*[3] 398; Flacelière 1937: 182; Rigsby 1996: 26; Habicht 1997: 138.

26 Paus. 1.3.5, 10.21.5; Habicht 1997: 138.

27 Scholten 2000: 41; cf. Tsangari 2002.

28 Scholten 2000: 102; cf. Tsangari 2002.

29 Nachtergael 1977: 295–304; Champion 1995; Scholten 2000: 99–100.

30 Nikandros: *Syll*[3] 452; *FGrH* 271, 272; Aristodama: *Syll*[3] 532.4–7; Poseidippos honoured at Thermon: *IG* IX.1[2] 1, 17.24 (see Klaffenbach 1932 *ad loc*). See Antonetti 1990b: 114–18.

31 Scholten 2000: 235–52; cf. *CID* IV.

32 *IG* IX.1[2] 1, 10a, b, 11a-c, 12a; Scholten 2000: 45–6.

33 *IG* IX.1[2] 1, 3A; Scholten 2000: 78–80.

34 E.g., *IG* IX.1[2] 1, 169A.2, 169B.3, 189.3, 190.2.

35 Klaffenbach 1932: 118, s.v. *koinon*.

36 Klaffenbach 1932: 106.

37 See Ager 1996; Rigsby 1996. See also Baker, chapter 15, and Eilers, chapter 9, both in this collection.

38 Walbank 1989; Scholten 2000: 170–3.

39 See the various papers collected in Malkin 2001, including Malkin's very helpful introduction, esp. those by Morgan, McInerny, and Hall. See also, in general, Hall 1997.

40 *SdA* III: no. 508 III = *IG* XII.5 532; IG IX.1[2] 654; *SdA* III: no. 508 I = IG IX.1[2] 169A. See also Reger and Risser 1991.

41 By the same token, Thucydides would have been surprised by Philip V/ Polybios's placement of the Agraioi of the central Acheloös river valley within the rubric of 'Aitolians' (see below) – although he would have heartily endorsed the view that these Agraioi were outside the bounds of the Hellenic. See Antonetti 1987.

42 *Hell.* 4.6.1. Cf. 4.6.14; Diod. Sic. 14.34.1–3; Bommeljé 1988.

43 Sacks 1975; Mendels 1984–6. It is difficult to evaluate Polybios's complaints about the excesses of Aitolian domestic life. Of those Aitolian sites that have

been surveyed or excavated, only Kallion/Kallipolis has had any attention paid to domestic zones – and the results remain largely unpublished. Cf., however, Bakhuizen 1993–4.

44 Diod. Sic. 28.1; Polyb. 13.3–5.6, 18.54.8–12; see Walbank 1967: 415–19, 625–6.
45 Rigsby 1996: 95–105, 164–9; Scholten 2000: 105–30.
46 Polyb. 13.1–2; 15.25.16; cf. 18.53–4; Livy 31.43.5–7; Walbank 1967: 413–15, 624–5.
47 Gómez-Pantoja and Hernández 2008.
48 On Aitolia and Aitolians in the late Hellenistic and Roman Imperial eras, see Bommeljé and Vroom 1995.

# 6

# Democracy in the Hellenistic World[1]

## GLENN BUGH

This paper addresses the question of the survival of democratic institutions in the Hellenistic world. The city of Athens and the Greek colonies on the north and west coast of the Black Sea offer a comparative case study from two distinct regions of the Greek world, one an old mainland site, the home of democracy, and the others on the periphery of the Greek *oikoumene*. Does the sense of isolation among a sea of barbarians diminish or strengthen traditional political institutions in the Black Sea, and are they different for Athens embedded within a purely Hellenic landscape? Whatever differences may be observed, there is sufficient literary, archaeological, and epigraphical evidence to affirm that democratic institutions were still viable into the second century BC, exhibiting a pragmatic blend of sortition (lot) and direct election, and a power sharing between elite and masses. The *demos* was still a player in this world, belonging integrally to the polis community, and not yet isolated or marginalized into political impotence. That day would come soon enough with the Romans.

### Athens

The Athenian democracy never ceases to fascinate us, in great part because every modern democracy claims to be heir to it in one form or the other. Sometimes we forget that Athens was not the only democracy in the Greek world, nor was it static over time. It has provided scholars with a wealth of information, literary, archaeological, epigraphical, not found in other *poleis*, and by that fact obscures the variety of political communities called 'democracies.' A reading of Aristotle's *Politics* should caution us against extrapolating the definition and nature of democracy solely from the classical (i.e., radical) Athenian experiment. Moreover, Aristotle and his students are purported to have penned over 170 constitutions, from which we have only one, the *Athenaion Politeia*, a serendipitous gift from the sands of Egypt. How might we view Athens's singularity if we possessed just ten other constitutions from different parts of the Greek *oikoumene*? And there are still scholars who mark the Battle of Chaironeia on their syllabuses as the beginning of the end of the polis and of democracy, or to be more generous, hold that Athenian democracy held on at least until after the Chremonidean War in the third century BC (Dreyer 2001: 27–66). If Athens could not sustain its democratic institutions in the face of Macedonian, and then Roman, power, how could we expect the hundreds of little democratic *poleis* to do otherwise? Obviously, I do not adhere to the view that democracies fell away in the Hellenistic period, whether to foreign powers or to an internal reallocation of power from the *demos* to the elite (the Notables, the Honoratioren, et al.), the last a very popular view these days. Rather, I hope to show that Athens retained its essential democratic institutions until the eve of the First Mithridatic War and that the Greek cities of the West and North Pontic regions followed a similar course and fate – not by any attempt to follow the Athenian model, but true to their own geographical settings and Milesian or Megarian heritage.

At the XIth International Congress of Greek and Latin Epigraphy held in Rome in 1997, Simone Follet sketched out changes in the Athenian constitution and political institutions during the second and first centuries BC (167/166–31 BC). Conceding the absence of a continuous historical narrative, she catalogued the epigraphical evidence that in her view demonstrated that the Athenian democracy had undergone fundamental changes during this period. This is not a novel thesis: nearly every scholar of Hellenistic Athens from William Ferguson to Christian Habicht to Volker Grieb[2] have argued that from the Third Macedonian War to the First Mithridatic War the Athenian constitution may have been superficially 'democratic,' but in reality the government rested in the hands of a propertied elite, a mix of old and new commercial families, and pro-Roman in their political sympathies. I would suggest, however, that the inscriptions of this period do not support the thesis of an enervated or superficial Athenian democracy.

What sort of democracy obtained in Athens on the eve of the First Mithridatic War? In his *Deipnosophistai*, Athenaios quotes a lengthy extract from the histories of Poseidonios of Apameia, reporting that when the Athenians were 'inclining towards Mithridates,' probably in 89/88 BC, they elected Athenion, a Peripatetic philosopher, as ambassador to the Pontic king. Athenion sent letters back to his fellow Athenians, encouraging them with the hope that through Mithridates, they 'would be able to live in harmony; rid themselves of fines imposed upon them (ἐπιφερομένων ὀφλημάτων); have their democracy restored (τὴν δημοκρατίαν ἀνακτησαμένους); and receive ample gifts for both individual and community' (Ath. 5.212a).

Probably early in 88 BC, after Mithridates had ordered the massacre of Italians and Romans (the so-called Asian Vespers) and had seized Asia Minor, Athenion returned to Athens in triumph. Athenian ships were sent to escort him, crowds lined his route, excitement and anticipation filled the air. Standing defiantly on the bema erected by Roman generals in front of the Stoa of Attalos, Athenion decried the current state of affairs imposed on Athens by the order of the Roman Senate: 'Let us no longer tolerate the anarchy created by the Roman Senate while it deliberates on what sort of government we should have. And let us not accept the current situation wherein our holy places are closed to us; the gymnasia in decay; our theatre without assemblies (ἀνεκκλεσίαστον); our courts (τὰ δικαστήρια) without voice; the Pnyx, once engaged in divine functions, taken away from the *demos*; the sacred voice of Iacchos quieted; the temple of Demeter and Persephone closed; and the schools of the philosophers without voice' (Ath. 5.213c-d). An incredible and problematic list, but there is no reason to dismiss it as rhetorical fiction.[3] The Athenians certainly took it to heart; they rushed to the theatre and elected Athenion as Hoplite General, the most important military official in this period.

Recent scholarship places these passages in the context of the unprecedented and seemingly unconstitutional three consecutive eponymous archonships, 91/90–89/88 BC, of one Medeios of the Peiraeus (*IG* II² 1713.9–11). Medeios had already held the eponymous archonship exactly ten years before, so his election in 91 BC is unlikely to have followed the traditional procedure of sortition, and re-election by the same method for the two subsequent years is mathematically impossible. Stephen Tracy (1991: 201–4) has noted that only once before had there been a repeated archonship, in the troubled 290s during the intervention of Demetrios Poliorketes. So, what is going on here? Various scenarios are possible, but there is agreement among most scholars that some sort of stasis was afflicting Athens at this time, Medeios having seized power and abrogated the democratic institutions, his opponents perhaps appealing to Rome. The Roman Senate, distracted after 91 BC by the Social War in Italy, ordered the status quo be maintained until such time as it chose to adjudicate the issue of the Athenian constitution. One point is undeniable: the second, and apparently unconstitutional, election to the archonship of Medeios predates the outbreak of the Social War and must therefore be initially unrelated to it.

However we interpret the Medeios episode, the Poseidonios fragment confirms that just before the outbreak of the First Mithridatic War the Athenians still possessed a democracy. The loss of the right of the *demos* to assemble and to serve in the popular courts confirms this. But Appian, our principal source for the Mithridatic Wars, suggests that the Romans had interfered with the Athenian constitution back in the second century BC.

The context of Appian's remarks is shortly after the fall of Athens to Sulla in the spring of 86 BC. Aristion, who had held out with his closest supporters on the Acropolis, surrendered to Sulla's lieutenant. Sulla ordered that Aristion and his bodyguard be executed, along with any who had held authority during the tyranny, or 'who had committed any wrong contrary to the arrangements laid down for them in the earlier capture of Hellas by the Romans' (*Mith.* 39). Appian goes on to say that Sulla pardoned all the others and 'gave to all of them essentially the same laws (νόμους) that had been previously established for them by the Romans.' Despite some ambiguity about the historical reference, it is likely that Appian meant the period of the Achaian War and its aftermath, that is, 146 BC. This would seem to be associated with a note in Pausanias, who provides our longest historical narrative of the Achaian War. At the conclusion of the war and the destruction of Corinth by the Roman commander Mummius, commissioners were dispatched to Greece to settle affairs. According to Pausanias their work included the abolition of democracies and the establishment of governments based on a property qualification (ἀπὸ τιμημάτων) (Paus. 7.16.9). In other words, oligarchies were set up. Tribute was imposed on Greece and it was forbidden to acquire possessions in foreign lands. But whatever Appian intended to mean, it is very unlikely that Athens, a free city, friend of Rome, and non-combatant in the Achaian War, would have suffered such interference in its internal affairs. This punishment was reserved for the defeated states. Moreover, Appian himself, discussing the fate of the survivors after the sack of the city – but before the surrender of Aristion – states that Sulla granted them freedom (*eleutheria*), but removed their rights as 'voters' and 'electors.' The terms *psephos* and *cheirotonia* should probably be understood to encompass the democratic principles of sortition and election. Thus, Sulla cannot be abolishing a democracy that does not exist. This fact is confirmed by Strabo, who observes that the Athenians preserved their democracy until the Roman conquest (*epikrateia*), and that the Romans, acknowledging this democracy, in turn safeguarded the autonomy and freedom of the Athenians (9.1.20 C398). Furthermore, Strabo adds that tyrants, presumably Athenion and most certainly Aristion, did not appear in Athens until the Mithridatic War. There is no hint here of a stasis involving Medeios, but it is only a brief account. I am inclined to think that Appian is either mistaken about so-called rules established specifically for Athens by the Romans in the second century BC, or that the *nomoi* mentioned were general rules of international conduct, stipulations of peace, law, and order in Greece, not an intrusion into the political institutions of Athens.

Still, the eminent scholar W.S. Ferguson argued that Athens underwent an oligarchic revolution inspired by a series of political crises between 106/105 and 101/100 BC and that this was encouraged, or at least sanctioned, by the Romans.[4] In his classic work *Hellenistic Athens*, he stated: 'The democracy was overthrown, and government of business men took its place. Not simply was the constitution altered in that the judicial control of magistrates was abandoned and, if any, senatorial control substituted for it; not simply was the lot discarded generally, and election, probably on a limited franchise, put in its place' (428–9). This thesis rooted itself deeply in the literature until the late 1970s. Then scholars like Ernst Badian and Stephen Tracy began to question Ferguson's reconstruction.[5] Tracy's detailed analysis of *IG* II[2] 2336, a list of contributors of 'first fruits' for the Pythaïs to Delphi between 103/102 and 97/96 BC, shows 'no anomalies in the constitutional process; instead sortition, tribal rotation, limitation on repeated tenure of archonships, the prohibition against simultaneous office holding are all very much in evidence' (Tracy 1982: 171). And his study of the Athenian archonship suggests that 'once a man had held one of the nine archonships, he could not constitutionally hold another,' and that these offices continued to be filled by sortition, perhaps not open, but initially screened by some sort of means test, since the offices required 'real expense' (Tracy 1991: 201–4).

This can hardly be much different from the Classical period. The *Athenaion Politeia* (26.2) informs us that the *zeugitai*, the third census class, became eligible for the archonship shortly after the reforms of Ephialtes (462/461 BC) and that the first occupant was a certain Mnesitheides (457/456); but inasmuch as the archonship was a non-salaried office and the admission ticket into the old aristocratic Areopagos, whose members served for life, it is unlikely that many Athenians of modest means presented themselves as candidates then or later. We have already seen that with the exception of Olympiodoros in the 290s and Medeios in the early 90s, there is no evidence that the prohibition of iteration of the eponymous archonship was violated. This is an impressive constitutional record.

So, if there is no evidence that the Romans intervened in Athens's internal political institutions or that an Athenian elite orchestrated an oligarchic revolution prior to the First Mithridatic War, and there is strong literary and epigraphical evidence that Athens retained its democratic institutions, at least with respect to the magistracies, then we are left with the question, what *is* different about Athenian democracy in the late Hellenistic period?

The essential characteristics of the Classical Athenian democracy have been described as sortition, rotation, and payment. The institutions that best exhibit these are the Council of 500 and the popular courts. Of course, in this period we are dealing with a Council of 600, not 500, because the tribes now number twelve. Even though our evidence is frustratingly incomplete at times, and it is dangerous to argue from silence, the inscriptions attest the continued functioning of the Council in conjunction with the *demos* in the issuance of various public decrees, like the prytany and ephebic decrees, and the use of sortition to fill this body.

Furthermore, there may be evidence that the councillors continued to be paid in this period: in the inscriptions detailing the festival of the Theseia for the years 161/160, 158/157, and 153/152,[6] the agonothete is honoured for his contribution of the *kathesimon*, a monetary payment to enable the members of the Council to attend the festival (*IG* II² 956.14–15; 957.9–10; 958.12).[7] P.J. Rhodes accepts Ferguson's assumption that 'there was still payment for councilors and jurors, since otherwise it would have been hard to find enough men to serve,' but he interprets the *kathesimon* payment merely as a benefaction, 'a special payment for attendance at a festival, not a regular stipend.'[8] So then, simply a grand – and expensive – gesture on the part of the agonothete. James O'Neil remarks: 'this is not a revival of pay for office, which the Athenians certainly could no longer afford, but a new form of liturgy, placed on magistrates' (1995: 107).

On the contrary, the Athenians could afford to pay their elected officials in this Athenian 'Renaissance,' as reflected in the reacquisition of their former cleruchies of Delos, Lemnos, Skyros, and Imbros, the minting of the famous New Style silver coinage, and the extensive building program in Athens,[9] but they did not do so on major festival days (Habicht 1997: 242). Furthermore, why would such compensatory payments be needed at all unless the members of the *boule* were still elected by lot from the non-elite population, as had been the case in the Classical period?

I am convinced that Ferguson was correct in linking the *kathesimon* to the survival of payment for public service, but that it embodies both liturgy and benefaction. The amounts listed for the *kathesimon* – a term unattested elsewhere in Attic epigraphy – for the three best-preserved Theseia festival documents represent two, one, and two drachmas for each of the six hundred members of the *boule* attending the Greater Theseia. I have argued elsewhere that the festival to Theseus was revived and reorganized on a grand scale consequent to the return to Athenian control of Skyros, the reputed site of Theseus's death, at the conclusion of the Third Macedonian War (Bugh 1990: 20–1). Although the actual festival day for Theseus was 8 Pyanopsion in the Athenian calendar (Plut. *Thes.* 36), it is now clear that the new festival, showcasing numerous athletic and cavalry events, must have take place over several days prior to 8 Pyanopsion. Tracy has joined *IG* II² 959 to *IG* II² 1014: a fragmentary decree securely dated to 109/108 by the archonship of Jason, and more importantly, whose preamble proves that there was a meeting of the *boule* and *demos* on 6 Pyanopsion (Tracy 1990: 183–5). Tracy comments that 'we now see that the elaborate games honoring Theseus, no doubt of several days duration, came during the week before the great sacrifice' (1990: 185). Jon Mikalson's study of the Athenian festival calendar has already demonstrated that the *boule* met for official business on 6 Pyanopsion (Mikalson 1975: 67–71); whether the preceding day, 5 Pyanopsion, was a meeting day is not known.

What I would like to suggest is that 5 and 6 Pyanopsion were normal meetings days for the Council of 600 and that the *kathesimon* contributed by the agonothete was not just a festival benefaction but a compensation for the loss of the drachma per day salary provided by the state. Thus, in 161/160 and 153/152 the *agonothetai* paid for two days of lost wages, and in 158/157, for reasons we do not know, the agonothete was asked (or volunteered) to compensate for only one day. A drachma per day per councillor seems too mathematically attractive to ignore, and the agonothete for the Theseia of 158/157, whose name begins with 'Theo . . .,' would surely have been criticized as penurious for reducing the amount from 1200 drachmas to 600 if it were merely a contributor's personal choice. Considering the hippic character of the festival and the Council's ancestral role in overseeing the Athenian cavalry (*Ath. Pol.* 61), I suggest that it was more than appropriate for the Council of 600 to be in attendance, and certainly they (along with the *demos*) officially honoured the agonothete for organizing successful games. Therefore, I propose that the *kathesimon* was in fact compensatory for lost wages, and this provides us with our only secure evidence that some form of state pay survived into the second century BC. It might serve as a useful *comparandum* that the island state of Rhodes did continue to pay wages for public service in this period.[10]

We know much less about the popular courts, the *dikasteria*, but the Poseidonios fragment attests their existence as late as 88 BC. We have ample epigraphical evidence from the late third to after the middle of the second century BC that these courts were still operating.[11] This series of inscriptions records that grants of citizenship to foreigners required a scrutiny (*dokimasia*) by the *dikasterion* of 501 members summoned by the *thesmothetai*. Homer Thompson, former director of the Agora excavations, commenting on the massive remodelling of the South Square complex in the second century BC, wrote that 'though it may seem strange that such a monumental provision should have been made for the law courts long after the great period of Attic oratory, we must remember that juries on the old scale are attested by inscriptions of the second century BC. Moreover, all the allotment machines (*kleroteria*) that can be dated were made within a few years around the middle of the second century, the very time the Middle Stoa was coming into use. Fragments of at least four of the *kleroteria* were found close along the north terrace of the stoa.'[12] Again, unless we assume a major change in their composition or appointment – for which there is no evidence – then the members of these courts must have continued to be paid for judicial service.[13]

If Athens had the will, it certainly had the resources to pay its citizens for political participation in this period. The Athenians did not even have to spend their own money on building projects. Royal benefaction was ubiquitous. The princes of the royal houses of the Hellenistic world all ended up in Athens. They journeyed from Ptolemaic Egypt, Seleukid Syria, Attalid Pergamon, Kappadokia, Pontos, even Numidia. Some came to study at the 'School of Hellas'; others came to participate in the festivals and games, most notably the Panathenaia, where the Pergamene house is prominently showcased in inscriptions.[14] With a keen sense of competition, the Hellenistic kings vied with one another to bequeath something special to Athens. Antiochos IV Epiphanes of Syria attempted to complete the Temple of Olympian Zeus, begun four centuries earlier by the Peisistratids; Eumenes II of Pergamon built an enormous stoa on the south slope of the Acropolis, so that theatregoers would have a place of refuge in the event of a sudden storm; and his younger brother Attalos II, not to be outdone, constructed a stoa in the Agora dedicated to the Athenian *demos*, which bears his name and was reconstructed by the American School of Classical Studies in the 1950s.

But the monuments – and the prosperity – came from other sources in addition to royal benefaction. The Athenians themselves began to finance a major building program in the Agora and its environs as early as the 170s, and extending perhaps as late as the 120s. This was made possible by the reopening of the silver mines at Laureion in Attika and the production of the so-called Athenian New Style silver coinage, which swept the markets of the Greek world from the 160s (although large-scale minting did not occur until after the Achaian War in the 140s) to the Mithridatic Wars.[15] A decree of the Amphiktyonic League late in the second century BC effectively recognized the Attic tetradrachm as the 'standard currency in Greece.'[16] The Athenian construction efforts in the Agora were centred on the South Square, which included the Middle Stoa, the East Building, and the South Stoa II, and around 140 BC the Metroon (state archives), on the west side of the Agora.[17] The Tower of the Winds, in the area of what would become the

Roman Agora, and a new theatre in the Peiraeus were built about this time (ca 150–125 BC).[18]

So, if the democratic institutions and principles of Athenian democracy still closely reflect their Classical antecedents, why is it that most scholars feel compelled to describe the democracy of Athens with some restrictive or qualifying adjective, like 'moderate' or Ferguson's archaic use of 'Tory'? This position is perhaps best summarized in the words of the British historian Geoffrey De Ste Croix: 'behind a usually democratic facade, with the Council and Assembly passing decrees as in old times, the real power is in the hands of the propertied class.'[19]

No political system is static. Institutional and personnel changes occur naturally over time to meet changed political, social, and military conditions. The author of the *Athenaion Politeia* concludes his survey of Athenian constitutional history in 401 BC and summarizes the eleven political changes (*metabolai*) that had occurred over the centuries (*Ath. Pol.* 41). His analysis of the Athenian democracy is situated in the time of Aristotle, the later fourth century BC. Institutional changes two centuries later would hardly be surprising. In this later period, two magistracies stand out in this regard: the Hoplite General and the Herald of the Areopagos.[20] The administration of the military was now sufficiently and efficiently concentrated in the office of Hoplite General (Geagan 1967: 18–31). As for the Herald of the Areopagos, the latter appears to have assumed an increasingly prominent political role in association with the nine traditional archons.[21] These two officers will become the 'principal civic magistrates of Roman Athens' (Geagan 1967: 57).[22] Correspondingly, the Areopagos will gain prominence in this period, but the evidence is sketchy, and the meaning we should attach to this development is problematic. It will certainly assume primacy over both the Council and Assembly in the Roman period,[23] but let us not be too hasty in attaching oligarchic intentions to the emergence of the Areopagos and its Herald in the second century BC. For instance, the Herald is duly recorded along with the other archons (except the eponymous archon) on an inscription that should date to 88/87, the very year Athenion was elected as hoplite general and was given the power to appoint the other magistrates (*archontes*).[24] Here he is viewed as just another archon, and we may assume that he served as liaison with the democratic-based regimes of first Athenion, then Aristion.[25] The conservative tradition associated with the Areopagos does not mean the Athenian *demos* in the late second century BC viewed these developments as some sort of threat to democratic institutions. Consider that the famous stele from the Agora, entrusting the Areopagos with guardianship over the Athenian constitution in the 330s, is surmounted with a relief of *Demokratia* crowning *Demos*. The Areopagos was, after all, recognized after 462/461 as the premier homicide court (*Ath. Pol.* 57.3). The Council, the Assembly, and the Areopagos were integral to the Athenian democracy. There is no reason to believe that the Athenians themselves thought that their government in the second century BC was not a democracy or that democratic institutions were being eroded.

Perhaps the argument for a *modified* democracy is to be situated in the leadership. It has become almost commonplace to refer to an illustrious group of Athenian propertied families in this period who seem to monopolize the most important political and military offices through individuals such as Ammonios, son of Demetrios; Buttakos, son of Pyrrhos and Pyrrhos, son of Pyrrhos; Medeios, son of Medeios; Sarapion, son of Sarapion; Charias, son of Charias, et al.[26] To be sure, they fared well, but is this a sign of oligarchic control? Did these families enjoy a greater degree of power than their counterparts in the Classical age, the age of the 'radical' democracy? After all, who but the *demos* elected Phokion to the generalship forty-five times (Plut. *Phoc.* 8.2) and Perikles nearly continuously over a span of twenty-five years? And who but the *demos* elected our aspiring late Hellenistic oligarchs? Has the partnership, the *synergasia*, between elite and the *demos* now dissolved? I think not. Shifted slightly, perhaps, but if there is now a 'moderate democracy,' it is because the *demos* has deferred to the propertied classes, not that the propertied classes have assumed power contrary to the letter or the spirit of democratic institutions. Christian Habicht, the foremost authority on Hellenistic Athens, urges caution: 'Der Beweis, dass eine neue Klasse von "Notabeln" die demokratischen Institutionen der Städte obsolete gemacht und die Masse der Bürger nach ihrem Willen gegängelt habe, scheint mir nicht gebracht' (1995: 92). The names have changed, but the story remains the same: the prerequisites for generalships and high offices are still wealth, pedigree, and leadership skills. And just as in the past, wealthy Athenians are now called upon to assume burdensome liturgical obligations. As I examine the inscriptions of this period, and see recorded there the names of hundreds of prominent and not-so-prominent Athenians, I am struck by the extent of citizen participation. This is a heady age of opportunity, an age of wealth, cultural status, and echoes of past glory. It is too soon to perform an autopsy on Athenian democracy. Sulla will see to that in the First Mithridatic War.

## The Black Sea

We turn our attention to the Black Sea, particularly the west Pontic cities of Apollonia, Mesembria, Odessos, Kallatis, Tomis, Istria, and the north

Pontic cities of Olbia and Chersonesos. It is not an exaggeration to say that since the collapse of the Soviet Union in 1989 interest in the region has led to increasingly fruitful collaborations between the East and West. There is usually an entire session devoted to new discoveries of the Black Sea at the annual meetings of the APA/AIA. Probably the most daunting challenge to a Western scholar who enters this world is dealing with a plethora of non-European languages. It is only marginally helpful that the commentaries for the first two volumes of the inscriptions of Scythia Minor are in Romanian – at least a Romance language (volume 3, gratefully, is in French). To complicate our efforts, contemporary historical narratives are almost entirely lacking – what we know must be gleaned from inscriptions and archaeology.[27] Particularly useful on the question of ancient political institutions are the publications of K. Nawotka.[28] For recent archaeological work, the two volumes edited by D.V. Grammenos and E.K. Petropoulos are valuable, although the separately authored chapters vary widely in quality.[29]

The obvious question remains: what do inscriptions reveal about the political institutions of the Black Sea cities? First of all, democracy flourished in the Pontos in the Hellenistic period, and the standard deliberative bodies, the *boule* and the *demos*, are operative, along with a variety of magistrates. The texts of the inscriptions tend to follow patterns familiar elsewhere in the Greek world. Several of the inscriptions provide fulsome enough biographical and historical detail for the third and second centuries BC to be included in collections of epigraphical *selectae* (e.g., for Apollonia, Mesembria, Kallatis, Istria, Olbia, and Chersonesos).[30] One of the most evocative documents attesting the dynamism of polis life in the Black Sea is the so-called Civic Oath of Chersonesos, dated to the early third century BC. I quote the beginning sections:

I swear by Zeus, Gaia, Helios, Parthenos, the Olympian gods and goddesses, and all the heroes who protect the polis, chora, and forts of the people of Chersonesos. I shall act in concord with my fellow citizens on behalf of the protection and freedom of the polis and its citizens. I shall not betray to anyone whomsoever, whether Greek or barbarian, Chersonesos, Kerkinitis, Kalos Limen, the other forts, and the rest of the chora, which the people of Chersonesos inhabit or inhabited. But I shall carefully guard all of these for the demos of the people of Chersonesos. I shall not put down the democracy. I shall neither rely upon nor help conceal either traitor or subverter, but I shall reveal them to the magistrates in the city. I shall oppose anyone who plots against, betrays, or revolts from Chersonesos, Kerkinitis, Kalos Limen, the forts, and the chora of the people of Chersonesos. I shall hold the office of *damiorgos*; I shall be, to the best of my ability and with the greatest fairness, a councilor to the city and its citizens. I shall guard carefully the *saster* for the demos; and I shall not reveal to

either a Hellene or a barbarian any secret that is likely to harm the city. I shall neither offer nor accept a gift to harm the city and its citizens.[31]

Besides the Civic Oath of Chersonesos, arguably the three most informa-
tive Pontic inscriptions take the form of decrees, all dated to the late third to
mid-second century BC, honouring the following individuals: 1) Protogenes,
son of Heroson of Olbia;[32] 2) Agathokles, son of Antiphilos of Istria;[33] and
3) Hegesagoras, son of Monimos of Istria.[34]

1) **Protogenes of Olbia** was honoured by the Council and People of
   Olbia for his extraordinary benefaction to the city in times of war and
   peace. He was one of the most illustrious and richest *euergetai* of the
   Greek world: he repeatedly loaned (or forgave) the city large quantities of money to pay the extortion tribute to one of the rapacious local
   barbarian kings; he handled the city's finances with great skill; and he
   paid for the strengthening of the city's fortifications against the barbarian attacks of the Scythians, Skiroi, and Gauls. About Protogenes, Paul
   Veyne has written: 'As we read the decree we realize that Protogenes
   is richer than the city, that he is its absolute master, just as Cosimo
   de'Medici's wealth made him master of Florence; that he maintains the
   city out of his own pocket, just as a feudal lord would with his manor.
   Yet nothing in the wording of the decree reveals that dependence. If
   we were to judge by the style alone (ignoring the content), we should
   see the community honouring a benefactor who has merely behaved
   as a good citizen' (Veyne 1990: 108). This characterization has elicited
   a good deal of comment, most scholars agreeing with the tenor but
   objecting to the exaggerated parallels. The most balanced and insightful
   critique comes from Philippe Gauthier's seminal study of euergetism
   (benefaction) in the Greek cities from the fourth to the first centuries
   BC (Gauthier 1985). All subsequent literature on the subject references Gauthier, and it anchors the argument that as the Hellenistic
   period progresses, Greek cities become increasingly dependent on the
   kindness and largess of their wealthy citizens (as they had done from
   the Hellenistic kings in the third century), to the point that by the late
   second century BC, the elite benefactors superseded the democratic
   institutions of their respective cities. They were for all intents and purposes, oligarchies. We will have more to say on this later.
2) **Agathokles of Istria,** whose father was a benefactor, was honoured by
   the *boule* and *demos* for his effective political office holding; his military leadership (as an elected commander of the archers and mercenaries, he led a force against Thracian pirates); and his role as ambassador

to the Scythian King Rhemaxos (Agathokles persuaded the king to dispatch cavalry forces in defence of Istria and its *chora* against King Zoltes, a Thracian chieftain).

3) **Hegesagoras of Istria** was honoured by the *boule* and *demos* of the southern-most Ionian city, Apollonia, for his military role in a dispute between Mesembria and Apollonia over possession of the port of Anchialos (uncomfortably situated between the two *poleis*). Apparently, the Mesembrians attacked and seized Anchialos; the Apollonians appealed to their sister Ionian city (against Doric Mesembria) for military assistance. Hegesagoras, leading a war fleet and troops, was elected admiral and commander-in-chief of the coalition army, recaptured Anchialos, and defeated a naval force sent by Mesembria. This is a good example of the fact that the threat to the safety of the Pontic cities was not limited to the neighbouring barbarians. Like typical Greeks of the Classical period, they squabbled amongst themselves over borders and land.

Much has been made of this euergetic activity, and it is clear that it played an important part in the civic life of the Greek cities in the Hellenistic period, including the cities of the Pontos. What makes me uneasy is to equate this phenomenon with the demise of democratic institutions, that political power no longer ultimately rested in the hands of the People, the *demos*, but in the hands of the Elite, the Notables, the *Honoratioren*. Manfred Oppermann, commenting on the early Hellenistic period, concludes that 'the West Pontic *poleis* continued to have in their outside institutional structure essentially a democratic base. In reality, the political and economic power was naturally situated in the hands of a few wealthy people, of whom some come down to us as *euergetai*,' and that 'little substantial modification in the basic structures of West Pontic *poleis* administrative development occurred in the Late Hellenistic period. Thus there were also documents for this epoch of a developed Euergetismos' (Oppermann 2004: 339, 341).

Nawotka has pointed out that the majority of decrees issued by the West Pontic cities were honorific in nature, as in the well-known examples mentioned above, and that we lack significant examples of legislative acts. Reasonably, he argues that routine legislation probably did not find its way onto stone with the same frequency as honours for benefactors (who might be called upon to pay for the setting up of the dedication). However, he is struck by the disparity in numbers between legislative acts and honorific decrees (2:84), and he adds, 'it betrays a growing dependence of all these cities on their citizens in providing free services and cash handouts' (Nawotka 1997: 202). He concludes, 'Euergetism seems to have been a very important factor in Hellenistic Istros, Tomis, Dionysopolis, Odessos; in fact they became dependent on their rich citizens in vital areas of civic life. The real power in these cities seems to be concentrated in the hands of the local elite of city notables even if the constitutions of these cities remained nominally democratic' (1997: 204). 'We have the impression that the Western and Northern Pontic cities were hardly capable of making any step without the involvement of wealthy benefactors.'[35]

Nawotka is simply following what has now become the party line: democracy is dead or dying by the second century BC. The *boule* and *demos* may continue to 'preamble' the inscriptions, but it is all a sham, just going through the motions out of conservative tradition. The real power rests in the hands of the local elite. I believe that this conclusion goes beyond our evidence. I would suggest that we have embraced euergetism too uncritically and have empowered honorific inscriptions at the expense of common sense. First of all, the fact that we have more honorific inscriptions than other types does not prove that this was now the only business of the *boule* and the *demos*. An honorand would naturally expect a public and lasting acknowledgment of his generosity; who bothers to read documents in the archives? Do we assume that the *boule* and the *demos* have no other business to attend to but honorific proclamations? What are they doing on the normal meeting schedule? Why bother to meet at all? The sad truth is that with certain exceptions, we know next to nothing about the 'discourse of democracy,' the ebb and flow of the discussions, the debate over the proper course of action, and even less about who is saying what at the Assembly or Council meeting. Is it some sort of mute Spartan-style assembly? The fact remains: decrees do not represent 'minutes' of a meeting. I am reminded of working in the Venetian archives, reading documents issued by the Senate: like Greek decrees there are formulaic points of detail (preambles, justifications) and then a vote on the motion (*parte*). At the bottom of the document are the words 'si, non, insinceri,' with numbers to indicate the vote. If we did not have the contemporary eyewitness diaries of the nobleman Marino Sanudo or the moralistic diatribes of Girolamo Priuli, how would we reconstruct the context of the text? The simple answer is, we could not, and neither can we with respect the Pontic cities.

This is not to diminish the place of the *euergetes*; I seek only to strike a balance consistent with what our sources tell us. As Habicht has noted about Hellenistic Athens, it is not a given that rich benefactors, as a new ruling class, sought political power outside the normal channels of the established democratic institutions. They belong as much to the civic landscape of the Greek city as do the former liturgists.

But can we go beyond just a cautionary note about reading too much into our enigmatic inscriptions? I offer an alternative model: the democracies of the Black Sea were more vibrant and self-aware than most cities in Old Greece because of the precarious circumstances of their location on the periphery of the Greek world. It was a dangerous and uncertain world to be surrounded by barbarians, be they Scythians, Sarmatians, Getai, Gauls, or Thracians. Greek and Roman writers from Herodotos to Polybios to Ovid to Dio Chrysostom, spanning six centuries, affirm the uncivilized and dangerous nature of the rough neighbours of the West and North Pontic cities. Ovid's pitiable poems from Tomis are surely exaggerated to elicit imperial sympathy, but they would have been credible to their readers. In the second century BC, Polybios, excursing on the city of Byzantion, acutely observes:

As Thrace encompasses their territory so effectually as to extend from one sea to the other, they are engaged in perpetual and most difficult warfare with its inhabitants. They cannot on the one hand rid themselves of the war once for all by a carefully prepared attack resulting in victory, owing to the great number of the chieftains and their followers. For if they get the better of one, three more powerful chieftains are sure to invade their territory. Nor are they at all better off if they give way and agree to terms and the payment of tribute; for the very fact of their making concessions to one chief raises against them enemies many times more numerous. So that they are, as I said, involved in a warfare both perpetual and most difficult; for what can be more full of peril, what more terrible than a war with near neighbors who are at the same time barbarians? (4.45.1–5; Loeb trans.)

These comments can be aptly applied to all of the West and North Pontic cities, and the Civic Oath of Chersonesos acknowledges this clear and present danger. It is telling that when Dio arrives in Olbia around AD 100AD, the city is in the midst of a military crisis and barbarians threaten its security.

Apart from the Gallic invasion in the early third century BC, the cities of mainland Greece and Asia Minor operated within an agreed-upon set of diplomatic and civic norms, playing one Hellenistic king off of another to ensure the highest degree of autonomy, freedom, and democracy. They all understood what a Greek polis meant. What did 'democracy' mean to the barbarians? The Pontic cities could not always match up against them militarily, but they could entice them to peace by tribute and honours. This required special skill sets, qualifications that led the citizens to the same pool of candidates that included benefactors. The *demos* is still 'in charge,' the fundamental Aristotelian definition of *demokratia*. Ambassadors do not elect themselves, nor do benefactors award honours to themselves. I propose that the sense of cultural and community difference between Greeks and barbarians elevated the desire on the part of citizens to preserve their democratic institutions, their ancestral constitutions. The constant military threat encouraged a greater degree of citizen participation and ensured the survival of those political institutions that heralded their Hellenicity. The barbarians were the new Cyclopes (echoes of the *Odyssey*). The peripheral 'isolation' of the Black Sea cities may in fact have generated a broader sense of communal 'belonging' amongst their citizens. Survival was at stake. All of this will change, of course, with the coming of the Romans and the imposition of the Pax Romana. But these developments will occur later than those in Greece or Asia Minor. Mithridates VI Eupator played the Hellenic card and championed the Greeks of the Crimea.[36] It is no surprise that the West Pontic cities, like Athens, keen to their illustrious democratic traditions, turned to Mithridates against the Romans.

## Notes

1  I wish to thank Professors Sheila Ager and Riemer Faber, the organizers of the Workshop 'Belonging and Isolation in the Hellenistic World,' for the invitation to present this paper and the hospitality provided by their colleagues and the University of Waterloo.

2  Ferguson 1911; Habicht 1997; Grieb 2008.

3  As does Kidd 1988: 2.876–877.

4  Ferguson 1911: 428; Day 1942: 110n346 on Ferguson's revision of his 103/2 thesis.

5  Badian 1976: 105–28; Tracy 1982.

6  For this date, see Bugh 1990: 20–37. Kennel 1999: 241–62 argues for 151/150.

7  See Ferguson 1911: 289–90; Habicht 1997: 241–2.

8  Rhodes and Lewis 1997: 43, 55.

9  See Camp 1986: 168–80.

10  Cic. *Rep.* 3.48 with Berthold 1984: 39–40.

11  *IG* II² 851 (redated to ca 190 BC by Tracy 1990: 261), 853, 855, 856 (redated to ca 185 BC by Tracy 1990: 261), 889, 893, 922, 923, 925, 954, 979–82. See O'Neil 1995: 107–8.

12  Thompson and Wycherley 1972: 70 (= *Agora* XIV). For courts, see now Boegehold 1995: vii, 41–2, 93–6, 230–1 (= *Agora* XXVIII).

13  See Ferguson 1911: 290.

14  For example, see Habicht 1990: 561–77; Tracy and Habicht 1991: 187–236.

15  See Habicht 1997: 242–5.

16  *FdeD* III.2 139 = *Syll.*[3] 729. For discussion, see Day 1942: 91–2; Habicht 1997: 291–2; Shipley 2000: 382; and translation, Austin 2006: no. 125.

17  See Camp 1986: 168–80.

18  See Kienast 1997: 53–65; Camp 2001: 176–80; Garland 1987: 55.

19  De Ste Croix 1981: 525–6. Cf. Touloumakos 1977; Bernhardt 1985; Quass 1979, 1993; Fernoux 2004; Fröhlich 2004; Fröhlich and Müller 2005; and Dmitriev 2005.

20  Of course, one might also include the Epimelete of Delos and the mint magistrates. For discussion, see Habicht 1997: 242–63, 287–90, 321–4.

21  *SEG* 21 469 (129/128 BC); *Syll.*[3] 697 (128/127 BC); *IG* II[2] 1714.12; in the Pythaïs: *IG* II[2] 2336.

22  Geagan 1967: 57.

23  Aristides, *Panathenaicus*; see Geagan 1967: 32–61.

24  *IG* II[2] 1714; Ath. 5 213e.

25  On Athenion and Aristion, see Bugh 1992: 108–23.

26  See Habicht 1997: 287–8 and passim.

27  For ancient Latin literary sources, at least for Ukraine, see now Mason 2008.

28  Nawotka 1997, 1999.

29  Grammenos and Petropoulos 2003. Sadly, the translations are almost incomprehensible in sections – closer oversight in the editing process was desperately needed.

30  For Greek texts, see *Syll.*[3] and Moretti II 1975; for translations, see Austin 2006: nos. 112, 114–16, 120.

31  *Syll.*[3] 360. Translated by T. Lytle in Carter et al. 2003: 136. Though dated, see Latyschev 1885: 265–300.

32  *Syll.*[3] 495; *IosPE* I[2] 32; Tarn and Griffith 1952: 109; Ogden 2002: 202–5; Anghel 1999–2000: 104, 111; Shipley 2000: 98; Austin 2006: no. 115; Braund and Kryzhitskiy 2008: 64–72.

33  Moretti II 131; *IScM* I 15; Pippidi 1984: 101–8; Nawotka 1999: 39–40; Anghel 1999–2000: 103–4; Austin 2006: no. 116.

34  Moretti II 129; *IScM* I 64; Chamoux 2003: 168–72.

35  Nawotka 1999: 173–4; cf. Avram 1999: 88: 'de certaines activités de notables "evergètes" qui se sont, semble-t-il, profondément impliqués en politique.'

36  See McGing 1986.

# PART THREE

---

# *Symploke*: Mediterranean Systems and Networks

The polities of the Hellenistic Mediterranean were remarkable for their number and variety: *poleis*, leagues, kingdoms, empires, and of course Rome. Such diversity was emblematic of the anarchy of a multipolar system; yet at the same time, as the papers in this section show, these polities were bound together in a complex network of interaction, or rather in a series of such networks. Mutual political and economic interests, ties of kinship, diplomatic relations, and of course conflict brought the states into contact with one another. It was in the Hellenistic age, Polybios argues, that the affairs of the two isolated halves of the Mediterranean first merged. From this point on, the affairs of the West and of the East were inextricably woven together, intertwined by a process of *symploke* (Polyb. 1.3; 4.28; 5.105).

Employing contemporary international relations theory – specifically, that of the Realist school – Arthur Eckstein demonstrates that patterns of integration, of *symploke*, in the Hellenistic Mediterranean were not necessarily harmonious. With the sudden collapse of Ptolemaic power at the end of the century, and the intrusion of Rome into eastern affairs, the entire Mediterranean system underwent a crucial shift, a 'power-transition crisis.' As Eckstein shows us, Polybios himself – an expatriate Greek living in Rome – was, like Thucydides, able to separate himself sufficiently from his own political loyalties that he could observe and record what was happening on a systemic level.

In spite of the political anarchy of the Hellenistic world, Gary Reger's contribution, drawing on contemporary network theory, illustrates well the interconnectedness of the peoples of the Mediterranean. His paper discusses economic networks, and illustrates vividly the mutuality of belonging that defines the threads of connectedness in these networks. It is worth noting that, as Reger points out, 'flow of information' was a crucial aspect of successful economic networks; such free exchanges of information were, by contrast, missing from the militarized political system, where it was precisely lack of trustworthy information about other states that exacerbated individual states' fear and security consciousness.

Claude Eilers's paper focuses on the complexity of diplomatic friendship and kinship networks in the Hellenistic Mediterranean. Diplomatic networks such as these – often with fictitious bases of shared past history and kinship relations – were perhaps the grease that allowed the anarchic system to function as peacefully as it on occasion did. An Athenian decree honouring Hyrkanos I, high priest of the Jewish people, demonstrates diplomatic (and perhaps trade) ties between the Hasmonean state and the Hellenistic polis. These diplomatic ties extended also to Pergamon and Rome, embracing each polity in a mutual network of international friendship.

Networks, as Reger points out, operate in various dimensions. Simultaneous and overlapping layers of relationships characterize any system, and the Hellenistic Mediterranean featured many ways of belonging: trade, intermarriage, diplomatic agreements of *asylia* or *sympoliteia*, honorary kinship, and so on. Ultimately, with the final victory of Rome and the establishment of a unipolar system, the peoples of the Mediterranean were able to engage in all these varied modes of connectedness without the fears and insecurity so typical of an anarchic system.

# 7

# Polybios and International Systems Theory

## ARTHUR ECKSTEIN

### Introduction

Allow me to begin this chapter with a statement of the obvious: Polybios was not a modern political scientist. He was a Hellenistic intellectual, and Hellenistic culture and the course of Hellenistic history led him to be impressed with the impact of Tyche (Fortune) in human affairs.[1] And Tyche is an idea – or a phenomenon – that makes modern political scientists, searching for their law-like patterns in interstate relations, shudder. Polybios wrote too with a moral as well as a pragmatic purpose. But this is a moral engagement that modern political scientists, who don the mask of cool objectivity, tend to shun.[2]

Nevertheless, and even admitting the powerful cultural complications, Polybios – like Thucydides before him – did evolve and employ the major insights that inform modern international systems theory. The most important modern school of thought here is called 'Realism.' Its fundamental insights are (1) that the presence or absence of international law is crucial in determining the behaviour of states; and (2) that in the absence of international law, the distribution of power capabilities across a state system – its dispersal among many states, or in a few states, or its concentration in one state – is crucial to the character of the system, to the behaviour of the states that make it up, and to understanding both.

Polybios was not alone in thinking in this Realist fashion in the Hellenistic age, that is, he was not an isolated or lonely figure; there were other intellectuals, both Greek and Roman, who analysed international relations in a similar Realist fashion, in that sense creating, as one of our colleagues at the conference put it, a connected 'garland' of Greek and Roman thinkers about international politics.[3] But Polybios is the most prominent surviving Hellenistic analyst along these lines, and has left us the most material.

This is an interdisciplinary topic, involving modern international relations studies and modern scholarship on antiquity, and one problem is that there has been so little contact between modern international relations studies and modern scholars of antiquity. Thus specialists in the rise of Rome mostly know the theories of the *internal* causes of imperial expansion and aggression as those theories were first propounded by John Hobson a century ago, and flourished in British universities in the 1950s. These theories focus on the social-economic-cultural pathologies that allegedly produce imperial expansion. They are then applied to Roman society (as in the work of W.V. Harris), or to the great Hellenistic states (as in the work of M.M. Austin).[4] Now, Polybios – like Thucydides before him – was highly interested in the internally generated causes of imperial expansion. But in the savage world in which both men lived, internalist explanations focused not on pathologies but on the internal *strengths* that enabled states to survive and to prevail. This is most obvious in Polybios's book 6, on the character of the Roman *politeia*. Despite Jacqueline de Romilly's comments on this point long ago, scholars of antiquity have been slow to realize what such an attitude implies about the harsh interstate environment (de Romilly 1977).

Specialists in ancient interstate politics also have almost no knowledge of current theories in political science that focus not on internal conditions but rather on the harsh nature of international relations itself as the cause both of war and of imperial expansion. Until a year ago, only one book made a major contribution to antiquity here, the good collection of essays edited by the political scientist Richard Ned Lebow and the ancient historian Barry Strauss – *Hegemonic Rivalry* – and it is out of print and almost unobtainable (Lebow and Strauss 1991). Yet Realist theories have been central to the modern analysis of international relations since at least 1945. This approach has much to tell scholars of ancient history, not least because its major insights can be traced to ancient writers.

This paper will proceed in a roundabout way, briefly laying out the Realist paradigm, and then addressing even more briefly – though inevitably – Thucydides, before showing how Polybios's view of interstate life correlates to the maxims of modern Realist theory. To repeat: all of this is with the caveat that Polybios was not a modern intellectual.

## The Realist Paradigm

Contemporary international systems Realism is founded on three pessimistic assertions. First is the prevalence of anarchy. The interstate world has typically consisted of a multiplicity of sovereign entities; they recognize little by way of international law, and have almost no way of enforcing it. There really are no enforceable rules of conduct – especially for strong states. This harsh anarchic environment dictates that the primary goals of all governments are simply survival and security.

There are two possible exits from anarchy. One is the emergence of a universal empire. That is, one state achieves universal and unchallenged power, and imposes a rough law and order everywhere, to suit its own purposes and as it sees fit. This, of course, was the Roman solution. But the emergence of universal empires is rare, and difficult to achieve (as the United States has now found out). The second exit is through acceptance of international law, especially by the strong states, administered – and enforced – by a neutral international institution such as a United Nations. But because the interstate world has always been so dangerous, the voluntary acceptance of restraints on state conduct is unlikely. This is especially true for the powerful, who do not wish to give up their hard-won advantages in the system. Historically, then, multipolar anarchy has been *the* prevalent form of interstate life.

The prevalence of anarchy leads to the second Realist assertion: anarchy results in ruthless self-seeking by all states. With no international law, states must provide for their own security. The interstate order is thus a self-help regime. That is, governments are unable to depend on the help of others or on the rule of law, so every government reserves the right to be sole arbiter of what constitutes justice for itself, and the right to take up arms to enforce it (Aron 1973: 64–5). Self-help leads naturally to power-maximizing behaviour – for in an anarchy power is the best way to be secure, and power-maximizing behaviour is thus the norm for *all* states. This aggressive, expansionist behaviour originates partly from greed, but mostly from fear: from the desire for self-preservation. In a fiercely competitive world, 'States must meet the demands of the political eco-system or court annihilation.'[5]

The combination of anarchy, ruthless self-help, and power-maximizing behaviour by all states leads to the third Realist assertion: war is normal. That is, war, or the threat of war, is a normative way by which states under anarchy resolve conflicts of interest. Those conflicts of interest are real, and not a mere matter of miscommunication.[6] Widespread internal cultures of militarism and bellicosity are simply a natural adaptation to the bleak international environment, though they in turn contribute to the prevalence of war.[7] This is true of all states: under anarchy they are all 'functionally similar' (Waltz 1979: 96–7).

Political scientists also posit that in an anarchic state system, there is a moment when the danger of large-scale war is most acute: when a sudden large shift in the distribution of power capabilities of states occurs within the system. Political scientists term this a power-transition crisis. The shift can be either a dramatic *increase* in the capabilities of one of the main actors, and/or a dramatic *decrease* in the capabilities of another main unit. When the existing distribution of privilege, influence, and territory in a system becomes mismatched to the changing realities of power, the result tends to be large-scale war that in turn creates a new structure, a new configuration of privilege and territory, one better matched to the actual distribution of power (Lemke and Kugler 1996). Thus realignments of power, influence, and status within anarchic state systems have tended to be accompanied by great violence: what political scientists call 'hegemonic war.' The First World War is a good example. Realists hold that power-transition crises and hegemonic wars often come from the attempt by a major state to preserve its deteriorating position; it acts while its governing elite feels it still can (Gilpin 1988). This is only a trend; individual moments of decision-making by governments are too idiosyncratic to be predictable. Hence the power-transition crisis caused by the collapse of the Soviet Union was handled without war, thanks to good diplomacy on both sides. Historically, however, a power-transition crisis tends to lead to hegemonic war to establish new leaders within the system.

## Thucydides

Modern Realists have no doubt that Thucydides is their intellectual ancestor.[8] And more: they employ Thucydides to argue that intellectuals perceived a world of fearful, ruthless, power-maximizing, and warlike states as soon as interstate politics itself came into existence in antiquity. Hence the Realist world view was (and is) a natural reaction to a real situation.[9]

It is clear why Realists like Thucydides. His is a world of fearful states living in conditions of danger – a world, he explicitly says, where each state must depend upon itself to survive (5.105.3, 113). There is of course no written international law, and even the few informal norms of state conduct are violated with impunity. Sworn treaties are meaningless (see the Corcyrean statement at 1.36.1). Distrust among states is pervasive. And, as Thucydides's Athenians tell the Melians, interstate politics is a deadly business in which the goal is physical survival (5.101). Indeed, the term *kindynos* (danger) appears more than two hundred times in Thucydides's text.[10]

So Thucydides's vision conforms to the grimmest aspects of the Realist model of anarchy. But in three passages (1.23.5–6, 1.88, and 1.118.2) Thucydides also indicates – to the delight of political scientists – that a power-transition crisis was the truest cause of a hegemonic war, namely, the Peloponnesian War.

Thucydides' analysis is as follows. At 1.88 and 1.118.2, he indicates that the growth of Athenian power is the destabilizing element in the interstate system, but that this general trend also eventually takes a specific form: Athenian actions against Sparta's allies. This is explicit in 1.118.2: as the power of Athens reached its height, 'the Athenians began to lay hands on Sparta's alliance.' This led the Spartans, previously passive in the face of growing Athenian power, to feel compelled to risk war.

This is also Thucydides's analysis in 1.23.5–6: Athenian pressure on Sparta's allies was a specific manifestation of the general growth of Athenian power. In 1.23.5, Thucydides says that he is going to lay out 'the complaints and disputes' between states so that no one will ever have to enquire 'from whence the war arose.' By the 'complaints and disputes' he means the conflicts between Athens and Sparta's allies Corinth and Megara. Then comes the famous sentence in 1.23.6, on the 'truest cause of the war,' an explanation which foregrounds *not* the complaints and disputes, but how the Athenians, by growing powerful, created fear at Sparta. This sentence begins with the Greek particle *gar*. Now, *gar* is not oppositive in meaning ('But . . .'), though it is often translated that way. Rather, *gar* is *explanatory*: 'For, indeed . . .' So for Thucydides the 'truest cause' *explains* his previous comment about the 'disputes and quarrels.' And 1.118.2 shows us how: the Athenian actions against Sparta's allies were a manifestation of the deeper shift of power in the Greek state system in favour of Athens. One must note, however, that for Thucydides these actions and the resulting war were *also* the result of contingent (if natural) decisions made by both the Athenians and the Spartans; there is no 'inevitability' in the Greek of 1.23.5–6.

If Thucydides is thus complex, the political scientists are still basically correct that he foregrounds a power-transition crisis as the truest cause of the war. Given this, and his pessimistic view of the harsh character of interstate relations in an anarchic world, Thucydides can indeed be seen as modern political scientists see him: as the founder of international systems theory in general and Realist theory in particular.[11]

## Polybios

How does all of this relate to Polybios? There are crucial parallels between the world view of the two ancient writers.

First, Polybios's world of states is a dangerous world; and *kindynos* (danger), one of Thucydides's favourite terms, appears in the extant text of Polybios no less than 455 times. Polybios's text is 50 per cent longer than Thucydides's, but this only partly explains the huge number. By contrast, Herodotos's long history only uses *kindynos* and related terms thirty-five times (Munson 2001). Polybios's employment of *kindynos* terminology in his discussions of interstate relations does not prove that he had read Thucydides (a controversial topic) – but this is an intriguing thought.

Second, Polybios posited that his interstate world was dangerous in good part because international law did *not* exist. He is explicit about this. In discussing the failed peace talks between Egypt and Syria over Lebanon in 219/218 BC, he comments: 'Claims and counter-arguments were constantly repeated by one side or the other in the course of the embassies and counter-embassies. But there was no possibility of actually arriving at any result, because there was no one to interpose between the two sides with the power to block or restrain the side disposed to transgress the boundaries of justice' (5.67.11). He concludes that in the absence of an overarching authority, the Lebanon issue could only be resolved by war – which it was (5.68.1).[12]

Indeed, in Polybios, perceived state interest renders meaningless even treaties sworn to the gods. Hence the obligations of a sworn treaty of alliance do not keep Philip V of Macedon from attacking his ally Messene in 214 BC (Polyb. 3.19.11 with 7.1.2), nor does a similar treaty keep King Nabis of Sparta from attacking Messene in 202 (16.13.3), nor does a sworn peace treaty with Egypt deter Antiochos III from attacking Egypt in 202 (15.23.13), nor does a written agreement keep Antiochos IV from attacking Egypt in 168 (29.26). And such conduct was not limited to great states: the Kydonians destroy the town of Apollonia in Crete in a surprise attack, even though they have mutual citizenship with the Apolloniates through a sworn treaty (28.14.4–5).

What was true of written treaties was naturally even more true of informal norms. Polybios condemns Philip V for habitually pillaging sacred sites that officially possessed *asylia*, immunity from violence. But he knows there was no way for Philip to be brought to book for his actions – except in Polybios's own negative comments half a century later. The Kydonians, too, were never punished for their atrocity (28.15). Similarly, Polybios condemns Philip's enslavements of Greek populations that surrendered to him peacefully, but he knows that the only response at the time to Philip's multiple violations of this alleged norm of Hellenistic conduct was increased international unpopularity. That was a political problem, yes, but Philip was prepared to live with it in exchange for the large financial gain he reaped (15.22–3).[13]

Now Polybios, unlike Thucydides, is barely known to modern political scientists: they know little about Classical Greece, but even less about Hellenistic writers. Yet he deserves a place alongside Thucydides as an ancient founder of international systems theory, with all its grim tenets. His interstate world is a lawless one, as is Thucydides's, where war is common and governments act harshly to advance their interests. And similarly to Thucydides, interstate politics – in the absence of international law – is shaped in good part by the distribution of power capabilities across the interstate system. This is my final topic. Because of space limitations, I can point out only a few examples of this Polybian analysis.

First, there is Polybios's Thucydidean-style view of how a power-transition crisis in the eastern Mediterranean initiated the large hegemonic war that transformed the Hellenistic state system at the end of the third century BC. This power-transition crisis was one of the central and most crucial events in his *Histories*.

The state system in the Greek East had been based since ca 280 BC on a tripolar balance of power: Antigonid Macedon, the Seleukid Empire, and the Ptolemaic regime. The situation had always been unstable (Ager 2005), but after 207 BC it began to undergo a dramatic upheaval. The Ptolemaic regime suddenly weakened: a massive indigenous rebellion in the Nile Valley that proved impossible to put down, the loss of governmental control over major tax-contributing regions, the premature death of Ptolemy IV in 204 and his succession by a child, with political chaos reigning thereafter in Alexandria itself – all this resulted in a sudden, unexpected, and profound redistribution of power across the Hellenistic system.[14] The weakening of the Ptolemies led to a decisive expansion in the power of Philip V and Antiochos III. The number of great powers was reduced from three to two. If we possessed Polybios's book 14, which dealt almost exclusively with the Egyptian crisis, we would see this process even more clearly (Walbank 1967: 424). The ruthless ambitions of Philip and Antiochos found expression in a treaty of alliance (ca winter 203/202) to divide between them the entire Ptolemaic realm, apparently including Egypt itself; there followed large-scale warfare against Ptolemaic holdings. The structure of the Hellenistic state system would never be the same.

Polybios made the 'Pact between the Kings' a centrepiece of his *Histories*, foregrounding its importance in two commentaries appended to his ongoing narrative, and describing its workings within the narrative itself.[15] Yet scholars have raised doubts about the real extent of the Pact, or even its historicity.[16] I think the proponents of the existence of the Pact have always had the better argument. But now we have an inscription indicating cooperation against the Ptolemies by Antigonid and Seleukid forces in Karia in 201 BC: Ptolemaic towns conquered by Philip were being turned over to Antiochos. In short, Polybios – what a surprise! – knew what he was talking about.[17]

The expansion of the power of the kings in turn triggered resistance from some second-tier states – notably the Republic of Rhodes and the Kingdom of Pergamon – as well as from Egypt itself. By the summer of 201 the East was ablaze from Gaza to the Aegean. It was a large-scale hegemonic war to determine the new structure of the state system; Polybios covered the fighting in detail (cf. 16.22a). But the resisters were hard-pressed. The result was an appeal for help to Rome in autumn 201 by no less than four Greek states: Egypt, Pergamon, Rhodes, and Athens. The Greek envoys presented the Senate with disturbing information about the kings. Though Polybios's account of the events in Rome is lost, we can know what he said the Greeks' information was. We have an important clue at 15.20.5–6. In the midst of his moral condemnation of Philip and Antiochos for their conduct, Polybios writes: 'For even while they were still breaking their pledged faith with each other, and destroying the kingdom of the child, Tyche (Fortune) alerted the Romans, and then very justly visited upon the kings the very evils they had planned in their total lawlessness to bring upon others.'

Polybios says that Tyche 'alerted the Romans' – ἐπιστήσασα ῾Ρωμαίους – to the bad conduct of the kings, which he had been discussing. He had been discussing the Pact. Walbank pointed out the correct translation of ἐφίστημι in this passage forty years ago, and I have recently sought to show just how correct Walbank was, and why this is so important for understanding what occurred at Rome in winter 201/200.[18]

Polybios often underlines the arbitrary conduct of Tyche (see 2.70.2–3). But in 15.20 Tyche is not arbitrary; she is retributive Justice. Tyche took her retribution on the kings' bad conduct by alerting the Romans. How? The obvious answer is through the Greek embassies to the Senate, which alerted the Romans specifically to the Pact (the only subject of 15.20), that is, to the danger it presented not merely to the Greeks, but ultimately to Rome. The Achaian envoys to Antigonos Doson in the Peloponnesian crisis of the 220s had made a similar point to the Macedonian king about the ultimate threat posed by Kleomenes III of Sparta not merely to themselves but ultimately to Macedon (Polyb. 2.49.6). The proper translation of 15.20.5–6 thus tells us much about how Polybios depicted the decision in Rome in 201/200 BC. The Greeks' pleas led the Senate to push the *comitia centuriata* into a conditional declaration of war against Philip, while simultaneously dispatching an embassy to warn Antiochos away from invading Egypt proper (Livy 31.6–7).

The Romans, like Philip, like Antiochos, and like the second-tier Greek states, were all ultimately responding here to the same real systemic crisis, the crisis ultimately caused by the Ptolemaic collapse.[19] All these states, including Rome but not only Rome, responded in the same way: by resort to force. Strictly speaking, they need not have done so; the governing elites possessed freedom of will. Philip and Antiochos could have decided not to take advantage of Ptolemaic weakness. The weaker Greek states could have decided to appease the newly emerging hegemons of the system, or even to bandwagon with them in hopes of gaining spoils from the Ptolemaic collapse, instead of resisting the kings militarily and then seeking help from a power on the periphery of the traditional Hellenistic system.

That latter point brings us to another aspect of the crisis – the one most relevant to the theme of this collection. Polybios foregrounds the rise of Roman power, but the other great theme in his *Histories* is the growing interconnectedness (*symploke*) between the eastern and western halves of the Mediterranean. The two halves of the Mediterranean had long been two separate state systems, and this was true, Polybios says, until things began to change in 217 BC when Philip began to look to attack Rome. The envoys of the Greek states at Rome in 201/200 were urging that major events in the *East* should have an impact on actions of the great state of the *West;* and indeed for Polybios this was a crucial event in the emergence of the *symploke.* In modern international relations terms, the Greek envoys were seeking to enlarge the traditional Greek diplomatic field by bringing the outsider Rome into their struggle against Philip and Antiochos. And by 150 BC the Mediterranean had indeed become one large unified system – under Roman domination. The Greek envoys thus played a catalytic role in the emergence of a single Mediterranean state system. Polybios's emphasis on the enlargement of the Greek diplomatic field and the emergence of the *symploke* is, of course, another example of his taste for system-level analysis.[20]

But Polybios must also have been well aware that he was dealing here with a contingent event. Rome was exhausted by the Hannibalic War, had serious trouble with the Celts just over the Apennines in northern Italy, and we know that many Romans opposed the decision to intervene in the East.[21] Polybios's emphasis on Tyche is thus perhaps a way of expressing the not-easy-to-predict decisions made by governments during the crisis, including Rome. He expresses in a Hellenistic way another Realist point: the anarchic nature and shifting power configurations of the interstate system (in this case, the dramatically changing distribution of power in the Hellenistic system) shape and shove the decision making of states but they do not *determine* their actions.[22] That is, while grim trends in behaviour are broadly predictable, individual state decisions are not, and Polybios expresses this indeterminacy through his use of Tyche.

A final example of Polybios at work: Rome's destruction of Antigonid Macedon in the Third Macedonian War (171–168 BC) transformed Roman-Greek relations as well as the entire Mediterranean state structure. Polybios praises Greek leaders who refrained from choosing sides in this war because they feared that *whichever* side won, the Greeks would fall under the domination of a single power (ὑπὸ μίαν ἀρχήν, 30.6.5). It is a given that before this the Greeks had not yet been under the domination of a single power, because the existence of a powerful Macedon somewhat balanced Rome, a situation these statesmen wished to preserve. Similarly, Polybios praises Kephalos of Epiros for his analysis of the situation ca 172: Kephalos wished to preserve the current status quo, which provided a reasonable situation for the smaller states (27.15.10–12); he feared a new war would establish the heavy-handed hegemony of either Rome or Macedon (27.15.11). In the view of both Kephalos and Polybios, then, in 172 BC no heavy-handed hegemony existed as yet in Greece, and this was because of the existence of *two* large powers. No wise man wanted to risk that number being reduced to one, whether it be Rome or Macedon.[23]

Livy, drawing on different Polybian material, presents a similar picture of Greek political leaders in this period (42.30.5–6). He says that the Greek leaders deserving praise were those responsible and intelligent men who, if forced to make a choice of a master who was superior in power, preferred being under Rome to being under the erratic Macedonian ruler Perseus, but who, if given a free choice, preferred neither Rome nor Perseus to become more powerful through the downfall of the other. They understood that a continuation of the current status quo was best for the free Greek states, since one power would always be there to protect the weak against wrongdoing by the other.[24] The passage seems overly theoretical, in that even with a powerful Macedon in existence, one may doubt its ability to balance Rome (perhaps the idea is Macedon at the head of a Greek coalition). Nevertheless, the passage indicates again that in Polybios's analysis, the general power configuration meant that the Greek states before the Third Macedonian War had no overpowering master, and that what had occurred by 168 BC was a catastrophic shift in that configuration in favour of Rome. This change, from two great powers in Greece to one, is precisely why Polybios dates the beginning of true Roman *arche* in the East to 168/167 BC (Polyb. 1.1.5).[25]

This system level of analysis is not limited to the later books of Polybios. It appears already in book 1. Here Polybios praises King Hieron II of Syracuse for providing aid to Carthage during its war with the Mercenaries in 241–238 BC. Polybios says that Hieron aided Carthage so that it would be preserved, and Syracuse would not have to face a (western) state system with only one power: namely, Rome (1.83.3–4). Polybios then makes Hieron's 'two powers' policy a general rule (1.83.4): second-tier states should never contribute to the attainment by one state of a power so unrivalled that one is helpless before a tyrant (Eckstein 1985).

Polybios's analysis of the political impact of the distribution of power capabilities across a state system is thus underlined right from book 1 of the *Histories*, which was written in the late 160s BC. We have just seen that he later indicates that the concept was widespread among Greek statesmen in the 170s. And this suggests that – while we admit Polybios's own genius – he is reflecting here a broad trend in Greek thinking. After all, he grew up among the political elite of the Achaian League; his father was *strategos* of the League twice. Perhaps he imbibed ideas about the impact of power capabilities from the circle of prominent statesmen who politically educated him in the 180s and 170s.[26]

To conclude: the above examples of Polybios's system-level and power-focused analysis of interstate relations show that he should be seen as a major early figure in international systems theory and Realism in all its aspects, right beside Thucydides. This is not to pat Polybios on the head for his 'modernism,' as if he were a bright child. The point, rather, is this: our two most profound ancient observers of interstate politics and war emphasize the savage nature of interstate politics under anarchy, and the impact of system-level distributions of power, as primary explanations for the violent events they describe (though not to the exclusion of other factors). This shows how early the Realist vision emerged, and suggests the enduring power of that vision. These experienced men, sober and sombre thinkers, are (both of them) convinced exponents of it.

## Notes

1  On Polybios and Tyche, see Walbank 1994.
2  On Polybios's moralism, see Eckstein 1995a.
3  See below, n. 25, on the Roman Cato the Elder.
4  See, e.g., Harris 1979; Austin 1986.
5  Sterling 1974: 336. See, e.g., Waltz 1988.
6  Waltz 1959: 160, 1979: 102, 1988: 620 (the quote), and 2000: 8. Regular warfare a fact of international life under anarchy: see the statistical study of Geller and Singer 1998.
7  On this fundamental and obvious point, see Gourevitch 1978.
8  See, e.g., Doyle 1990: 223.
9  See, e.g., Doyle 1991: 169.
10  On the theme of distrust in Thucydides, see Leppin 1999.
11  On Thuc. 1.23.5–6, see Eckstein 2003.
12  Eckstein 1995a: 195–6 and 2006: 100–1.
13  Discussion in Eckstein 2006: 102–3.
14  On the Egyptian revolt, see Veïsse 2004. On the unstable situation in Alexandria, see Mittag 2003.
15  See Polyb. 3.2.8 (emphatic); 14.1a.1 (with Walbank); 15.20 (emphatic); 16.1 and 16.24.

16 See, e.g. Magie 1939; Errington 1971 and 1986: 8 and n15.

17 On the inscription, see Dreyer 2002. For a general defence of the historicity of the Pact between Philip and Antiochos, see Eckstein 2008: chapter 4.

18 Walbank 1967: 474. In greater detail: Eckstein 2005.

19 Cf. Mommsen 1903: 696–701.

20 Aron 1973: 87–8, on the occasional unforeseeable 'enlargement of the diplomatic field' to include major states not previously within a system; cf. Eckstein 2008: chapters 5 and 6.

21 Detailed discussion and sources in Eckstein 2008: chapter 6.

22 Waltz 2000: 24. On Polybios's two-track approach here, at the secular and the metaphysical level, see Walbank 1994.

23 See Eckstein 1995a: 206 and 209n58 and 2008: 369–71.

24 Livy working here from Polybian material: see discussion in Gruen 1975: 62–3.

25 Note too the way Polybios's Roman friend Cato the Elder in 167 BC defended the Rhodian lack of support for Rome in Third Macedonian War: they did not want to fall under the control of a single state, namely Rome; the earlier power configuration was better for *libertas*: Gell. 6.1.3 = Cato *ORF*, fr. 164: *ne sub sole imperio nostro in servitute nostra essent. libertatis causa in ea sententia fuisse arbitror.*

26 On Polybios's aristocratic background and political heritage, see Eckstein 1995a: 4 and 197–203.

# 8

# Networks in the Hellenistic Economy

## GARY REGER

In 1967 the sociologist Stanley Milgram published a short paper report-ing the results of a clever experiment. Milgram gave individuals living in Boston, Massachusetts, and Omaha, Nebraska, copies of a letter addressed to a stockbroker in Boston. He instructed his subjects to try to pass the letter to the stockbroker not directly but by sending it to someone they knew on a first-name basis with a request to pass the letter on to another person that person knew on a first-name basis. The idea was to test a proposition that had been circulating in the sociological community: that the social world is 'small' in the sense that you can get from any given person to another in only a few steps. Milgram discovered that on average, his subjects were able to get the letter delivered to the stockbroker in 5.5 steps, and he concluded that the social world was indeed 'small' in the sense that no one was more than about six steps, or links, away from anyone else.[1]

Milgram and his students repeated this experiment with variations a few times and confirmed the results (Korte and Milgram 1970). The no-tion that the world is small entered the idiom, spawning games like 'Six Degrees of Kevin Bacon,' which links actors to Bacon through films in which they appeared. Recently Milgram's basic claim received striking confirma-tion through a study of instant messaging that looked at 30 billion messages dispatched globally by 240 million people in the month of June 2006; the in-vestigators found an average distance between all participants in this study of 6.6 steps (Leskovec and Horvitz 2008: 922).

Milgram's results surprised not only because of the unexpected closeness they implied for all people in the world population, but also because social groups tend to be clustered: that is, the members of any given social group connected with a given individual tend to be connected to each other as well.

My friends are likely to know each other; my co-workers are likely to know each other. This clustering seems to suggest that most social groupings are fairly closed, and that in turn raises a conundrum: if social groups tend to be clustered, how is it possible to get from any individual to any other – remembering that the world population today is over 7 billion – in so few steps? This problem turned out to be a good deal harder than it may seem, and the work done on it by sociologists, mathematicians, and physicists in the forty years following Milgram's initial paper has flowered into the formal study of networks – a science that has now found a home in a bewildering variety of academic fields.

This is not the place for a full review of the development of the field or its applications.[2] For our purposes the most immediately relevant result relates to the resolution of the small-world problem in connection with clustering. Social groups within networks are indeed clustered, as one would expect. But it is possible for people in a network to find a short path to some other given person because people do not construct their social identity on a single dimension but simultaneously on multiple dimensions (Watts 2003: 150). Consider for example the Athenian poet Philippides. To his identity as a poet he owed his honoured place in the court of Lysimachos and access to the king. One of the networks to which he belonged, then, was that of the courtiers of Lysimachos. But another dimension of his personal identity, his Athenian citizenship, motivated him to use his access repeatedly to the benefit of his homeland.[3] Recent work on the small-world problem in this context of identity has shown that people tend typically to look at two different dimensions of their identity in seeking paths through their networks to reach an unknown party – in modern-day groups, usually geography and occupation.[4]

We need to add two last descriptors to the picture of small-world networks drawn so far. The earliest mathematical approaches to network problems had assumed, as a simplification, that all nodes in a network enjoyed the same number of connections and that randomness determined to which other node(s) any given node was connected. In fact, most networks do not follow this script. Instead, they tend to display clustering (as already mentioned) and to have some nodes that are substantially better connected than others. These nodes László Barabási christened 'hubs,' and their heavy connectedness allows us to understand how a network can display both clustering and small-worldedness: the hubs provide most of the long-distance connections that enable short paths.

Finally, the explanation for clustering is found in homophily – the tendency for like people to connect with each other. You are more likely to know someone picked at random in your neighbourhood than someone picked at random from Beijing because you and your neighbour are homophilous for residence. Likewise, I am far more likely to know a German picked at random who happens to be a Greek historian than a German who is not because she and I are homophilous for profession. The recent instant messaging experiment mentioned earlier has also offered striking confirmation of the operation of homophily in the exchange of instant messages except on one dimension – sex: people are somewhat more likely to instant message with a member of the opposite sex than the same (Leskovec and Horvitz 2008: 919).

Let me summarize the characteristics of small-world networks, as worked out in the recent literature. The typical small-world network displays *clustering*, that is, the tendency for there to be small groups of interconnected nodes within the larger network; *homophily*, the tendency for nodes that share a characteristic to be more likely to be connected than those that do not; *short-pathedness*, that is, the ability to get from any given node to another given node by relatively few steps, as in the 6.6-step instant-messaging network; and the presence of *hubs*, that is, nodes that are substantially better connected than the typical node. Finally, in networks composed of nodes with agency – like human beings – the nodes deploy dimensions of their *social identity*, itself multifarious, when asked to locate a path from themselves to another node.

When Milgram designed his experiment he was not stepping into unexplored territory. The idea of networks had been in use for many decades in sociology and social anthropology, under the designation of social network analysis.[5] Networks can be difficult to understand and use as tools of analysis in part because they can be regarded both as quite specific phenomena, identified by particular rules and applied in particular ways – this is the approach of social network analysis, which deploys statistical methods to identify network membership and track the movement of data and interconnections – or as metaphors for social interaction and connectivity, an approach that has been more typical both of social anthropology and the more generalized use of 'networks as methodological tools, as metaphors for understanding forms of relations and as descriptors of social forms.'[6]

The application of network theory, mainly in its socio-anthropological sense, to the Graeco-Roman world has burgeoned in recent years.[7] For instance, social network analysis has been applied to theoric networks connecting *poleis* with festival centres and arguing that such an optic can identify features of these networks that would have otherwise gone unremarked; to reconceptualizing Greek history as a world system that reaches beyond an 'orthodox model of writing Greek history'; or to understanding the social world of the fourth-century AD rhetor Libanios.[8] Network analysis has also been deployed to address a host of economic questions, particularly in commerce and trade.[9] This interest in networks no doubt converged with the idea of 'connectivity' as a model for explaining movement and interrelationships among different parts of the Mediterranean world, following the work of Peregrine Horden and Nicholas Purcell.[10]

The past decade or two has seen an efflorescence of new work on the economy of the Hellenistic world specifically and the Graeco-Roman world more generally. The appearance of this work partly coincided with and was partly a reaction to a sense that the terms that had framed debate on the Graeco-Roman economy up into the 1980s had played themselves out. I refer to the so-called primitivist-modernist debate, which pitted against each other two different models of economic activity in the ancient Mediterranean world: one, associated especially with Moses Finley, seeing that world as essentially 'non-economic' in twentieth-century terms of neoclassical economic theory; the other arguing that modern economic concepts could be applied to antiquity to explain economic activity. It became increasingly clear, I think, that neither model was really satisfactory, as both failed to capture important aspects of the ancient economy. Thus the outpouring of work to which I refer served both to critique the reigning bipolar model and to grapple for new ways of thinking about the economy that would avoid the pitfalls newer research was continually revealing.[11]

As yet no single model has emerged to replace the old paradigms, but one has attracted a good deal of attention: the so-called New Institutional Economics.[12] This approach was pioneered by Douglass North and his collaborators as a way to think about economies for which we lack the kind of hard data necessary to undertake analysis of modern economies. North's work is supple and compelling, too much so to characterize fully here. Let me instead draw attention to two components that have proven especially attractive to a number of historians. First, as the name implies, the New Institutional Economics looks closely at the ways institutions affect economic activity. Institutions, in North's formulation, are fundamentally the rules that govern economic activity, whether formal as in the case of laws or informal as in the case of ideology about appropriate wealth-generating activities for respectable people. (These are simply examples.) Institutions are much easier to find in the evidence we tend to have about economic activity in the ancient Mediterranean world than the kinds of data needed for strict neoclassical analysis. Second, the New Institutional Economics focuses special attention on the role of transaction costs. Such costs include actual 'costs of transaction,' like the fee we pay every time we change dollars to Euros, but also much more broadly any cost that can facilitate or hinder economic activity, like the cost of having to deal with an unresponsive bureaucracy. In many cases, the level of transaction costs is a function of institutions, so that these aspects of the New Institutional Economics are interrelated. One of the chief goals of the model is to assess the presence or absence of economic growth and to attempt to explain this.

The New Institutional Economics appeals to historians of the ancient economy in part because it finesses some of the insuperable barriers that bedevilled the old paradigms. It does not depend on reams of data, something that, with a few possible exceptions, Hellenistic historians simply will never have. Its attentiveness to institutions looks toward one aspect of the Hellenistic world about which we happen to know, relatively, a good deal (thanks especially to the rich epigraphy and papyrology), and which clearly exercised influence over economic activities. We see *sympoliteiai* agreements that linked up *poleis* formerly separate and independent, and in the process deconstructed barriers to the movement of goods and people between them; we see *asylia* agreements that secured protection for fairs and festivals run by civic sanctuaries, and so reduced transaction costs for persons engaged in economic activity connected with them; we see coinage systems like the Attalid *cistophori* that established closed circles of monetary movement. The New Institutional Economics encourages us to think about these institutions in new ways, as barriers to or facilitators of economic activity and, perhaps, growth.

I myself find this approach extremely intriguing, and I think, with one major caveat (to follow), that the New Institutional Economics will be a crucial component of an emergent new model for thinking about the Hellenistic economy. But I also see a couple of areas to which I would like to suggest that network theory, outlined above, can make its own, perhaps equally fundamental, contribution.

That first area has to do with the crucial matter of the *flow of information*. Economic activity depends on access to information.[13] Some recent work on red-figure pottery, for instance, has argued that Athenian potters produced decorative motifs on their pots in response to changes in tastes among customers in Etruria in the fifth century BC. If this claim is correct, Athenians must have had access to information about the tastes of those Etrurians several hundred kilometres away (Williams forthcoming). In terms of trade, reliable, up-to-date information could spell the difference between profit and loss. According to a late fourth-century BC indictment against one Parmeniskos, the latter relied on letters circulated among merchants in the Aegean world to determine the prices of grain at different locations and exploit the differentials for gain (Demos. 56.3). In the *De officiis* Cicero presents the moral conundrum of a grain merchant who arrives from Egypt at Rhodes during a terrible famine and grain shortage ('fame summaque annonae caritate'). The merchant can command a high price, but he knows that more ships are on the way and so the price will fall soon – should he seize the profit or share the information? Cicero concludes that his merchant – whom he stipulates to be an 'honourable man,' a *vir bonus* – must reveal his full knowledge to the buyers.[14]

How, exactly, did that information about grain prices and local demand get transmitted? It is axiomatic that – again, with an exception I will address in a few moments – all movement of information in history before the invention of the telegraph presupposed the movement of people.[15] No letter bearing news from the Rhodian market, say, was delivered but in the hands of a human being. This reality comes through with amusing clarity on a papyrus of the third century AD bearing explicit instructions for delivery: 'From the gate of Seleniake,' it reads, 'walk toward the treasuries and, if you please, turn left behind the baths.' More detailed directions through the neighbourhood end finally: 'Shout out . . . [someone] will answer you' (*P Oxy.* 2719).

It seems to me that network theory offers an attractive model for helping us understand and explain that flow of information, especially over distances greater than the local. It helps to answer a puzzling question: given that the vast majority of the population of the Hellenistic world surely never travelled more than a few dozen kilometres from home, how could the information necessary for a regional or long-distance economy to function have moved and found its targets? A small-world network, in which most nodes (people) are clustered but a few serve as hubs, and where the people involved are homophilous for profession (trade), would seem to offer a model answer.

A second respect in which network theory strikes me as especially useful to the historian of the Hellenistic economy lies in its focus on individuals. The nodes of a human network are people, and the most important of those nodes are the well-connected hubs. Just as our sources tell us far more about institutions than, say, the tax receipts of Athens in the third century, so likewise do they have a great deal to say about individual people, and precisely about people who are often not ordinary individuals but wealthy, well-placed men and women. They appear in the hundreds of honorary decrees passed by the Hellenistic *poleis*, and as political and military actors in the literary sources.

Some recent work on the flow of knowledge may offer models for thinking about the ways this process could have worked in the Hellenistic and Roman worlds. Olav Sorenson and his colleagues have identified three social/physical groupings that, they argue, help determine the structure and connectedness of people within social networks through which information can be transmitted: organizational membership, geographic regions, and technical communities (Sorenson, Rivkin, and Fleming 2007: 152). By 'organizational membership' they mean typically employment in the same firm.

Such employment creates opportunities for communication and exchange of information and reduces the likelihood of suspicion of others' motives (a fellow employee is not stealing proprietary information). Geographic proximity, of course, likewise increases the likelihood of contact – it is simply easier for people close to each other to communicate than for people farther apart. Finally, members of a technical community – people who have the same technical interests and skills – are again more likely not only to talk to each other and to understand technical lingo and share interests in problems but also to see the world in similar ways. This is, of course, another instance of homophily.

Consider, for example, Athenian relations in the second quarter of the fourth century BC with Sidon in Phoenicia. The Athenians passed a decree honouring the Sidonian king Straton because of his positive disposition to the Athenians. During the assembly when the decree was debated, it was amended to grant Sidonian merchants living in Sidon and exercising citizenship there exemption from various Athenian taxes while visiting Athens for purposes of trade (ἐπιδημῶσιν κατ' ἐμπορίαν).[16] From a network point of view, the relations created between Straton and the Athenians by Straton's beneficence spilled over to benefit the less well-connected members of Straton's network of fellow Sidonian citizens – who realized a substantial reduction in transaction costs in doing business with Athens. Such examples could easily be multiplied.

Moreover, our sources not infrequently connect individuals and institutions. Straton, as king of Sidon, sat at the centre of an institution – the Sidonian state – whose operations must have affected economic life in many ways. Another telling example comes from a recent study by Vincent Gabrielsen of the so-called private associations of the Hellenistic world. These associations ranged from clubs providing entertainment and burial insurance to their members to groups of merchants domiciled in a foreign land. In their organization they mimicked the polis in its Hellenistic, democratic form, replicating offices and institutions and passing decrees and awarding honours. As Gabrielsen stresses, by bringing together people who might otherwise be separated by 'social distance,' these associations created new links between individuals that could then serve as conduits for the transfer of information (Gabrielsen 2009). For instance, around 153/152 BC the *koinon* of the Poseidoniastai of Berytos on Delos passed a decree honouring the Roman Marcus Minatius Sextus (*IDélos* 1520). This *koinon* consisted of 'merchants and ship-owners and warehouse owners' ([ἐμπόρω]ν καὶ ναυκλήρων [καὶ ἐ]γδοχέων, line 2). In the inscription they honour Marcus because he has contributed a substantial sum of money to the cost of construction of a headquarters (*oikos*) for the *koinon*.

The *koinon* also honoured as its benefactor (*euergetes*) the Roman praetor Gnaius Octavius (*IDélos* 1782) and the goddess Roma (*IDélos* 1778).[17] The *koinon* enabled a link with a wealthy Roman, but just as important, provided a nexus for citizens of Berytos residing or sojourning on Delos for purposes of commerce to come together, share meals, worship – and certainly pass on information useful professionally. Moreover, the presence of warehouse owners in the *koinon* offered access to fellow countrymen who provided a necessary local service.[18] Delos preserves evidence of another such *koinon* of the Herakleistai of Tyre (*IDélos* 1519). A sense of the networks into which these citizens of Tyre were plugged is conveyed by a number of inscriptions from Delos. A good example is the family in which the name Dies appears in several generations. Originally from Tyre, the two brothers Dies and Basileides received Athenian citizenship by 100 BC. A descendant, also called Dies, played an important role in the Delians' decision to support Mithridates in 88 BC; he is described as a 'man rich thanks to his income from Delos' (πλουντοῦντος ἀνθρώπου ταῖς ἐκ Δήλου προσόδοις).[19]

Finally, in explaining how people in a network manipulate their connections to transfer information, network theory places considerable stress on social identity. The path out of the trap of clustered homophily runs through a careful consideration of the various modes of identity within which the individual operates. Here again, work in the past decade or so, beginning notably with Jonathan Hall's book on Greek ethnic identity,[20] has explored in considerable detail the question of the construction of identity in antiquity, and we can now trace some of the ways in which multifarious individual identities – as an Acharnian, an Athenian, an Ionian, for example – were negotiated and deployed. This optic brings into focus the situation of people like our Poseidoniastai on Delos, who were simultaneously citizens of Berytos, foreigners on Delos, merchants, and members of this club.

I noted above the existence of one form of information transfer not wholly dependent on the movement of people. I am thinking of the written text as a mechanism for transferring information – not letters, but literary or subliterary sources, most particularly the *periplous*. The *Periplous of the Red Sea*, an anonymous text written around the middle of the first century AD, describes the routes merchants follow in the Arabian Sea, with information about ports, trade, and so forth. It mentions by name the king of Adoulis, Zoskales, who is (the *Periplous* tells us) stingy and a tough trader, but familiar with Greek.[21] The author provides information about Zoskales and the trading opportunities at Adoulis to anyone who happens to acquire a copy of the *Periplous*, and in so doing also opens to those people access to a network of acquaintances, including King Zoskales, not mediated by personal contact but through the anonymous transmission of information through the

*Periplous*. Another example is the well-known fragment attributed to one Herakleides describing the land route from Athens to Thebes. The author provides information about distances, accommodations, and other details useful to the traveller.[22] Less detailed travel information appears in the form of *itineraria*, the best known of which is perhaps the *Antonine Itinerary*, reflecting the state of the Roman Empire in the last quarter of the third century AD and rendered into its present form by AD 324. Benet Salway has recently argued that these texts may derive from regional itineraries drawn up on the basis of *tabellaria*, monuments laying out routes from a particular central node. The recently published *Stadiasmos Provinciae Lyciae* would present the most striking example of this genre.[23]

A glimpse of another kind of network may perhaps be afforded by a series of inscriptions from Miletos listing new citizens. In some cases the texts include the names and ethnics of a man and his wife (along with their minor children, if any). In ten cases where the ethnics of both spouses are preserved, seven couples originate from neighbouring cities, such as Ephesos and Samos, Mylasa and Halikarnassos, Magnesia and Ephesos, or Apollonia on the Maiandros and Tralleis. Only one couple clearly originated in cities far apart, a husband and wife from Cyrene and Ephesos.[24] Statistically, of course, these data are meaningless, but as an indication of a tendency to depend on local networks for finding spouses they are suggestive. We know nothing about the interconnections that brought into marriage any of these men and women, but it is fair to suppose that pre-existing local networks – previously intertwined families, business partnerships – must have served to help their families find each other.

The intertwining of network and institution that these few examples illustrate suggest, I hope, how powerful an analytic tool might be built from a model of the Hellenistic economy that borrowed from both the New Institutional Economics and network theory. The great virtues of such a model lie especially in its applicability to a past without lots of good hard data; its focus on the kinds of institutional and human information that our sources provide; and the fact that it has been developed and tested outside the small world of Hellenistic historians – so that its formal value has been established independently of our use. This seems to me particularly advantageous in a world like ours of lacunose sources, where a model constructed purely on the information we have can be demolished by the discovery of a single piece of new evidence.

I would like to add, however, one caveat, or perhaps rather qualification. Hopes that discoveries in the Mediterranean world will reveal documentary evidence providing the kinds of quantitative data modern economic historians relish remain, alas, vanishingly small. But there is certainly one arena in which hopes have been rising: ceramics, and most particularly, amphoras. Recent work by many archaeologists, notably among them John Lund and Mark Lawall, has contributed to the compilation of large databases of amphora distribution and typology, a project that we may hope will ultimately result in enough data to support some meaningful statistical tests. That is, at a moment in time when, I think, a new model is emerging for the Hellenistic economy that will enable us finally to break out of the old primitivist-modernist debate, we are also looking toward the possibility of a completely different, independent mechanism for describing the activity of the economy. In effect, in a few years we may have two separate and independent approaches to the Hellenistic economy that can be deployed each to test the other and to generate new questions. It is, in my view, a particularly exciting time to be working on the Hellenistic economy.

At the same time, it is important to remember both that network analysis arising out of the social network analysis school has been deployed already in the study of the Graeco-Roman world and that the fundamental connectedness that network theory seeks to explain and elucidate has already entered the discussion. As an example of the former I note simply the 1990 study by two sociologists of Cicero's personal network, derived from a study of his letters. They used a network analysis of the contacts between members of the senatorial and equestrian orders documented in the letters to show that no clear social distinctions could be drawn between the two groups. This result confirmed the view of historians that 'the two groups were not monolithic blocks in opposition' via a completely independent channel.[25] Connectivity forms, of course, one of the central leitmotifs of Peregrine Horden and Nicholas Purcell's *The Corrupting Sea*. Indeed, the model of the Mediterranean world they draw, with many little microregions interconnected by trade and the movement of people, looks much like a small-world network: homophilous clusters interconnected through well-connected hubs.[26] Other scholars have also begun to deploy a network model to explain various aspects of Greek history. Irad Malkin, who counts as perhaps the true pioneer of the application of network theory to Greek history, has argued that the emergence of Greek identity in the Archaic and Classical periods can be accounted for by uncovering the effects of the network of colonies and mother-cities in the greater Graeco-Mediterranean world (Malkin 2003).

In a massive study called *The Information Age*, Manuel Castels argues that the networked society is the new model for the world of the twenty-first century; the rise of networks, in his view, represents a change as fundamental as industrialization by creating a world in which virtually instantaneous communication and international connectivity reshape the ground on which individuals seek to erect their personal identities. Castels's grand scheme has come in for critique.[27] However that may be, it should be clear that networks have been a feature of human society since the deep past, and that they provide a model for understanding the ways people interconnect for all sorts of reasons, including economic activity. The characteristics that recent research on network systems has identified can be applied to the Hellenistic economic world to uncover and explain centrally important aspects of economic activity. In combination with the focus on institutions pushed by the New Institutional Economics, this approach may help us draw a more textured, more personalized, and more complex picture of the economic bustle of the Hellenistic world.

## Notes

1 Milgram 1967, reprinted in revised form in Milgram 1992: 259–75; see also Travers and Milgram 1969. The story is retold in every book on networks; see, for example, Watts 2003: 37–42.

2 Or an explication of the mathematics, a task beyond my capabilities in any case. There are now several excellent general guides written by central participants in the emergence of networks science in the late 1990s and first years of the twenty-first century: Barabási 2003, Strogatz 2003, Watts 2003 (a particularly clear and readable account, in my view); see also Buchanan 2002.

3 *IG* II² 657; Bielman 1994: 74–80 no. 20; Habicht 1993: 253; Fittschen 1995: 67n135.

4 Killworth and Bernard 1978; Watts 2003: 154.

5 Knox, Savage, and Harvey 2006. I am very grateful to Hannah Knox for providing me with a pre-publication copy of this article. Knoke and Yang 2008.

6 Knox, Savage, and Harvey 2006: 114. See also the cautionary remarks of Knappett 2005: 64. Knappett applies network theory to the nexus of archaeological objects and actors in the past, an interesting application of the theory in a different but related sphere.

7 A good introduction now in the essays in Malkin, Constantakopoulou, and Panagopoulou 2011; see also Malkin 2011.

8 Rutherford 2009: esp. 28; Vlassopoulos 2009: 12; Sandwell 2009.

9 Osborne 2009; Sommer 2009; Paleothodoros 2009; Lolos 2009; Rathbone 2009.

10 Horden and Purcell 2000, with the essays in Harris 2005.

11 For a good summary, see Morley 2007: 2–9.

12 A good place to start is North 1991 and for further extensions of the project, especially attempting to explain growth, North 2005. For some recent work using the approach of the New Institutional Economics, see Bresson 2007 and 2008; Frier and Kehoe 2007 and Lo Cascio 2007: 626–7, both in the massive

recent *Cambridge Economic History of the Greco-Roman World*, edited by
Walter Scheidel, Ian Morris, and Richard Saller, many of the contributors to
which apply the model in various ways. There are however other models worth
considering; I explore some briefly in Reger forthcoming.

13  See Reger 2007: 469–470.

14  Cic., *De off.* 3.50–7 with Erdkamp 2005: 189 and Morley 2007: 79–89 on morality. For a striking parallel, see the case of the Alexandrian merchant who beat
his competitors to Old Cairo, only to have the customs officials there impound
his goods for five days until the rest of the merchants transporting the same
commodity had arrived: Goitein 1967: 201.

15  Perhaps I should add that we do hear of course of signalling towers and other
such mechanisms for transmitting limited amounts of information much faster
than human movements, but the kinds of information that could be transmitted in such ways were limited, and required pre-agreements between parties of
what the signals meant.

16  *IG* II² 141.29–36 for the amendment.

17  Probably in 131 BC: Badian 1990: 405–6n22, followed by Brennan 2000:
1.348–9n85.

18  See further Roussel 1987: 90–2.

19  Athen. 5 212d; Le Dinahet-Couilloud 1997: 636–8.

20  Hall 1997; see also Hall 2002.

21  *Peripl. M. Rubr.* 5; see Reger 2007: 261.

22  Pfister 1951; *Brill's New Jacoby* (online by subscription only): Herakleides
Kritikos (369A) F1 5–13. In his biographical essay on Herakleides in *Brill's New
Jacoby*, Jeremy McInerney now suggests that the author of this text was the
master of a travelling troop of actors.

23  Salway 2001: 39–43, 45–58. For the Lykian inscription, see Şahin and
Adak 2007.

24  *Milet* I 3 41 II.1–2, 45 I.8–9 (222/221 BC), 46.3–4 (212/211 BC), and 74.2–4;
57.6–8. In some cases it is not possible to be sure about distances, since one or
both ethnics apply to more than one city.

25  Alexander and Danowksi 1990: quotation at 330. See also, but less formally,
Rauh 1986.

26  Horden and Purcell 2000; Malkin 2003: 57.

27  Castels 1998, 2000a, and 2000b; see 2004a for a brief précis of his views;
critique, briefly, at Doukellis 2009: 287.

# 9

# Diplomacy and the Integration of the Hasmonean State

## CLAUDE EILERS

Questions of integration and isolation are applicable to many aspects of Hellenistic literature, society, and history, as can be seen in the other contributions to this volume. They are important, too, in the case of Jews, for whom the Hellenistic age was marked both by increasing Hellenization of various parts of their state and society and by strong reactions against it.

My paper will focus on two documents quoted by Josephus in his *Jewish Antiquities*. Both also illustrate an important point about Josephus's handling of documentary material that his readers should understand at the outset: he is not very good at it, at least if we hold him to the standards that we apply to ourselves and to our students. To put it bluntly, Josephus almost never successfully places a document into a correct chronological context. Consider: Josephus presents a large dossier of documents in book 14 (190–264) at the moment when the ambassadors of the Jewish high priest Hyrkanos arrive in Rome to seek a renewal of the long-standing peace treaty between the Jews and Romans in 46 BC. None of the quoted documents, however, belongs to 46 BC. A pair (14.190–5) dates to 47 BC; seven documents (14.228–32, 234–40) belong to 49 BC; and there are five fragmentary documents that date to the years of Caesar's dominance (14.196–212), but these are probably fragments of Caesar's decisions of 47 and 44 that had become embedded in an Antonian decree of April 44 BC.[1] In short, none of these documents seems to belong to 46 BC, the year in which Josephus has placed them.[2]

To make matters worse, the pair of documents quoted at 14.190–5 (which are an edict of Caesar and its covering letter), which Josephus places in 46, in fact do belong to 47 BC and recognize Hyrkanos as high priest and ethnarch of the Jews – recognition that Josephus had himself narrated in the correct year (47 BC) thirty sections earlier. But what do we find in Josephus's narrative there? Two other documents: a decree of the Roman senate of ca 140 BC (14.145–8)[3] and a decree of Athens (14.150–5) to which we now turn.

## Decree of Athens

The Athenians passed a decree to honour Hyrkanos, high priest of the Jews, a decree quoted by Josephus. From his handling of the document, it is clear that he has assumed the honorand to be Hyrkanos II, a contemporary of Caesar. Our knowledge of Athenian chronology and prosopography, however, is especially good for these years,[4] and these make it possible to rule out such an identification. The decree dates itself to the archonship of Agathokles, which can with confidence be dated to 105 BC,[5] specifically to the month of Mounychion, roughly April or May.[6] The date is corroborated by the identification of other individuals in the decree.[7] Given the date, the honorand must be Hyrkanos I (135–104 BC). Again, Josephus has mishandled a document, though in this case to our benefit since the decree so nicely illustrates our theme.

The decree praises the goodwill and helpfulness that Hyrkanos had always shown towards the Athenians collectively and individually, receiving them hospitably and providing for their safe passage homeward. It therefore attests to ongoing diplomatic relations between the Athenian polis and Hyrkanos, which presumably (as Habicht suggests) arose out of trade (1997: 283). The decree itself, of course, is a concrete expression of an ongoing relationship and illustrates the deepening integration of Hyrkanos's Judaea into the wider Mediterranean network, as do the other honours it describes: a bronze statue of Hyrkanos is to be erected in the *temenos* of the Demos and the Graces, and a golden crown is to be announced at several festivals. All of these honours are to be communicated to Hyrkanos via an embassy that the decree approves (*AJ* 14.153) – an embassy that is again both an honour in its own right and a mechanism by which the relationship would be perpetuated and strengthened. The whole interaction is typical of what we find attested elsewhere and assumes that Hyrkanos was part of the Hellenistic world. Indeed, the honours are nicely paralleled by those awarded to contemporary monarchs and royal officials.[8]

All this speaks to the integration of the Hasmonean court into the Hellenistic world: typically, Greek honours are awarded by a Greek city because of the honorand's interaction with the Greek world.[9] This integration, however, may be even deeper than it first appears, since this decree was itself circulated elsewhere in the Greek world, as is shown by the words immediately preceding the document. The decree proper opens with an archon date, as expected. Right before this, however, in the immediately preceding line in Josephus's text, is another dating formula:

In the prytany and priesthood of Dionysios the son of Asklepiades, on the fifth day before the end of the month of Panemos, the decree of the Athenians was delivered to the magistrates. In the archonship of Agathokles, etc. (*AJ* 14.149–50)

These words report the delivery of the decree to another city in the year in which Dionysios the son of Asklepiades was the eponymous magistrate of that city, a notation that was apparently added to the decree on its delivery and subsequently became embedded in the copy that Josephus eventually inherited (Eilers 2008: 212–13). The formula, it is important to note, reveals a provenance: for although dating by eponymous *prytaneis* is attested in many cities, the eponymous magistrate '*prytanis* and priest' is found only in Pergamon.[10] The Pergamene venue is corroborated by constitutional and prosopographical details in the text that are consistent with Pergamon.[11] This can only mean that the decree of Athens honouring Hyrkanos was subsequently delivered to Pergamon.

By itself, of course, the delivery of a decree honouring Hyrkanos to a point elsewhere in the Mediterranean implies a deeper integration of the Hasmoneans into the Mediterranean network – not only was Hyrkanos honoured in Athens, but those honours were relevant to someone else and delivered to them to be archived there. That the delivery was to Pergamon, however, is also noteworthy, in that a decree of Pergamon is included among other documents quoted by Josephus in book 14 of the *Jewish Antiquities*. This document may clarify what lay behind the Athenian decree.

### Decree of Pergamon

The Pergamene eecree (*AJ* 14.247–56) records the recent arrival in Pergamon of a Judaean embassy, apparently returning to their homeland from Rome. In their possession was a decree of the Roman senate that instructed King Antiochos to cease harassing the Jews. All of this, of course, again speaks to the interconnectedness of the various parties – not only do the Pergamenes receive a Judaean embassy, but they make (and presumably ratify) a proposal to send their own embassy back (14.254). In addition there are assertions of Pergamon's admiration of the Romans and their eagerness to follow the Roman example. Pergamon also claims an ancient relationship with the Jews: Abraham had been a friend of their ancestors, a fact that they claim is proved by documents in their archives (14.255). This was clearly fictional – but it was the kind of fiction to which ancient states occasionally resorted in their diplomatic manoeuvring.[12]

The fact that a reference to a mythical connection between Pergamon and Abraham could be found in Pergamon's civic archives probably implies earlier contact. We find a similar phenomenon in an exchange of letters between the Spartans and the Jews recorded in 1 Maccabees and Josephus. The fiction was created (as seems likely) when the Jewish high priest Jonathan sent an embassy to Sparta in the 140s BC to establish diplomatic relations with the Spartans (1 Macc. 12.6–18). Jonathan claimed to have discovered an old letter in the archives from the Spartan king Areus, who in turn claimed to have discovered evidence that the two peoples were kin (1 Macc. 12.20–3; AJ 12.225–7). The letter of Areus was certainly a forgery – its form and content as provided in 1 Maccabees and Josephus are highly suspect (Gruen 1996: 257). But from the perspective of the participants, the falsehood was useful: both parties could use it to justify the creation of a real relationship between them. Jonathan's letter (possibly authentic) in turn became the pretext for a Spartan reply (probably authentic; 1 Macc. 14.16–23; cf. AJ 13.164–70). A new diplomatic relationship is made possible through the acceptance of the fictional one.[13] A similar discovery of convenience probably lies behind Pergamon's claim to have found documents referring to ancient relations between the two peoples. All this, of course, furthered the integration of the Hasmoneans into the Hellenistic *oikoumene*.

When, however, did the visit to Pergamon take place? Josephus has again included this document in his *Caesarian* narrative – but this must be another mistake, since at 14.249 the decree refers to 'King Antiochos, son of Antiochos,' and a reference to a Seleukid monarch requires a date before the final end of the Seleukid kingdom during the Mithridatic Wars. Again Josephus is wrong, and he seems to have made the same mistake as with the decree of Athens, considered above: that is, he has attributed a document pertaining to Hyrkanos I to Hyrkanos II, as many commentators have recognized.[14]

Can we be more specific about the date? By itself, 'King Antiochos, son of Antiochos' should refer to refer Antiochos IX Philopator, nicknamed Kyzikenos (114–195 BC). Many scholars, however, reject this identification and the date that goes with it.[15] They point to the narrative of Josephus, where the civil war between Antiochos IX Kyzikenos and his half-brother, Antiochos VIII Grypos, is said to have allowed Hyrkanos to flourish and to show complete disdain for both of them (AJ 13.273), and where Kyzikenos's efforts are presented as only a minor irritant to Hyrkanos: the former could (according to Josephus) only ravage the countryside like a brigand and never dared to face Hyrkanos in set battle (13.277–8). By contrast, the King Antiochos of the Pergamene decree is said to have captured fortresses, harbours, and territories and installed a garrison at Joppa (14.249–50). That is not much like what Josephus describes.

Ritschl (followed by Mendelssohn, Schürer, and others) therefore argued for a different Antiochos, dating the Pergamene decree to the mid–130s BC, when Antiochos VII Sidetes invaded Judaea and besieged Jerusalem.[16] The problem is that in the decree the offending Seleukid monarch is called 'Antiochos, son of Antiochos'; Sidetes was a son of Demetrios, which requires an emendation from *Antiochou* to *Demetriou*. The text of the *Jewish Antiquities* is highly corrupt, especially when it comes to names, and there are dozens of places where the text of Josephus's documents can be improved to make it consistent with documentary parallels and chronological or prosopographical necessity. In *this* case, however, an examination of the numismatic evidence of Kyzikenos's achievements – mostly unavailable when this argument was first developed – shows that the emendation is unnecessary.

As a youth, Antiochos IX had been sent to be raised in the city of Kyzikos (hence the nickname Kyzikenos). According to Appian, the young man had had no ambitions to the Seleukid throne until his half-brother (Antiochos VIII Grypos) conspired unsuccessfully against his life (App. *Syr.* 69). Kyzikenos then collected an army and started a civil that was to last for decades. He invaded Syria in 114 BC, and to judge from his coin mints, he seems to have met with success at first: his coins appear in most of Syria's cities.[17] Grypos, however, was able to regain most of these territories in the following years, coming to control most of Syria, while Kyzikenos remained strong on the coast.[18] In Ake-Ptolemaïs, for example, Kyzikenos's coinage is attested from 113/112 down to 107/106 BC,[19] and his coinage in Tripolis implies his control there until 105/104 BC (Houghton 1983: no. 693). Askalon, by contrast, remained in Grypos's hands except for a short period in the years 114/113 and 113/112 BC, when Kyzikenos's coins were minted there, revealing his control of the city for several months (Houghton and Spaer 1998: nos. 2751–4).

The decree of Pergamon reports that Kyzikenos had managed to gain control over Judaean fortresses, harbours, and territory on the coast and had installed a garrison at Joppa. Since these territories were situated between Askalon, which Kyzikenos seems to have occupied in 113/112 BC, and his power base further up the coast,[20] which he held for much of this period, the decree's claim is not especially hard to believe. Rather than redate the Pergamene decree because of Josephus's assertion that Kyzikenos had presented little threat to Judaea, then, we should dismiss Josephus's characterization itself in light of the Pergamene decree. Josephus was presumably reflecting later propaganda or post-victory chauvinism. With it, however, goes the only justification for the early date or the emendation to *Demetriou*.

There are other problems with the early date that I plan to discuss in another context. It should be sufficient here to note that the decree mentions a speech before the council praising Hyrkanos for conferring 'benefits upon all men generally and in particular upon those who come to him' (*AJ* 14.253). This is hardly consistent with the early date that some propose for the decree: the first two years of Hyrkanos I's reign had been spent under siege, which will have prevented him from performing the kinds of hospitality referred to here. In any case, Hyrkanos's long rule had only just begun at that point and he would not yet have acquired any Mediterranean-wide reputation for generosity. No, this reference comes later, at the end of a long rule, during which time diplomatic contact in the wider Mediterranean had brought him a reputation for hospitality.

In any case, we know that Hyrkanos I had indeed gained a reputation for hospitality by the end of his life – he is praised for it in the Athenian decree of 105 BC discussed above. And given that we now know that the latter had been delivered to Pergamon, it is no doubt important to note that the Athenian decree makes a similar point about the reception of visitors: 'When any Athenians come to him either on an embassy or on a private matter, he receives them in a friendly manner and sends them on their way with precautions for their safe return' (*AJ* 14.151). Since we now know that this decree was actually delivered to Pergamon, it seems a safe assumption that it was somehow related to what was discussed there and that the Judaean embassy that visited Pergamon on its homewards journey had also visited Athens.

Together these documents provide a glimpse of the shifting fortunes in the East at the end of the second century BC, and the ways in which these shifts isolated Judaea, compelling its inhabitants to reach out diplomatically to the Mediterranean cities of Rome, Athens, and Pergamon. The two documents reflect only one moment of these events, but they are striking for the ways in which they invoke the interconnectedness between the parties. They also have implications for the broader workings and goals of Hasmonean diplomacy. The Hasmoneans had been cultivating western cities from their earliest days.

## *SC Fannianum*

The most important Mediterranean power was Rome, of course, and from the outset of the Maccabean movement, the Hasmoneans had worked hard to create and maintain good relations with the Romans. In light of this, it is not surprising to see that the diplomatic connection with Pergamon arose as a by-product of a Judaean embassy to Rome; nor should we be surprised that

Pergamon was keen to follow Rome's lead in a matter like this. The embassy mentioned in the Pergamon decree, however, seems not to have been the first mission to seek Rome's support against Antiochos. An earlier attempt is attested in another of Josephus's documents: a senatorial decree passed under the presidency of a certain Fannius, which is typically referred to in the literature as the *senatus consultum Fannianum* (*AJ* 13.260–6).

Josephus placed this decree in the aftermath of the death of Antiochos VII Sidetes (reported at 13.253), which we know occurred in 129 BC,[21] and in the midst of his summary of an expansion occurring in the last decade of Hyrkanos's reign. As has been noted, however, Josephus's placement of documents is not a reliable indicator of date: he usually gets it wrong, as we have seen, and this seems to be the case here, though it should be admitted that his chronology of the events of the reign of Hyrkanos I is not completely clear.[22]

The dating of this decree has also proved problematic for historians, who have offered dates of 134/133,[23] 132,[24] 125,[25] 122,[26] and ca 110 BC (which must be correct).[27] Clearly the *SC Fannianum* is reacting to the same events as the Decree of Pergamon: both documents react to the aggressions of a King Antiochos; both mention his control of Joppa (13.261; 14.250) and his capture of territory (*chora, choria* 13.261, 14.249), strongholds (*phrouria* at 14.249; *poleis*, including Gazara and Pegai,[28] at 13.361), and ports (*limenes* 13.261, 14.249); the *SC Fannianum* records the renewal of Judaea's treaty with Rome (13.264, cf. 261), a treaty that is assumed by the Pergamon decree (14.249); and both documents mention Apollonios son of Alexander as one of the ambassadors (13.260, 14.248). The *SC Fannianum* clearly comes first. It renewed the treaty to which the Pergamene decree alludes, and its decision is less favourable than that in the senate decree mentioned in the Pergamon decree. Indeed, the *SC Fannianum* defers discussion of the Jewish complaints, and we should perhaps suppose that the Pergamene decree reflects a decision made in that later discussion.

The most important point here is that the *SC Fannianum* and the Pergamene decree belong together, and since the Pergamene decree belongs at the end of Hyrkanos's reign, together with the Athenian decree of 105 BC, so, too, must the *SC Fannianum*. Such a date is consistent with all of the evidence and contradicts none of it. The situation described is consistent with the numismatic evidence that implies that Antiochos IX Kyzikenos (ruled ca 114–96 BC) controlled most of the Levantine coast in the first years of his reign.

This reconstruction fits well in any case with the prosopography. The two senatorial witnesses of the *SC Fannianum* can also be identified. The first, called Mannius in Josephus's manuscripts, is probably L. Manlius

Torquatus, whose quaestorship can be dated to 113 or 112 BC.[29] The second is C. Sempronius C. f. of the tribe Falerna, who should be the ninth witness listed in the *SC de agris Pergamenis* of 101 BC (the name, filiation, and tribe are identical).[30] Both were apparently quite junior when the *SC Fannianum* was passed, probably around 110 BC.[31]

Such a date is also required by another reference in the *SC Fannianum*. Rome had been asked to forbid Seleukid soldiers from crossing not only Judaean territory, but also the territory of 'their subjects.'[32] This provision also points to a date later in Hyrkanos's reign. The Hasmonean state had begun to expand beyond its Judaean heartland only very recently. Such expansion obviously could not begin until the Hasmoneans threw off Seleukid vassalage, an act which their own traditions dated to 142/141 BC.[33] Some expansion into neighbouring territories took place under Simon and Jonathan, but it was marked by expropriation of territory and expulsion of native populations.[34] An important development under Hyrkanos was the practice of granting to conquered districts a degree of political autonomy provided that they undergo religious and social acculturation.[35] This innovation was already in place at the time of the *SC Fannianum*, as is clear from the request that Antiochos be instructed to leave Judaean *subjects* alone. Since having such subjects will have been the product of the imperialist program that began under Hyrkanos and gained momentum in the latter part of his reign, the reference and the senate decree require a later date.

Taken together, the three documents reveal an evolution in Rome's policy in the region. It seems that Rome had at first backed Antiochos Kyzikenos: the *SC Fannianum* seems to allude to earlier decisions made in his favour, though the text here is problematic.[36] In several stages Hyrkanos seems through diplomacy to have managed first to move the Romans away from actively supporting Kyzikenos and towards neutrality, as is evidenced by the *SC Fannianum*, probably ca 110 BC. A few years later, in 105 BC, we see from another embassy that the Romans decided to support the Jews against Kyzikenos more forcefully. This is the embassy reported in the Pergamene decree and reflected in the Athenian decree.

The documents also illustrate the ongoing integration of the Hasmonean state into the wider Mediterranean world. The importance of Rome in the geopolitics of the eastern Mediterranean had been growing dramatically over the course of the second century BC. It is therefore not surprising to find that Judaean efforts to buttress their position centred on Rome. An important stage in this policy had come already in 161 BC when a treaty between Rome and the Jews was finalized,[37] and much of the Judaean diplomatic effort during the rest of the century centred on the renewal of this treaty.[38] We see too that Judaean diplomacy also reached out to the Greek cities of

Mediterranean. This strategy resulted in the outreach to Sparta in the mid-second century and the discovery of a fictional kinship, and to Pergamon at the end of the century and the 'rediscovery' of a friendship going back to mythical times. It is important to note, however, that these attempts to reach out to Rome and the West were motivated by an external threat from a Seleukid king who had successfully occupied the Hasmoneans' chief harbour (Joppa) and threatened to cut them off from the Mediterranean world of which they had become a part. It was this threat of isolation, then, that caused them to draw themselves closer to the Romans.

## Notes

1 See now Ward and Eilers, forthcoming in *Phoenix*.
2 The documents have a vast bibliography, which has been conveniently collected in Pucci Ben Zeev 1998.
3 The decree seems to refer to the same events as 1 Maccabees (15.16–21): Giovannini and Müller 1971: 160–5; Schürer et al. 1973–87: 1.194–7; Timpe 1974: 146–7; Gruen 1984: 748–51; Schwartz 1993: 114–26; Canali De Rossi 1997: 551–4, no. 600.
4 As noted by Tracy 1979: 216 and n.10.
5 Dinsmoor 1931: 240–4; Meritt and Pritchett 1940: xxxiv; Meritt 1977: 187.
6 The Athenian civil year normally began on the new moon following the summer solstice, which would place Mounychion (the tenth month) in April or May. Hence Aristotle (*Hist. An.* 543b) wrote that most fish spawn in the three months beginning in Mounychion, a process that Pliny (*HN* 9.162) assigned to the Julian months of April, May, and June.
7 The presiding secretary, Eukles, son of Xenandros, is attested in two ephebic decrees of 106/105 BC (*IG* II² 1011); also attested is Theodotos son of Diodoros of the deme Sounion, who spoke in favour of the decree honouring Hyrkanos. (The slight corruption of the names is no barrier: Eilers 2008: 212–13.)
8 E.g., Habicht 1997: 281; cf. Tracy 1988: 383–8. Such parallels, of course, argue against fraud: Eilers 2008.
9 Habicht 1997: 283; cf. Rajak 1994: 296–9.
10 Cf. Sherk 1992: 238–9; Allen 1983: 161–5; Wörrle 2000: 550–1.
11 'Asklepiades' is a name common in an important Pergamene family (*IvPergamon* II 251). The *strategoi* in Pergamon were responsible for introducing public business, so it makes sense that the documents would be delivered to them (Allen 1983: 165–7).
12 Jones 1999; Battistoni 2008: 73–97.

13 Gruen 1996; Jones 1999: 73–80.

14 Juster 1914: 134–35, 148; Smallwood 1976: 10n23, 559; Rajak 1984: 111n14; Pucci Ben Zeev 1996: 214–16; Pucci Ben Zeev 1998: 22, 400–1, and the works cited in the next note.

15 Ritschl 1873: 586–614 at 610–11n31; Mendelssohn 1875: 135–43; Hatzfeld 1907: 6–9; Schürer et al. 1973–87: 1.205–6n7; (cautiously) Rajak 1981: 78–9 = Rajak 2001: 94–5; Rhodes 1997: 419, 547.

16 Joseph. *AJ* 13.235–46; *BJ* 1.61; Diod. Sic. 34.1.

17 The numismatic evidence is especially important, on which see Houghton and Müseler 1990 and Houghton 1993, superseding Bellinger 1949: 87–91.

18 Bellinger 1949: 66 and n. 37, 87–91.

19 See the chart at Houghton and Müseler 1990: 60; for the coins, Houghton and Spaer 1998: nos. 2745–50.

20 Kasher 1990: 124, following Stern 1961 and Stern 1965: 162–5 (*non vidi*), dates the Pergamon decree to 113/12 BC on the basis of this coinage. Kyzikenos's capture of Joppa, however, provides only a *terminus post quem* for the Pergamon decree, since diplomatic efforts to roll back his control of Joppa need not have been immediate (military options might have been exhausted first), and Grypos's almost immediate recapture of Askalon does not require that Kyzikenos had also lost control of Joppa.

21 For 129 as the date of Sidetes's death, see Helm 1956: 146.

22 Josephus seems to place the conquest of the Idumaeans and Samaritans very soon after the death of Antiochos Sidetes (*AJ* 14.254–258) and before the *SC Fannianum*; the archaeological evidence now suggests that this conquest did not occur until rather late in Hyrkanos's reign, probably beginning in ca 112 BC: Barag 1992–3; Finkielstejn 1998: 34–42, 45; Schwartz 2001: 36–8.

23 Best argued by Rajak 1981: 72–8 = Rajak 2001: 88–94; cf. also Bevan 1930: 530, Smallwood 1976: 9–10.

24 Münzer (*RE* 6 [1909] *s.v.* Fannius no. 7: 1988); Marcus 1943: 353 n. (d), commenting on *AJ* 13.249; cf. 359 n. (c); Klausner 1972: esp. 333–4n27.

25 Broughton *MRR* 1: 509n2; Schürer et al. 1973–87: 1.204–6 and nn. 6–7; Timpe 1974: 147–8 and n. 37; Canali De Rossi 1997: 561–2no612; Baltrusch 2002: 105–8.

26 Brennan 2000: 1.119 with 295n169 (adumbrated by Meyer 1925: 275).

27 Reinach 1899, followed by Willrich 1924: 63–4 (whose position is mischaracterized by Broughton *MRR* 1: 509n2); Giovannini and Müller 1971: 159–60.

28 The fact that Gazara and Pegai are not mentioned at 14.249 need not be significant (*pace* Finkielstejn 1998: 46), though it could signal the recovery of these sites in the interim.

29 The manuscripts report the name as *Manniou* or *Maniou*, neither of which is attested as a *gentilicium* for any senator in the Republican period; the Latin

versions report the name as 'Mallius' (very rare) and 'Manlius.'A convenient summary of the family is found at Mitchell 1966: 23–31. For the date of Manlius's quaestorship, see Crawford 1974: no. 295.

30 *RDGE* 12 ( = IGR IV 262), lines 26–7: *Gaios Sempronios Gaiou Phalernai*. For the date, see Mattingly 1972, with the important observations of Badian 1986: 14–16.

31 Reinach 1899; Giovannini and Müller 1971: 159–60.

32 *AJ* 13.262: ἵνα τε τοῖς στρατιώταις τοῖς βασιλικοῖς μὴ ἐξῇ διὰ τῆς χώρας τῆς αὐτῶν καὶ τῶν ὑπηκόων αὐτῶν διέρχεσθαι ('that the royal troops not be allowed to the territory of them and their subjects').

33 1 Macc. 13.41 with Goldstein 1976: 477–9.

34 Gazara (1 Macc. 13.43–48 and 14.34); Joppa (1 Macc. 13.11; Joseph. *AJ* 13.202); Beth Zur (1 Macc. 11.66).

35 Cohen 1999: 116–19, 138–9; Schwartz 2001: 38–9.

36 13.262: ὅπως τὰ κατὰ τὸν πόλεμον ἐκεῖνον †ψηφισθέντα ὑπὲρ (ms. ὑπὸ) Ἀντιόχου παρὰ τὸ τῆς συγκλήτου δόγμα ἄκυρα γένηται ('that the motions passed on behalf of Antiochos during that war contrary to the decree of the senate be annulled'). The most sensible reconstruction of its text and significance is that of Rajak 1981: 74–8 = Rajak 2001: 90–4.

37 1 Macc. 8.1–30; Joseph. *AJ* 12.414–19. Gruen 1984: 748–51; Baltrusch 2002: 92–8.

38 Renewal in ca 143 BC: *AJ* 13.163–70; *BJ* 1.48; 1 Macc. 12.1–4, 16; in ca 139: *AJ* 14.145–8; 1 Macc. 14.16–18, 24; 15.15–24; under Hyrkanos I: *AJ* 13.259, with the *SC Fannianum* (*AJ* 13.260–9), discussed above.

# PART FOUR

# Alexandria: The Invention of a City

Alexandria was an 'invention,' an artificial construct founded by a Macedonian general near the Egyptian settlement of Rhakotis on the Nile River. Unlike many Greek and other Mediterranean cities that boasted mythical origins, Alexandria had been established in the living memory of its Hellenistic inhabitants. This unique characteristic permitted the fabrication of a self-representation that reflected the diversity of people who constituted the population. It was a multicultural city of native Egyptians, North Africans, Jews, and other Semitic groups, mercenaries from Macedonia and elsewhere, and Greek-speaking people.

Andrew Erskine argues that the inconsistencies in Alexandria's foundation accounts reveal the interests of these diverse 'stakeholders.' Though superficially historical, the stories function as means whereby various groups assert their legitimacy and right of presence in the city. As such, they reveal more about the people for whom the stories are told than the characters in them: contemporary political, social, and economic concerns all contribute to the story. Thus, for example, the inclusion in some accounts of Alexander's visit to the oracle of Zeus Ammon in Siwah may have added a typically Egyptian feature. Also the Ptolemies' seemingly contradictory self-portrayal as both pharaonic and Greek may be explained by the competing social interests.

The perception of the role of Ptolemy Soter and the dynasty he established must have been effected purposefully through a multiform representation of the ruling dynasty in religion, literature, and art. Gaining credibility and authority by association with Alexander, the Ptolemaic dynasty also depicted itself as representative of the Egyptian civilization that it ruled. Daniel Ogden demonstrates that the stories of the different paternities of Ptolemy Soter served to adapt the legacy of the Macedonian clan to a distinctly Egyptian context. For example, the image of the Zeus-eagle that was employed by Soter even before he became ruler established a link with Alexander; meanwhile, the image of Zeus-Ammon as snake connected Ptolemy to native North African religion.

The 'invention' of Alexandria was not restricted to the Hellenistic period, as Craig Hardiman reminds us in his paper. Until very recently, many modern art historians premised their interpretations upon the notion of regionalism, according to which distinctive styles were attributed to aesthetic forces at work in particular centres such as Pergamon or Rhodes. For Alexandria, these forces produced sculptures and other artworks that seemed suited to interpretations of allegory, symbol, or metaphor. The features of this so-called Alexandrian school seemed to be corroborated by similar themes in the literary production associated with the Mouseion. Such artistic themes and styles, however, occur in works disbursed throughout the Mediterranean world, so that the assumptions of 'Alexandrianism' in particular and 'regionalism' in general are proven to be no more than inventions.

# 10

# Founding Alexandria in the Alexandrian Imagination

## ANDREW ERSKINE

### Introduction

The foundation of Alexandria in 331 BC is one of the best-documented foundation stories that survives from antiquity. Unlike that of its Mediterranean rival Rome, the story occurs in historical time with known historical figures involved, primarily Alexander but also other secondary characters such as Kleomenes of Naukratis and the architect Deinokrates. Rome, in contrast, offers figures whose very existence is questionable, as is the case with Romulus and Remus.[1] Contemporary or near-contemporary records of the foundation of Alexandria, however, are now lost with the result that scholars must rely on accounts written much later, none earlier than the closing years of the Ptolemaic dynasty. Among the more substantial are those of Diodoros, Strabo, Plutarch, Arrian, Quintus Curtius Rufus, Stephanos of Byzantion, and the *Alexander Romance*.[2]

Yet there is frequent disagreement between the accounts. There is no doubting that Alexander is the founder in all cases, but what he did, why he did it, and when he did it are more debatable, much to the frustration of modern Alexander historians. For instance, was it a spur-of-the-moment decision or was he planning to found a city? Did the foundation occur before or after his visit to Siwah? Scholars in their search for the historical truth try to amalgamate the more plausible parts of these stories, a procedure which often means taking Arrian and supplementing his account with elements extracted from the accounts of the other authorities where necessary. But if we want to look for a historical truth in these stories it might lie not in a vain attempt to extract what happened but paradoxically in the inconsistencies.

What I want to suggest in this paper is that the inconsistencies are what matter – that they are reflections, in part at least, of the multiple person-alities of Alexandria itself. Cities, and nations too, use foundation stories to express and shape their identity in the present. Consequently, the stories change depending on who is speaking and to whom and when.[3] Alexandria is no different.

## Multiple Personalities

In many ways the stories of the foundation of Alexandria are as much myth as those of Rome. They say more about later Alexandrian identity than they do about Alexander or about the circumstances of the city's founda-tion. Before examining these stories, however, it is important to consider the city itself and the multiple personalities that may have given rise to them. Depending on what aspect we focus on, a different city emerges.[4]

At the forefront there is Alexandria as a Greek cultural centre, the succes-sor to Athens, attracting the leading poets of the time (Apollonios Rhodios, Theokritos of Syracuse, Kallimachos of Cyrene), home to the largest collec-tion of Greek books in the world, and as such the embodiment of the Greek literary tradition – its memory, so to speak. All this was happening through the patronage of the ruling dynasty, the Ptolemies. Alexandria, although in Egypt, was thus advertising itself as a Greek city to the rest of the Greek world.[5] There was, of course, a large Greek population; some were citizens of Alexandria, others lived there but maintained an affiliation with a home state. Yet Alexandria also seems to fall short of what we expect from a proper Greek polis: it conforms to the Greek model in having a tribe and deme system and in its careful regulation of citizenship, but when we look for the council and an assembly, these fundamental elements seem strangely absent, as is evident from the argument amongst scholars over whether or not the city had a council and if it did when it ceased to exist. Certainly it did not have one in the first century AD when the Roman emperor Claudius turned down the Alexandrians' request for one.[6] Nor does Strabo point out a *bouleterion* in his description of late first-century BC Alexandria; instead, the institutions he draws attention to are the gymnasium and the law court.[7]

But Alexandria was also a city founded by a Macedonian, leading an in-vading Macedonian army. It was ruled by a dynasty established by a man who had been a commander in that army. Even at the end of the third cen-tury BC Macedonian forms and traditions can be observed in the relation-ship between monarch and army. After the death of Ptolemy IV Philopator, for example, when Agathokles is trying to seize power for himself through the regency of Ptolemy's infant son, appeal is made to an assembly of the Macedonians to support the new king, which recalls the way kings in Macedon itself were proclaimed by the army.[8] Alexandria's military character is nicely picked up by Theokritos in *Idyll* 15, written around the 270s: it is the day of a royal festival and two Syracusan women living in Alexandria are talking with each other, yet there is no escaping the presence of the army. One of the women, Gorgo, after making her way through the city to the house of her friend Praxinoa, sums up the crowded streets as 'everywhere army boots and men in military cloaks' (Theok. *Id*. 15.6.). The term for the latter is *chlamys*, the Macedonian cloak to which it will be necessary to return as it has particularly Alexandrian connotations. The Macedonian identity of Alexandria and Alexandrians continues even when the city has fallen under Roman rule, as Dio Chrysostom shows in his *Alexandrian Oration*.[9]

But there is also a third Alexandria. This is after all a city in Egypt on the Nile, albeit one sometime known as Alexandria-by-Egypt, a phrasing of which perhaps too much is made.[10] Greek literature written in Alexandria may often avoid explicit reference to the city's Egyptian setting,[11] but archaeology is increasingly showing that the Egyptian element was important to the visual make-up of the city. Underwater archaeology in the harbour has produced a considerable amount of Egyptian-style material from near the area where the lighthouse of Pharos once stood, including several colossal statues of Ptolemaic rulers in the guise of Pharaohs. These statues show that even within such an apparently Greek city as Alexandria the Ptolemies sought to present themselves in an Egyptian manner, perhaps for a native audience, perhaps as a way of expressing rule over Egypt.[12] Alexandria may have been at its most Egyptian in its population, with the native Egyptians and their language a prominent feature of the city's streets and markets.[13] This Egyptian population does not make a significant impact on our sources, but one recent estimate suggests that the Egyptians may have been the largest group in this multicultural city (Scheidel 2004: 24–7).

If our attention is focussed, then, on the palace and the grandiose displays of power such as the great procession described by Kallixeinos of Rhodes or the building of absurdly large ships, it is evident that this is also a royal city.[14] Indeed, Strabo in his account of late Hellenistic Alexandria wrote that the royal palaces covered 'a fourth or even a third of the whole city area' and so must have gone some way towards defining the whole character of the city.[15] Inhabitants of Alexandria provided services for the court, were observers of royal processions through the city, and participated in festivals sponsored by the court; thus, for example, the two women in Theokritos *Idyll* 15, Gorgo and Praxinoa, attend a festival of Adonis put on in the palace grounds by the queen, Arsinoë II. No doubt the royal presence overshadowed any other political institutions and helps to account for the dearth of information on such bodies as the council and the assembly.⁻

These various elements are apparent in a brief and negative notice attributed to Polybios, who had been a visitor to the city around the mid-second century BC. Polybios's original text and its context are no longer extant; instead, what survives is Polybios as reported by Strabo, who had himself spent time in Alexandria in the 20s BC, shortly after the end of the Ptolemaic dynasty. It is possible that the description is coloured by Strabo's own experience and his need to explain the failure of the regime. What is important, however, is the analysis of the city's population. Polybios distinguished three groups: the native Egyptians, the mercenaries, and the Alexandrians. Of the latter the passage reports that 'though mixed (μιγάδες) they were by origin Greeks and remembered their common Greek heritage (τοῦ κοινοῦ τῶν Ἑλλήνων ἔθους).' Exactly in what sense the Alexandrian Greeks are 'mixed' is unclear. The tendency among scholars has been to assume that it is through intermarriage with other ethnic groups, such as the Egyptians, hence the common and rather loaded translation 'mongrels' or the term 'mixed race.' This mixing might also be understood as the result of cultural contact, so many peoples inhabiting the same city.[16] There is, however, another less widely canvassed possibility that is more in keeping with the text and explains why the adjective 'common' is used to describe their Greek heritage. Polybios (or Strabo) may here be thinking of the Alexandrian Greeks as having migrated to Alexandria from many different cities and parts of the Greek world; they are therefore mixed in that sense but what they share is a common Greekness.[17]

The city, therefore, can be conceived in different ways depending on which element is highlighted. The maintenance of these separate identities over time was helped by the fact that so many residents were not Alexandrian citizens and thus they identified themselves by a non-Alexandrian affiliation. There were as a result different immigrant communities that often formed themselves into semi-autonomous organizations (politeumata) that were able to run their own affairs; there is evidence, albeit of varying quality, for bodies of Boiotians, Jews, Lykians, and Phrygians, among others.[18] Moreover, anyone resident in Egypt had by law to indicate deme or place of origin, further reinforcing an alternative identity for those living in Alexandria. As Daniel Selden puts it: 'In effect, every time a person signed his name, he reacknowledged that he was an alien, and in this way the foreign sources of the population, the composite make-up of the city, and its eclectic character were kept constantly in view' (1998: 298). The somewhat laissez-faire attitude of the Ptolemies to different groups subject to them may have been inherited from Macedon; N.G.L. Hammond has pointed out how Philip II and Alexander tended to leave the peoples in the Macedonian kingdom, whether they be Illyrians, Thracians, or Greeks, to look after their own local government (Hammond 1993: 20–1). It should also be noted that individuals could change identities depending on context; they might, for instance, have both Greek and Egyptian names which they would use at different times, but what is significant is that these distinct identities continue to exist and can have potency, hence the value of signalling belonging to one or the other or both.[19]

One common identity for Alexandrians would lie in the acknowledgment of Ptolemy as ruler, but even here multiple personalities persist. The Ptolemaic king is both Greek *basileus* and Egyptian pharaoh; as Ludwig Koenen puts it in the opening of his influential paper on the Ptolemaic king as a religious figure, 'Ptolemaic kingship has a Janus-like character,' or in the words of Willy Peremans, it is a 'monarchie bicéphale.'[20] Images of the king reflect this distinction; some are conventional Greek portraits that would not be out of place in Athens; others, such as the colossal statues recovered from the harbour, are very clearly pharaonic.[21] Yet even these Egyptian-style images show traces of Greek influence: the use of a diadem around the Egyptian crown, for example, or the hints of the tangled hair associated with Alexander.[22] This is something that continues right to the end of the dynasty; there is no emergence of a single unified concept of ruler, even though the Egyptian and Greek sides of Ptolemaic kingship may have influenced and informed each other (Koenen 1993).

Alexander as founder might be closer to a common point of contact for all Alexandrians, but here we see different versions of the foundation that reflect the different elements of the city as each told the story of the foundation in their own way.

## Foundation Stories

Alexander's conquest of Egypt is marked not only by the foundation of Alexandria but also by his visit to the sanctuary of Ammon at Siwah. Accounts of these events suggest that they attracted the interest not only of historians but also the imagination of storytellers and may have become increasingly elaborated in oral tradition. The focus of this paper is on the foundation, but some attention will also be given to the trip to Siwah insofar as it helps to illuminate the various foundation stories.

The account of the foundation of Alexandria that is treated most seriously by scholars is that of Arrian. This is partly because it is believed to have the authority of Ptolemy behind it as the most likely source and so be derived directly from someone on the campaign with a good knowledge of

Alexandria. But its general character also adds to its credibility; it is the least elaborate and lacks the supernatural paraphernalia found in other accounts:

From Memphis Alexander sailed downstream towards the sea, taking on board the hypaspists, archers and Agrianians, and from the cavalry the royal squadron of the Companions. When he reached Kanobos and sailed round Lake Mareotis, he went ashore where the city of Alexandria, named after him, is now situated. It struck him that the position was admirable for founding a city there and it would prosper. A longing for the work therefore seized him; he himself marked out where the city's marketplace was to be built, how many temples there were to be and the gods, some Greek, and Isis the Egyptian, for whom they were to be erected, and where the wall was to be built round it. With this in view he offered sacrifice and the sacrifice proved to be favourable.[23]

This reads as a very matter-of-fact account, but it is not one without subtext. The spur of the moment decision draws attention to Alexander's brilliance and insight – he lands and instantly realizes its potential. Then he lays out the ground himself. This is an account that emphasizes Alexander's initiative and his role as founder: he takes responsibility for everything. Alexandria is defined for the future by decisions taken by Alexander in what comes across as a single burst of activity with the result that the site, the walls, the agora, and the temples all have his imprimatur. It is not merely the city that owes its existence to Alexander but the very layout and conception of the city. Significantly, he is in effect the founder of both Greek and Egyptian temples within the city, thus making Alexandria from the beginning a city that encompassed both Greek and Egyptian traditions.

It must be remembered, however, that all this is based on the memoirs of the man who brought Alexander's body to Alexandria (with no little difficulty given the bodysnatching character of its acquisition) and who highlighted Alexander's role as founder by burying him within Alexandria. Moreover, if it is true that Alexander's body was first kept in Memphis, this was a very deliberate decision on the part of Ptolemy.[24] It is little wonder then that Alexander should here take his role as founder so seriously and be so personally involved with every aspect. Factual though this account of Arrian may appear, it is very much in keeping with an image of Alexander and his relation to the city (and to Ptolemy) that Ptolemy himself was seeking to project. First and foremost this would have been to the Macedonian soldiers, the people for whom Alexander meant most and upon whom the maintenance of Ptolemy's power in Egypt depended. According to Diodoros (18.28.3–5), Ptolemy's possession of Alexander's body encouraged soldiers to come to Egypt to enlist with him. Furthermore, the marking out of a temple of the Egyptian goddess Isis in Alexandria gives Alexander's authority to the coexistence of Greek and Egyptian gods within the city and by extension to the Janus-like character of Ptolemaic kingship.[25] Even the idea that the city was founded at the place where Alexander went ashore is not without significance. It is as if in some way he sanctified the land just as the spot in Athens where Demetrios Poliorketes dismounted from his chariot became the site of the altar of the Descending Demetrios (Plut. *Demetr.* 10). In reading this account of the foundation of the city it is important to realize that Alexandria was as much the creation of Ptolemy as it was of Alexander, but it was in Ptolemy's interests to portray himself as the protector of Alexander's legacy. To think that 'Alexandria was, first and last, Alexander's creation' is to be led astray by Ptolemy's formidable public relations skills.[26] If Alexander had not founded Alexandria, it might have been necessary to create the myth anyway as Seleukos appears to have done with Antioch, where he presented the foundation as a fulfilment of Alexander's own wishes.[27]

Other versions whose audience (and whose narrators) may have been different have less emphasis on the agency of Alexander. Plutarch in his *Life of Alexander* (26) presents a very different story.[28] This time there is no impulsive decision after seeing a great plot of land. Alexander conquers Egypt and then decides he wants to build a large and well-populated Greek city. For this he turns to architects who advise him on the site and is on the verge of preparing the ground when he has a remarkable dream that changes everything. A grey-haired old man appears to him reciting lines from the *Odyssey*: 'Now there is an island in the heavy surging sea / In front of Egypt, and Pharos is what men call it' (4.354–5). Was this meant to be Homer himself appearing to Alexander? Whoever it is, he points Alexander towards Pharos. Immediately, Alexander gets up and goes to visit Pharos, no doubt aware that had the old man recited more he would have continued as Homer did to praise the harbour there. When he sees the site, he realizes that it is exactly what he needs and says that not only is Homer amazing in other respects but that he is also a very wise architect. In the rest of the account Alexander himself is not depicted as playing a direct role in the laying out of the city itself in the way he does in Arrian's version. Plutarch instead has Alexander delegate that task to others.

In Plutarch then while the decision to build the city is again Alexander's, the choice of site belongs to Homer; here the emphasis is very much on things Greek. It is not *any* guide but Greece's greatest poet, nor is it *any* city but a Greek city (πόλις Ἑλληνίς) that is to be founded. So this story shares the Greek cultural predominance that is evident in the Library of Alexandria, where editing the text of Homer as well as other works of Greek literature was a major activity.[29] Alexander famously carried a copy of Homer's *Iliad* around with him (and clearly pondered its implications while he slept), but the story related by Plutarch is a version of the foundation that may have appealed especially to Greeks. It is no surprise then that Plutarch prefaces his account by saying that it is one told by the Alexandrians, by which we should understand Alexandrian Greeks; they tell it, he says, trusting in Herakleides. Plutarch, however, gives no further indication as to who this Herakleides might be; the most plausible suggestion is that it is the second-century BC Alexandrian writer Herakleides Lembos.[30] Homer's supposed participation in the foundation of the city may have been one of the reasons that he came to be especially venerated in Alexandria. In the late third century Ptolemy IV Philopator is known to have set up a cult of Homer there; a statue of Homer was seated in a sanctuary and around it in a circle were placed representations of all the cities that laid claim to the poet. Alternatively, Homer's role in the foundation story may have been a consequence of the emergence of a cult of Homer in Alexandria, an aetiological myth for the cult as well as the city.[31]

One Macedonian element might seem to intrude into this very Greek account of Plutarch. The plan of the city, sketched out in sprinkled barley meal, is in the shape of a *chlamys*, that military cloak associated with the Macedonians and so much a feature of the crowded streets as observed in the previous section. The analogy between the shape of Alexandria and the *chlamys* is a relatively common one, appearing also in Diodoros, Strabo, and Pliny the Elder; Pliny, perhaps because he is not Greek, explicitly qualifies it with the adjective Macedonian (*ad effigiem Macedonicae chlamydis*). It is tempting to see in this description of Alexandria's ground plan a claim of Macedonian ownership of the land or an acknowledgment of the Macedonian basis of the city. In the second book of Strabo's *Geography* the *oikoumene*, the known world, is several times described as shaped like a *chlamys*. If, as is probable, this description goes back to the geographical writings of the Alexandrian scholar and head of the royal library, Eratosthenes, we should perhaps see here some kind of statement about the Macedonian character of the world or indeed of Ptolemaic aspirations. It is true that a more prosaic explanation might be that Alexandria did indeed look like *chlamys*, whatever shape that is supposed to be, but the choice of description can still be significant.[32]

### Enter Ammon

But there are other versions of the foundation of Alexandria and they add an important twist to the story. In contrast to Arrian and Plutarch, the accounts of Justin, Diodoros, and Q. Curtius Rufus all place the foundation of Alexandria after Alexander's visit to Siwah rather than before, but they make no explicit connection between the two events. Justin's epitome of Pompeius Trogus has only the briefest of mentions, but Diodoros, who had visited Egypt in the latter days of Ptolemaic rule, and Curtius are fuller; both of them give Alexander himself a role in marking out the site.[33] It is the *Alexander Romance*, however, that is most interesting; it also puts the visit to Siwah before the foundation but in this case explicitly connects the two events. Alexander first learns that he is indeed the son of Ammon and then the Romance continues:

He asked also to receive an oracle from the god as to where he should found a city that would allow his name to be remembered forever. Then, in his sleep he saw the god speaking to him:

> O king, I the horned Phoibos address you:
> If you want to be young and forever ageless,
> Found a famous city opposite the island of Proteus. (1.30)

C. Bradford Welles argued, contrary to the prevailing scholarly opinion at the time, that this was the true order of events, first the visit to Siwah and then the foundation of Alexandria. He suggested that Alexander needed to follow Greek practice and consult an oracle before founding his city; this, therefore, would have been one of his reasons for visiting Siwah.[34] A.B. Bosworth tries to smooth out the scholarly and source differences by proposing that Alexander made the decision about the site of Alexandria before going to Siwah but only put it into practice after his return.[35] But all this fails to pay sufficient attention to the nature of the stories themselves, in particular to their likely origins as local stories about the foundation of a city, complete with inconsistencies that reflect their varying perspectives.

So in the *Alexander Romance* Alexander receives another visitation in his sleep to advise him on the foundation of his city, but on this occasion it is the Egyptian god Ammon, marked out by his characteristic ram's horns. The passage quoted is from the earliest extant version of the *Alexander Romance*, the A-text; the β-recension is fuller and describes the god as an old man, albeit one with golden hair.[36] The role of dreams and old men in directing Alexander towards his goal, both here and in Plutarch's account, may not be coincidental. It is possible that these represent linked traditions; this is not to say that one had priority but that they developed alongside each other.

Whereas Alexander's unique insight in Arrian's account might point to a Macedonian perspective, and Homer's guiding hand in Plutarch to a Greek one, the authority of Ammon, an Egyptian god, suggests that this element of the *Alexander Romance* should be read as in some sense an Egyptian story, either for an Egyptian audience or told by Egyptians for whom Alexandria was their city (as opposed to the hostile sentiments behind the *Potter's Oracle*, which impatiently predicted the end of Alexandria). Mostafa El-Abbadi has recently pointed out that there are similarities between Ammon's role in the *Alexander Romance* story and his role in earlier Egyptian tradition, in which after proclaiming paternity to an Egyptian ruler he indicated a course of action to their offspring; thus it is in the life of the female Pharaoh Hatshepsut as told on the walls of her temple at Deir-el-Bahary. Hatshepsut, however, was far from recent, ruling over a thousand years earlier, so the likelihood of continuity here might be slim; however, it may be that the conservative nature of Egyptian religion did enable such ideas of Ammon to be handed down through successive generations of priests.[37]

Even without this tentative analogy between Alexander's encounter with Ammon and earlier pharaonic tradition it is possible to see a variety of ways in which the Egyptian god's intervention in the foundation of Alexandria might suggest a story that circulated among Egyptians. It could have been told as a means of legitimating the foundation of Alexandria to the Egyptian population or perhaps in order to justify the move from the traditional centre of Memphis to this new site by the sea (in these cases its origins may lie with the Macedonian authorities), but it could also have been a means by which Egyptians could themselves lay claim to Alexandria as their city, a way of offsetting its alienness. The *Alexander Romance* may seem to be a source that should be treated with extreme scepticism, but I am not concerned here with whether what it says is true or not, at least not in the way in which Welles and other scholars have tried to extract those parts that are true. Rather, I am interested in its perspective, its value as a bearer of traditions about Alexandria. Although written in Greek and concerned with Alexander's adventures throughout the world, there is a distinctly Egyptian dimension to it. There is, for instance, the bizarre story at the beginning that Alexander's father was not Philip or some deity but the last Egyptian pharaoh Nectanebo, who somehow has ended up at the Macedonian court. He uses his magical skills to sneak into Olympias's bed in the guise of Ammon – on a regular basis (*Alexander Romance* 1.1–14). What the *Alexander Romance* presents might be best understood as a merging of Greek and Egyptian traditions, a particular strain of local Alexandrian tradition, although it must be conceded that the circumstances of the composition of the Romance are something of a puzzle.[38] Diodoros and Curtius, on the other hand, both place the foundation after the visit to Siwah but say nothing of any assistance that Ammon gives in identifying the site of the city. Perhaps they knew nothing of it, but it may also be that they preferred to focus on the paternity issue, Alexander as the son of Ammon, and in comparison with this the god's role in the foundation of the city was of little interest to them, the one a major historical issue, the other of merely local significance.

Some believe that these foundation stories were already being publicized by Alexander himself,[39] but, although Alexander was an enthusiastic self-mythologizer, the roots of these stories are most likely to be found later. Alexander founded the city and moved on; these are the stories of those who lived in Alexandria, people whose identity within this huge city mattered and who shaped their stories of the city's foundation accordingly. But it was such a divided city that the stories reflected its component parts: Macedonian soldiers, Greeks, Egyptians. These roughly are the groups picked out by Polybios, although the Macedonian soldiers of the early days would have been replaced by a more disparate mix of mercenaries by the second century. Nonetheless, with his mainland perspective Polybios omitted one important group. Significantly, there is no mention of a Jewish population, although clearly there was a sizeable one by that date; one estimate suggests that around a third of the population at the time Polybios was writing may have been Jewish.[40] They too had their own mythology of the foundation of the city. According to Josephus, writing in the *Jewish War* in the first century AD, the Jews had been granted certain privileges by Alexander for helping him against the Egyptians; these privileges included (on the most likely reading of the text) permission to live in the city on equal terms with the Greeks, a privilege confirmed by Alexander's successors, who extended it to give them a special quarter of their own. Here Josephus, though not an Alexandrian himself, explicitly incorporates the Jews into the very beginnings of Alexandria and projects Alexander as a quasi-founder of the Jewish community; in the *Contra Apionem* he goes even further and credits Alexander himself with giving them their own quarter. Some of this may reflect the circumstances of the later first century AD, not least the recent Roman crushing of the Jewish revolt, but nonetheless it is in keeping with the type of stories told by other groups within Alexandria.[41]

The foundation was not simply a story (or stories) passed down through the generations, it was also part of the religious calendar of Alexandria. The *Alexander Romance* reports that every year on the Egyptian date of Tybi 25 the Alexandrians celebrated a festival. According to tradition this was the day on which Alexander founded not only the city but also the sanctuary of Agathos Daimon, the latter supposedly marking the burial place of a snake that had repeatedly frightened the workmen during the city's construction.[42] There has been some debate among scholars as to whether this is a Ptolemaic date, therefore April, or a date consequent on Augustus's calendar reforms, therefore January, and if the former whether Alexander could have reached Gaugamela in time.[43] It seems optimistic to imagine that this is the real date of Alexandria's foundation (insofar as a city can be founded on a single day). It could equally be that the day for the celebration of the cult of Agathos Daimon came to be identified as the foundation day of the city and an appropriate aetiological story developed accordingly, perhaps as early as the rule of Ptolemy when he was shaping Alexander's image as a founder of Alexandria. Daniel Ogden in chapter 11 of this volume points out the close association there appears to have been between the emerging cult of Agathos Daimon and Alexander the founder.[44] This passage of the *Alexander Romance* shows that for Alexandrians the commemoration of the city's foundation was part of their religious calendar, and we can expect stories, no doubt changing over time, to have been told to accompany this. It may be that the foundation was celebrated in different ways by the different communities of this diverse and multi-ethnic city as reflected in the stories examined in this paper, but such celebrations and no doubt others sponsored by the Ptolemies themselves shared a common focus.

This paper has concentrated on those aspects of the foundation stories that reveal something of the various identities of the people who lived in or round Alexandria. There are other features that have not been covered, notably the common story of the use of barley meal to mark out the site. This essentially simple tale is found in most of our sources but in a surprising number of different permutations: there are different reasons for using barley meal (Macedonian custom, no chalk, not enough chalk, nothing else available); mostly, not always, it is eaten by birds; the omen is sometimes the use of barley meal, sometimes the birds eating it; for the most part Alexander is disturbed but on one occasion it is he who sees it as a sign of future prosperity; the interpreters of the omen differ as indeed do their interpretations.[45] That there is such variety here is partly in the nature of Alexander histories but it is also, I would suggest, because in this case these are stories that are handed down often orally as part of local Alexandrian tradition. We should think of these not so much as stories of Alexander as stories of Alexandria and its people.

### Notes

1  For the foundation of Rome, see, for instance, Erskine 2001; Wiseman 1995.
2  Diod. Sic. 17.52; Strabo 17.1.6 (C792); Plut. *Alex.* 26; Arr. *Anab.* 3.1.4–2.2; Curt. 4.8.1–6; Steph. Byz., s.v. Ἀλεξάνδρεια; *Alexander Romance* 1.30–3 (Kroll 1926 for A-text, Bergson 1965 for β-recension); cf. also Just. *Epit.* 11.11.13; Val. Max.

1.4, ext. 1, *Itinerarium Alexandri* 20. In the modern literature, see, in particular, de Polignac 2000; Green 1996; Fraser 1972: 1.3–7, with notes; Welles 1962. Cohen surveys the evidence and secondary literature for many of the key topics in the scholarship on Hellenistic Alexandria (2006: 355–81, with 360–3 on the foundation). For Alexander's other foundations, see Fraser 1996.

3 For the foundation traditions of Greek cities during the period of archaic colonization, see Malkin 1987 and 1994; Dougherty 1993, with 2009 on Syracuse. On the changing character of the foundation story of Rome, see Erskine 2001. For the role of the classical past in modern foundation myths, see Erskine 2009.

4 Fraser (1972) is fundamental but note also the various recent collections of essays that all give a sense of Alexandria's diverse character: Walsh and Reese 1996; Jacob and de Polignac 2000; Harris and Ruffini 2004; Hirst and Silk 2004.

5 Weber (1993) and Fraser (1972: 1.part 2) collect the evidence for intellectual and literary patronage in Alexandria; on the projection of Greek identity, see Erskine 1995.

6 The fullest and most up-to-date discussion of the vexed question of the *boule* (and with less accumulated bibliography, the *ekklesia*) is now Cohen (2006: 368–71), where the evidence and contending parties are lucidly laid out; for an earlier review, see Fraser (1972: 1.93–6, I.175–6); Claudius's letter, *P. Lond.* VI = *Select Papyri* 212.

7 Strabo 17.1.10 (C795); Rowlandson 2005: 252–3.

8 Polyb. 15.25.3–12 (note the oath at 12), 15.26 (Agathokles addresses the Macedonians), on which see Hammond 1993: 16–17; Fraser 1972: 1.80.

9 Dio Chrys. 32.63–5; cf. Joseph. *BJ* 2.387; Spawforth 2006.

10 This was the official designation in the Roman period, *Alexandrea ad Aegyptum* or Ἀλεξάνδρεια ἡ πρὸς Αἰγύπτωι, but it is rarely and not consistently attested in the Ptolemaic period; see Fraser 1972: 1.107–108; Lloyd 2011: 87; for the idea, see Clarysse 2000: 29.

11 Weber 1993: 369–99, though to be read now with Stephens 2003.

12 Stanwick 2002: 15–20; on recent archaeological work, see Goddio and Clauss 2008; Goddio et al. 1998; Empereur 1998; for its implications, see Bagnall 2001: 229–30, though note also the cautionary remarks of McKenzie (2006: x). For an Egyptian audience, see Ashton 2004.

13 Abd-el-Ghani 2004: 161–163; Riad 1996; Fraser 1972: 1.54; for the Roman period, see Delia 1988.

14 Procession: Ath. 5.197–203; Rice 1983 with text; ships: Plut. *Demetr.* 43; Ath. 5.203e–204d; Bugh 2006: 276; royal city: Fraser 1972: 1.93–131.

15 Strabo 17.793–4; Pliny *HN* 5.62 says a fifth, though what period he is talking of is unclear.

16 Polyb. 34.14 in Strabo 17.1.12 (C797). Polybios's visit to Egypt: Walbank 1979b: 180–1; translation 'mongrel' for μιγάδες appears in Paton's Loeb, followed in Spawforth 2006: 13; Goudriaan 1988: 118; Momigliano 1975: 37; for 'mixed race,' see Ogden 1996: 354. Walbank (1979a: 629) draws a comparison with

μιξέλληνες; cf. also Walbank 1979b: 182. On the negative image of Egyptians in modern interpretations of this chapter, see Ritner 1992. For effects of cultural contact, see Joseph. *BJ* 2.488, where the Jews are able to preserve their way of life because they mix (ἐπιμισγομένων) less with other peoples.

17  Cf. Lane Fox 1973: 543: 'Greeks of mixed Greek origin, not Greco-Egyptians'; for μιγάδες as coming together from different sources, cf. Isoc. *Panath.* 124, *Paneg.* 2.

18  Selden 1998: 294–295, Fraser 1972: 1.59–60; much discussion on *politeumata* focuses on the Jews, cf. Smallwood 1981: 225–6, with n.23 on *politeumata* more generally; Honigman 2003: 99–101. The best-documented is the Jewish *politeuma* of Herakleopolis; see Cowey and Maresch 2001.

19  See the examples in Baines 2004; cf. also Koenen 1993: 34–6. For ethnicity in Egypt, see Goudriaan (1988) and the essays in Bilde et al. (1992). The large Greek population and the urban environment may have made this issue rather different in Alexandria; see Thompson 2001: 303–4; Goudriaan 1988, 118–19.

20  Koenen 1993: 25; Peremans 1987; Hölbl 2001: 77–123.

21  Stanwick 2002; Ashton 2001; Smith 1988.

22  Diadem: Koenen 1993: 25–6; hair: Stanwick 2002: 16, 27; Ma 2005: 189–90.

23  Arr. *Anab.* 3.1.4–5 (trans. Brunt); it is followed by a more fanciful story from the vulgate about the marking out of the site with barley meal, see n.45 below.

24  For the removal of the body to Alexandria, see Erskine 2002.

25  The representation of Isis in Alexandria came to develop in different ways from the image traditionally found in Egypt; see Dunand 2007 with Dunand 2000.

26  Green 1990: 84; contrast Tacitus who gives Ptolemy credit for the creation of Alexandria (*Hist.* 4.83.1).

27  Lib. *Or.* 11.72–93, and perhaps in imitation of Alexander Seleukos was said to have laid out the ground with wheat, see further n.45 below. For foundations myths of Antioch, see Buraselis 2010: 269–71; Ogden 2011: 89–102.

28  See Hamilton (1969: 66–8).

29  On Alexandrian scholarship, see Pfeiffer 1968: 87–233; Fraser 1972: 1.447–79.

30  Hamilton (1969: 66), who also notes the suggestion of F. Pfister (1956: 13n2) that an Alexandrian history may have cited Herakleides of Pontos. On Herakleides Lembos, see Fraser (1972: 1.514–15, II.741–3), though he says that the Herakleides of Plutarch is unidentifiable.

31  For the cult, see Aelian, *VH* 13.22; Erskine 2001: 49–50; and Brink 1972: 549–52.

32  Shape of Alexandria: Plut. *Alex.* 26.8; Diod. Sic. 17.52.3; Strabo 17.1.8 (C793); Pliny *HN* 5.62; of *oikoumene*: Strabo 2.5.6 (C113), 2.5.9 (C116), 2.5.14 (C118), 2.5.18 (122); for a detailed examination of the *chlamys* and Eratosthenes's use of it, see Zimmermann 2002; cf. also Fraser 1972: 2.26n64; for its political significance, see Jacob 1999: 31.

33  Just. *Epit.* 11.11.13; Diod. Sic. 17.52 (where he mentions his own visit); Curt. 4.8.1–6.

34 Welles (1962), rejected by Fraser (1967: 30); on religion and the foundation of Alexandria, see Malkin 1987: 106–9.

35 Bosworth 1980: 263–4; cf. Atkinson (1980: 361–2).

36 For the A-text, see Kroll 1926; for β-recension, see Bergson 1965; for the multiple receptions of the *Romance*, see Stoneman 2008.

37 El-Abbadi (2004: 263–5), although he mistakenly seems to think that the *Alexander Romance* is the only history to place the Siwah visit before the foundation; rather, it is the only one to connect the two.

38 For Egypt and the *Romance*, see Jouanno 2002: 57–125.

39 Cf. El-Abbadi 2004: 265.

40 Paget 2004: 146; cf. Delia (1988) for the Roman period, though in the early third century the Jewish population may have been quite small (Honigman 2003: 100–1).

41 Joseph. *BJ* 2.487–8; *Ap.* 2.35; for the Jews in Alexandria, see Fraser 1972: 54–8; Barclay 1996: 27–34; on Alexander and the Jews, see Stoneman 1994.

42 *Alexander Romance* 1.32, the various recensions differ quite considerably in detail if not in the main point, see further Ogden, this volume, chapter 11.

43 Fraser 1972: 1.3n9; Bagnall 1979; Green 1996: 23n98.

44 See Ogden, this volume, chapter 11 and the bibliography there, cf. also Goukowsky 1978: 331n235.

45 Sources: *Alexander Romance* 1.32; Amm. Marc. 22.16.7; Arr. *Anab.* 3.2.1–2; Curt. 4.8.6, *Itinerarium Alexandri* 20; Plut. *Alex.* 26; Steph. Byz., s.v. Ἀλεξάνδρεια; Strabo 17.1.6 (C792); Val. Max. 1.4, ext. 1; it does not appear in Diodoros or Justin. Reasons: Macedonian custom (Curtius), no or not enough chalk (Ammianus, *Itinerarium*, Plutarch, Stephanos, Strabo, Valerius Maximus), nothing available (Arrian); in the *Romance* wheat meal is used instead; eaten by birds (with the exception of Ammianus, Arrian and Strabo, for whom therefore the omen is the use of barley meal rather than its being eaten); Alexander disturbed (Plutarch, *Romance*, Stephanos), positive (*Itinerarium*); interpreters: Egyptian priests (Valerius Maximus), Aristander of Telmessos (Arrian), unspecified seers or prophets (Curtius, Plutarch, Stephanos), Alexander (*Itinerarium*); interpretations tend to overlap, stressing prosperity of various sorts, growing population, especially of immigrants, and the ability to feed both the city and beyond the city. Bosworth (1980: 265–6) reviews some of the main differences, cf. Atkinson (1980: 367–8) for commentary on Curtius. Buraselis (2010) stresses the way the stories fulfil the need for divine participation in the foundation. The story appears to be part of the vulgate and may not have been recorded by Ptolemy. Lib. 11.90 tells a story that when Seleukos was founding Antioch he marked out the land with wheat, which, if true, may suggest that the Alexandrian grain story was early in the tradition. On the other hand, it could be one foundation story borrowing from another.

# 11

# The Birth Myths of Ptolemy Soter[1]

## DANIEL OGDEN

How did the Ptolemies present themselves as belonging to or with the dynasty of Philip and Alexander on the one hand, and as belonging in Egypt on the other? The principal means was the generation of a rich birth mythology for the dynasty's founder, Ptolemy Soter. Alexander had been the son of Philip and the son of Zeus. If Ptolemy wished to emulate Alexander and claim some of his aura, then he would be obliged to appropriate at least one of these for himself – or those writing on his behalf had to do it for him. In fact, he – or they – went for both.

Let us consider the appropriation of Philip first.[2] Alexander himself had had to be careful to retain his claim to be the blood son of Philip, the mortal sire upon whom his earthly title to the Macedonian throne depended, whilst enhancing his credentials by also claiming direct descent from Zeus.[3] For Ptolemy, or for those working on his behalf, the case was almost the inverse; his own sire, Lagos, could offer nothing to which he might aspire to succeed, and so he was shunted aside in favour of that same earthly father whose position Alexander had, willy-nilly, compromised in his own case: Philip himself. Plutarch and Justin may well exaggerate in portraying Lagos as a man of humble origin, but an anecdote preserved by the former serves well to express his perceived obscurity: 'Ptolemy was making fun of a scholar for his ignorance, and asked him who the father of Peleus was. He replied that he would tell him, "If you first tell me who the father of Lagos was." The joke referred to the poor birth of the king, and all were angry at it as tactless and inappropriate. But Ptolemy said, "As it is the part of a king not to endure being mocked, so it is the part of a king not to make mock"' (Plutarch *Moralia* 458ab).[4] In default of further specification on Plutarch's part, we must assume that the Ptolemy making the joke was Soter, and this would, after all, render the scholar's joke the most pointed.[5] It may or may not be significant that Ptolemy was not concerned to apply to himself – or that others were not concerned to apply to him – the patronymic phrase 'son of Lagos' in the formal inscriptions of his own era.[6]

In official contexts Ptolemy and his heirs may have kept his claim to Argead descent discreetly vague. In an unpublished inscription the Ptolemies refer to their ancestors as 'Heraklid Argeads.'[7] It is in fact possible that Ptolemy did have some tenuous family link with the Argeads, and indeed through his mother: Arsinoë may have been a descendant of Amyntas I and cousin to Philip II.[8] But evidently closer ties to Philip himself were felt desirable. We learn the mechanics of a more direct claim to the best of Argead blood first from Curtius: 'In particular Ptolemy ... drew the king's [Alexander's] concerned attention. He was a blood-relative, and some believe he had been born of Philip. At any rate it was established that he was the son of a concubine of his' (Curtius 9.8.22). It is not clear whether Curtius identified this concubine with Arsinoë, whom the *Souda*, to which we will turn shortly, plausibly names as Ptolemy's mother. Pausanias seemingly preserves a politer version of the same tradition in two adjacent passages:

The Macedonians hold that Ptolemy is the son of Philip the son of Amyntas, although nominally the son of Lagos. For they say that his mother was given to Lagos by Philip with him already in her belly. (Pausanias 1.6.2)

If this Ptolemy truly was the son of Philip, the son of Amyntas, he should know that he inherited his craziness about women from his father. This is because although he was married to Eurydike the daughter of Antipater and they had children, he fell in love with Berenike, whom Antipater had sent with Eurydike to Egypt. He fell in love with her and had children by her, and when his end was near, he left that Ptolemy to rule Egypt after whom the Athenians name one of their tribes, the boy born from Berenike [i.e., II Philadelphos] but not from the daughter of Antipater [i.e., Keraunos]. (Pausanias 1.6.8)

Comparison of the first Pausanias passage here with the second, which shortly follows it, suggests that Pausanias's source may have been one specializing in Macedonian sexual musical chairs, although the wry moralizing may be Pausanias's own. The Pausanian tale constitutes the mirror image of the *delegitimating* tale sponsored in Sparta by the enemies of King Demaratos. It was alleged against him, as Herodotos tells, that he was not, as was initially believed, the son of King Ariston, but the son of the commoner Agetos, with whose child Ariston's wife had already been pregnant when the king took her from his friend.[9]

And a yet politer version is preserved by the *Alexander Romance*, as it speaks of Perdikkas's expectations as the dying Alexander sets his affairs in order: 'Perdikkas suspected that Alexander had bequeathed the succession to Ptolemy, since he had often spoken to him about Ptolemy's birth, and since Olympias had made it clear that Ptolemy was born of Philip. So he took Ptolemy aside and made him swear that if he was made Alexander's successor, he would divide the succession with him and share it. Ptolemy took the oath without any inkling of Perdikkas' suspicions, for he himself believed that Perdikkas would be the successor' (*Alexander Romance* 3.32 [A]).[10] The Egypt-slanted *Romance* is wholehearted in its advocacy of Ptolemy. Charles Edson and Peter Brunt, a little quaintly perhaps, assess the chances of Ptolemy actually having been the illegitimate son of Philip, and find them slim. They note that if we take the Lucianic *Long-lived Men* seriously, then Ptolemy will have been born in 367/366 BC when Philip was himself sixteen and a captive in Thebes.[11] When was this claim first made? We have little basis for certainty, since all the sources that preserve it were themselves composed long after the extinction of the Ptolemaic dynasty. The *communis opinio*, however, seems to be that it was first made by Ptolemy himself close to the Year of the Kings, 306 BC.[12]

And so to Ptolemy's appropriation of Zeus. He appropriated Zeus not directly as sire or as co-sire, as Alexander had done, but indirectly as a foster father, and perhaps in more than one way. Zeus is shown in this role, working through the agency of his eagle, in the most elaborate version of Ptolemy's dynastic foundation myth to survive, a fragment of Aelian preserved by the *Souda*: 'Lagos, proper name. He married Arsinoë the mother of Ptolemy Soter. Lagos exposed this Ptolemy in a bronze shield as having no relationship with him. A tradition comes down from Macedonia to the effect that an eagle visited him and stretched its wings over him and, hovering over him, shielded him from the direct rays of the sun, and from excessive rain, whenever it rained. It frightened off the flock-birds, tore up quails, and provided him with their blood as nourishment in place of milk' (*Souda* s.v. Λάγος = Aelian F283 Domingo-Forasté).[13] The baby suckled on blood, even the blood of unintimidating quails, is surely a fiercer and hardier proposition than one suckled on milk. The shield-cradle too is no doubt an anticipation of the baby's future martial prowess.[14] But it is aggravating that this tale is not preserved at fuller length. Whom did Lagos imagine the father to be? Who was it in fact? Zeus? Lagos himself after all? How did Ptolemy return to favour within Lagos's family, if indeed he did?

It is of course theoretically possible to combine Aelian's tale of the eagle with those of Curtius and Pausanias about the paternity of Philip. The Pausanias tale to a certain extent explains why Lagos regards Ptolemy as nothing to do with him and so exposes him, although one might wonder why he should knowingly seek to expose the son of the king (or for that matter of a god), and we might wonder even more why such a compelling detail should be omitted from even the hastiest summary of the story. But a narrative of this sort, even without the key detail of royal descent, could serve meaningfully as a dynastic foundation myth. The narrative pattern in accordance with which a baby, illegitimate or deformed, is subjected to exposure but survives and returns to become a king is a common one in the Greek world. It is found famously in the myth of Oidipous and is associated with the legends of the rise of a great many of the Greek tyrants, such as Kypselos of Corinth and Agathokles of Syracuse, and those of the founders of colonies, such as Battos of Cyrene.[15] And the simpler motif of the child-hood exposure of a future great ruler is even more widespread: we have only to think of Moses, Romulus, and Cyrus.[16]

The motif of the Zeus-eagle establishes a legitimating link for Ptolemy back to the Zeus-eagle symbolism promulgated by Alexander himself. Almost immediately upon his accession Alexander began to decorate some of his coin reverses with the striking iconic image of a Zeus-eagle perching on the thunderbolt of which it had been the traditional bearer since the age of the Hesiodic *Shield*.[17] Already for Alexander himself this symbolism probably functioned as an allusion to or in conjunction with the first of his birth myths preserved by Plutarch: 'Anyway the bride [i.e., Olympias], before the night on which they were closeted into the bridal chamber, thought that there was a peal of thunder and that a thunderbolt struck her womb, and that a great fire was kindled from the point of the strike, which then broke into flames that surged all around before being extinguished' (Plutarch *Alexander* 2). We cannot be sure that this birth myth originated in Alexander's own lifetime, though the second birth myth that Plutarch goes on to relate – that in accordance with which Philip dreamed that he sealed Olympias's womb with a lion signet ring – can be traced back to Ephoros, who is thought to have stopped writing ca 330 B.C.[18] Alexander further advertised this myth, it seems, by having himself portrayed as a brandisher of a thunderbolt in his own person. Kallisthenes described Alexander himself as a thunderbolt bearer before whom even waves did obeisance at some point before his death in 327 BC.[19] Towards the end of his reign Alexander's 'Poros' decadrachms, minted 326–323 BC, portrayed him in armour brandishing the thunderbolt in person.[20] Apelles too painted Alexander brandishing a thunderbolt ('Alexander Keraunophoros') for the temple of Artemis at Ephesos, seemingly in the king's own lifetime.[21] His picture may be reflected in the fine 'Neisos' gem in the Hermitage, normally dated to the earlier third century BC, on which a nude Alexander brandishes a thunderbolt as a well-drawn eagle sits beside him.[22] What did all this mean for Ptolemy? The eagle that (we presume) delivered the thunderbolt to sire Alexander for Zeus now takes on a nursing role for Ptolemy.

When did the Ptolemies first decide that Soter had been reared by the Zeus-eagle in this way? It is difficult to tell, but the Zeus-eagle was emphatically prominent in Soter's own imagery from the period ca 321–315 BC, long, therefore, before his actual assumption of kingship. His Alexandrian silver tetradrachms from this period offer a head of Alexander on the obverse. The reverses offer either a seated Zeus or a standing Athena. The seated Zeus, in the normal fashion of the 'Alexanders,' holds an eagle, whilst shown in the field is either a thunderbolt or an eagle on a thunderbolt. The standing Athena brandishes her spear and holds her shield out horizontally to protect an eagle perching on a thunderbolt below.[23] The combination of eagle with a seemingly protective shield here is highly suggestive, in a kaleidoscoped way, for the Ptolemaic birth myth.[24] Subsequently, from ca 300 BC, now within the regal period, Ptolemaic tetradrachm reverses are decorated with the most magnificent series of full-frame eagles perching on thunderbolts, in a triumphant embellishment of Alexander's style.[25] These reverses were to remain highly popular with Ptolemy's successors.[26] Werner Huss guesses that it was these coins that inspired the birth myth.[27] By the time Theokritos came to write his *Encomium of Ptolemy* for Philadelphos in ca 275–270 BC, he knew that a great eagle had cried out three times from the clouds to mark the latter's birth, and that 'this was the sign of Zeus.'[28] The remains of a relief of Zeus with an eagle at his feet decorate the fragmentary circular white marble base of an altar of the late third or early second century BC discovered in the heart of the Alexandrian palace district.[29] And it is noteworthy too that the emphatically Ptolemaic *Alexander Romance*, the roots of which may be early Hellenistic, has Nectanebo, here the earthly father of Alexander, transform himself from serpent (*drakon*) to eagle after making his magical demonstration before Philip, and then has an eagle escort Alexander's soul to the heavens as he dies.[30] It is probable that the notion that Soter was reared by the eagle was developed significantly in advance of the formal promulgation of his divinity by the Ptolemaic state. Philadelphos first seems to have proclaimed his father Soter's divinity in around 280 BC, but he had to wait until 215 BC in the reign of his great-grandson Philopator before actually being incorporated into Alexander's cult, so as to be able to receive worship as a god. In the meantime Philadelphos had incorporated himself and his sister-wife Arsinoë II into Alexander's cult ca 272 BC.[31]

At some point before he was killed by the Gauls in 279 BC, after having enjoyed the kingship of Macedon for a mere two years, the son, another Ptolemy, whom Soter had initially groomed to succeed himself, before

disinheriting him, acquired the surname Keraunos, 'Thunderbolt.' Memnon
and Pausanias venture to offer explanations of the name: it was, Memnon
says, 'on account of his stupidity and insanity.' If this were true, it would
suggest that Keraunos only acquired his name subsequent to one or both of
his signally stupid and insane actions, namely, his murder of Seleukos in 281
BC and his brief bloodbath of a marriage to Arsinoë II ca 280 BC. But the explanation is wholly implausible: a thunderbolt is hardly a pellucid metaphor
for either stupidity or insanity. Pausanias, a little more plausibly, tells us that
he acquired the surname because he was bold and proactive. But at any rate
it is likely that the surname, whether bestowed by his father at or close to his
birth (which would have been shortly after ca 322–321 BC, when Soter married his mother Eurydike), or taken on by the prince himself in adulthood,
in rebellion, or in coronation, primarily saluted the thunderbolt so closely
associated with the Zeus-eagle in Alexander's iconography. And it is tempting, though it can not be proven, to think that it more specifically saluted
Alexander's already established thunderbolt birth myth. Between them, it
seems, Ptolemy Soter and his son appropriated for themselves, in different
ways, the two elements of Alexander's eagle-thunderbolt coin reverses.[32]

Interaction between kingly myths is not a one-way street. Although
Alexander clearly had himself promulgated the symbol of the thunderbolt
in his own lifetime, it is possible that its subsequent prominence in his tradition owes much to the Ptolemies' decision to appropriate it and its eagle
bearer for their own purposes.

I now turn to something that may be regarded as a quasi-birth myth, or
perhaps better a rebirth myth, for Ptolemy Soter, one which bears a striking structural parallel with the myth of the fostering Zeus-eagle. In the
third of Alexander's birth myths recorded by Plutarch, Alexander is sired
not through the agency of an eagle, but by the agency of a serpent: 'And
once too a serpent (*drakon*) was seen stretched out beside Olympias' body
as she slept. And they say that this most of all blunted Philip's desire for and
fond feelings towards his wife, so that he no longer visited her frequently to
sleep with her, either because he feared that some kind of magic was being
performed against himself, and he feared the woman's spells, or because he
avoided her company out of religious scruple since she was having congress
with a higher power' (Plutarch *Alexander* 2). In subsequent tradition this
serpent came to be identified as Zeus Ammon, curiously, since Ammon was a
ram god, but never really a serpent god.[33] Almost certainly the serpent was a
more indigenous variety of Zeus in origin, most probably Zeus Meilichios.[34]
But, identity aside, Ptolemy seems to have made a gesture with this creature
parallel to that made with the Zeus-eagle. A number of vulgate sources relate the tale of Ptolemy's near-fatal wounding by an arrow tipped with snake

venom at Harmatelia in India; the implication is that the tale goes back to the Alexandrian Kleitarchos, now usually thought to have published soon after 310.[35] Diodoros and Curtius tell how Alexander, dreadfully anxious about the fate of his favourite lieutenant, slept by his side, and was visited in a dream by a serpent (*drakon*) that brought him a herb with which to cure Ptolemy and showed him where in the local area he could find it growing. Upon awaking Alexander had the herb brought to him, and Ptolemy was duly cured. But it is Cicero who makes explicit the identity of this healing serpent:

When Ptolemy, Alexander's associate, had been struck in battle by a poisoned arrow and was dying from that wound in the greatest pain, Alexander, sitting by him, fell asleep. Then, in his slumbers, he saw a vision of that serpent (*draco*) that his mother Olympias used to keep carrying a root in its mouth and at the same time telling him where it grew (nor was it far from that place). It told him that it had such great power that it would easily cure Ptolemy. When Alexander awoke he told his dream to his friends and men were sent to find that root. It is said that it was found and that Ptolemy was cured, as were many soldiers who had been wounded by that type of weapon. (Cicero *On Divination* 2.135)

In other words, the serpent that had sired Alexander becomes the serpent that heals Ptolemy. The parallel with Ptolemy's appropriation of the Zeus-eagle is clear: once again Alexander's siring divine animal becomes Ptolemy's nursing divine animal.

But Ptolemy did not stop there with his appropriation of Alexander's serpent imagery. Arrian, in a well-known passage, gives us an intriguing insight into Ptolemy's own unique account of Alexander's visit to Siwah:

But Alexander's army lost its way, and the guides were doubtful as to which route to take. Ptolemy son of Lagos [*FGrH* 138 F8] says that two serpents (*drakontes*) went before the army giving forth voice [i.e., human speech?] and Alexander ordered his guides to follow these, trusting in the [or 'his'] divinity, and they led him all the way to the oracle and back again. But Aristoboulos, and this is the predominant story, says that two crows flew before the army, and that these were guides for Alexander. I am able to confirm that some divinity helped him, because this is likely, but the possibility of supplying an accurate account has been closed down because people have told such diverse stories about him. (Arrian *Anabasis* 3.3.4–6)

Arrian's observation that the crows' version predominated is borne out by all other extant accounts of the episode, which do indeed give us crows.[36] Why, specifically, might Ptolemy have made this change in the tale? Presumably because he saw here an opportunity to exploit the serpent imagery he had appropriated from Alexander to predestine his own future rule of Egypt.

This becomes clear again in the myth of the foundation of the city of Alexandria preserved in the *Alexander Romance*.[37] Alexander's architects have marked out the projected city to extend between the rivers 'Serpent' (*Drakon*) and 'Agathodaimon.'[38] The *Romance* continues:

They began to build Alexandria from the Middle plain and so the place took on the additional name of 'Beginning,' on account of the fact that the building of the city had begun from that point. A serpent (*drakon*) which was in the habit of presenting itself to people in the area kept frightening the workmen, and they would break off their work upon the creature's arrival. News of this was given to Alexander. He gave the order that on the following day the serpent should be killed wherever it was caught. On receipt of this permission, they got the better of the beast when it presented itself at the place now called the Stoa and killed it. Alexander gave the order that it should have a precinct there, and buried the serpent. And he gave the command that the neighbourhood should be garlanded in memory of the sighting of Agathos Daimon . . . When the heroon was being built + one architrave . . . + there leaped out from it a large host [of snakes], and, crawling off, they ran into the four [?] houses that were already there. Alexander, who was still present, founded the city and the heroon itself on the 25th Tybi. From that point the doorkeepers admitted these snakes (*opheis*) to the houses as Agathoi Daimones. These snakes are not poisonous, but they do ward off those snakes that do seem to be poisonous, and sacrifices are given to the hero himself <,as serpent-born>. (*Alexander Romance* 1.32.5–7 and 10–13 [A; Armenian §§ 86–8])[39]

The public cult of Agathos Daimon ('Good Demon')was probably established at a very early stage. At any rate, it is clearly reflected in the famous *Oracle of the Potter*, probably third-century BC in origin, perhaps second, a unique piece of native-Egyptian-derived propaganda against the Macedonian regime, originally composed in Demotic but surviving only in Greek. This prophesies that Agathos Daimon will abandon the city that is currently being built (Alexandria) for the native-Egyptian city of Memphis. In other words, it seems, Alexandria will be deprived of its protecting deity.[40]

But the Ptolemies' embrace of Agathos Daimon – and therefore probably of his public cult – can almost certainly be taken back to the 320–300 BC period under Soter himself. This is the period to which Andrew Stewart assigns the original of the lost Alexander Aigiochos ('Aegis-bearing') statue that is held to have decorated Alexander's tomb in Alexandria, and to have represented Alexander in his role as founder of the city.[41] In this statue Alexander wore an aegis decorated with a small gorgoneion, or Gorgon head; in his right hand he held a spear; in his left he held a palladion, a small statuette of the goddess Athena. The statue is attested by seventeen copies in various states of repair – statues, statuettes and cameos – all, where provenance is known, deriving from Egypt. In one severely damaged statuette copy, now in the Louvre, Alexander's leg is supported by a tree trunk around which winds a serpent.[42] Despite its vestigial attestation, the serpent presumably did feature in the original. This is further suggested by the Aigiochos's strong allusions to Pheidias's famous chryselephantine Athena Parthenos in the Athenian Parthenon, allusions supported, of course, by the featured palladion: the Parthenos statue too wore the aegis and held a spear and a female statuette, in this case of Nike, Victory.[43] And nestling under the Parthenos's shield was a magnificent serpent: the anguiform Erichthonios, protective spirit of the city of Athens, much as Agathos Daimon was the protective spirit of the city of Alexandria.[44]

The Alexander Aigiochos statue seems to have suggested a tight association at least between Alexander and Agathos Daimon. Might it actually have expressed a degree of identification? The phrase 'and sacrifices are given to the hero himself, as serpent-born' in the *Alexander Romance* quotation above is reconstituted into the A-text on the reliable basis of the ancient Armenian translation. The Armenian term used here for 'serpent,' *višap*, is apparently a good match for Greek *drakon*, 'serpent' in that it refers particularly to large snakes.[45] But who receives the sacrifices? The singular and great Agathos Daimon, as immediate context seems to suggest, or Alexander, whom the description 'as serpent-born' fits better? Alexander on the one hand, we know, was serpent-born, whilst, on the other, it is difficult to see why one should feel the need to describe the anguiform Agathos Daimon as 'serpent-born.' There may lurk beneath this curious phraseology an attempt, at some level, actually to merge Agathos Daimon and the dead Alexander. Lily Ross Taylor guessed so and sought support for her notion in the serpent that Virgil speaks of at Anchises's tomb: this offered her a paradigm of a serpent that at once constitutes the spirit of a dead hero and a protecting *genius loci*.[46] Her contention may draw some support from Ammianus Marcellinus, who seemingly identifies Alexander's tomb with the shrine of Agathos Daimon; his unsympathetic bishop Georgios arrogantly threatens the magnificent temple to the 'Genius of the city,' scoffing 'How long will this tomb stand?'[47] At any rate, we find here a connection of some sort between the serpent rivers, the serpent spirit that protected Alexandria, and the figure of Alexander himself.

Agathos Daimon almost certainly came to be identified, similarly, with the Ptolemaic kings in turn. At any rate, his native-Egyptian counterpart, Šaï, is found identified with the kings in Egyptian-language evidence from the reigns of Polemies III, IV, IX and XII,[48] and the title bestowed upon Nero in a Greek inscription adjacent to the Sphinx, 'Agathos Daimon (Good Demon) of the Known World' almost certainly harks back to Ptolemaic usage.[49] One may wonder whether Ptolemy II Philadelphos had not already been claiming some sort of identity with Agathos Daimon for himself before his son. A fragment of Manetho's *History of Egypt*, which was compiled during his reign (282–246 BC), incorporates the principal Egyptian gods, some under their *interpretatio Graeca* names, into a mythical First Dynasty of pharaohs, and Agathos Daimon is already amongst them, in second place, no less: Hephaestos, Agathos Daimon, Helios, Kronos, Osiris and Isis, Typhon, Horos, Ares, Anoubis, Herakles, Apollo, Ammon, Tithoes, Sosos, Zeus.[50]

Ptolemy's birth myths legitimated him and his dynasty and enabled them to belong in a number of ways: he was the son of the best of Argead blood, Philip's, in a fashion that in part saluted and in part reversed Alexander's own birth mythology; he was the foster-son of Zeus himself; his eagle-nurse saluted Alexander's eagle-and-thunderbolt imagery; and he expanded Alexander's serpent imagery to embrace himself directly within it (the Harmatelia story) before then focusing it on the land that he himself was destined to rule, in the figures of the serpents of the Western Desert and in the figure of Agathos Daimon. Ptolemy's birth imagery entered into a retrospective dialogue with Alexander's.

Alexander was not in a position to object to the appropriation of his imagery, but Ptolemy's claims upon it were made in a competitive context; others wanted it too. Most notably, Seleukos claimed Alexander's eagle-and-thunderbolt imagery for the elaborately linked foundation myths of his great cities of Seleukeia in Pieria and Antioch. For expansive versions of these myths we depend principally on late sources, Libanios and John Malalas, though the coins seem to anchor their origins before 300 BC and to suggest that they were generated in the same age as Ptolemy's myths – and, therefore, seemingly in dialogue with them. Zeus brought him to Seleukeia with a thunderbolt, according to one account, or with an eagle carrying sacrificial meat, according to another. And Zeus brought him to Antioch by sending his eagle to seize flaming ox thighs (ersatz thunderbolts, of course) from a sacrifice, and depositing them at the site of the future city. And with these two thunderbolt-led foundations he metaphorically subdued the great Orontes river that connected them, the river that had, it was said, once been called the *Drakon*, the Serpent. It had originally been created when Zeus blasted the primeval serpent Typhon with his thunderbolt, and the latter had carved out its serpentine channel with his coils as he fled beneath the earth. Like Ptolemy's empire, Seleukos's too rested upon an appropriation of Alexander's eagle and serpent imagery, rearranged with a different shake of the kaleidoscope.[51]

## Notes

1 This piece originated in a 'Vorstudie' for Ogden 2011, and corresponds in part to 57–78 therein.

2 Collins 1997 offers a helpfully well-referenced discussion of Ptolemy's claim to be a son of Philip, but an impossible argument. Her case is compromised by, inter alia, an unsophisticated understanding of the workings and representations of illegitimacy in the Macedonian courts and the wider Greek world, for which see Ogden 1999 and 1997b respectively.

3 See in particular Strabo C814 (incorporating Kallisthenes *FGrH* 124 F14); Livy 26.19.7–8; Justin 11.11.2–13; Valerius Maximus 9.5.ext. 1; Curtius 4.7.8, 4.25–7; Plutarch *Alexander* 2–3 (incorporating Eratosthenes *FGrH* 241 F28), 27–8, 33 (incorporating Kallisthenes *FGrH* 124 F36); Tertullian *De anima* 46 (incorporating Ephoros *FGrH* 70 F217); Arrian *Anabasis* 3.3.1–2, 4.7.4, 4.10.1–2; Lucian *Dialogues of the dead* 13; Aulus Gellius 6.1.1, 13.4.2; Eunapios *FHG* iv p.24, F24; *Alexander Romance* 1.6–7. Discussion at Balsdon 1950; Bosworth 1977; Badian 1981, 1996; Kienast 1987–8; Anson 2003; Fredricksmeyer 2003; Chaniotis 2005b; Ogden 2011: 1–28.

4 Cf. Justin 13.4.10.

5 But Collins 1997: 448–50 believes that either Philadelphos or Euergetes is intended.

6 'Ptolemy' without patronymic at:*SEG* ix.1 (constitution of Cyrene, 321 BC); *OGIS* 5 lines 9. 29 and 59 (311 BC), *OGIS* 6 line 6 (311 BC); *Syll.*³ 314 (308–307 BC). By contrast, the patronymic is prominent in the literary tradition and not least Arrian (from the opening phrase of the *Anabasis* onwards). See Collins 1997: 442, 445–7.

7 Errington 1990: 265n6: Ἡρακλείδας Ἀργεάδας.

8 Satyros *FGrH* 631 F1 = F27 Kumaniecki: the line of descent is Amyntas I, Bokros, Meleager, Arsinoë. Cf. Beloch 1912–27:iv.2 177; Edson 1934: 224; Fraser 1972: II.123; Brunt 1976–83: I:478; Errington 1976: 155; Heckel 1992: 222; Bingen 2007: 18. Tarn 1933 is too speculative to take seriously.

9 Herodotos 6.61–9.

10 Cf. also the Armenian version, §269 Wolohojian. Bouché-Leclerq 1903–7: I.4n1 wondered whether a further trace of the tradition that Ptolemy was a son of Philip might be found in Arrian's passing reference at *Anabasis* 1.14.6 to a 'Ptolemy, son of Philip' commanding the cavalry at the Granicus. Had Arrian's source at this point (Timagenes?) identified the future Soter in this way, without any indication of controversy, and so misled Arrian into thinking that this Ptolemy was being identified as the son of a common Philip and so into differentiating him from Soter? But it is hard to believe that Arrian, who depended so heavily on Soter's own history, could have made such a gross error in relation

to his role in such in a key battle. For this Ptolemy, son of a common Philip, see Berve 1926: no. 671 and Heckel 2006: 234 (Ptolemy [2]).

11 [Lucian] *Long-lived Men* 12; Edson 1934: 225; Brunt 1976–83: I.478–9; Heckel (1992: 222) dismisses this birthdate for Ptolemy, preferring to see him as a coeval of Alexander. Quainter still is Chugg's repeated insistence on the actuality of this claim (2006: 198–9, etc.).

12 For the context of the claim that Ptolemy I was a son of Philip II, see Berve 1922: II.330 no. 668; Errington 1976: 155–6; Heckel 1992: 222; and Collins 1997: 437, with further citations.

13 Collins 1997: 462 thinks the image of the shield made appeal to Alexander's own shield of Athena, mentioned at Diodoros 17.18.1,'21.2, 17.98.2–17.99.4; Curtius 9.4.26–9.5.18; Plutarch *Moralia* 327b; Arrian *Anabasis* 1.11.7–8, 6.9.3, 6.10.1–2, 6.11.1. See Fraser 1972: II.295n275 for the rejection of a notion that the shield may have found illustration on the coins of Corone.

14 For the combination of protective shield and supernatural eagle, cf. also the myth of Aristomenes of Messene. When thrown thrown into the Kaiadas crevasse by the Spartans he was seemingly saved by the eagle blazon on his shield, which came to life and bore him gently to the ground: Pausanias 4.18.4–4.19.1; discussion at Ogden 2004: 70–4 and Vincent 2007.

15 Oedipus: Sophokles *Oedipus Tyrannus*. Cypselus: Herodotos 5.92. Agathokles: Diodoros 19.2. Battus: Herodotos 4.150–7. Cf. Ogden 1997a passim and, for the Hellenistic monarchs in particular, Préaux (1978: I.192–4), oddly making no mention of either Ptolemy or Seleukos! Other motifs from Herodotos's rich tale of Kypselos recur in the tale of Pyrrhos's childhood, as recounted at Plutarch *Pyrrhus* 3. Just as the natural smile of baby Kypselos saves him by melting the heart of his executioners, so the child's play of baby Pyrrhos persuades the Illyrian king Glaukias, with whom he has been deposited in refuge, not to give him up to Cassander, and to certain death.

16 Moses: Exodus 2.1–11. Romulus: Livy 1.4. Cyrus: Herodotos 1.107–30.

17 Mørkholm 1991: figs. 5–6 (cf. also fig. 202); le Rider 1996: plate 9, nos. 10, 11, and 12 (the reverse is paired with obverses of both Zeus's head and of Alexander's). Discussion at Mørkholm 1991: 42; le Rider 1996: 91–4; le Bohec 2002: 43. [Hesiod] *Shield* 135.

18 Tertullian *De anima* 46, incorporating Ephoros *FGrH* 70 F217. *Terminus ante* for Ephoros's work: Barber 1935:12–13.

19 Kallisthenes *FGrH* 124 F40 (at Polybios 12.12b3); cf. Stewart 1993: 97 and 193.

20 Mørkholm 1991: fig. 44; Stewart 1993: 194, 201–6, 433, with figs. 68–9; they were perhaps intended as '5 shekel' pieces.

21 Cicero *Verrines* 4.60; Pliny *Natural History* 35.92; Plutarch *Alexander* 4, *Moralia* 335a, 360d; Stewart 1993: 191–209, 363–4 (192 for the dating of the picture); and le Bohec 2002: 43.

22  St Petersburg, Hermitage inv. no. 609; see discussion and references at Stewart
1993: 199–201 and 436, with illustrations at figs. 66–7 and colour fig. 8a.
Alternatively, Apelles's picture may be reflected in a fresco in the House of the
Vettii in Pompeii: see Stewart 1993: 198–9 and fig. 65.

23  Mørkholm 1991: figs. 90–2; cf. also figs. 93–5; and Stewart 1993: figs. 76, 77–9
and colour plate 8c for the same Athena image from other mints or from a
slightly later period.

24  We may think of Phidias's Athena Parthenos statue (emphatically saluted in the
Alexandrian Alexander Aigiochos statue of ca 320–300), in which the goddess
protects with her shield the serpent Ericthonios.

25  Mørkholm 1991: figs. 97–100, 127 (cf. 485).

26  Ptolemy II: Mørkholm 1991: figs. 284–6, 291–3, 296, 300–4, 306 (302 has a
wonderful *pair* of eagles perched on the thunderbolt); cf. also fig. 494. Ptolemy
III: figs. 309–10, 312, 314–15. Ptolemy IV: figs. 317–18. Ptolemy V: figs. 319, 321,
324–6, 328. Cleopatra Thea: fig. 635.

27  Huss 2001: 90.

28  Theokritos *Idylls* 17.71–3. For the date, Hunter 2003: 3–7. The same poem,
131–4, projects Philadelphos himself as a new Zeus by comparing his marriage
to his full sister Arsinoë II to that between Zeus and Hera; cf. also *SH* 961, embracing Arsinoë and Hera in the language of weddings. Discussion at Gow 1952:
II.345–6; Ogden 1999: 79; Hunter 2003: 192–3.

29  Fraser 1972: I.208, describing the eagle as 'very Ptolemaic.'

30  *Alexander Romance* 1.10 (Armenian at §21 Wolohojian; β) and 3.33 (β; however, Kroll 1926 seems to think that this material antedated the A text, even
though omitted by it). Dating of the *Alexander Romance* tradition: Stoneman
2008: 6–26.

31  Cerfaux and Tondriau 1957: 189–208; Taeger 1957: I.287–309; Fraser 1972:
I.216–19; Préaux 1978: I.256–7; Koenen 1993: 50–66; Samuel 1993: 181–3,
with response by Delia at 196–200; Dunand 2007: 261–2. Cf., more generally,
Hazzard 2000.

32  Memnon *FGrH* 434 F8. Pausanias 1.16.2 (τολμῆσαι πρόχειρος) and 10.19.7
(διὰ τὸ ἄγαν τολμηρόν). The surname Keraunos (Κεραυνός) is also attested at
Trogus *Prologues* 17 and 24 and Plutarch *Pyrrhos* 22. The notion that the surname might salute Zeus's thunderbolt, or even the eagle that was the traditional
bearer of Zeus's thunderbolt, was suggested by Mahaffy (1895: 105n2) and
treated at least half-seriously by Bouché-Leclerq (1903–7: I.95n2. For Ptolemy
Keraunos, see above all Heinen 1972; Hammond and Walbank 1988: 243–9,
252–3; Collins 1997: 464–73; Ogden 1999: 68–73; Huss 2001: 254–60.

33  See the references in note 3 above.

34  The case is laid out in Ogden 2011: 29–56. For Zeus Meilichios, see especially
Mitropoulou 1977: 97–155 and Jameson, Jordan, and Kotansky 1993: 81–103

(cf. 137–41). The former offers copious illustrations of the god, but his angui-form representations are most comprehensively listed at Jameson, Jordan, and Kotansky 1993: 94–5, with references back to their catalogue at 81–91. See also Cook 1914–40: II.1091–1160. For the intriguing possibility that there was a colossal statue of this god in the Hellenistic temple of Eukleia at Aegae, see Saatsoglou-Paliadeli 1991: 12–21.

35 Diodoros 17.103.4–8; Curtius 9.8.22–8. Cf. also Strabo C723; Justin 12.10.2–3; and Orosius 3.19.11. Date of Kleitarchos: Heckel 2006: 237.

36 Strabo C814 = Kallisthenes *FGrH* 124 F14; Diodoros 17.49.5; Curtius 4.7.15; Plutarch *Alexander* 27, *Itinerarium* 21 (crows, but acknowledging the variant of serpents).

37 For other aspects of Alexandrian foundation mythology, see Andrew Erskine's piece in this volume.

38 *Alexander Romance* 1.31.7 (A). For Agathos Daimon in this context, see above all Fraser 1972: I.209–11; Dunand 1969, 1981, with bibliography; and Pietrzykowski 1978.

39 The text is heavily corrupt and disputable throughout: see Fraser 1972: II.356n162–3. Stoneman (1994 and 2007: 533) intriguingly contrasts the subsequent Christian tale of [Epiphanios] 61.11–12, in accordance with which Alexander had the mortal remains of Jeremiah transported to Alexandria, with the result that all serpents were banished from the city.

40 *P.Oxy.* 2332 lines 51–3: κατά τε ὁ ἀγαθὸς / δαίμων καταλείψει τὴν κτιζομένην πόλειν καὶ ἀ/πελεύσεται εἰς τὴν θεοτόκον Μέμφειν καὶ ἐξερημώσηται. For this text, see Tarn 1928: 215; Fraser 1972: I.683–4.

41 Stewart 1993: 246–53, 421–2, with figs. 82–3.

42 Louvre, Collection Lambros-Dattari; cf. Schwarzenberg 1976: 235 with fig. 8; Stewart 1993: 247; Stoneman 2007: 533.

43 Cf. Stewart 1993: 248–50.

44 For Erichthonios-Erechtheus, see Kron 1988.

45 *Alexander Romance* 1.32.11 (A): καὶ θυσία τελεῖται αὐτῷ τῷ ἥρωι <ὡς ὀφιογενεῖ>, as reconstituted by Kroll. The Armenian translation: §87 Wolohojian. The signifiance of *višap*: Taylor 1930: 376–7.

46 Taylor 1930: 376–7; Virgil *Aeneid* 5.84–103 (*anguis, serpens, genius loci*). Taylor speculated further that Ptolemy Soter may similarly have had himself identified, qua founding hero, with Agathos Daimon, in the city he built and named after himself, Ptolemais. The Egyptian name for the city was Psoi, which she read as a variant of Šaï. However, the latter claim no longer seems tenable: Visser 1938: 5–7 and 65–6; Fraser 1972: II.356–6n164; Eggermont 1975: 114n454; Quaegebeur 1975: 111.

47 Ammianus Marcellinus 22.16.15. See Fraser 1972: II.356–7n164; and Saunders 2006: 100–1.

48 Evidence and discussion at Quaegebeur 1975: 111–13.
49 *OGIS* ii 666 lines 3–4: ἀγαθὸς δαίμων τῆς οἰκουμένης; Quaegebeur 1975: 113, 170.
50 Manetho *FGrH* 609 F3; cf. Quaegebeur 1975: 174–5.
51 Strabo C750–1; Appian *Syrian Wars* 299; Libanius *Orations* 11.85–8 (Förster i.2 pp. 464–5); John Malalas *Chronicle* 198–200 Dindorf. During Seleukos's reign Antioch issued coins decorated with a Zeus-head on the obverse and a thunderbolt on the reverse (Mørkholm 1991: fig. 153, ca 300–286 BC), whilst Seleukeia issued coins decorated with a Zeus-head on the obverse and an eagle-winged thunderbolt on the reverse (Newell 1941: plate xv nos. 5–10, 12–18; Mørkholm 1991: fig. 154; Houghton and Lorber 2002: II.figs. 32–3, ca 290–80 BC). More detailed discussion of this material in Ogden 2011: 79–110.

# 12

# 'Alexandrianism' Again: Regionalism, Alexandria, and Aesthetics

## CRAIG I. HARDIMAN

It has been a long-held belief on the part of many classical art historians that the diversity that so characterizes the art and aesthetic of the Hellenistic period can be analysed by examining certain regions of production that are the prime champions of any given element of a panhellenic 'style.' Thus, while one can understand the multiplicity of styles under the umbrella term 'Hellenistic' (in fact, this multiplicity defines Hellenistic style), any one style was often seen as emanating from one particular region. This was, perhaps, most famously espoused in the late nineteenth century when Heinrich Brunn postulated a Pergamene school of sculpture after his 'discovery' of the *Lesser Attalid Dedication* from the Athenian Acropolis that also encompassed the *Capitoline* and *Ludovisi Gauls* and the *Altar of Zeus*. Stylistically, this Pergamene School came to be the prime exponent of the 'Baroque' style of Hellenistic art, so called as it looked like material produced during the Baroque phase of the Italian Renaissance. In time, this link became so explicit that the scholarship on the *Altar*, and by association similar-looking pieces, would describe its sculptural style as either 'High Baroque' or 'High Pergamene' interchangeably.[1]

Although aspects of such a 'regional' approach to the material remains were surely tied to the archaeological record, over time this method of categorization became an entrenched interpretive tool and means through which one should understand the art of the period. Though this methodology had been employed by early scholars such as Gerhard Krahmer (1924) and Rhys Carpenter (1960), it was when Margarete Bieber produced her landmark book *Sculpture in the Hellenistic Age* (1961) that she became the de facto source among English scholars and students for the use of regionalism as a way of viewing the art of the period. Although she notes that 'it is astonishing how homogeneous Hellenistic art is in comparison to Classical art,' she goes on to say: 'On the other hand, it has till now not been possible to attribute definite styles to the different schools of artists working in Pergamon, Antioch, Alexandria, the island of Rhodes and other important centres of Hellenistic art.'[2] Implicit in this statement, of course, is the notion that each of these individual centres had a distinctive and unique style of art, that this style was codified into something as formal and didactic as a 'school,' and that the examination of these centres as distinct entities would provide the best method for evaluating the art of the period. Thus her book is carefully structured to present chapters that not only examine questions of style, but also chapters that delve into the prime centres of Hellenistic art as she saw them, namely, Alexandria, Priene, Pergamon, and Rhodes. While in these initial stages of investigation it may have been as valuable an analytic method as any other, the unfortunate outgrowth of this championing of the regional has been to entrench the notion that any individual centre had an art that was unique in the face of the rest of the Hellenistic world, that the characteristics of this style can be carefully elucidated, and that this individuality points to a conscious development of 'style' that could only be the outgrowth of something as formal as a school.[3]

The importance of Bieber's work was to have a lasting effect on the field of sculptural studies and led to many adopting her view of regionalism as being a prime characteristic of the Hellenistic age.[4] This fact was made fully tangible by a conference held in Athens in 1996 that specifically dealt with the topic of regional schools in Hellenistic sculpture that, while addressing some of the underlying assumptions of regionalism, took as its starting point attempts to define and understand regionalism in the Hellenistic period more fully.[5] What became apparent in much of the scholarship, however, is that while one can use geographical delineations in the study of ancient art, as it makes both the size and the focus of one's research manageable, to then make the jump to stylistic notions of regionalism is fraught with problems and, in general, does not hold under the light of further investigation.[6] Thus, while stylistic analysis was (and is) an investigative tool by which scholars attempt to understand the chief artistic and cultural characteristics of a given region, attempts at limiting a particular style to a given period or region often illustrate that such a position cannot be maintained. Part of the difficulty lies in the nature of the evidence. Scholars have now come to identify many of the styles traditionally associated with the Hellenistic period as having Classical precedents, while styles or even motifs and subjects that have been associated with one particular area are now known throughout much of the Hellenistic world.[7] The other major difficulty lies in an understanding of just what the term 'style' means. Implicitly, notions of style have to centre around a series of identifiable characteristics or techniques that can be found in the artistic works of a given area and thus provide a homogeneous collectivity of characteristics.[8] Given the plurality of styles that existed in the Hellenistic period, simultaneously, diachronically, and geographically, it becomes difficult to assign specific, homogeneous styles to a given region to the exclusion of others. Thus it is that many scholars have attempted to describe the style of a given region as 'eclectic' in an attempt to circumvent the issue of homogeneity, but this becomes an exercise in obfuscation as eclecticism runs counter to the notion of specificity.[9] Eclecticism may reflect the plurality of styles that was the *koine* of Hellenistic artistic aesthetics, but its application as a descriptive term of a style in art illustrates the lengths to which some scholars will attempt to fit 'square' evidence into 'round' categorization schemes.

## An Alexandrian Style?

Such categorization schemes are even more difficult to come to terms with at a site like Hellenistic Alexandria, given the paucity of evidence owing to the vagaries of time and minimal excavations. This lack of excavation, due to reasons both man made and natural, has left scholars in the dubious position of coming to conclusions about an Alexandrian 'style' through the literary, epigraphical, and papyrological records and by making inferences from the very few material remains that have been unearthed.[10] Such a situation, however, can, and in some cases has, led to a number of models and classification schemes that in reality become exercises *ex silentio*. Much more is known of the literary situation at Alexandria and so this situation can be used in an attempt to make parallel arguments or speculations about the city's artistic production. The difficulty of this posture lies in assumptions regarding not only the links between the literary and artistic models, but an assumption as to the uniqueness of the literary model in the first place. In addition, scholars can also use those few remains we have to make grandiose pronouncements about the corpus of Alexandrian art on the whole. While not suggesting that scholars throw up their hands in exasperation, it can be seen how one can make conclusions about Alexandrian art and its style based on a house of cards.[11]

This difficulty is clearly visible in the useful history of the scholarship on Alexandrian style that Andrew Stewart (1996: 231) provided to ask his question: 'is an Alexandrian style a mirage?' In his summary, Stewart shows the two distinct traditions within the scholarship. The more prevalent and older suggests that there is indeed a specific Alexandrian style with definitive characteristics, while the less prevalent and newer tradition suggests that a determination of an all-encompassing style is impossible to achieve. Throughout the nineteenth century, under the auspices of such scholars as Heinrich Brunn, the attitude had been that Alexandria had produced nothing comparable to the other great Hellenistic centres, primarily owing to the lack of available quality stone.[12] In 1885, however, under the influence of contemporary notions of regionalism, Theodor Schreiber decided to prove the critics wrong and advance the idea of Alexandria's originality in art, based primarily upon her literary achievements and the descriptions in ancient testimonia.[13] His analysis revolved around the 'cosmopolitan' aspects of Alexandrian culture, and he attempted to frame the art within this overall structure (Schreiber 1885: 391–9). Thus, while insisting on certain cosmopolitan aspects of the art, such as an Atticizing (i.e., Praxitelean) style, he then began to add more and more to the innovative Alexandrians over the next twenty-five years. Although there were those who both supported and opposed his thesis in general, it was not until Arnold Lawrence in 1925 that a systematic challenge to very notion of Alexandria's greatness in the field of sculpture was made.[14] His article, devoted to all of the arts but primarily sculpture, attempted to show how the style and quality of the work was actually inferior to that in existence elsewhere in the Mediterranean.[15] Though coloured by a general colonial attitude, Lawrence's thesis held sway until Frederik Poulsen (1939) refined it with a new chronology based on the partial separation of genres, though he too looked to Schreiber for Alexandria's importance in the field of the grotesque and in the all-pervasive influence of Praxiteles. Finally, Achille Adriani (1958) took up the colonialist attitudes of Lawrence, denying any interaction or cohesion between Greek and Egyptian elements, but he adopted Schreiber's overall attitude, ascribing many innovations to Alexandrian art. Indeed, he seems to find Alexandrian art to encompass the entire spectrum of artistic styles and so labels the material 'eclectic,' a descriptor that insinuates that the style could encompass anything.[16]

Such was the positivistic attitude by the middle of the twentieth century that Alexandria's 'style' could be all things to all people. By the end of the century, however, little had changed. Although there had been a switch from cultural imperialism to multiculturalism and an understanding of Egyptian influence in the art, the importance of local styles and a sense of the regional importance of Alexandria still dominated.[17] Although there are still some dissenters, by and large the notion of pan-Alexandrianism is still alive and well, albeit in a lesser form than that of the early twentieth century that now takes a back seat to questions of genre, and it is couched in a cautious language that still champions the century-old notions of an Alexandrian style, full of Praxitelean *sfumato* and Egyptian elements.[18] Though different in form, the same questions persist, and despite changes in biases, investigative methodologies, and even in the corpus under study, many of the findings of scholars have simply become reworked or parallel versions of hundred-year-old arguments. It begs the question: if the history of Alexandrian scholarship is based on so many assumptions, can a re-evaluation of the notion of an Alexandrian style be used as a test case to bring to light the inherent problems with regional studies in Hellenistic art, especially sculpture?

As has been stated, the prime method through which scholars have attempted to get at a sense of Alexandrian art has been through an analysis of style. Within the confines of studies on sculpture, one of the prime characteristics that was determined to be Alexandrian was an emphasis on Praxitelean *sfumato*. Thought to relate to a style in the manner of the fourth-century Athenian sculptor, this *sfumato* consists of a soft and smooth treatment to the surface and overall modelling of a figure.[19] This particular analysis of the Alexandrian material can be traced as far back as Schreiber and was carried through to Bieber.[20] Even in more contemporary scholarship, this ideology finds echoes in scholars such as R.R.R. Smith, who, while rejecting *sfumato* specifically, describes the style of Ptolemaic portraiture as 'calm, impassive, mannered in form and refined in effect' (Classical) versus the 'baroque' (Hellenistic) stylings of the Antigonids and Seleukids.[21] While a certain softness in the modelling can be seen in such works as the *Statue of Isis* in the Uffizi (Bieber 1961: fig. 330), the *Bust of a Ptolemy* in Naples (fig. 12.1) and in much of the Ptolemaic female portraiture, there is nothing to suggest that this modelling was a primary characteristic of Alexandrian sculpture. This 'Praxitelean' style sits side by side with such 'Lysippan' features as the parted lip and the upturned head in works like the *Head of Ptolemy VI* in Alexandria (fig. 12.2) and in the *Gallic Head* from Gizeh (Bieber 1961: fig. 373).[22] Such characteristics suggest that Smith's dichotomy is not as clear as he puts forth. Indeed, while some non-Praxitelean styles made their way into Alexandrian art, so the 'Praxitelean' *sfumato* can be found in numerous Hellenistic pieces from around the Mediterranean.[23] It may be that Praxitelean *sfumato* was a preferred style at Alexandria – only future finds will tell – but that this style is found elsewhere in significant numbers suggests that questions of style cannot be broken down by region or even by time period. What scholars are becoming increasingly aware of is the notion of stylistic preference over a formalized structure of style consciousness. Though dealing with a different set of stylistic concerns, commentators such

12.1. Bust of a Ptolemy (II? III?), Naples, Museo Archeologico Nazionale, NM 6158.
Photograph © 2012 Vanni/Art Resource, NY.

12.2. Head of Ptolemy VI, Alexandria, Graeco-Roman Museum 24092.
Photograph © 2012 DeA Picture Library/Art Resource, NY.

as Brunilde Ridgway (1990: 374 and 2000: 268–88) and Mark Fullerton have suggested that once a style has come into existence, it becomes a general source for future artists to draw upon, as much or as little as they like.[24] Although the style may show itself in many examples, the most one can say is that the style existed, and perhaps was even a preferred style, in a given area, but arguments for generation quickly fall in light of evidence from the rest of the Hellenistic world.

This would also appear to be the case for genre pieces as well. As an outgrowth of Schreiber's attitudes regarding the cosmopolitan qualities of Alexandria, it has been suggested that such tastes for the multiple were characteristic of the city's art as well. Such subject matter as children, dwarves, non-Greek racial types, grotesques, and deformed individuals would fit this notion of plurality, and all were types not usually associated with Classical Greek art.[25] Relying heavily on some rather spurious interpretations of Hellenistic social, literary, and ethnographic studies, it was thought that these types were first produced in Alexandria and then spread to the rest of the Hellenistic world owing to their inventiveness.[26] What scholars have since shown is that such genre scenes were in fact popular throughout the Hellenistic world, and evidence such as the material recovered from the Mahdia wreck illustrates that there was likely a brisk trade in such material, suggesting a common language of experience, for the intended buyers would have had to understand the 'Alexandrianism' behind such figures. While individual works by scholars have contributed much to our understanding of genres within the Hellenistic period, any privileging of Alexandria's place within the tradition is complicated by the lack of evidence, the preponderance of the material elsewhere, and the assigning of unattributed works to Alexandria based on style.[27] John Pollitt most likely comes closest to the mark when he suggests that Alexandria may have played an important role in genre figures, though not a generative one.[28]

Although such genre scenes fall into the same category as the *sfumato* with regard to their supposed impact upon an Alexandrian style, the one aspect of this style that would seem to properly be local would be any native Egyptian elements that make up a fusion of Graeco-Egyptian styles. Begun with Lawrence, who saw the final phase of a declining Ptolemaic art as a 'revival in native sculpture,' and formalized by Ibrahim Noshy, who believed that Egyptian elements overtook the Greek on account of intermarriage, this notion did not last overly long as by the time of Adriani, most scholars saw the art of Ptolemaic Egypt as seminally Greek with little interaction with native Egyptian work.[29] By the 1980s a change had occurred, however, and scholars such as Helmut Kyrieleis and Günter Grimm saw more and more Egyptian influence in the material of the period, and Egyptologists began to appropriate some of the Ptolemaic material as solely native.[30] So the state of scholarship now suggests that there was indeed a strong element of native Egyptian styles incorporated into Ptolemaic art, but as one examines the evidence, what seems to emerge is more a case that the two styles coexisted without any deep interaction.

Portraits such as that of *Arsinoë II* in the Vatican (fig. 12.3, middle figure) and the *Statue of a Princess as Isis* in the Glyptothek (Bieber 1961: fig. 350) clearly show attempts to depict the ruling family in an Egyptian style through a purely native vocabulary. These pieces contain no Greek elements in the figures and can be viewed as wholesale attempts to Egyptianize (i.e., legitimize) the ruling family to the native population in a familiar form. These statues then sit side by side with material that is stylistically, in the main, Greek. Portraits of *Ptolemy I* (fig. 12.4), *Ptolemy VI* (fig. 12.5), *Ptolemaic Queen* (fig. 12.6), in addition to numerous coin portraits and statues of divinities, all show a marked preference for sculpture created in a thoroughly Greek vocabulary. There is nothing Egyptian at all about these works. There are occasions when a combination of the two styles can be observed, but when used the Egyptian elements tend to be iconographic alone. A ruler may be presented with a completely Greek portrait type but wearing Egyptian headgear, as in the *Head of Ptolemy VI* (fig. 12.5) or the portrait of a Ptolemaic queen in Rome (fig. 12.7). When one can compare two heads of the same ruler, as in the heads of *Ptolemy VIII*, the faces themselves show very little differentiation in style (though there is some in the modelling of the cheeks) and only the crown of Upper Egypt marks the primary difference (fig. 12.8).[31] In the end, there seems to have been no Graeco-Egyptian style, or even a mixture on any serious scale between the two styles; there was simply a Greek and an Egyptian style that coexisted and that, on occasion, intruded into the other with its own iconography.[32]

One final element has often been discussed as being exemplary of the Alexandrian style in sculpture – allegory. Allegory, symbolism, and metaphor all bore rich fruit in the Hellenistic period, but, like the numerous styles that pervade the art of this time, these elements too have a Panhellenic disbursement both across geographic regions and across time. Numerous monographs and studies have taken up this idea in Hellenistic art and placed this within the overall cultural context of the age.[33] While allegory and personification are hallmarks of Greek art of many ages, an increase in appreciation for the allegorical seems to come to the fore in the fourth century, possibly allied to changes in traditional religious beliefs and cultural-political outlooks.[34] The *Eirene with Baby Ploutos* by Kephisodotos would be a prime example, as would the numerous personifications of abstract ideas like Tyche and Kairos that became popular over the course of the fourth century.[35] It is with the advent of Alexander that such allegorical practices are first attached to a specific individual, however, when he had himself portrayed with the attributes of Zeus-Ammon and Herakles on coinage and in the image of Zeus

12.3. Statue inscribed for Arsinoë II, Vatican, Rome, Museo Gregoriano Egizio 22682.
Photograph © 2012 Scala/Art Resource.

12.4. Head of Ptolemy I, Paris, Musée du Louvre, Ma 849.
Photograph © 2012 Réunion des Musées Nationaux/Art Resource, NY.

12.5. Head of Ptolemy VI, Alexandria, Graeco-Roman Museum 3357.
Photograph © 2012 DeA Picture Library/Art Resource, NY.

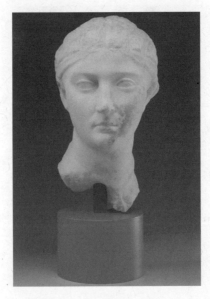

12.6. Head of a Ptolemaic Queen (Arisnoë III?), Boston, Museum of Fine Arts, Henry
and Lillie Pierce Fund 01.8207. Photograph © 2012 Museum of Fine Arts, Boston.

12.7. Head of a Ptolemaic Queen, Rome, Musei Capitolini, 354.
Photograph © 2012 Alinari/Art Resource, NY.

12.8. Head of Ptolemy VIII, Brussels, Musées Royaux d'Art et d'Histoire, E1839.
Photograph © 2012 Musées Royaux d'Art et d'Histoire (Photothèque), Brussels.

in the famed portrait by Apelles. It is therefore not surprising that personal allegory comes into the art of his followers soon after. While the Ptolemies may have been aided by an Egyptian tradition that had long seen its rulers as allegorical representations of Horos, Osiris, and Isis, coin portraits of Demetrios Poliorketes and Seleukos I show the rulers wearing the horns of Poseidon Taureos, and Demetrios may have commissioned a sculpture of himself as Poseidon.[36] The pride of place for Alexandrian art in the field of allusion likely derives from the *Tazza Farnese*, a justly famous Ptolemiac sardonyx cameo bowl once in the collection of Lorenzo de'Medici. An allegorical work with historical overtones that illustrates the fertility of the Nile, this

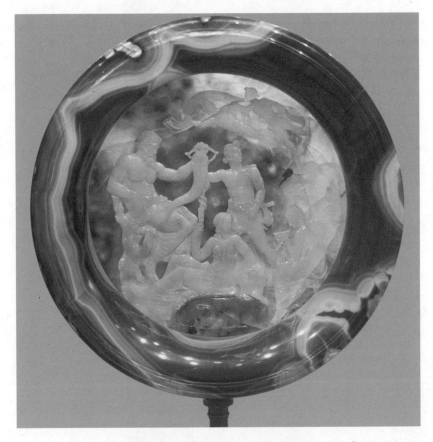

12.9. Tazza Farnese, Naples, Museo Archeologico Nazionale.
Photograph © 2012 Vanni/Art Resource, NY.

piece reflects figural types and allegorical representations that, as was shown in sculpture, are fully in line with the rest of the art of the period (fig. 12.9).[37]

It is clear that allusive monuments like the *Tychaion* and works like the *Tazza Farnese* point to a strong tradition at Alexandria, but like most elements of the Alexandrian style, this characteristic is well within the overall framework of Hellenistic aesthetics and artistic practices. It may be that a combination of such material, the literary record, and the long tradition in Egypt of allusive representations in art provide a skewed view of the place of Alexandria within the overall tradition of allusion in Hellenistic art.[38] If the case is put forward for the particular importance of Alexandrian art in the field of allusion and that this is closely tied to the poetry and general literary output produced in Ptolemaic Alexandria, then it is this final issue that must be addressed.

## Alexandrianism and Aesthetics

It is very easy, and in many ways very appropriate, to link the literary culture of Alexandria to broader issues in Hellenistic art. Barbara Fowler (1989) did just this when she analysed Hellenistic poetry and its subjects and compared them to genre art of the period to illustrate similar interests in notions like realism, the grotesque, and the erotic. One can even examine the very dense and learned poetry of writers like Kallimachos and Apollonios and conclude that they seem to reflect a general love of allegory in the period, be it literary or artistic. Such questions revolving around matters of style and taste work very well when one examines the whole of Hellenistic culture and the numerous styles and tastes of the period. It is no wonder that if one can determine an artistic *koine* (or perhaps more appropriately *koinai*), then one should see such cultural reflections in the writing of the period as well. The difficulty in using the literary material specifically from Alexandria comes to the fore, however, when one tries to extrapolate an Alexandrian context within the broader Hellenistic context. A close examination reveals how special the situation at Alexandria is, how little is known about literary traditions outside of the city, and how dangerous it is to draw parallels to the artistic realm when philologists cannot fully agree on the model that the city presents. I shall not delve into the generalities of Hellenistic literary aesthetics or the specifics of any author per se, but rather illustrate the difficulties of using the Alexandrian literary situation as a model on which to graft a parallel and allied Alexandrian artistic 'style.'[39]

The overriding image that dominates all discussions of an Alexandrian literary culture is that of the Mouseion. Though not unique in the Hellenistic world, the Ptolemies attempted to gather the best scholars, poets, and collections of material for their 'cage of the Muses' with a voracity to match no other ruling house.[40] Here the best minds of the age came to sit in a building devoted to their craft and debate the scholarly issues of the day. To this end the great Library that housed all of the source material that these literati would need was created in order to facilitate the scholarly activities that formed the raison d'être of the institution.[41] It has thus become standard to associate this new intellectual activity with Alexandria, even if this basic scholarly function may have been a direct outgrowth of critical assessments carried out by Aristotle and his students at the Lykeion and owes its basic form to the late fourth-century scholar-poet Philitas of Kos.[42] To be sure, the list of famous intellectuals and scholar-poets that came out of Hellenistic Alexandria is remarkable, but as with the art of Alexandria, it is very difficult to surmise how much of what was done in the Mouseion was unique to the city itself.

Whether Athenian or Koan, it does seem clear that the initial steps of the type of critical enquiry that became the hallmark of the Alexandrians actually began in the mid-to late fourth century and outside of Egypt proper. Whether altruistic or not, Ptolemy I seems to have been instrumental in personally fostering the type of scholarship in which Philitas was engaged and then in creating the Mouseion in order to promote and further this activity. Ptolemy I chose Philitas to tutor his son, the future Ptolemy II, who was born on Kos, and when done, Philitas's pupil Zenodotos took over the duties. While in Alexandria and tutoring both Ptolemy II and Arsinoë II, Zenodotos seems to have been the first to actively initiate Homeric studies that emphasized editorial and lexicographic methodologies.[43] With this new spirit of investigation and critical appraisal, the Mouseion became something of a community in which those scholars interested in such investigation could gather, and the Library was created as an attachment to serve as an instrument of research.[44] Indeed, such scholars came as part of the waves of new immigrants to the city and helped foster this 'new intellectualism' for several generations. These new scholars came from several areas, but especially from the south-eastern Greek world, places such as Kos, Samos, Kolophon, and Kilicia. The implication is that perhaps this type of scholarship was not an Alexandrian invention but was already 'in the air' in the later part of the fourth century, and that the Mouseion helped to nurture an approach or methodology to literature and scholarship that may have become dominant at Alexandria, but which certainly was not the sole provenance of the city.[45]

This new literary style, then, seemingly took its form from a method of enquiry into the world popularized by Aristotle where investigation was the key and the Library allowed for serious examination and analysis of previous models, hence the so-called bookishness of the age.[46] This methodology had its greatest impact upon the scholarship of the period, where categorization schemata like Kallimachos's *Pinakes* became popular, as did critical analysis evidenced by the numerous editions of a 'true' Homer, but it is within the field of the poetic arts that this methodology has held the greatest attention. More so than in previous ages, the style of the poetry produced during this period has been described as learned and recherché. Authors now had texts before them to consult and so could craft their works in a style that was more consciously 'constructed' than ever before. Authors could refer to numerous versions of a given text, to both well-known and obscure versions of a myth and to lesser known authors in order to create poems that were, in the depth of sources examined, denser than the poetry of previous generations. While this type of poetry was certainly new with regard to how far it took the notion of source use, it is also clear that this type of retrospection on the part of authors seems to have been an intrinsic element in the mindset of Greek writers.[47] The novelty at Alexandria, however, seems to have been the lengths to which such allusion was carried out, owing most likely to the availability of source material, and the connection of such poetic undertakings with the concurrent notion of scholarly criticism. Even then, the notion does not seem to have belonged to Alexandria alone, as Pergamon later set up a system that was very similar.

In an attempt to claim a complete Hellenic past, the Attalids themselves created a library, likely on the Alexandrian model, in order to establish a centre for literary debate and creation. Unlike Alexandria, the library at Pergamon did not attract the cream of Panhellenistic poets and writers, but instead drew scholars that seem to have concentrated heavily on matters philosophical, something that was surprisingly lacking at Alexandria. Being primarily Stoics and not Peripatetics, the scholars who came to Pergamon seem to have been less interested in the creation of poetry and its scholarly criticism, but they still had an intense interest in matters philological.[48] 'Grammar,' in its loosest sense, was a common link between the two, a shared heritage from Aristotle's interest in etymology and language perhaps, though the forms of each school's grammatical analysis differed.[49] At Alexandria, the emphasis seems to have been a systematic approach to matters grammatical and textual that relied upon an *ekdosis*, loosely, a critical edition of a text.[50] It seems that the Alexandrian scholars always saw their work as *grammatikoi* in relation to their earliest, Peripatetic work as *kritikoi*, even though they abandoned this earlier term for the newer *grammatikoi*[51] At Pergamon, however, there seems to have been no direct concern for the production of critical editions of texts, and their own sense of the term *grammatikoi* had a more general and holistic meaning. The first leader of the library, Krates of Mallos, was more concerned with allegory in his interpretations of texts and was seemingly opposed to Alexandrian techniques, preferring to find 'correct' Greek through anomaly, rather than analogy. Although there do seem to be distinct differences between the two schools, both seem to have taken critical analysis of matters literary as their starting point, the one simply doing so through a Peripatetic lens and the other through a Stoic one.[52]

Though there was a difference in execution, the function of the two libraries was largely similar. The major distinction between the two schools, however, seems to have been with regard to their external referents and not with their antecedents. One element within the tradition and creation of the Library and with its scholarly concerns that has achieved little attention is the very nature of the self-fashioning that it engenders. To an extent this is a natural outgrowth of retrospection, whether poetic or critical, as one both defines and becomes defined by the author quoted or studied, but the nature of the self-fashioning can still differ.[53] Though the two schools shared a common heritage but differed in their theoretical approaches and philosophical applications, it is important to keep in mind that Alexandria was starting fresh. Literary centres had existed prior to her founding, but the Library at Alexandria was trying to place itself within a tradition in a new manner, perhaps using the Lykeion as the model. The idea may have been borrowed, but the city seems to have attempted to carve out its own niche in the intellectual history of the Hellenic community by collecting the best material and brightest minds to create a locus for intellectual activity. Pergamon, however, not only had the benefit of using Alexandria as a model, but the city seems to have been preoccupied not with carving its own niche, but becoming the second coming of Athens, something made manifest by the city's attempts to entice both the leaders of the Academy and the Lykeion before obtaining the leader of the Stoics.[54]

Such an analysis seems to fit well with much of the artistic program of the Attalids, which clearly echoes and invokes material at Athens. As such, it is the overall construction of Pergamon that seems so surprising, given that a single vision of its own making and representation may well have been the driving force behind much of its success and cultural definition. This would seem out of the norm in the Hellenistic Age, when such retrospection and cultural cohesion was not so overtly programmatic, yet contemporary scholars are quite content to say that there was no such thing as a Pergamene 'style.'[55] When Alexandria's own fashioning was much less programmatic, is it then fair to say that the Mouseion provides an adequate model on which to posit the notion of an Alexandrian style? Perhaps their lack of retrospection and allusion in their fashioning negated the possibility of any unity that would allow for a cohesive style to develop, but given that the scholarship produced at the Mouseion was full of allusion and retrospection, this lack of a programmatic direction for such material, other than the promotion and the celebration of the Ptolemaic regime, should illustrate how difficult it is to use the Mouseion and its culture as a model for artistic production. And yet it was Shreiber's devotion to the literary tradition of Alexandria and the belief that the city must have been as prolific and programmatic in its art through a shared 'artistic' aesthetic that started much of the problem. Underlying the whole notion of Alexandria as a supreme centre of artistic production is the fundamental notion of Alexandria as a construct through its literary heritage, a construct that still survives in large part to today.

## Conclusion

If the Mouseion now falls as a strong parallel for which one can attempt to formulate an Alexandrian style, it seems fairly clear that such a style becomes untenable. It does not appear in the artistic record, and the literary record shows that, while the city was unique in its execution, much of the material it produced was not an invention of the city itself. The difficulty with attempting to get at an Alexandrian style and precisely what that style would be lies primarily with the nature of the city itself and how odd it was. In general, Alexandria seems to have been a rather isolated and isolationist city, despite being an international Hellenic centre and important trade port. The city may have had a multicultural population, but it was in its day-to-day affairs Greek, with Greek institutions and cults that cut it off from the rest of Egypt, while the Mouseion kept the city looking inward, with foreign interaction limiting itself to conquest, trade, and occasional patronage. Perhaps this is why there was little integration in Ptolemaic art, as there seems to have been two sets of art – the one for Alexandria (mainly Greek in style) and the other for the country (mainly Egyptian in style). Of course, such a division would not have been absolute with material of both types found in both areas, but, like the portraiture discussed, the two seemed to live separately with little interaction. Even in Memphis, where there had been a tradition of attempting to fuse the Greek and Egyptian cultures into something more cohesive, an artistic style that was clearly in the main tradition of contemporary Greek art was in place. Recent population and ethnographic studies have suggested that there may have been a greater interaction between the Greek and Egyptian populations than previously thought, especially over time, but these interactions tend to be located outside of Alexandria proper and to suggest socio-cultural and not artistic integration.[56] This would also seem to be the suggestions of others in this volume, as both Andrew Erskine (chapter 10) and Daniel Ogden (chapter 11) have attempted to mediate aspects of use and integration between the Macedonian rulers and their Egyptian subjects.

While what has been presented is not necessarily new or unique in the history of Alexandrian studies, it should be reiterated, especially in light of much new material over recent years. The excavations at Alexandria, major exhibits that attempt a greater synthetic understanding of the material, and new studies that both show the differentiation between Egyptian and Greek art of the age yet still attempt an overarching stylistic framework unique to the city necessitate another look at the interpretive tradition. It is difficult to properly come to terms with Alexandria as an entity in the first place, let alone attempt any kind of analysis with regard to a style of art that was unique to the city. Among philologists it is a giant, owing to the city's rightful rank as a literary centre, its effusive fame in the literary tradition, and by the luck of climactic conditions that help to preserve texts. Among archaeologists it is still mostly unknown, though recent excavations have helped somewhat. Among art historians it is an enigma, frequently eliciting strong reactions both for and against its uniqueness in the hopes of recovering what was, one assumes, one of the great production centres of the Hellenistic era. If the city is so many things to so many people, it is no wonder that unification schemes, which ultimately is what an attempt at style definition is, usually fail. Perhaps Carol Mattusch (1998) can serve as a model in her rejection of the notion of Rhodes as a regional 'school,' seeing rather a series of production facilities that made the island simply a production centre. This may be the best way of thinking of Alexandria. Certainly, the historical record chronicles a great deal of material wealth that should be reflected in the physical record, but its paucity should make us appropriately cautious. In light of these issues, let us hope that entirely subjective and emotive responses such as 'Alexandrian style [is its] quality of craftsmanship' do not again bring back the 'dismal failure' of regionalism.[57]

## Notes

1  The older view that the two are synonymous is best summarized by Bieber (1961: 113–14). A more recent treatment of the topic is Ridgway (2000: 39–42). Both have extensive bibliographies. On Brunn, see Stewart 2005: 500–7.

2  Bieber 1961: 4–5.

3  This is an understandable by-product of the source material (epigraphical or literary) that often uses a locative to delineate one artist from another suggesting an importance of regionalism (Pliny, *NH* 34.37. with the artists of the Laokoön suggesting a Rhodian 'school'). Ridgway (1990: 6–11) notes the reservations of this methodology in light of conflicting literary testimonia and archaeological finds.

4  Two major examples that actively promote this 'geographical' approach would be Gualandi (1976) and Marcadé (1969).

5  See Palagia-Coulson 1998: v.

6  Thus while Geominy (1998: 66) finds certain technical differences among various Attic schools, those scholars focusing more on broader stylistic analyses (as opposed to the more specific focus on style after Lysippos alone by Palagia [1998: 22–3]), such as Sturgeon (1998: 10), von Prittwitz (1998: 73), Marszal (1998: 123), Mattusch (1998: 155–6), and Mark (1998: 162–3), find little evidence for styles that are unique to any given region or school. Although he deals with material at the end of the period that must also take Roman values into consideration, Smith (1998: 258–9) would seem one of the few dissenters.

7  For specific examples, see Marszal (1998) and his analysis of the 'Early Baroque' and Pergamon and Ridgway (2000: 39–47) for the Classical precedents for the Altar of Zeus. Indeed, it has become increasingly clear that much of what is Hellenistic in style took shape in the fourth century; see Ridway 1997: 364–71. One can clearly see in works like those of Ghisellini (1999) on Athena and the Ptolemaic court and of Himmelmann (1983) on Grotesques how subjects and genres thought to relate to one area have a much wider field of reference. See Stewart (1979: 17–21, 146–7) for a view of regionalism as a driving force.

8  For an overview of 'style' as an aesthetic notion, with a convenient appendix that details the evaluative process, see Lang (1987).

9  So Lawrence (1925: 181–5, 189) first used the term for early Alexandrian art, which was then followed by Adriani (1946: 7) and Bieber (1961: 89) and still holds sway in more current literature, as in Bonacasa (2004).

10  For a brief historical overview of these difficulties, with references, see Green 1996: 4–6, esp. n23); Empereur 1998.

11  Such a process is best exemplified by the attempt of many scholars to attribute many innovations in the field of Hellenistic painting to Alexandria. The ancient sources talk of Alexandria as a centre that created a possible abstract 'shorthand' (compendiaria – Petronius Sat. 2). Analysis of the surviving material shows that Egyptian painting of the period is well within the tradition of the rest of the Hellenistic world, and perhaps even conservative, in light of the finds from Macedonia. See Brown 1957: 1–2, 45–51, 83–95; and Pollitt 1986: 252–5. For the interpretation of compendiaria and the ancient sources, see Pollitt 1974: 327–34.

12  Brunn (1889: 595) was unquestioningly followed by Overbeck (1882: 199) and Mitchell (1883: 606) in their handbooks.

13  Schreiber (1885: 386). See Himmelmann's analysis (1983: 21).

14  Among his supporters were Courbaud (1899: 251) and Weissbach (1910: 9–15). His detractors included Gardner (1915: 475–6) in the main, while Wickhoff (1895: 17–20), Wace (1902–3: 228–9; 1903/4: 113–14), and Ruffer (1910: 174–5) objected respectively to the supposed Alexandrian supremacy in the field of painting and the genre of the grotesques. For a more extensive bibliography, see Stewart 1996: notes 9–13.

15 Lawrence (1925: 179–80): 'I have therefore collected what remains of Greco-Egyptian work in the round, and I wish people to look at the collection and see that it is bad.'

16 Adriani 1958: 231–2; Stewart 1996: 237–8.

17 Most notable in Kyrieleis (1975: 126–8) and Grimm (1981). See Stewart 1996: 238–9.

18 See Bonacasa 2004. Dissenting is Pollitt 1986: 250–259. On the cultural effects on the art, see Schmidt 2005a. Stewart (1996: 239) is perhaps overly cautious.

19 Though generally credited to Praxiteles, there are discrepancies of modelling throughout the sculptor's tentative corpus, and problems with the literary tradition and Roman copies may suggest that this *sfumato* cannot be directly associated with this sculptor. See Ajootian 1996: 109–29. Ashmole (1972: 147) is correct, however, when he recognizes a distinctive Praxitelean style, even if one cannot define it.

20 Schreiber (1885: 138) was the first to hint at the idea with notions of Atticism in the works of Alexandria, but it was Amelung (1897) who first attempted to see specifically 'lo sfumato delle forme' in his analysis. The difficulty lies in the fact that much of the material he studied was not actually from Alexandria and was identified as Alexandrian based on style alone. His view then entered the mainstream and in the middle of the century was supported by Adriani (1948: 14–19), whose views were then picked up and brought to a wider audience by Bieber.

21 See Smith (1996: 204), who sees these 'classical' forms in the portraiture of the Ptolemies, despite rejecting a Praxitelean *sfumato* in his survey (1991: 205). See Kyrieleis 1975; Smith 1988: 86–98.

22 Pollitt 1986: 251.

23 Most notably from the Agora in Athens and from Delos; see Stewart 1996: 239.

24 In general, see Fullerton 1996: 93; Fullerton 1998a: 70–1. The ideology is indebted to the work of Ridgway.

25 After Schreiber 1885: 394. See the summary by Noshy 1937: 97–101; and Bieber 1961: 95–7.

26 See Noshy 1937: 98.

27 Such is the case with Himmelmann and Kyrieleis. See Stewart 1996: 239–43.

28 Pollitt 1986: 252.

29 Lawrence 1925: 190; Noshy (1937: 146), who found this mixture distasteful; Adriani 1958: 231–2.

30 Kyrieleis 1975: 126–8; Grimm 1981 in general. For a discussion with references, see Stewart 1996: 236–9.

31 For an image of Ptolemy VIII without the crown, see Stanwick 2002: 229, figs. 258–9 (now in a private collection). This is *contra* Smith (1996: 208), who sees an Egyptian influence. The modelling is clearly different and may attest to an

individual style of an (Egyptian?) artist, but the overall physiognomy is the same with respect to the full cheeks, the pouting lips, and the large, close eyes. If this is a reflection of a Pharaonic form, then there is little to distinguish it from the Greek other than a general 'smoothing' of the features and poor workmanship.

32  Smith (1988: 87) sets up a convenient four-part schemata for the types of portraiture: (1) Purely Pharaonic, (2) More or Less Greek with Pharaonic Regalia, (3) Clearly Greek with Pharaonic Regalia, and (4) Purely Greek. The majority of works that survive are in the first two categories. Although some native elements such as material and statue type (with a backing pillar) can creep in, it is clear that there was little stylistic mingling between the Greek and the Egyptian typologies. See Smith (1988: 88–9) for a defence of the separateness of the two traditions, against Kyrieleis (1975: 129, 136). These parallel but separate traditions are generally supported by Stanwick (2002) and Ashton (2004).

33  Most notable are Hinks (1939); Onians (1979: esp. ch. 3); and Fowler (1989), whose work on aesthetics in poetry has, as a basic assumption, the allusive quality of the works, which she then relates to many of the Hellenistic genre sculptures; Stewart 1995.

34  In general, see Nilsson 1948.

35  On personifications in general, see Shapiro (1993). On the *Eirene*, see Schultz (2003). On *Tyche*, see Matheson et al. 1994; Palagia 1982.

36  See Pollitt (1986: 31–2) for Demetrios. See Smith (1991: 224) for Seleukos.

37  A convenient summary with references may be found in Pollitt (1986: 255–9). For the *Tazza Farnese*, see Plantzos (2007) with bibliography to previous interpretations. Bianchi (1996) makes it clear that he finds no evidence for a 'mixed school' of artistic styles in the minor arts. This is in line with other Alexandrian material, and it is suggested that the minor arts of Alexandria are distinguished by their quality and innovation of technique.

38  Thus all of Stewart's questions concerning future investigations of the material are valid (1996: 243), though one should add: 'Is there a significant difference between Alexandrian allusion and that from elsewhere?' As Mark Fullerton (personal communication) has suggested – allusion is essentially a literary device and Alexandria is a literary place and there may be no more to it than that.

39  For a recent summary, see Gutzwiller 2007.

40  For a convenient collection of the source material on the ancient Library at Alexandria, see Canfora 1990: 109–97.

41  Seminal to the understanding of the activities in the Library is Pfeiffer (1968: 95–151). See also Maehler (2004) and Schmidt (2005a: 268–70), for its role within Alexandria.

42  Although Pfeiffer's view (1968: 88–9) that the links between the traditions at the Lykeion and the work done at Alexandria were minimal and that the work

of the Alexandrians was new and unique is still widely popular, Richardson (1994: 14–17) has re-evaluated the evidence and suggests that the link is much stronger, especially in the fields of antiquarian studies, biography, and, in its broadest humanistic sense, grammar. On Philitas of Kos and his links to Alexandria, see Pfeiffer 1968: 88–93. In a list of famous Koans, Strabo (14.2.19 c657) refers to Philitas as poet and critic.

43 It is unknown whether Philitas tutored the future king on Kos or in Alexandria (Souda, s.v. Philitas), but Zenodotos does seem to have been the first of the new 'scholars' to have come to Alexandria and established and promulgated his analytical methodologies. See Pfeiffer 1968: 92–3.

44 Plutarch, *Mor*.13.1095d; Strabo, 17.1.8c793–794. Strabo refers to the museum as a σύνοδος, a 'community,' and because the Mouseion had a general religious character, as it was run by a priest nominated by the King, might even suggest the term 'commune.' See Pfeiffer 1968: 96–7; esp. 97n4.

45 In the first half of the third century, authors in the 'Alexandrian Style' included Alexander of Aetolis, Anyte of Tegea, Apollonios of Rhodes, Aratos of Soloi, Asklepiades of Samos, Kallimachos of Cyrene, Hedylos of Samos, Hermesianax of Kolophon, Herodas, Leonidas of Tarentum, Lykophron of Chalkis, Mnasalkes of Sikyon, Nikander of Kolophon, Nossis of Lokroi, Philitas of Kos, Poseidippos of Pella, Rhianos of Lebena, Simias of Rhodes, and Theokritos of Syracuse. These are but the best of the known authors (though often their poetry remains a mystery), whose origins illustrate the geographical diversity of the 'Alexandrian' style. Given this, coupled with the fact that not all of these went to Alexandria and that there is evidence for even fewer working at the Mouseion proper, the term 'Alexandrian' for the style of literature seems too narrow. See Cameron 1995: 24–5. Though some scholars have attempted to limit the term to the poetry of Kallimachos, his teachers, and his followers, this too would seem problematic. See Zanker 1987: 1–3.Thus the standard is now to describe the poetics as Hellenistic and not Alexandrian. On the history of the terms and their use to describe the poetry of the period, see Kassel 1987.

46 The starting points seem to have been the critical analysis of Aristotle and his followers, while the transmission may have as its link Theophrastos and Peripatetic philosophies in general. See Richardson 1994; Nagy 1998: 189–90, esp. n. 13. On the bookish culture, see Bing 1988: 15–48. Opposing is Cameron 1995: 33–8.

47 As early as the Archaic period poets were making direct comments upon and references to Homer and Homeric poetry, while later authors would quote and allude to all noted previous authors in an attempt to invoke the other work or engage in a dialogue with the theme, story, or idea presented. See Pfeiffer (1968: 8–9), with references.

48 Although Peripatetic philosophy may have been the underpinnings for the methodology of scholarship at Alexandria, the scholars themselves seem not to have been concerned with philosophy as a science. This may have been since the leading Peripatetics were still in Athens, carrying on the work at the Lykeion. Stoicism had no strong tradition linking it to a paternal land and so it may have been easier for its adherents to move about. On the library at Pergamon, see Pfeiffer (1968: 233–51); Nagy (1998: 190) agrees but downplays this division.

49 Thus the broad definition of *grammatike* by Dionysios Thrax (*Ars Grammatica* 1.1).

50 As Nagy (1998: 192–204) understands the term.

51 Strabo, 13.1.54 c609; Plutarch, *Sul.* 26.1–2; Athenaios, 5.214d. Each makes it clear that the type of critical analyses that Alexandrian scholars were concerned with was, at heart, Peripatetic in its outlook and execution. Although the terminology changed to incorporate a more stringent and exacting sense of one's interest in matters philological and linguistic, the sense of a critical analysis remained. See Nagy 1998: 200–6. In fact, the Library may even have retroactively created a history for itself with a direct link to Aristotle. See Strabo, 13.1.54 c508.

52 Dio Chrysostom seems to make it clear that the two were to be conceptually, if not formally, linked (*Or.* 53.1). Pfeiffer (1968: 67) objects to this view, in that he sees the two systems as consciously opposed to one another, whereas Nagy (1998: 213–32) attempts to show that the two are different applications of essentially the same system. On allegory in Hellenistic literature, see Bing 1988: 95, 141. On allegory among the Pergamene scholars, see Pfeiffer 1968: 140, 167, 237.

53 On the notion of literary self-fashioning through retrospection prior to the Hellenistic age, see Pfeiffer (1968: 1–86), though he uses the term 'self-interpretation.'

54 For Alexandria's and Pergamon's fashioning in general, see Nagy (1998), who uses Richardson as his starting point. Maehler (2004) feels that that the Library was used in an Hellenic/Egyptian divide in Ptolemaic cultural policy.

55 Formerly seen as the High Hellenistic, but enough fifth- and fourth-century precedents for the Baroque style are known that the notion of a Pergamene style is no longer tenable. See n.1.

56 On the ethnicity of Ptolemaic Alexandria, see Fraser 1972: 1.38–92; La'da 2003; Scheidel 2004. For its consequences, especially for the Jewish population, see Bilde et al. 1992. See Baines (2004) for examples of Egyptian elites living under Ptolemaic rule who may have mixed Egyptian or Greek elements based on circumstance, but who largely held to an Egyptian tradition, especially outside Alexandria. On the Greek cults of Ptolemaic Egypt, see Fraser (1972: 1.189–304); Kahil (1996), who notes how adaptable these cults were to the native

population, but how very Greek they were. For the Serapeion and its Greek sculptures, see Bergmann 2007. Kahil (1996: 78) notes how religion was used at Memphis in a more integrated form. On Memphis under the Ptolemies in general, see Thompson 1988. On the poetry and art of Memphis in the Hellenistic age, see Maehler 1988.

57 Kozloff 1996: 258; Fullerton 1998a: 75n15.

# PART FIVE

# Integration: Social In-Groups and Out-Groups

During the Hellenistic era the movement of people from one civic community to another strained the traditional criteria for membership within the *oikos* and the *polis*. And as the public expression of a person's bond with household or community shifted, opportunities arose for gaining entry into a particular social group; so too did the risks of being removed from one.

Christina Vester draws attention to the discourse in Menander's play about the difference between the norms and customs encoded in the city's laws and the behaviour of the human beings who are expected to uphold and promote them. Even those who are legally non-members of the city state – in the case of *Samia*, a foreign concubine – may effect a member's legitimacy, while those who are members according to law may fail to keep or advance the city's social values. Thus it is shown that the moral virtues of honesty, goodness, and usefulness are more important than the laws that encode them, and that real citizenship exists in good actions. According to this ideological (rather than political) reading, the members in the audience are prompted to reflect on their roles in shaping social norms.

The place of the *oikos* within the polis is most concretely expressed by the architecture of the dwelling itself. Ruth Westgate argues that domestic architecture and decoration could be employed to express cultural belonging or isolation. Using the evidence for domestic design in Delos and in Crete, Westgate demonstrates that the architectural strategy of similarity served to bring together the multicultural population of Delos into a socially homogeneous in-group. Both the design of the homes and the decorations in them fostered social interaction and a sense of belonging. On Crete, by contrast, the architectural strategy suggests an 'opting out' from the trends that prevailed elsewhere. Perhaps due to their long-standing reputation for austerity, or to their uncomfortable situation amidst competing Hellenistic kingdoms, Cretans effected internal cohesion through architectural exclusivism.

The interrelationship between cities in the Hellenistic era was further complicated by the movements of 'professionals,' individuals or groups who participated in the activities of communities to which they did not belong. Patrick Baker's paper, in which he concentrates on the well-documented case of the Cretan military mercenaries in Miletos, demonstrates the isolation that came upon those who were not integrated into Milesian society nor welcomed back into the Cretan communities from which they had departed. The evidence – inscriptions – is an important medium for the public expression of civic belonging. Though details about the identity, civic roles, and interactions of the mercenaries are scanty, the inscriptions do reveal that the dubious social and political associations of the mercenaries placed them in an awkward position of being neither an in-group nor an out-group.

# 13

# Staging the *Oikos*: Character and Belonging in Menander's *Samia*

## CHRISTINA VESTER

In arguing that Menander[1] is more important than wine at a symposion, a character in Plutarch's *Moralia* musters an impressive array of evidence.[2] He cites the playwright's pleasant style, judicious mixture of gravity and levity, and carefully calibrated storyline carrying both sober and tipsy along (*Mor.* 712b). A lack of homoerotic desire and the provision of marriage for violated virgins make the plays fitting fare for married men. Sex workers do appear in Menandrean dramas, but relationships with them are governed by suitable endings. Erotic entanglements with *hetairai* ('courtesans') conclude swiftly in the case of an overbold one, or humanely for the one who is good (712d). In concluding his praise of Menander's comedies as the most fitting fare for a drinking party, Plutarch's symposiast asserts that his plays improve moral character (712d).

This is a remarkable claim, and not simply because Menandrean drama is recognized as possessing didactic value.[3] Instead, it is the symposiast's vocabulary of normative appropriateness that demands attention. When discussing fitting entertainment for dinner guests who will soon return to their wives, tragedy is struck from the roster, marked as it is by weighty themes, misfortune, and grief. So too Aristophanic comedy on account of its directness, obscenity, and obscure learnedness, and Pyladic dancing with its arrogance and emotions (711f–g, 711e). Menander's balance, charm, and benefits are chosen instead. His style and action plot a middle course between difficulty and condescending ease. His sentiments improve morals (τὰ ἤθη, 712b) to a more proper degree (πρὸς τὸ ἐποεικέστερον, 712b). Given the space dedicated to describing them, erotic pursuits are important but they are also appropriate (καιρόν, 712c). Raped virgins are properly married (ἐπιεικῶς, 712c). The bad *hetaira* is finished with while her opposite either finds her biological citizen father or some bit of time, an accommodation of humane decency (συμπεριφορὰν αἰδοῦς ἔχων φιλάνθρωπον, 712c) is allotted to the affair with her. Finally, Menander's polished charm raises moral character (τὰ ἤθη) to be fitting and humane (ἐπιεικῆ, φιλάνθρωπα, 712d).

When Plutarch's symposiast declares Menander's dramas balanced and proper, he is not offering an in-depth commentary on the moral principles underlying these terms. Because he is himself trying to teach and persuade, he uses his description as evidence and capitalizes upon the links created between himself and the playwright. Both he and Menander focus on the *oikos* ('home'), marriage, and heterosexual desire, and both are balanced, appropriate, and offer lessons. And the symposiast's use of Menander makes a persuasive argument. He forcefully deploys antithesis, yoking together elements as follows: the sober and the inebriated, individuals at work or leisure, virgins and sex workers, good and bad *hetairai*,[4] and marriage or the end of a relationship, to list but a few. To describe the excellence of Menander, he often modifies his nouns with two adjectives. For example, his speech is sweet and grounded (ἡδεῖα καὶ πεζή), maxims both useful and simple (τε χρησταὶ καὶ ἀφελεῖς, 712b), and *hetairai* eager and overbold or good and loving (ἰταμαὶ καὶ θρασεῖαι, χρησταὶ καὶ ἀντερῶσαι, 712c). The wealth of description is further increased by metaphor. Menander's maxims flow imperceptibly and soften and bend the most unyielding of character – as if in a forge – to a more moderate degree (γνωμολογίαι τε χρησταὶ καὶ ἀφελεῖς ὑπορρέουσι καὶ τὰ σκληρότατα τῶν ἠθῶν ὥσπερ ἐν πυρὶ τῷ οἴνῳ μαλάττουσι καὶ κάμπτουσι πρὸς τὸ ἐπιεικέστερον, 712b). This balanced presentation, focused upon appropriate content and context, and replete with antitheses, double adjectives, and metaphor, makes the symposiast's case – rhetorically underscoring the lesson that Menander's carefully worked grace improves character by making it more proper (712b), fitting and humane (712d).

In light of this passage, it might well be asked if such fulsome praise is deserved. Was a play such as *Samia* reasonably perceived by the ancients to improve moral character? This is, after all, a comedy in which the young citizen male is guilty of rape, cowardice, and the shirking of responsibility with respect to his child and future wife. It depicts a relationship of fear and mistrust between father and son. And a crucial role is given to a foreign *hetaira* who poses as the infant's mother, thereby keeping biological father, mother, and child in close proximity to one another and ensuring the legitimate perpetuation of a citizen *oikos*. The relationship with her is not severed at the close of the play. So brief a summary demonstrates that *Samia* does not map cleanly onto the Menander described in Plutarch. Of greater importance, though, is the insight shown in deeming elements of Menandrean drama 'appropriate,' 'proper,' and 'fitting.' In making such a characterization, the symposiast draws attention to the underlying set of moral principles that determine 'good' and 'bad' individuals, choices, norms, and practices. He directs us to community and the rules and the obligations that govern belonging to it. And in this Menander's plays are rich, being long understood as *the* ancient authority on life as lived,[5] replete with shared ritual, custom, morals, characters, situations, and emotions.

Menander's *Samia* forcefully engages with what is 'appropriate' within a community. Yet another domestic comedy, it represents Athenians and a foreigner responding to the birth of a baby. Moschion became its father by raping his neighbour at a night-time festival and now desires to marry the mother. Too intimidated to seek the support of his father Demeas, who has just returned from a lengthy trip abroad, he diligently avoids confessing and thereby endangers his child's claim to belong to the *polis*. Demeas's concubine Chrysis pretends to be the mother of the baby and thereby supports his plan to keep the baby in the household. Demeas thus first believes that he and Chrysis are the parents, but after overhearing a nurse talking to the infant, he pursues the suspicion that his son and concubine are the actual parents. As at the end of other plays, the infant is reconciled with its biological parents, both Athenian, and they are properly married.

*Samia* ends with the marriage of two citizens and the addition of a legitimate citizen to both *oikos* and *polis*. This conclusion should function as a guarantee that all is well and flourishing within the city state. However, this union is not brought about by Moschion, the infant's father, or by his father Demeas, both Athenians. The impetus driving all towards disclosure and union is instead an outsider. By safeguarding the infant, the foreign concubine Chrysis enacts the role of wife and mother and adds a legitimate citizen to the *oikos* (and *polis*). All of this raises awkward issues. First, as the infant's situation demonstrates, laws, customs, and norms (νομοί) do not sufficiently safeguard status. Second, they do not ensure that citizens will live by and propagate the community customs and rules that conferred citizenship upon them. Status is arbitrarily granted to both good and bad. Third, outsiders can and do enact Athenian values and customs more convincingly than those who possess full citizenship. *Samia* addresses the diminishment of marriage and the double endogamy requirements of the Periclean citizenship law by suggesting revised parameters of status. Early in the drama it is stated that a man who proves himself χρηστός – useful, good, honest, worthy – is legitimate, and the bastard and slave is he who is πονηρός – bad, worthless, and a rogue (*Sam.* 140–143*a*). Demonstrated good moral character, or ἦθος, becomes preferable to legal requirements in determining who belongs. As such, good moral character is invested with political import for it suggests that full status can and should be enacted and not simply acquired from two parents. Performing good and appropriate behaviour in the *polis* – and perpetuating the community's rules and norms of belonging – is, in *Samia*, crucial for determining citizenship.

The interpretation of *Samia* as a suggested corrective to citizenship requirements by means of enacting good moral values is an ideological reading. Like other recent work on Menander, it sees a drama (or any literary text) as staging characters, morals, or norms inviting consideration or self-identification of the audience.[6] In so doing, a play such as *Samia* participates in the shaping of societal issues. As Susan Lape explains, Menander's plays 'provide stories that enable audience members to identify as democratic citizens without reference to the political regime actually in power' (2001: 12). New Comedy is particularly suited for negotiating identity. Set before an audience composed of *polis* members, each play stages a marriage or reunion within households composed of husbands, wives, sons, daughters, and slaves, all existing outside the drama. Being of a mild, balanced, and stereotypical nature, Menandrean drama can take up the subjects of identity and status and examine, rework, and perform them. *Samia* is fully engaged in this process, possessing a narrative depicting an infant whose status is in danger. In resolving the plot, the play inverts commonly held notions regarding citizens and foreigners, parents and strangers. It makes the young citizen-father look unworthy of status and a foreign concubine and former sex worker deserving of it.

*Samia*'s reworking of citizenship requirements is relevant within its historical context. As in all Menander's comedies, the democratic *oikos* expands in a very specific way in *Samia*. As if unaware of the significant political and military upheavals of the early Hellenistic age, Menandrean comedy identifies as citizens exposed or unclaimed infants and young women about to become *hetairai*. It strengthens and enlarges the *oikos* by uniting estranged wives and husbands, rapists and victims, parents and lost children,[7] always in strict accordance with the requirements of the Periclean citizenship law of 451/450 BC. In doing so, it declares the *polis* a flourishing entity and downplays or dismisses its diminished status under Macedonian rule.[8] On stage, citizen identity means belonging to and participating in the perpetuation of an *oikos* and *polis*, a timely lesson given the inability of Athens to define citizenship after Macedon imposed an oligarchic constitution upon it.[9] In Menandrean comedy the *polis* still matters. By staging a flourishing self-governing and self-perpetuating culture it states that it belongs, that it is still a place in the new political order of the Macedonian kingdoms.

## First Impressions, Great Expectations

Two main characters take on the role of keeping the infant close to its biological parents: Moschion the Athenian, and Chrysis the Samian. They will maintain the fiction that Chrysis is the child's mother until Moschion marries Plangon and makes the legitimacy of his son public. Both debut in the opening scene and both create significant expectations as to conduct and its underlying moral conduct. The opening scene, furthermore, foregrounds the following equation: one who belongs to the *polis* will have good moral character whereas a foreigner will have a more ambiguous moral colouring.

From the beginning, Moschion situates himself within the polis as one seeking exoneration. He begins a long monologue by acknowledging some sort of misdeed, stating 'I have erred' (ἡμάρτηκα, 3). Forty lines later he reticently describes his actions:

> ὀκν]ῶ λέγειν τὰ λοίπ᾽· ἴσως δ᾽ αἰσχύνομαι
> ὅτ᾽] οὐδὲν ὄφελος· ἀλλ᾽ ὅμως αἰσχύνομαι.
> ἐκύ]ησεν ἡ παῖς. (*Sam.* 47–9)

> ([I] hesitate
> To say what happened next – ashamed, perhaps
> [When] there's no need, but still I am ashamed.
> The girl got [pregnant].)[10]

He recounts his rape and impregnation of his neighbour regretfully and admits shame,[11] thereby acknowledging that he has acted contrary to community values.[12] He uses the same verb in responding to Parmenon's injunction to take responsibility ('I feel shame before my father,' αἰσχύνομαι τὸν πατέρα, 67). In the first sixty-seven lines of the drama, Moschion employs the verb 'to feel shame' three times and uses another that marks hesitance (ὀκνέω). More strikingly, his father is likewise marked by feelings of shame in erotic matters:

> Σαμίας ἑταίρας εἰς ἐ<πι>θυμίαν τινὸς
> ἐλθεῖν ἐκεῖνον, πρᾶγμ᾽ ἴσως ἀνθρώπινον.
> ἔκρυπτε τοῦτ᾽, ᾐσχύνετ᾽· ᾐσθόμην ἐγὼ
> ἄκοντος αὐτοῦ, διελογιζόμην θ᾽ ὅτι,
> ἂν μὴ γένηται τῆς ἑταίρας ἐγκρατής,
> ὑ[π᾽] ἀντεραστῶν μειρακίων ἐνοχλήσεται·
> τοῦτο <δὲ> ποῆσαι δι᾽ ἔμ᾽ ἴσως αἰσχύνεται· (*Sam.* 21–7)

(He pursued his desire for a *hetaira* from Samos,
Something that's human, possibly. He kept
It secret – he was ashamed. I found out,
Against his wishes, and I judged that if
He didn't take her under his protection,
He'd then be plagued by younger rivals, [but]
He was ashamed to do this, perhaps because of me.)[13]

Moschion's description of his father's desire seems to suggest that the shame of the father has been reproduced in his son. Both share a clear tendency to conceal their erotic undertakings. At the beginning of his monologue Moschion confesses to having erred and then takes rather a long time to explain his misdeed. Instead, he first recounts his upbringing (8–18), refers again to the incident (19), and then describes his father's feeling for the Samian courtesan (21–7). Moschion does indeed hesitate (ὀκνῶ, 47). He avoids explicitly disclosing his deed but then elliptically confesses by mentioning that his beloved got pregnant at a night-time festival hosted at his home. Demeas is likewise unwilling to admit to his desires before his son. He concealed the affair (23), did not want his son to know of it (24), and was ashamed to do what his son advised (27). The very order of the narrative placing the actions and shame of the father before those of the son suggests shared hereditary traits.

The shame of Moschion and Demeas, while related, are of a different scale. Moschion's actions are the more serious, as his confession acknowledges. Yet in providing a lineage for his desire, actions, and shame, there is the suggestion of an argument that he is not inherently bad but that he learned some negative lessons. He is persuading the audience that he knows that he has broken community codes of behaviour. In describing the night, he twice refers to his shame (47, 48) before stating that the girl got pregnant. After this he went to the girl's mother, took responsibility (50–1), and swore to marry her daughter. That Moschion fears censure with respect to the child is commendable, and understandable, for Menandrean comedies adhere to the strictures of the Periclean citizenship law.[14] When the term *nothos* ('bastard') is raised (136), it recalls the citizenship requirements of double endogamy. Every audience member must have recognized that a well-established set of privileges and rights would be lost if the parents remained unmarried. Being barred from full participation in the city's political, legal, and religious affairs, not inheriting his father's full estate, nor being able to marry an Athenian or maintain his family's cult site and funerary monuments were the reality of *nothoi*.[15] Moschion's use of the verb 'to be ashamed' is thus understandable, for his actions may strip a citizen of significant and highly guarded benefits.

In order to further contextualize his deed, Moschion prefaces his account of that night with a history of his life in his *oikos* and *polis*:

εἶτ᾽ ἐν]εγράφηνοὐδὲν διαφέρων οὐδενός,
τὸ λεγό]μενον δὴ τοῦτο, τῶν πολλῶν τις ὤν·
ὃς γέγον]α μέντοι, νὴ Δί᾽, ἀθλιώτερος·
παχεῖς] γάρ ἐσμεν. τῷ χορηγεῖν διέφερον
καὶ τῇ φιλοτιμίᾳ· κύνας γὰρ ἔτρεφέ μοι,
ἵππο]υς· ἐφυλάρχησα λαμπρῶς· τῶν φίλων
τοῖς] δεομένοις τὰ μέτρι᾽ ἐπαρκεῖν ἐδυνάμην.
δι᾽ ἐκεῖνον ἦν ἄνθρωπο. ἀστείαν δ᾽ ὅμως
τούτων χάριν τιν᾽ ἀπεδίδουν· ἦν κόσμιος. (*Sam*. 10–18)

([Next], I was registered – an average chap,
[That's how the] phrase goes, just like any other.
And I've [become] in fact more wretched – all
Because we're [loaded]. I shone with my payments
For choruses [and] public service. He kept hounds
For me, and [horses]. I starred as a colonel of
Hussars! I could give modest help to needy
Friends. Through him, I was a man. I paid my debt
For that, though, nobly: I behaved myself.)[16]

Moschion acquits himself admirably as a young male citizen and under-scores his belonging in the community. In recalling his deme registration, an enrolment confirming citizenship, he states that he was at that point no different from any other. He thus both stakes a claim to be one of the many and presents an upgrade to the common Athenian by suggesting all citizens had money to pay for a liturgy, the maintenance of horses and dogs, and the aiding of friends. Wealth did not mire him in personal pursuits. Instead, he recounts his role as *choregos* ('chorus producer'), a commission assigned to a wealthy Athenian to meet the expenses of training and costuming a tragic, comic, or dithyrambic chorus, usually after the age of forty.[17] He discharged this duty and then served in a military office. This young dynamo also served his friends, offering modest help to those in need. This brief account serves as a short version of what prosecutors or defendants offer up in forensic speeches when they seek to align themselves with cultural norms held as true and important by the citizen body. Moschion's linking of finances and duties is duplicated, for example, in the speech of Lysias wherein he accuses Eratosthenes and his fellow members of the Thirty for their actions taken against his own upstanding and civic-minded family:[18] 'We were not deserving of these things at the hands of the city, for we undertook the duties of the choregos (πάσας <μὲν> τὰς χορηγίας χορηγήσαντας), we paid into many special tax levies (πολλὰς δ' εἰσφορὰς εἰσενεγκόντας), we showed ourselves to be well ordered (κοσμίους δ' ἡμᾶς παρέχοντας), we did everything required of us (πᾶν τὸ προσταττόμενον ποιοῦντας), we acquired no enemy (ἐχθρὸν δ' οὐδενα κεκτημένους), and we ransomed many Athenians from enemies (πολλοὺς δ' Ἀθηναίων ἐκ τῶν πολεμίων λυσαμένους)' (12. 20–1). Vocabulary is shared. Lysias makes the claim that he and his family were well-behaved (κοσμίους, 12.20) and so too does Moschion (κόσμιος, 18). Similarly, both refer to military duties, Lysias by ransoming some Athenians and Moschion by serving as *phylarch* ('cavalry commander'). Both characterize themselves as orderly, recall their public benefactions, underscore their good sense by mentioning their friends and allies,[19] and suggest that their wealth was put to work on behalf of the state. Moschion caps his history by referring to the debt he owed his father. In closing with recognizing the important father-son bond, our protagonist links what is owed to the *polis* and the *oikos*. As he states, he became a man on account of his father (ἦν ἄνθρωπος, 17), and a modest and orderly one at that (ἦν κόσμιος, 18).

Alternatively, Chrysis receives little such colouring in the opening narrative. For the first fifty lines, the audience receives little information other than that she possesses connections to prostitution for she is a *hetaira* from Samos (21).[20] She is called 'the Samian' until the fifty-sixth line, a move that depersonalizes her, underlines her foreignness, and links her to sex work. She is the host of the Adonia, a festival celebrating sexuality. Although attended by wives, mothers, and daughters, courtesans and concubines were particularly known for observing its rituals.[21] When her name Chrysis is first used (56), it only adds to the supposition that she may be a typically expensive courtesan. As David Wiles (1991: 179) points out, her 'name means "golden" and this suggests that she should wear the mask of the "golden courtesan."' Wiles also notes (1991: 179) that in the Mytilenean mosaic depicting Chrysis with the baby held to her breast, the courtesan appears to be wearing a bejewelled headdress – golden headgear that is appropriate for a woman who is living with a very rich man. Her name, appearance, and provenance may well have led the ancient spectator to expect Chrysis to be a physical manifestation of the costly and beautiful courtesan upon whom money and goods are lavished.[22] In the few words granted to her, Chrysis does little to dispel such expectations. When affirming that she will pretend to be the child's mother until Moschion speaks to his father, she dismisses his concerns with playful condescension. As she confidently asserts, Demeas will calm down after finding out that he is a father. He is, after all, 'terribly in love' (ἐρᾷ γάρ, ὦ βέλτιστε, κἀκεῖνος κακῶς, 81), a statement implying she possesses the power to make Demeas disregard cultural norms.[23] His love will allow her to keep his bastard in the house, and further, will grant her the authority to function as the authority determining who is introduced into the *oikos*. At the end of the first scene, she has been coloured with some negative characteristics of the sex worker: expense, manipulation, confidence, and consumption – literal and figurative.

The monologue, heavily used in *Samia*,[24] grants Moschion (and Demeas) the ability to transmit their immediate thoughts, feelings, and plans, thereby giving them significant control over their reception.[25] However, through monologue the audience also acquires the means by which to challenge a speaker's self-presentation. Lengthy lectures replete with narrative, justification, and plans seed the expectation that deeds will reinforce words. In Moschion, the bastard's father, a young man with the greatest potential reward for ensuring that his son acquires status, words and deeds do not coincide. His moral character emerges as weak when he is judged by his deeds. By contrast, Chrysis, a foreigner and former sex worker with precious little to gain from safeguarding Moschion's child, speaks few words throughout yet contradicts all negative stereotypes through her deeds.

## Words and Deeds, πονηρός ('Useless') and χρηστά ('Worthy')

Moschion, the public citizen of Athens, is κόσμιος ('well-behaved'). Moschion the father is not, a failing that diminishes his public record and upbringing. His actions garner him no recognition of 'goodness.' When the slave Parmenon informs him that the fathers have returned to Athens and that the time has come when he must 'be a man' (63–4), he immediately mentions his fear (65) and cites his shame before his father (65). Parmenon then sharply asks why he does not fear the young woman he wronged or her mother, and calls him a 'girly-boy' (ἀνδρόγυνε, 69). As in other scenes, Moschion here is anything but a man. He earlier swore to marry Plangon, an oath declaring he would soon be a *kyrios* ('household head') in his own *oikos*. Yet as Parmenon's next rebuke shows, Moschion does little to realize the wedding. Instead of preparing for the ceremony by sacrificing, putting on garlands, and cutting up cake (74–5),[26] Parmenon describes the young man as wailing at the doors of Plangon and then recalls the oath sworn to Plangon's mother (73–4). By speaking thusly, Parmenon foregrounds his master's inability to fulfil the demands of the community. In declaring that he wants the marriage to happen immediately, he shows a resolve far greater than that of his young master. In expressing his desire that Moschion cease crying and keep his oath true, Parmenon – a slave – casts doubt upon his master's manliness, resolve, and honesty. That Moschion does not rebuke the slave for calling him a girly-boy and casting aspersions upon his willingness to maintain his word underlines what an ἀνδρόγυνε ('girly-man') Moschion is and how ill-prepared the young Moschion is in claiming his role as *kyrios*. In response to the orders of the slave, he sullenly gives way and states: 'I'll do all that – why must you preach?' (πάντα ποιήσω· τί δεῖ / λέγειν; 76–7).

The exercise of authority and capacity for action required for discharging the office of *choregos* and *phylarch* are nowhere evidenced. Rather than meet up with his father, Moschion asks himself if it isn't necessary to hold a practice for the contest, citing the seriousness of his contest (94–5). For the three middle acts, he makes brief appearances and thereby assiduously avoids confrontation. The weakest of pretences serve. He sets off to prepare for the wedding and recounts that he sacrificed, invited friends, bathed, and distributed the cake – in his head (120–5). When his father states that he understands his situation and will thus arrange his marriage, Moschion does not probe this unexpected statement and ensure the truth of it. He instead praises Demeas's plan and then says he must set off to take a ritual bath, pour a libation, and offer incense (156–8). And when his father asks him to wait for the approval of the bride's father, Nikeratos, he says that he will be in the way and then runs off (161–2). When this young man next appears he is lamenting the slow passage of time (428) and discloses he is off to take his third bath as he can find nothing else to do (429–30). Opportunities to correct misapprehensions are studiously avoided. When Nikeratos tells him that Demeas has thrown out Chrysis (434, 435–6), when he sees Demeas shouting at the servants about household events and the wedding (440–51), and finally, when Demeas demands he tell Nikeratos who the baby's mother is (488–90), Moschion avoids disclosure. This increases the ire of Demeas and Nikeratos, both of whom believe that he had sex with Chrysis. When he finally explains to his father that Chrysis is doing him a favour (522–3), he admits his wrongdoing. Hard on the heels of this confession, Nikeratos bursts in and tells them that he found his daughter nursing. Moschion flees (539).

All in all, Moschion does precious little unless forced into a corner. Rather than reconciling himself to his father and to his future father-in-law, from whom assent is desired, he avoids them. Confession of wrongdoing to male authority figures appears beyond him. At the play's end, Moschion cannot even carry out the pretence that he is setting off to enlist in a mercenary army. He wastes an extraordinary amount of time describing his upset over his father's suspicions (619–22), mooning over Plangon (630–2), imagining the rewards and pitfalls of his ruse (636–40, 664–9, 681–6), and ordering the slave Parmenon in and out of the house to secretively fetch his cloak and spear (658–63, 678–80) – military gear he barely has time to don in order to deceive his father. If we return to Moschion's definition of a citizen, we are compelled to ask if Moschion is χρηστός ('worthy') and therefore γνήσιος ('legitimate'). The problem in the drama as Moschion framed it is the birth of a child due to rape. The resolution to his predicament is marriage and nothing blocks it except his incapacity to face his father and potential father-in-law. Displays of *philotimia* ('political generosity'), discharging military command, and the outlay of monies and organization so as to fulfil the office of the *choregos* all testify to the citizen status of the one undertaking them, but do not, in this drama, provide resolution to the problem by showing that he has a character worthy of such status.

The actions of Chrysis drive the events within the play to resolution. Because of her resolve marriage closes the drama – a ceremony in which the baby's citizen status can be asserted. In representing Chrysis, good moral character takes centre stage, not the duties, displays, and rituals of the citizen, and is posited as a foundation for guaranteeing status. Chrysis has far more at stake than the loss of face that Moschion so strongly rails against while trying to deceive his father at the end of the drama. She also has far less to gain from sheltering the child as she lacks citizen status, a point that is made repeatedly throughout *Samia*. Moschion can pass on his wealth and estate to his son, ensure the continuation of the family name, and protect the familial cult site and funerary monuments. He has every reason to see that his child, a very real investment for the future of his *oikos*, is entered into the deme registry. Legally, Chrysis can do none of these things and is under no such pressure. Furthermore, as she can never be Demeas's legal wife and participate fully in reproducing the *oikos* and protect its inhabitants, her actions in doing just that are all the more significant. Lack of status does not stop Chrysis from acting much as an Athenian matron would in trying to safeguard a child with civic status. Her success in assuming this role and its responsibilities ultimately results in a newly formed official union producing another citizen for Athens. While Chrysis is no biological mother, she enacts this role and invests it with a value that outstrips its legal definition as well as its biological substrate.

Chrysis is clearly embedded in the *oikos* of Demeas. Furthermore, her standing is not as simple as the men represent it. While the fathers repeatedly use terms that reveal her non-Athenian status, other characters reveal that she is de facto mistress of the household. In the opening monologue, she appears to have the support and friendship of the neighbours, and even of Nikeratos's formidable wife:

φ]ιλανθρώπως δὲ πρὸς τὴν τοῦ πατρὸς
Σαμί]αν διέκειθ᾽ ἡ τῆς κόρης μήτηρ, τά τε
πλεῖ]στ᾽ ἦν παρ᾽ αὐταῖς ἥδε, καὶ πάλιν ποτὲ

αὐτ]αι παρ' ἡμῖν. ἐξ ἀγροῦ δὴ καταδραμών
ὡς ἔτυ]χ[έ] γ', εἰς Ἀδώνι' αὐτὰς κατέλαβον
συν]ηγ[μ]ένας ἐνθάδε πρὸς ἡμᾶς μετά τινων
ἄλλω]ν γυναικῶν. (35–41)

(The girl's mother got on well with
Father's Samian. She spent
[A lot of time] with them and [they] in turn
With us. Well, [as it happened(?)], I had rushed
Back from the farm, and found them [gathered] in
Our house here for the Adonis revels, with
Some [other] women.)

Ariana Traill explains the importance of her neighbours as follows: '[T]he women have no personal stake in defending Chrysis and they have a unique authority to sanction her position in a respectable oikos' (2008: 158). Athenian women frequently shared their home, belongings, and company with friends and neighbours, as Lysias, Demosthenes, and Aristophanes attest.[27] To the neighbours and other Athenian women of the community, Chrysis has the authority to invite guests and host ritual celebrations. At the very least she is a *pallake* ('concubine') of considerable standing within the *oikos* and not seen as a working *hetaira*.[28]

In addition to the women of the community, members of the household see her as responsible for the household workings. When the maid refers to Chrysis as αὐτή (258) she essentially acknowledges her standing as mistress. Αὐτός was used by slaves to refer to their master, as when Demeas is mentioned (256).[29] The fact that they are called αὐτός ('himself') and αὐτή ('herself') within a few lines by the slaves suggests that they are seen as a couple, as partners. When Chrysis calls for one of the household servants, the message is quickly passed on and imperatives used to fulfil her request (258–9). After she is thrown out of the house, the slaves are caught weeping by Demeas. Ordering them back to work, Demeas shouts at them: 'Yes indeed, you've every reason to lament and weep. For a mighty benefactor to you all has left the house' (πάνυ γάρ ἐστιν ἄξιον, νὴ τὸν Δία, / ἐπιδακρῦσαι· μέγα γὰρ ὑμῖν ᾤχετ' ἐκ τῆς οἰκίας ἀγαθόν, 442–4). Chrysis seemingly possesses a good relationship with the servants (or slaves), and has the power to affect their lives for good or ill.

It is not only slaves and servants who recognize Chrysis as mistress of the household. Just as Nikeratos tells his wife to ready the things for the wedding (196–7), so Demeas assigns this to Chrysis (729–31). Just as the wife of Nikeratos is called γυναῖκα ('wife,' 197, 558) by her husband, so too is Chrysis by her common-law partner (561, 577, 585). Moschion tells his father that he wants Chrysis present at the wedding, an occasion for family and presumably not for *hetairai*, former or not. The neighbour women ally with Chrysis, protecting her and the child until the reconciliations all take place. When the truth is out, Demeas takes his concubine back into the house and acknowledges his grandson. He also takes on the role of *kyrios* for her when Nikeratos threatens her, shouting: 'And you too have raised a stick against a woman of free birth, and chased her!' (σὺ δ' ἐπ' ἐλευθέραν γυναῖκα λαμβάνεις βακτηρίαν / καὶ διώκεις, 577–8). At the end of the drama she disappears into the house for the wedding preparations. She is not seen again on stage and this is fitting – Athenian women with *kyrioi* were to stay inside and have as few meetings with people outside as possible.

In assuming the role as the mother of the abandoned baby, Chrysis acquires standing within the house. The terms used to describe her provisions for the baby are telling. Unlike Moschion, who states that he 'took' the child (εἴληφα, 54), a verb meaning little more than 'I picked it up,' Chrysis's relationship with the baby is constructed as far more permanent. Chrysis, Moschion, Plangon, and others feign the biological link, presumably because they believe that this will protect the child and keep it nearby until the marriage occurs. The pretend mother of the baby is believable, a point underlined by having Chrysis appear for most of the play with the infant in her arms. Thus is the verb τίκτω ('to give birth') twice used in connection with Chrysis (79, 651). The fact that Chrysis has given birth and is lactating qualifies her as fertile, a 'real' mother, and in a sense Moschion's baby takes her own baby's place (i.e., at her breast).[30] When faced with eviction, Chrysis asks Demeas if it was because she accepted the baby (374). Soon after, she is told by Nikeratos that he heard she had kept the child (410). The verb used in both of these contexts is ἀναιρέω ('to claim'), a term that carries the meaning 'to take up new born children, to own.'[31] This verb has a rather more permanent sense to it than Moschion's simple use of λαμβάνω ('to take,' 54), for it is used when a father picks up his child so as to acknowledge it as legitimate and his own. This latter point is substantiated by the use of yet one more verb in connection with Chrysis. She is twice described as rearing the child (τρέφω, 'to rear,' 318, 410) and not simply nursing it, another point marking the commitment she is making. When Demeas says to her, 'But you have made a son, you have everything' (ἀλλὰ σὺ / υἱὸν πεποίησαι· πάντ' ἔχεις, 386–7), he uses Greek adoption terminology. As Alick Harrison explains: 'The adoptive father is said εἰσποιεῖσθαι or ποιεῖσθαι, either with or without the word υἱόν' (1968: 84). Demeas's statement to Chrysis raises two points: first, Demeas thinks that Chrysis is adopting the child and committing herself to rearing it, and second, he is sarcastically rebuking her for her act of adoption, for overstepping boundaries of gender, status, and station. The text builds a strong and permanent link between the baby and its voluntary mother.[32]

Chrysis has no legal right to undertake the course she chooses as she has no legal position within the *oikos*. Only a man could acknowledge his child as legitimate. It was *his* decision whether to expose it or 'take it up' (ἀναιρέω). For much of the play, it would seem that Plutarch is right in reading Menander's courtesans as properly situated outside the household. Chrysis's status as a foreigner and sex worker is often and explicitly raised. Her place of origin is also mentioned more than once (21, 36, 265, 354) and this underlines her lack of status. In addition to mentioning her foreignness, which locates her legally on the periphery of the *oikos*, individuals also mention her occupation. Moschion first refers to her as a *hetaira* (21), a woman who makes a living from maintaining a relationship with one or more men and who serves (ideally) as a witty, beautiful, and knowledgeable companion. Moschion's usage of the term here is in no way negative. However, when Demeas discovers that his Chrysis has a child, he too mentions her position as a *hetaira*, stating sarcastically: 'It has escaped my attention, or so it would seem, that my mistress has become my wife' (γ]αμετὴν ἑταίραν, ὡς ἔοικ', ἐλάνθανον / ἔχ]ων, 131–2). The tone of Demeas's designation is decidedly hostile as are two later sentences: '[A secret son's] been born to me, it seems; she'll take him now and leave my house – to hell with her' (λάθ]ριό[ς τι]ς ὑ<ός>, ὡς ἔοικε, γέγονέ μοι, / ὅν γ'] ἐς [κόρ]ακας ἄπεισιν ἐκ τῆς οἰκίας / ἤ]δη λαβ[ο]ῦσα, 132–4). First the phrase γαμετὴν ἑταίραν. This is an oxymoron, equivalent to saying: 'My mistress, my kept woman, legally married to me.' In Athens, the two nouns γαμετή ('married woman') and γυνή ('wife') were paired to mean 'legally married wife,' and to say that a γαμετὴν ἑταίραν ('legally married courtesan') has had a child is to imply that a bastard has been born. Demeas makes this point explicitly by asking his son: 'But do I look like I would bring up a bastard son inside my house?' (ἀλλ' ἦ μ[ε θ]ρέψειν ἔνδον υὸν προσδοκᾷς / νόθον, 134–5). Furthermore, linking γαμετή with ἑταίρα is dangerous for it mixes erotics with procreation, confuses the issue of status, and potentially surrenders some of the rights of a wife or mother to a courtesan. In this context, Demeas's description of Chrysis as a *hetaira*, as well as his threat to eject her, is a way of locating her properly outside of the *oikos*, reaffirming her status as sex worker, and stripping her of the claim to wifely status implied in the word γαμετή.

When Demeas mistakenly believes that Chrysis and Moschion are the parents, the Samian is downgraded. She is now a Helen, the prime example in Athenian thought of a faithless and seductive wife (337). Curiously, invoking Helen at this point actually reveals that Chrysis is much more than a sex worker to Demeas. By using that analogy, Demeas implicitly declares that Chrysis is his wife, even as he excoriates her for being a whore. Unlike Helen, who left with her lover for Troy, Chrysis can and must be thrown out so as to establish that she is not a wife. Demeas next calls her a χαμαιτύπη, a 'ground-pounder,' a term affixed to the most common of whores in antiquity (348). It is not insignificant that Demeas uses her place of birth and the term 'whore' in the following passage, for he is convincing himself that he must eject her from his house:

χαμαιτύπη δ᾽ ἄνθρωπος, ὄλεθρος. ἀλλά τί;
οὐ γὰρ περίεσται. Δημέα, νῦν ἄνδρα χρὴ
εἶναι σ᾽. ἐπιλαθοῦ τοῦ πόθου, πέπαυσ᾽ ἐρῶν,
καὶ τἀτύχημα μὲν τὸ γεγονὸς κρύφθ᾽ ὅσον
ἔνεστι διὰ τὸν ὑόν, ἐκ τῆς δ᾽ οἰκίας
ἐπὶ κεφαλὴν ἐς κόρακας ὦσον τὴν καλὴν
Σαμίαν. (348–54)

(That woman is a whore, a bitch!
So what? She'll not last long. Now, Demeas, you've got
To be a man. Forget your ardour, stop
Desiring her. Conceal the glitch that's happened
As best you can, for your son's sake. Eject
The lovely Samian woman from your house –
Headfirst to hell!)

In making her foreign and exceedingly common, Demeas gives himself the justification to hurl Chrysis out of his *oikos*. This denigration of her sexual behaviour continues when Demeas characterizes her as a knockabout *hetaira*, one who hires herself out for parties, and who dies of strong drink or starvation if she does not put out quickly enough:

τὸ μέγα πρᾶγμ᾽. ἐν τῇ πόλει
ὄψει σεαυτὴν νῦν ἀκριβῶς ἥτις εἶ.
αἱ κατά σε, Χρυσί, πραττόμεναι δράχμας δέκα
μόνας ἕτεραι τρέχουσιν ἐπὶ τὰ δεῖπνα καὶ
πίνουσ᾽ ἄκρατον ἄχρι ἂν ἀποθάνωσιν, ἢ
πεινῶσιν, ἂν μὴ τοῦθ᾽ ἑτοίμως καὶ ταχὺ
πoῶσιν. (390–5)

(Superstar! In town,
You'll see exactly what you are! The others of
Your type dash down to their parties, where they charge
A mere ten drachmas and knock back strong wine

Until they die – or else they starve, if what they
Do is not quick and willing.)

The more common Demeas makes her, the less likely it is that she is his
ἑταίρα γαμετή.

It is not only Demeas who uses the terminology of sex workers to distance himself from Chrysis. When Nikeratos is led to believe that Chrysis
and Moschion were lovers, he even strips her of her freedom, swearing,
'I'd have been the first man to sell off mistress on the morrow' (508–9).
Furthermore, by virtue of Demeas and Moschion's previously close relationship with Chrysis, they are likewise characterized as slaves (506–9). Her
status as foreigner, *hetaira*, common whore, concubine, and slave, devalues
all around her. On account of her status and social standing, Chrysis cannot beget a citizen-child as she cannot legally be married. However, on account of her goodness, assertiveness, and admirable actions, Demeas, and
even Nikeratos, must work hard to distance themselves from Chrysis, thus
underlining the threat she poses through her ambiguous status as ἑταίρα
γαμετή.

While the storyline dealing with Chrysis and the baby whose protection
she has assumed takes up but a small part of the drama, her steadfastness
drives the reconciliations that occur between the two households, between
father and son, and between bride and groom. Chrysis's connection with
the infant goads Demeas into throwing her out and declaring repeatedly
that she can go to hell (133–4, 353–4, 372). It is this unrelenting harshness
towards the *hetaira* that compels the son to confess to his father. With father
and son working in tandem towards the wedding, only Nikeratos remains to
be persuaded. When he discovers his daughter nursing the baby, he knows
he has been wronged and shouts for fire so that he can burn up the baby
(553–5). Nikeratos then threatens to kill Chrysis. Again her protection of
the child forces the issue and compels reconciliation. The threats and pun-
ishments meted out to Chrysis fail to dislodge the baby from her care. In
fact, they ultimately serve to bring about the marriage that will provide the
infant with status.

This is an interesting stance to take, especially since *Samia* was likely
produced during the oligarchic regime of Demetrios of Phaleron (317–307
BC).[33] Moschion's claim to wealth, to dogs and horses, could be read as
Menander's construction of a rich young man as a Macedonian-approved
Athenian. It was during the ten years of Demetrios that citizenship was
no longer determined by bilateral Athenian parentage but by measure of
wealth. In this decade, one thousand drachmas were required for citizenship,

an easing of the two thousand drachmas required in 322 BC.[34] The shifting parameters of citizenship register strongly in *Samia*, in which traditional status requirements are measured against character and found arbitrary and weak. There appears to be the suggestion that status needs to be substantiated by actions that are evidence of strong and good character, and that this could be the way to establish belonging. Performed in theatres across vast empires, the staged good Athenian could call upon immense numbers to model themselves after it. The production of New Comedy throughout the Macedonian kingdoms could arguably have drawn many to complicate their identity. By appropriating and enacting Athenian identity as constructed by Menander, individuals throughout the Hellenistic empires could stake a claim to belonging to a Greek *polis*.

Unlike Moschion, the *choregos*, cavalry soldier, hunter, and citizen, Chrysis does meet and surpass significant challenges: she is stripped of home, seriously diminished in standing, threatened with fire and beatings, and truly insulted. Unlike Moschion, her resolve never seems to waver. Her actions suggest the actions of the ideal wife or mother in Athens – perpetuator and safeguarder of an *oikos*. If we return just once more to the equation that Moschion voiced in constructing legitimacy, we must conclude that Chrysis is, in the deepest sense, legitimate, because she is not *ponera* ('useless'). And she is, admittedly, a good character on to which to pin a new construction of belonging to a Greek *polis*. Because she inhabits a space both within and without the *oikos*, weaving between former independence and current reliance upon the goodwill and support of her household's *kyrios*, her claim of the role of mother and protector is less threatening. Because she is a non-citizen, foreigner, and former sex worker, her claim can be dismissed. Along with other *hetairai*, concubines, slaves, and children, individuals who fall into that liminal space between belonging and isolation, Chrysis can negotiate her past and present to striking effect. Even as she maintains fifth-and fourth-century Athenian familial norms, she nonetheless suggests a new way of defining status. Ultimately subordinate to Demeas, the household's *kyrios*, she acts as a legitimate wife in Athens would have, succeeds in her assumed role of mother, and belies the negative stereotype of sex workers. The moral lessons to be learned from Menander might just consist in this: be good, be really good, and you will be proven good, despite your past. Laws, customs, and civic ritual do not safeguard the citizen status of the baby in *Samia*, whereas the goodness, determination, and actions of an individual on the margins of Athenian culture do. Moral character and its manifestations matter immensely. What better foundation for determining who belongs, who is a citizen?

## Notes

1 Unless otherwise noted, all references and citations of Menander are to Arnott 2000.
2 This need not mean that reading or performing entire plays of Menander was the norm in Plutarch's time (ca 46–120 AD). Evidence suggests that sections rather than complete dramas were more often recited or performed in symptotic settings. See Fantham (1984: 299–309) for the circumstances and ways in which Romans encountered Menander in the late Republic and early Empire. Supporting the notion that Menander was more often than not experienced in excerpted form is Green 1994: 142–65. Interpreting the material remains of New Comedy, he argues that images on sarcophagi, vessels, mosaics etc., were part of a trend that moved from representing 'key moments from the plays in question, often the name-scenes' to become 'simple illustrations of Menander or even the Classics' (165).
3 Often reserved for Greek tragedy. For Greek tragedy as a didactic genre, see Gregory 1997. For a brief but excellent discussion of approaches to Greek tragedy, see Goldhill 1997: 324–47, particularly 343–7.
4 Although Brown (1990: 251–3) states that Plutarch is discussing two types of women, not three as Gilula (1987: 513–14) suggests, neither critic is reading Plutarch as providing a comprehensive typology of Menander's plots or sex workers. Both focus upon the moral lessons gained from encountering Menander.
5 So Aristophanes of Byzantion could rhetorically ask: 'Oh Menander! Oh life! Which of you mimicked the other?' (Kassel-Austin *PCG*, Test. 170). This question still echoes in works of a social-historical bent. Menander is mined for details of ancient daily life, physical, psychological, and moral, often to excellent result.
6 For different ideological interpretations, see Konstan 1995: 4–7; Major 1997: 59–73; Rosivach 1998: 140–3; Lape 2004: 10–12.
7 The one complete comedy of Menander (*Dyskolos*) and the six plays that we have in large parts (*Aspis, Epitrepontes, Misoumenos, Perikeiromene, Samia,* and *Sikyonios*) either close with a legitimate union being (re-)established or suggest this. Fragments, some substantial, bear out this tendency. See Webster (1974: 111–93) for a description of all of Menander's plays, presented by scene and act, as far as can be established from papyrus remains. Gomme and Sandbach's (1973) commentary likewise provides plot descriptions whenever the remains warrant.
8 For which see Lape: 2004, passim. Lape's is the strongest argument to date for a political aspect to Menander.
9 Davies (1978: 113–14) comments on the pervasiveness of citizenship topics in Menander: 'Since so much depends on citizenship, while for fifteen years of

Menandros' adult lifetime Athens was powerless to determine her own citizenship criteria, his obsession with the theme is understandable: he was dealing with something of crucial contemporary importance.'

10 Arnott's translation adapted slightly.

11 I read Moschion's act as a rape. He might not have sexually assaulted Plangon, but he has then committed statutory rape. So Cohen 1993: 14: 'In particular, females below a certain age are seen as incapable of consenting to sexual intercourse.' Further, as women were the responsibility of a *kyrios*, they may have been seen as unable to consent regardless of their age. For reading Moschion's act as rape, see Konstan 1995: 121; Zagagi 1996: 114–15; Rosivach 1997: 20–1; Lape 2001: 93. Lape (2004: 144–7) provides the strongest argument for reading this as seduction. On rape in Menander, see Fantham 1975: 53–7, 67–71; Konstan 1995: 141–52; Pierce 1997: 163–84; Rosivach 1998: 13–50. On rape in fifth-and fourth-century Athens, see Harrison 1968: 34–6; Cole 1984; Harris 1990; Cohen 1991, 1993: 5–16; Carey 1995; Ogden 1997b: 25–41; Lape 2001: 84–9.

12 Rape and seduction were political. Lape (2004: 85–91) convincingly argues that seducers and rapists could have been seen as anti-democratic as they attacked the authority of another Athenian *kyrios*.

13 Arnott's translation adapted slightly.

14 In New Comedy, it is usually the child's lack of status rather than the act of rape that causes distress in fathers. See Pierce 1997: 166–8 and Konstan 1995: 145–52.

15 For which see Harrison 1968: 61–8. For other links with bastardy, see Ogden 1996: 197–208.

16 Arnott's translation adapted slightly.

17 *Ath. Pol.* 56.3; Aeschin. *in Tim.* 11. See Pickard-Cambridge 1968: 86–93; Wilson 2000: 55, 150, and for the requirements of the office see 50–103.

18 Lists of actions undertaken on behalf of the city can take up considerably more space. See, for example, Demosthenes *Meid.* 154–61, in which the orator's list of benefactions runs to several pages.

19 See Connor (1971: 26, 35–43) for a discussion of political friendship in which gifts and money were given by one to another political 'friend.'

20 Defining sex workers is problematic. For the vocabulary of prostitution, see Davidson 1997: 109–27 and McClure 2003: 9–24. For a brief introduction to the study of prostitution, including its terminology, see McClure 2006: 3–8.

21 See Detienne 1981: 101–2. Rituals included feasting, dancing, the burning of aromatics, and the carrying of plants up to hot rooftops for quick withering.

22 See Henry (1985: 8–18, 32–48) and Davidson (1997: 109–36) for the relationship between *hetaira* and expense.

23  So Traill 2008: 162: 'Chrysis is not alone in harboring a certain pride. All of the professional types spoofed in Middle and New Comedy . . . brag about their specialized skills.'

24  See Blundell 1980: 44: 'When we make allowances for lacunae, monologue can hardly count for less than 370 lines in a play of about 900.' See also Bain (1983: xxi), and Gomme-Sandbach (1973: 543), who briefly discuss the monologue and attempts by earlier scholars to use it as evidence that *Samia* is among Menander's earlier plays.

25  So Gomme-Sandbach 1973: 543 and Bain 1983: xxi.

26  For a description of the wedding day ceremony, see Oakley and Sinos 1993: 11–37 and Garland 1990: 217–25.

27  In the first speech of Lysias, Euphiletos's wife claims that she went to the neighbour's to rekindle a lamp (1.14). Demosthenes describes two mothers visiting one another frequently before their sons fall out (*Call.* 23–4). In Aristophanes's *Lysistrata* a mother speaks of inviting two women to attend a celebration honouring Hekate (700–2).

28  Fear of being characterized as a sex worker probably kept citizen-women from visiting *hetairai*. In both written and visual evidence, it is only men who are pictured with *hetairai* and *pornai* ('prostitutes').

29  Αὐτός LSJ s.v. 1.1.

30  On account of the fragmentary state of *Samia*, it is inconclusive as to whether Chrysis bore a baby. Dedoussi (1970: 177) argues that Chrysis feigns nursing the infant. Most critics accept that Chrysis had a miscarriage or that the baby was stillborn. See Bain 1983: xiii and xiv n.2; Keuls 1973: 15–16 and n.47.

31  LSJ B.I.4.

32  I do not, however, think that Chrysis and the baby are to be envisioned as remaining together. A great deal of pressure is put upon Moschion to marry, Plangon is also nursing the child (535–6), and the women in Nikeratos's house support Chrysis. These three circumstances suggest that they are all in on the plan of marriage.

33  There is no specific internal evidence establishing a date for this play, nor is there preserved a hypothesis or didascalic notice. Arnott (2000: 7–12) discusses style and internal references and concludes that it was likely produced around 314 BC Gomme-Sandbach (1973: 542–3) suggest 309 BC, the year Ptolemy occupied Karia. Bain (1983: xii) says only that it is a good bet that the play was performed during the regency of Demetrios of Phaleron. See Habicht (1997: 42–66) for the years under Demetrios of Phaleron.

34  Plutarch *Phokion* xxvii.3; Diod. Sic. xviii 74.3 (1,000 drachmai), xviii 18.4–5 (2,000 drachmai).

# 14

# Making Yourself at Home in the Hellenistic World[1]

## RUTH WESTGATE

Home is a place where we define ourselves. More or less consciously, we use the architecture, decoration, and contents of our homes to express our status and affiliations, to show others what kind of person we are, or would like to be. But at a deeper level, home is also where we first learn who we are, what our role in society is, and how to behave appropriately for that role; the household is one of the central contexts in which we articulate fundamental social distinctions of gender, age, and status. Our homes are therefore designed not only to show others where we belong, but also to teach us our place: the layout of the house shapes the ways in which we move around and interact with other people, and its decoration and furnishings subtly reinforce the conditioning that we receive from other sources. The central role of the home in forming and expressing identity means that changes in society are likely to be reflected by changes within the household, though not necessarily in ways that are easily identifiable from the gutted, depopulated shells of houses that are left for us to study.

An increase in social and geographical mobility in the Hellenistic period, and the shift from the small, relatively closed Classical city states to larger, more complex, and more diverse communities are often thought to have led to a sense of dislocation or isolation. This paper explores the repercussions of these developments in the home, and identifies some of the ways in which the architecture and decoration of Hellenistic houses were shaped by the occupants' need to establish their place in this expanded and transformed world. It will centre on a case study of Delos, not only because it is the site with the largest number of excavated houses of Hellenistic date (about a hundred) whose decor was left undisturbed when they were abandoned in the early first century BC,[2] but also because it was like the Hellenistic world

in microcosm, a cultural melting pot where a wide range of ethnic groups –
Athenians, Greeks from all over the eastern Mediterranean and Magna
Graecia, Italians and Romans, Syrians, and Jews, including many slaves and
ex-slaves – came together to take advantage of the economic opportunities
offered by one of the busiest trading centres in the Mediterranean.[3]

I will start by assessing what we can tell from the remains of the houses
about how the residents of Delos responded to living in such a cosmopolitan
community: to what extent did they assimilate to the society and culture of
their new home, or cling to the ways of their native cultures? How did they
use the architecture and decoration of their homes to help them form connections in this diverse, mobile society? The observations from Delos will be
illuminated by a brief comparison with the very different domestic culture
of Hellenistic Crete, where the prevailing fashions seem to have been rejected or regarded as irrelevant. Finally, as for some people to belong inevitably means that others are excluded, I will also look at some of the ways in
which the architecture and decoration of Hellenistic houses were designed to
differentiate between those who belonged and those who did not.

## Belonging on Delos

It has often been noted that despite the diversity of the population, the architecture and decoration of the Delian houses are surprisingly uniform.[4]
Although there is no standard 'house type' of the sort found in planned cities
like Olynthos, certain types and combinations of rooms appear repeatedly,
such as the open-fronted *exedra* (e.g., fig. 14.1, room I; fig. 14.7, room R), or
the large 'broad room' with a door in the centre of a long side, which often
has two smaller rooms opening off it (e.g., fig. 14.1, room K; fig. 14.7, rooms
N and AE).[5] The walls are almost invariably decorated in the Masonry Style,
which imitates the structure of ashlar masonry in moulded and painted
stucco (fig. 14.2), and almost all of the decorated mosaics have a rug-like design, consisting of concentric bands of decoration framing a plain, patterned,
or figured central field (figs. 14.3, 14.4); the same motifs – waves, meanders,
rosettes, perspective cubes – appear over and over again. Philippe Bruneau
suggested that a shared, Greek style of interior decoration served as a means
of integrating the cosmopolitan community on Delos, in the same way as
they all used the Greek language in their public dealings with each other
(Bruneau 1994–5: 107–8), but although this seems plausible, no one has really explored how it might have worked.

. Certainly there is very little evidence that the foreign residents adapted
the housing to reflect their native ways of life. For example, the population included a large and economically powerful contingent of Roman and
Italian businessmen, but they do not seem to have reproduced their own

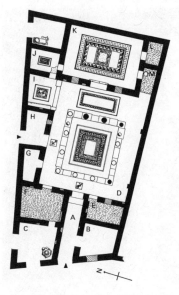

14.1. Delos, Maison du trident. Plan by Ruth Westgate.

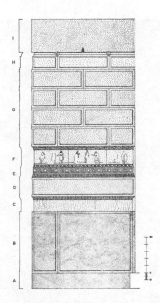

14.2. Masonry Style wall painting in room N of the Maison des comédiens, with frieze of comic scenes (after Bruneau, Vatin et al. 1970: fig. 110 © École française d'Athènes).

14.3. Vestibule mosaic in the Maison des dauphins, with the 'sign of Tanit.'
Photo by Ruth Westgate.

14.4. Panathenaic amphora mosaic in the *exedra* (I) of the Maison du trident.
Photo by Ruth Westgate.

styles of domestic architecture and decoration, which are well known to us from Pompeii and other sites, and from Roman writers such as Vitruvius. The houses all follow the typical Greek pattern of rooms arranged around a courtyard, often with a peristyle; none has the axial sequence of *fauces*, atrium, and *tablinum* that Vitruvius saw as the key feature differentiating Roman domestic architecture from Greek (*De arch.* VI, 7.1). Some scholars have seen Italian influence in the four-columned peristyles found in some houses, which bear a superficial resemblance to a tetrastyle atrium, and in the axial alignment of the vestibule, peristyle, and main room in some of the grander houses, which appears to create an impressive view of the interior from the entrance, as in an atrium house (e.g., the Maison du trident: fig. 14.1, rooms A, D, K).[6] However, axial arrangements could equally well be intended to emulate Hellenistic monumental architecture, and the sight lines into the house were usually closed off by doors at the inner end of the vestibule.[7] Moreover, the four-columned peristyles never lead into an open-fronted room like a Roman *tablinum*, but typically to a closed broad room, a type that is ubiquitous in the Greek East.[8]

There is also little sign of Italian influence on the interior decoration of the houses. The Delian version of the Masonry Style conforms to the standard scheme found in the eastern Mediterranean, which resembles the structure of real stonework, with tall orthostat blocks set on a low plinth; it lacks the high socle that was usually added in Italy when it was translated into the First Pompeian Style.[9] The concentric, rug-like design of the mosaics, with a small 'doormat' in front of the entrance, is also typical of the Greek East; contemporary Italian pavements tend to have all-over patterns that fill the space, with decorated strips marking divisions between and within rooms.[10] *Opus signinum*, the most common type of pavement in Italy at this time, is used for only six of the 350 or so surviving pavements on Delos.[11] It is hard to see any Italian influence even in houses whose last occupants have been identified as Italian by modern scholars, such as House I C in the Quartier du Stade, which contained a statue base dedicated to Q. Tullius by three of his freedmen (Rauh 1993: 195–205), or the Maison de l'hermès, which takes its name from a herm inscribed by a freedman of the Italian Paconii (Rauh 1993: 219–31).[12]

Only a handful of the houses contain features that might be identified as evidence of the occupants' non-Greek cultural or religious affiliations. In some cases this is plausible, such as House II A of the Quartier du Stade, which had an installation that may be a Jewish ritual bath,[13] or the Maison des dauphins, where a mosaic in the vestibule features the symbol of the Phoenician goddess Tanit (fig. 14.3);[14] the signature of a Phoenician craftsman, [Askle]piades of Arados, on a mosaic in the peristyle adds weight to the idea that the house was occupied by a Syrian.[15] But other cases are more questionable. For example, it has also been argued that the Maison du trident belonged to a Syrian, because its peristyle has two sculpted consoles in the form of crouching animals, a pair of lions and a pair of bulls, which may be linked to the Syrian deities Atargatis and Hadad.[16] However, it has also been suggested that the house was occupied by an Athenian, because one of the mosaics depicts a Panathenaic amphora (fig. 14.4).[17] It is possible that both theories are right, as the house probably had a succession of occupants, who may have added their own touches to the decor,[18] but it is equally possible that the house was never occupied by either a Syrian or an Athenian. This kind of argument is problematic not only for the obvious reason that it relies on a simplistic equation of particular motifs with specific ethnic identities, but also because it involves singling out individual elements of the decor and interpreting them in isolation, rather than considering them in the context of the whole ensemble and of Hellenistic domestic decoration in general. Both motifs are paralleled in other houses, and it is more profitable to interpret them as part of a common decorative vocabulary intended to convey particular meanings (Westgate 2010: 504–11). The mosaic belongs to a popular genre of motifs in Hellenistic interior decoration, such as crowns, palms, moneybags, and Nikai driving chariots, which are associated with victory and success, and were presumably intended to project a favourable impression of the householder and his family.[19] Too many copies, imitations, and images of Panathenaic amphorae have been found throughout the Mediterranean for them all to belong to Athenians, although it is possible that they were intended to advertise admiration for Athens or Athenian culture.[20] Similarly, the animal consoles are not unique: consoles in the form of bulls were sometimes used to support the elaborate stucco cornices that crowned Masonry Style wall decorations, including one in the house next door to the Maison du trident and a miniature version in the Maison des comédiens, which probably framed an ornate niche.[21] It is possible that the motif was chosen precisely because it was foreign and therefore exotic, perhaps because it evoked the power and luxury of the East. Even in the Maison des dauphins, the decor includes elements related to more than one culture: the peristyle mosaic has a border of griffin heads linked by a snaky body, a rare motif derived from the decorative arts of Scythia, far away from the house-owner's – and Asklepiades's – presumed birthplace in Syria (Guimier-Sorbets 1994: 261–2); again, the intention was perhaps to evoke an exotic and opulent culture. This idea of decoration as a common language is one way of interpreting Bruneau's suggestion that a shared style of decoration served to bring the diverse residents of Delos together, following his analogy with their use of the Greek language.

However, we cannot conclude from the prevalence of Greek architectural forms and decorative styles that the foreign residents of Delos abandoned their native traditions and assimilated to a Greek lifestyle and culture. Their ability to create a 'home away from home' would have been limited by the relative permanence of architecture, wall plaster, and mosaics, and probably by the need to rely on local craftsmen or workshops. The latter point is difficult to substantiate because no paintings and only a handful of mosaics are signed, and attributing them to individuals or groups by style or technique is not straightforward, but it is telling that in the few cases where the work of foreign craftsmen can be identified, it is in highly prestigious contexts, where it looks as if no expense was spared. The mosaic signed by Asklepiades, for example, is one of the most elaborate on the island, and the Maison des dauphins is one of the grandest houses.[22] At least four of the six *opus signinum* pavements on Delos may have been the work of Italian craftsmen, as they have been found in particularly lavish buildings where there are other indications of Italian influence, namely, the Agora of the Italians and the Maison de Fourni.[23] But most of the residents probably had to make do with local workshops; this was certainly the case with domestic sculpture, as attested by numerous unfinished statuettes found on the island, which closely resemble the finished pieces in the houses.[24] Given these limitations, if the foreign residents on Delos wished to express their native identity at home, they may have done so through other means that are less archaeologically visible, such as furnishings, clothing, and food, or by using the space in different ways. They may also have maintained their bonds to their native culture and compatriots in contexts outside the home, for example, through participation in the many religious and ethnic associations that are attested on Delos.[25]

There are, however, some areas of domestic life where we can see foreign residents bringing their native practices with them, and even influencing the lifestyle of the rest of the community. About a quarter of the houses have paintings on the exterior walls depicting sacrifices and games, which are thought to represent the rituals of the Compitalia, an Italian cult associated with slaves and freedmen.[26] The cult was clearly brought to Delos by Italians, although Claire Hasenohr has recently shown that they adapted it to suit their new circumstances: the relationship of the paintings to house doors suggests that what had been a communal cult in Italy had become a domestic one on Delos (Hasenohr 2003). Furthermore, although most of the paintings depict sacrifices conducted by participants in Roman dress, a few show the celebrants unveiled in the Greek fashion, some of the figures are labelled with Greek names, and there are other features that seem to have been influenced by Greek ritual; either the Italians had adopted some elements of Greek practice, or some non-Italian households had adopted the cult, or both (Hasenohr 2003: 207–8). The cult was a means of integrating the servile members of the household, an aim that might have appealed to non-Italian as well as Italian residents. From the point of view of the slaves and freedmen themselves, participation may have had advantages beyond assimilating them to their master's household: the gymnasium and other social institutions were closed to them, so the Compitalia would have offered them a valuable opportunity to form social or business networks of their own.[27] This may have been especially important on Delos, as it is thought that much of the community consisted of slaves or freedmen acting as agents for their masters (Rauh 1993). There is other evidence that the diverse community on Delos was developing its own local domestic culture that combined elements from different ethnic groups. The cooking- and tablewares found in the houses – which are more likely than fixed structures and decoration to reflect the actual behaviour of the occupants – are dominated by similar types to those found elsewhere in Greece at this time, even in houses like the Maison des sceaux, whose last occupants may well have been Roman.[28] But households throughout the community had also adopted certain Italian types of cooking and drinking vessels that were not yet common in other areas of Greece (Peignard-Giros 2000).

Both the Compitalia paintings and the pottery formed part of activities – cult and commensality – that enabled the residents of Delos to make connections within the community. Considering domestic architecture, mosaics, and paintings as essential elements in such social activities, rather than as objects that simply assert belonging by imitation, offers another way of approaching Bruneau's suggestion that the uniformity of the houses helped to assimilate the diverse community.[29] The repetition of certain room types, for example, can be seen as a product of the need to reciprocate invitations in an appropriate fashion, which made it desirable to have spaces suitable for the prevailing forms of social occasion. Rooms decorated with mosaics and wall paintings commonly belong to one of three types, the large broad room, a smaller room (the so-called *oecus minor*), and the *exedra*, which Trümper has identified as forming a standard 'set' (e.g., Maison des comédiens, fig. 14.7, rooms N, Q, R).[30] The desirability of these standard rooms is shown by the fact that they were often added when houses were remodelled, a fashion that was not confined to Delos: the proprietor of a house on Rhodes updated his square *andron* by converting it into a broad room and having a tessellated floor laid over the original pebble mosaic.[31] It seems likely that their characteristic shapes are related to particular types of social occasion: *oeci minores*, for example, are often about the right size for three dining couches, so might have been used for more intimate dinner parties than the broad room.[32] The mosaic designs might reflect a general preference for Greek modes of hospitality, as the undecorated outer border is often about the right width for Greek-style symposium couches, which were about 80–100 cm wide. Only a couple of rooms have a broad, U-shaped border that might have been intended to accommodate the wider couches of a Roman-style *triclinium*, although of course there are plenty of rooms where a *triclinium* could have been used if the host did not mind it resting on the decorated area of the mosaic.[33]

The Delians' somewhat monotonous choice of decorative styles and motifs may have been determined by a need to conform to established patterns of decoration in order to ensure that social events were 'right,' in the same way as the menus and accoutrements of formal occasions today tend to follow highly standardized patterns (Douglas and Isherwood 1996: 106). Presumably the Masonry Style remained the dominant form of domestic wall painting for almost four centuries because it was felt to create an appropriate ambience for entertaining, probably because it lent the proceedings a flattering air of importance and formality through its associations with monumental architecture. Similarly, mosaics draw on a fairly limited repertoire of motifs, often connected with drinking, abundance, luxury, and pleasure, which presumably helped to create a convivial atmosphere; other popular motifs were drawn from architecture, and probably evoked the same kind of prestigious associations as the Masonry Style (Westgate 2010: 505–10). A preference for themes related to pleasure and beauty can also be observed in domestic sculpture: Aphrodite is by far the most common subject, and once again the same types are repeated endlessly, often on a small and thus relatively affordable scale.[34] Unfinished statuettes found on Delos show that the sculptors blocked out the poses roughly by eye, rather than producing exact copies: as Philippe Jockey puts it, 'a general look is enough' to send out the right signals.[35]

Thus, while on one level possessing the standard room types and other 'prestige' features such as peristyles, mosaics, wall paintings, and sculptures was a means of displaying wealth and setting oneself apart from others, from a different point of view, keeping up with the neighbours was a way of maintaining connections within one's social circle (Douglas and Isherwood 1996: 90–1). But the demands of reciprocal hospitality may also have encouraged standardization in a different way, by placing limits on competitive display, which risked straining social bonds by seeming to place the host too much above his guests: there may have been a tension between standing out and fitting in.[36] Such social pressure might help to explain the near-universal repetition of the Masonry Style scheme, despite the existence of alternative styles that might have allowed greater freedom and flexibility of expression. One house, the Maison de l'épée, did have a more elaborate decoration, with a trompe l'oeil colonnade, garlands, and birds in the upper zone, but this was apparently a new innovation in the early first century BC, although a similar illusionistic style had been used in tombs over a century earlier.[37] Large-scale figured frescoes also appear in tombs from the fourth century onwards, but although figured scenes were clearly a prestigious feature in the Masonry Style, for some reason it never seemed appropriate to expand them beyond the narrow frieze band. Paradoxically, such restraint may actually be a product of intense competition for status, enabling close comparisons of value to be made easily (Douglas and Isherwood 1996: 106); the relative uniformity of the Masonry Style probably meant that small details such as expensive pigments, multiple friezes, or ornate cornices made a big difference.[38]

As well as contributing to the success of social networking, decorative motifs may have been chosen to assert or claim associations with particular groups in society. For example, one of the most widespread fashions in Hellenistic interior decor, at Delos and elsewhere, is for motifs related to drama, including masks in mosaics, theatrical scenes in wall painting (fig. 14.2), and terracotta masks and figurines of actors.[39] Such objects and motifs were probably intended to imply that the householder belonged to the educated class who were familiar with Greek literature, but they may also have claimed fellowship with his guests (who probably had similar items in their homes) on the basis of a shared enjoyment of the theatre. As the masks and scenes are most often drawn from comedy, they might also have appealed to a shared sense of humour, in much the same way that we might buy a mug or a T-shirt bearing a popular catchphrase.

The motif of the prize amphora, as well as projecting an aura of success and good fortune, may have been intended more specifically to suggest membership of the leisured elite who engaged in sport and frequented the gymnasium. Similar amphorae also appear in funerary contexts, where they are sometimes juxtaposed with more explicit references to the gymnasium, such as herms, strigils, and oil flasks.[40] Grave *stelai* from Rheneia showing the deceased leaning on a herm or accompanied by a slave carrying a strigil indicate that gymnastic activities (whether actual or aspired to) were an important status marker for male residents of Delos;[41] it would not be surprising if they chose the decoration of their houses to advertise this too. In the Maison du trident, the architecture and decoration may have been designed as a co-ordinated ensemble to suggest membership of this privileged group (figs. 14.1, 14.4): not only does the Panathenaic amphora mosaic allude to the pursuit of athletics, but it decorates the floor of an *exedra* (I), a type of room that is characteristic of gymnasia; the allusion was probably enhanced by a pair of marble pilasters and a central column framing the opening at the front of the room.[42] In the gymnasium, the *exedra* was a place for sitting and thinking or talking (Vitruvius, *De arch.* V, 11.2), and the smaller versions in houses were probably built with a similar purpose in mind: in Cicero's dialogues, for instance, which are set in various wealthy Italian villas, the speakers sometimes come to rest in an *exedra* for part of their discussions.[43] It seems likely that the *exedra* in the Maison du trident was intended for a similar function, as the mosaic is (unusually) oriented towards the back of the room, and was thus seen to best advantage by someone sitting inside looking outwards. Adding an *exedra* was a popular home improvement on Delos, not only because it provided a fashionable and pleasant venue for informal socializing and conversation, but also because it suggested a leisured lifestyle, athletic prowess, and perhaps an interest in philosophy.[44]

So although Bruneau's suggestion that the cosmopolitan residents of Delos assimilated to a Greek lifestyle and domestic culture may not be entirely justifiable, the uniformity of the houses can be linked in various ways to their desire to integrate themselves into the community. But perhaps the most powerful evidence of the Delians' need to communicate their place in society is the extraordinary quantity of domestic decoration found on the island. Despite the fact that the houses are relatively small – and many are only apartments, as the upper floors were occupied independently – they account for almost half the mosaics known from the entire Greek world in this period.[45] This is surely the product not only of the good preservation of the site, but of the exceptional social pressures caused by the unusual diversity and mobility of the population. Amos Rapoport has argued that living in large, heterogeneous communities intensifies the need for people to signal where they belong, as it is less likely that the inhabitants will know each other and how to behave appropriately towards each other; this tends to result in the multiplication of social and behavioural 'cues' in the environment, which typically include decoration.[46] The anonymity of the big city also makes it easier for the upwardly mobile to reinvent themselves, and the resulting fluidity of relationships tends to further increase the importance of material display (Cannon 1998, esp. 26–7). The connection between the mass of decoration on Delos and the pressures caused by social and geographical mobility becomes clearer if we turn to a society that seems to have rejected the proliferation of domestic display.

### Isolation? The Case of Crete

Not everyone wanted to belong to this world of leisured, cultured luxury. At a time when people all over the Hellenistic world were installing monumental features and elaborate decoration in their houses, the inhabitants of Crete seem to opt out of the prevailing trends in domestic architecture. Hellenistic houses at some Cretan sites, notably Lato and Trypetos (figs. 14.5, 14.6), are very different from the houses found on Delos and elsewhere, with much simpler plans of two or three rooms, often dominated by a large living room with a central hearth, and lacking the courtyard that is generally seen as the defining feature of the Greek house. Even at sites such as Phaistos where there are more complex courtyard houses, the prestigious features such as columns, sculptures, mosaics, and wall paintings that are increasingly common elsewhere seem to be virtually absent.[47]

This is unlikely to be the result of genuine isolation from the mainstream of Greek culture: Crete's strategic position meant that it was a pawn in the power politics between the Hellenistic kingdoms, and Cretan mercenaries were involved in wars all over the Greek world. The island also lay at the intersection of major transport routes, and there is growing evidence for external trading contacts.[48] Even so, it is difficult to be sure how far the distinctive simplicity of Cretan housing was the product of choice rather than economic necessity, but it seems consistent with ancient descriptions of the peculiar social structure of Cretan cities, where the men's lives are said to have centred around communal messes (*andreia*).[49] These accounts suggest two possible explanations for the plainness of Cretan houses, which are not mutually exclusive. Most obviously, if the *andreion* was the principal venue for male social networking in Cretan communities, it might have been less important to have elaborately decorated spaces for entertaining in the house. However, it may not be quite as simple as this, as there is evidence for formal drinking in some houses, and the extent and nature of the *andreion* system by the late Hellenistic period is a matter of some debate (Westgate 2007b: 446, 448, 452–3).

Secondly, if the proliferation of domestic decoration elsewhere was a response to the social pressures created by social and geographical mobility, the absence of decoration in Cretan houses might indicate either that the Cretans were not affected by these developments, or that they wanted to appear unaffected. This possibility is too complex to examine in detail here, but it is suggestive that the Hellenistic houses at Lato and Trypetos are strikingly similar to houses of the Early Iron Age, to the extent that those at Lato were once assumed to date from the Archaic period. It is possible that this was a conscious archaism, designed to project an impression of deep traditionalism, in the same way as the Hellenistic Cretans incorporated remains from the Bronze and Iron Ages into their sanctuaries and houses, and preserved ornate Archaic *pithoi* in their homes.[50] The intention was perhaps to suggest that their lifestyle and values had not been corrupted by change and external influences, just as they proudly claimed to trace their laws back to the legendary King Minos.[51]

But of course what looks from the outside like isolation, when seen from a different perspective, may actually be a way of belonging. The simplicity of the Cretan houses is also part of an ethos of restraint in the private

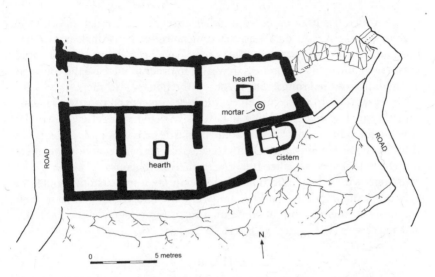

14.5. Lato, houses above the Prytaneion. Plan by Howard Mason.

14.6. Trypetos, House B1–3, viewed from the entrance. Photo by Ruth Westgate.

sphere, which has been observed in other areas of Cretan material culture, such as epigraphy.[52] As on Delos, this reluctance for individuals or families to stand out through material display may have been the product of social pressure to downplay differences in wealth in order to increase the cohesion and stability of the group.[53] The layout of the houses also suggests a desire for integration into the community: the lack of a central courtyard means that they are less inward-looking and exclusive than houses elsewhere in the Greek world, and it appears that some domestic activities took place at the front of the house, in sight of communal space, perhaps enabling members of the household to socialize freely with their neighbours.[54] This would be consistent with other indications that Cretan laws and customs tended to play down the importance of the family and the household, in favour of an emphasis on membership of communal institutions, such as the *andreion* and age classes (Westgate 2007b: 451–2).

## Exclusion

Some people may have chosen isolation as a statement of identity, but many occupants of the Hellenistic world did not have a choice. The architecture and decoration of Hellenistic houses seem to reflect a growing desire to reinforce the exclusion of those who did not belong – and hence, of course, the inclusion of those who did. In the houses at Delos, service rooms are much more sharply differentiated from living and reception rooms than in Classical houses, where there is usually no clear architectural or decorative distinction between living and service areas, apart from the elaborately decorated dining rooms that are found in a minority of homes. At Delos, service rooms are usually easily recognizable by their poor decoration, small size, and marginal position, typically in the dark, inconspicuous corners of the house (e.g., fig. 14.1, rooms E, F, G, L, M), or in a narrow range adjacent to the entrance (e.g., fig. 14.7, rooms A – H, AI – AM).[55] The Delian houses are also more likely than Classical houses to have a second entrance (e.g., fig. 14.1, room H) and alternative circulation routes, which often pass through the service area (as in the Maison des comédiens and Maison des tritons, fig. 14.7), enabling domestic activities to be carried out without intruding on the rest of the house (Nevett 2002: 84–8). A second vestibule and a service wing were often created when houses were modified, suggesting that these facilities were becoming increasingly desirable in the late Hellenistic period.[56]

One intention behind these arrangements was doubtless to keep menial activities out of sight, in order to present a good impression to visitors, but they also permitted stricter differentiation between members of

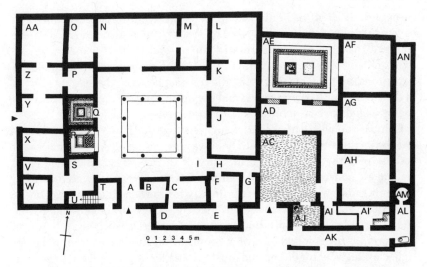

14.7. Delos, Ilot de la Maison des comédiens (Maison des comédiens, entrance at A; Maison des tritons, entrance at AC; Maison aux frontons, entrance at Y). Plan by Ruth Westgate.

the household, by keeping the people who performed menial functions apart from the other inhabitants, like the servants' quarters, back stairs, and tradesmen's entrances of well-to-do houses in the recent past. This may have helped to shape the slaves' sense of their subordinate status, as the habitual patterns in which people move around their homes and interact with other members of the household are a fundamental means by which their social identities are formed. The disposition of space within the house is a powerful tool for reinforcing social roles, and for defining who belongs and who does not. It was not simply a matter of confining slaves to dedicated 'slave quarters,' which would have been impractical, as they needed to move all over the house in order to carry out their duties. Rather, the menial and dirty activities associated with slaves were banished to more remote and less comfortable areas of the house; slaves were likely to spend more of their time in these areas, and to feel that this was, literally, their place. Their awareness of their inferiority would have been reinforced by the lack of decoration in the service rooms: in the Maison du trident, for instance (fig. 14.1), the courtyard and rooms I, J, and K had fine mosaics and polychrome wall plaster with the 'blocks' moulded in relief, but the rooms alongside the entrance and in the corners (E, F, L, M) had only flat, white plaster with incised divisions, and pavements of rough stone chips.[57] The service rooms also tend to be more cramped than the grander decorated rooms, and to have poorer access to light and air from the courtyard: in the Maison des comédiens and Maison des tritons, for example (fig. 14.7), the contrast between the spacious rooms in the sunny south-facing ranges and the much smaller, north-facing service rooms would have been obvious to the occupants.

Comparison with earlier houses suggests that the desire to emphasise social distinctions within the household was increasing, despite – or perhaps because of – the greater social mobility of the age. In Classical and early Hellenistic houses, mosaics and wall paintings are typically concentrated in the dining area, where they were primarily for the benefit of the head of the household and his guests; the rooms used by the rest of the household, free and slave alike, are usually undecorated.[58] In the Delian houses, however, decoration is often found in several rooms, which no longer seem to be designed exclusively for dining and must (in smaller houses at least) have been used for day-to-day living as well as for entertaining; if the decoration was now intended for the comfort of the householder's family, as well as their guests, the plainer areas that were the preserve of the slaves would be downgraded by comparison. Moreover, in Classical houses, domestic tasks often seem to have been carried out in the light and air of the courtyard, which is usually relatively plain,[59] whereas at Delos the presence of columns, mosaics, and elaborate wall plaster suggests that the court was now intended primarily as a display area and domestic activities were confined to enclosed rooms, which Lisa Nevett has interpreted as evidence that there was less concern for the comfort of the people who did domestic chores (Nevett 1999: 165–6). This may indicate not only that the division of labour within the household was shifting, as Nevett suggests, so that more of the menial work was done by slaves rather than free women, but also that people were more concerned to keep their distance from their slaves. This concern may have been especially pressing on Delos, where the many ex-slave residents are likely to have been particularly anxious to make it clear that they now belonged.

## Conclusion

The social pressures of the age were probably unusually intense on Delos, but the developments in housing observed there can be paralleled at many other sites in the period. Although no other site has yet yielded a concentration of domestic decoration to match Delos, the increase in the elaboration of houses is reflected throughout the Hellenistic world in a proliferation of mosaics, sculpture, painted wall plaster, and monumental architectural features (Westgate 1997–8: 111–15). The trend towards more pronounced spatial differentiation within the house is manifested even more strongly at other, less cramped sites, such as Morgantina, where some houses have second courtyards or service corridors (Westgate 2000a: 424–6). Both trends form part of a long-term process of increasing segmentation and specialization of space in Greek houses, which can be observed from the early Archaic period onwards and is probably related to the growing scale and complexity of society over this period.[60] At some level these developments may be the product of economic growth, but they can also be seen as responses to the social dislocations resulting from the movement of people, both socially and geographically, and from the development of great cosmopolitan cities. In such conditions, relationships and hierarchies become more fluid, creating a need for people to signal more explicitly where they belong and to delineate more clearly the boundaries between themselves and others, a need that is intensified by the fact of change itself (Cannon 1998: 25–6).

On the other hand, the hybrid elements observed in the domestic culture of Delos seem to be local developments, arising from the particular social and economic circumstances on the island; every community will have been affected by and responded to the social changes of the period in its own way.[61] But the cultural syncretism seen at Delos does reflect an important general phenomenon, namely, the potential for identities to become more complex as a result of geographical and social mobility. Many of the 'Romans' attested on Delos were actually slaves or freedmen of Greek or oriental origin (Rauh 1993: 33–4), like the freedmen who dedicated the statues in the 'House of Q Tullius' and the Maison de l'hermès, and other residents may have had multiple ethnic affiliations as a result of mixed marriages or adoptions (Baslez 2002). In this expanded and mobile world, it was possible to belong in more than one place.

There are limits to our ability to reconstruct people's behaviour and identities from the mute remains of their homes, but we can observe some of the ways in which the occupants of the Hellenistic world used the architecture and decor of their houses to associate themselves with others through imitation or emulation, to reinforce their place in society by excluding those who did not belong, or to set themselves apart, as the Cretans seem to have done; belonging to one group may mean not belonging to another. But as well as simply asserting claims to belonging, the house was also a means of achieving it, through its use as a setting for social occasions at which relationships could be formed and maintained; its rooms, decorated in an appropriate style, were a key element in the successful exchange of hospitality. The growing elaboration of houses in the Hellenistic period is probably a reflection of a trend towards greater use of the home for socializing, and thus of the need to make connections in the large, diverse communities of a changing world.

## Notes

1 I would like to thank the organizers for inviting me to participate in such a stimulating and friendly workshop, and the other participants for their helpful comments on the original version of this paper. The work presented here derives from the British Academy/AHRB-funded project 'Strategies, Structures, and Ideologies of the Built Environment' at Cardiff University. I am also grateful to the Leverhulme Trust for a Research Fellowship in 2008–9, which enabled me to develop some of these ideas in greater depth.

2 For the Delian houses, see Chamonard 1922–4; Bruneau 1994–5; Trümper 1998; Tang 2005; for their decoration, also Bulard 1908; Bruneau 1972; Bezerra de Meneses 1984; Kreeb 1988; Westgate 2000a, 2010: 504–12.

3 Couilloud (1974: 307–35) reconstructs the ethnic composition of the community from the funerary monuments of Rheneia and other epigraphic evidence.

4 E.g., by Bezerra de Meneses 1984: 86; Bruneau 1994–5: 106–8; Trümper 1998: 136–7. Tang (2005) is more confident about the possibility of identifying influences from different ethnic groups.

5 This type of room is also often described by the invented Latin term *oecus maior* (Chamonard 1922–4: 169–74).

6 Wallace-Hadrill 1994: 45 and fig. 3.12; Tang 2005: 43, 177; Nevett 2010: 76–8, 87. Nevett (1995) outlines the characteristics of the typical Greek 'single-entrance courtyard house.'

7 Chamonard 1922–4: 109. In the Maison du trident, the view from the entrance through to room K was obscured not only by doors, but also by a flight of steps at the far end of the vestibule.

8 Tang (2005: 43) identifies the broad room as a feature borrowed from Near Eastern architecture, although a rectangular room with two smaller rooms opening off the back is a common feature of Greek houses from the Late Geometric period onwards (Krause 1977).

9 For the differences between the Greek and Italian versions of the style, see Bruno 1969: 309–11; Ling 1991: 12–17, figs. 8, 9; Guldager Bilde 1995.

10 See Westgate 2000b: 256–62 for this and other differences between eastern and western mosaics.

11 Bruneau 1972: nos. 8, 17, 316, 326, 327, 339. *Opus signinum* is a red mortar containing crushed terracotta, often decorated with patterns in tesserae or stone chips.

12 Both houses did, however, have external paintings related to the Italian cult of the Lares Compitales (see below pp. 251–2). The occupants are generally

identified from inscribed statue bases or altars found in the houses (listed by Tang 2005: 56–7), but it is not always certain that the person named actually lived in the house. Some of the inscribed objects were portable, and even in the case of the fixed statue-bases mentioned here, it is not clear whether the house was occupied by the recipient of the statue or by his freedmen; in any case they were probably only the last of a series of occupants. The graffiti found in the houses are similarly inconclusive, because we do not know who wrote them or under what circumstances.

13 The case may be strengthened by the find of a Jewish dedicatory inscription in the house, although the 'bath' went out of use before the final phase of occupation: Trümper 1998: 135, 222–3, fig. 24.

14 Bruneau 1972: no. 209 and p. 71, 116–17.

15 Bruneau 1972: no. 210 and p. 111.

16 Bruneau 1970: 473. The consoles formed the junction between the higher columns of the north colonnade and the lower entablature on the east and west sides: Chamonard 1922–4: 143–4, figs. 65, 67.

17 Valavanis 2001: 169. For the mosaic, see Bruneau 1972: no. 234.

18 It is not certain whether the mosaic was installed when the house was built or at a later date, as there has been no investigation below the floors.

19 The theme occurs in several mosaics on Delos (Bruneau 1972: nos. 25, 214, 217, 234, 325), and friezes of Nikai in chariots appear twice in domestic wall paintings there (Maison des tritons: Bruneau, Vatin et al. 1970: 165, fig. 122 183–5, pls. 25.9, 26.1–5; Quartier du Stade, House I A: Plassart 1916: 164), as well as on Rhodes (Michaud 1973: 389, figs. 303, 304; Konstantinopoulos 1986: pl. 30).

20 Westgate 2010: 506–7. It is even less likely that they all commemorate actual victories in the Panathenaic Games, as there are too many fantastic variants on the theme. For imitations and images of Panathenaic amphorae, see Bentz 1998: 18–22; Valavanis 2001.

21 Quartier du Théâtre, House II B, peristyle, Bulard 1908: 156, fig. 52 a, a'; Maison des comédiens, room N, Bruneau, Vatin et al. 1970: 157, fig. 113.

22 Nevertheless, we cannot entirely rule out the possibility that Asklepiades was permanently based on Delos, or a regular visitor, although no other mosaic has been convincingly attributed to him.

23 One *opus signinum* floor was found in the Agora of the Italians (niche of Ofellius, Bruneau 1972: no. 17), and three in the Maison de Fourni (rooms AC, AH, and upper floor: Bruneau 1972: nos. 326, 327, 339), where Italian influence has also been detected in the plan and the mosaic decoration (Trümper 1998: 317–18; Westgate 2000b: 261–2; below, n.33), although other elements of the decor have a more oriental flavour (Trümper 2006: 126–8, who suspects that the building was a clubhouse rather than a private residence).

24 Jockey 1998, 2000.

25 The architecture and decoration of these associations' clubhouses also do not necessarily reflect the ethnicity of the members or the origin of the cult: Trümper 2006.

26 Bulard 1926a, 1926b; Bruneau 1970: 589–620.

27 It is not certain whether the Delian gymnasia were open to freedmen (Baslez 2002: 56–7).

28 Among the finds in the house were two portrait busts in the veristic style, which is generally associated with Romans: Rose 2008: 106–7, fig. 10, with references.

29 This approach owes a great deal to the ideas of Douglas and Isherwood (1996).

30 Trümper 1998: 52–63. For the distribution of mosaics and paintings, see Westgate 1997–8: 108, with fig. 1 and table 2.

31 Skaros plot, House Δ: Konstantinopoulos 1967: 526–8, with figs. 4, 5.

32 In practice the proportions and sizes of all three types vary, and they were probably used for a range of activities (Westgate 2007a: 321; Trümper 2007: 326–30).

33 Roman dining couches were typically about 1.2 x 2.2–2.4 m, large enough for three diners to recline at an oblique angle and eat from a communal table; Dunbabin (2003: 36–50) explains the differences between Greek and Roman practice. Room E of House IV B in the Quartier du Théâtre and room AN of the Maison de Fourni are roughly the right size for a *triclinium* to fit snugly, and have a small decorated mosaic with a broad plain surround on three sides (Bruneau 1972: nos. 276, 328), although this may be accidental, at least in the relatively modest House IV B, where the plain border may have been intended to save money (Westgate 2010: 510–11); in the Maison de Fourni, however, this was not the only Italian-style element (see above, n.23). In many Delian rooms the border varies in width or is too narrow for couches of any kind, which Hoepfner (1999: 516–20) takes as evidence that they were used for one or more *triclinia*; but he sees the *triclinium* as a Greek innovation, originating in the Hellenistic royal courts, rather than a Roman import. In any case, how closely the width of the border reflects the arrangement of furniture is debatable, as the concentric design had clearly become conventional in rooms of all types (Westgate 2007a: 316–19).

34 Kreeb 1988: 58–60. At least 37 statuettes of Aphrodite have been found on Delos, 29 of which represent only 4 different poses (13 removing her sandal, 6 topless, 5 Knidian, and 5 washing her hair). The need to mass-produce a limited range of types is clearly reflected in the unfinished statuettes found around the Portico of Philip, which may have been practice pieces: the 'Sandal-binding,' Knidian, and *Pudica* types predominate (Jockey 2000).

35 Jockey 1998: 182 with n.44.

36 Douglas and Isherwood (1996: 123–6) discuss an illuminating case, a community of Yorkshire miners whose consumption patterns were strictly regulated
   by the need to maintain solidarity with their colleagues: any attempt at ostenta-
   tion was met with disapproval, but at the same time the principle of reciprocity
   meant that any man whose income dropped was forced to move down to a less
   well-off social circle.

37 E.g., in the late third-century Tomb of Lyson and Kallikles at Lefkadia. The
   fragments from the Maison de l'épée were initially identified as belonging
   to the Second Pompeian Style, but it is now clear that they surmounted a
   conventional Masonry Style decoration (Alabe 2007).

38 For a possible hierarchy of values expressed by these elements, see Westgate
   2000a: 397–400.

39 Comic masks, often linked by a garland, appear on numerous mosaics, e.g., at
   Delos (Bruneau 1972: nos. 68, 215, 347), Rhodes (Konstantinopoulos 1986: pls.
   27, 50), and Tel Dor (Stewart and Martin 2003). For the painted frieze of comic
   scenes in the Maison des comédiens, see Bruneau, Vatin et al. 1970: 155–7, fig.
   110, 168–83, pls. 21–5.

40 E.g., Valavanis 2001: 165, pl. 43; the most illuminating is the third-century *stele*
   of Metrodoros, from Chios, which includes gymnastic motifs alongside other
   imagery relating to elite pursuits: the dead man is depicted hunting, framed
   by Panathenaic amphorae on columns, and by friezes of Nikai in chariots and
   heroic Lapiths fighting centaurs, while on the back of the *stele* his gymnasium
   kit is shown hanging from a nail (Berlin, Pergamon Museum Sk. 766 A: Pfuhl
   and Möbius 1979: II, 566–7, no. XXI, pl. 331).

41 Herms: Couilloud 1974: nos. 90, 118, 141, 167, 219, 296–300, 473; slaves
   with strigils (e.g.) Couilloud 1974: nos. 75, 180, 274, 277, 281, 287, 301–3.
   Couilloud (1974: 278) rejects the idea that herms represented the gymnasium,
   partly because one of the Delian males thus commemorated was only a baby
   (Noumenios, no. 141), but the point was surely to show that the child and his
   family belonged to the social class who attended the gymnasium; this is made
   more explicit in another child's *stele*, that of twelve-year-old Themistokles
   (no. 473), who is shown leaning on a herm, holding a ball and a book roll, along
   with a slave carrying his strigil, and a dog, a favourite companion of high-status
   males (cf. Menander, *Sam.* 14, quoted by Christina Vester in this volume).

42 The marble elements were not in situ, but Chamonard thought they were from
   room I (1922–4: 152, 277, fig. 145).

43 *Nat. D.* 1.6; *De or.* 3.5.

44 Indeed, as Trümper (1998: 56) notes, some *exedrai* are barely big enough to use,
   and must have been created for their prestigious associations alone.

45 Westgate 2010: 110. Many upper floors were accessible independently (Trümper
   1998: 92–106).

46  Rapoport 1990: 16–17. By 'cues' I mean information encoded in the built environment or conveyed by people (through their behaviour or dress, for example), which helps us to 'place' other people or identify situations, and to behave accordingly.

47  Westgate 2007b. The houses at Lato were probably built in the late fourth or early third century, those at Trypetos and Phaistos in the later third century; all three sites were abandoned in the second century BC.

48  E.g., Perlman 1999: 146–51; Vogeikoff-Brogan and Apostolakou 2004; though Chaniotis (2005c) is more cautious about the scale of Cretan trade. Crete clearly did not lack economic potential (de Souza 1998), even if it was not fully exploited in the Hellenistic period.

49  E.g., Aristotle, *Pol.* 1272a, and the fragmentary Aristotelian Cretan *politeia* (fr. 611.14–15 Rose); Athenaeus, *Deipnosophistae* IV, 143, quoting Dosiadas and Pyrgion; Strabo, *Geog.* X, 4.16–21.

50  For the reuse of earlier monuments, see Alcock 2002: 108–17. There is also some evidence for imitation of earlier buildings: a Hellenistic sanctuary at Syme seems to have been designed to resemble a Late Minoan house shrine (see Alcock 2002: 108–17). Numerous Archaic *pithoi* have been found in Hellenistic houses on Crete, for example at Phaistos, Lyttos, and Trypetos.

51  Plato, *Laws* 624; Aristotle, *Pol.* 1271b; Strabo, *Geog.* X, 4.8. I hope to pursue this question at greater length elsewhere.

52  Chaniotis 2004a; Westgate 2007b: 453.

53  As suggested by Strabo, *Geog.* X, 4.16.

54  Note, for example, the stone mortars in the front rooms in figs. 14.5 and 14.6, and the forecourts and cistern in front of the houses in fig. 14.5.

55  Westgate 2000a, esp. 426; Westgate 2007a: 313–15; Trümper 2007: 323–31.

56  For example, in Quartier du Théâtre House IV B: Trümper 1998: 287–9.

57  Chamonard 1922–4: 366–8, 390, figs. 224, 225.

58  Westgate 1997–8: 95–102, with fig. 1 and table 1.

59  Nevett 1999: 65, 69; Cahill 2002: 161–93.

60  Susan Kent (1990a) observed that there is a correlation between the scale and complexity of societies, and their tendency to partition space and create discrete areas for different activities. In Greece, the typical house plan evolves from a single multifunctional room in the early Archaic period, perhaps with a porch in front and a smaller chamber at the rear, to the complex houses of the Classical period, with multiple rooms around a courtyard, often including specialized rooms for dining and bathing. Particularly rapid increases in the number and specialisation of spaces seem to coincide with periods when social boundaries were proliferating or hardening, such as the early Archaic period when concepts of citizenship, gender, and slavery were crystallizing and the courtyard house makes its first appearance, or the late Classical period, when

the first double-courtyard houses appear. These ideas are explored more fully in Westgate, forthcoming.

61 As shown, for example, by Tang's (2005) comparison of housing in the trading communities of Delos, Carthage, and Ampurias, or Papaioannou's (2007) analysis of how the housing of various Greek cities reflects their differing responses to Roman rule.

# 15

# Mère-patrie et patrie d'adoption à l'époque hellénistique: Réflexions à partir du cas des mercenaires crétois de Milet

PATRICK BAKER

### Introduction

L'époque hellénistique fut une période d'innovations, de changements, de transition, pour reprendre la formule des éditeurs du présent ouvrage. Période importante pour la suite de l'histoire occidentale et complexe en raison des proportions que prit alors le monde de culture hellénique, elle fut parfois rapprochée du monde actuel, notamment lorsque le concept de mondialisation (*globalization*) a suscité l'intérêt des historiens.[1] Marqué par la mobilité des personnes d'abord, mais également des biens, des idées, etc., le monde hellénistique présente en effet des caractères qui font que l'historien d'aujourd'hui peut sentir une proximité avec certains des phénomènes qui le composèrent. À l'heure où le sentiment d'appartenance à la communauté est mis à mal et qu'il est pointé du doigt dans la détresse que vivent quantité de gens, toutes catégories d'âges, de sexe, d'origine ethnique ou de pratiques religieuses confondues, le thème de l'isolement et de l'appartenance apparaît à la fois comme actuel et très hellénistique.

Un dossier d'inscriptions permet de l'aborder sous l'angle de l'épigraphie et de l'histoire dans les cités, groupe social structurant indissociable de la civilisation grecque. Il concerne un groupe de mercenaires crétois recrutés par la cité ionienne de Milet, puis naturalisés en deux vagues successives. Ces nouveaux citoyens implantés sur le territoire durent cependant envisager de rentrer dans la mère-patrie lorsque le territoire où se trouvaient les lots qui leur avaient été concédés passa aux mains des Magnètes, dont la cité était située en amont de la vallée du Méandre. Mais l'appartenance d'origine des Crétois de Milet était sérieusement remise en cause lorsque les cités de Crète exprimèrent une fin de non-recevoir catégorique empêchant littéralement ceux-ci de rentrer dans ce qu'ils pensaient être ou espéraient encore être 'chez eux.'

Le cas de figure de ces mercenaires crétois apparaît donc comme exemplaire pour le thème *belonging and isolation*. Les Crétois avaient fait le choix d'*appartenir* désormais à la cité de Milet renonçant à leur appartenance d'origine; ils se trouvèrent *isolés* lorsqu'ils furent coupés de leur patrie d'adoption et qu'ils n'étaient plus les bienvenus dans leur mère-patrie.[2] Ce cas fournit en outre un prétexte pour se pencher sur l'utilisation conjointe et peut-être un peu contradictoire par les cités hellénistiques des mercenaires et des citoyens-soldats et pour chercher à éclaircir le rapport des uns et des autres à la défense de la communauté à laquelle ils n'appartenaient pas de la même façon, mais dont ils constituaient des éléments clés.

On peut à bon droit se demander s'il est justifié de revenir à nouveau sur la question des mercenaires hellénistiques qui, il est vrai, a suscité une riche historiographie. Depuis les études fondatrices de H.W. Parke, W.W. Tarn et G.T. Griffith, portant sur les mercenaires eux-mêmes ou sur les armées royales hellénistiques avec un traitement parallèle de la question des mercenaires, jusqu'à l'imposante étude de M. Launey sur les armées royales, les travaux, articles ou monographies ne manquent pas; et ceci est sans compter les parutions plus récentes, soit sur la guerre à l'époque hellénistique ou sur l'époque hellénistique elle-même.[3] Seulement, il semble que la distinction entre citoyens-soldats et mercenaires n'est pas encore parfaitement acquise et que les textes demandent à être analysés dans cette perspective. Un article récent confirme qu'il n'est pas superflu de reprendre l'exercice, fût-ce, comme ici, dans la perspective ciblée du thème 'appartenance et isolement à l'époque hellénistique' (Couvenhes 2004).

### Le cas des mercenaires crétois à Milet: les documents, les faits

Dans le dernier tiers du III<sup>e</sup> s. a.C., Milet engagea un nombre important de mercenaires crétois qu'elle installa sur le territoire de la petite ville de Myonte. Ces terres avaient été nouvellement acquises par Milet grâce à l'incorporation de Myonte au territoire civique. Les Crétois au service de

Milet ne demeurèrent pas longtemps des mercenaires étrangers puisqu'en deux vagues successives, la plupart furent enregistrés dans les listes civiques.

Les inscriptions qui permettent de suivre, au moins en partie, la destinée des mercenaires crétois de Milet constituent un ensemble réunissant d'abord et principalement des textes de Milet,[4] puis de Magnésie-du-Méandre et de Crète (textes de Knossos et de Gortyne).[5] Ils constituent la trame de fond d'un épisode couvrant plus de trente ans de la vie milésienne à la fin du IIIe s. Plusieurs aspects de la mobilité et du statut des personnes y sont évoqués, principalement en ce qui concerne les étrangers (les conditions et restrictions liées à l'octroi de la citoyenneté, les liens des résidents étrangers *naturalisés* avec leur cité d'origine, etc.), sans compter les questions de démographie,[6] du mercenariat, etc. Devant une telle richesse d'informations, on ne sera pas surpris que les textes en question et la petite tranche d'histoire qu'ils relatent, aient suscité de multiples études et commentaires dans l'historiographie hellénistique.[7]

Dans ce dossier, les documents milésiens concernent l'enregistrement de Crétois comme nouveaux citoyens de Milet. Les Milésiens firent donc venir chez eux, en deux vagues successives espacées d'environ cinq ans, un nombre indéterminé, mais certainement important, de soldats crétois, qu'ils installèrent sur une partie du territoire. Il semble que ceux de la première vague étaient déjà sur place, employés par la cité comme mercenaires sous les ordres de condottieres.[8] Quant à ceux de la seconde vague, ils seraient venus spécialement depuis la Crète.[9] La datation des deux vagues – 228/227 et 223/222 – établie par A. Rehm et longtemps acceptée reposait sur sa datation de la liste de stéphanéphores milésiens (Rehm 1914: 124). Mais des arguments présentés par M. Wörrle firent remonter de six ans cette liste; la première vague daterait donc de 234/233 et la seconde de 229/228.[10]

De cette immigration organisée, les Milésiens conservèrent non seulement les listes des nouveaux citoyens inscrits, mais aussi les décisions du peuple: celles-ci sont d'ordre politique (octroi de la citoyenneté à ceux qui le désiraient: [. . .τοῖς βουλομένοις πολιτεύε]σθαι μετὰ Μιλησίων [*Milet* I.3 37b.30–1], pleine jouissance des droits civiques et des charges), d'ordre judiciaire (interdiction d'être en procès avec qui que ce soit et pour aucune raison, etc.), d'ordre civique (répartition dans les tribus, attribution des lots) et d'ordre religieux (participation aux cultes, jouissance des sanctuaires nationaux, etc.). Les textes furent gravés sur les murs du portique délimitant l'enclos sacré du Delphinion, dont le hasard du temps n'a préservé que quelques blocs.[11] Les décisions du peuple ne se laissent deviner qu'aux prix de substantielles restitutions laissant le champ libre à de multiples interprétations. Quant aux politographies elles-mêmes, elles sont aussi fort lacunaires: de la première vague qu'A. Rehm évaluait à probablement plus de deux cents nouveaux citoyens inscrits, quelques dizaines de noms seulement sont conservées;[12] de la seconde, deux cent dix noms subsistent du millier supposé par le même éditeur. En ajoutant à cela le nombre des femmes dont quelques-unes sont inscrites avec leur mari, et des enfants dont les noms figuraient parfois aussi à la suite de ceux de leurs parents, l'éditeur évaluait à trois ou quatre mille personnes l'exode crétois vers le territoire milésien.[13] La présence de femmes que l'onomastique rapproche des soldats recrutés indique un lien de dépendance entre elles et ceux-ci. Les périodes de service prolongées incitaient naturellement les mercenaires à se déplacer avec leur famille.[14]

De ceux de la première vague, on sait qu'ils avaient reçu des lots de terre et des habitations (cantonnement) en Hybandis[15] et à Myonte: [δια]∥κλήρωσιν, suivi de τῆς δὲ ['Υβ]ανδίδος (1.12) et 33e: 1.11–14: δεδόσθαι δὲ αὐτοῖς καὶ σκ[ευά]∥ριον. Μυο[υσίων δὲ τοὺς κ]ε[κτημ]ένους τὰς οἰκίας ἐν τῶι χωρίωι δέ[ξασ]∥θαι αὐτούς. δοῦναι δὲ καὶ] ἀπὸ τῶν ὑπαρχόντων στεγνῶν[16] τῶ[ν]∥ ἐφ' ἑτ[έρων οἰκημάτων, ὅ]σοι ἐπαγγέ[λλ]ονται. (Milet I.3 33d.9–10 [très mutilé]). Je comprends l'argument de P. Brulé (1978: 166n2) selon lequel les terres de la plaine, certes fertiles, étaient les 'confins marécageux, paludéens' du territoire milésien 'où le seul animal bien adapté devait être le moustique' et qui, partant, suggérait de voir dans cette plaine leur 'terrain de parcours' bien plus que celui d'installation qui dut être plutôt l'île d'Hybanda mentionnée par Pline ([HN] 2.91). Cette île se présentait donc, selon lui, comme le 'point fort de la plaine'; le texte ne dit-il pas d'ailleurs ἐν τῶι χωρίωι (ligne 12)? Mais cela ne va pas sans poser un problème sur lequel je reviens un peu plus loin.[17] De toutes les façons, le texte spécifiait au préalable qu'il leur serait interdit de vendre le lot à l'intérieur d'une période de vingt ans sous peine de poursuites impliquant le vendeur aussi bien que l'acheteur (Milet I.3 33e.6–11). Dans le cas où une telle infraction eût été commise, les Milésiens de préciser, la 'loi sur les étrangers' servirait de code de référence pour appliquer la sanction (33e.11: κατ[ὰ τὸν] ξενικ[ὸν] νόμον).[18]

Dans les sources de la seconde vague, rien n'indique l'endroit où furent installés les colons-soldats, dont un groupe choisit tout de suite de s'inscrire sur les listes de nouveaux citoyens,[19] mais il est probable que ce fût au même endroit que le premier contingent. À cet égard, seule subsiste la décision au sujet de l'affectation des nouveaux citoyens à une tribu déterminée par le peuple: la formalité incombait au collège des prytanes: ἐπικληρωσάτωσαν δὲ | [αὐτοὺς οἱ πρ]υτάγ[ει]ς καὶ ἐπὶ φυλάς, ἃς ἂν ὁ δῆμος ἀποδείξηι (Milet I.3 37d.63–4).[20] Pour la suite de l'histoire, il faut se reporter une trentaine d'années plus tard.

Vers 201, après plusieurs années de dépendance à Milet, le territoire de la petite ville de Myonte passa aux mains des Magnètes.[21] Philippe V leur en avait fait cadeau pour les remercier d'avoir approvisionné son armée qui battait désespérément la campagne en quête de ravitaillement (Polyb. 16.24.9), une largesse effectuée au détriment des Milésiens malgré l'accueil favorable qu'ils avaient réservé au roi au lendemain de sa victoire à Ladè.[22] Les Crétois, désormais en territoire magnète, étaient devenus indésirables parce que la plupart d'entre eux étaient citoyens milésiens; à ceux qui n'avaient pas fait ce choix, c'est-à-dire celui de renoncer à leur citoyenneté d'origine, on peut se surprendre que les Magnètes aient réservé le même accueil. Mais au delà du fait que les terres arables de la plaine fluviale suscitaient évidemment l'intérêt des Magnètes, on ne peut manquer de noter, à la suite de Brulé, que les Magnètes n'étaient de toute façon pas liés par une décision politique prise par les Milésiens et qu'ils n'avaient aucun engagement à respecter vis-à-vis les colons-soldats crétois (Brulé 1978: 170), et ce même s'ils pouvaient, à leur tour, bénéficier de leurs services et de leur présence sur le territoire en question.

Une correspondance diplomatique s'établit alors entre Magnésie et quelques cités crétoises – Gortyne, Knossos et peut-être Éleutherne – au sujet du rapatriement des colons. Mais parce qu'ils avaient accepté la citoyenneté milésienne, la plupart des colons étaient également devenus indésirables dans leur patrie d'origine. Sur cette question 'des Crétois qui avaient émigré' (διαλεχθέ[ντων δὲ τῶν πρεσ]|βευτῶν καὶ περὶ τῶν Κρηται[έων τῶν εἰς Μίλητον]| ἀποικιζομένων), les réponses des Gortyniens et des Knossiens marquèrent une différence nette entre ceux qui avaient gardé le statut d'étrangers résidents (métèques) et ceux qui avaient choisi la citoyenneté milésienne, modifiant par cela leur appartenance à une communauté: ὅσοι ἐμ Μι[λήτωι Γορτύνιοι]| ὄντες μετῴι[κη]σαν εἰς Μίλ[ητον ἢ – – – –]|αν ἢ ἄλλω[ς, εἶμ]εν Γορτυνίο[υς, ὅσοι δὲ πολι]|τεύουσιν ἐμ Μιλήτωι, μὴ εἶμεν [ἐπάνοδον εἰς]| τὰν ἰδίαν, ἀλλὰ τὰ ὑπάρχον[τα αὐτοῖς εἶμεν δα]|μόσια καὶ εἶμεν αὐτοῖς τὰ ἐπ[ιτίμια ἅπερ τοῖς ἐπὶ]| τὰν ἰδίαν στρατευσαμένοις.[23] Les premiers pouvaient rentrer chez eux sans être inquiétés; quant aux autres, le droit d'accès à leur patrie était supprimé, leurs biens devenaient propriétés publiques et ils étaient passibles du même châtiment que celui qui était infligé aux traîtres coupables de s'être battus contre leur propre cité. Dans ses dernières lignes conservées, le décret de Gortyne renforce la position des Gortyniens à l'égard de ceux qui sont tenus pour 'être passés à l'ennemi.' Il prévoit en effet qu'une copie 'des décrets' soit envoyée 'aux Milésiens et à ceux (des Crétois) passés à Milet': δ[έδοχθαι τὰ ψαφίσ]|ματα ἀποστεῖλαι πρός τε Μιλ]ησίους καὶ πρὸς | το]ὺς μετελθόντας εἰς Μίλητ[ον. . . ] (IC IV 176.39–41). Le verbe μετέρχομαι, employé ici dans un sens négatif, souligne le fait qu'ils sont 'passés' dans le camp de quelqu'un d'autre, qu'ils ont 'fait défection.'[24] Un point demeure à mon avis encore ambigu et aucun commentateur ne paraît l'avoir relevé. S'il est clair que de telles mesures ont valeur d'une 'véritable proscription'[25] pour les Milésiens d'origine crétoise, je m'interroge sur la portée de la clause selon laquelle 'leurs biens devenaient propriétés publiques.' Qu'est-ce à dire? Après un quart de siècle de résidence et d'appartenance à la cité de Milet, certains de ces Crétois qui avaient quitté la mère-patrie comme mercenaires, détenaient encore des biens 'au pays'? Ou bien ne s'agit-il que d'une licence dont le but est de renforcer l'interdiction de rentrer? On ne peut guère conjecturer sur le sens de l'expression presque banale de τὰ ὑπάρχοντα pour trouver la solution de cette énigme.

De tous les mercenaires crétois, on ne sait pas ce qu'il advint, car il n'est plus fait mention de cette histoire dans les sources. À cet égard, il est frappant de constater l'absence des citoyens d'origine crétoise dans l'épigraphie milésienne postérieure. Les réponses des cités crétoises confirment cependant que plus de trente ans après, il se trouvait encore sur le territoire de Milet – devenu magnète – des colons-soldats crétois qui n'avaient pas souhaité changer de nationalité. Ceux-là rentrèrent peut-être dans leur patrie d'origine, bien que l'on n'en ait aucune certitude. Il est clair en tout cas que la région ou les Milésiens les avaient installés (et peut-être la ville de Myonte elle-même) faisait toujours l'objet d'un contentieux entre Milet et Magnésie quelques années plus tard, car une guerre éclata entre les deux cités et, bien que le nom de Myonte soit absent du traité de paix qui suivit (197/196 a.C.), on a généralement admis qu'il s'agissait de la portion de territoire en cause.[26]

### Les colons – soldats crétois et la défense de la cité

Un aspect fondamental passé sous silence par les documents du dossier est celui des raisons exactes de ce recrutement en masse par les Milésiens.[27] Certes, plusieurs hypothèses ont été formulées quant au contexte historique général de cette intégration de nouveaux citoyens. R. Lonis, par exemple, décrivait en ces termes le contexte historique et politique de cette fin du IIIᵉ s. telle qu'elle aurait été vécue par les Milésiens:

C'est dès le début du conflit entre Séleucos II et son frère Antiochos Hiérax, commencé en 241/0, que ces soldats furent engagés. Pour être plus précis, ils l'ont sans doute été après l'écrasante défaite subie par Séleucos II à Ancyre, en 240 ou 239, défaite à la suite de laquelle le Séleucide se retira en Cilicie, laissant l'Asie Mineure comme une proie offerte à Hiérax. On imagine dans ces conditions l'affolement de Milet. Ces événements ont dû faire apparaître la tragique insuffisance des troupes propres à Milet, dès lors que cette cité ne pouvait plus compter sur les troupes royales, d'où son recours à des troupes d'appoint. Mais en 234/3, le danger n'est pas écarté. Certes la menace des Galates est éloignée, grâce à la victoire éclatante d'Attale de Pergame sur ces derniers en 238/7, mais le danger d'une attaque de Hiérax persiste. Il faut donc s'attacher les mercenaires engagés quelques années plus tôt en en faisant des citoyens. Quant au second train de mesures prises en 229/8, il pourrait se situer lors de l'expédition d'Antigonos Doson en Carie. (Lonis 1992: 264–5)[28]

Les efforts, comme celui-ci, de rattacher à la grande histoire l'intégration de mercenaires crétois à Milet perdent cependant en pertinence si l'on se penche sur le contexte local, voire régional. S'il est légitime de chercher à replacer les cités du vieux monde grec au cœur des interactions entre les grands royaumes, cela ne doit pas faire oublier qu'elles maintenaient, comme depuis toujours, des relations avec leurs voisines, des relations qui n'étaient pas nécessairement paisibles et qui nécessitaient, dès lors, que soit mis en place un appareil militaire efficace pour défendre leurs intérêts, principalement économiques il va sans dire, puisqu'il s'agissait généralement de la possession et de la jouissance de territoires.[29]

La documentation épigraphique de la fin du IIIe siècle et du début du IIe siècle illustre bien les initiatives des Milésiens dans le renforcement de relations commerciales et politiques avec les cités d'Ionie et de Carie. Ainsi, pour le contexte de l'implantation de mercenaires en Hybandis, puis de leur politographie, il faut songer davantage à des causes locales, à savoir les conflits récurrents qui ont opposé les cités de la basse vallée du Méandre et portant sur les terres fertiles de la grande plaine fluviale. Profitant de ce que la bourgade de Myonte et son territoire étaient désormais intégrés au territoire civique, les Milésiens souhaitèrent y installer des effectifs de manière à créer un glacis protecteur dans la région contre toute poussée ennemie venant de l'intérieur du pays, plus haut dans la vallée.[30] Mais cela n'éclaircit pas le contexte de la politographie des soldats crétois et des avantages qui leur furent octroyés par les Milésiens. Quel que fût le contexte, est-ce que l'inscription massive de colons-soldats crétois correspondait, comme l'écrivait R. Lonis, à une grave pénurie de troupes locales, ou s'agissait-il plutôt de mesures visant à résoudre un problème de repeuplement rural, comme l'avait d'abord pensé M. Launey et plusieurs à sa suite?[31] Les textes, du moins ce qu'il en reste, présentent une contradiction qui peut être expliquée: d'un côté, les nouveaux citoyens étaient exclus des services de garde et de la charge importante de phrourarque pour une période de vingt ans suivant leur inscription et, de l'autre, ils devaient jurer de défendre et de protéger la cité et ses forts *du mieux* qu'ils pouvaient;[32] d'une part, ils étaient exclus des forts, d'autre part ils semblent y avoir été installés ou en tout cas avoir reçu des habitations associées à un fort (Μυρ[υσίων δὲ τοὺς κ]ε[κτημ]ένους τὰς οἰκίας ἐν τῶι χωρίωι δέ.[ξασ]]θαι αὐ[τούς) [*Milet* I.3 33e.12–13]), car c'est bien le sens qu'il faut donner à *chorion*.[33]

Les Milésiens ont peut-être essayé de résoudre plusieurs problèmes à la fois, c'est-à-dire celui de peupler une partie du territoire avec des colons accoutumés au métier de la guerre qui présentaient l'avantage, tout en participant à la vie économique de la cité, de constituer un obstacle efficace contre les ennemis qui essaieraient de s'emparer de cette portion de leur territoire, isolée du reste du territoire et de la ville par le Golfe Latmique; en s'assurant par ailleurs que les mercenaires crétois devenaient milésiens, la cité réglait en soi le problème de l'occupation de ce territoire nouvellement acquis, comme de la protection de son bourg, qui demeurait cependant aux mains des Milésiens.

Dans ces conditions, la clause excluant pour vingt ans les nouveaux citoyens des services ordinaires de défense de la cité, par 'défiance envers ces gens guerriers et volontiers séditieux' comme l'écrivaient J. et L. Robert (Robert 1976: 199), ne constituait pas un obstacle à leur utilisation à des fins strictement militaires. Les mercenaires crétois occupaient et cultivaient une zone du territoire, en même temps qu'ils formaient un actif de troupes utilisable en campagne ou en cas d'invasion venant de l'arrière-pays; quant au service de garde des forts nationaux, qu'il s'agisse du commandement ou des garnisaires, il restait sous le contrôle étroit du peuple milésien, du moins durant les vingt années que l'on peut qualifier de délai 'probatoire.' En obligeant les mercenaires à résider toutes ces années avant de participer à la garde des forts nationaux, les Milésiens s'assuraient qu'ils se seraient créé suffisamment d'attaches dans la cité pour la servir en toute loyauté.[34] Les Crétois reçurent des lots de terre et devinrent par là même des colons-soldats qui défendirent désormais 'leur' patrie. Mais ils ne servirent pas dans les forts comme garnisaires avant vingt ans. Les deux missions étaient tout à fait différentes. En conséquence, peut-on affirmer qu'ils avaient été installés sur l'île d'Hybanda, comme le suggérait Brulé, car celle-ci, bien que cela ne soit pas archéologiquement vérifié à ma connaissance, constituait le 'point fort,' le verrou, de ce secteur de la vallée et il devait donc s'y trouver une place forte? Conformément au dispositif du texte, la garde de ces endroits demeurait sous le contrôle de Milésiens de souche, 'di antica data' pour reprendre l'expression d'I. Savalli (1985: 395).[35]

Il faut se garder de pousser trop loin l'interprétation, car il manque beaucoup d'informations sur cet épisode, spécialement pour les débuts de l'affaire et pour ce qui se produisit après la perte de Myonte aux mains des Magnètes; des Crétois qui essayèrent peut-être de rentrer dans ce qu'ils croyaient encore être 'chez eux,' on ne sait ce qu'il advint; quant aux autres, qui demeurèrent à Milet, ils sont absents du traité de paix entre Milet et Magnésie survenu quelques années plus tard, ce qui se conçoit puisqu'ils étaient désormais intégrés au corps civique milésien. Mais cela interdit toute interprétation définitive quant aux motifs milésiens de cet enrôlement collectif tout comme de l'exode de centaines de Crétois. Il est en tout cas clair que, lors de la première politographie, les soldats crétois étaient déjà présents sur le territoire myontais, et probablement même depuis quelques années au service de Milet elle-même, à titre de mercenaires employés par la cité. À cet égard, ils avaient été recrutés sur la base d'un contrat comme l'épigraphie en fournit des attestations sous diverses formes (contrats, clauses d'un traité, etc.).[36]

En outre, le texte de la première politographie, comme on la vu plus haut, laissait ambigu le statut de ceux des Crétois qui avaient choisi d'adopter la citoyenneté milésienne. Toute infraction à la règle de ne pas vendre le lot qui leur était octroyé à l'intérieur du même délai 'probatoire' de vingt ans serait sanctionné par la 'loi sur les étrangers.' À la différence d'autres exemples d'octroi du droit de cité et aux yeux des Milésiens, ces nouveaux citoyens demeuraient limités dans leur droit pour une période suffisamment longue pour que l'on puisse imaginer que leur enracinement dans la communauté serait achevé; il m'apparaît difficile de ne pas considérer cela comme un élément de discrimination important créant, fût-ce pour une durée déterminée, une catégorie à part de citoyens, de citoyens *minoris iuris*. Mais selon Savalli (1985: 395), le fait que l'acheteur potentiel de la terre était aussi susceptible d'être jugé par cette même loi constituait un argument suffisant pour ne pas voir dans la mesure une discrimination des nouveaux citoyens, l'acheteur pouvant être lui-même un Milésien de souche.

### Citoyens-soldats à Milet

La discussion sur les mercenaires crétois de Milet doit être faite en parallèle à l'étude des attestations de citoyens-soldats. Sans chercher à répondre textuellement à la question, il convient en effet de se demander si ce dossier – exceptionnel, il est vrai – est le signe d'une participation plus effacée des Milésiens d'origine à la défense de leur cité. L'étude du corpus milésien permet de voir que les citoyens comptaient aussi parmi les forces militaires de la cité.

Ce que l'on sait des soldats composant les effectifs militaires proprement milésiens, c'est-à-dire milésiens d'origine, concerne essentiellement les garnisons des *phrouria* du territoire et leur chef, les phrourarques.[37] On trouve cette information dans plusieurs traités conclus entre Milet et d'autres cités à la fin du IIIᵉ s. et au début du IIᵉ s., à la même époque donc que le dossier des mercenaires crétois ce qui, en soi, est un heureux hasard de la conservation des documents. Une clause récurrente y interdit, pour un délai de dix ans (vingt dans le cas des Crétois), l'exercice de la phrourarchie ou la participation au service de garde aux citoyens des cités traitantes qui choisiraient de venir s'installer à Milet ou sur son territoire et de se faire enregistrer dans les listes civiques. La clause figure dans les traités d'isopolitie avec Séleucie-Tralleis (*Milet* I.3 143), ville de la moyenne vallée du Méandre, avec Mylasa en Carie (*Milet* I.3 146) et, surtout, du traité d'alliance avec l'autre cité du Golfe Latmique, Héraclée-du-Latmos (*Milet* I.3 150); un traité de sympolitie avec la bourgade de Pidasa impliquait des dispositions similaires à celles mises en œuvre par une autre cité ionienne, Téos, lors de son incorporation de la bourgade de Kyrbissos (Robert 1976); les Milésiens se chargeraient désormais d'envoyer un phrourarque et une garnison pour contrôler le fort de Pidasa, ce qui confirme la participation des citoyens à la défense et à l'occupation des forts (*Milet* I.3 149). À ces textes, s'ajoute la série concernant la politographie de soldats crétois étudiée plus haut.

D'autres textes encore concernent des phrourarques milésiens, mais en fonction hors de la ville et même hors du territoire de la péninsule milésienne: à haute époque, la dédicace d'un phrourarque en poste dans un petit fortin du Mykale (*IPriene* 365)[38] et quelques textes provenant des îles dites 'milésiennes.'[39] De l'île de Lepsia, on a conservé un décret honorifique pour le phrourarque Timothéos envoyé par la cité de Milet, aux environs de 170 a.C.[40] et deux dédicaces de phrourarques sortant de charge (Ier s. a.C.);[41] de Léros, un décret honorifique pour le phrourarque Apollonios, daté du IIIe-II[e] s. a.C.[42] Pour achever ce survol des sources, de courtes dédicaces concernent enfin la marine milésienne de basse époque hellénistique (Ier s. a.C.). Deux d'entre elles ont été offertes par l'équipage de navires en escale à Cos et présentent un intitulé semblable: Μιλησίων οἱ στρατευσάμενοι;[43] les équipages comptaient sinon en totalité du moins en majorité des citoyens milésiens.[44] Une autre est la dédicace par le peuple des Milésiens d'une statue au citoyen Hégémôn fils de Philodémos, qui avait exercé la navarchie (*Milet* I.3 167). Deux autres dédicaces enfin, datées de 69 a.C., sont le fait d'équipages milésiens ayant participé à l'effort de guerre de Rome contre Mithridate, lorsque Délos subit de graves dommages causés par la bande de pirates d'Athénodôros au service du roi pontique (*IDélos* 1855 et 1856).[45] C. Valerius C. f. Triarius, un légat de Lucullus engagé dans cette guerre (en 73 et en 69),[46] avait entrepris la réparation des dégâts et notamment la construction d'un rempart autour de la ville, dont les vestiges sont désignés aujourd'hui par le nom de 'muraille de Triarius.'[47] Les équipages s'y présentent par la formule: οἱ συνστρατευσάμενοι Μιλησίων ἐν νηῖ δικρότωι.

Dans les traités conclus avec Séleucie-Tralleis et avec Mylasa, la clause probatoire dont il vient d'être question est rédigée en des termes identiques: φυλακὴν δὲ καὶ φρουραρχίαν συγκληροῦσθαι διελθόντων ἐτῶν δέκα ἀφ' ἑκάστης ἐπικληρώσεως (respectivement lignes 30–1 et 39–40). La même clause apparaît sous une forme légèrement différente dans la politographie de soldats crétois: [λαγχ]αγέτ[ω]σαν δὲ φυλακὴν καὶ φρουραρχίαν ἐτῶν παρελ||[θόντων . . . εἴ]κοσι (*Milet* I.3 37d.65–6). Dans le traité d'alliance conclu avec les citoyens d'Héraclée-du-Latmos, la formule employée pour limiter l'accès des nouveaux citoyens à la charge reste d'abord assez discrète sur les conditions d'attribution: φρο[υ]||ραρχίας δὲ καὶ φυλακῆς τῆς κατὰ πόλιν καὶ φρουρικῆς μετεῖναι αὐτοῖς διελθόντων | ἐτῶν δέκα, ἀφ' οὗ ἂν ἕκαστοι ἐπικληρωθῶσιν (50–2); mais elle est immédiatement suivie de la précision suivante: τὰ δὲ ἄλλα τὰ περὶ τὸν κλῆρον τὸν ἐν ἀρχαιρεσ[ί]|αις ὑπάρχειν κατὰ τὸν βουλευτικὸν νόμον (52–3). Les Héracléotes ne pouvaient pas 'obtenir' la charge de phrourarque, ni une responsabilité concernant la garde de la cité (ville et territoire), ni même jouir du droit de participer au service de garnison avant un délai de dix ans suivant leur enregistrement éventuel dans les listes civiques à Milet; mais 'pour les autres charges attribuées par tirage au sort dans les assemblées électorales,' la procédure demeurait conforme à la loi du conseil.[48] Enfin, dans le traité d'incorporation du petit bourg de Pidasa, il était convenu 'que les Milésiens envoient (régulièrement) à Pidasa celui des citoyens désigné par le sort pour occuper la fonction de phrourarque, ainsi que des garnisaires (τὸν λαχόντα τῶν πολιτῶν | φρούραρχον καὶ φρουρούς) aussi nombreux que nécessaire, et qu'ils prennent soin que les remparts soient restaurés, qu'ils restent en l'état, et qu'ils veillent à la garde, de la manière qu'ils jugent profitable' (15–18).[49] À Lepsia, les considérants du décret pour le phrourarque Timothéos, Milésien de la ville envoyé dans l'île pour commander le petit fort local, laissent tout ignorer des conditions de la désignation: ἐπειδὴ Τιμόθεος Ἀρήτου γεν[ό]|μενος φρούραρχος ἐν τῶι ἐνιαυτῶι |τῶι ἐπὶ στεφανηφόρου Εὐκράτου κτλ. (4–6). Quant au décret de Léros pour le phrourarque Apollonios, la partie perdue de la pierre a emporté avec elle l'information.

Le formulaire des textes ne précise pas si la phrourarchie s'appliquait autant à la garde de la citadelle et des remparts de la ville qu'à celle des fortins du territoire, ou bien seulement à l'une ou à l'autre,[50] mais l'intérêt ici reste le même. Les témoignages indiquent hors de tout doute que le tirage au sort parmi les citoyens permettait l'attribution des magistratures en question et que la tâche de garnison concernait les citoyens. Dans la clause probatoire incluse dans les traités conclus entre Milet et d'autres cités, ce qui intéresse surtout ici n'est pas tant la clause elle-même que ce qu'elle enseigne sur la manière de choisir les citoyens pour le service de garnison à Milet: comme les phrourarques, les garnisaires n'étaient pas élus mais désignés ou assignés par le sort. Les termes utilisés sont λαγχάνειν dans la politographie de soldats crétois, συνκληροῦσθαι dans les traités avec Séleucie-Tralleis et avec Mylasa, et ἐπικληροῦσθαι dans le traité avec Héraclée-du-Latmos. En incorporant le petit bourg de Pidasa, le peuple de Milet prévoyait de choisir par le sort (λαχεῖν *Milet* I.3 149.15–16) un phrourarque, puis de recruter une garnison pour prendre le contrôle du fort local.

À Milet, les remarques faites à propos des phrourarques s'appliquent aussi aux garnisons qu'ils commandaient. Tout citoyen était susceptible d'être désigné pour participer à la protection du territoire et de la ville, sans que le choix fût influencé par des critères précis de sélection. Le détail ne manque pas d'intérêt, car il sous-entend qu'une majorité de citoyens étaient aptes à assumer des tâches militaires; en tout état de causes, que cela allait de soi. Mais force est de constater que beaucoup de précisions demeurent inconnues. N'est-ce pas là une interprétation trop littérale des termes employés? Y avait-il des nuances qu'il n'est aujourd'hui plus possible de saisir? On peut penser par exemple que les garnisaires 'tirés au sort' l'étaient à partir de listes préétablies de citoyens mobilisables ou de citoyens volontaires. Des listes de citoyens mobilisables existaient à Athènes, au IVe s. a.C., mais elles étaient le plus souvent dressées en vue de campagnes militaires à l'étranger. Nous n'en connaissons pas dans les cités d'Asie Mineure.[51]

Les parallèles peuvent être multipliés. Dans la guerre qui avait opposé les Milésiens et leurs alliés héracléotes aux Magnètes et leurs alliés priéniens, au début du IIe s. a.C., une guerre dont l'enjeu était l'éternelle pomme de discorde que constituaient pour ces cités les terres arables de la basse vallée du Méandre, de nombreux citoyens avaient été faits prisonniers d'un côté comme de l'autre.[52] Ces prisonniers étaient bel et bien des citoyens-soldats qui avaient combattu dans les troupes de leur cité et non des prisonniers civils capturés en cours de campagne comme ceux que les Galates, moins d'un siècle plus tôt, avaient capturés à Érythrées et à Priène et qu'ils utilisaient comme otages ou qu'ils destinaient aux marchés d'esclaves.

### Mercenaires et citoyens: cas parallèles d'Érythrées et de Priène

Malgré son caractère particulier, par le nombre de personnes concernées et les conditions du recrutement et de l'implantation, le cas des mercenaires crétois n'est évidemment pas le seul d'une cité recourant à des services professionnels pour les questions militaires à l'époque hellénistique. Quelques documents d'autres cités d'Ionie, pour ne citer que des exemples proches de Milet, attestent, à divers moments de l'époque hellénistique, de la présence de contingents de mercenaires parmi les effectifs de la cité. En nombre plus ou moins important selon les cas, il reste cependant difficile de quantifier les proportions des uns comme des autres, c'est-à-dire des mercenaires par rapport aux effectifs civiques. Devant l'idée reçue selon laquelle, les cités s'adonnaient à cette pratique de manière généralisée, et ce depuis le IV<sup>e</sup> siècle a.C., on s'étonnera cependant que les cas n'abondent pas. Voyons deux exemples de haute et de basse époque.

Lors de l'invasion galate en Asie Mineure, au premier quart du III<sup>e</sup> s., la cité d'Érythrées et particulièrement son territoire furent touchés par les déprédations des envahisseurs. Un collège de stratèges en fonction à ce moment dut traiter avec les mercenaires qu'employait la cité au sujet de leur solde en souffrance. Les magistrats avancèrent les fonds nécessaires pour régler les sommes dues (*IErythrai* 24.18–20). Le texte ne dit rien sur la longueur du retard, détail qui fournirait un indice sur la durée du contrat passé entre la cité et les mercenaires.[53] Faisaient-ils partie d'une armée régulière employée toute l'année, ou n'étaient-ils engagés que pour de courtes périodes quand le besoin s'en faisait sentir? Malgré le laconisme qui la caractérise, cette mention d'effectifs professionnels dans l'armée d'une cité compte parmi les plus explicites, du moins dans les textes émanant des cités d'Ionie.[54] Un siècle et demi plus tard, un passage du long décret de Priène pour l'évergète Moschiôn, daté d'après 129 a.C., mentionne la solde de mercenaires (*IPriene* 108.150–2: Μοσχίων μετὰ τῶν συν[υ]ποςτάντ[ω]ν [π]ολ[ιτῶν]‖ το[ὺς σ]τρατίωτας εἰς μῆνας δύο, τὴν εἰς αὐτοὺς μισθοφορὰν ‖[ἐ]κ [τῶ]ν ἰδίων χορηγῶν·). Avec des concitoyens,[55] le Priénien honoré avait fourni des fonds pour payer deux mois de solde aux soldats. L'expression τὴν εἰς τοὺς στρατίωτας μισθοφορὰν ne fait pas de doute: ces soldats étaient des mercenaires au service de la cité.[56] Il faut probablement penser à une avance de fonds, comme celle qu'avaient faite les stratèges érythréens honorés dans l'année 275 a.C.

Que révèle d'autre part la documentation sur les effectifs civiques dans ces deux cités? Les informations concernent surtout les officiers, c'est-à-dire les magistrats militaires susceptibles de recevoir des honneurs de leurs concitoyens; tel est le cas, par exemple, du dossier épigraphique érythréen où le collège des stratèges est principalement représenté dans des textes datant généralement du III<sup>e</sup> siècle.[57] D'un autre côté, les inscriptions sont moins nombreuses et moins révélatrices pour les effectifs eux-mêmes. Souvent en effet la présence ou l'absence d'effectifs civiques se devine sans pouvoir être définitivement prouvée; de même, la cohabitation toujours possible de citoyens-soldats et de mercenaires employés par la cité sur une base permanente ou temporaire est rarement repérable sauf dans quelques cas particuliers où, pour différentes raisons, les textes marquent la distinction entre les deux types de soldats. Il n'en demeure pas moins que les documents disponibles permettent d'affirmer avec certitude l'existence de milices civiques dans les cités. Parfois la formule employée pour désigner un corps de troupe ne laisse aucun doute quant au statut des soldats, comme à Skepsis ou à Chrysè en Troade.[58] Mais cela est loin d'être la règle et il faut la plupart du temps chercher ailleurs ces informations précieuses.

Le fait que certaines garnisons aient voté des décrets honorifiques pour leur chef, parfois connus seulement sous la forme abrégée (inscriptions honorifiques), en calquant le modèle des décrets de la cité, suggère naturellement qu'elles étaient composées de citoyens. À cela on doit ajouter l'existence d'une copie inscrite du texte exposée dans les lieux publics de la cité, signe que l'assemblée du peuple avait entériné les honneurs accordés par les membres de la garnison. Certes, l'on pourrait objecter que la garnison fût mixte, qu'il pût y avoir en son sein un détachement de mercenaires, sans que les textes ne le laissent entrevoir. Des inscriptions honorifiques, par exemple, votées par des garnisons pour leur supérieur ne présentent parfois aucun caractère public, c'est-à-dire officiel.[59] Mais ce serait fermer les yeux sur le soin jaloux que les cités mettaient à préserver leurs places fortes, citadelle (acropole), remparts, forts sur le territoire, etc.

À propos des garnisaires en poste dans la citadelle de Télôneia à Priène, A. Asboeck écrivait jadis qu'ils formaient dans leur isolement – *Abgeschlossenheit* – une sorte de *koinon* et qu'ils pouvaient ainsi voter leurs propres décrets honorifiques (Asboeck 1913: 123). Prenons l'exemple d'Hélikôn à Priène (*IPriene* 19). Le décret mentionne des honneurs antérieurement accordés au magistrat: 'Déjà deux fois dans le passé . . . il avait été couronné par les garnisaires de couronnes d'or, et ils lui avaient accordé l'éloge' (20–4). Ces honneurs étaient demeurés en quelque sorte des honneurs 'privés,' en ce sens qu'ils n'avaient pas été reconnus officiellement par la cité, non pas qu'elle les ait refusés, mais parce que la garnison ne lui en avait point fait la demande expresse. C'est grâce à la troisième occasion que l'on a connaissance de la brillante carrière du Priénien. Les garnisaires, bien décidés à faire savoir aux autres citoyens les mérites du concitoyen qu'ils avaient élu pour la troisième fois consécutive, dépêchèrent deux des leurs auprès du conseil et de l'assemblée du peuple pour demander que le décret fût inscrit à un endroit précis du sanctuaire urbain d'Asklépios ainsi que sur une stèle posée dans le sanctuaire dédié à Télôn, héros éponyme de la citadelle. La démarche, bien qu'unique dans les documents conservés de Priène, n'était certainement pas exceptionnelle. Un moment précis était prévu dans l'ordre du jour des assemblées pour les requêtes de ce genre[60] et d'autres stèles pour des particuliers étaient déjà posées dans la citadelle: avec la permission de l'assemblée, la stèle d'Hélikôn devait en effet être posée 'dans le sanctuaire de Télôn, près de la stèle d'Aristippos fils de Philios' (47–9).

On peut ainsi imaginer que des garnisons rendaient – régulièrement (?) – hommage à leur chef lors des célébrations du culte local, et que dans quelques cas exemplaires une procédure était entreprise pour élever ces honneurs au rang d'honneurs civiques. Cet exemple est remarquable bien que, *stricto sensu*, il renseigne peu sur les effectifs civiques comme tels, c'est-à-dire leur nature, leur nombre, leur organisation, etc. Mais le dossier priénien contient plusieurs documents similaires de contenu et la série qu'ils constituent témoigne de la participation des citoyens à la défense de la cité.[61]

Ainsi, il ne fait pas de doute que les garnisons affectées à la garde de la citadelle ou des forts du territoire étaient composées de citoyens. Ce que suggère fortement le décret honorifique pour Hélikôn trouve confirmation dans les autres décrets pour des phrourarques priéniens.[62] Dans le décret pour Bias, à la suite de la mention de son attitude zélée et de la manière intègre et juste avec laquelle il avait commandé le fort et la garnison (?), il est question 'des autres citoyens.'[63] Le décret évoque également l'équité dont il fit preuve à l'égard des soldats 'pendant tout le temps où il avait autorité sur eux.'[64] Pareil énoncé de qualités se retrouve dans les décrets pour Hélikôn et pour Nymphôn, qui étaient loués pour leur rigueur et leur sens de la justice à l'endroit des garnisaires. Qui plus est, Hélikôn, précise le décret, haranguait ses hommes pour les encourager à ne pas faillir à leur tâche. À première vue, cela renseigne davantage sur l'attitude des citoyens élus à la charge de phrourarque. En revanche, il est clair qu'aux yeux du peuple, l'attitude des magistrats honorés ne prenait tout son sens que si les garnisaires étaient eux aussi des citoyens et que le comportement louable d'un concitoyen élu au poste de commandement avait été de respecter ses pairs et de ne pas abuser de son pouvoir. À Érythrées, un collège de stratèges honoré vers 260, 'alors qu'une guerre frappait le territoire,' avait 'contribué au maintien de la démocratie pour le peuple et avait rendu la cité libre à ses successeurs' (*IErythrai* 29.7–8 et 12–14).

Lorsque le territoire de Priène fut envahi par les Galates, vers 275, le peuple essaya tant bien que mal de repousser l'ennemi en envoyant contre lui les corps civiques d'infanterie et de cavalerie.[65] Mais ces efforts ne suffisaient pas. C'est à ce moment que Sôtas intervint à la tête d'une troupe de citoyens, 'les meilleurs' dit le texte.[66] Certes, il n'est pas possible de faire la lumière complète sur l'information apportée, car s'il est clair qu'il s'agissait de citoyens, donc de personnes potentiellement mobilisables, on ne sait pas s'ils formaient à l'origine un corps de troupe régulier ou si, au contraire, il s'agissait d'une troupe de fortune. Dans le premier cas, le qualificatif pourrait signifier qu'il s'agissait d'un corps d'élite comme les citoyens de Chersonèsos recrutés en hâte par Diophantos, alors que, dans le second cas, il désignerait plutôt l'ensemble des hommes encore valides et prêts à combattre. Le décret pour

Sôtas confirme en tout cas l'existence de corps civiques d'infanterie et de cavalerie opérationnels à Priène.[67] À pareille époque, alors que 'de grandes peurs et de grands dangers' menaçaient leur cité, les stratèges d'Érythrées avaient été honorés pour avoir 'conservé en toutes circonstances la cité et le territoire intacts' (*IErythrai* 24.10–13). Et à l'instar de Sôtas, l'Érythréen Polykritos avait trouvé là l'occasion de participer à l'effort de guerre.[68]

## Conclusion

Au terme de cette analyse, il convient de formuler un certain nombre de remarques conclusives. Les deux catégories, bien distinctes, des mercenaires et des citoyens-soldats, ne doivent pas être envisagées l'une au détriment de l'autre dans les cités, petites, moyennes ou grandes, de l'époque hellénistique. Les mercenaires étaient assurément présents, sans doute parfois en nombre important, dans les effectifs des cités; le dossier des mercenaires crétois de Milet (comme d'autres) le montre bien. De leur côté, les effectifs civiques sont rarement quantifiables pour ne pas dire identifiables. Mais ce fait dépend de la nature des textes parvenus jusqu'à nous, bien plus qu'il n'est le signe d'une désaffection des citoyens pour la pratique militaire en général et la défense nationale en particulier. Seule la lecture fine des textes permet de ne douter de la présence ni des uns ni des autres. Si l'appartenance à la communauté qu'ils défendaient ne pose aucun problème dans le cas des citoyens, les cas des mercenaires crétois illustre pour sa part toutes les variables qu'elle pouvait adopter.

Sur la constitution des troupes, leur organisation, etc., les documents apportent peu de lumière. Nous ne disposons, par exemple, pas de listes de citoyens mobilisables comme à Athènes, ni de listes de garnisaires ou de combattants qui permettent une étude des 'populations militaires' ou l'établissement de statistiques comparatives entre les cités. Il n'est pas possible non plus, à partir des textes, de reconnaître les proportions de citoyens mobilisés par rapport au nombre de citoyens dans le corps civique entier et impossible également de procéder à un classement par armes, même sommaire, des effectifs civiques, pour observer d'éventuelles distinctions entre les corps de mercenaires et ceux de citoyens, ceux-là employés pour leurs aptitudes spécifiques dans telle technique de combat et ceux-ci remplissant un rôle propre à leur qualité de citoyens.[69] Le mercenaire était un mal nécessaire pour les cités. S'il apportait dans certains cas une expertise qui pouvait faire défaut aux troupes civiques, sans que cela constitue le seul motif de son recrutement, il arrivait aussi avec son contingent de problèmes.

Et si le dossier des Crétois de Milet présente des caractères singuliers, on peut imaginer sans glisser dans la spéculation que des situations

similaires sont survenues dans d'autres cités grecques de l'époque hellénistique. Comme à l'époque classique, et ce même s'il se déplaçait en groupe,
le mercenaire demeurait un électron libre, parfois rattaché pour de longues
périodes à une cité, mais sans doute condamné, dans le long terme, à une
forme d'isolement, dans la mesure où il renonçait à la mère patrie, sa mère
patrie. De même, la nouvelle appartenance qu'il pouvait se voir offrir avait
bien des chances de se révéler un cadeau de Grec si certaines données politiques changeaient, telle la cession des possessions milésiennes de la vallée aux Magnètes par un roi hellénistique. À l'instar de Savalli (1985: 426),
on ne manquera pas de voir le cas des mercenaires crétois de Milet comme
'un possibile compromesso fra la tradizione della democrazia greca, fondata
sull'identità del cittadino-soldato, e l'innovazione del mercenariato,'[70] même
si tout porte à penser que la décision prise par les Milésiens n'allait pas de soi
(n. 244). On remarquera enfin que ce sont les Magnètes, non les Milésiens,
qui négocièrent le retour éventuel des Crétois chez eux. 'Nos émigrés sont
donc partout indésirables: comment s'en débarrasser?,' de remarquer Brulé
(1978: 170), l'histoire ne le dit pas.


## Notes

1 À cet égard, plusieurs écrits de l'historien Ed. Will restent des classiques et une
source d'inspiration pour l'étudiant comme pour l'érudit. On consultera, en premier lieu, Will (1979a), avec les pistes de réflexion qu'il propose, mais également
les limites qu'il ne manque pas de rappeler ('comparaison n'est pas raison': 95);
à lire, également, sur les cités Will 1985 et 1988; cf. enfin Ferrary 1998.

2 '[T]he best documented case,'Chaniotis 2002: 100 et 2004b: 485.

3 Pour ne citer que celui-là, je pense, par exemple, à Chaniotis (2005a: 82–8) sur
les conditions de service.

4 Les textes ou plutôt ce qu'il en reste, car ils sont malheureusement fort lacunaires, sont présentés à la suite par Rehm (1914), ci-après *Milet* I.3 33 à 35 pour
la première vague et 36 à 38 pour la seconde. L'ensemble est accompagné d'un
commentaire, p. 166–202. En dernier lieu, Herrmann (1997: 160–3), pour une
mise à jour bibliographique et la traduction allemande des textes.

5 Gortyne: *IC* IV 176 (antérieurement *I. Magnesia*, 65a + 75); Knossos, *IC* I 9\*
(antérieurement *I. Magnesia*, 65b + 76).

6 Cf., par exemple, Pomeroy 1983.

7 Chaque fois abordés sous l'un de ces aspects, ils n'ont pas encore fait l'objet
d'une étude complète qui offrirait une compréhension d'ensemble des événements. P. Brulé, dans son étude sur la piraterie crétoise hellénistique (1978: 165),
formulait déjà cette remarque; il étudia par la suite le dossier dans la perspective

d'une 'enquête démographique sur la famille grecque antique' (Brulé 1990). Quelques années auparavant, I. Savalli utilisa ce cas dans sa brillante étude de la concession et de l'acquisition de la citoyenneté à l'époque hellénistique (Savalli 1985); R. van Bremen, pour ne citer encore qu'un exemple, s'est brièvement intéressée au même dossier (van Bremen 2005: spéc. 319–20).

8 On identifie peut-être trois d'entre eux: Lichas, dont on a retrouvé la base d'une statue honorifique (Fredrich 1908: 115–17) liée aux événements de la campagne d'Asie Mineure de Philippe V en 201 a.C. (cf. Haussoullier 1902 :140–2; Launey 1987: 256n 2: il était peut-être ξενολόγος); Philanôr, Sô[. . .] et [?], *Milet* I.3 33g.7–8 [. . . ἄνδρας τοὺς περὶ . . . ca 6 . . .]| καὶ Φιλάν[ο]ρα καὶ Σω[. . .]. Cf. Launey (1987: 33 et postface: xii) pour quelques références supplémentaires sur le mercenariat crétois à cette époque; et voir Boulay 2011: 216–25.

9 Identification possible d'un quatrième condottiere: *Milet* I.3 380.6 τῶν μετὰ Ἐχεβούλου. Cet Échéboulos était milésien selon A. Rehm et vraisemblablement un des fils de Lichas. Le rapprochement prosopographique avec l'Ἐχέβουλος Λίχα figurant un demi-siècle plus tôt dans la liste des garants de l'emprunt de Milet à Knide n'est pas interdit (*Milet* I.3 138.64; cf. Migeotte 1984: 303–4). Pour ces chefs de mercenaires de la première et de la seconde vague, cf. *Milet* I.3: 199–200.

10 Wörrle 1988: 444. Plus récemment encore, M. Wörrle est revenu sur les événements de la toute fin du IIIe et du début du IIe s. qui marquèrent la destinée des cités de la vallée du Méandre (Wörrle 2004). Il a montré de façon convaincante que la datation retenue depuis Errington (1989) pour le traité de paix entre Milet et Magnésie du Méandre (*Milet* I.3 148) ne résistait plus à l'analyse (cf. *infra*, n.26).

11 Pour une reconstitution, cf. Rehm 1914: 168, fig. 54, 174, fig. 56 et le dépliant entre 180–1.

12 Ils étaient originaires des cités de Dréros et de Milatos (*Milet* I.3 33f.8).

13 Je relève sommairement dans les fragments des listes de la deuxième vague (38a à 38mm): 43 femmes, γυνή; 4 fils, υἱοί; 8 fils ayant atteint l'âge de la puberté, υἱοὶ ἐβῶντες; au moins 21 garçons impubères (les noms ne sont pas toujours donnés), υἱοὶ ἄνηβοι et 13 filles, θυγάτηρ ou θυγάτηρ κόρη. Cette fois, les Crétois provenaient de plusieurs cités (dans l'ordre d'apparition): Priansos, Dréros, Knossos, Phaistos, Lappa, Rithymna, Hiérapytna, Éleutherne, Arkadès, Gortyne, Lyttos, Oaxa, Hyrtakina, et Rhaukos. Brulé 1978: 168 ajoutait à cette liste des citoyens de Kydonia, Lato, Elyros, Olonte, Héraklion, et Malla qu'il put identifier malgré la disparition de l'ethnique par des rapprochements prosopographiques. Pomeroy (1983) a fait l'étude de la composition de ces familles crétoises; voir, en dernier lieu, Brulé (1990), fondé sur l'étude de cette liste de politographie. Dans le traité d'isopolitie entre Milet et Héraclée-du-Latmos (*Milet* I.3 150), il était prévu que les citoyens de l'une et l'autre cité choisissant de se faire inscrire comme nouveaux citoyens dans l'autre cité, inscrivent aussi

femmes et enfants (46–7 et 55–6); telle précision ne figure pas (ou n'est pas conservée) dans la politographie de soldats crétois.

14 Chaniotis 2004b: 486 (déjà Chaniotis 2002: 111).

15 À mettre en relation avec la rivière Hybandos qui servit, une quarantaine d'années plus tard, de frontière entre Milet et Magnésie dans la plaine du Méandre (*Milet* I.3 148 [*Syll*³ 588; Ager 1996: n° 109]); en dernier lieu Wörrle 2004: 47 ('*Mit der Lokalisierung dieses Flusses beginnen unsere Probleme*').

16 Τὰ στεγνὰ désignent des logements pour les soldats, cf. Cohen 1978: 70–1 (s.v. ΣΤΕΓΝΟΠΟΙΕΩ). Launey (1987: 694) traduisait par 'baraquements.' Voir aussi Robert, *BÉ* 1968: no. 247, p. 459.

17 Voir déjà Savalli 1985: 426.

18 Cf. l'étude de cette question par Savalli 1985: 395.

19 Cf. *Milet* I.3 37b.

20 Même procédure dans le traité avec Séleucie-Tralleis (*Milet* I.3 143.28–9) et dans le traité avec Mylasa (*Milet* I.3 146.36–8). Des Crétois de la première vague, un fragment concerne peut-être l'affectation (*Milet* I.3 33d.5). Cf. Savalli 1985: 387–92.

21 S'il est impossible de déterminer le moment exact où elle fut incorporée au territoire milésien, le texte relatif à la première vague cité ci-dessus en fixe indéniablement le *terminus ante quem* à 234/233 a.C. Par ailleurs, elle était absente de la liste des cités ioniennes contenue dans un décret de Klazomènes trouvé à Magnésie et daté de 205–200 (*IMagn.* 53), mais le texte comporte une lacune (cf. Ruge 1935: col. 1432). Seules les sources relatives aux mercenaires crétois et l'anecdote relatée ci-après renseignent sur son appartenance à Milet. Cf. Herrmann 1975: 92–103 et, en dernier lieu, Wörrle 2004: 48.

22 Polyb. 16.15.6; cf. Haussoullier 1902: 139–42.

23 *IC* IV 176.29–31 et 32–7 (antérieurement *IMagn.* 65a + 75); réponse similaire des Knossiens, *IC* I 9*.25–32 (antérieurement *IMagn.* 65b + 76).

24 Cf. LSJ s.v. μετέρχομαι.

25 Launey 1987: 681 (déjà cité par Brulé 1978: 170).

26 Le territoire au centre du litige est désigné ἡ χώρα τῆς περαίας, *Milet* I.3 148.28–9. Holleaux (1952: 230–1n1 et 331) doutait de l'identification certes 'plausible et séduisante' de Myonte avec ce territoire de la pérée (même opinion chez Ruge 1935: 1433). Il faudrait parvenir à identifier hors de tout doute le lien entre cette ville et le fleuve Hybandos (et l'île Hybanda), car c'est celui-ci qui est utilisé dans la nouvelle délimitation de frontière prenant effet avec le traité de paix (lignes 29–38), ce qui laisse supposer qu'il se trouvait au cœur de la 'pérée.' Cf. Robert 1959 ( = *OMS* III: 1423–8). Pour une édition récente du traité (*Milet* I.3 148 = *Syll*³ 588), cf. Baker 2001: 71–5. En dernier lieu, sur l'Hybandis, la rivière Hybandos, l'île Hybanda, et Myonte, Wörrle (2004: 47–8 et passim) pour la discussion critique sur les documents et les événements en question, et la

justification probante d'un retour à la date proposée naguère par Rehm (contra Errington 1989: 286–8).

27  Savalli 1985: 426n244: 'Le circostanze della concessione della cittadinanza milesia ai Cretesi sono, purtroppo, misteriose.'

28  Voir aussi, avec l'ancienne datation, Launey 1987: 255–6. Menace d'une attaque d'Antiochos Hiérax comme justification de la première vague de Crétois, Launey 1987: 661; expédition d'Antigonos Dôsôn en Carie pour la seconde, Rehm 1914: 199 et 267.

29  Herrmann (1997: 161) a réfuté quelques-unes des hypothèses jusqu'ici admises. Comme on le verra ensuite, le conflit de longue date opposant les cités de la basse vallée du Méandre, et notamment Milet et Magnésie, pour la possession des terres fertiles de la vallée est sûrement à la source de cette décision (Brulé 1978: 165–6, le premier, avait supposé cela).

30  Je reste cependant sceptique devant l'explication de Chaniotis (2004b: 486), selon qui les Milésiens enrôlèrent les Crétois parce qu'ils 'had to man numerous forts in Hybandis (on the former territory of Myous) and on the islands, Patmos, Leros and Lepsia' (même formule Chaniotis 2002: 100). L'analyse fine des textes montrera que dans ces îles milésiennes, comme dans le reste des forts milésiens d'ailleurs, les effectifs étaient tous civiques.

31  Launey 1987: 42. Pour son étude ethnique, L. a choisi d'écarter, entre autres, les listes de soldats provenant tous du même endroit et représentant davantage une communauté étrangère fixée sur le sol d'une cité, ainsi les Crétois d'Hermionè *IG* IV 729 et les Crétois naturalisés à Milet (Launey 1987: 66–7).

32  Le passage est cependant lacunaire, *Milet* I.3 37e.83–5: [. . . συνδιατηρήσω τὴν πόλιν] καὶ τὰ φρούρια, ἅ τε | [νῦν κατέχει ὁ δῆμος καὶ ὅσα ἂν ὕστερον πρὸς α]ὐτὰ προσγίνηται,| [ἀεὶ κατὰ δύναμιν τὴν ἐμήν· Un fragment mutilé relatif à la première vague d'immigration – et, il faut admettre, largement restitué lui aussi – contenait peut-être les termes d'un serment semblable, par lequel les Crétois juraient de défendre de *toutes leurs forces* la cité de Milet (*Milet* I.3 33f.1–4). L'expression παντὶ σθένει se retrouve dans le traité avec Héraclée-du-Latmos, *Milet* I.3 150.41 et 43, mais la restitution κατὰ δύναμιν, 37e.85, est équivalente.

33  On lui reconnaît ce sens depuis les commentaires de L. Robert à ce sujet, cf. Baker 2000: 37–8n23 avec les références; également Schuler 1998: 49–53; et Savalli 1985: 425n239; mais Herrmann (1997: 161) a traduit l'expression par 'auf dem Land,' ce qui efface toute ambiguïté, mais n'offre pas le sens attendu.

34  Cf. Aen. Tact. 12, qui mettait en garde les cités à propos du recours aux troupes alliées ou à des troupes de mercenaires: jamais en nombre supérieur à l'intérieur des murs, sans quoi la ville tombait littéralement à leur merci; 12.5: exemple d'Héraclée-du-Pont où les dirigeants firent appel à un trop grand nombre de mercenaires. Cela leur servit bien d'abord à détruire leurs adversaires politiques, mais la cité tomba ensuite aux mains des mercenaires soulevés par leur chef

Kléarque (cf. Pseudo-Souda s.v. Κλέαρχος). Les événements sont également relatés par Diod. Sic. 15.81.5; Just. *Epit.* 16.4 et Polyaenus, *Strat.* 2.30.

35  Voir encore Savalli (1985: 426n243), qui pensait de même mais pour d'autres raisons (l'interprétation contestée de la lecture οἰνοφυλάξι *Milet* I.3 33e, avec discussion et références).

36  On pensera d'abord au règlement militaire d'Amphipolis: en dernier lieu Nieto (1997) (mais voir aussi les premières éditions: Roussel 1934; De Sanctis 1934; et Feyel 1935); également aux traités attalides avec des cités crétoises (Ducrey 1970; Virgilio 1982) ou à celui entre Eupolémos et Théangela (Robert 1936: 69–86), etc.

37  Les travaux archéologiques menés sur le site dès le début du XXe siècle ont permis de dégager les restes d'une acropole fortifiée d'époque hellénistique (*phrourion*) située sur la hauteur entre les deux ports principaux de Milet: le 'port du théâtre'et la 'baie des lions' (*Löwenbucht*), laquelle donne immédiate-ment sur le sanctuaire d'Apollon Delphinios. C'est précisément la forteresse qui était tenue, en 313 a.C., par Asandros, le satrape de Carie, et qu'Antigonos libéra à la suite d'un siège (Diod. Sic. 19. 7. 4). Outre la citadelle, le site était doté d'un solide rempart garni de puissantes tours carrées d'époque hellénistique blo-quant, au sud, l'accès à toute la péninsule milésienne (illustré dans Garlan 1974: 360, fig. 16). Pour une courte description des fortifications de la ville, cf. Kleiner 1968: 27–32 et, sur le rempart, von Gerkan 1935. En des temps plus anciens (les restes remontent à l'époque mycénienne), une forteresse était installée au sud de la petite péninsule occupée par la ville de Milet, sur une colline désignée aujourd'hui Kalabaktepe (von Gerkan 1925).

38  Attribué à tort à la cité de Priène par Kortenbeutel 1941: 780.

39  Ces îles étaient situées au large du Golfe Latmique, en direction ouest, à l'intérieur d'un triangle formé par les îles d'Ikaria, d'Amorgos, et de Cos et of-fraient une sorte d'avant-garde au large de la ville et du territoire de Milet.

40  Manganaro 1963–4: 318–20 n° 18; on peut ajouter le fragment d'un texte sem-blable, mais dont ne subsistent que les premières lignes sans mention du titre de phrourarque.

41  Manganaro 1963–4: 322–3 n° 21 et n° 22.

42  Manganaro 1963–4: 306–8 n° 3.

43  Segre 1993: EV 14, EV 192.

44  Même observation à propos des dédicaces de marins chiotes en escale à Samothrace au sanctuaire des Grands Dieux (Skarlatidou 1990–1). Mais si les dédicaces portent l'intitulé 'χίων' et contiennent certains noms typiquement chiotes, la présence de plusieurs autres noms *atypiques* peut suggérer pour sa part que des étrangers comptaient parmi l'équipage.

45  On notera la dédicace similaire de citoyens marins de Smyrne: IDélos 1857. Pour la piraterie organisée ou soutenue par Mithridate, dès le début du I$^{er}$ s. a.C., cf. Appien *Mith.* 63 et 92.

46  Tite live *Per.* 98: *C. Triarius, legatus Luculli, aduersus Mithridaten parum prospere pugnauit.*

47  Événement raconté par Phlégon de Tralleis (*FHG* III: 606, fr. 12): καὶ Ἀθηνόδωρος πειρατὴς ἐξανδραποδισάμενος Δηλίους τὰ τῶν λεγομένων θεῶν ξόανα διελυμήνατο· Γαῖος δὲ Τριάριος τὰ λελωβημένα τῆς πόλεως ἐπισκευάσας ἐτείχισε τὴν Δῆλον.

48  Selon Rehm (1914: 365), cette clause n'évoquait pas un traitement particulier des Héracléotes qui choisissaient de devenir citoyens milésiens, mais constituait un simple rappel de ce qui figurait déjà à la ligne 50 à l'effet que tous les nouveaux citoyens étaient sur un pied d'égalité avec les Milésiens de souche (à l'exception bien entendu de ce qui relevait du domaine de la défense nationale).

49  Cf. Gauthier 2001: 123.

50  En effet, le traité entre Milet et Héraclée-du-Latmos ajoutait à la phrourarchie non seulement le service de garnison mais aussi 'ce qui concernait la défense pour toute la cité et pour les garnisons' (*Milet* I.3 150.51: ἡ φυλακή ἡ κατὰ πόλιν καὶ φρουρική).

51  Cf. Baker 2001: 67–9. Labarre (2004: 239) présente mon interprétation comme 'non satisfaisante,' mais il me cite hors contexte et finit par dire, quelques lignes plus loin, exactement ce que je dis moi-même. Je profite de l'occasion pour me surprendre de lire, plus loin dans son article (241n108), au sujet d'une restitution que j'ai proposée en 1996, mais qu'il reprend à son compte: 'Cette restitution a été *également* proposée par P. Baker (suit la référence à ma thèse inédite).' Bien qu'inédite, cette thèse est en accès libre; ma proposition précède de huit ans la sienne.

52  Voir la discussion à ce sujet dans Baker 2001.

53  Cf. Robert 1936: 78–9: exemple de Théangela, assiégée par Eupolémos, qui se résout à conclure un traité avec l'ennemi, et ce malgré la position inexpugnable de sa ville. Elle redoutait probablement un soulèvement des troupes mercenaires à l'intérieur des murs: le traité nous apprend en effet qu'Eupolémos, qui prit sous son commandement ces soldats, paya leur solde en retard de quatre mois et leur offrit une avance de deux mois.

54  Le citoyen Phanès avait été honoré, entre 323 et 315, pour avoir avancé les sommes nécessaires au 'renvoi des soldats et la démolition de l'acropole' (*IErythrai* 21.7–10). Les soldats en question ici constituaient évidemment une garnison royale occupant l'acropole.

55  Lecture συν[υ]ποστάντ[ω]ν suggérée à Hiller par Wilamowitz: συνυφίσταμαι à l'aoriste second de sens moyen, 'aider, soutenir.' S'agissant de Moschiôn et d'autres citoyens, l'expression τῶν συν[υ]ποστάντ[ω]ν [π]ολ[ιτῶν] exprime des actes d'évergétisme concertés ('avec les citoyens qui contribuaient à assumer ces charges'). Voir, par exemple, Polyb. 4.32.7: φίλους . . . συνυποστησόμενους, 'des amis . . . qui pussent les aider' (trad. de Foucault, les Belles Lettres). Voir également le commentaire de Robert (1963: 487–8), au sujet d'un décret d'Hanisa.

56 Cf. Launey 1987: 29–36 et 724–50 (spécialement 731–2).

57 *IErythrai* 24, 29 (décrets); *IErythrai* 32, 33, 214, 215 et Engelmann 1987: 140–1 (dédicaces de stratèges sortant de charge).

58 Judeich 1898: 231–2 n° 2 avec copie de la pierre, fig. 4 (Barth et Stauber 1993: 380); cf. Robert 1926: 511n4 ( = *OMS* I: 74n4), qui se demandait s'il ne s'agissait pas d'un décret pour un phrourarque et proposait la restitution (7–8): τῶν πολιτῶν [τοῖς τεταγμέν]οις ἐν τῶι ὀχ[υρώματι]. Dans une inscription honorifique pour un phrourarque de Chrysè en Troade, on lit οἱ ἐν χρυσῆι πολεῖται (*IAlexandreia Troas* 4). Selon Robert 1926: 501–11 ( = *OMS* I: 65–74), la formule employée désignait sans aucun doute possible la garnison et il la rapprochait de l'expression οἱ τεταγμένοι τῶν πολιτῶν ἐν τοῖς φρουρίοις courante dans les textes athéniens (*e.g. IG* II² 1299.18).

59 Telles sont, par exemple, des inscriptions honorifiques gravées à même le roc le long du sentier escarpé conduisant à un petit fort du territoire de Smyrne (*ISmyrna* II 1.611–12).

60 *IPriene* 19.41–3: οἵτινες [les envoyés] παραγενό|μενοι ἐπί τε τὴν βουλὴν καὶ τὸν δῆμο[ν] | [ἐν] τῶι ἐννόμωι χρόνωι ἀξιώσουσιν, κτλ.

61 Plusieurs décrets pour des phrourarques de Télôneia, *IPriene* 4 (Apellis), 19 (Helikôn), 20–21–22 (Nymphôn), 23 (Bias); décret pour Ménarès, un citoyen qui s'est démarqué (militairement?) lors d'une guerre contre les Milésiens, *IPriene* 26; une base de statue pour un citoyen phrourarque de Télôneia, *IPriene* 252a; le célèbre arbitrage de Rhodes entre Priène et Samos, en guerre pour la possession d'un territoire et d'un fort, le Karion, *IPriene* 37; le décret pour l'évergète Moschiôn, *IPriene* 108, qui a notamment fournit des fonds pour la solde de mercenaires (lignes 150–2) et participé à la garde de la citadelle (209–12).

62 Et les exemples se multiplient en visitant les corpus des autres cités: e.g., l'inscription honorifique d'une garnison pour le commandant de fort Démétrios ὁ καλούμενος Γερῦς (*ISmyrna* II 1.609; cf. Gauthier, *BÉ* 2005: 140), où les garnisaires libérés de leur service sont désignés par plusieurs expressions (lignes 4–7).

63 *IPriene* 23.6–9: περὶ | [πλείστου ποιούμενος τό τε διαφ]υλάξαι τὸ φρούριον καὶ πρὸς τε[[ – – καὶ μὴ τῶν ἄ]λλων πολιτῶν ἐν τούτοις καθ[υ]]στερεῖν].

64 *IPriene* 23.4–5: [διὰ πάντα] τὸγ χρόνον ἐν ὧι τὴν ἀρχὴν αὐ[[τῶν εἶχε].

65 *IPriene* 17.18–19 (Bielman 1994: 86–90 n° 22): ἐκπέμψας μισθοφόρους τῶν πολιτῶν πεζοὺς καὶ [ἄλ]λους ἱππ]οτρόφους.

66 De fait, le texte est corrompu à cet endroit, lignes 19–20: Σωτᾶς δὲ συνα[γα]|γὼν τῶ[μ] πολιτῶν τοὺς [κρατίστ]ο[υ]ς. La restitution de Dittenberger [ἐθέλοντα]ς (reprise par Bielman), 'ceux des citoyens qui se portaient volontaires,' n'est pas incorrecte. Mais cf. le décret de Potidée de Karpathos pour Pamphilidas, Maier 1959: n° 50.16–18: [αὐτὸς δὲ μετὰ τῶν]| μάλιστα δυναμέγ[ων τῶν πολιτᾶν καὶ

τῶν ξέ]|νων ὑπ᾽ αὐτοῦ συ[λλεξθέντων] κτλ. ; ou le décret du dème d'Halasarna pour Dioklès, Baker 1991: n° 2a.10–11 (en dernier lieu Hallof-Habicht 1998: n° 12a.17–18): ἑλόμενος κατὰ ψάφισμα τὸς μάλιστα δυνασομένος [ἐπιμ]ελειθῆ[μεν τᾶς φυλακᾶς. Devant l'urgence de la situation, l'idée était de rassembler les plus 'capables' des citoyens ou, généralement, des hommes disponibles citoyens ou non, et non d'essayer seulement de regrouper les volontaires. Autres exemples dans le décret de Chersonèsos pour Diophantos, le général de Mithridate (107 a.C.), *IPE* I² 352.18: Διό|[φα]ντος ἀναλαβὼν τοὺς ἰδίους καὶ τῶν πολιτᾶν τοὺς δυνατωτάτους et l. 37–8: παραλαβὼν δὲ καὶ τῶν πολιτᾶν ἐπιλέ|[κ]τους ('ayant recruté l'élite des citoyens'); la même idée de corps 'd'élite' se retrouve dans un décret de Tomi, *Syll*³ 731.31 et 40.

67 De même, durant la crise qu'avait traversée la cité sous le tyran Hiéron, ce sont des citoyens du parti au pouvoir qui tenaient le fort appelé Karion, et ce sont également des citoyens, des démocrates ceux-là, qui s'étaient enfuis de la ville, qui avaient délogé la garnison en place et s'étaient maintenus dans le fort pendant les trois années de la tyrannie (*IPriene* 37). Ce sont aussi des citoyens en fuite qui se sont réfugiés dans un autre fort du territoire, le Charax. Un décret d'Éphèse voté à leur sujet les désignait par la formule: 'ceux des Priéniens qui sont dans le Charax,' *IEphesos* 2001.1: τῶμ πολιτῶν <τῶν> ἐκ Πριήν[ης οἱ] ἐν τῶι χάρακι; 1.6: τῶμ πολιτῶν τῶν ἐκ Πριήνης τοὺς ἐν τῶι χάρακι ὄντας; également lignes 13 et 15.

68 *IErythrai* 28 (Bielman 1994: 80–5 n° 21), lignes 1–18.

69 Cf. par exemple le traité entre le dynaste de Carie Eupolémos et la cité de Théangéla, qui capitula après un siège, Robert 1936: 69–86 (sauf pour le passage où il est question d'une exemption d'impôt sur les ruches, cf. Rostovtzeff 1931: 7–21 'qui a toute la valeur d'une *editio princeps*'). Eupolémos avait réussi à gagner à sa cause les mercenaires employés par Théangela en payant les arriérés de leur solde. Plusieurs corps de mercenaires, identifiés par le nom de leur chef comme c'était l'usage, se trouvaient à l'intérieur de la cité. Certains de ces mercenaires étaient des artilleurs et l'on peut penser qu'ils avaient été engagés pour pallier l'incompétence de la milice locale en ce domaine; ἀποδοθῆναι δὲ | καὶ τοῖς καταπαλταφέταις ὀψώνια μηνῶν τεσσαρῶν (14–15). Mais, comme je l'ai expliqué ailleurs (Baker 2003: 394), il ne fait pas de doute non plus que les cités ont suivi les développements techniques de leur temps.

70 Cas qu'elle rapproche de celui des soldats de Palaimagnésie dans le dossier de l'incorporation de Magnésie-du-Sipyle par Smyrne (*OGI* 229).

# PART SIX

# *Insulae*: Geopolitics and Geopoetics

The idea of insularity links the papers in this section. Islands – like the sea in which they float – are symbolic of both isolation and belonging. The sea both divides and facilitates movement; islands are set apart, and yet act as hubs of human contact. The island of Delos in the southern Aegean is a particularly striking example of this paradox. Small and politically insignificant, yet centrally located, and important in both religious and economic terms, Delos brought together the traders of the Mediterranean and inspired the imagination of the poets.

Ephraim Lytle's essay challenges conventional notions of belonging. His examination of the role of fishermen and fishing in the economy and society of Hellenistic Delos starts from the traditional view of fishermen as outsiders, 'entirely ignorant of the agora,' that is, of regular polis life. But, as Lytle goes on to demonstrate, fishermen and their activities played a vital role in the interconnectedness of the Hellenistic Mediterranean. Those on the margins, whose work took them far from the hub of the polis, such as fishermen or mercenaries, functioned as strands in the web that connected the polities of this world. As Lytle points out, sea routes lay at the heart of Mediterranean interconnectedness – and yet those who navigated these routes, like fishermen, did so in lonely isolation.

Léopold Migeotte examines another kind of isolation in his paper: the deliberate self-isolation of an economy that turns inward to prevent the risks and losses attendant on engagement with others. Migeotte surveys the accounts of the Apollo treasury on Delos during the period of Hellenistic independence, and outlines a significant shift in monetary policy. Under Athenian domination in the Classical period, the Apollo treasury had been the source of major contributions to the regional economy in the form of loans. Much of the debt was still outstanding upon

Delos's independence in 314 BC, and the islanders seem to have decided against future risk by retiring their capital into the treasury and making only small loans to the polis of Delos and individual Delians. In spite of the significant role played by Delos in the economy and trade networks of the Hellenistic period, the islanders became truly 'insular' when it came to their own monetary policy.

The poet Kallimachos intimates through his poetic personae that he is grateful to be ignorant of seafaring. The direct opposite of the fishermen of Delos, Kallimachos nevertheless creates an elaborate construction of connectedness in his poetry. Mary Depew's paper analyses Kallimachos's poetic use of geography, in particular streams and rivers, to link Alexandria and the Ptolemies with the Greek homeland. The Nile, the source of Egypt's wealth and power, not only links Alexandria (almost an island itself) with Egypt; it also dives beneath the sea and joins with the River Inopos on the island of Delos. Apollo's birthplace is thus linked to the Ptolemaic monarchy and provides a putative claim that the sacred island – and other places in Greece – belong to the new Macedonian dynasty.

# 16

# 'Entirely Ignorant of the Agora' (Alkiphron 1.14.3): Fishing and the Economy of Hellenistic Delos

## EPHRAIM LYTLE

Both with regard to its role in the Hellenistic economy and specifically in relation to this volume's themes, marine fishing poses a number of fundamental problems. On the one hand, as Mikhail Rostovtzeff long ago noted, the Greeks' knowledge of seafood and how to procure it seems to have been well developed from an early date, and it is doubtful that technological innovation could have contributed much to the growth of fishing industries during the Hellenistic period.[1] On the other hand, the viability of ancient Greek fishing economies depended not only on Aegean ecologies but also on social factors such as the availability of sufficient demand and the efficient functioning of markets. Here Hellenistic social and economic developments could have had real effects, but the evidence is usually insufficient to allow us to draw confident conclusions. Similarly, with respect to the central themes of belonging and isolation, in a certain sense the Hellenistic period marked little change in the lives of Greek fishermen who had always, or at least since the emergence of the polis as the institution of primary cultural importance, existed at the margins.[2]

Ancient literary sources depict fishermen toiling in isolation, living along remote beaches, 'as unlike the residents of cities and villages as the sea is foreign to the land' (Alkiphron 1.4.1). To a certain degree, these portraits reflect basic realities. But at the same time we might observe that they rely on a viewpoint that peers outward from insular poleis. Ironically, this viewpoint obscures the degree to which a greater belonging, the connectivity that allowed for the existence of a shared Greek identity, a society of cities, was owed in large part to those living on the margins.[3] This volume offers abundant examples of Hellenistic interconnectivity, from cosmopolitan poets and sculptors to interstate relations to migrant mercenaries. But this abundant cultural contact occurred across a network of sea routes oriented only by memory of headlands and stars, an invisible infrastructure charted by largely unattested men. Even if we are sceptical of John Bintliff's theory that the rise of an interconnected Aegean began with the seasonal transmerance of prehistoric fishermen, it is impossible to deny the close relationships, historically, between fishing and maritime trade.[4] Here again the part played by ancient Greek fishermen remains underappreciated.

This irony inherent in the polis-centric view of the fisherman's isolation is heightened by the fact that the fruit of his toil, seafood, can be described as residing at the very centre of sympotic culture, a symbol of the conspicuous consumption perhaps most characteristic of Hellenistic, like modern, belonging.[5] It is only the (fish)market at the intersection between economy and culture, and between centre and periphery, that allows us to resolve these paradoxes, a pivotal role highlighted, albeit in a slightly different context, by the comic poet Anaxandrides: 'Is not the market rich in fish (εὔοψος ἀγορά) alone responsible for lovers? . . . And tell me, what choice little piece of salt fish will be captured by whom, with what spells or entreaties, when you take away the fisherman's craft?'[6] While Anaxandrides's *euopsos agora* invites a more general investigation into the economics of sex, the particular focus of this paper is rather more prosaic: it is my hope that some of the problems and suggested links between ancient fishing and trade can be brought into better focus by concentrating on the specific case of Hellenistic Delos. Here the temple accounts preserve data that, although sparse and often difficult, are potentially profitable. If properly contextualized, they suggest a dense fabric of relationships between the fishing industry and maritime trade, demographic change, economic growth, and Hellenistic 'elegant living.'

The key piece of evidence for much of what follows is a single temple account for the year 250 BC. In it, an entry appears for an *ichthuon dekate* in the amount of 1,850 drachmas. Although this 'tithe on fish' has occasionally been construed as a kind of tax on fishing rights, it is best interpreted, as the Greek would suggest, as a simple ten per cent duty assessed on the value of the delivered catch.[7] In 250 BC, it appears together with the *enoikion dekate*, or tithe on rents, the *sitou dekate*, a tithe on grain, and the *pentekoste he astia*, the 2 per cent customs duty, here enigmatically delimited 'of the city.'[8] The testimony of two earlier accounts from 279 and 278 BC reveals that these are civic revenues, appearing in temple accounts as repayments of silver loaned to the city by Apollo.[9] An account from 274 BC preserves additional, albeit fragmentary, evidence for these revenues. All four entries are presented chronologically here (divergences from *IG* readings and proposed restorations are discussed in the notes):

1) *IG* XI.2 161A.25–27 (279 BC):[10] καὶ τάδε ἄλλα εἰσῆλθεν· εἰς τὴν ἀπόδοσιν τοῦ ἀργυρίου οὗ ἡ πόλις ὀφείλει τῶι θεῶι, παρὰ βουλευτῶν τῶν ἐπ᾽ ἄρχοντος Ὑψοκλέους,/ ἐκ τῆς πεντηκοστῆς σὺν τοῖς ἐπωνίοις· ΜΧΧΧΧΡΗΗΗΗΔ· τῶν ἐνοικίων τῆς δεκάτης ὑπὲρ Τεισικλέο<υ>ς· ΡΗ· τοῦ ὑποτροπίου ὑπὲρ Φίλλιος/ ΡΔΔΔ· τῆς δεκτης τοῦ σίτου ὑπὲρ Γνωσιδίκου· ΗΡΔ· ἐπώνια τούτων δραχμὰς ΡΔΗΙΙΙ·

(Also these additional funds were deposited: for the repayment of the silver which the city owes to the god, from the council during the archonship of Hypsokleos: from the *pentekoste* with the surcharges: 14,910 drachmas; from the tithe on rents farmed by Teisikleos: 600 drachmas; from the *hypotropion* farmed by Phillis: 530 drachmas; from the tithe on grain farmed by Gnosidikos: 160 drachmas; the surcharges on these: 61 drachmas, 3 obols.)

2) *IG* XI.2 162A.29–30 (278 BC):[11] ἄλλο εἰσῆλθεν ἀργύριον εἰς τὴν ἀπόδοσιν τοῦ ἀργυρίου οὗ ἡ πόλις ὤφειλεν τῶι θεῶι παρὰ βου[λευτῶν τῶν ἐπ᾽ ἄρχοντος Μενεκράτου? ἐκ τῆς πεντηκοστῆς μετὰ τοῦ]/ ἐπωνίου· ΜΡΧΧΧΡΗΗΗΗ· καὶ τοῦ ὑποτροπίου· ΡΔΔΔΔΓ· σίτου τῆς δεκάτης ΗΗΗΗΔΙΙΙ· ἐνοικίων τῆς δε[κάτης ———·

(Additional silver was deposited as repayment for the silver which the city owes to the god, by the council [under the archonship of Menekrates: from the 2% customs duty], together with the surcharge: 18,900 drachmas; also from the *hypotropion*: 540 drachmas and 5 obols; from the tithe on grain: 410 drachmas, three obols; from the tithe on rents [. . .])

3) *IG* XI.2 199A.15–16 (274 BC):[12] ——————]/ ΗΝ . . . . ΕΙ τῶν ἐνοικίων ΡΗΗΗΔΔΓ· τοῦ ὑποτροπίου ΡΗΔΔΔ· ἐπώνια τούτων ΗΔΔΙ.

(From the tithe on rents 835 drachmas; from the *hypotropion* 630 drachmas; the surcharges on these: 120 drachmas, 1 obol.)

4) *IG* XI.2 287.8–10 (250 BC): καὶ παρὰ βουλῆς τῆς ἐπὶ Σωσισθένου καὶ ταμίου Πιστοῦ/ πεντηκοστῆς τῆς ἀστίας δραχμαὶ ΡΗΗΡ· ἰχθύων δεκάτης δραχμαὶ ΧΡΗΗΗΡ· ἐνοικίων δεκάτη[ς] ΧΡΗΡΔΔΔ· σίτου δεκά/της ΗΔ· καὶ τὸ ἐπώνιον τούτων δραχμαὶ ΗΗΗΗΔΔΔΓ·

(From the council under Sosisthenes and Pistos the treasurer: 5,250 drachmas from the *pentekoste* of the city; 1,850 drachmas from the tithe on fish; 1,690 drachmas from the tithe on rents; 110 drachmas from the tithe on grains; also the surcharge on these, 445 drachmas.)

These figures do not represent the total revenues collected from each tax but rather the sums paid by tax farmers for the contracts to collect each duty. The actual tax revenues likely stood somewhat higher. But we can be fairly certain that the sums recorded represent the total value of each contract in a given year.[13] A bidder was required to pay a tax or surcharge of 5 per cent, *to eponion*, assessed on the value of his winning bid. The bids themselves represented only obligations, but the surcharge was likely collected by the city soon after the auction (probably in part as a way of discouraging unqualified bids), with the sums recorded separately in civic accounts. Hence, it is no coincidence that in 250 BC the 445 drachmas collected in surcharges represent precisely 5 per cent of the total value of the contracts: it is far more reasonable to assume that the city handed over to the temple the total proceeds from the sale of each tax contract, as well as the surcharges, than it is to assume the alternative, that the city paid over partial proceeds and then calculated a partial sales tax, paying that over as well.

This brings us to a second point: the surcharge was not a security deposit. This has important consequences when estimating the total value of the catch represented by the *ichthuon dekate* in 250 BC. For example, it has been suggested that 'the 10 percent tax on fish from 250 BC represents the sale of fish worth 17,575 dr.' (Reger 1994a: 254). That is, the 5 per cent surcharge of 92 drachmas, 3 obols has been subtracted from the 1,850 drachmas recorded for the tithe before calculating the corresponding value. In fact, the surcharge represents a non-refundable cost; the only way for the tax farmer to meet his obligations, altogether 1,942 drachmas, 3 obols, was by collecting a tithe on fish, the anticipated total value of which cannot have been less than 19,425 drachmas. The real figure is likely to have stood considerably higher still. Certainly, the tax farmer would have bid with the expectation of securing profit. Even a paltry 5 per cent profit margin, or a return of roughly 100 drachmas on the value of his bid, would have required that he collect a tithe on an additional 1000 drachmas worth of fish. This ignores some obvious additional considerations, such as that collecting the duty probably entailed costs borne directly by the tax farmer. In short, we can be confident that in 250 BC the farmer of the *ichthuon dekate* anticipated collecting duties on fish worth well in excess of 20,000 drachmas.[14]

This figure, by itself, does not tell us much about the nature and scale of the Delian fishing industry. If conger eel literally cost its weight in gold as alleged in a fragment of Diphilos, 20,000 drachmas might buy only a few large specimens.[15] In other words, the significance of the sum recorded for the *ichthuon dekate* depends in large part on the extremely tricky question of price. The now standard view is that fish was, for the most part, prohibitively expensive. This notion is owed in part to Thomas Gallant, who introduces the high price of fish as the crowning argument in his oft-cited attack on Rostovtzeff, concluding that fish was on average thirteen times more expensive than wheat and would have remained a luxury item, eaten only on special occasions by a privileged few (Gallant 1985: 39–40). Others have followed suit.[16]

The claim rests on thin evidence. Gallant's ratio, which equates the caloric content of a drachma's worth of wheat to a drachma's worth of fish, has been justly criticized by a number of scholars, both because fish is a food low in energy but high in nutrients and because a strictly caloric interpretation ignores the sometimes considerable cultural value of food.[17] But, in fact, Gallant's price data are fundamentally flawed. For the cost of fish, he relies exclusively on the prices recorded in a fascinating but poorly understood Hellenistic inscription from the Boiotian town of Akraiphia. It chiefly consists of a long list of fish names accompanied by acrophonic numerals inscribed over two blocks.[18]

It is agreed by all that the acrophonic numerals represent maximum prices per mina. The numeral system employed in the inscription uses four symbols in descending order: I, H, Π, and X. Three are easily construed: the first is an obol, the second a hemi-obol, and the fourth a chalk, which, in Boiotia, is one-twelfth of an obol. The evidence afforded by other acrophonic systems suggests that Π should simply stand for *pente* and indicate five chalks. In this inscription, however, that would introduce anomalies (e.g., both ΠX and H indicating six chalks), leading scholars, beginning already with Michel Feyel, to suggest alternative solutions. The most recent word on the subject suggests that Π, if it cannot stand for *pente*, is likely to stand for *pettares*, Boiotian for 'four,' and here indicating four chalks (Sosin 2004). Unfortunately, few of the entries are entirely legible, and in his calculation Gallant employs prices for only a dozen fishes. For eight of these, the price recorded by Claude Vatin is IΠX, which Gallant follows Vatin in construing as one obol, six chalks. But Vatin's reconstruction of the Akraiphian numeral system is the least likely of all those proposed, and not simply because one obol, six chalks could more simply be written IH. This price is actually inscribed with the first two symbols in ligature: ᴴIX Elsewhere in epigraphic Greek the ligature ᴴI always represents HΠ, but if Π stands for five chalks, then ᴴIX would represent a truly bizarre way of writing one obol. Vatin has chosen instead simply to erase the horizontal and read IΠX. Restoring the ligature and following Joshua Sosin's interpretation of the sign Π as four chalks gives a price of eleven chalks, which not only removes apparent inconsistencies but also reduces the most common price by seven chalks.[19] In other words, in fully two-thirds of his sample Gallant appears to have overestimated the price of fish by 65 per cent. Add to this the likelihood that Gallant's ratio of cost to caloric content assumes too light a mina, and it is clear that the figures preserved at Akraiphia represent better values for fish than scholars have assumed.[20]

A more difficult task is to try to infer from the sums recorded at Akraiphia a plausible estimate for the price of fish at Delos. The most commonly recorded price at Akraiphia is 11 chalks per mina. But this price generally corresponds to those fishes most praised in our ancient sources, the same fishes categorized as *pesce nobile* or *fino* in nineteenth-century Adriatic markets, for which we have remarkably good data, thanks to George Faber's richly documented account (Faber 1883). In Adriatic markets, the lesser species, *pesce ordinario* or *pesce populo*, could usually be had for half the price of the better varieties, and we find the same phenomenon in the Akraiphian list, where some cheaper varieties can be had for less than half an obol per mina. The average maximum price at Akraiphia is roughly nine obols per local mina. But this price cannot represent the average price paid for a mina of fish even at Akraiphia. As comparative data from the Adriatic and more recently from the Greek Aegean demonstrate, the fishes accompanied by the highest prices at Akraiphia are generally captured in lesser quantities. Indeed, it is worth noting that at Akraiphia no prices are preserved for the species that ancient and comparative sources suggest would have been most affordable and captured in the largest quantities, the small fry (*lepton ichthudion*, Ath. 7 303a) that still represent for many the only affordable fresh fish in modern Greek markets and tavernas. In short, even at Akraiphia the average (maximum) price of a mina of seafood likely stood somewhere between half an obol and nine chalks.

We have good reason to suspect that the fish tithed at Delos would have been valued based on prices that are lower still, and not simply because the island poleis of the Aegean are frequently associated in our ancient sources with the ready availability of seafood (Brun 1996: 131–16). Even if the distance of roughly twenty kilometres from Akraiphia to the coast at Anthedon would not have prevented a regular supply of fish, the cost of overland transportation, often cited as one of the most important restraints on ancient economic growth, would have added markedly to the price of fish.[21] A related problem is addressed directly by Hadrian in a letter to Athens in which the emperor blames the high price of fish on the costs imposed by middlemen, one layer of whom he attempts simply to abolish (*IG* II[2] 1103; Lytle 2007a).

An even more important consideration is that the prices recorded at Akraiphia are maximum retail prices. Although this is not the place to review the question in detail, the evidence suggests that at Delos the *ichthuon dekate* represents not a tithe on the retail value of fish but on the wholesale or ex-vessel value.[22] This point is perhaps illustrated by a fragment of Diphilos that has not received the special attention it deserves: 'I have never seen fish more expensive. Poseidon, if you were collecting a tithe on fish *from the price each day* (*apo tes times hekastes hemeras*), you would be by far the richest of the gods.'[23] In my view, the speaker is best understood as proposing not an altogether new tithe but rather that an existing tithe be assessed based *on the actual retail price*. The passage takes for granted what the audience would already know: tithes and similar duties on fish, ubiquitous in Greek ports, were collected long before the fish arrived on the fishmonger's tables, and they would have been assessed based on values that had no direct relationship to eventual retail prices.

The upshot of all this? In my view half an obol per (Akraiphian) mina is a reasonable estimate for the average wholesale price of seafood at Hellenistic Delos. Assuming an expected ex-vessel value in 250 BC of at least 20,000 drachmas, a conservatively low figure, we are left with at least 240,000 minas of fish arriving annually on the docks at Delos in the mid-third century BC. Converting this figure into more meaningful measures depends in part on the weight of an Akraiphia mina, but we are left with a broad range of roughly 110,000 to 192,000 kilos, with a mina of approximately 600 grams suggesting a total catch in the neighbourhood of 144,000 kilos, or 300,000 pounds. Comparative data suggest that these figures are not impossible, but they *are* clearly incompatible with a view of ancient fishing as a part-time subsistence strategy, practised not by professionals but by peasant farmers trying to scare up an extra bit of protein, without, it would appear, much success, since 'far too often the solitary fisherman with his reed pole would return home with an empty creel.'[24] The Delian market could only have been supplied fish in such volumes by scores of professional fishermen engaged in what can be described as an artisanal industry. Not surprisingly, the temple inventories include fishing implements and other items that might reasonably be interpreted as dedications made by fishermen, while the archaeological record preserves abundant evidence of the trade.[25]

The temple accounts likewise suggest that Delians enjoyed limited quantites of fish in the context of a religious festival.[26] But most fresh fish would have been purchased privately, and here it is clear that the inhabitants of Hellenistic Delos were consuming fresh seafood in considerable quantities. It is important to remember that Delos was hardly a great metropolis in the third century; its population was, as Gary Reger stresses, sizeable only by regional standards. The best demographic evidence comes only from the last years of independence in the early second century BC. Various arguments and figures have been proposed, but they range from a total population of an impossibly low 2,600 to Claude Vial's most recent estimate of a total population of at most 8,000.[27] But these figures correspond to the last decades of independence, and even if we accept the highest estimate, it is clear just from the archaeological record that the island's population, which stood at perhaps a mere 500 male citizens in the mid-fourth century, had undergone considerable expansion in the latter half of the third and the first decade of the second centuries. The total population in 250 BC is unlikely to have exceeded 6,000.[28] For the sake of comparison we will include a reasonable low estimate of 4,000 as well as an upward limit of 8,000. Again, assuming a total catch of 144,000 kilograms, these figures give a range for annual per capita consumption of fresh seafood of between 18 and 36 kilograms (38 and 76 pounds) by whole weight, suggesting that fish, far from being merely 'a short-term solution to the problem of periodic dearth,' constituted an important element in the Delian diet.[29] Given that these figures exclude not only fish procured by extra-market means but also, in all likelihood, imported salt fish, total seafood consumption may have stood even higher.[30]

It is entirely possible that stable-isotope analysis studies will in the future confirm these findings. Similar studies have been published suggesting surprisingly limited fish consumption in the Aegean, primarily at Bronze and Early Iron Age sites. More intriguing is a very recent study suggesting that the Mycenaeans buried in Grave Circles A and B had diets rich in marine foods. For certain individuals it made up as much as 25 per cent of the total intake (Richards and Hedges 2008). These results correspond well to a model in which the consumption of seafood in sizeable quantities is entirely an elite phenomenon. Scholars such as Gallant and James Davidson have assumed that a similar pattern prevailed even in the late Classical and Hellenistic periods. But, as John Wilkins has recently observed, the literary sources strongly suggest that, already by the Hellenistic period, sympotic culture and the consumption of seafood were no longer restricted to a narrow class of traditional elites.[31] The data from Delos similarly suggest that, at least as far as the consumption of fresh fish is concerned, Hellenistic 'elegant living' included a somewhat broader cross section of society than previously assumed. Obviously, not every Greek could afford to purchase fresh seafood. But here we might cite not just the apparently widespread phenomenon of eating clubs, but also the emergence, especially in urban centres, of a class of people whose wealth derived largely from various forms of market exchange, those skilled in what Aristotle describes as *he ktetike chrematistike techne*, loosely translated: 'the art of making money.'[32] These individuals contributed in turn to monetized exchange in ancient fish markets, a dynamic that lies behind a fragment of the comic poet Kriton, in which it is suggested that early second-century Delos, with its 'market rich in fish' and its 'throng of spendthrifts' would for the parasite offer even better hunting grounds than the Peiraeus.[33] On Delos, at least, this dynamic of trade, population growth, and increasing consumption is a decidedly Hellenistic phenomenon, and here again it is possible that the account entries reproduced above can offer additional insight.[34]

The *ichthuon dekate* appears only in the account for 250 BC. For the years 279, 278, and 274, the *pentekoste*, the *enoikion dekate*, and the *sitou dekate* are accompanied not by the *ichthuon dekate* but by an *hypotropion*. The adjective *hypotropios* appears twice in poetry with the expected sense of 'beneath the keel,' but the word is otherwise unattested.[35] In the Delian accounts it is clearly an idiomatic designation for a particular tax that is either synonymous with or subsequently replaced by the *ichthuon dekate*. Théophile Homolle (1890: 442) surveys the evidence and concludes that the two are likely to be identical. Nevertheless, he remained troubled by the disparity in recorded revenues. The sums for the *hypotropion* in 279, 278, and 274 are 530 drachmas, 540 drachmas, 5 obols, and 630 drachmas, respectively, with the 1,850 drachmas from the *ichthuon dekate* in 250 BC representing more than a threefold increase over the average of the sums recorded for the *hypotropion* just a few decades earlier. Largely in an attempt to explain this disparity, subsequent scholars have offered various alternative theories that assume a change in the basic nature of the tax.[36] None of these theories are particularly convincing, and one might ask instead whether a threefold increase in revenues is really that surprising.

Interestingly, the sums recorded for the *enoikion dekate* show a nearly identical rate of increase. It is generally agreed that since foreigners normally could not own property, their domiciles were rented, and a tithe was paid on the value of these rents. The accounts show an increase from 600 drachmas in 279 BC to 1,690 drachmas in 250 BC. Homolle (1890: 440–1), assuming an average annual rent of 50 drachmas and an average household size of five, suggests that the metic population increased from about 600 individuals in 279 BC to 1,690 in 250. Reger is perhaps right to question the reliability of these estimates (1994a: 256–7n14), but, for our purposes, precise population figures are not necessary. The temple accounts suggest that in the first half of the third century house rent prices on Delos were remarkably stable, with the average hovering right around 55 drachmas per annum. Reger agrees with Homolle that these data can be used to calculate the number of rented properties, suggesting that the sum recorded in 250 BC represents a tithe on the rents of some 290 domiciles (1994: 256). This figure needs to be revised upward to at least 323 households.[37] Yet in 279 the minimum figure for rented domiciles is only 115. In other words, setting aside the question of calculating a precise figure for the metic population, we are still left with a 280 per cent increase in rented domiciles in less than forty years.

In my view, these data are difficult to square with Reger's larger theory that the population and economy of Delos hardly grew at all in the first eighty-five years of independence, remaining remarkably stable until circa 230 BC, when a period of true Delian independence ushered in the first period of increased prosperity. The argument for a negligible level of trade is based chiefly on data that can be very differently interpreted.[38] The archaeological and epigraphic evidence better agrees, in my view, with the model suggested already by Rostovtzeff, specifically that, although Independent Delos did indeed have a very modest beginning, by the mid-third century it was 'a small but prosperous city, rapidly growing and attracting steadily increasing numbers of foreigners.'[39]

Increased commercial activity accompanied by population growth suggests an obvious explanation for a proportional increase in revenues from the *ichthuon dekate*. Here we might cite any number of modern comparative examples demonstrating the close correlation between fishing economies and growth in monetized markets. Susan Sutton, for example, discussing the fishing village of Vourkari on Keos, notes that it supported a population of only twenty-six in 1896, but that that figure had grown to over one hundred by 1920, chiefly because 'the villagers' catch entered the growing cash economy of the island' (1991: 394–5). At Delos, as the population grew, especially its population of cash-carrying urban-dwelling merchants and artisans, the demand for fresh seafood grew proportionately. Demand and the attendant potential for securing profits, however modest, would have attracted additional fishermen. This, the central role of the profit motive in the fisherman's endeavours, is everywhere attested in our ancient sources. It resides, for example, at the heart of Oppian's masterful proem, which opens with an image of a fisherman alone at sea on the heaving swells, pursuing an unseen quarry over a fathomless void, guided only by 'the manifold devices of a profit-seeking art' (*Hal.* 1.7–8).

In the fluid landscape of the Hellenistic Aegean there was very little to prevent fishermen from pursuing their craft wherever it was most profitable. Ancient Greek marine fisheries were generally open access, a principle Plato codifies in his *Laws* (7 824b–c). Although a host of scholars have followed Jacques Dumont in suggesting that this is merely a convenient philosophical construct, contradicted by quotidian practice, his argument rests on evidence that is for the most part misinterpreted.[40] Indeed, the ancient literary sources routinely attest the mobility of fishermen, and it is no accident that refugee populations are frequently depicted as engaging in this activity.[41] Here we might cite the letter of Alkiphron quoted in the title of this article, which brings us back full circle to the unique status of marine fishermen residing on the periphery of the polis. The fisherman Thynnaios writes to his fellow fisherman Skopelos about yet another impending Athenian naval expedition, for which their skills at sea will no doubt be put to use pulling oars in the bowels of a trireme. Why, he wonders, should we, 'who are entirely ignorant of the agora,'·risk a pointless death when we can simply practice our trade elsewhere? For Thynnaios's part, he tells us that he plans to choose a course that is *lusitelesteron*, 'more profitable' (1.14). Many of the Delian 'seafaring fishermen' familiar to Kallimachos in the mid-third century would have been natives of that island. Many too would have originated in villages on Rheneia or Mykonos, but often have chosen to sell their catches at Delos. Others would have been migrants from even further afield, attracted by the availability of a rich market and the potential for profits, however modest.[42] We might imagine Alkiphron's Thynnaios mending his nets on a beach in the Kyklades.

The reality, however, is that the connections between Delos's growing commercial activity and its fishing economy were more complex than a fishing effort simply chasing demand. The skills ancient fishermen possessed were useful in a whole range of maritime activities. In the twenty-first century these relationships are no longer always obvious, but not so long ago it was possible for the naturalist Bernard de Lacépède to write, without risk of being accused of hyperbole, that without fishermen 'there is for a nation no sure navigation, no prosperous commerce, no maritime force, and by consequence no wealth, no power.'[43] We have already seen how easily a fisherman like Thynnaios might find himself employed in the Athenian navy, but he would as easily have found work as a pilot or as crew of a commercial vessel, or even on the docks and shipyards.[44] It is for this reason that our sources routinely employ phrases such as *thalattourgoi* that can apply to fishermen or sponge divers, but just as easily to sailors or salt workers. This point is driven home in Herakleides Kritikos's description of the small city of Anthedon, whose inhabitants, we are told, are virtually all fishermen, although many have also laboured as ferrymen or in shipyards.[45] Nor should we ignore another kind of economic activity closely linked with fishing in antiquity: piracy. In another of Alkiphron's letters (1.8), Eukolymbos weighs the guiltless hardship of fishing against the more profitable but bloody life of the pirate, a career choice that many fisherman would have faced in antiquity, even as they apparently often continue to do so now.[46] Recent scholarship has rightly stressed the degree to which piracy depended on and contributed to other more 'legitimate' economic activities, and it certainly would have played some role at Delos.[47]

In other words, we ought to avoid the temptations both to minimize the scale and importance of marine fishing economies in their own right and to see this kind of economic activity as essentially non-productive, merely transferring extra disposable income from the pockets of the wealthy to the needy hands of the marginal classes. The pool of skilled labour afforded by Delian *thalattourgoi* would itself have contributed to commercial growth, attracting not only parasites but, more importantly, their merchant prey. Some of that growing commercial wealth is likely to have been reinvested in fishing and related activities. In the third century, a certain Apemantos, son of Leophon, is recorded together with his son, whom he appears to have named Sponge (*IG* XI.2 161 D.69–72). While Vial concedes that the space Apemantos is recorded as having rented is likely to have been used for commercial purposes, he doubts that the name Apemantos gave his son indicates a link to sponge diving, chiefly because there is little ancient or modern evidence for that trade in the region. But this ignores ecological and historical complexities, as well as the fact that ancient sponge divers could have ranged far from their home ports.[48] The two primary obstacles would have been finding the requisite capital to fund a boat, equipment, provisions, and wages, and the availability of skilled divers. The former was available in abundance on Hellenistic Delos, and the fact that the 'Delian diver' became proverbial in antiquity not only proves the presence of the latter but also can be best explained, in my view, by the existence of a Delian sponge-diving industry.[49]

Otherwise, fishermen are not easily identified in the local prosopographic record, despite the fact that Athenaios cites the name Ichthybolos as one of those characteristically Delian (4 173a).[50] But we might conclude by noting that better evidence for the presence of fishermen, and possibly too their influence, is afforded by an account recording a loan ca 240 BC to the Ichthypolidai, the only phratry attested on Independent Delos.[51] This temple loan has been interpreted as suggesting the phratry suffered financial difficulties that have in turn been linked to the *ichthuon dekate*, which, it is suggested, constituted an impossible burden.[52] Although the evidence is admittedly scarce, this argument could easily be turned on its head.

Interestingly, the loan appears to have been backed by Delian officials, suggesting a particular public interest.[53] And if we must link this evidence with that afforded by the *ichthuon dekate*, we could as easily cite as an analogy an inscription from Ephesos attesting the construction in the first century AD of a designated customs house to collect the duty on fish.[54] The city bore part of the costs of the project by donating valuable real estate on the waterfront, but the construction itself was paid for by private contributions and through funds provided by a joint association of fishermen and fishmongers. This circumstance can be best explained in the context of commercial growth at Ephesos and a desire on the part of the association to have a dedicated space allowing for the more efficient collection of duties and subsequent wholesale of its product. In other words, the loan attested at Delos need in no way imply financial hardship on the part of the local association of fishermen (and possibly fishmongers too); it can as easily be interpreted as a simple advance to cover short-term costs resulting from some infrastructure project that, albeit unattested, is easily imagined in a context of demographic and commercial growth, with a corresponding increase in activity in its 'market rich in fish.'

In many respects, Hellenistic Delos is unique, and it remains to be seen how broadly this particular model can be applied to the Hellenistic period. No doubt there were coastal poleis with poorly monetized markets and correspondingly underdeveloped fishing industries, while other cities would perhaps have seen analogous growth already in the fourth century. But where economic development did occur, it would have derived chiefly from growth in trade, giving rise to the same essential paradox whereby connectivity, or greater belonging, was mediated chiefly by isolated actors – *thalattourgoi* – pursuing economic interests at the margins of the polis.

## Notes

1 1941: 2.1179. Better evidence would perhaps complicate this conclusion; see, for example, although slightly earlier, the development of a dredge that Aristotle suggests may have been partly responsible for decimating scallop stocks at Pyrrha (*Hist. an.* 7 602a22–24).

2 See most recently Mylona 2008: 67–9.

3 On this question of connectivity Horden and Purcell (2000) is fundamental. More recently, see Bresson (2005) and especially his two-volume treatment of the economy of the Greek poleis (2007 and 2008), which emphasizes the relationships between a 'société des cités' and growth in trade and the market.

4 Bintliff (1977: 117–22), criticized by, e.g., Efstratiou (1985: 7), and Jameson, Runnels, and van Andel (1994: 314–15).

5 The cultural significance of seafood and its consumption has, thanks in part to Davidson's popular *Courtesans and Fishcakes* (1997), gained much deserved attention, but less so the methods and markets that evolved to satisfy a seemingly insatiable demand for seafood. As Davies has recently noted, in general the economics of Hellenistic 'elegant living' remain sadly understudied (2001: 33).

6 Kassel-Austin, *PCG* fr. 34.9–10 and 12–15.

7 The more general works on Delos have virtually nothing to say about marine fishing or the *ichthuon dekate* (see, e.g., von Schoeffer 1901; Roussel 1925;

Laidlaw 1933). The tax is mentioned only in passing by Larsen (1938: 355: 'tithe on fisheries'), Deonna (1938: 200: 'un droit sur la pêche'), Rostovtzeff (1941: 1.235: 'fishing rights'), and Vial (1984: 338). Most references continue to rely on Homolle 1890: 438–44. The *ichthuon dekate* receives more careful attention in the overlooked dissertation of Höppener (1931: 163–4), who interprets it as a simple 10% duty on the delivered catch. Much of his discussion is reprised by Dumont (1977b: 137). Brun includes a number of useful observations (1996: 136) on this tax and on the role of fishing in the Kyklades more generally.

8 The precise meaning of the designation remains obscure. Although various solutions have been proposed, most scholars agree that it designates only a portion of the city's total customs revenues: see, for example, Dürrbach's commentary to *IG* XI.2 161.A.26; Larsen 1938: 355; Vélissaropoulos 1980: 210; Vial 1984: 339–40.

9 It is possible that the city regularly earmarked tax revenues to cover transfers from Apollo to the city. On these loans see Homolle 1890: 438–44; also Larsen 1938: 338–40.

10 For Dürrbach's figure for the surtax, Lacroix (1924: 404) proposed ⟦ΡΔΗΗΙΙΙ⟧, 62 drachmas, 3 obols, a sum that would compute precisely if Dürrbach's ΗΔΔ were retained for the tithe on grain. But in fact that sum is corrected by Chankoswki-Sable and Feyel (1997: 119) to ΗΡΔ, 160 drachmas, a reading that has to be retained, meaning the expected sum for the surtax should be 64 drachmas, 3 obols. The figure recorded on the stone is probably an error, and we should read ΡΔΗ<ΗΗ>ΙΙΙ.

11 In line 30 Dürrbach read ΜΡΧΧΧΡΗΗΗ, 18,800 drachmas, corrected by Chankoswki-Sable and Feyel (1997: 120) to 18,900 drachmas, a sum that also offers better sense (the contract auctioned for 18,000 drachmas, plus a 5% surcharge of 900).

12 The 5% surcharge raised 120 drachmas, 1 obol. This is 5% of approximately 2,403 drachmas. Subtract 1,465 for the *hypotropion* and the tithe on rents leaves approximately 938 drachmas for the tithe on grain. We should perhaps restore something like: τοῦ σίτου ΡΗΗΗ]/ΗΔ[ΔΔΓΗ]ΗΗ· τῶν ἐνοικίων ΡΗΗΗΔΔΔΓ· τοῦ ὑποτροπίου ΡΗΔΔΔ· ἐπώνια τούτων ΗΔΔΙ.

13 Reger expresses reservations on this point (1994a: 254).

14 Although hesitant to extrapolate, Brun follows Vial (1984: 338) in noting that the recorded sum represents a total value of fish of more than three talents, which, he suggests, corresponds to an average annual expenditure per citizen of approximately 15 drachmas (1996: 136).

15 Kassel-Austin, *PCG* fr. 32.

16 Schaps, for example, concludes that the evidence 'strongly suggests that there was nothing intrinsically inflationary about the dialogue of Attic comedy'

(1985–8: 69–70). And Davidson cites both Gallant and Schaps in comparing the consumption of fish to 'a bottle of champagne' (1997: 187).

17  See, e.g., Powell 1996: 14–15; Rose 2000: 517; Bekker-Nielsen 2002: 32; Wilkins 2005: 22.

18  Feyel published one stone in 1936, and Vatin a second, together with a new edition of the first, in 1971 [SEG 32 [1982] 450]. In 1974 Roesch republished the inscription's prescript [SEG 38 [1988] 377]. A new edition and study has recently appeared in Hesperia (Lytle 2010); the following discussion reprises some of the arguments treated in greater detail there.

19  Sosin's solution has the advantage of introducing incongruities at only two points, one of which I found, upon examining the stone, does not in fact exist; the former is probably the product of a similar error by Vatin, but the block on which it resides could not be located. Sosin's suggestion has the additional advantage of construing the most common price, HIX, as eleven chalks, which in an inscription regulating prices could suggest an attempt to keep prices below a psychologically significant barrier (one obol).

20  Citing work on Boiotian coinage, Gallant concludes that the Akraiphia mina would have been calibrated on a prevailing silver standard equal to approximately 430 grams (1985: 35). But coin standards and retail weights need not agree and, as noted by Feyel (1936: 31) and subsequently Schaps (1988: 67), an Aeginetan mina equal to approximately 630 grams is more likely. It seems that also at Athens an 'emporic mina' was standard during this period and equivalent to 138 drachmas, or roughly 600 grams (see IG II$^2$ 1013). Feyel, mentioning the possibility of a Boiotian mina attested by Epiphanios (De mensuris et ponderibus 314) as equivalent to 2.5 Roman pounds, concludes that the mina specified in our inscription likely equaled not 430 but between roughly 600 and 800 grams (1936: 32–3). I am sceptical of the testimony of Epiphanios, but even a mina of 600 grams would mean that Gallant has overestimated the cost of fish by an additional 40%.

21  On the costs of land transport, see Bresson's recent discussion (2007: 88–91).

22  In the epigraphic evidence, dekatai ichthuon are occasionally paired with regular customs duties. A decree from Hellenistic Crete issued by the city of Praisos records civic revenues at Stalai, naming a tithe on fish together with the regular customs duties, much like at Delos (Syll.$^3$ 524 = IC III vi 7 = Chaniotis 1996: 64.4–8). Likewise, our ancient sources regularly equate dekatai and those who collect them with customs duties and agents. Pollux, for example, includes dekatai in a list of terms for duties assessed in harbors (Onom. 9.30), and together with other terms for customs houses he offers dekatelogia, dekateuteria, and dekatonia, attributing the last of these specifically to a comedy by Antiphanes called The Fisherwoman (Halieuomene, Kassel-Austin, PCG fr. 28). It has

recently been argued that in an inscription from Athens (*IG* II² 1103) Hadrian directly equates a tax on fish with revenues from import duties, *eisagogia* (Lytle 2007a). A first-century AD inscription from Ephesos (*IEphesos* Ia 20, discussed below) attests a designated customs house to collect a local duty on seafood, and the peculiar arrangement of our Hellenistic price decree from Akraiphia can be explained by the hypothesis that it contains a document borrowed from just such a customs house, probably, in this case, at nearby Anthedon (Lytle 2010). Additional evidence suggests that fish were routinely taxed in Hellenistic harbors, including at Delos's neighbour Mykonos, where a sacred law perhaps dating to the end of the third century BC mentions sacrifices that are to be offered by the council 'from the duty on fish' (*Syll.*³ 1024.10). Similarly, in the late fourth-century BC a 20% duty on fish is attested at Kolophon (Meritt 1935: 372–7 [+ Wilhelm 1939: 352–65] line 31; the same duty is probably alluded to in line 81: see Migeotte 1984: 282–5), and it has been suggested that a similar tax lies behind the 20% duty attested at Kalymna (*Syll.*³ 953.61 = Segre 1944–5: 79 B.9).

23  Kassel-Austin, *PCG* fr. 32.1–4.

24  Gallant 1991: 120–1. We have very little historical catch data for the Aegean, but see again the figures given for the northeast Adriatic by Faber (1883). More recent data suggests the Aegean would have offered comparably rich resources: in 2002 Greek fishermen captured nearly 86,000 metric tons of seafood, about 90 per cent of which was caught in the Aegean. These statistics are published by the Fishery Information, Data and Statistics Unit of the Food and Agriculture Organization of the United Nations (Yearbook of Fishery Statistics, Vol. 94/1, Rome 2004). FAO data can also be searched online at http://www.fao.org/fishery/statistics/global-capture-production/en [accessed 24 August 2009]. Likewise, as Bintliff notes, Delos, Mykonos, and Rheneia sit in a relatively rich fishing zone within the Aegean (1977: 2.594–6).

25  Fishing spears or *triainai* appear in the accounts (*IDélos* 354.60) and inventories (see, e.g., *IDélos* 421.20), as do various shells, whether of silver (*IDélos* 442.B.179), gilded (*IDélos* 1417.A.II.31–2) or erected on wooden columns (*IDélos* 1417.A.II.36). Deonna discusses this material in the context of the abundant archaeological evidence from Delos and Rheneia for fishing, which includes, among other items, spears, hooks, weights and net mending tools (1938: 200–3).

26  Temple accounts suggest salt fish (*tarichos*) and probably fresh fish too (*opson*) was consumed at the annual Eileithyiaia festival; see, e.g., *IDélos* 401.24 (190 BC); 442.A.223 (179 BC); 440.70 (173 BC). The sums are typically small, for example three drachmas for *tarichos* and six drachmas for *opson* in 190 BC. On these 'sacred menus,' see Linders 1994. It has been suggested that the widespread consumption of seafood on Delos is also acknowledged in a very different religious context: *IDélos* 2530 attests that those entering the sanctuary

of Atargatis were required to have abstained from fish only for a period of two days, which Deonna (1938: 200) follows previous scholars in describing as a concession to the culinary habits of the local population.

27 Vial (1984: 17–20) revised Bruneau's estimates (1970: 262–3) of a population of 1,800–2,000 adult males downward on good grounds, suggesting that in the last years of independence that figure stood at only 1,200, which would correspond to a total population, including non-citizen residents, of somewhere in the neighbourhood of 5,200–6,500. Reger, promising to justify his figures elsewhere, suggests that even this number is too high and that the total Delian population including metics, slaves, women, children, and transient visitors ranged between 2,600 and 3,900 (1994: 83–5). Vial argues that this is impossible, suggesting that, if one includes a sizeable number of slaves, the island's total population may have stood as high as 8,000 in the last years of independence (1997: 342).

28 The best estimates derive from public provisions for the Posideia recorded in the accounts of 190 (IDélos 401.17) and 173 BC (IDélos 440 A.60–1).

29 By comparison, FAO statistics give 50 pounds, by whole weight, for the annual per capita consumption of fish and shellfish by modern Greeks. On the other hand, Americans annually consume only about 15 pounds of fish, shellfish, and processed fish products annually (for the years 2000–3 the figures are 15.2, 14.8, 15.6, and 16.3 pounds), but the residents of Hong Kong over 100. Figures for annual fish consumption are calculated by the National Marine Fisheries Service (U.S. consumption) and the FAO (world consumption), and they are collected in the annual report of the Fisheries Statistics Division of the Office of Science and Technology of the NMFS, *Fisheries of the United States, 2003* (Silver Spring 2004). The chapter on per capita consumption is available at www.st.nmfs.gov/st1fus03/08_perita2003.pdf [accessed 24 August 2009].

30 A perhaps considerable quantity of the total catch would never have arrived in the marketplace. Some would have been consumed directly by fishermen and their families (Alk. 1.1) or their patrons (Antiphanes, Kassel-Austin, *PCG* fr. 188; Alk. 1.9), some distributed to hired hands in lieu of cash (Alk. 1.20), and some offered in barter (Alk. 1.7) or sold directly to consumers (Plato Comicus, Kassel-Austin, *PCG* fr. 28; *Anth. Pal.* 6.304). This fresh fish probably avoided duties altogether. More significantly, imported salt fish is likely to have been subject only to the regular 2% customs duty. Ancient literary, epigraphic, and archaeological data all agree in suggesting distinct trades in, and taxes on, fresh and salted fish (Lytle 2010: 291–2). At Delos too, it would appear that salt fish was retailed in dedicated shops: fourth-century accounts record a *tarichopolion* among the properties owned by the god; see, e.g., *IDélos* 104(18).15. The figures for the tithe may even have excluded the fish captured in Delos's sacred *limne*, the rights to which were leased directly by the temple, for 60 drachmas in 278 BC (*IG* XI.2 161 A.36) but for only ten drachmas a half-century later (*IDélos*

353 A.35–6 [219 BC]), and 10 drachmas, 1 obol in 179 BC (*IDélos* 442 A.151–2). This decline in value perhaps reflects urban development and consequent changes to the *limne*, on which see Brunet et al. 2001: 622–7.

31  2005: 22. Based in part on a survey of the material evidence, Collin-Bouffier has even more recently arrived at a similar conclusion (2008).

32  *Pol.* 1256b40–1. On this passage and Aristotle's attitude towards trade, see especially Bresson 2000 [1987].

33  Kassel-Austin, *PCG* fr. 3.4–8. This Kriton is likely to have been one of the two attested as victors at the Dionysia (*IG* II² 2323.151 [183 BC] and 210 [167 BC]).

34  For much of the rest of the Aegean world the third century is frequently seen as a period of relative economic stagnation; see, e.g., Reger 2007: 481–3.

35  The root *tropis* is well attested as referring to a ship's keel, but the adjective *hypotropios* occurs only in the Orphic *Argonautica* (267) and Oppian's *Halieutica* (1.224). Höppener (1931: 163–4) suggests that *hypotropion* derives instead from the verb *hypotrepomai* and refers to the right of using the harbour, arguing that both the sense and the form are analogous to the *eisagogion* mentioned in a letter from Hadrian to Athens (*IG* II² 1103), which he interprets as a harbour tax on fishing vessels. The three-fold increase in revenues is then due to the replacing of a direct tax on fishing vessels with the *ichthuon dekate*, intended to replace lost revenues from the *pentekoste*. But his proposed etymology is unlikely and various harbour taxes already appear among the taxes leased out by the temple, on which see Homolle 1882: 66–8. Furthermore, the *eisagogion* mentioned in the inscription from Athens likely refers specifically to import duties on fish, for which the *ichthuon dekate* offers a much better analogy (Lytle 2007a). And there is no evidence to suggest a drop in customs revenues ca 250 BC.

36  Höppener's theory has already been discussed above. Dürrbach suggests the possibility of a tax on fishing rights (*ius piscatus*) but admits the meaning of the term is obscure (see his commentary at *IG* XI.2 161 A.26–7). Most subsequent scholars have either passed over the question in silence or assumed a tax on fishing rights (Rostovtzeff 1941: 1234–5; Étienne 1985: 61–2; Vial 1984: 214n100; and Reger 1994a: 254). Comparanda for a tax on marine fishing rights are difficult to find. Reger suggests it may have been 'analogous to the funds collected from leasing porphyry fields' (1994: 256). In my view, the Delian *porphyra* is better interpreted as a duty assessed on the murex delivered to dyeworks (Lytle 2007b). Finally, Dumont proposes (1977b: 137) that the change in designation from *hypotropion* to *ichthuon dekate* can be explained by a doubling of the rate of the duty from 5% to 10%. But his argument rests only on the attested increase in revenues and Höppener's unlikely theory that increased funds were necessary to replace a drop in customs revenues.

37 The tax farmer could only recover the cost of his bid (1,690 drachmas) plus the surcharge (84 drachmas, 3 obols) by collecting tithes on rents worth 17,745 drachmas. At 55 drachmas per annum, this would require 323 houses, again with the likelihood of profits suggesting an actual total somewhat higher still.

38 Reger's argument for 'a piddling trade' depends in large measure on the evidence for the *pentekoste* (1994: 253–7). Following Vial in suggesting that the sum (5,250 drachmas) given for the *pentekoste he astia* in 250 BC represents only a third of the total customs duties, he concludes that 'the total annual value of goods in transit on Delos would have remained fairly stable across the first half of the third century' (255). But even if we accept Vial's thesis (1984: 339–40) that the *pentekoste he astia* (for which we have no additional evidence) corresponds to duties on terminal rather than transit trade, Vial's conclusion that roughly two-thirds of the customs duties in any given year were assessed on goods in transit relies entirely on the assumption that the total revenues for the *pentekoste* were the same in 250 BC as three decades earlier. In fact, the total value of the *pentekoste* in 250 BC may have been far higher than the 18,900 drachmas attested in 278, and there is no evidence in the accounts to suggest otherwise. Even the sums for 279 and 278 may well represent only a portion of the island's total trade: Bresson has recently suggested that all Delians enjoyed the same exemptions from customs duties attested in honorary decrees for certain foreigners (2008: 81–3). Nor is there any reason to believe that gradual growth in the first half of the third century need have been accompanied by stark changes in local rent or other prices. Price changes in the second half of the third century are a different matter; see here Bresson's recent re-examination of the data for charcoal, wood, pork, oil and grain (2006).

39 1941: 1.236. On the archaeological record, Rostovtzeff defers to Roussel 1925. The problems are too complex to detail here, but much of the archaeological evidence for growth around the Delian harbour can only be roughly dated to the mid- and late third century. In my view, it is more logical to follow Rostovtzeff in interpreting building projects like the South Stoa as a response to, rather than a leading indicator of, demographic and commercial growth.

40 See Dumont 1977a. His arguments are reprised most recently by Bresson 2008: 189–90. I treat this question at length in a recent article (Lytle, 2012: 1–55).

41 For example, a letter of Alkiphron clearly attests Rhodian fishermen working in Attic waters (1.2, the setting is assured by a reference to Mounychia). Plutarch includes an anecdote (*Sulla* 26.3–4) in which Sulla encounters fishermen on the beach near Aidepsos on the northwest coast of Euboia, and they turn out to be refugees from Lokrian Halai. Similarly, many of the fishermen of Halieis in the southern Argolid are reported to have been refugees from Tiryns, destroyed by

Argos in the mid-fifth century (Herodotus 7.137; Ephoros *FGrH* 70 F 56; Strabo 8.6.11 C373).

42  *Hymn to Delos* 15: *ichthubolees haliplooi*. *IG* II² 1103 makes it clear that fishermen from as far away as Eleusis, rather than selling their catch in local ports, were pursuing better prices in Peiraeus. Similarly, we are told that the Spartan Teleutias's raid on Peiraeus in 388 BC captured 'a great number of fishing vessels and crowded ferryboats sailing in from the islands' (Xen. *Hell*. 5.1.23).

43  1798: cxli ('sans lui, il n'y a pour une nation ni navigation sûre, ni commerce prospère, ni force maritime, et par conséquent ni richesse, ni pouvoir!'). A similar view underlies Faber's description of Austro-Hungarian policy in the Adriatic: 'Lastly, an attempt is being made to organise and develop the fisheries, which have always proved a most important branch of industry to every country which has the good fortune to be in the possession of a seaboard, not only on account of the immediate profits it brings to those personally engaged in the exercise, but for the highest State reasons, as it is the best school for training seamen' (1883: 41–2).

44  The seizing of fishing vessels and the drafting of fishermen into service is well attested in the sources, e.g., Plut. *Sol*. 9.2, *Tim*. 18.1; and Livy 25.23.6.

45  Fr. 1.23–4, Arenz 2006; *Brill's New Jacoby* (online): Herakleides Kritikos (369A) F1 23–4. Given Anthedon's orientation facing Euboia and that island's close regional connections with the Kyklades it is likely that a number of Anthedonians were among the fishermen and sailors who migrated to Hellenistic Delos. An Anthedonian is named in a list of ephebes from the last quarter of the second century (*IDélos* 2598.31), but far more interesting, given the frequency of kinship ties among fishermen and the well-attested dangers of ancient seafaring, is a first-century BC epitaph from Rheneia bidding farewell to five Anthedonians, all sons of Apollodoros (Couilloud 1974: no. 160). Although Couilloud follows Roussel in suggesting that these Anthedonians are citizens of the Anthedon in Palestine, Knoepfler argues persuasively for Boiotia (1986: 608–12), and is followed by Reger 1994b: 77.

46  Fittingly symbolic of this close relationship is a clause prohibiting piracy in *IG* I³ 67.7–8 (427–424 BC), a treaty between Athens and the southern Argolid community of Halieis, a town that, not surprisingly, took its name from the chief occupation of its inhabitants (Strabo 8.6.12 C373). Links between fishing and piracy are widespread and enduring, as witnessed by the now famous Somali pirates, frequently described in news reports as former fishermen (e.g., 'seasoned fishermen-turned-hijackers' in the 5 November 2005 *Agence France-Presse* article 'Cruise Liner Narrowly Escapes Hijack in Pirate-Infested Somali Waters').

47  Noted by Reger specifically in the context of Delos (1994: 262), and discussed in greater detail by Gabrielsen (2001).

48 Already in the nineteenth century the overharvesting of sponges, thanks in part to the development of diving helmets, led Greek sponge divers to range increasingly farther afield, and by the end of the century most Mediterranean sponges were being harvested off the coast of North Africa. More recently, sponge blight has taken its toll. Ethnographic studies suggest that even in antiquity sponge diving boats would have been highly specialized operations, and because sponges could be cleaned, dried, and stored on board, these vessels need not have been bound to local ports (Bernard 1967 and 1972).

49 On the Delian diver see, e.g., *AP* 9.578; Diogenes Laertius 2.22 and 9.12. Although scholars have followed Bruneau (1969) in suggesting a reference to divers in the local murex industry, there were far more efficient methods of capturing murex, as the ancient sources clearly indicate (Aristotle *Hist. an.* 5.547a; Sophokles fr. 504 Radt, *TrGF* IV; Poll. *Onom.* 1.47–48; Oppian *Hal.* 5.598–611; Ael. *NA* 7.34; Plin. *HN* 9.132). Likewise, the scale of the murex industry in the region during the Hellenistic period was decidedly modest (see Lytle 2007b).

50 As Vial notes (1984: 338n95), three individuals bear the name Ostakos, 'Lobster,' but this name is not uncommon (although more usually Astakos). One local fisherman, albeit legendary, is known by name: a popular story held that Pythagoras's soul had previously inhabited a Delian fisherman named Pyrrhos (Herakleides Pontikos *apud* Diog. Laert. 8.4).

51 *IDélos* 298 A.197–199 + *SEG* 34 [1984] 778[d]. On this phratry and the etymology of the name, which suggests a direct connection to fishing, see Vial 1984: 23.

52 Bogaert 1968: 137; Dumont 1977b: 137–8. This argument relies, as we have seen, on the (improbable) suggestion that the sums recorded for 250 BC represent a doubling of the duty.

53 On the role of *prodaneistai* at Delos, see Migeotte 1984: 26.

54 *IEphesos* Ia 20. This document is discussed by Horsley (1989), but deserves a detailed reappraisal.

# 17

# De l'ouverture au repli: Les prêts du sanctuaire de Délos

## LÉOPOLD MIGEOTTE

Le sanctuaire d'Apollon, à Délos, a pratiqué pendant plusieurs siècles différents types de crédit, d'abord durant la période classique, lorsque les Athéniens contrôlaient l'administration des biens sacrés, ensuite pendant les 150 ans de l'Indépendance de l'île (314–167 a.C.), enfin au temps de l'occupation athénienne, non seulement jusque vers 145 avant J.-C., date à laquelle les documents commencent à nous faire défaut, mais sans doute encore au-delà. Il y a plus de quarante ans, R. Bogaert a analysé en détail l'ensemble de ces opérations et, tout récemment, V. Chankowski est revenue sur celles de la période classique.[1] Ces études conservent toute leur valeur et me permettent de reprendre la question aujourd'hui pour la situer dans un contexte plus large, en la comparant aux pratiques habituelles du monde grec dans le même domaine, et pour proposer des réflexions sur la portée du phénomène. En effet, d'une période à l'autre, les activités de crédit présentent de forts contrastes qui illustrent, à leur manière, le double thème du colloque.

Pour éviter toute ambiguïté, précisons qu'il ne s'agit pas des fondations. Certes, comme dans la plupart des cités hellénistiques, il y avait à Délos un bon nombre de fondations pieuses. Leur fonctionnement est bien connu: le capital initial venait en général de la générosité d'un bienfaiteur, roi ou particulier, il était considéré comme inaliénable et offert en prêt à la population locale, de manière à produire régulièrement des intérêts qui étaient strictement assignés, dans la longue durée, à l'objectif défini au départ. Les fondations déliennes n'avaient donc rien d'original en soi, sauf peut-être leur grand nombre, et elles se sont maintenues sans changement pendant de nombreuses générations.[2]

Il en allait tout autrement du crédit offert librement par la caisse sacrée. En effet, ses capitaux ne provenaient pas de générosités privées ou royales et les intérêts faisaient partie des revenus courants du dieu. Le système n'était donc pas programmé à l'avance et obéissait en fait à la loi de l'offre et de la demande, tout en suivant lui aussi des règles strictes concernant les garanties, le paiement des intérêts et le remboursement des capitaux. Pour bien comprendre son fonctionnement et sa portée durant la période hellénistique, il faut remonter brièvement en arrière.

En effet, dès la seconde moitié du V$^e$ siècle, puis au siècle suivant, les Athéniens ont utilisé une partie de la fortune d'Apollon pour accorder des prêts à des particuliers et surtout à des cités étrangères situées en majorité dans les Cyclades. D'après les comptes des années 434/433–431/430, 54,020 drachmes (un peu plus de neuf talents) étaient déjà placées en prêts pour cinq ans, au taux de 10%.[3] Ces opérations ont graduellement pris de l'ampleur au point que, dans les années 370, le capital en circulation était cinq fois plus élevé:[4] il dépassait 282,000 drachmes (plus de 47 talents), dont plus de 92% (260,600 drachmes) étaient prêtés à une douzaine de cités au moins, parmi lesquelles on reconnaît Mykonos, Ténos, Andros, Kéos, Sériphos, Siphnos, Syros, Paros, Naxos, Karystos, etc. Trente ans plus tard, d'après les comptes de 341/340, malheureusement très incomplets, le sanctuaire accordait encore des avances importantes à Paros (30,000 drachmes), à Sériphos (4,000 drachmes), à Karystos (de 18,000 à 30,000 drachmes) et à une autre cité dont le nom a disparu (18,000 ou 24,000 drachmes).[5] Les textes manquent pour les décennies suivantes, mais il est clair que le crédit du dieu est resté ouvert en permanence jusqu'en 314. Ces opérations, on le voit, mettaient en jeu des sommes considérables, qui contribuaient fortement à la circulation monétaire dans la région.

Or, des sommes aussi élevées ne pouvaient pas provenir des revenus courants du dieu, car la moyenne annuelle de ces derniers, qui peut être calculée grâce aux comptes de 377/376–374/373, était d'environ 17,300 drachmes, donc de moins de trois talents.[6] D'après l'interprétation séduisante de V. Chankowski, elles venaient d'un capital de réserve qui s'était constitué peu à peu grâce à l'*aparchè* d'un soixantième prélevée sur le *phoros* des alliés de la première Confédération athénienne (Chankowski 2008: 317–19). On sait en effet que le trésor de cette alliance fut déposé à Délos de 478/477 à 454/453 et que, durant ce quart de siècle, l'*aparchè* fut régulièrement consacrée à Apollon.[7] Si le *phoros* rapportait déjà 400 talents par an, comme par la suite, le dieu disposait donc d'une réserve de l'ordre de 160 talents (plus de 900,000 drachmes).[8] Il se peut que cet argent ait été en partie thésaurisé, mais les Athéniens en ont soustrait un tiers environ (50 talents ou 300,000 drachmes), semble-t-il, pour le consacrer au crédit, tout en allouant le reste à des constructions et à des célébrations religieuses.

En mettant ce capital à la disposition d'autres cités, les Athéniens faisaient évidemment preuve d'ouverture, et même d'audace, car ce type de crédit était pratiquement inconnu à l'époque et est demeuré très rare par la suite.[9] Les Athéniens eux-mêmes ne l'ont jamais pratiqué à partir de leurs propres fonds sacrés, à notre connaissance, et une dizaine d'exemples à peine sont attestés ailleurs. Il mettait souvent en jeu des sommes élevées, qui pouvaient poser des problèmes de remboursement et créer des risques pour les cités prêteuses. Il avait généralement des motifs politiques et ne pouvait être négocié et conclu qu'entre des cités amies ou alliées. Par son ambition et sa durée, l'expérience athénienne fut donc unique.

Or, les comptes du IVe siècle montrent, malgré leurs lacunes, que les amphictyons athéniens ont eu du mal à percevoir les intérêts et à récupérer les sommes prêtées. Ainsi, les comptes de 377/376–374/373, déjà cités, permettent de calculer que, pour ces quatre années, les débiteurs ont payé en tout un peu plus de 33,300 drachmes d'intérêts, mais ont laissé en souffrance environ 80,250 drachmes, soit plus du double. L'endettement des cités était beaucoup plus élevé que celui des particuliers, on l'a vu, et tout porte à croire qu'il a traîné durant plusieurs décennies, au point qu'une partie des dettes n'a sans doute pas été remboursée avant l'expulsion des Athéniens en 314. La proportion des sommes impayées nous échappe, mais il paraît clair que les Déliens en ont hérité quand ils ont retrouvé leur Indépendance. En effet, ils n'ont réussi à les recouvrer, au moins en bonne partie, semble-t-il, que dans les années 280 grâce à l'intervention du roi Ptolémée et de son grand officier Philoklès, roi de Sidon, auprès des cités de la Confédération des Nésiotes.[10] Ils ont alors tiré la leçon de ces difficultés, selon toute apparence, car ils ont retiré de la circulation la majeure partie du capital et l'ont immobilisée durant un siècle, sans y toucher et sans la comptabiliser dans la caisse sacrée (ou du moins sans faire transcrire dans la pierre les documents qui en faisaient état).[11] Une thésaurisation aussi longue et aussi massive peut étonner, mais elle n'était pas inhabituelle dans les sanctuaires grecs.

En outre, elle était liée à la nouvelle politique de crédit des Déliens. Ceux-ci, en effet, ont bientôt décidé de mettre fin aux prêts à des cités étrangères,[12] de réserver les avances de fonds sacrés à deux clientèles internes, la cité de Délos et les particuliers, presque tous Déliens, et d'y consacrer des sommes beaucoup plus modiques qu'auparavant. Celles-ci sont difficiles à évaluer, mais elles semblent avoir été d'une douzaine de talents seulement, auxquels une partie des surplus courants pouvait être jointe à l'occasion.[13] En tout cas, il est certain que ce double crédit ne pouvait pas être assuré, lui non plus, par les surplus des revenus sacrés, car ces derniers tournaient autour de trois talents par année[14] et servaient naturellement aux dépenses du culte, aux travaux de construction, de restauration et d'entretien des lieux sacrés et au fonctionnement de l'administration religieuse. En d'autres termes, les Déliens ont réservé à cet usage une fraction des capitaux légués par les Athéniens en 314. Or, même si leur cité n'avait pas l'envergure ni l'autorité d'Athènes, ils auraient pu profiter de sa position privilégiée dans la Confédération des Nésiotes, créée par Antigonos le Borgne en 315–14,[15] pour continuer à servir de banque à des cités voisines. Par prudence ou par conformisme, ils ont choisi une position de repli et d'isolement, qui rompait radicalement avec la politique précédente.

La cité de Délos avait donc désormais à sa disposition une ouverture permanente de crédit.[16] On constate en effet que les prêts et les remboursements ont laissé, dans les comptes des hiéropes, des traces nombreuses et continues durant 130 ans environ, de 301 à 169. Leurs montants ont beaucoup fluctué selon les années, manifestement selon les besoins de la cité et les disponibilités du sanctuaire. Mais ces emprunts étaient chaque fois décrétés par l'Assemblée des citoyens, comme les dépenses non routinières. Lors de ces réunions, l'un des hiéropes (au moins) devait donc, au nom du collège, faire état de la fortune du dieu et suggérer la solution la plus équilibrée pour ne pas y puiser inconsidérément. C'étaient des emprunts à court terme: la cité commençait parfois à les rembourser durant l'année, puis s'efforçait de régler le solde sans trop tarder.[17] On le constate de manière particulièrement précise dans les comptes détaillés des années 195–170, qui rapportaient non seulement de multiples emprunts contractés pour offrir des couronnes et des cadeaux à des rois et à des peuples étrangers, mais aussi de nombreux remboursements effectués rapidement.[18] En outre, dans l'ensemble, la fréquence des remboursements montre que la cité tenait à payer ses dettes au mieux de ses possibilités.

Il est évidemment impossible de savoir si elle y a toujours réussi, mais les textes n'ont conservé aucune trace de saisie ou d'exécution. Nous savons également que ces opérations étaient régies par une loi et que chaque prêt, consigné dans un contrat, était accompagné de plusieurs garanties qui ont été renforcées du IIIe au IIe siècle: engagement des revenus publics et surtout présence, à titre de cautions personnelles, de citoyens fortunés dont certains agissaient comme *prodaneistai*, c'est-à-dire à la fois comme garants et comme intermédiaires.[19] Jusqu'en 250, ces derniers ont été de simples citoyens, puis ils furent remplacés par les membres du Conseil, auxquels se sont ajoutés les trésoriers (en 246) et le secrétaire de la cité (en 218). Leur rôle était important, car ils s'engageaient comme s'ils étaient les emprunteurs, recevaient l'argent des mains des hiéropes et devaient le rembourser de leur poche, au nom de la cité, quand celle-ci tardait à le faire ou en était incapable.[20] Grâce à eux, la fortune d'Apollon ne paraît donc pas avoir souffert de ces avances. Mais elle n'en a guère profité non plus grâce aux intérêts, puisque les remboursements ne tardaient pas. En fait, plutôt que de faire fructifier une partie de l'argent sacré, l'intention des Déliens fut simplement, selon toute apparence, de mettre à la disposition de la cité une source commode de crédit sans nuire à la fortune du dieu. C'est donc en pensant aux besoins publics que l'Assemblée a créé le système.

Or, tout en maintenant fermement cette politique de repli, les Déliens ont également fait preuve d'originalité. En effet, ce type de crédit était peu courant, lui aussi. Il n'est connu dans d'autres cités que durant de courtes périodes et par un très petit nombre d'exemples, qui se comptent presque sur les doigts d'une seule main pour les époques classique et hellénistique.[21] L'un de ces cas est celui d'Athènes, qui fut exceptionnel lui aussi, car il a permis à la cité de faire face à des dépenses colossales avant et pendant la guerre du Péloponnèse: de 433/432 à 423/422, donc pendant onze ans, elle a accumulé une dette de près de 5,600 talents (environ 33 millions de drachmes) auprès d'Athéna et des autres dieux de l'Attique.[22]

Les prêts d'Apollon aux particuliers, attestés de 313 à 169, obéissaient à la même politique de repli, puisqu'ils ont été presque tous consentis à des citoyens déliens.[23] Certes, une partie au moins des intérêts payés en 313 (4,768 drachmes [*IG* XI.2 135.16–22]) remontait sans aucun doute au dernier exercice des amphictyons athéniens, donc à des dettes dont les Déliens ont également hérité. Multipliée par dix, la somme donne une idée du capital alors en circulation: près de 48,000 drachmes ou huit talents, ce qui n'était pas négligeable. Mais les choses ont beaucoup changé par la suite. Les prêts ont évidemment varié en nombre et en importance d'une année à l'autre, selon les besoins des individus et les disponibilités de la caisse. Mais la plupart étaient modiques: ils dépassaient rarement 1,500 drachmes par individu et leur moyenne était de 300 à 345 drachmes. En pratique, chaque année, les hiéropes ne prêtaient jamais plus de quelques milliers de drachmes à la fois et la moyenne du capital en circulation était, semble-t-il, d'un peu plus de deux talents.[24]

Dans l'ensemble, d'après R. Bogaert, la plupart des remboursements ont été partiels et Apollon perdait régulièrement 20% de son avoir. Les hiéropes semblent donc s'être montrés plus complaisants envers leurs concitoyens qu'envers la cité elle-même. Mais les chiffres conservés ne sont probablement pas tout à fait représentatifs et nous savons aussi que les Déliens ont imposé à ces opérations des règles sévères (contrats écrits, garanties réelles et personnelles) et que beaucoup de paiements ont été effectués par des garants au nom de débiteurs défaillants. En fait, contrairement aux prêts publics, ces petites avances étaient consenties à long terme: elles s'étendaient parfois sur vingt ou trente ans, voire davantage, donc jusqu'aux héritiers des emprunteurs. Si les Déliens se sont contentés de recouvrer 80% des capitaux, ils ont probablement tenté de compenser ces pertes grâce aux intérêts. En fin de compte, ici encore, ils semblent avoir voulu se donner à eux-mêmes, à titre individuel, une source de crédit pour leurs dépenses ou leurs affaires personnelles, sans nuire outre mesure à l'avoir d'Apollon et sans vouloir non plus le faire fructifier. Or, ces prêts avaient eux aussi leur originalité. Certes, on en trouve des équivalents dans d'autres cités, du IVᵉ au Iᵉʳ siècle a.C., mais leur nombre total n'atteint pas la dizaine et ils n'ont jamais été pratiqués durant de longues périodes ni en même temps qu'un autre type de crédit.[25] À Délos, au contraire, c'est durant près d'un siècle et demi qu'ils ont côtoyé, sans discontinuer, les avances de la caisse sacrée à la cité.

Les textes postérieurs à 167, beaucoup plus rares et plus délabrés que ceux de la période précédente, n'ont conservé aucune trace de prêts à la communauté locale en tant qu'entité politique. Nous ne connaissons pas les motifs de ce choix et nous ignorons même si la colonie des Athéniens s'est considérée comme l'héritière des dettes impayées de la cité de Délos, s'il y en avait. Mais l'abandon de ce type de crédit confirme à la fois l'originalité de la pratique antérieure et la bonne santé financière de la nouvelle communauté. Les textes ne mentionnent pas non plus de prêts à des cités étrangères, mais cette absence s'explique aisément: les Athéniens gardaient sans doute un mauvais souvenir de leur expérience du IVᵉ siècle et la domination romaine bouleversait désormais le contexte politique. En fait, les Athéniens eux-mêmes ont procédé à une thésaurisation massive en décidant de ne plus donner cours qu'à leur propre monnaie et à celles de même étalon. Pour cela, ils ont inventorié et trié les monnaies entreposées dans le sanctuaire, y compris sans doute une partie des capitaux immobilisés durant l'Indépendance, et alloti toutes celles qui n'étaient pas d'étalon attique ou d'Alexandre dans cinquante jarres de contenu homogène dont ils ont fait un dépôt sacré et intangible. Or, même s'il n'atteignait pas 50 talents, ce capital était assez considérable: on l'a évalué à une somme variant de 82,000 à 100,000, voire à 130,000 drachmes.[26] Seules deux activités de crédit se sont donc poursuivies, toutes deux dans le domaine privé: celle des fondations, intangibles à cause de leur caractère religieux, et celle des prêts aux particuliers. Les premières ont laissé très peu de traces,[27] mais les secondes sont un peu mieux connues, du moins entre les années 162/161 et 146/145. On y constate quelques changements: les Athéniens leur ont consacré des sommes plus élevées que les Déliens et ont resserré les conditions des prêts, notamment en les limitant à cinq ans.[28]

Le contraste est donc frappant entre l'esprit d'entreprise des Athéniens, sans doute un peu téméraire à la période classique, et la politique prudente et pragmatique des Déliens. Chacune de ces attitudes avait de bons motifs, on l'a vu, mais leur évolution contraste à son tour avec celle de la fonction économique de Délos. En effet, probablement dès la période archaïque, l'île et surtout le sanctuaire d'Apollon, qui était un gros acheteur et un gros employeur, ont joué un rôle moteur dans l'économie de la région. À la période hellénistique, le commerce extérieur s'est développé: les étrangers ont commencé à affluer à partir du dernier tiers du IIIe siècle et, après 167, la franchise fiscale octroyée par le Sénat romain a encore élargi le rayonnement des échanges et contribué à enrichir la communauté installée sur place, qui était de plus en plus cosmopolite.[29] L'évolution des activités de crédit s'est donc faite en sens contraire. Mais des traits contradictoires cohabitaient souvent dans les cités grecques. À l'affairisme qui se répandait de plus en plus s'opposaient des traditions conservatrices qui considéraient les fonds des dieux comme un domaine à part, qu'il fallait protéger et qu'il n'était pas toujours convenable de mettre sur le marché.

## Notes

1  Bogaert 1968: 126–69; Chankowski 2001 et Chankowski 2008: 309–22. Je fais moi-même le point sur la question dans un livre en cours de rédaction (chapitre VI, section IV).

2  Voir les relevés et les commentaires de Roussel 1916: 174–5; Ziebarth 1917: 425–41; et R. Bogaert 1968: 153–61.

3  *IDélos* 89 ; *IG* I[3] 402 (Prêtre 2002: 25–7) ; Chankowski 2008: 399–400 n° 1.12–14.

4  D'après les comptes bien conservés des années 377/376–374/373: *IDélos* 98 (Migeotte 1984: n° 45-II; Prêtre 2002: 29–37; Rhodes-Osborne 2003: n° 28) ; Chankowski 2008: 417–24 n° 13. Pour le détail des chiffres, voir le commentaire de *IDélos* n° 98, Bogaert (1968: 126–30), et Migeotte (1984: 141–57), avec les tableaux récapitulatifs des avances aux cités.

5  *IDélos* 104(28) (Migeotte 1984, n° 45-VI); Chankowski 2008: 486–491 n° 43 bA.19–22.

6  Voir les références à la note 4 et le commentaire de *IDélos* 98. Outre une moyenne de 8,329 drachmes perçues en intérêts, les revenus annuels comprenaient un peu plus de 8,000 drachmes venant des fermages et des loyers et environ 830 drachmes tirées notamment de recours d'ordre judiciaire.

7  L'accord est très large sur ce point: voir entre autres, avec des références à des études antérieures, Giovannini 1997: 152; Samons 2000: 36; Chankowski 2008: 39–40. La date de 454/453 est controversée, mais admise comme probable par de nombreux savants.

8  Cf. Chankowski 2008: 318.

9  À ce sujet, voir Migeotte 1984: 363–6 et 393–400.

10  Cf. Migeotte 1984: 161–5. Cette interprétation a convaincu Étienne 1990: 111; Chankowski 2002: 46–47; et Chankowski 2008: 328–9. Dreher (1995: 254n307) et Vial (2002: 258–9) se sont montrés plus réservés.

11  Sur la réapparition d'une partie de ce capital dans les comptes du début du IIe siècle, voir Chankowski 2002: 42–9.

12  Les rares exceptions semblent toutes se situer à la fin du IVe siècle. Cf. Migeotte 1984: 156–7 et Vial 1988: 58.

13  Ce chiffre n'a qu'une valeur indicative. Pour les prêts à la cité, le mieux est de retenir le plus élevé, celui de l'année 218, qui a atteint 61,634 drachmes 3 oboles (*IDélos* 354.10–15), car il représente sans doute le maximum des disponibilités de la caisse sacrée (les dix talents n'étaient certes pas toujours prêtés au complet). Pour les avances aux particuliers, voir la note 23.

14  Cf. Chankowski 2008: 324–5.

15  Cf. Will 1979b: 57–8.

16  Voir l'analyse détaillée de Bogaert (1968: 131–8), avec des tableaux récapitulatifs.

17  Cf. Bogaert 1968: 133–4. Du compte de l'année 269 (*IG* XI.2 203.78) on a généralement conclu que la perception des intérêts ne commençait qu'au début de l'année suivante, donc que les prêts étaient gratuits jusque-là. Mais Vial (2002: 250–60) a combattu cette interprétation avec de bons arguments: la clause de 269 était une exception.

18  Voir Baslez-Vial 1987: notamment 282–3.

19  Pour les détails, voir Bogaert 1968: 134–7; et Vial 1984: 107–11 (rôle du Conseil et des *prodaneistai*) et 357–67 (analyse prosopographique).

20  Mais ils n'intervenaient pas systématiquement pour tous les remboursements, comme le pensait Gabrielsen (2005: 153), car beaucoup de remboursements ont été effectués par les trésoriers.

21  Cf. Chankowski 2005, dans une analyse plus large des activités financières des sanctuaires, et Migeotte 2006: 119–25, chaque fois avec les références. On peut maintenant ajouter, grâce à Kritzas (2006: 413–24), le cas d'Argos où le Trésor de Pallas, au début du IVe siècle, a avancé des sommes à la cité pour la guerre et des besoins courants, de même qu'aux cinq stratèges pour les cavaliers et au collège des Quatre-Vingts.

22  D'après *IG* I³ 369, comptes récapitulatifs des logistes des années 426/425– 423/422. Le total, restitué grâce aux indications éparses de ce long texte, est indiqué aux lignes 122–3. Voir les tableaux et le commentaire de D. Lewis à la fois *ad loc.* et dans Meiggs-Lewis 1989: 214–17.

23  Ici encore, voir l'analyse minutieuse de Bogaert (1968: 138–53), avec quatre tableaux récapitulatifs. Vial (1984: 367–83) s'est placée avant tout du point de vue social, étudiant le rôle des emprunteurs les plus riches et les motifs de leurs emprunts; elle a résumé plusieurs de ces points dans Vial (2002: 260–2).

24 Cette estimation est fondée sur les listes, assez longues, des intérêts versés et dus (cf. Bogaert 1968: 139–40), dont la moyenne était de 1,250 à 1,300 drachmes (car plusieurs sommes sont incomplètes): le capital, dix fois plus élevé, tournait donc habituellement autour de 12,500 ou de 13,000 drachmes, soit un peu plus de deux talents.

25 Voir Bogaert 1968: 288–94; et Chankowski 2005.

26 Cf. Roussel 1916: 168–73; Bogaert 1968: 167–9; Tréheux 1991: 349–52.

27 Des paiements liés à des fondations apparaissent par exemple dans *IDélos* 1408 AII.33–35.

28 Cf. *IDélos* 1408 AII.36–50; 1415.13–15; 1416 BII.68–118 et C.1–53; 1419.4, 9, 15 et 17; 1442 B. 73–74. Voir les commentaires de F. Dürrbach et P. Roussel, *ad loc.*, et de Bogaert 1968: 165–6.

29 Cf. Reger 1994 et Roussel 1916: 1–96.

# 18

# Connections, Origins, and the Construction of Belonging in the Poetry of Kallimachos

## MARY DEPEW

Of all the major third-century poets, Kallimachos may have had the best claim to 'belong' to Egypt and the culture established by the Ptolemies. In his second *Hymn* he proudly refers to his Cyrenaean, and thus Spartan, heritage, even as he acknowledges that Cyrene is now 'Egyptian.'[1] He was a favoured member of the court, and was commissioned to catalogue the great Library's collection. As if aware of his privileged status and point of view in Alexandria, in various passages throughout his poetry Kallimachos represents himself – or the poem's implied speaker – as someone who has either never left Egypt, or who has no desire to travel beyond its borders.

In this paper I will consider several passages in Kallimachos's poetry, most of which are fairly well known, from a different perspective, that of belonging. I am interested in how each passage represents the speaker as positioned in Egypt, and what this positioning implies both for Kallimachean poetics and for Ptolemaic claims to political and cultural territory. With regard to this latter point, I will also briefly examine how Kallimachos uses the theme of rivers and springs in his poetry to articulate the connections between Greece and Egypt. These themes are traditional in Greek poetry, but Kallimachos takes them up to provide his monarchs with a justification for their claims to cultural and political hegemony over Greece. Far from representing Egypt as isolated from Greece, Kallimachos establishes, through these themes, a series of validating connections that authorize both his own and his monarchs' claims to own the Greek past as well as its landscape.

## Belonging: Kallimachos's Self-Positioning in Egypt

Throughout his poetry, Kallimachos repeatedly represents the poem's first-person speaker as positioned in Egypt and as belonging to the world created by the Ptolemies. Sometimes this sense of belonging appears as a kind of provincialism. In the fragmentary thirteenth *Iambos*, for example, the speaker defends his right to compose iambic poetry even though he has 'never come to Ephesos, nor mixed with the Ionians' (12, 64). This poem ends the collection of *Iamboi*; in the first poem in the collection Hipponax, the sixth-century Ionian iambic poet, had been represented as travelling from the underworld to Alexandria to criticize the *philologoi*, the poets and scholars resident at the palace's Mouseion, for their contentiousness. In the thirteenth *Iambos* that contentiousness has turned against Kallimachos himself, and his answer to it forms the body of the extant poem. Not only has Kallimachos never been to Ionia, the accusing voice continues, but he mixes iambic verse with various Greek dialects – a fair description of the experimentation with genre that the poet has accomplished with *Iambos* 2 through 12.[2] In the last extant lines of the poem, the speaker takes up his critic's words and defiantly makes this claim: 'I do sing, neither having visited Ephesos nor mixed with the Ionians' (63–4). Kallimachos's claim to do this is based here and elsewhere in his poetry on his appropriation of the traditional notion of *techne*, or skill.[3] Cultural specificity, the fact that traditional poetic genres arose in places outside of Egypt, is dismissed as a determining factor in the continuing viability of these genres.[4] What replaces such 'belonging' is the skill the poet-scholar comes to possess through his hard work in the Library and through his role as a scholar.

In the first *Iambos*, which, like the thirteenth (and unlike most of 2–12) is composed in a traditional metre and dialect (choliambics, Ionic) associated with the genre, Hipponax is represented as having made a significant journey: he has left the underworld and has arrived at a sanctuary near Alexandria. The Diegesis identifies the sanctuary as the Sarapeion of Parmenion, one of many unidentified sanctuaries outside the city proper. The temple of Sarapis in this sanctuary is said to have held a statue of Zeus modelled on the same Homeric lines that were supposed to have inspired Pheidias's statue of Olympian Zeus.[5] So it is even more impious that the site is described as the place where 'that old man who thought up Panchaian Zeus of old babbles and scribbles his impious books' (9–11). The reference is to Euhemeros of Messene's *Hiera Anagraphe*, 'Sacred Scripture,' in which the fourth-century author denied the divinity of the Olympian gods. They were, he claimed, merely kings who were worshipped after their death for their beneficence to their people. The scene that Kallimachos sets at the Sarapeion represents Hipponax mingling with *philologoi*, scholars and poets, who, like Kallimachos himself, were privileged to work in the Ptolemies' Library and Mouseion. In their poetry, Kallimachos, along with Theokritos and others, overtly identified Ptolemy with Zeus.[6] The purported site of the meeting between Hipponax and the *grammatikoi* sets the tone of moral outrage and instruction that was a traditional element of the iambic genre. But the description here of Euhemeros as impious has a particular point: to direct criticism to the Olympians, as Euhemeros did, is to direct it to the beneficent monarchs, and in this particular case, to deny their divinity.

As if emphasizing this point of contention, Kallimachos represents Hipponax as having come to harangue the scholar-poets, Kallimachos included, and to forbid them to criticize one another (Kerkhecker 1999: 34). Their aim, after all, is a common one. In good iambic fashion, he tells a moral tale, the story of the Cup of Bathykles, which was left to the wisest of the seven Sages, who one by one refused it and sent it on to the next, until it returned to the first recipient, who dedicated it to Apollo.[7] The poem's revival of this ancient poet may seem bizarre, but, along with everything else in the extant text, it is quite relevant to Kallimachos's situation in Alexandria. As Kerkhecker puts it: 'Hipponax returns from Hades, and breaks through the barrier between then and now. He presents himself as a figure of the past, a literary classic . . . But this old poet becomes an active part of the present. He enters a world precisely defined in time and space. The scholars, Euhemeros, the sanctuary – this is the world of Callimachus. He mocks "you, hoi nun"' (1999: 32). The first and last poems in the collection of *Iamboi* emphatically locate the book's concerns in Alexandria. Like Kallimachos in the final *Iambos* of the collection, here at its beginning Hipponax is speaking from and for an Alexandrian context. The fact that *he* is represented as coming to *them* fits a pattern that, as we shall see, is duplicated throughout Kallimachos's poetry.

Another passage that privileges the speaker's situation in Alexandria comes from the *Aitia* (frs. 178–85). The speaker is reclining at a symposium hosted by a displaced Athenian, Pollis, who has brought one of his city's religious festivals, the Anthesteria, to Alexandria. The Ptolemies had fostered this sort of religious diversity and importation of their citizens' cults. Next to the speaker is seated one Theugenes, who is described as a *xeinos* (178.6), a visitor to Alexandria from Ikos, an island in the northern Sporades. Taking up the theme introduced by the setting, the speaker questions the Ikian about the religious practices of his own home: 'Why is it the tradition of your country to worship Peleus, king of the Myrmidons? What has Thessaly to do with Ikos?' (178.23–4). He continues: 'What my heart yearns to hear from you, do tell me in answer to my question' (178.21–2). The Ikian's reply is lost except for its opening lines, but they are noteworthy. He congratulates the speaker for having avoided seafaring, and laments his own life of business travel:

τρις μάκαρ, ἢ παύρων ὄλβιός ἐσσι μέτα,
ναυτίλίης εἰ νῆιν ἔχεις βίον· ἀλλ᾽ ἐμὸς αἰόν
κύμασιν αἰθυίης μᾶλλον ἐσῳκίσατο. (fr. 178.32–4)

(Three times blessed you are, and happy (*olbios*) as few are,
if you lead a life that is ignorant of seafaring. But I live
more among the waves than the sea gull.)

Scholars have approached the *bios* tradition regarding Kallimachos in basically two ways. On the one hand, Kallimachos's extensive knowledge of customs originating throughout Greece and the Mediterranean has led some to argue that he had travelled widely, for example to Athens, whose topography he describes in some detail in the *Hekale*.[8] The Ikos episode, however, has prompted others to conclude that Kallimachos was 'ignorant of seafaring.'[9] These issues cannot be resolved, nor do they need to be. We should instead ask why Kallimachos represents his poetic personae in the way he does with regard to travel, distance, and the Greek poetic tradition. The Ikian's address to 'the poet,' for example, recalls Hesiod's statement at *Works and Days* (650), in which he represents himself as never having left Thebes to travel by sea. There was one exception, he says: he once sailed to the island of Euboia to take part in a poetic contest (*Works and Days* 651–62). The reference here to Hesiod's *Works and Days* would be natural in the quasi-didactic context of the *Aitia*, with its accounts of the origin of cults and institutions from the Greek world.

This view is given weight when we note that the speaker's address to the Ikian ('What my heart yearns to hear from you, do tell me in answer to my question,' 21–2) takes the form of a traditional invocation of the Muses, the ultimate authority on origins. This, however, is a strikingly new model of inspiration. The Ikian is a reliable, 'pure' source just because he is a native of the 'distant' area in question; he can offer the unmediated access to the truth that the Muses' inspiration had always provided to poets.[10] The important point for this paper, however, is this: Kallimachos represents himself, or the speaker in his poem, as not having to leave Alexandria to access information about distant cults and their origins. Like the myriad religious traditions that the Ptolemies invited into their diverse city, reliable information comes *to* the guest reclining at the celebration of an Athenian cult celebrated in Alexandria. There is no need to leave the great city.

The Ikos episode, like the *Aitia* as a whole, is not so much about the practice or performance of rituals as it is about their *origins*, all of which are at a considerable distance from Egypt. This distance, however, is not represented as problematic, as some would argue.[11] On the contrary, Alexandria is portrayed as the ultimate destination of all knowledge, as of all diversity in religious practice.

Another episode in the *Aitia* represents a similar refashioning of the traditional model of poetic inspiration and knowledge by privileging the speaker's standpoint in Egypt. Near the end of the Akontios and Kydippe episode in *Aitia* Book 3 the speaker cites his source for the tale:

> Κεῖε, τεὸν δ' ἡμεῖς ἐκλύομεν
> τόνδε παρ' ἀρχαίου Ξενομήδεος, ὅς ποτε πᾶσαν
>   νῆσον ἐνὶ μνήμῃ κάτθετο μυθολόγῳ.

> Ξυγκραθέντ' αὐταῖς ὀξὺν ἔρωτα σέθεν
> πρέσβυς ἐτητυμίῃ μεμελημένος, ἔνθεν ὁ πα[ι]δός
>   μῦθος ἐς ἡμετέρην ἔδραμε Καλλιόπην. (fr. 75.53–5; 75.75–7)

(Kean, we heard about your love
from old Xenomedes, who once set down all
the island in a mythological history.

And blended with it, that old man,
mindful of the truth, told of your passionate love.
From there the maidens' story came to my Muse.)

Like the Ikian, the Kean mythographer Xenomedes is characterized in terms traditionally used of the Muses. He is 'mindful of truth' and the source of Kallimachos's own true knowledge about Keos. Also like the Ikian, Xenomedes is a credible, 'pure' source of information just because he is a native of the place whose inhabitants and customs he describes. It is because Xenomedes is from 'there' that he is a reliable, 'pure' source for the Alexandrian poet.

There is an important difference, however, between this description of inspiration and that described in the Ikian episode. The speaker in the *Aitia* says that he heard about the origin of the Akontiadai clan from Xenomedes. But then we are told that Xenomedes wrote this information down in his mythological treatise (κάτθετο ἐνὶ μνήμῃ . . . μυθολόγῳ, 55). The speaker would have heard it only insofar as he, or another, read it out loud.[12] Kallimachos himself catalogued the scrolls in the Library, and Xenomedes's mythography would have been among them. Like the Ikian, these scrolls would have arrived in Alexandria on ships, having travelled from Greece, in many cases from the original location their contents described, or whose institutions they accounted for. These original scrolls, as the famous account of Galen tells us, were, on Ptolemy's order, seized from ships arriving in Alexandria and copied. It was these copies, rather than the original scrolls, that were returned to the original owners.[13]

The Library itself, built in the palace grounds by Ptolemy I, would, along with the Library at Pergamon, begin a long tradition of grand civic monuments that announced a regent's appropriation of cultural capital. Peter Bing (2005: 123) has detected in the newly discovered poetic book of Poseidippos a repeated theme that coincides with this effort: the flowing into the Ptolemies' domain of both material wealth (olbos) and information. Looking in particular at the section of the Milan papyrus entitled 'lithika,' or 'Stone Poems,' Bing examines 'how the stones exemplify in their geographical distribution and social construction both the territorial and cultural/artistic aims of the Ptolemies and of their poet, Poseidippos' (2005: 120).

Bing cites other passages from Poseidippos's contemporaries, including Kallimachos, in which the poets set out a 'political landscape reflecting certain aspirations of sovereignty' (2005: 121). One example, Theokritos Id. 17. 95–7 is particularly relevant to the themes that I am examining in this paper: 'In wealth Ptolemy could outweigh all other kings, so much comes each day to his sumptuous house from everywhere' (italics are Bing's).[14] As Bing points out (2005: 133), however, Poseidippos's lithika poems describe not only finely wrought and expensive gemstones whose sources reveal the extent of the wealth flowing into the Ptolemies' city, but stones whose interest lay in their marvellous qualities.[15] Poems such as these suggest 'that the Ptolemies were not simply interested in claiming the wealth of the world, but also in gathering together its wonders.'[16] There are many examples of this directing of the interest in the marvels of distant lands, which had been so much a part of Alexander's project, to the glorification of Alexandria. Ptolemy Philadelphos, for example, had a zoo built in the palace grounds where, among other animals, exotic birds were on display.[17] The fascination that Kallimachos and his colleagues had for paradoxography, 'the objective and rational presentation of an item which appears to break the laws of nature,' is in accord with the impulse to bring to Alexandria the symbols of dominion over both Greece and the expanse of Alexander's conquests.[18]

Kallimachos himself composed a prose treatise entitled Collection of Marvels Throughout the World by Location (frs. 407–11), and like Apollonios of Rhodes and other court poets, included this sort of material throughout his poetic oeuvre. In all these cases, whether it is wealth, scrolls, marvellous accounts, animals, or stones, the direction of movement is to the city of Alexandria, where the monarchs' collections display the extent and the vast wealth of their rule, a rule which did not in fact reach as far as the origins of these wonders, but could still be claimed through their possession. No wonder Kallimachos represents himself as never having to leave Egypt.

For Kallimachos in particular the most obvious metaphor for mastery and control over the Greek world is his status as a scholar, a *grammatikos*, who in his catalogues and editions, as well as in his poetry and his official capacity as cataloguer of the Library, controls the currency of the tradition.[19] The same could be said, of course, for Apollonios of Rhodes, the second Director of the Library. Throughout his poetry, Kallimachos figures the skills of the *grammatikos* as offering to the monarchs a powerful, elitist model of control that is explicitly set in contrast to popular spectacle. It is in this context that we might interpret the way the Ikian guest fragment connects the ideas of purity and origins, of both rituals and knowledge. The fragment describes the cameraderie between the two men in this way: 'Like calls to like,' the speaker says in line 10. Both he and the Ikian guest find drinking *chalepos* 'difficult' or 'tiresome' (11–12, 20), and for this reason they turn to their discussion of cults and their origins. This is a surprising turn of events in a festival whose main point was to honour Dionysus. The rather surprising lack of interest in wine in this context may suggest an opposition on the poet's part to the *Technitai*, 'Artisans of Dionysus,' who were largely responsible for the monarchs' representation of their divinity for public consumption.[20] In contrast, here and in other passages throughout his work, Kallimachos represents the monarch's dominion as mirroring the universal command that the scholar has over the collected traditions stored in the Library.

These same themes of the *xeinos*, source, and of the arrival in Egypt of the currency of the Greek cultural tradition are also central to the 'Victory of Sosibios' (fr. 384 Pf.), an encomiastic elegy composed by Kallimachos either for the powerful minister of Ptolemy IV or for someone living under Soter. The text is fragmentary, but it preserves a glancing reference to the sort of aitiology proper to a victory ode. Cataloguing Sosibios's victories, lines 21–6 read: 'swiftly he took more celery ... so that the people of Alexandria and those living on the banks of the river Kinyps may learn that Sosibios received two crowns nearby the two sons – the brother of Learchos and the child that the woman of Myrina suckled.' The references, typically oblique, are to the sepulchral origins of the Isthmian and Nemean games, which were founded to honour Melikertes and Opheltes-Arkhemoros, respectively. Kallimachos extends the reach of Sosibios's fame to the boundary of the Ptolemaic kingdom, which was marked in the west by the River Kinyps. In lines 44–5, Sosibios is described as 'the stranger (*xeinos*) [who] has been victorious in both [the Nemean and Isthmian Games],' and then there is a reference to dedications made in the Argive *Heraion*. It is unclear who is speaking, but, since it would be to a mainland Greek that this Egyptian-born Greek would be a 'stranger,' we may be justified in imagining that it is an Argive or some other native of the mainland, from whom the announcement of Sosibios's victory would have to travel far to reach Egypt. In a similar way, lines 35–9 describe a victory *komos* sung in Sosibios's honour in Athens, after his wrestling victory in the Panathenaia.

A few lines later, Kallimachos's 'stay-at-home' persona emerges as the speaker describes himself in the following terms: 'I heard from others about that offering [the one made in Argos in Sosibios' honour], but I myself saw the one Sosibios dedicated on the outermost branch of the mouth of the Nile on a visit to the Kasian Sea' (47–9). He then quotes the dedicatory inscription, placing himself in memory before the dedicated object.[21] This striking image overturns the assumption of most Hellenistic epigrams, which emphasize not the act of reading an *object*, but the migration of a text *from* an inscribed object to a scroll. The speaker is quoting an inscription that he himself has seen. In 48–9 he says that he himself saw the dedication πὰρ ποδὶ . . . Νείλου /νειατίῳ. Pfeiffer (1985: ad fr. 384, 1) glosses the phrase, *in extrema parte*, 'at the furthest part.' There is another sense, then, in which this encounter with the inscription is represented as 'going to the source.' Although earlier, in lines 31–2, the Nile had said that no one knows 'from whence' it travels, the Kasian Sea was nonetheless in this period one of several candidates for the river's origin.[22] In traditional epinician poetry, the poet often represents his own point of view as coinciding with that of the victor: both are present at the site of the victor.[23] In Kallimachos, the speaker's source of knowledge about Sosibios's victory comes not from being at that victory's site, but from travelling to the sanctuary of Zeus Kasios, a site where the Nile may have originated. The Nile was thought to be the source of Egypt's wealth and fertility, and it was also imagined as the pharoah's – and the Ptolemies' – counterpart.[24]

In this poem, then, Kallimachos takes up the traditional epinician theme of representing the poet as mirroring qualities of the victor: Sosibios is a native Egyptian (a 'nursling [θρεπτός] of the Nile,' 28). He therefore dedicated his trophy at what may have been thought of as the source of the great river. The speaker represents himself as an unimpeachable source just insofar as he stands at this point in Egypt. The fact that both victor and poet are *xeinoi* with respect to Greece is less important than their relation to their homeland and to the source of its wealth and power: the Nile River.

The bond between Sosibios and the poet is actually alluded to when, a few lines later, the Nile itself speaks. The river says of Sosibios's accomplishment: 'A beautiful reward has my nursling paid back to me . . . for till now no one had brought a trophy to the city from these sepulchral festivals ... and, great though I am [πουλύς, 31], I, whose sources no mortal man knows, in this one thing alone was more insignificant [than those streams which] the white ankles of women cross without difficulty and children pass over on foot without wetting their knees' (28–34). The great river lacks only thing: a connection to the Greek past. The means of obtaining such a connection is figured in the poem as twofold: Sosibios travels from Egypt to Greece and brings home crowns from the Greek games, and the scholar-poet 'brings home' the Greek past not by leaving Egypt, but by creating poetry that takes up the earlier Greek tradition. This endeavour presses the claims of Egyptian Greeks such as Sosibios by re-appropriating the status of Greek institutions by a form of literary control. Moreover, if the Nile is identifiable, as it always was in Egyptian tradition, with the kings, can it be that they too, in all their greatness, lack only one thing: a connection to the Greek past and to its landscape?

## Sources and Connections

The way that Kallimachos forges this connection between the kings and the Greek tradition is easiest to see in his *Hymns*.[25] The first *Hymn* begins the collection by making the connection between the kings and the Olympian gods explicit: ἐκ δὲ Διὸς βασιλῆες, 'from Zeus come kings' (89, quoting Hesiod *Theogony* 96). For the Ptolemies this is just a statement of 'fact'; they legitimated their claims to rule by claiming descent from two sons of Zeus, Herakles in their paternal line and Dionysus on their maternal side. While other human beings 'belong' to one god or an other insofar as they share in their attributes or actions (75–7), the genitive of source implied in ἐκ δὲ Διὸς βασιλῆες declares that kings actually descend from Zeus. This meaning is reinforced by the rest of the period: 'Nothing is more divine than the kings of Zeus' (78–9), a statement that attributes to the Ptolemies divinity itself.

Since the hymn is so explicit in claiming the kings' origin in Zeus, the reader might assume that Kallimachos will develop the traditionally hymnic theme of a god's origin or birth. In fact, he spends only two lines (10–11) on the god's birth, and instead devotes twenty-four lines (17–41) to the birth of Arkadia's rivers. Since she has no water to wash the newborn Zeus, Rhea asks the earth to help her by also giving birth: 'Gaia *phile* (dear Earth), you give birth too! Your birth pangs are light' (29). The line endings of 28 and 29 ('Ρείη, ἐλαφραί) emphasize the conflation of Rhea and Gaia that often occurred in the tradition: Gaia (Rheia) brings forth *rheia* ('easily,' i.e., her labour pains are *elaphrai*, 'light'). By representing the earth as giving birth, Kallimachos not only conflates the mother figures here, but also their offspring. The birth of Arkadia's rivers and the birth of Zeus are in effect the same thing, since, as both etymology and prosody suggest, the two have the 'same' mother (Rhea ~ Gaia).[26]

What does this mean, both for this hymn and for the collection of hymns? If kings 'are from Zeus,' and Zeus's birth is figured as the equivalent of the rivers that spring from the oldest spot in Greece (cf. 40, *palaiotaton . . . hydor*, of the Arkadian river Neda), then are we to conclude that Egypt's Greek kings belong to, and are the autochthonous descendents of, Greek land? I would argue that this is just what Kallimachos is suggesting.

It is important to remember in this regard that the first *Hymn* begins a theogony that develops throughout the collection of six *Hymns*.[27] The first *Hymn's* narrative about Zeus's birth and about rivers emerging from their underground streams is a metaphor for the origin of a new world order. But Kallimachos's readers would recall that the world's rivers have a more distant source – they are there already, after all, as the first hymn describes it, flowing beneath the ground (20–7). In the *Theogony*, Gaia ('Earth') produces Pontos ('Sea,' *Th.* 126–32), and she then mates with her other offspring, Ouranos ('Sky'), to produce Okeanos and the other Titans (*Th.* 132–8). Okeanos mates with his sister Tethys, and the rivers are their offspring. Hesiod's catalogue of rivers then begins, with the Nile taking first place. Okeanos is the original source of the earth's rivers, and this great river that was thought to encircle the earth also plays a recurring role in Kallimachos's book of *Hymns*. For example, Kallimachos unites the portrayals of the three virgin deities the collection honours by portraying each goddess (or nymph, in one case) as travelling to Okeanos.[28] Especially after the first *Hymn's* portrayal of Zeus's birth as parallel to the birth of Arkadia's rivers, this repetition implies a connection between these three hymns and their representation of female divinity, suggesting as it does that these two daughters of Zeus, as well as the nymph and *choregos* Asteria, whose own qualities of purity link her to Artemis and Athena, are returning to their own source. Okeanos's association with the Nile further suggests these goddesses' identification with Isis, and thus with the Ptolemaic queens. In *Hymns* 3 and 6 the goddesses are in fact overtly linked with Isis.

The importance of Okeanos in the *Hymns* may be related to its traditional role as the parent of the Nile as well as the rivers of Greece. As early as Hesiod this genealogy represents Egypt as belonging to the same line as the Greek landscape. That this Greek genealogy was taken up in the Greek-Egyptian imagination is clear from a fourth-century AD papyrus that preserves an invocation to the Nile as part of a school exercise (Cribiore 1995: 100). As Raffaelle Cribiore points out, the theme of invoking the Nile is ancient, appearing as it does in Pharaonic hymns, and Greeks knew of such hymns to the Nile as early as Aeschylus and Herodotos. What is interesting about this text is the conventional association it illustrates between this ancient Egyptian tradition and Greek traditions of theogony. It begins:

[Νεῖλον +8]ϲϙν ἀναμέλψετε .... γονοιτε
τὸν ποταμῶν πρέσβιστον ἐγίνατο πότνια Τηθύς
ἢ τῶν ἐξ ἱερῶν /ἀψορρόου Ὠκεανοῖο ///
Αἰγύπτου ζαθείης φυσίζοον ὄλβιον ὕδωρ.

(Celebrate, O . . . the Nile with song,
The oldest river which queen Tethys begot
Or one of the sacred waters of encircling Ocean,
Blessed, life-giving water of holy Egypt.)

As Cribiore (1995: 100) points out, the tradition of the Nile originating from Okeanos came from the Egyptians, and in one Egyptian cosmogony the Nile was regarded as Okeanos itself: 'The world had originated from Ocean and the flooding Nile was called Ὠκεανός.'[29]

If such hymns, and their relevance to Greek notions of cosmogony, were at all current in the third century BC, the equivalence of Zeus's birth with the birth of Arkadia's rivers takes on a deeper relevance. Greece's most ancient land, as well as Zeus's birth, are connected at this foundational moment to Egypt via the genesis of rivers from Okeanos – which is also the Nile, the symbol of the Egyptian king's power and beneficence. The 'blessed, life-giving water of holy Egypt' of the Nile hymn's fourth line is described in terms that are echoed in the last lines of Kallimachos's first *Hymn* (94–6): 'Give *arete* and *aphenos*; *olbos* without *arete* cannot increase men, nor can *arete* without *aphenos*; give *arete* and *olbos*' (δίδου δ' ἀρετήν τ' ἄφενός τε. /οὔτ' ἀρετῆς ἄτερ ὄλβος ἐπίσταται ἄνδρας ἀέξειν /οὔτ' ἀρετὴ ἀφένοιο· δίδου δ' ἀρετήν τε καὶ ὄλβον). The insistence on the *olbos*, the wealth, joy, and hope that Zeus can grant, matches the same qualities supplied by the Nile's summer flooding. Zeus himself was identified with the Nile as early as Pindar.[30] In Kallimachos's hymn, the invocation applies equally to Zeus and to Ptolemy. Here at the beginning of his *Hymns* Kallimachos has marked out a foundational moment for the origin of the king of the gods and of rivers, and so he is able to apply to Zeus the importance that rivers have as symbols of origination, connection, and territorial claims.

Elsewhere in his *Hymns* Kallimachos takes up the theme of rivers to connect Greece to Egypt and Egypt's new kings to the landscape of Greece. In the fourth *Hymn*, for example, the birth of Apollo is explicitly – even

literally – connected with Egypt. Asteria, the nymph/island who will become Delos, has just invited Leto to give birth on her shores:

ἔννεπες· ἡ δ' ἀρητὸν ἄλης ἀπεπαύσατο λυγρῆς,
ἕζετο δ' Ἰνωποῖο παρὰ ῥόον ὅν τε βάθιστον
γαῖα τότ' ἐξανίησιν, ὅτε πλήθοντι ῥεέθρῳ
Νεῖλος ἀπὸ κρημνοῖο κατέρχεται Αἰθιοπῆος· (205–8)

(So you spoke. And she gladly ceased her grievous journeying
And sat down by the water of the Inopos, which the ground sends forth
In abundance at the time when the Nile
Descends in full spate from the Ethiopian Banks.)

Some sixty lines later the same imagery recurs. Asteria's transformation
occurs in tandem with Apollo's birth. The passage emphasizes the island's
famous features by line-initial anaphora: lines 260–3 each begin with a de-
clensional form of 'gold' and end with features of the Delian landscape (in
the translation I reproduce the order of the line-initial and line-end order):

χρύσεά τοι τότε πάντα θεμείλια γείνετο Δῆλε,
χρυσῷ δὲ τροχόεσσα πανήμερος ἔρρεε λίμνη,
χρύσειον δ' ἐκόμησε γενέθλιον ὄρνος ἐλαίης,
χρυσῷ δὲ πλήμυρε βαθὺς Ἰνωπὸς ἑλιχθείς. (260–3)

(Golden, then, all your foundations (themeilia) became, Delos;
with gold flowed all day your round lake,
golden foliage put forth your native olive tree,
with gold flowed in deep flood the coiled Inopos.)

The Inopos's connection with the Nile, the most ancient of rivers, is also ref-
erenced in Kallimachos's description of the *Nymphai Deliades*, the 'Delian
Nymphs,' who feature also in the *Homeric Hymn to Apollo*'s post-birth
description. In *Hymn* 4. 256–8 they are portrayed as singing a hymn to
Eileithyia after the god is born. Kallimachos calls the nymphs *potamou
genos archaioio*, 'offspring of an ancient river' (256), emphasizing the antiquity of the Inopos, which by virtue only of its connection to the Nile can be
called 'ancient' (Mineur 1984: 212).

The tradition that the Nile and the Inopos were linked by a subterra-
nean channel allows Kallimachos to emphasize the link between Apollo's
birthplace and Egypt, a link which in turn signifies the Greek past and the
Ptolemaic present.[31] In the hymn's long central narrative it is the fact that

Asteria fled the advances of Zeus, and so remained pure, that allows her transformation into the island that the pure god, Apollo, will consent to be born on.[32] The narrative thus inverts the traditional colonization theme that involves movement across the sea via the rape of a nymph.[33] Kallimachos enlists instead the close relation to nymphs that rivers have to construct the foundation of Ptolemaic rule and legitimacy. The River Inopos is already Greek, springing as it does from the Delian soil. It is also already native to Egypt, since its flow is connected to the inundation of the Nile. By 280/279 Delos had become particularly important to Ptolemaic claims of rule. Egypt had assumed leadership of the Nesiotic ('[Cycladic] Island') League, and had established a presence along the Ionian coast.[34] The fourth *Hymn* is making a wide-ranging point: with the birth of Apollo, the counterpart of Ptolemy, and with Asteria's transformation into the now rooted-down island of Delos, the world has settled into its present order. The connections between Greece and Egypt that undergird that new order have been made and sanctioned by their connection to the god's birth. The congruence of names seals the connection: Asteria may now receive her name of Delos 'because she no longer wanders unseen' (53).[35] The role that rivers play in this geopoetic use of the Greek tradition is both pervasive and crucial in Kallimachos's poetry.

Rivers are metaphors for both source and connection, and provide a means for Greece to 'belong' to Egypt's new Macedonian monarchs. The offspring of Okeanos, rivers and springs are important themes throughout Kallimachos's poetry. Susan Stephens (2003: 25) has noted that the first *Hymn*'s narrative of the origin of Arkadia's rivers parallels the tradition of the origin of Argos's water supply. The daughters of Danaos either discovered or dug the area's springs, and many were named after them. This myth appears quite often in Kallimachos's poetry. For example, fr. 66 (book 3) of the *Aitia*, Argos's springs are conflated with the Danaids: 'Heroines . . . children of . . . Io' (1); later on their water is identified with the Danaids Amymone, Physadea, Hippe, and Automate (7–8), who are called 'Pelasgiades' in line 9. Kallimachos's interest in this myth is not surprising: Danaus is at the very centre of the generational relationship between Egypt and Greece. Moreover, the Danaid line itself emerges from flowing water. The Argive river Inachos was the progenitor of Io, Libya, Aegyptos, and Danaos. It is the site of Athena's bath in *Hymn* 5.

Stephens succinctly sums up the kernel of this double migration narrative: 'The Greek Io wanders to Egypt where she becomes the ancestor of Libya, Danaos, Aegyptos, and Phoinix. In a later generation Danaus, with his daughters, returns to Argos.' 'Greek Io may be figured as the ancestor of Egypt, and in turn, her descendant Danaus may be figured as Egyptian as he returns to Greece with his daughters. However it plays out, the family genealogy was inextricably intertwined with Egypt.'[36] Throughout his poetry Kallimachos makes this important link via the theme of rivers and springs.

Io would have been an important figure to the queens in their own claims to divinity. She was identified with Isis as early as Herodotos, and Kallimachos himself wrote a poem called *The Arrival of Io*. Kallimachos Epigram 57 refers to a statue of a girl, Aeschylis, daughter of Thales, which was set up in the temple of 'Inachian Isis' in fulfilment of the vow of her mother, Eirene. The epithet of Isis identifies her with Io, and while no queen is mentioned in this short poem, it suggests that the conflation of Isis and Io, as well as the tradition that both descended from the Argive river Inachos, was common enough to be alluded to in such a passing way.[37] Berenike II achieved chariot victories at Olympia and the Isthmia as well as at Nemea, but it is her Nemean, or Argive, victory which is celebrated at the beginning of *Aitia* 3. The queens' identification with Isis involved imagining them not only as related to the Nile, but as descended from the very earth of Argos. Kallimachos's sustained interest in these myths suggests an attempt to write the female monarchs into this collection of myths, and to suggest by means of river imagery a very fluid – and yet secure – connection both to the landscape of Greece and to Egypt.

As I have noted, Kallimachos was the author of several prose treatises that cover a range of topics: the foundation of islands and cities, the local names of fish and rivers, nymphs, marvels, winds, and birds. These works fit in well with the Peripatetic tradition, but given his use of some of this material, Kallimachos may have had reasons beyond an interest in anything arcane for choosing the topics he did.[38] Rivers, at least, had a relevance for the politics of the Ptolemaic court. Prudence Jones (2005: 59–60) has shown how rivers traditionally offered to Greek, and later to Roman, poets various metaphors for narratives themselves. Their flowing offers a spatial geography for the flow of a narrative, as well as the source of a poet's inspiration. They also mark off territory, and feature in myths of origin, source, connection, and movement. The sort of colonization myths we find in the epinician tradition was unavailable for use in the diverse context of Alexandria. But for a poet or a monarch looking north to Greece, and already possessing the claim of a 'native' to the Nile and its ancient myths, rivers would offer the richest source of connection and belonging, not only to Greece and Egypt, but the whole of the known world.

## Notes

1  *Hymn* 2.65–8, 70–3. All references to Kallimachos are to the text of R. Pfeiffer (1985: 1, 2).

2 The Diegesis takes Kallimachos to be responding to a charge of *polyeideia*, or composing in too many genres, and this is what the poet responds to in line 41. He asks what law there is that says: 'You must write elegy, you epic, or that you were allotted by the gods tragedy?'

3 E.g., fr. 1.17.

4 I discuss these issues more fully in Depew 1992.

5 Ps.-Kallisth. I 33, 13 (37, 13–20 Kroll), Kerkhecker 1999: 23. In *Ia*. 6 the speaker describes this very statue of Zeus at Olympia (Dieg. VII 25–9).

6 E.g., Theok. *Id.* 17.

7 The aitiological aspect of the myth would have appealed to Kallimachos: it was because he received it twice that Thales dedicated the cup to Didymaian Apollo. Cf. Dieg. VI. 18–19.

8 The assumption originates with a statement in the Latin *Vita Arati* (in Maass 1898: 149.3), that Kallimachos resided in Athens for a time. Fraser (1972: 2a.463n15) discusses the statement and later scholars who accept it, but concludes from the fragment under discussion (178.31–4) that Kallimachos cannot have travelled to Athens.

9 Cf. Pfeiffer (1985: 2.xxxix): 'at revera se numquam mare periculosum transiisse expressis verbis dicit, fr. 178, 27 sqq.'

10 The speaker's questions end with a fragmentary (and textually problematic) line that preserves something like the phrase 'holding ears ready for those who want to tell a story' (30).

11 E.g., Selden 1998: 290–306.

12 Peter Bing (1988: 27–31) cites this passage as evidence for the fundamentally literary character of third-century Alexandrian poetry.

13 Galen *Comm. in Hipp. Epidem.* iii; Fraser 1972: 325–6, and n.147; 2a.480.

14 The flip side of this wealth is the onerous burden it gave to the Egyptian community. For a discussion of how the wealth that supported Ptolemaic spectacles such as the Ptolemaieia and the Procession of Philadelphos derived primarily from the collection of rents and personal poll taxes, see Mori 2008: 149.

15 E.g., Epigram 17 AB.

16 Bing 2005: 133.

17 The information is preserved in Strabo's account of Euergetes II's *Memoirs, FGrH* 234 F 2.

18 Krevans 2004: 175. Krevans notes that the genre survives 'in modern culture in sub-literary works such as Ripley's *Believe it or Not* and in tabloid news stories of monsters and marvels.'

19 On the transformation of this term's meaning in the third century from 'school-teacher' to 'scholar-poet,' see Pfeiffer 1968: I, 157.

20 On this point see Le Guen 2001.

21 Κυπρόθι Σιδόνιός με κατήαγεν ἐνθάδε γαῦλος ('from Cyprus a Sidonian merchant-ship brought me here') can be read for line 50, but the text is fragmentary thereafter.

22 The dedication may have been meant to be understood as having been set up in the temple of Zeus Kasios (Pfeiffer 1968: *ad loc*).

23 The identity of the first-person narrator of victory odes is a contentious issue (does it belong to Pindar or to the chorus?), but the 'I' is very often placed either at the place of victory or in the celebration in the victor's home town. A good summary of the discussion may be found in Morgan 1993: 1n1.

24 For discussion of this aspect of the Ptolemies's rule, see Koenen 1993 and Stephens 2003.

25 I develop the arguments in this section about Kallimachos's book of *Hymns* in Depew, forthcoming.

26 This is true particularly in Hesiodic terms, since in the *Theogony* all births evolve from a mother.

27 I develop this argument in Depew, forthcoming.

28 *Hymn to Artemis*, 42; *Hymn to Delos*, 17; *Hymn to Athena*, 10.

29 Diod. Sic. 1.12.4–6, drawing on Hekataios. In 1.37.7 Diodoros says that the priests of Egypt say the Nile has its origin in Okeanos, τοῦ περιρέοντος τὴν οἰκουμένην ὠκεανοῦ.

30 *Pyth.* 4. 56, Νείλοιο . . . Κρονίδα. Bing (1988: 137n90) also refers to Parmenon of Byzantion (*Suppl. Hell.* 604 A, 1): Αἰγύπτιε Ζεῦ Νεῖλ᾽.

31 The connection is not attested before the Hellenistic period, but may have been as old as the seventh century BC when, as Mineur (1984: 186) points out, Egyptian influence on Delos had grown. At *Hymn* 3.171 the Inopos is called 'Egyptian.' The scholiast to this line notes: Ἰνωπὸς ποταμός Δήλου· Αἰγύπτιος δὲ διὰ τὸν Νεῖλον, ὅτι καὶ αὐτὸς ἐκεῖ πλημυρεῖ. Bing (1988: 137n90) notes that πλημυρέω is a term used for the Nile flood. Also Lykophr. 575–6: Ἰνωποῦ πέλας, /Αἰγύπτιον Τρίτωνος ἕλκοντες ποτόν; Strabo 6.2.4.272a.

32 At *Hymn* 4. 98 the unborn Apollo utters from his mother's womb: εὐαγέων δὲ καὶ εὐαγέεσσι μελοίμην, 'pure am I and may I be the care of them that are pure.'

33 For discussion of this theme in Pindar and other early Greek poetry, see Dougherty 1993: 136–56, and passim.

34 For a recent discussion of the evidence and scholarly debate about the date of this assumption, see Ager 2005: 38.

35 As she herself confirms at the end of the myth: καὶ ἔσσομαι οὐκέτε πλαγκτή (273).

36 Stephens 2003: 25, citing Vasunia 2001: 33–58.

37 Ἰναχίης ἕστηκεν ἐν Ἴσιδος ἥ θάλεω παῖς.

38 Aristotle's list of Olympic victors, for example, was the model for Kallimachos's own catalogue of athletic victors (fr. 403).

# REFERENCES

Abd-el-Ghani, M. 2004. 'Alexandria and Middle Egypt: Some Aspects of Social and Economic Contacts under Roman Rule.' In Harris and Ruffini 2004: 161–78.

Acosta-Hughes, B. 2002. *Polyeideia: The* Iambi *of Callimachus and the Archaic Iambic Tradition*. Berkeley.

Adriani, A. 1946. *Documenti e ricerche d'arte alessandrina 1*. Rome.

– 1948. *Testimoniaze e monumenti di scultura alessandrina. Documenti e ricerche d'arte alessandrina 2*. Rome.

– 1958. 'Alesandrina, arte,' *Enciclopedia dell'arte antica, classica e orientale 1*, 232–5. Rome.

Ager, S. 1996. *Interstate Arbitrations in the Greek World 337–90 B.C.* Berkeley.

– 2005. 'An Uneasy Balance: from the Death of Seleukos to the Battle of Raphia.' In Erskine 2005: 35–50.

Ajootian, A. 1996. 'Praxiteles.' In *Personal Styles in Greek Sculpture*, edited by O. Palagia and J.J. Pollitt, 91–129. Cambridge.

Alabe, F. 2007. 'Routines hellénistiques et normes romaines? À propos du décor de quelques maisons déliennes.' In *Villas, maisons, sanctuaires et tombeaux tardo-républicains: découvertes et relectures récentes*, edited by B. Perrier, 405–15. Rome.

Alcock, S.E. 2002. *Archaeologies of the Greek Past: Landscape, Monuments, and Memories*. Cambridge.

Alexander, M.C., and J.A. Danowski. 1990. 'Analysis of an Ancient Network: Personal Communication and the Study of Social Structure in a Past Society,' *Social Networks* 12: 313–35.

Allen, R.E. 1983. *The Attalid Kingdom: A Constitutional History*. Oxford.

Amandry, P. 1978. 'Consécration d'armes galates à Delphes,' *BCH* 102: 571–81.

Amelung, W. 1897. 'Dell' arte Alessandrino a proposito di due teste rinvenute in Roma,' *BullCom*: 110–42.

Andreae, B. 2001. *Skulptur des Hellenismus*. Munich.

Aneziri, S. 1994. 'Zwischen Musen und Hof: Die dionysischen Techniten auf Zypern,' *ZPE* 104: 179–98.

– 2003. *Die Vereine der dionysischen Techniten im Kontext der hellenistischen Gesellschaft*. Historia Einzelschrift 163. Stuttgart.

Anghel, S. 1999–2000. 'Euergetai in the Greek Cities in the Black Sea during the Hellenistic Age,' *Il Mar Nero* 4: 89–115.

Anson, E.M. 2003. 'Alexander and Siwah,' *AncW* 34: 117–30.

Antonetti, C. 1987. '*Agraioi* et *Agrioi*. Montagnards et bergers: un prototype diachronique de sauvagerie,' *Dialogues d'histoire ancienne* 13: 199–236.

– 1990a. 'Il santuario apollineo di Termo in Etolia.' In *Mélanges P. Lévêque* 4, edited by M.-M. Mactoux and E. Geny, 1–28. Paris.

– 1990b. *Les étoliens: image et religion*. Paris.

Archibald, Z.H., J.K. Davies, and V. Gabrielsen, eds. 2006. *Making, Moving, and Managing. The New World of Ancient Economies, 323–31B.C.* Oxford.

Arenz, A. 2006. *Herakleides Kritikos 'Über die Städte in Hellas': Eine Periegese Griechenlands am Vorabend des Chremonideischen Krieges*. Quellen und Forschungen zur Antiken Welt 49. Munich.

Argentieri, L. 1998. 'Epigramma e libro: Morfologia delle raccolte epigrammatiche premeleagree,' *ZPE* 121: 1–20.

– 2003. *Gli epigrammi degli Antipatri*. Bari.

Arnott, W.G., trans. 2000. *Menander*. Volume III. The Loeb Classical Library 460. Cambridge.

Aron, R. 1973. *War and Peace*. Paris.

Arslan, M. 2004. *The Coinage of Ancyra*. Ankara.

Asboeck, A. 1913. *Das Staatswesen von Priene in hellenistischer Zeit*. Munich.

Ashmole, B. 1972. *Architect and Sculptor in Classical Greece*. London.

Ashton, S.-A. 2001. *Ptolemaic Royal Sculpture from Egypt*. Oxford.

– 2004. 'Ptolemaic Alexandria and the Egyptian Tradition.' In Hirst and Silk 2004: 15–40.

Atkinson, J.E. 1980. *A Commentary on Q. Curtius Rufus* Historiae Alexandri Magni, *Books 3 and 4*. Amsterdam.

Aubreton, R., J. Irigoin, and F. Buffière, eds. 1994. *Anthologie grecque, première partie: Anthologie Palatine*. Tome 11, livre 12. Paris.

Austin, M.M. 1986. 'Hellenistic Kings, War, and the Economy,' *CQ* 36: 450–66.

– 2006. *The Hellenistic World from Alexander to the Roman Conquest. A Selection of Ancient Sources in Translation*. Second edition. Cambridge.

Avram, A. 1999. *Inscriptions grecques et latines de Scythie Mineure* III: *Callatis et son territoire*. Paris.

Badian, E. 1976. 'Rome, Athens and Mithridates,' *AJAH* 1: 105–28.

– 1981. 'The Deification of Alexander the Great.' In *Ancient Macedonian Studies in Honor of Charles F. Edson*, edited by H. Dell, 27–71. Thessaloniki.

– 1986. 'Two Notes on Senatus Consulta concerning Pergamum,' *LCM* 11: 14–16.

– 1990. 'The Consuls, 179–49 B.C.,' *Chiron* 20: 371–413.

Bagnall, R.S. 1979. 'The Date of the Foundation of Alexandria,' *AJAH* 4: 46–9 (reprinted in Bagnall 2006: 46–9).

– 2001. 'Archaeological Work on Hellenistic and Roman Egypt 1995–2000,' *AJA* 105: 227–43 (reprinted in Bagnall 2006: 1–31).

– 2006. *Hellenistic and Roman Egypt: Sources and Approaches*. Aldershot.

Bagnall, R.S., and P. Derow, eds. 2004. *The Hellenistic Period*. Malden and Oxford.

Bain, D.M. 1983. *Menander: Samia*. Warminster.

Baines, J. 2004. 'Egyptian Elite Self-Presentation in the Context of Ptolemaic Rule.' In Harris and Ruffini 2004: 33–62.

Baker, P. 1991. *Cos et Calymna, 205–200 a.C.: esprit civique et défense nationale*. Québec.

– 2000. 'La cause du conflit entre Mélitéa et Narthakion : une note à propos de *IG* IX 2, 89.' In *Philokupros. Mélanges de philologie et d'antiquités grecques et proche-orientales en mémoire d'Olivier Masson*, edited by L. Dubois and É. Masson, 33–47. Minos Supplément 16. Salamanca.

– 2001. 'La Vallée du Méandre au II$^e$ siècle: relations entre les cités et institutions militaires.' In *Les cités d'Asie Mineure occidentale au II$^e$ siècle*, edited by A. Bresson and R. Descat, 61–75. Paris.

– 2003. 'La guerre à l'époque hellénistique.' In *L'Orient méditerranéen de la mort d'Alexandre aux campagnes de Pompée. Cités et royaumes à l'époque hellénistique. Actes du colloque international de la Sophau, 4–6 avril 2003*, edited by F. Prost, 381–401. Rennes.

Bakhuizen, S.C. 1987. 'De Vikingen van Hellas – Strooptochten van de Aetoliërs, een Grieks bergvolk,' *Utrechste Historische Cahiers* 3: 21–39.

– 1993–4. 'Veloukhovo,' *AR*: 33–5.

Baldry, H.C. 1965. *The Unity of Mankind in Greek Thought*. Cambridge.

Balsdon, J.P.V.D. 1950. 'The Divinity of Alexander,' *Historia* 1: 368–88.

Baltrusch, E. 2002. *Die Juden und das Römische Reich: Geschichte einer konfliktreichen Beziehung*. Darmstadt.

Barabási, L. 2002. *Linked. The New Science of Networks*. Cambridge, MA.

Barag, D. 1992–3. 'New Evidence on the Foreign Policy of John Hyrcanus I,' *INJ* 12: 1–12.

Barbantani, S. 2001. *Phatis Nikephoros. Frammenti di elegia encomiastica nell'età delle Guerre Galatiche: Supplementum Hellenisticum 958 e 969*. Milan.

– 2005. 'Goddess of Love and Mistress of the Sea: Notes on a Hellenistic Hymn to Arsinoe-Aphrodite (P. Lit. Goodsp. 2, I–IV),' *Ancient Society* 35: 135–65.

Barber, G.L. 1935. *The Historian Ephorus*. Cambridge.

Barclay, J. 1996. *Jews in the Mediterranean Diaspora*. Edinburgh.

Barth, M., and J. Stauber. 1993. *Inschriften Mysia und Troas*. Munich.

Baslez, M.-F. 2002. 'Mobilité et ouverture de la communauté "romaine" à Délos: amitiés, marriages mixtes, adoptions.' In *Les Italiens dans le monde grec, IIe siècle av. J.-C. – Ier siècle ap. J.-C.: circulation, activités, intégration,* edited by C. Müller and C. Hasenohr, 55–65. BCH Supplement 41. Paris.

Baslez, M.-F., and C. Vial. 1987. 'La diplomatie de Délos dans le premier tiers du IIe siècle,' *BCH* 111: 281–312.

Battistoni, F. 2008. 'Rome, Kinship, and Diplomacy.' In *Diplomats and Diplomacy in the Roman World,* edited by C. Eilers, 73–97. Leiden.

– 1997. *Polis und Koinon: Untersuchungen zur Geschichte und Struktur der griechischen Bundesstaaten im 4. Jahrhundert v. Chr.* Stuttgart.

Beck, H., P. Bol, and M. Bückling, eds. 2005. *Ägypten Griechenland Rom: Abwehr und Berührung.* Frankfurt.

Bekker-Nielsen, T. 2002. 'Fish in the Ancient Economy.' In *Ancient History Matters: Studies Presented to Jens Erik Skydsgaard on His Seventieth Birthday,* edited by K. Ascani et al., 29–37. Analecta Romana Instituti Danici Supplement 30. Rome.

Belke, K. 1984. *Tabula Imperii Byzantini 4: Galatien und Lykaonien.* Vienna.

Bellinger, A.R. 1949. 'The End of the Seleucids,' *Transactions of the Connecticut Academy of Arts and Sciences* 38: 51–102.

Beloch, K.J. 1912–27. *Griechische Geschichte.* Second edition. Strassburg, Berlin, and Leipzig.

Bengtson, H. 1977. *Griechische Geschichte von den Anfängen bis in die römische Kaiserzeit.* Fifth edition. Munich.

Bennett, J. 2003. 'Ancyra, *Metropolis Provinciae Galatiae.*' In *The Archaeology of Roman Towns,* edited by P.R. Wilson and J.S. Wacher, 1–12. Oxford.

Bentz, M. 1998. *Panathenaïsche Preisamphoren: Eine athenische Vasengattung und ihre Funktion vom 6.–4. Jahrhundert v. Chr.* AntK Beiheft 18. Basel.

Bergmann, M. 2007. 'The Philosophers and Poets in the Serapieion at Memphis.' In *Early Hellenistic Portraiture: Image, Style, Context,* edited by P. Schultz and R. von den Hoff, 246–63. Cambridge.

Bergson, L. 1965. *Der griechische Alexanderroman Rezension β.* Stockholm.

Bernard, H.R. 1967. 'Kalymnian Sponge Diving,' *Human Biology* 39, no. 2: 103–30.

– 1972. 'Kalymnos, Island of the Sponge Fishermen.' In *Technology and Social Change,* edited by H.R. Bernard and P. Pelto, 277–316. New York.

Bernhardt, R. 1985. *Polis und römische Herrschaft in der späten Republik (149–31 v. Chr.).* Berlin.

Berthold, R.M. 1984. *Rhodes in the Hellenistic Age.* Ithaca.

Berve, H. 1926. *Das Alexanderreich auf prosopographischer Grundlage.* Munich.

Bevan, E.R. 1930. 'Syria and the Jews.' In *The Cambridge Ancient History 8: Rome and the Mediterranean 218–133 B.C.,* edited by S.A. Cook, F.E. Adcock, and M.P. Charlesworth, 495–533. Cambridge.

Bezerra de Meneses, U.T. 1984. 'Essai de lecture sociologique de la décoration murale des maisons d'habitation hellénistiques à Délos,' *DialArch* (series 3) 2: 77–88.

Bianchi, R.S. 1996. 'Pharaonic Egyptian Elements in the Decorative Arts of Alexandria during the Hellenistic and Roman Periods.' In Hamma 1996, 191–202.

Bieber, M. 1961. *The Sculpture of the Hellenistic Age*. Second edition. New York.

Bielman, A. 1994. *Retour à la liberté. Libération et sauvetage des prisonniers en Grèce ancienne. Recueil d'inscriptions honorant des sauveteurs et analyse critique*. Athens.

Biers, W. 1996. *The Archaeology of Greece: An Introduction*. Second edition. Ithaca.

Bilde, P., et al., eds. 1992. *Ethnicity in Hellenistic Egypt*. Studies in Hellenistic Civilization 3. Aarhus.

Billows, R.A. 1995. *Kings and Colonists: Aspects of Macedonian Imperialism*. Leiden, New York, and Cologne.

Bing, P. 1988. *The Well-Read Muse: Present and Past in Callimachus and the Hellenistic Poets*. Göttingen (reprinted Ann Arbor 2008).

– 1993. 'The *Bios* and Poets' Lives as a Theme of Hellenistic Poetry.' In *Nomodeiktes, Festschrift M. Ostwald*, edited by R. Rosen and J. Farrell, 619–31. Ann Arbor.

– 2003. 'The Unruly Tongue: Philitas of Cos as Scholar and Poet,' *CP* 98: 330–48.

– 2005. 'The Politics and Poetics of Geography in the Milan Posidippus Section One: On Stones (AB 1–20).' In *The New Posidippus: A Hellenistic Poetry Book*, edited by K. Gutzwiller, 119–40. Oxford.

Bingen, J. 2007. *Hellenistic Egypt. Monarchy, Society, Economy, Culture*. Edinburgh.

Bintliff, J.L. 1977. *Natural Environment and Human Settlement in Prehistoric Greece*. BAR Supplement 28. Oxford.

Birkhan, H. 1997. *Kelten. Versuch einer Gesamtdarstellung ihrer Kultur*. Second edition. Vienna.

Birnbaum, E. 2004. 'Portrayals of the Wise and Virtuous in Alexandrian Jewish Works: Jews' Perceptions of Themselves and Others.' In Harris and Ruffini 2004: 125–60.

Bittel, K. 1976. 'Die Galater in Kleinasien, archäologisch gesehen.' In *Assimilation et résistance à la culture gréco-romaine dans le monde ancient*, edited by D.M. Pippidi, 241–9. Travaux du VIᵉ Congrès International d'Études Classiques (Madrid, Septembre 1974). Paris.

Blundell, J. 1980. *Menander and the Monologue*. Göttingen.

Boegehold, A.L. 1995. *The Lawcourts at Athens: Sites, Buildings, Equipment, Procedure, and Testimonia*. Athenian Agora 28. Princeton.

Bogaert, R. 1968. *Banques et banquiers dans les cités grecques*. Leiden.

Bollansée, J. 1999. *Hermippos of Smyrna and his Biographical Writings: A Reappraisal.* Studia Hellenistica 35. Leuven.

Bommeljé, L.S. 1988. 'Aeolis in Aetolia: Thuc. 3.102.5 and the Origins of the Aetolian *Ethnos*,' *Historia* 37: 297–316.

Bommeljé, L.S., et al. 1987. *Aetolia and the Aetolians.* Utrecht.

– Forthcoming. *An Inland Polity: The Spatial Organization of Eastern Aetolia in Antiquity.* Amsterdam.

Bommeljé, L.S., and J. Vroom. 1995. 'Deserted and Untilled Land: Aetolia in Roman Times,' *Pharos* 3: 67–130.

Bonacasa, N. 2004. 'Realismo ed eclettismo nell'arte alessandrina.' In Harris and Ruffini 2004: 87–98.

Borg, B., ed. 2004. *Paideia: The World of the Second Sophistic.* Millenium-Studien 2. Berlin.

Bornmann, F. 1973. 'Meleagro e la corona delle Muse,' *SIFC* 45: 223–32.

– 1975. 'Ancora sulla corona di Meleagro,' *Maia* 27: 45–6.

Bosch, E. 1967. *Quellen zur Geschichte der Stadt Ankara im Altertum.* Ankara.

Bosworth, A.B. 1976. 'Early Relations between Aetolia and Macedon,' *AJAH* 1: 164–81.

– 1977. 'Alexander and Ammon.' In *Greece and the Eastern Mediterranean in Ancient History and Prehistory. Studies presented to F. Schachermeyr on the Occasion of His Eightieth Birthday*, edited by K.H. Kinzl, 51–75. Berlin and New York.

– 1980. *A Historical Commentary on Arrian's History of Alexander* 1. Oxford.

– 1996. 'Alexander, Euripides and Dionysos: the Motivation for Apotheosis.' In *Transitions to Empire: Essays in Greco-Roman History 360–146 BC, in Honor of E. Badian*, edited by R.W. Wallace and E.M. Harris, 140–66. Norman, OK.

Bouché-Leclercq, A. 1903–7. *Histoire des Lagides.* Paris.

Boulay, T. 2011. 'La mémoire des faits d'armes dans les cites d'Asie Mineure à l'époque hellénistique: un *polyandrion* à Milet et Lichas fils d'Hermophantos.' In *Pratiques et identités culturelles des armées hellénistiques du monde méditerranéen*, edited by J.-C. Couvenhes, S. Crouzet, and S. Péré-Noguès, 213–25. Bordeaux.

Bousquet, J. 1985. 'L'hoplothèque de Delphes,' *BCH* 109: 718–26.

– 1988. 'La stèle des kyténiens au Letôon de Xanthos,' *REG* 101: 12–53.

Braund, D. 1984. *Rome and the Friendly King. The Character of the Client Kingship.* London.

– 2002. 'Steppe and Sea: The Hellenistic North in the Black Sea Region before the First Century B.C.' In Odgen 2002, 199–219.

Braund, D., and S.D. Kryzhitskiy. 2008. *Classical Olbia and the Scythian World from the Sixth Century B.C. to the Second Century A.D.* ProcBritAc 142. Oxford.

Brennan, T.C. 2000. *The Praetorship in the Roman Republic.* Oxford.

Bresson, A. 2000. 'Aristote et le commerce extérieur.' In *La cité marchande*, edited by A. Bresson, 109–30. Scripta Antiqua 2. Bordeaux (reprint of *REA* 89 [1987]: 217–38).

– 2005. 'Ecology and Beyond.' In *Rethinking the Mediterranean*, edited by W.V. Harris, 94–114. Oxford.

– 2006. 'Marché et prix à Délos: charbon, bois, porcs, huile et grains.' In *L'économie hellénistique*, edited by R. Descat, 311–39. Entretiens d'archéologie et d'histoire 7. Saint-Bertrand-de-Comminges.

– 2007. *L'économie de la Grèce des cités (fin VI^e-I^er siècle a.C.) 1: Les structures et la production.* Paris.

– 2008. *L'économie de la Grèce des cités (fin VI^e-I^er siècle a.C.) 2: Les espaces de l'échange.* Paris.

Bringmann, K. 2002. 'Tetrarches, Tetrarchia (I./III.),' *Der Neue Pauly* 12, no. 1: 196–9.

Bringmann, K., and H. von Steuben, eds. 1995. *Schenkungen hellenistischer Herrscher an griechische Städte und Heiligtümer* 1. Berlin.

Brink, C.O. 1972. 'Ennius and the Hellenistic Worship of Homer,' *AJP* 93: 547–67.

Brown, B. 1957. *Ptolemaic Paintings and Mosaics and the Alexandrian Style.* Cambridge, MA.

Brown, P.G.McC. 1990. 'Plots and Prostitutes in Greek New Comedy,' *Papers of the Leeds International Latin Seminar* 6: 241–66.

Brûlé, P. 1978. *La piraterie crétoise hellénistique.* Paris.

– 1990. 'Enquête démographique sur la famille grecque antique. Étude de listes de politographie d'Asie Mineure d'époque hellénistique,' *REA* 92: 233–58.

Brun, P. 1996. *Les archipels égéens dans l'antiquité grecque (V^e-II^e siècles av. notre ère).* Paris.

Bruneau, P. 1969. 'Documents sur l'industrie délienne de la pourpre,' *BCH* 93: 759–91.

– 1970. *Recherches sur les cultes de Délos a l'époque hellénistique et à l'époque impériale.* BÉFAR 217. Paris.

– 1972. *Les mosaïques.* Exploration archéologique de Délos 29. Paris.

– 1994–5. 'La maison délienne,' *Revue d'archéologie moderne et d'archéologie générale* 12: 77–118 (reprinted in *Études d'archéologie délienne.* BCH Supplement 47: 873–914. Paris, 2006).

Bruneau, P., C. Vatin, et al. 1970. *L'îlot de la Maison des Comédiens.* Exploration archéologique de Délos 27. Paris.

Brunet, M., et al. 2001. 'L'eau à Délos, un milieu naturel et son aménagement durant l'Antiquité,' *BCH* 125: 620–7.

Brunn, H. 1889. *Geschichte der griechischen Künstler* 1. Second edition. Stuttgart.

Bruno, V.J. 1969. 'Antecedents of the Pompeian First Style,' *AJA* 73: 305–17.

Brunt, P.A. 1976–83. *Arrian. History of Alexander and Indica.* Cambridge, MA.

Buchanan, M. 2002. *Nexus. Small Worlds and the Groundbreaking Theory of Networks.* New York.

Buck, C.D., and W. Petersen. 1945. *A Reverse Index of Greek Nouns and Adjectives.* Chicago.

Bugh, G.R. 1990. 'The Theseia in Late Hellenistic Athens,' *ZPE* 83: 20–37.

– 1992. 'Athenion and Aristion of Athens,' *Phoenix* 46: 108–23.

– 2006. 'Hellenistic Military Developments.' In *The Cambridge Companion to the Hellenistic World,* edited by G.R. Bugh, 265–94. Cambridge.

Bulard, M. 1908. *Peintures murales et mosaïques de Délos.* MonPiot 14. Paris.

– 1926a. *Description des revêtements peints à sujets religieux.* Exploration archéologique de Délos 9. Paris.

– 1926b. *Le religion domestique dans la colonie italienne de Délos d'après les peintures murales et les autels historiés.* BÉFAR 131. Paris.

Buraselis, K. 2010. 'God and King as Synoikists: Divine Disposition and Monarchic Wishes Combined in the Traditions of City Foundations for Alexander's and Hellenistic Times.' In *Intentional History: Spinning Time in Ancient Greece,* edited by L. Foxhall, H.-J. Gehrke, and N. Luraghi, 265–74. Stuttgart.

Burton, P.J. 2003. '*Clientela* or *Amicitia*? Modeling Roman International Behavior in the Middle Republic (264–146 B.C.),' *Klio* 85, no. 2: 333–69.

Cahill, N. 2002. *Household and City Organization at Olynthus.* New Haven and London.

Calder, W.M., and J. Keil, eds. 1939. *Anatolian Studies Presented to William Hepburn Buckler.* Manchester.

Cameron, A. 1993. *The Greek Anthology from Meleager to Planudes.* Oxford.

– 1995. *Callimachus and his Critics.* Princeton.

Camp, J.M. 1986. *The Athenian Agora. Excavations in the Heart of Classical Athens.* London.

– 2001. *The Archaeology of Athens.* New Haven.

Canali De Rossi, F. 1997. *Le ambascerie dal mondo Greco a Roma in età repubblicana.* Studi pubblicati dall'Istituto Italiano per la storia antica 63. Rome.

Canfora, L. 1990. *The Vanished Library.* Translated by M. Ryle. Berkeley.

– ed. 2001. *Ateneo, I Deipnosofisti.* Rome.

Cannon, A. 1998. 'The Social and Historical Contexts of Fashion.' In *Consuming Fashion: Adorning the Transnational Body,* edited by A. Brydon and S. Niessen, 23–38. Oxford.

Carey, C. 1995. 'Rape and Adultery in Athenian Law,' *CQ* 45: 407–17.

Carpenter, R. 1960. *Greek Sculpture: A Critical Review.* Chicago.

Carter, J.C., et al. 2003. *Crimean Chersonesos. City, Chora, Museum and Environs.* Austin.

Castels, M. 1998. *The Information Age. Economy, Society and Culture* 2: *The Power of Identity*. Oxford.

– 2000a. *The Information Age. Economy, Society and Culture* 1: *The Rise of the Network Society*. Second edition. Oxford.

– 2000b. *The Information Age. Economy, Society and Culture* 3: *End of Millennium*. Second edition. Oxford.

– 2004a. 'Informationalism, Networks, and the Network Society. A Theoretical Blueprint.' In Castels 2004b: 3–45.

– ed. 2004b. *The Network Society. A Cross-Cultural Perspective*. Cheltenham-Northampton.

Cerfaux, L., and J. Tondriau. 1957. *Le culte des souverains dans la civilisation gréco-romaine*. Tournai.

Chamonard, J. 1922–4. *Le quartier du Théâtre*. Exploration archéologique de Délos 8. Paris.

Chamoux, F. 2003. *Hellenistic Civilization*. Translated by M. Roussel. London.

Champion, C. 1995. 'The Soteria at Delphi: Aetolian Propaganda in the Epigraphical Record,' *AJPh* 116: 213–20.

– 1996. 'Polybius, Aetolia and the Gallic Attack on Delphi (279 B.C.),' *Historia* 45: 315–28.

Chaniotis, A. 1996. *Die Verträge zwischen kretischen Poleis in der hellenistischen Zeit*. Stuttgart.

– 2002. 'Foreign Soldiers – Native Girls? Constructing and Crossing Boundaries in Hellenistic Cities with Foreign Garrisons.' In *Army and Power in the Ancient World*, edited by A. Chaniotis and P. Ducrey, 99–113. Stuttgart.

– 2004a. 'From Communal Spirit to Individuality: the Epigraphic Habit in Hellenistic and Roman Crete.' In *Creta romana e protobizantina 1*, edited by M. Livadiotti and I. Simiakaki, 75–87. Padua.

– 2004b. 'Mobility of Persons during the Hellenistic Wars. State Control and Personal Relations.' In *La mobilité des personnes en Méditerranée de l'Antiquité à l'époque moderne: procédures de contrôle et documents d'identification*, edited by C. Moatti, 481–500. Rome.

– 2005a. *War in the Hellenistic World*. Oxford.

– 2005b. 'The Divinity of Hellenistic Rulers.' In Erskine 2005: 431–46.

– 2005c. 'Inscribed Instrumenta Domestica and the Economy of Hellenistic and Roman Crete.' In Archibald, Davies, and Gabrielsen 2005: 92–116.

Chankowski, V. 2001. 'Athènes, Délos et les Cyclades à l'époque classique: un réseau économique?' *REA* 103: 83–102.

– 2002. 'De l'argent jeté dans les fontaines? La "Minoé" de Délos et les jarres du trésor sacré à la fin de l'Indépendance.' In Ευεργεσίας χάριν. *Studies presented to Benedetto Bravo and Ewa Wipszycka by Their Disciples*, edited by T. Derda et al., 37–49. Warsaw.

– 2005. 'Techniques financières, influences, performances dans les activités bancaires des sanctuaires grecs,' *Topoi. Orient-Occident* 12–13, no. 1: 69–93.

– 2008. *Athènes et Délos à l'époque classique. Recherches sur l'administration du sanctuaire d'Apollon délien.* Athens.

Chankowski-Sable, V., and C. Feyel. 1997. 'Comptes de la fin de l'indépendance délienne,' *BCH* 121: 103–24.

Chantraine, P. 1933. *La formation des noms en grec ancien.* Paris.

Chugg, A.M. 2006. *Alexander's Lovers.* No place of publication declared.

Claerhout, I., and J. Devreker. 2008. *Pessinous: An Archaeological Guide.* Istanbul.

Clarysse, W. 2000. 'Ptolemies visiting the Egyptian Chora.' In *Politics, Administration and Society in the Hellenistic and Roman World,* edited by L. Mooren, 29–53. Leuven.

Clauss, J.J. 1986. 'Lies and Allusions: The Address and Date of Callimachus' Hymn to Zeus,' *ClAnt* 2: 155–70.

Coffey, M. 1989. *Roman Satire.* Second edition. Bristol.

Cohen, B. 2001. 'Ethnic Identity in Democratic Athens and the Visual Vocabulary of Male Costume.' In Malkin 2001a: 235–74.

Cohen, D. 1991. 'Sexuality, Violence, and the Athenian Law of "Hubris",' *GaR* 38: 171–88.

– 1993. 'Consent and Sexual Relations in Classical Athens.' In *Consent and Coercion to Sex and Marriage in Ancient and Medieval Societies,* edited by A. Laiou, 5–16. Washington, DC.

Cohen, G.M. 1978. *The Seleucid Colonies. Studies in Founding, Administration and Organization.* Wiesbaden.

– 2006. *The Hellenistic Settlements in Syria, the Red Sea Basin, and North Africa.* Berkeley.

Cohen, S.J.D. 1999. *The Beginnings of Jewishness: Boundaries, Varieties, Uncertainties.* Berkeley.

Cole, S.G. 1984. 'Greek Sanctions against Sexual Assault,' *CP* 79: 97–113.

Collin-Bouffier, S. 2008. 'Les poisson dans le monde grec, mets d'élites?' In *Pratiques et discours alimentaires en Méditerranée de l'Antiquité a la Renaissance,* edited by J. Leclant, A. Vauchez, and M. Sartre, 91–121. Cahiers de la Villa Kérylos 19. Paris.

Collins, N.L. 1997. 'The Various Fathers of Ptolemy I,' *Mnemosyne* 50: 436–76.

Connor, W.R. 1971. *The New Politicians of Fifth-Century Athens.* Princeton.

Cook, A.B. 1914–40. *Zeus. A Study in Ancient Religion.* Cambridge.

Coşkun, A. 2004. 'Die tetrarchische Verfassung der Galater und die Neuordnung des Ostens durch Pompeius.' In *Ad fontes! Festschrift für Gerhard Dobesch,* edited by H. Heftner and K. Tomaschitz, 687–711. Vienna.

– ed. 2005. *Roms auswärtige Freunde in der späten Republik und im frühen Prinzipat.* Göttingen.

– ed. 2008a. *Freundschaft und Gefolgschaft in den auswärtigen Beziehungen der Römer (2. Jh. v.Chr. – 1. Jh. n.Chr.)*. Frankfurt.
– 2008b. 'Interkulturelle Ortsnamen in Zentralkleinasien und Galatische Geschichte,' in NIO-GaRo 2008.1. URL: http://www.uni-trier.de/fileadmin/ fb3/AGY/NIO-GaRo_2008.1.pdf. Revised version in *Names in Multi-Lingual, Multi-Cultural and Multi-Ethnic Contact. International Congress of Onomastic Sciences 23*, edited by W. Ahrens, S. Embleton, and A. Lapierre, 243–53. 2009. Toronto.
– 2008c. 'Galatische Legionäre in Ägypten: die Konstituierung der *legio XXII Deiotariana* in der frühen Kaiserzeit,' *Tyche* 23: 21–46.
– 2009a. 'Das Edikt des Sex. Sotidius Strabo Libuscidianus und die Fasten der Statthalter Galatiens in augusteischer und tiberischer Zeit,' *Gephyra* 6: 159–64.
– 2009b. 'Grosszügige Praxis der Bürgerrechtsvergabe in Rom? Zwischen Mythos und Wirklichkeit.' In the series *Colloquia Academica*, edited by the *Mainzer Akademie der Wissenschaft und Literatur – Akademievorträge junger Wissenschaftler*, Stuttgart.
– 2009c. 'Der Ankyraner Kaiserkult und die Transformation galatischer und phrygisch-galatischer Identitäten in Zentralanatolien im Spiegel der Münzquellen.' In *Repräsentation von Identität und Zugehörigkeit im Osten der griechisch-römischen Welt*, edited by A. Coşkun, H. Heinen, and S. Pfeiffer, 173–211. Frankfurt.
– 2010. *Amici Populi Romani (APR). Prosopography of the Foreign Friends of Rome*. Published by the Waterloo Institute for Hellenistic Studies (WIHS). Waterloo, ON, April 2010. URL: http://apr.uwaterloo.ca (accessed 16 April 2011).
– 2011. 'Galatians and Seleukids: a Century of Conflict and Cooperation.' In *Seleukid Dissolution: Fragmentation and Transformation of Empire*, edited by K. Erickson and G. Ramsey. Wiesbaden: 86–105.
– 2012a. 'Deconstructing a Myth of Seleucid History: The So-Called "Elephant Victory" Re-Visited,' *Phoenix* 66.1–2: 57–73.
– 2012b. 'Intercultural Anthroponomy in Hellenistic and Roman Galatia,' *Gephyra* 9: 51–68.
– 2013a. 'Die Tetrarchie als hellenistisch-römisches Herrschaftsinstrument.' In *Client Kings between Centre and Periphery*, edited by Ernst Baltrusch and Julia Wilker. Exzellenzcluster TOPOI & Friedrich-Meinecke Institut, FU Berlin, 18.–19.2.2011.
– 2013b. 'Neue Forschungen zum Kaiserkult in Galatien. Edition der Priester-Inschriften des Ankyraner Sebasteions (*OGIS* 533 = Bosch 51) und Revision der frühen Provinzialgeschichte.' In *Der Beitrag Kleinasiens zur Kultur- und Geistesgeschichte der griechisch-römischen Antike*, edited by Gerhard Dobesch and Joseph Fischer. Kleinasiatische Kommission der Österreichischen Akademie der Wissenschaften, Wien, 3–5 Nov. 2010.

Couilloud, M.-T. 1974. *Les monuments funéraires de Rhénée*. Exploration archéologique de Délos 30. Paris.

Courbaud, E. 1899. *Le Bas-relief romain à représentations historiques*. BÉFAR 81. Paris.

Couvenhes, J.-C. 2004. 'Les cités grecques d'Asie Mineure et le mercenariat à l'époque hellénistique.' In Couvenhes and Fernoux 2004: 77–113.

Couvenhes, J.-C., and H.-L. Fernoux, eds. 2004. *Les cités d'Asie Mineure en guerre à l'époque hellénistique*. Tours.

Cowey, J.M.S., and K. Maresch. 2001. *Urkunden des Politeuma der Juden von Herakleopolis (144/3–133/2 v.Chr.)*. Wiesbaden.

Crawford, M.H. 1974. *Roman Republican Coinage*. Cambridge.

Cribiore, R. 1995. 'A Hymn to the Nile,' *ZPE* 106: 97–106.

Darbyshire, G., S. Mitchell, and L. Vardar. 2000. 'The Galatian Settlement in Asia Minor,' *AnatSt* 50: 75–97.

Davidson, J. 1997. *Courtesans and Fishcakes: The Consuming Passions of Classical Athens*. New York.

Davies, J.K. 1978. 'Athenian Citizenship: The Descent Group and the Alternatives,' *CJ* 73: 105–21.

Davies, J.K. 2001. 'Hellenistic Economies in the Post-Finley Era.' In *Hellenistic Economies*, edited by Z.H. Archibald, J. Davies, V. Gabrielsen, and G.J. Oliver, 11–62. London.

Day, J. 1942. *An Economic History of Athens under Roman Domination*. New York.

De Lacépède, B.G. 1798. *Histoire naturelle des poissons* 1. Paris.

De Polignac, F. 2000. 'The Shadow of Alexander.' In *Alexandria, Third Century B.C.: the Knowledge of the World in a Single City*, edited by C. Jacob and F. de Polignac, 32–42. Alexandria.

De Romilly, J. 1977. *The Rise and Fall of States According to Greek Authors*. Ann Arbor.

De Ste Croix, G.E.M. 1981. *The Class Struggle in the Ancient Greek World*. London.

De Sanctis, G. 1934. 'Il regolamento militare dei Macedoni,' *RivFil*. 62: 515–21.

De Souza, P. 1998. 'Late Hellenistic Crete and the Roman Conquest.' In *Post-Minoan Crete*, edited by W.G. Cavanagh, M. Curtis et al., 112–16. BSA Studies 2. London.

Dedoussi, C. 1970. 'The *Samia*. Discussion.' In *Ménandre*, edited by E.G. Turner, 159–80. Geneva.

Delamarre, X. 2003. *Dictionnaire de la langue gauloise*. Second Edition. Paris.

Delia, D. 1988. 'The Population of Roman Alexandria,' *TAPA* 118: 275–92.

Dench, E. 2005. *Romulus' Asylum. Roman Identities from the Age of Alexander to the Age of Hadrian.* Oxford.

Deonna, W. 1938. *Les mobilier Délien.* Exploration archéologique de Délos 18. Paris.

Depew, M. 1992. '"*Iambeion kaleitai nun.*" Genre, Occasion, and Imitation in Callimachus, frr. 191 and 203 Pf.,' *TAPA* 122: 313–30.

– Forthcoming. *Callimachus' Book of Hymns: A Political Study.*

Derow, P. 2005. 'The Arrival of Rome: from the Illyrian Wars to the Fall of Macedon.' In Erskine 2005: 51–70.

Detienne, M. 1981. 'The Myth of 'Honeyed Orpheus.' In *Myth, Religion, and Society,* edited by M. Detienne and R.L. Gordon, 95–110. Cambridge.

Devreker, J. 1984. 'Les monnaies de Pessinonte.' In *Les Fouilles de la Rijksuniversiteit te Gent a Pessinonte, 1967–1973 1,* edited by J. Devreker and M. Waelkens, 173–215, with 2, 142–57 and plates 254–69. Brussels.

Di Marco, M. 1989. *Timone di Fliunte: Silli.* Rome.

– 1998. 'Hermeias 2,' *Der Neue Pauly* 5: 422.

Dietz, S., et al. 1998. 'Surveys and Excavations in Chalkis, Aetolias, 1995–1996. First Preliminary Report,' *PDIA* 2: 233–315.

Dinsmoor, W.B. 1931. *The Archons of Athens in the Hellenistic Age.* Cambridge.

Dmitriev, S. 2005. *City Government in Hellenistic and Roman Asia Minor.* Oxford.

Dorandi, T. 1982. 'Filodemo. Gli Stoici (PHerc. 155 e 399),' *CronErcol* 12: 91–133.

Dougherty, C. 1993. *The Poetics of Colonization: From City to Text in Archaic Greece.* New York and Oxford.

– 2009. 'Interpreting Myth.' In *A Companion to Ancient History,* edited by A. Erskine, 154–63. Oxford.

Douglas, M., and B. Isherwood. 1996. *The World of Goods: Towards an Anthropology of Consumption.* Second edition. London and New York.

Doukellis, P.N. 2009. 'Hadrian's *Panhellenion*: A Network of Cities?' In Malkin, Constantakopoulou, and Panagopoulou 2009: 285–98.

Doyle, M. 1990. 'Thucydidean Realism,'*Review of International Studies* 16, no. 3: 223–37.

– 1991. 'Thucydides: A Realist?' In Lebow and Strauss 1991: 169–88.

Dreher, M. 1995. *Hegemon und Symmachoi. Untersuchungen zum Zweiten Athenischen Bund.* Berlin and New York.

Dreyer, B. 2001. 'Wann endet die klassische Demokratie Athens?' *Ancient Society* 31: 27–66.

– 2002. 'Der "Raubvertrag" des Jahres 203/2 v. Chr.: Das Inschriftenfragment von Bargylia und der Brief von Amyzon,' *EpigAnat* 34: 119–38.

Ducrey, P. 1970, 'Nouvelles remarques sur des traités attalides avec deux cités crétoises,' *BCH* 94: 637–59.

Dumont, J. 1977a. 'Liberté des mers et territoire de pêche en droit grec,' *Revue historique de droit français et étranger* 55: 53–7.

– 1977b. 'La pêche dans le Fayoum hellénistique; traditions et nouveautés d'après le Papyrus Tebtynis 701,' *ChrÉg* 52: 125–42.

Dunand, F. 1969. 'Les representations de l'Agathodémon; à propos de quelques bas-reliefs du Musée d'Alexandrie,' *BIFAO* 67: 9–48.

– 1981. 'Agathodaimon,' *LIMC* 1, no. 1: 277–82.

– 2000. *Isis, mère des dieux*. Paris.

– 2007. 'The Religious System at Alexandria.' In *A Companion to Greek Religion*, edited by D. Ogden, 253–63. Oxford.

Dunbabin, K.M.D. 2003. *The Roman Banquet: Images of Conviviality*. Cambridge.

Eckstein, A.M. 1985. 'Polybius, Syracuse, and the Politics of Accommodation,' *GRBS* 26: 265–82.

– 1995a. *Moral Vision in the Histories of Polybius*. Berkeley and Los Angeles.

– 1995b. 'Glabrio and the Aetolians: a Note on *Deditio*,' *TAPA* 125: 271–89.

– 2003. 'Thucydides, the Outbreak of the Peloponnesian War, and the Foundation of International Systems Theory,' *International History Review* 25: 757–74.

– 2005. 'The Pact between the Kings, Polybius 15.20.6, and Polybius' View of the Outbreak of the Second Macedonian War,' *CP* 100: 228–42.

– 2006. *Mediterranean Anarchy, Interstate War, and the Rise of Rome*. Berkeley and Los Angeles.

– 2008. *Rome Enters the Greek East: From Anarchy to Hierarchy in the Hellenistic Mediteranean*. Oxford.

Edson, C.F. 1934. 'The Antigonids, Heracles and Beroea,' *HSCP* 45: 213–46.

Efstratiou, N. 1985. *Ayios Petros: A Neolithic Site in the Northern Sporades* [BAR Int. Series 241]. Oxford.

Eggermont, P.H.L. 1975. *Alexander's Campaigns in the Sind and Baluchistan and the Siege of the Brahmin Town of Harmatelia*. Leuven.

Eilers, C. 2008. 'Forgery, Dishonesty, and Incompetence in Josephus' Acta: The Decree of Athens (AJ 14. 149–55),' *ZPE* 166: 211–17.

El-Abbadi, M. 2004. 'The Island of Pharos in Myth and History.' In Harris and Ruffini 2004: 259–67.

Empereur, J.-Y. 1998. *Alexandria Rediscovered*. Translated by M. Maehler. New York.

Engelmann, H. 1987. 'Inschriften von Erythrai,' *EpigAnat* 9: 133–52.

Erdkamp, P. 2005. *The Grain Market in the Roman Empire. A Social, Political, and Economic Study*. Cambridge.

Ernout, A., and A. Meillet. 1959. *Dictionnaire étymologique de la langue latine*. Fourth edition. Paris.

Errington, R.M. 1971. 'The Alleged Syro-Macedonian Pact and the Origins of the Second Macedonian War,' *Athenaeum* 49: 336–54.

– 1976. 'Alexander in the Hellenistic World.' In *Alexandre le grand. Image et réalité*, Entretiens Hardt 22, edited by E. Badian, 137–79. Geneva.

– 1986. 'Antiochos III., Zeuxis, und Euromus,' *EpigAnat* 17: 1–8.

– 1989. 'The Peace Treaty between Miletus and Magnesia (I. Milet, 148),' *Chiron* 19: 279–88.

– 1990. *A History of Macedonia*. Berkeley.

Erskine, A. 1995. 'Culture and Power in Ptolemaic Egypt: the Museum and Library of Alexandria,' *GaR* 42: 38–48.

– 2001. *Troy between Greece and Rome: Local Tradition and Imperial Power*. Oxford.

– 2002. 'Life after Death: Alexandria and the Body of Alexander,' *GaR* 49: 163–79.

– ed. 2005. *A Companion to the Hellenistic World*. Originally published 2003. Oxford.

– 2009. 'Ancient History and National Identity.' In *A Companion to Ancient History*, edited by A. Erskine, 555–63. Oxford.

Étienne, R. 1985. 'Le Capital immobilier dans les Cyclades à l'époque hellénistique.' In *L'Origine des richesses dépensées dans la ville antique*, edited by P. Leveau, 55–67. Aix-en-Provence and Marseilles.

Étienne, R. 1990. *Ténos II. Ténos et les Cyclades du milieu du IV$^e$ siècle av. J.-C. au milieu du III$^e$ siècle ap. J.-C.* Athens.

Faber, G.L. 1883. *The Fisheries of the Adriatic and the Fish Thereof: A Report of the Austro-Hungarian Sea-Fisheries, with a Detailed Description of the Marine Fauna of the Adriatic Gulf.* London.

Fantham, E. 1975. 'Sex, Status and Survival in Hellenistic Athens: A Study of Women in New Comedy,' *Phoenix* 29: 44–74.

– 1984. 'Roman Experience of Menander in the Late Republic and Early Empire,' *TAPA* 114: 299–309.

Ferguson, W.S. 1911. *Hellenistic Athens*. London.

Fernoux, H.-L. 2004. *Notables et elites de Bithynie aux époques hellénistique et romaine) III$^e$ siècle av. J.-C. – III$^e$ siècle apr. J.-C.* Lyon.

Ferrary, J.L. 1998. 'L'"oikoumène", l'Orient et l'Occident d'Alexandre le Grand à Auguste: Histoire et historiographie.' In *Convegno per Santo Mazzarino, Roma 9–11 maggio, 1991*, 97–132. Rome.

Feyel, M. 1935. 'Un nouveau fragment du règlement militaire trouvé à Amphipolis,' *RA*: 29–68.

– 1936. 'Nouvelles inscriptions d'Akraiphia,' *BCH* 60: 11–36.

Finkielstejn, G. 1998. 'More Evidence on John Hyrcanus I's Conquests: Lead Weights and Rhodian Amphora Stamps,' *Bulletin of the Anglo-Israel Archaeological Society* 16: 33–60.

Fittschen, K. 1995. 'Eine Stadt für Schaulustige und Müssiggänger: Athen im 3. und 2. Jh. v. Chr.' In Wörrle and Zanker 1995: 55–77.

Fitzgerald, J.T. 2004. 'Gadara: Philodemus' Native City.' In *Philodemus and the New Testament World*, edited by J.T. Fitzgerald, D. Obbink, and G.S. Holland, 343–97. Leiden.

Flacelière, R. 1937. *Les Aitoliens à Delphes. Contribution à l'histoire de la Grèce centrale au III<sup>e</sup> siècle av. J.-C.* Paris.

Fowler, B.H. 1989. *The Hellenistic Aesthetic*. Madison.

Fraser, P.M. 1967. 'Current Problems concerning the Early History of the Cult of Sarapis,' *OpAth* 7: 23–45.

– 1972. *Ptolemaic Alexandria*. 3 volumes. Oxford. Reprint 1984.

– 1996. *Cities of Alexander the Great*. Oxford.

Fredrich, C., et al. 1908. *Milet I, 2. Das Rathaus von Milet*. Berlin.

Fredricksmeyer, E.A. 2003. 'Alexander's Religion and Divinity.' In *Brill's Companion to Alexander the Great*, edited by J. Roisman, 253–78. Leiden.

Freeman, P. 2001. *The Galatian Language. A Comprehensive Survey of the Language of the Ancient Celts in Greco-Roman Asia Minor*. Lewiston and New York.

Freitag, K. 2000. *Der Golf von Korinth. Historisch-topographische Untersuchungen von der Archaik bis in das 1. Jh. v. Chr.* Munich.

French, D. 2003. *Roman, Late Roman and Byzantine Inscriptions of Ankara*. Ankara.

Frenken, K., ed. 2007. *Economics and Economic Geography*. Cheltenham-Northampton.

Freudenburg, K. 2005. 'Introduction.' In *The Cambridge Companion to Roman Satire*, edited by Kirk Freudenburg, 1–30. Cambridge.

Frier, Bruce W., and Dennis P. Kehoe. 2007. 'Law and Economic Institutions.' In Scheidel, Morris, and Saller: 113–43.

Frings, I. 1998. 'Mantua me genuit – Vergils Grabepigramm auf Stein und Pergament,' *ZPE* 123: 89–100.

Fröhlich, P. 2004. *Les cités grecques et le contrôle des magistrats (IV<sup>e</sup>–I<sup>er</sup> siècle avant J.-C.)*. Geneva.

Fröhlich, P., and C. Müller. 2005. *Citoyenneté et participation à la basse époque hellénistique*. Geneva.

Fullerton, M.D. 1998a. 'Atticism, Classicism and the Origins of Neo-Attic Sculpture.' In Palagia and Coulson 1998: 93–9.

– 1998b. 'Description vs. Prescription: A Semantics of Sculptural Style.' In ΣΤΕΦΑΝΟΣ: *Essays in Honor of Brunilde Sismondo Ridgway*, edited by K. Hartswick and M. Sturgeon, 69–77. Philadelphia.

Funke, P. 1985. *Untersuchungen zur Geschichte und Struktur des aitolischen Bundes*. Habilitationschrift. Cologne.

Gabrielsen, V. 2001. 'Economic Activity, Maritime Trade and Piracy in the Hellenistic Aegean,' *RÉA* 103: 219–40.

- 2005. 'Banking and Credit Operations in Hellenistic Times.' In Archibald, Davies, and Gabrielsen 2005: 136–64.
- 2009. 'Brotherhoods of Faith and Provident Planning: The Non-Public Associations of the Greek World.' In Malkin, Constantakopoulou, and Panagopoulou 2009: 176–203.

Gallant, T.W. 1985. *A Fisherman's Tale: Analyzing the Potential Productivity of Fishing in the Ancient World*. Gent.
- 1991. *Risk and Survival in Ancient Greece: Reconstructing the Rural Domestic Economy*. Stanford.

Gallo, I. 1981. *Teatro ellenistico minore*. Rome.

Gardner, E.A. 1915. *A Handbook of Greek Sculpture*. Second edition. London.

Garlan, Y. 1974. *Recherches de poliorcétique grecque*. BÉFAR 223. Athens and Paris.

Garland, R. 1987. *The Piraeus from the Fifth to the First Century B.C.* Ithaca.
- 1990. *The Greek Way of Life*. London.

Gauthier, P. 1985. *Les cités grecques et leurs bienfaiteurs (IVe – Ier siècle avant J.-C.)*. BCH Supplement 12. Paris and Athens.
- 1993. 'Les cités hellénistiques.' In *The Ancient Greek City-State*, edited by M.H. Hansen, 211–31. Copenhagen.
- 2001. 'Les Pidaséens entrent en sympolitie avec les Milésiens: la procédure et les modalités institutionnelles.' In *Les cités d'Asie Mineure occidentale au IIe siècle*, edited by A. Bresson and R. Descat, 117–27. Paris.

Geagan, D.J. 1967. *The Athenian Constitution after Sulla*. Hesperia Supplement 12. Princeton.

Geiger, J. 1986. 'Eros und Anteros, der Blonde und der Dunkelhaarige,' *Hermes* 114: 375–6.

Geller, D.S., and J.D. Singer. 1998. *Nations at War: A Scientific Study of International Conflict*. Cambridge.

Geominy, W. 1998. 'The So-Called Delphi Philosopher and his Context.' In Palagia and Coulson 1998: 61–8.

Gerber, J. 1998. 'Hellenisierung,' *Der Neue Pauly* 5: 301–9.

Gerhard, G.A. 1909. *Phoinix von Kolophon*. Leipzig.

Ghisellini, E. 1999. *Atene e la Corte Tolemaica*. Rome.

Gilpin, R. 1988. 'The Theory of Hegemonic War,' *Journal of Interdisciplinary Studies* 17: 591–613.

Gilula, D. 1987. 'Menander's Comedies Best with Dessert and Wine,' *Athenaeum* 65: 511–16.

Giovannini, A. 1971. *Untersuchungen über die Natur und die Anfänge der bundesstaatlichen Sympolitie in Griechenland*. Göttingen.
- 1993. 'Greek Cities and Greek Commonwealth.' In *Images and Ideologies: Self-Definition in the Hellenistic World*, edited by A. Bulloch et al., 265–86. Berkeley.

– 1997. 'La participation des alliés au financement du Parthénon: *aparchè* ou tribut?' *Historia* 46: 145–57.

Giovannini, A., and H. Müller. 1971. 'Die Beziehungen zwischen Rom und den Juden im 2. Jh. v. Chr.,' *MusHelv* 28: 156–71.

Goddio, F., et al. 1998. *Alexandria: the Submerged Royal Quarters*. London.

Goddio, F., and M. Clauss, eds. 2008. *Egypt's Sunken Treasures*. Second edition. Munich.

Goitein, S.D. 1967. *A Mediterranean Society. The Jewish Communities of the Arab World as Portrayed in the Documents of the Cairo Geniza. Volume I. Economic Foundations*. Berkeley and Los Angeles.

Goldhill, S. 1997. 'Modern Critical Approaches to Greek Tragedy.' In *The Cambridge Companion to Greek Tragedy*, edited by P. Easterling, 324–47. Cambridge.

– ed. 2001. *Being Greek under Rome. Cultural Identity, the Second Sophistic and the Development of Empire*. Cambridge.

Goldstein, J.A. 1976. *I Maccabees: A New Translation with Introduction and Commentary*. The Anchor Bible 41. Garden City.

Gómez Espelosín, F.-J. 1989. 'Estrategía política y supervivencia: Consideraciones sobre una valoración histórica del fenómeno etolio en el siglo III a. de C.,' *Polis* 1: 63–80.

Gómez-Pantoja, J.L., and F. Morales Hernández. 2008. 'Los etolios en Numancia.' In *La guerre et ses traces dans la péninsule Ibérique à l'époque de la conquête romaine: approches méthodologiques*, edited by F. Cadiou, M. Ángeles Magallón Botaya, and M. Navarro Caballero, 37–58. Madrid.

Gomme, A.W., and F.H. Sandbach. 1973. *Menander: A Commentary*. Oxford.

Goudriaan, K. 1988. *Ethnicity in Ptolemaic Egypt*. Amsterdam.

Goukowsky, P. 1978. *Essai sur les origines du mythe d'Alexandre (336–270 av. J.-C.) I. Les origines politiques*. Nancy.

Gourevitch, P. 1978. 'The Second Image Reversed: The International Sources of Domestic Politics,' *International Organization* 32: 881–911.

Gow, A.S.F. 1952. *Theocritus*. Second edition. Oxford.

– 1958. *The Greek Anthology: Sources and Ascriptions*. London.

Gow, A.S.F., and D.L. Page, eds. 1965. *The Greek Anthology: Hellenistic Epigrams*. Cambridge.

Gowers, E. 1993. *The Loaded Table: Representations of Food in Roman Literature*. Oxford.

Grainger, J.D. 1991. *Hellenistic Phoenicia*. Oxford.

– 1999. *The League of the Aitolians*. Leiden.

– 2000. *Aitolian Prosopographical Studies*. Leiden.

Grammenos, D.V., and E.K Petropoulos, eds. 2003. *Ancient Greek Colonies in the Black Sea*. Thessaloniki.

Gratwick, A.S. 1982. 'The Satires of Ennius and Lucilius.' In *The Cambridge History of Classical Literature II: Latin Literature*, edited by E.J. Kenny and W.V. Clausen, 156–71. Cambridge.

Green, J.R. 1994. *Theatre in Ancient Greek Society*. London.

Green, P. 1990. *Alexander to Actium: the Hellenistic Age*. Berkeley.

– ed. 1993. *Hellenistic History and Culture*. Berkeley.

– 1996. 'Alexander's Alexandria.' In Hamma 1996: 3–25. Reprinted in P. Green, *From Ikaria to the Stars: Classical Mythification, Ancient and Modern*, 172–96, 2004. Austin.

Gregory, J. 1997. *Euripides and the Instruction of the Athenians*. Ann Arbor.

Greif, A. 2006. *Institutions and the Path to the Modern Economy. Lessons from Medieval Trade*. Cambridge.

Grieb, V. 2008. *Hellenistische Demokratie. Politische Organisation und Struktur in freien griechischen Poleis nach Alexander dem Grossen*. Stuttgart.

Griffith, G.T. 1935. *The Mercenaries of the Hellenistic World*. Cambridge.

Grimm, G. 1981. 'Orient und Okzident in der Kunst Alexandriens.' In *Alexandrien: Kulturbegenungen drier Jahrtausende im Schmelztiegel einer mediterranen Groszstadt*, edited by G. Grimm, H. Heinen, and E. Winter, 22–5. Mainz.

Gruen, E.S. 1975. 'Rome and Rhodes in the Second Century B.C.: a Historiographical Inquiry,' *CQ* 25: 58–81.

– 1984. *The Hellenistic World and the Coming of Rome*. Berkeley.

– 1990. *Studies in Greek Culture and Roman Policy*. Leiden.

– 1993. 'The Polis in the Hellenistic World.' In *Nomodeiktes: Greek Studies in Honor of Martin Ostwald*, edited by R. Rosen and J. Farrell, 339–54. Ann Arbor.

– 1996. 'The Purported Jewish-Spartan Affiliation.' In *Transitions to Empire: Essays in Greco-Roman History, 360–146 B.C. in Honor of E. Badian*, edited by R.W. Wallace and E.M. Harris, 255–69. Norman.

Gualandi, G. 1976. 'Sculture di Rodi,' *ASAtene* 54: 7–259.

Guichard, L.A. 2000. 'Intertextualidad y antologación en la *Corona* de Meleagro.' In *Intertextualidad en las literaturas griega y latina*, edited by V. Bécares et al., 105–19. Madrid and Salamanca.

Guimier-Sorbets, A.-M. 1994. 'Les postes, décor privilégié de la mosaïque grecque et ses enrichissements à l'époque hellénistique.' In *Tranquillitas: Mélanges en l'honneur de Tran tam Tinh*, edited by M.-O. Jentel and G. Deschênes-Wagner, 255–67. Québec.

Guldager Bilde, P. 1995. 'The International Style: Aspects of Pompeian First Style and its Eastern Equivalents.' In *Aspects of Hellenism in Italy: Towards a Cultural Unity?*, edited by P. Guldager Bilde, I. Nielsen, and M. Nielsen, 151–77. Acta Hyperborea 5. Copenhagen.

Gutzwiller, K. 1997. 'The Poetics of Editing in Meleager's *Garland*,' *TAPA* 127: 169–200.

– 1998a. 'Meleager: From Menippean to Epigrammatist.' In *Genre in Hellenistic Poetry*, edited by M.A. Harder, R.F. Regtuit, and G.C. Wakker, 81–93. Hellenistica Groningana 3. Groningen.

– 1998b. *Poetic Garlands: Hellenistic Epigrams in Context*. Berkeley, Los Angeles, and London.

– 2007. *A Guide to Hellenistic Literature*. Malden and Oxford.

– 2012. 'Catullus and the *Garland* of Meleager.' In *Catullus: Poems, Books, Readers*, edited by T. Woodman and I.M. duQuesnay. Cambridge.

Habicht, C. 1990. 'Athens and the Attalids in the Second Century B.C.,' *Hesperia* 59: 561–77.

– 1993. 'The Comic Poet Archidikos,' *Hesperia* 62: 253–6.

– 1995. *Athen. Die Geschichte der Stadt in hellenistischer Zeit*. Munich.

– 1997. *Athens from Alexander to Antony*. Translated by D.L. Schneider. Cambridge, MA.

– 2006. *Athènes hellénistique. Histoire de la cite d'Alexandre le Grand à Marc Antoine*. Translated by M. and D. Knoepfler. Second edition. Paris.

Halfmann, H. 1986. 'Zur Datierung und Deutung der Priesterliste am Augustus-Roma-Tempel in Ankara,' *Chiron* 16: 35–42.

Hall, J. 1997. *Ethnic Identity in Greek Antiquity*. Cambridge.

– 2001. 'Contested Ethnicities: Perceptions of Macedonia within Evolving Definitions of Greek Identity.' In Malkin 2001a: 159–86.

– 2002. *Hellenicity. Between Ethnicity and Culture*. Chicago.

Hallof, L. and K., and C. Habicht. 1998. 'Aus der Arbeit der *Inscriptiones Graecae* II. Ehrendekrete aus dem Asklepieion von Kos,' *Chiron* 28: 101–42.

Hamilton, J.R. 1969. *Plutarch Alexander: a Commentary*. Oxford.

Hamma, K., ed. 1996. *Alexandria and Alexandrianism*. Malibu.

Hammond, N.G.L. 1993. 'The Macedonian Imprint on the Hellenistic World.' In Green 1993: 12–23.

Hammond, N.G.L., and F.W. Walbank. 1988. *A History of Macedonia 3*. Oxford.

Harris, E.M. 1990. 'Did the Athenians Regard Seduction as a Worse Crime than Rape?' *CQ* 40: 370–7.

Harris, W.V. 1979. *War and Imperialism in Republican Rome, 327–70 BC*. Oxford (reprinted with revisions 1985; 1991).

– ed. 2005. *Rethinking the Mediterranean*. Oxford.

Harris, W.V., and G. Ruffini, eds. 2004. *Ancient Alexandria between Egypt and Greece*. Leiden and Boston.

Harrison, A.R.W. 1968. *The Law of Athens 1*. London.

Hasenohr, C. 2003. 'Les *Compitalia* à Délos,' *BCH* 127: 167–249.

Hatzfeld, J. 1907. 'Une ambassade juive à Pergame,' *Revue des Études Juives* 53: 1–13.

Hauben, H. 1987. 'Philocles, King of the Sidonians and General of the Ptolemies.' In *Studia Phoenicia* 5, edited by E. Lipiński, 413–27. Leuven.

Haussoullier, B. 1902. *Études sur l'histoire de Milet et du Didymeion*. Paris.

Hazzard, R.A. 2000. *Imagination of a Monarchy: Studies in Ptolemaic Propaganda*. Phoenix Supplement 37. Toronto.

Heath, M. 1998. 'Was Homer a Roman?' *Papers of the Leeds International Latin Seminar* 10: 23–56.

Heckel, W. 1992. *The Marshals of Alexander's Empire*. London.

– 2006. *Who's Who in the Age of Alexander the Great*. Oxford.

Heinen, H. 1972. *Untersuchungen zur hellenistichen Geschichte des 3. hunderts v. Chr.: zur Geschichte der Zeit des Ptolemaios Keraunos und zum Chremonideischen Krieg*. Historia Einzelschrift 20. Wiesbaden.

– 1984. 'The Syrian-Egyptian Wars and the New Kingdoms of Asia Minor,' *CAH* 7, no. 1, 412–45. Second edition. Cambridge.

Helm, R. 1956. *Eusebius Werke 7: Die Chronik des Hieronymus*. Leipzig and Berlin.

Henderson, J. 1975. *The Maculate Muse: Obscene Language in Attic Comedy*. New Haven.

– 1990. 'The Demos and the Comic Competition.' In *Nothing to do with Dionysos? Athenian Drama in its Social Context*, edited by J.J. Winkler and F.I. Zeitlin, 271–313. Princeton.

– 1991. *The Maculate Muse: Obscene Language in Attic Comedy*. Second edition. New York and Oxford.

Henry, M.M. 1985. *Menander's Courtesans and the Greek Tradition*. Frankfurt, Bern, and New York.

Herrmann, P. 1975. 'Neue Urkunden zur Geschichte von Milet im 2. Jahr.,' *IstMitt* 25: 71–117.

– 1997. *Milet VI, 1. Inschriften von Milet*. Berlin.

Hiller von Gaertringen, F. 1906. *Inschriften von Priene*. Berlin.

Himmelmann, N. 1983. *Alexandria und der Realismus in der griechischen Kunst*. Tübingen.

Hinge, G., and J. Krasilnikoff, eds. 2010. *Alexandria. A Cultural and Religious Melting Pot*. Copenhagen.

Hinks, R. 1939. *Myth and Allegory in Ancient Art*. London.

Hirst, A., and M. Silk, eds. 2004. *Alexandria Real and Imagined*. Aldershot.

Hirzel, R. 1895. *Der Dialog 1*. Leipzig.

Hoben, W. 1969. *Untersuchungen zur Stellung kleinasiatischer Dynasten in den Machtkämpfen der ausgehenden römischen Republik*. Diss. Mainz.

Hoepfner, W., ed. 1999. *Geschichte des Wohnens, Band 1: 5000 v. Chr.–500 n. Chr. Vorgeschichte – Frühgeschichte – Antike*. Stuttgart.

Hölbl, G. 2001. *A History of the Ptolemaic Empire*. Translated by T. Saavedra. London. German edition, Darmstadt, 1994.

Holleaux, M. 1952. *Études d'épigraphie et d'histoire grecques 4: Rome, la Macédoine et l'Orient grec*. Paris.

Homolle, T. 1882. 'Comptes des hiéropes du temple d'Apollon délien,' *BCH* 6: 1–167.

– 1890. 'Comptes et inventaires des temples déliens en l'année 279,' *BCH* 14: 389–511.

Honigman, S. 2003. *The Septuagint and Homeric Scholarship in Alexandria: A Study in the Narrative of the Letter of Aristeas*. London.

Hooley, D.M. 2007. *Roman Satire*. Malden and Oxford.

Höppener, H. 1931. *Halieutica: Bijdrage tot de Kennis der oud-grieksche Visscherij*. Amsterdam.

Horden, P., and N. Purcell. 2000. *The Corrupting Sea: A Study of Mediterranean History*. Oxford.

Horsley, G.H.R. 1989. 'A Fishing Cartel in First Century Ephesus.' In *New Documents Illustrating Early Christianity 5: Linguistic Essays*, edited by G.H.R. Horsley, 95–114. Marrickville.

Höschele, R. 2010. *Die blütenlesende Muse: Poetik und Textualität antiker Epigrammsammlungen*. Tübingen.

Houghton, A. 1983. *Coins from the Seleucid Empire from the Collection of Arthur Houghton*. Ancient Coins in North American Collections 4. New York.

– 1993. 'The Reigns of Antiochus VIII and Antiochus IX at Antioch and Tarsus,' *SNR* 72: 87–106.

Houghton, A., and C.C. Lorber. 2002. *Seleucid Coins. A Comprehensive Catalogue 1: Seleucus through Antiochus*. Lancaster.

Houghton, A., and W. Müseler 1990. 'The Reigns of Antiochus VIII and Antiochus IX at Damascus,' *SchwMbll* 40, no. 195: 57–62.

Houghton, A., and A. Spaer 1998. *Sylloge Nummorum Graecorum, Israel 1: The Arnold Spaer Collection of Seleucid Coins*. Jerusalem.

Hudson, N.A. 1989. 'Food in Roman Satire.' In *Satire and Society in Ancient Rome*, edited by S.H. Braund, 69–87. Exeter.

Hunter, R. 2003. *Theocritus. Encomium of Ptolemy Philadelphus*. Berkeley, Los Angeles, and London.

Huss, W. 2001. *Ägypten in hellenistischer Zeit 332–30 v. Chr*. Munich.

Jacob, C. 1999. 'Mapping in the Mind: the Earth from Ancient Alexandria.' In *Mapping*, edited by D. Cosgrave, 19–49. London.

Jacob, C., and F. de Polignac, eds. 2000. *Alexandria, Third Century BC: the Knowledge of the World in a Single City*. Alexandria. French editon, Paris 1992.

Jacobson, H. 1977. 'Demo and the Sabbath,' *Mnemosyne* 30: 71–2.

Jacquemin, A. 1985. 'Aitolia et Aristaineta: offrandes monumentales étolienne à Delphes au III$^e$ s. av. J.-C.,' *Ktèma* 10: 27–35.

Jameson, M.H., D.R. Jordan, and R.D Kotansky. 1993. *A Lex Sacra from Selinous*. Durham.

Jameson, M.H., C.N. Runnels, and T.H. van Andel. 1994. *A Greek Countryside: the Southern Argolid from Prehistory to the Present Day.* Stanford.

Jockey, P. 1998. 'Neither School nor *Koine*: The Local Workshops of Delos and their Unfinished Sculptures.' In Palagia and Coulson 1998: 177–84.

– 2000. ' "Aphrodite Express": À propos d'une école (?) délienne de sculpture.' In *L'artisanat en Grèce ancienne: Les productions, les diffusions,* edited by F. Blondé and A. Muller, 75–90. Lille.

Jones, A.H.M. 1971. *The Cities of the Eastern Roman Provinces.* Second edition. Oxford.

Jones, C.P. 1999. *Kinship Diplomacy in the Ancient World.* Cambridge MA.

Jones, P.J. 2005. *Reading Rivers in Roman Literature and Culture.* Lanham.

Jouanno, C. 2002. *Naissance et métamophoses du Roman d'Alexandre.* Paris.

Judeich, W. 1898. 'Skepsis.' In *Beiträge zur alten Geschichte und Geographie: Festschrift für Heinrich Kiepert,* edited by O. Benndorf, 225–40. Berlin.

Juster, J. 1914. *Les Juifs dans l'empire romain: leur condition juridique, économique et sociale.* Paris.

Kadıoğlu, M., and K. Görkay. 2007. 'Yeni arkeolojik araştırmalar ışığında ΜΗΤΡΟΠΟΛΙΣ ΤΗΣ ΓΑΛΑΤΙΑΣ: ΑΝΚΥΡΑ,' *Anadolu* 32: 21–151.

Kadıoğlu, M., K. Görkay, and S. Mitchell. 2011. *Roman Ancyra.* Istanbul.

Kahil, L. 1996. 'Cults in Hellenistic Alexandria.' In Hamma 1996: 75–84.

Kallet-Marx, R. 1995. *Hegemony to Empire. The Development of the Roman Imperium in the East from 148 to 62 B.C.* Berkeley.

Kasher, A. 1990. *The Jews and Hellenistic Cities in Eretz-Israel: Relations of the Jews in Eretz-Israel with the Hellenistic Cities during the Second Temple Period (332 BCE–70 CE).* Texte und Studien zum Antiken Judentum 21. Tübingen.

Kassel, R. 1987. *Die Abgrenzung des Hellenismus in der griechischen Literaturgeschichte.* Berlin.

Kennell, N.M. 1999. 'Age Categories and Chronology in the Hellenistic Theseia,' *Phoenix* 53: 249–62.

Kent, S. 1990a. 'A Cross-Cultural Study of Segmentation, Architecture, and the Use of Space.' In Kent 1990b: 127–52.

– ed. 1990b. *Domestic Architecture and the Use of Space: An Interdisciplinary Cross-Cultural Study.* Cambridge.

Kerkhecker, A. 1999. *Callimachus' Book of Iambi.* Oxford.

Keuls, E. 1973. 'The Samia of Menander,' *ZPE* 10: 1–20.

Kidd, I.G. 1988. *Posidonius. The Commentary (2.1), the Fragments (2.2).* Cambridge.

Kienast, D. 1987–8. 'Alexander, Zeus und Ammon.' In *Zu Alexander d. Gr.: Festschrift G. Wirth zum 60. Geburtstag 1,* edited by W. Will and J. Hienrichs, 309–33. Amsterdam.

Kienast, H.J. 1997. 'The Tower of the Winds in Athens: Hellenistic or Roman.' In *The Romanization of Athens,* edited by M.C. Hoff and S.I. Rotroff, 53–65. Oxford.

Killworth, P.D., and H.R. Bernard. 1978. 'The Reverse Small World Experiment,' *Social Networks* 1: 159–92.

Kim, L. 2010. *Homer between History and Fiction in Imperial Greek Literature.* Cambridge.

Kirstein, R. 2002. 'Companion Pieces in the Hellenistic Epigram.' In *Hellenistic Epigrams*, edited by M.A. Harder, R.F. Regtuit, and G.C. Wakker, 113–35. Hellenistica Groningana 6. Groningen.

Kistler, E. 2010. *Funktionalisierte Keltenbilder. Die Indienstname der Kelten zur Vermittlung von Normen und Werten in der hellenistischen Welt.* Frankfurt.

Klaffenbach, G., ed. 1932. *Inscriptiones Aetoliae* (= *Inscriptiones Graecae* IX.1$^2$ 1). Berlin.

Klausner, J. 1972. 'John Hyrcanus I.' In *The World History of the Jewish People 6: The Hellenistic Age*, edited by A. Schalit, 211–21, 333–4. New Brunswick.

Kleiner, G. 1968. *Die Ruinen von Milet.* Berlin.

Kleinfeld, J.S. 2002. 'The Small World Problem,' *Society* 30: 61–6.

Knappett, C. 2005. *Thinking through Material Culture. An Interdisciplinary Perspective.* Philadelphia.

Knoepfler, D. 1986. 'Inscriptions de la Béotie orientale. II. Anthédon.' In *Studien zur alten Geschichte. Siegfried Lauffer zum 70. Gerburstag 2*, edited by H. Kalcyk, B. Gullath, and A. Graeber, 593–630. Rome.

Knoke, D., and S. Yang. 2008. *Social Network Analysis.* Second edition. Los Angeles.

Knox, A.D. 1929. *Theophrastus Characters, Herodes, Cercidas and the Choliambic Poets.* Loeb Classical Library 225. Cambridge.

Knox, H., M. Savage, and P. Harvey. 2006. 'Social Networks and the Study of Relations: Networks as Method, Metaphor and Form,' *Economy and Society* 35: 113–40.

Koch, J.T. 2007. *An Atlas for Celtic Studies: Archaeology and Names in Ancient Europe and Early Medieval Ireland, Britain, and Brittany.* Oxford.

Koehn, C. 2007. *Krieg – Diplomatie – Ideologie. Zur Aussenpolitik hellenistischer Mittelstaaten.* Stuttgart.

Koenen, L. 1977. *Eine agonistische Inschrift aus Ägypten und frühptolemäische Königsfeste.* Meisenham am Glan.

– 1983. 'Die Adaptation ägyptischer Königsideologie am Ptolemäerhof.' In *Egypt and the Hellenistic World*, edited by E. Van't Dack et al., 143–90. Leuven.

– 1993. 'The Ptolemaic King as a Religious Figure.' In *Images and Ideologies: Self-Definition in the Hellenistic World*, edited by A. Bulloch et al., 25–115. Berkeley and Los Angeles.

Konstan, D. 1995. *Greek Comedy and Ideology.* New York.

– 2001. 'To Hellēnikon ethnos: Ethnicity and the Construction of Ancient Greek Identity.' In Malkin 2001a: 29–50.

- 2009. 'Cosmopolitan Traditions.' In *A Companion to Greek and Roman Political Thought*, edited by R.K. Balot, 473–84. Oxford.

Konstantinopoulos, G. 1967. Ἀρχαία οἰκία ἐντὸς οἰκοπέδου Ἀντ. καὶ Μαρίας Σκάρου ἐπὶ παρόδου τῆς ὁδοῦ Ἁγίας Ἀναστασίας,' *ArchDelt* 22 B: 523–9.

- 1986. Ἀρχαία Ρόδος: Ἐπισκόπηση τῆς ἱστορίας καί τῆς τέχνης. Athens.

Korte, C., and S. Milgram. 1970. 'Acquaintance Networks between Racial Groups – Application of the Small-World Method,' *Journal of Personality and Social Psychology* 15: 101.

Kortenbeutel, H. 1941. 'Phrurarchos,' *RE* 20, no. 1: 773–81.

Kozloff, A.P. 1996 'Is There an Alexandrian Style – What is Egyptian About it?' In Hamma 1996: 247–60.

Krahmer, G. 1924. 'Stilphasen der hellenistischen Plastik,' *RM* 39: 138–84.

Kralli, I. 1999. 'Athens and her Leading Citizens in the Early Hellenistic Period (338–261 B.C.): The Evidence of the Decrees Awarding the Highest Honours,' *Archaiognosia* 10: 133–62.

Krause, C. 1977. 'Grundformen des griechischen Pastashauses,' *AA*: 164–79.

Kreeb, M. 1988. *Untersuchungen zur figürlichen Ausstattung delischer Privathäuser*. Chicago.

Krencker, D., and M. Schede. 1936. *Der Tempel in Ankara*. Berlin.

Krevans, N. 2004. 'Callimachus and the Pedestrian Muse.' In *Callimachus 2*, edited by M.A. Harder, R.F. Regtuit, and G.C. Wakker, 173–83. Hellenistica Groningana 7. Leuven.

Kritzas, C. 2006. 'Nouvelles inscriptions d'Argos: les archives des comptes du Trésor sacré (IVᵉ s. av. J.-C.),' *CRAI* 2006 1: 397–434.

Kroll, W. 1926. *Historia Alexandri Magni*. Berlin.

Kron, U. 1988. 'Erechtheus,' *LIMC* 4, no. 1: 923–51.

Kurke, L. 1999. *Coins, Bodies, Games, and Gold. The Politics of Meaning in Archaic Greece*. Princeton.

Kyrieleis, H. 1975. *Die Bildnisse der Ptolemaier*. Berlin.

Labarre, G. 2004. 'Phrourarques et *phrouroi* des cités grecques d'Asie Mineure à l'époque hellénistique.' In Couvenhes and Fernoux 2004: 221–48.

Lacroix, M. 1924. 'Notes sur diverses inscriptions de Délos,' *BCH* 48: 399–410.

La'da, C. 2003. 'Encounters with Ancient Egypt: The Hellenistic Greek Experience.' In *Ancient Perspectives on Egypt*, edited by R. Matthews and C. Roemer, 157–69. London.

Laidlaw, W.A. 1933. *A History of Delos*. Oxford.

Lane Fox, R. 1973. *Alexander the Great*. London.

Lang, B., ed. 1987. *The Concept of Style*. Ithaca.

Lape, S. 2001. 'Democratic Ideology and the Poetics of Rape in Menandrian Comedy,' *ClAnt* 20: 79–119.

– 2004. *Reproducing Athens: Menander's Comedy, Democratic Culture, and the Hellenistic City*. Princeton.

Larsen, J.A.O. 1938. 'Roman Greece.' In *An Economic Survey of Ancient Rome 4*, edited by T. Frank, 259–498. Baltimore.

Latyschev, V. 1885. 'La Constitution de Chersonésos en Tauride d'après des documents épigraphiques,' *BCH* 9: 265–300.

– 1916. *Inscriptiones antiquae orae septentrionalis Ponti Euxini Graecae et Latinae I².* Saint Petersburg.

Launey, M. 1987. *Recherches sur les armées hellénistiques*, Paris.

Lawrence, A.W. 1925. 'Greek Sculpture in Ptolemaic Egypt,' *JEA* 11: 179–90.

Le Bohec, S. 2002. 'The Kings of Macedon and the Cult of Zeus in the Hellenistic Period.' In Ogden 2002: 41–57.

Le Dinahet-Couilloud, M.-T. 1997. 'Une famille de notables tyriens à Délos,' *BCH* 121: 617–66.

Le Guen, B. 2001. *Les Associations de Technites dionysiaques à l'époque hellénistique*. Études d'Archéologie Classique 11–12. Nancy.

Le Rider, G. 1996. *Monayage et finances de Philippe II. Un état de question*. Meletemata 23. Athens.

Lebow, R.N., and B.S. Strauss, eds. 1991. *Hegemonic Rivalry: From Thucydides to the Nuclear Age*. Boulder and Oxford.

Lefèvre, F. 1995. 'La chronologie du IIIᵉ siècle à Delphes, d'après les actes amphictioniques (280–200),' *BCH* 119: 161–206.

– 1998a. *L'Amphictionie pyléo-delphique. Histoire et institutions*. Paris.

– 1998b. 'Traité de paix entre Démétrios Poliorcète et la confédération étolienne (fin 289?),' *BCH* 122: 109–41.

– 2002. *Documents amphictioniques*. Corpus des Inscriptions de Delphes 4. Paris.

Leppin, H. 1999. *Thukydides und der Verfassung der Polis.* Berlin.

Lemke, D., and J. Kugler. 1996. 'The Evolution of the Power Transition Perspective.' In *Parity and War: Evaluations and Extensions of 'The War Ledger'*, edited by J. Kugler and D. Lemke, 3–33. Ann Arbor.

Leskovec, J., and E. Horvitz. 2008. 'Planetary-Scale Views on a Large Instant-Messaging Network.' In *WWW 2008. Alternate Track: Industrial Practice and Experience, April 21–25, 2008, Beijing, China*, edited by J. Leskovec, E. Horvitz, 915–24. URL: http://arxiv.org/abs/0803.0939v1 (26 May 2010).

Linders, T. 1994. 'The Sacred Menus on Delos.' In *Ancient Greek Cult Practice from the Epigraphical Evidence*, edited by R. Hägg, 71–9. Stockholm.

Ling, R. 1991. *Roman Painting*. Cambridge.

Livrea, E. 1986. *Studi Cercidei*. Bonn.

Lloyd, A.B. 2011. 'From Satrapy to Hellenistic Kingdom: the Case of Egypt.' In *Creating a Hellenistic World*, edited by A. Erskine and L. Llewellyn-Jones, 83–105. Swansea.

Lo Cascio, E. 2007. 'The Early Roman Empire. Trade and the Economy.' In Scheidel, Morris, and Saller 2007: 619–47.

Lob, M. 1968. *Cicéron, Discours 18*. Paris.

Lolos, Y. 2009. 'Via Egnatia after Egnatius. Imperial Policy and Inter-Regional Contacts.' In Malkin, Constantakopoulou, and Panagopoulou 2009: 264–84.

Loman, P. 2005. 'Mercenaries, Their Women, and Colonisation,' *Klio* 87: 346–65.

Long, A.A. 2008. 'The Concept of the Cosmopolitan in Greek and Roman Thought,' *Daedalus* 137: 50–8.

Lonis, R. 1992. 'L'anaplèrôsis ou la reconstitution du corps civique avec des étrangers.' In *L'Étranger dans le monde grec 2*, 245–70. Nancy.

Luck, G. 1967. Review of *The Greek Anthology: Hellenistic Epigrams*, edited by A.S.F. Gow and D.L. Page, *GGA* 219: 23–61.

Lund, H.S. 1992. *Lysimachus: A Study in Early Hellenistic Kingship*. London and New York.

Lytle, E. 2007a. 'Fishless Mysteries or High Prices at Athens? Re-examining *IG* II² 1103,' *MusHelv* 64: 100–11.

– 2007b. 'The Delian Purple and the *lex portus Asiae*,' *Phoenix* 61: 247–69.

– 2010. 'Fish Lists in the Wilderness: the Social and Economic History of a Boiotian Price Decree,' *Hesperia* 79: 253–303.

– 2012. 'Ἡ θάλασσα κοινή: Fishermen, the Sea and the Limits of Ancient Greek Regulatory Reach,' *ClAnt* 31: 1–55.

Ma, J. 1999. *Antiochus III and the Cities of Western Asia Minor*. Oxford.

– 2005. 'Kings,' in Erskine 2005: 177–95.

Maas, P. 1912. 'Hermeias 10,' *RE* 8, no. 1: 732.

MacKendrick, P. 1975. *The Dacian Stones Speak*. Chapel Hill.

Macro, A.D. 2007. 'Galatian Connections with the Celtic West in the Hellenistic Era.' In *Regionalism in Hellenistic and Roman Asia Minor*, edited by H. Elton and G. Reger, 169–77. Bordeaux.

Maehler, H. 1988. 'Poésie alexandrine et art hellénistique à memphis,' *ChrÉg* 63: 112–36.

– 2004. 'Alexandria, the Mouseion, and Cultural Identity.' In Hirst and Silk 2004: 1–14.

Magie, D. 1939. 'The "Agreement" between Philip V and Antiochus III for the Partition of the Egyptian Empire,' *JRS* 29: 32–44.

Magie, D. 1950. *Roman Rule in Asia Minor to the End of the Third Century after Christ*. Princeton.

Mahaffy, J.P. 1895. *Empire of the Ptolemies*. London.

Maier, B. 2000. *Die Kelten. Ihre Geschichte von den Anfängen bis zur Gegenwart*. Munich.

Maier, F.G. 1959. *Griechische Mauerbauinschriften 1. Texte und Kommentare*. Heidelberg.

– 1961. *Griechische Mauerbauinschriften 2. Untersuchungen.* Heidelberg.

Major, W.E. 1997. 'Menander in a Macedonian World,' *GRBS* 38: 41–73.

Malkin, I. 1987. *Religion and Colonization in Ancient Greece.* Leiden.

– 1994. *Myth and Territory in the Spartan Mediterranean.* Cambridge.

– ed. 2001a. *Ancient Perceptions of Greek Ethnicity.* Center for Hellenic Studies
Colloquia 5. Cambridge, MA, and London.

– 2001b. 'Greek Ambiguities: Between "Ancient Hellas" and "Barbarian Epirus".'
In Malkin 2001a: 187–212.

– 2003. 'Networks and the Emergence of Greek Identity,' *Mediterranean Historical
Review* 18: 56–74.

– 2011. *A Small Greek World: Networks in the Ancient Mediterranean.* New York
and Oxford.

Malkin, I., C. Constantakopoulou, and K. Panagopoulou. 2007. 'Preface: Networks
in the Ancient Mediterranean,' *Mediterranean Historical Review* 22: 1–10.

Malkin, I., C. Constantakopoulou, and K. Panagopoulou, eds. 2011. *Greek and
Roman Networks in the Mediterranean.* London.

Manganaro, G. 1963–4. 'Le iscrizioni delle isole Milesie,' *ASAtene* 25–6: 293–349.

Männlein-Robert, I. 2007a. *Stimme, Schrift und Bild: Zum Verhältnis der Künste in
der hellenistischen Dichtung.* Heidelberg.

– 2007b. 'Hellenistische Selbstepitaphien: Zwischen Autobiographie und Poetik.' In
*Die griechische Biographie in hellenistischer Zeit,* edited by M. Erler and
S. Schorn, 363–80. Berlin and New York.

Marcadé, J. 1969. *Au Musée de Délos: Essai sur la sculpture hellénistique en ronde
bosse.* Paris.

Marcus, R. 1943. *Josephus, Jewish Antiquities 7: Books 12–14.* Loeb Classical
Library 365. London and Cambridge, MA.

Mark, I.S. 1998. 'The Victory of Samothrace.' In Palagia and Coulson 1998: 157–65.

Marszal, J. 1998. 'Tradition and Innovation in Early Pergamene Sculpture.' In
Palagia and Coulson 1998: 117–27.

Mason, R.A. 2008. *The Ancient Sources on the History, Geography, and
Ethnography of Ukraine. Latin Authors 1.* Vancouver.

Mass, E. 1898. *Commentariorum in Aratum Reliquiae.* Berlin.

Matheson, S.B., ed. 1994. *An Obsession with Fortune: Tyche in Greek and Roman
Art.* New Haven.

Mattingly, H.B. 1972. 'The Date of the Senatus Consultum de Agro Pergameno,'
*AJP* 93: 412–23.

Mattusch, C.C. 1998. 'Rhodian Sculpture: A School, a Style, or Many Workshops?'
In Palagia and Coulson 1998: 149–56.

McClure, L.K. 2003. *Courtesans at Table: Gender and Greek Literary Culture in
Athenaeus.* New York.

– 2006. 'Introduction.' In *Prostitutes and Courtesans in the Ancient World,* edited
by C.A. Faraone and L.K. McClure, 3–18. Madison.

McGing, B.C. 1986. *The Foreign Policy of Mithridates* VI *Eupator King of Pontus*. Mnemosyne Supplement 89. Leiden.

McInerney, J. 1999. *The Folds of Parnassos: Land and Ethnicity in Ancient Phokis*. Austin.

– 2001. 'Ethnos and Ethnicity in Early Greece.' In Malkin 2001a: 51–74.

McKenzie, J. 2006. *The Architecture of Alexandria and Egypt, c. 300 B.C. to A.D. 700*. New Haven.

Meid, W. 2007. *Die Kelten*. Stuttgart.

Meiggs, R., and D. Lewis. 1989. *A Selection of Greek Historical Inscriptions to the End of the Fifth Century B.C.* Second edition. Oxford.

Mellor, R. 1975. ΘΕΑ ΡΟΜΗ. *The Worship of the Goddess Roma in the Greek World*. Göttingen.

Mendels, D. 1984. 'Aetolia 331–301: Frustration, Political Power and Survival,' *Historia* 33: 129–80.

– 1984–6. 'Did Polybius Have "Another" View of the Aetolian League?' *Ancient Society* 15–17: 63–73.

Mendelssohn, L. 1875. 'Senati Consulta Romanorum quae sunt in Josephi Antiquitatibus,' *Acta Societatis Philologiae Lipsiensis* 5: 87–288.

Meritt, B.D. 1935. 'The Inscriptions of Colophon,' *AJPh* 56: 358–97.

– 1977. 'Athenian Archons, 347/46–48/47 B.C.,' *Historia* 26: 161–91.

Meritt, B.D., and W.K. Pritchett. 1940. *The Chronology of Hellenistic Athens*. Cambridge, MA.

Merker, I.L. 1989. 'The Achaians in Naupaktos and Kalydon in the Fourth Century,' *Hesperia* 58: 303–11.

Meyer, E. 1925. *Ursprung und Anfänge des Christentums*. Stuttgart.

Michaud, J.-P. 1973. 'Chronique des fouilles et découvertes archéologiques en Grèce en 1972,' *BCH* 97: 253–412.

Migeotte, L. 1984. *L'emprunt public dans les cités grecques. Recueil de documents et analyse critique*. Québec and Paris.

– 1992. *Les souscriptions publiques dans les cités grecques*. Geneva.

– 2006. 'L'endettement des cités grecques dans l'Antiquité.' In *La dette publique dans l'histoire*, edited by J. Andreau, G. Béaur, and J.-Y. Grenier, 115–28. Paris.

Mihailov, G. 1970. *Inscriptiones Graecae in Bulgaria Repertae I: Inscriptiones Orae Ponti Euxini*. Second edition. Sofia.

Mikalson, J.D. 1975. *The Sacred and Civil Calendar of the Athenian Year*. Princeton.

Milgram, S. 1967. 'The Small World Problem,' *Psychology Today* 2: 60–7.

– 1992. *The Individual in a Social World. Essays and Experiments*. Second edition (J. Sabini and M. Silver [eds.]). New York.

Millar, F. 1983. 'The Phoenician Cities: A Case-Study of Hellenisation,' *PCPS* 209: 55–71.

Mineur, W.H. 1984. *Callimachus, Hymn to Delos: Introduction and Commentary*. Leiden.

Mitchell, J.F. 1966. 'The Torquati,' *Historia* 15: 23–31.

Mitchell, L.M. 1883. *A History of Ancient Sculpture*. London and New York.

Mitchell, S. 1986. 'Galatia under Tiberius,' *Chiron* 16: 17–33.

– 1993. *Anatolia. Land, Men, and Gods in Asia Minor*. Oxford.

– 2007. 'Römische Macht im frühkaiserzeitlichen Ankara – Verwaltung oder Herrschaft?' In *Herrschen und Verwalten. Der Alltag der römischen Administration in der Hohen Kaiserzeit*, edited by R. Haensch and J. Heinrichs, 366–77. Cologne.

– 2008a. 'The Imperial Cult in Galatia from Claudius to Trajan.' In *Vom Euphrat bis zum Bosporus. Kleinasien in der Antike. Festschrift für Elmar Schwertheim*, 471–83. Bonn.

– 2008b. *The Imperial Temple at Ankara and The Res Gestae of the Emperor Augustus. A Historical Guide*. Ankara.

Mitchell, S., and D. French. 2012. *The Greek and Latin Inscriptions of Ankara I: From Augustus to the End of the Third Century AD*. Munich. (*I. Ankara* I).

Mitropoulou, E. 1977. *Deities and Heroes in the Form of Snakes*. Second edition. Athens.

– 1993. 'The Origin and Significance of the Vergina Symbol,' *Ancient Macedonia* 5: 843–958.

Mittag, P.F. 2003. 'Unruhen im hellenistischen Alexandreia,' *Historia* 52: 161–208.

Moles, J.L. 1996. 'Cynic Cosmopolitanism.' In *The Cynic Movement in Antiquity and its Legacy*, edited by B. Branham and M.-O. Goulet-Cazé, 105–20. Berkeley.

Möller, M. 2004. *Talis Oratio – Qualis Vita: Zu Theorie und Praxis mimetischer Verfahren in der griechisch-römischen Literaturkritik*. Heidelberg.

Momigliano, A. 1975. *Alien Wisdom: the Limits of Hellenization*. Cambridge.

Mommsen, T. 1884. 'Die keltischen Pagi,' *Hermes* 19: 316–21.

– 1903. *Römische Geschichte 1*. Ninth edition. Berlin.

Moraux, P. 1957. 'L'établissement des Galates en Asie Mineure,' *IstMitt* 7: 56–75.

Moretti, L. 1967–75. *Iscrizioni storiche ellenistiche*. Firenze.

Morgan, C. 2001. 'Ethne, Ethnicity, and Early Greek States, ca. 1200–480 B.C.: An Archaeological Perspective.' In Malkin 2001a: 75–112.

– 2003. *Early Greek States Beyond the Polis*. London and New York.

Morgan, K.A. 1993. 'Pindar the Professional and the Rhetoric of the ΚΩΜΟΣ,' *CP* 88: 1–15.

Mori, A. 2008. *The Politics of Apollonius Rhodius' Argonautica*. Cambridge.

Mørkholm, O. 1991. *Early Hellenistic Coinage from the Accession of Alexander to the Peace of Apamea (336–186 BC)*. Cambridge.

Morley, N. 2007. *Trade in Classical Antiquity*. Cambridge.

Müller, H. 1995. 'Bemerkungen zu Funktion und Bedeutung des Rats in den hellenistischen Städten.' In Wörrle and Zanker 1995: 41–54.

Müller-Karpe, A. 1988. 'Neue galatische Funde aus Anatolien,' *IstMitt* 38: 189–99.

Munson, R.V. 2001. '*Ananke* in Herodotus,' *JHS* 121: 30–50.

Mylona, D. 2008. *Fish-Eating in Greece from the Fifth Century B.C. to the Seventh Century A.D.: A Story of Impoverished Fishermen or Luxurious Fish Banquets.* Oxford.

Nachtergael, G. 1977. *Les Galates en Grèce et les Sôtéria de Delphes.* Brussels.

Nagle, D.B. 2006. *The Household as the Foundation of Aristotle's Polis.* Cambridge.

Nagy, G. 1998. 'The Library at Pergamon as Classical Model.' In *Pergamon: Citadel of the Gods,* edited by H. Koester, 185–232. Harvard Theological Studies 46. Harrisburg.

Nawotka, K. 1997. *The Western Pontic Cities. History and Political Organization.* Amsterdam.

– 1999. *Boule and Demos in Miletus and Its Pontic Colonies from the Classical Age until the Third Century A.D.* Krakow.

Nesselrath, H.-G. 2005. 'Comic Fragments: Transmission and Textual Criticism.' In *Brill's Companion to the Study of Greek Comedy,* edited by G.W. Dobrov, 423–53. Leiden.

Nevett, L.C. 1995. 'The Organisation of Space in Classical and Hellenistic Houses from Mainland Greece and the Western Colonies.' In *Time, Tradition and Society in Greek Archaeology,* edited by N. Spencer, 89–108. London.

– 1999. *House and Society in the Ancient Greek World.* Cambridge.

– 2002. 'Continuity and Change in Greek Households under Roman Rule: The Role of Women in the Domestic Context.' In *Greek Romans and Roman Greeks: Studies in Cultural Interaction,* edited by E.N. Ostenfeld, K. Blomqvist, and L.C. Nevett, 81–97. Aarhus Studies in Mediterranean Antiquity 3. Aarhus.

– 2010. *Domestic Space in Classical Antiquity.* Cambridge.

Newell, E.T. 1941. *The Coinages of the Western Seleucid Mints from Seleucus I to Antiochus III.* American Numismatic Society Numismatic Studies 4. New York.

Niese, B. 1898. 'Zur Geschichte der keltischen Wanderungen,' *Zeitschrift für deutsches Altertum und deutsche Literatur* 42: 129–61.

Nieto, F.J.F. 1997. 'Los reglamentos militares griegos y la justicia castrense en época helenística.' In *Symposion 1995. Vorträge zur griechischen und hellenistischen Rechtsgeschichte,* edited by G. Thür, J. Vélissaropoulos-Karakostas, 221–44. Cologne, Weimar, and Vienna.

Nilsson, M.P. 1948. *Greek Piety.* Translated by H.J. Rose. Oxford.

North, D.C. 1991. *Institutions, Institutional Change and Economic Performance.* Cambridge.

– 2005. *Understanding the Process of Economic Change.* Princeton.

Noshy, I. 1937. *The Arts in Ptolemaic Egypt.* London.

Oakley, J., and R. Sinos. 1993. *The Wedding in Ancient Athens.* Madison.

Ogden, D. 1996. *Greek Bastardy in the Classical and Hellenistic Periods.* Oxford.

– 1997a. *The Crooked Kings of Ancient Greece.* London.

– 1997b. 'Rape, Adultery, and Protection of Bloodlines in Classical Athens.' In *Rape in Antiquity*, edited by S. Deacy and K.F. Pierce, 25–42. London.

– 1999. *Polygamy, Prostitutes and Death. The Hellenistic Dynasties*. London.

– ed. 2002. *The Hellenistic World: New Perspectives*. London.

– 2004. *Aristomenes of Messene. Legends of Sparta's Nemesis*. Swansea.

– 2011. *Alexander the Great: Myth, Genesis, and Sexuality*. Exeter.

Olson, S.D., and A. Sens. 2000. *Archestratos of Gela*. Oxford.

O'Neil, J.L. 1995. *The Origins and Development of Ancient Greek Democracy*. Lanham.

Onians, J. 1979. *Art and Thought in the Hellenistic Age*. London.

Oppermann, M. 2004. *Die westpontischen Poleis und ihr indigenes Umfeld in vorrömischer Zeit*. Langenweissbach.

Osborne, R. 2009. 'What Travelled with Greek Pottery?' In Malkin, Constantakopoulou, and Panagopoulou 2009: 83–93.

Otto, W. 1931. 'Zu den Syrischen Kriegen der Ptolemäer,' *Philologus* 86: 400–18.

Overbeck, J. 1882. *Geschichte der griechischen Plastik 2*. Third edition. Leipzig.

Owen, G.E.L. 1983. 'Philosophical Invective,' *Oxford Studies in Ancient Philosophy* 1: 1–25.

Page, D. 1975. *Epigrammata Graeca*. Oxford.

Paget, J.C. 2004. 'Jews and Christians in Ancient Alexandria from the Ptolemies to Caracalla.' In Hirst and Silk 2004: 143–66.

Palagia, O. 1982. 'A Colossal Statue of a Personification from the Agora of Athens,' *Hesperia* 51: 99–113.

– 1998. 'The Enemy Within: A Macedonian in Piraeus.' In Palagia and Coulson 1998: 15–26.

Palagia, O., and W. Coulson, eds. 1998. *Regional Schools in Hellenistic Sculpture*. Oxford.

Paleothodoros, D. 2009. 'Commercial Networks in the Mediterranean and the Diffusion of Early Attic Red-Figure Pottery (525–490 BCE).' In Malkin, Constantakopoulou, and Panagopoulou 2009: 158–75.

Papaioannou, M. 2007. 'The Roman *Domus* in the Greek World.' In *Building Communities: House, Settlement and Society in the Aegean and Beyond. BSA Studies 15*, edited by R. Westgate, N. Fisher, and J. Whitley, 351–61. London.

Papapostolou, I.A. 1987–90. 'Ἀνασκαφὴ Θέρμου,' *Praktika*: 142–5.

– 1983–98. 'Θέρμος,' *Ergon*.

Parke, H.W. 1933. *Greek Mercenary Soldiers*. Oxford.

Pedzopoulos, E.A. 1931. 'Συμβολαὶ κριτικαὶ καὶ ἑρμενευτικαὶ εἰς Ἑλληνικὰ ἐπιγράμματα,' *Byzantinisch-Neugriechische Jahrbücher* 8: 171–88.

Peignard-Giros, A. 2000. 'Habitudes alimentaires grecques et romaines à Délos à l'époque hellénistique: le témoignage de la céramique,' *Pallas* 52: 209–20.

Peremans, W. 1987. 'Les Lagides, les élites indigènes et la monarchie bicéphale.' In *Le système palatial en Orient, en Grèce et à Rome*, edited by E. Lévy, 327–43. Strasbourg.

Perlman, P. 1999. '*Krētes aei lēistai?* The Marginalization of Crete in Greek Thought and the Role of Piracy in the Outbreak of the First Cretan War.' In *Hellenistic Rhodes: Politics, Culture, and Society*, edited by V. Gabrielsen et al., 132–61. Studies in Hellenistic Civilization 9. Aarhus.

Petzl, G. 1987. *Die Inschriften von Smyrna II, 1.* Bonn.

Pfeiffer, R. 1968. *History of Classical Scholarship 1. From the Beginnings to the End of the Hellenistic Age.* Oxford.

– 1985. *Callimachus.* Oxford.

Pfister, F. 1951. *Die Reisebilder des Herakleides.* Vienna.

– 1956. *Alexander der Grosse in den Offenbarungen der Griechen, Juden, Mohammedaner und Christen.* Berlin. Reprinted in F. Pfister, *Kleine Schriften zum Alexanderroman*, 301–37. 1976. Meisenheim am Glan.

Pfuhl, E., and H. Möbius. 1979. *Die ostgriechischen Grabreliefs.* Mainz.

Picard, C. 1920. 'Observations sur la société des Poseidoniastes de Bérytos et sur son histoire,' *BCH* 44: 263–311.

Pickard-Cambridge, A. 1988. *The Dramatic Festivals of Athens.* Second edition; revised by J. Gould and D. Lewis. Oxford.

Pierce, K.F. 1997. 'The Portrayal of Rape in New Comedy.' In *Rape in Antiquity*, edited by S. Deacy and K.F. Pierce, 163–84. London.

Pietrzykowski, M. 1978. 'Sarapis-Agathos Daimon.' In *Hommages à Maarten J. Vermaseren 3*, edited by M.B. de Boer and T.A. Edridge, 959–66. ÉPRO 68. Leiden.

Pippidi, D.M. 1963. 'Note sur l'organisation militaire d'Istros à l'époque hellénistique,' *Klio* 41: 158–67.

– 1965. 'Les colonies grecques de Scythe Mineure à l'époque hellénistique,' *BalkSt* 6: 99–118 (=Pippidi, *Parerga*, 118–34).

– 1971. *I greci nel basso danubio dall'età arcaica alla conquista romana.* Milan.

– 1975. *Scythica Minora. Recherches sur les colonies grecques du littoral roumain de la Mer Noire.* Amsterdam.

– 1983. *Inscriptiones Scythiae Minoris Graecae et Latinae I: Histria.* Bucharest.

– 1984. *Parerga. Écrits de Philologie, d'Epigraphie et d'Histoire ancienne.* Paris.

Pippidi, D.M., and E. Popescu. 1959. 'Les relations d'Istros et d'Apollonie du Pont à l'époque hellénistique,' *Dacia* 3: 235–58.

Plantzos, D. 2007. 'Ptolemaic Cameos of the Second and First Centuries BC,' *OJA* 15: 39–61.

Plassart, A. 1916. 'Fouilles de Délos, exécutées aux frais de M. le Duc de Loubat (1912–1913): Quartier d'habitations privées à l'est du stade,' *BCH* 40: 145–256.

Pollitt, J.J. 1974. *The Ancient View of Greek Art: Criticism, History, and Terminology.* New Haven.

– 1986. *Art in the Hellenistic Age.* Cambridge.

Pomeroy, S.B. 1983. 'Infanticide in Hellenistic Greece.' In *Images of Women in Antiquity*, edited by A. Cameron and A. Kuhrt, 207–22. London.

Pottier, E., and S. Reinach. 1888. *La nécropole de Myrina. Recherches archéologiques exécutées au nom et au frais de l'École Française d'Athènes*. Paris.

Poulsen, V. 1939. 'Gab es eine Alexandrinische Kunst?' *From the Collections of the Ny Carlsberg Glyptotek 2*, 1–52. Copenhagen.

Powell, J. 1996. *Fishing in the Prehistoric Aegean*. Jonsered.

Préaux, C. 1978. *Le monde hellénistique*. Paris.

Prêtre, C., et al. 2002. *Nouveau choix d'inscriptions de Délos. Lois, comptes et inventaires*. Athens.

Price, M.J. 1968. 'Mithradates vi Eupator, Dionysus, and the Coinages of the Black Sea,' *NNM* 7: 1–12.

Pritchett, W.K. 1991. *Studies in Ancient Greek Topography 7*. Amsterdam.

Pucci Ben Zeev, M. 1996. 'Ant. XIV, 185–267: A Problem of Authenticity.' In *Classical Studies in Honor of David Sohlberg*, edited by R. Katzoff, Y. Petroff, and D. Schaps, 193–221. Ramat Gan.

– 1998. *Jewish Rights in the Roman World: The Greek and Roman Documents Quoted by Josephus Flavius*. Texts and Studies in Ancient Judaism 74. Tübingen.

Purcell, N. 1995. 'Eating Fish: The Paradoxes of Seafood.' In *Food in Antiquity*, edited by J. Wilkins, D. Harvey, and N. Dobson, 132–48. Exeter.

Quaegebeur, J. 1975. *Le dieu égyptien Shaï dans la religion et l'onomastique*. Orientalia Lovaniensia Analecta 2. Leuven.

Quass, F. 1979. 'Zur Verfassung der griechischen Städte im Hellenismus,' *Chiron* 9: 37–52.

– 1993. *Die Honoratiorenschicht in den Städten des griechischen Ostens*. Stuttgart.

Raddatz, G. 1913. 'Homeros,' *RE* 8, no. 2: 2188–99.

Radinger, C. 1895. *Meleagros von Gadara: Eine litterargeschichtliche Skizze*. Innsbruck.

Radt, S. 2008. *Strabons Geographika 7*. Göttingen.

Rajak, T. 1981. 'Roman Intervention in a Seleucid Siege of Jerusalem?' *GRBS* 22: 65–81.

– 1984. 'Was there a Roman Charter for the Jews?' *JRS* 74: 107–23.

– 1994. 'The Jews under Hasmonean Rule.' In *Cambridge Ancient History 9: The Last Age of the Roman Republic, 146–43 B.C.*, edited by J.A. Crook, A. Lintott, and E. Rawson, 274–309. Cambridge.

– 2001. *The Jewish Dialogue with Greece and Rome: Studies in Cultural and Social Interaction*. Boston and Leiden.

Ramsay, W.M. 1897. *The Cities and Bishoprics of Phrygia 1*. Oxford.

– 1900. *Historical Commentary on St. Paul's Epistle to the Galatians*. Second edition. London.

– 1922. 'Studies in the Roman Province of Galatia III,' *JRS* 12: 147–86.

– 1939. 'Early History of the Province of Galatia.' In Calder and Keil 1939: 201–25.

Rapoport, A. 1990. 'Systems of Activities and Systems of Settings.' In Kent 1990b: 9–20.

Rathbone, D. 2009. 'Merchant Networks in the Greek World. The Impact of Rome.' In Malkin, Constantakopoulou, and Panagopoulou 2009: 299–310.

Rauh, N.K. 1986. 'Cicero's Business Friendships. Economics and Politics in the Late Roman Republic,' *Aevum* 60: 3–30.

– 1993. *The Sacred Bonds of Commerce: Religion, Economy, and Trade Society at Hellenistic Roman Delos.* Amsterdam.

Redondo, J. 1993. 'On a *vox nihili* of Hermeias: Ath. XIII 563 d ὑποκριτῆρες,' *Glotta* 71: 167–70.

Reger, G. 1994a. *Regionalism and Change in the Economy of Independent Delos, 314–167 B.C.* Berkeley, Los Angeles, and Oxford.

– 1994b. 'Some Boiotians in the Hellenistic Kyklades.' In *Boiotia Antiqua 4. Proceedings of the 7th International Congress on Boiotian Antiquities*, edited by J. Fossey, 71–99. Amsterdam.

– 2007. 'Hellenistic Greece and Western Asia Minor.' In Scheidel, Morris, and Saller 2007: 459–83.

– Forthcoming. 'Economic Regionalism in Theory and Practice.' In Viviers and Tsingarida forthcoming.

Reger, G., and M.K. Risser. 1991. 'Coinage and Federation on Hellenistic Keos.' In *Landscape Archaeology as Long-term History: Northern Keos in the Cycladic Islands*, edited by J.F. Cherry, J.L. Davis, and E. Mantzourani, 305–17. Monumenta Archaeologica 16. Los Angeles.

Rehm, A. 1914. *Milet I, 3. Das Delphinion in Milet.* Berlin.

Reinach, A.J. 1911. 'Un monument delphien: L'Étolie sur les trophées Gaulois de Kallion,' *JIAN* 13: 177–240.

Reinach, T. 1899. 'Antiochus Cyzicène et les Juifs,' *REJ* 38: 161–71.

Reitzenstein, R. 1893. *Epigramm und Skolion.* Giessen.

Relihan, Joel C. 1993. *Ancient Menippean Satire.* Baltimore.

Rémy, B. 1986. *L'évolution administrative de l'Anatolie aux trois premiers siècles de notre ère.* Paris.

– 1989. *Les carrières sénatoriales dans les provinces romaines d'Anatolie au Haut-Empire (31 av. J.-C.–284 ap. J.-C.) (Pont-Bithynie, Galatie, Cappadoce, Lycie-Pamphylie et Cilicie).* Istanbul.

Renfrew, C., and J. Cherry, eds. 1986. *Peer Polity Interaction and Socio-Political Change.* Cambridge.

Rey-Coquais, J.-P. 1994. 'Du sanctuaire de Pan à la "Guirlande" de Méléagre.' In *Aspetti e problemi dell'ellenismo: atti del convegno di studi, Pisa, 6–7 novembre 1992*, edited by B. Virgilio, 47–90. Pisa.

– 2006. *Inscriptions grecques et latines de Tyr.* Bulletin d'Archéologie et d'Architecture Libanaises, Hors Série 3. Beirut.

Rhodes, P.J., and D.M. Lewis. 1997. *The Decrees of the Greek States*. Oxford.

Rhodes, P.J., and R. Osborne. 2003. *Greek Historical Inscriptions 404–323 BC*. Oxford.

Riad, H. 1996. 'Egyptian Influence on Daily Life in Ancient Alexandria.' In Hamma 1996: 29–39.

Ribichini, S. 1983. 'Mito e storia: L'immagine dei fenici nelle fonti classiche.' In *Atti del 1. Congresso Internazionale di studi fenici e punice*, edited by P. Bartolini and S.F. Bondi, 443–8. Rome.

Rice, E.E. 1983. *The Grand Procession of Ptolemy Philadelphus*. Oxford.

Richards, M.P., and R.E.M. Hedges. 2008. 'Stable Isotope Evidence of Past Human Diet at the Sites of the Neolithic Cave of Gerani et al.' In *Archaeology Meets Science: Biomolecular Investigations in Bronze Age Greece*, edited by Y. Tzedakis, H. Martlew, and M.K. Jones, 220–30. Oxford.

Richardson, N.J. 1994. 'Aristotle and Hellenistic Scholarship.' In *La philologie greque à l'époque hellénistique et romaine*, edited by F. Montanari, 7–28. Entretiens sur l'antiquité classique 40. Geneva.

Ricl, M. 1997. *The Inscriptions of Alexandreia Troas*. Bonn.

Ridgway, B.S. 1990. *Hellenistic Sculpture 1: The Styles of ca. 323–200 B.C.* Madison.

– 1997. *Fourth-Century Styles in Greek Sculpture*. Madison.

– 2000. *Hellenistic Sculpture 2: The Styles of ca. 200–100 B.C.* Madison.

Rigsby, K. 1996. *Asylia: Territorial Inviolability in the Hellenistic Period*. Berkeley and Los Angeles.

Rist, J.M. 1969. *Stoic Philosophy*. Cambridge.

Ritner, R. 1992. 'Implicit Models of Cross-Cultural Interaction: A Question of Noses, Soap, and Prejudice.' In *Life in a Multi-Cultural Society: Egypt from Cambyses to Constantine and Beyond*, edited by J.H. Johnson, 283–90. Chicago.

Ritschl, F. 1873. 'Eine Berichtigung der republikanischen Consularfasten: Zugleich als Beitrag zur Geschichte der römisch-jüdischen internationalen Beziehungen,' *RhM* 28: 586–614.

Robert, L. 1926. 'Notes d'épigraphie hellénistique,' *BCH* 50: 469–522 (=*OMS* 1: 33–86).

– 1936. *Collection Frœhner 1: les inscriptions grecques*. Paris.

– 1948. *Hellenica 4*. Paris.

– 1959. 'Philologie et géographie II. Sur Pline l'Ancien, livre II,' *Anatolia* 4: 1–26 (=*OMS* 3: 1423–8).

– 1963. *Noms indigènes dans l'Asie Mineure gréco-romaine*. Paris.

Robert, L., and J. Robert. 1976. 'Une nouvelle inscription grecque de Téos en Ionie. L'union de Téos et de Kyrbissos,' *JSav* 1976: 153–235.

Roesch, P. 1974. 'Sur le tarif des poissons d'Akraiphia,' *ZPE* 14: 5–9.

Rose, C.B. 2008. 'Forging Identity in the Roman Republic: Trojan Ancestry and Veristic Portraiture.' In *Role Models in the Roman World: Identity and*

*Assimilation*. Edited by S. Bell and I.L. Hansen, 97–131. MAAR Supplement 7, Ann Arbor.

Rose, M.J. 2000. 'The Fish Remains.' In *Kommos 4. The Greek Sanctuary*, edited by J.W. Shaw and M.C. Shaw, 495–560. Princeton.

Rosen, R. 1988. *Old Comedy and the Iambographic Tradition*. Atlanta.

– 2007. *Making Mockery. The Poetics of Ancient Satire*. Oxford.

Rosivach, V.J. 1998. *When a Young Man Falls in Love: The Sexual Exploitation of Women in New Comedy*. London.

Rostovtzeff, M.I. 1931. 'Trois inscriptions d'époque hellénistique de Théangela en Carie,' *REA* 33: 5–25.

– 1941. *The Social and Economic History of the Hellenistic World*. Oxford.

Roussel, P. 1916. *Délos colonie athénienne*. Paris.

– 1925. *Délos*. Paris.

– 1934. 'Un règlement militaire de l'époque macédonienne,' *RA*: 39–47.

– 1987. *Délos colonie athénienne. Réimpression augmentée de complements bibliographiques et de concordances épigraphiques par Philippe Bruneau, Marie-Thérèse Couilloud-Ledinahet, Roland Étienne*. Paris.

Rowlandson, J. 2005. 'Town and Country in Ptolemaic Egypt.' In Erskine 2005: 249–63.

Rübekeil, L. 1992. *Suebica. Völkernamen und Ethnos*. Innsbruck.

Ruffer, M.A. 1910. 'On Dwarves and Other Deformed Persons in Ancient Egypt,' *BSAA* 13: 162–75.

Ruge, W. 1935. 'Myus 2,' *RE* 16, no. 2: 1430–7.

Rutherford, I. 2009. 'Network Theory and Theoric Networks.' In Malkin, Constantakopoulou, and Panagopoulou 2009: 24–38.

Saatsoglou-Paliadeli, C. 1991. 'Βεργίνα 1991. ανασκαφή στο ιερό της Εύκλειας,' Το αρχαιολογικο έργο στη Μακεδονία και Θράκη 5: 9–21.

Sacks, K.S. 1975. 'Polybius' Other View of the Aetolians,' *JHS* 95: 92–106.

Saddington, D.B. 1993. 'Preparing to Become Roman. The "Romanisation" of Deiotarus in Cicero.' In *Charistion, C.P.T. Naudé*, edited by U. Vogel-Weidmann, 87–96. Pretoria.

Şahin, S., and M. Adak. 2007. *Stadiasmus Patarensis Itinera Romana Rovinciae Lyciae*. Istanbul.

Saïd, S. 2001. 'Discourse of Identity in Greek Rhetoric from Isocrates to Aristides.' In Malkin 2001a: 275–99.

Salway, B. 2001. 'Travel, *Itineraria*, and *Tabellaria*.' In *Travel and Geography in the Roman Empire*, edited by C. Adams and R. Laurence, 22–66. London and New York.

Samons II, L.J. 2000. *Empire of the Owl. Athenian Imperial Finance*. Stuttgart.

Samuel, A.E. 1993. 'The Ptolemies and the Ideology of Kingship.' In Green 1993: 168–210.

Sánchez, P. 2001. *L'Amphictionie des Pyles et de Delphes. Recherches sur son rôle historique des origines au IIe siècle de notre ère.* Stuttgart.

Sandwell, I. 2009. 'Libanius' Social Networks. Understanding the Social Structure of the Later Roman Empire.' In Malkin, Constantakopoulou, and Panagopoulou 2009: 129–43.

Saunders, N.J. 2006. *Alexander's Tomb. The Two-Thousand Year Obsession to Find the Lost Conqueror.* New York.

Savalli, I. 1985. 'I neocittadini nelle città ellenistiche. Note sulla concessione e l'acquisizione della *politeia*,' *Historia* 34: 387–431.

Schalles, H.-J. 1985. *Untersuchungen zur Kulturpolitik der pergamenischen Herrscher im dritten Jahrhundert vor Christus.* Tübingen.

Schaps, D.M. 1985–8. 'Comic Inflation in the Market-Place,' *Scripta Classica Israelica* 8–9: 66–73.

– 1987. 'Small Change in Boeotia,' *ZPE* 69: 293–6.

Scheidel, W. 2004. 'Creating a Metropolis: a Comparative Demographic Perspective,' in Harris and Ruffini 2004: 1–31.

Scheidel, W., I. Morris, and R. Saller, eds. 2007. *The Cambridge Economic History of the Greco-Roman World.* Cambridge.

Schmidt, S. 2005a. 'Das hellenistische Alexandria als Drehschiebe des kulturellen Austausches?' In Beck, Bol, and Bückling 2005: 267–78.

– 2005b. 'Serapis – ein neuer Gott für die griechen in Ägypten,' in Beck, Bol, and Bückling 2005: 291–304.

Schmidt-Dounas, B. 2000. *Geschenke erhalten die Freundschaft. Politik und Selbstdarstellung im Spiegel der Monumente.* Berlin.

Schmitt, H.H. 1969. *Die Staatsverträge des Altertums 3: Die Verträge der griechisch-römischen Welt von 338 bis 200 v.Chr.* Munich.

Schmitz, T. 1997. *Bildung und Macht: Zur sozialen und politischen Funktion der Zweiten Sophistik in der griechischen Welt der Kaiserzeit.* Munich.

Scholten, J.B. 2000. *The Politics of Plunder. Aitolians and their Koinon in the Early Hellenistic Era, ca. 279–217 B.C.* Berkeley and Los Angeles.

– 2005. 'Macedonia and the Mainland, 280–221.' In Erskine 2005: 135–58.

Schreiber, T. 1885. 'Alexandrinische Skulpturen in Athen?' *AM* 10: 380–400.

Schuler, C. 1998. *Ländliche Siedlung und Gemeinden im hellenistischen und römischen Kleinasien.* Vestigia 50. Munich.

Schultz, P. 2003. 'Kephisodotos the Younger.' In *The Macedonians in Athens, 323–229 B.C.*, edited by S. Tracy and O. Palagia, 186–93. Oxford.

Schürer, E. et al. 1973–87. *The History of the Jewish People in the Age of Jesus Christ.* Edinburgh.

Schwabl, H. 1978. *Zeus.* Munich (=*RE* 10A and Supplementband 15).

Schwartz, D.R. 1993. 'Scipio's Embassy and Simon's Ambassadors,' *Scripta Classica Israelica* 12: 114–26.

Schwartz, S. 2001. *Imperialism and Jewish Society: 200 B.C.E. to 640 C.E. Jews, Christians, and Muslims from the Ancient to the Modern World*. Princeton.

Schwarzenberg, E. 1976. 'The portraiture of Alexander.' In *Alexandre le grand. Image et réalité*, edited by E. Badian, 223–67. Entretiens Hardt 22. Geneva.

Segre, M. 1930. 'Per la storia di Antioco I° Sotere,' *Athenaeum* 8: 488–507.

– 1944–5. 'Tituli Calymnii,' *ASAtene* 22–3 (n.s. 6–7).

– 1993. *Iscrizioni di Cos*. Rome.

Selden, D. 1998. 'Alibis,' *Classical Antiquity* 17: 289–412.

Shapiro, H.A. 1993. *Personifications in Greek Art*. Zurich.

Sherk, R.K. 1992. 'The Eponymous Officials of Greek Cities: IV,' *ZPE* 93: 223–72.

Sherwin-White, A.N. 1983. *Roman Foreign Policy in the East. 168 B.C. to A.D. 1*. Norman.

Shipley, G. 2000. *The Greek World after Alexander, 323–30 BC*. London and New York.

Skarlatidou, E.K. 1990–1. 'Κατάλογος μύστων και εποπτών από τη Σαμοθράκη,' *Horos* 8–9: 153–72.

Smallwood, E.M. 1976. *The Jews under Roman Rule: From Pompey to Diocletian*. Studies in Judaism in Late Antiquity 20. Leiden.

– 1981. *The Jews under Roman Rule: From Pompey to Diocletian: A Study in Political Relations*. Second edition. Leiden.

Smith, R.R.R. 1988. *Hellenistic Royal Portraits*. Oxford.

– 1991. *Hellenistic Sculpture: A Handbook*. London.

– 1996. 'Ptolemaic Portraits: Alexandrian Types, Egyptian Versions.' In Hamma 1996: 203–13.

– 1998. 'Hellenistic Sculpture under the Roman Empire: Fishermen and Satyrs at Aphrodisias.' In Palagia and Coulson 1998: 253–60.

Smyth, H.W. 1956. *Greek Grammar*. Cambridge, MA.

Snodgrass, A.M. 1980. *Archaic Greece. The Age of Experiment*. London, Melbourne, and Toronto.

Sommer, M. 2009. 'Networks of Commerce and Knowledge in the Iron Age. The Case of the Phoenicians.' In Malkin, Constantakopoulou, and Panagopoulou 2009: 94–108.

Sorenson, O., J.W. Rivkin, and L. Fleming. 2007. 'Informational Complexity and the Flow of Knowledge Across Social Boundaries.' In Frenken 2007: 147–60.

Sosin, J.D. 2004. 'Acraephia Counts: Π for Π(ΕΤΤΑΡΕΣ),' *ZPE* 148: 193–5.

Sparkes, B.A., and L. Talcott. 1958. *Pots and Pans of Classical Athens*. Princeton.

Spawforth, A.J. 2006. '"Macedonian Times": Hellenistic Memories in the Provinces of the Roman Near East.' In *Greeks on Greekness: Viewing the Greek Past under the Roman Empire*, edited by D. Konstan and S. Said, 1–26. Cambridge.

Stähelin, F. 1907–73. *Geschichte der kleinasiatischen Galater*. Reprint of the second edition. Osnabrück.

Stanwick, P. 2002. *Portraits of the Ptolemies: Greek Kings as Egyptian Pharaohs.* Austin.

Stephens, S.A. 2003. *Seeing Double: Intercultural Poetics in Ptolemaic Alexandria.* Berkeley.

Sterling, R.W. 1974. *Macropolitics: International Security in a Global Society.* New York.

Stern, M. 1961. 'The Relations between Judaea and Rome during the Rule of John Hyrcanus,' *Zion* 26: 1–22. In Hebrew.

– 1965. *The Documents on the History of the Hasmonaean Revolt with a Commentary and Introductions.* Tel Aviv. In Hebrew.

Stewart, A. 1979. *Attika: Studies in Athenian Sculpture of the Hellenistic Age.* London.

– 1993. *Faces of Power. Alexander's Image and Hellenistic Politics.* Berkeley.

– 1995. 'Narration and Allusion in the Hellenistic Baroque.' In *Narrative and Event in Ancient Art,* edited by P. Holliday, 130–74. Cambridge.

– 1996. 'The Alexandrian Style: A Mirage?' In Hamma 1996: 231–46.

– 2005. 'Hellenistic Art, AD 1500–2000.' In Erskine 2005: 494–514.

Stewart, A., and S.R. Martin. 2003. 'Hellenistic Discoveries at Tel Dor, Israel,' *Hesperia* 72: 121–45.

Stoian, I. 1961. 'La città pontica di Tomis,' *Dacia* 5: 233–74.

– 1987. *Inscriptiones Scythiae Minoris Graecae et Latinae II: Tomis.* Bucharest.

Stoneman, R. 1994. 'Jewish Traditions on Alexander the Great,' *The Studia Philonica Annual* 6: 37–53.

– ed. and trans. 2007. *Il romanzo di Alessandro.* Milan.

– 2008. *Alexander the Great: A Life in Legend.* New Haven.

Strobel, K. 1994. 'Keltensieg und Galatersieger.' In *Forschungen in Galatien,* edited by E. Schwertheim, 67–96. Bonn.

– 1996. *Die Galater 1: Geschichte und Eigenart der keltischen Staatenbildung auf dem Boden des hellenistischen Kleinasien.* Berlin.

– 1999. 'Kelten III.: Kelten im Osten,' *Der Neue Pauly* 6: 393–400.

– 2002. 'Die Staatenbildung bei den kleinasiatischen Galatern. Politisch-historische und kulturelle Prozesse im hellenistischen Zentralanatolien.' In *Brückenland Anatolien? Ursachen, Extensität und Modi des Kulturaustausches zwischen Anatolien und seinen Nachbarn,* edited by H. Blum et al., 231–293. Tübingen. (In English [2002]: 'State Formation by the Galatians of Asia Minor,' *Anatolica* 28: 1–44.)

– 2007. 'Die Galater und Galatien: Historische Identität und ethnische Tradition im Imperium Romanum,' *Klio* 89: 356–402.

Strobel, K., and C. Gerber. 2000. 'Tavium (Büyüknefes, Provinz Yozgat). Ein regionales Zentrum Anatoliens. Bericht über den Stand der Forschungen nach den ersten drei Kampagnen (1997–1999),' *IstMitt* 50: 215–65.

Strogatz, S. 2003. *Sync: How Order Emerges from Chaos in the Universe, Nature, and Daily Life.* New York.

Strootman, R. 2005. 'Kings against Celts: Deliverance from Barbarians as a Theme in Hellenistic Royal Propaganda.' In *The Manipulative Mode,* edited by K.A.E. Enenkel and I.L. Pfeijffer, 101–41. Leiden.

Strubbe, J. 2005. *The Inscriptions of Pessinous.* Bonn.

Stucky, R. 1988. 'Die Tonmetope mit den drei sitzenden Frauen von Thermos, ein Dokument hellenistischer Denkmalpflege,' *AntK* 31: 71–8.

Sturgeon, M. 'Hellenistic Sculpture at Corinth: The State of the Question.' In Palagia and Coulson 1998: 1–13.

Sutton, S.B. 1991. 'Population, Economy, and Settlement in Post-Revolutionary Keos: A Cultural Anthropological Study.' In *Landscape Archaeology as Long-Term History: Northern Keos in the Cycladic Islands from Earliest Settlement until Modern Times,* edited by J.F. Cherry, J.L. Davis, and E. Mantzourani, 382–402. Los Angeles.

Syme, R. 1995. *Anatolica. Studies in Strabo.* Oxford.

Szabó, M. 1991. 'The Celts and their Movements in the Third Century B.C.' In *The Celts,* edited by M. Szabó, C. Tanzi, and M. Andreose, 303–19. Milan.

Taeger, F. 1957. *Charisma. Studien zur Geschichte des antiken Herrscherkultes.* Stuttgart.

Tang, B. 2005. *Delos, Carthage, Ampurias: The Housing of Three Mediterranean Trading Centres.* AnalRom Supplement 36. Rome.

Tarán, S.L. 1979. *The Art of Variation in the Hellenistic Epigram.* Leiden.

– ed. 1987. *The Greek Anthology.* New York.

Tarn, W.W. 1930. *Hellenistic Military and Naval Developments.* Cambridge.

– 1933. 'Two Notes on Ptolemaic History,' *JHS* 53: 57–68.

Tarn, W.W., and G.T. Griffith. 1952. *Hellenistic Civilisation.* Third edition. London.

Taylor, L.R. 1930. 'Alexander and the Serpent of Alexandria,' *CP* 25: 375–8.

Thomas, R. 2001. 'Ethnicity, Genealogy, and Hellenism in Herodotus.' In Malkin 2001a: 213–34.

Thompson, D.J. 1988. *Memphis under the Ptolemies.* Princeton.

– 2001. 'Hellenistic Hellenes: the Case of Ptolemaic Egypt.' In Malkin 2001a: 301–22.

Thompson, H., and R.E. Wycherley. 1972. *The Agora of Athens.* Athenian Agora 14. Princeton.

Timpe, D. 1974. 'Der römische Vertrag mit den Juden von 161 v. Chr.,' *Chiron* 4: 133–52.

Tomaschitz, K. 2002. *Die Wanderungen der Kelten in der antiken literarischen Überlieferung.* Vienna.

Touloumakos, J. 1977. *Der Einfluss Roms auf die Staatsform der griechischen Stadtstaaten des Festlandes und der Inseln im ersten und zweiten Jahrhundert v. Chr.* Göttingen.

Tracy, S.V. 1979. 'Athens in 100 B.C.,' *HSCP* 83: 213–35.

– 1982. *IG II² 2336. Contributors of First Fruits for the Pythais.* Meisenheim.

– 1988. 'IG II² 937: Athens and the Seleucids,' *GRBS* 29: 383–8.

– 1990. *Attic Letter-Cutters of 229 to 86 B.C.* Berkeley.

– 1991. 'ΤΟ ΜΗ ΔΙΣ ΑΡΧΕΙΝ,' *CP* 86: 201–4.

Tracy, S.V., and C. Habicht. 1991. 'New and Old Panathenaic Victor Lists,' *Hesperia* 60: 187–236.

Traill, A. 2008. *Women and the Comic Plot in Menander.* Cambridge.

Travers, J., and S. Milgram. 1969. 'An Experimental Study of the Small World Problem,' *Sociometry* 32: 425–43.

Tréheux, J. 1991. 'L'administration financière des ΕΠΙ ΤΑ ΙΕΡΑ à Délos: une théorie nouvelle,' *BCH* 115: 349–52.

Trümper, M. 1998. *Wohnen in Delos: Eine baugeschichtliche Untersuchung zum Wandel der Wohnkultur in hellenistischer Zeit.* Internationale Archäologie 46. Rahden.

– 2006. 'Negotiating Religious and Ethnic Identity: The Case of Clubhouses in Late Hellenistic Delos,' *Hephaistos* 24: 113–50 (Special issue: I. Nielsen (ed.), *Zwischen Kult und Gesellschaft: Kosmopolitische Zentren des antiken Mittelmeerraums als Aktionsraum von Kultvereinen und Religionsgemeinschafte*).

– 2007. 'Differentiation in the Hellenistic Houses of Delos: The Question of Functional Areas.' In Westgate, Fisher, and Whitley 2007: 323–34.

Tsangari, D. 2002. 'Corpus des monnaies d'or, d'argent et de bronze du Koinon étolien.' Dissertation, Paris.

Valavanis, P. 2001. 'Panathenaïsche Amphoren auf Monumenten spätklassischer, hellenistischer und römischer Zeit.' In *Panathenaïka: Symposion zu den Panathenaïschen Preisamphoren,* edited by M. Bentz and N. Eschbach, 161–73. Mainz.

Van Bremen, R. 2005. 'Family Structures.' In Erskine 2005: 313–30.

Van Rooy, C.A. 1965. *Studies in Classical Satire and Related Literary Theory.* Leiden.

Vanderspoel, J. 1995. *Themistius and the Imperial Court. Oratory, Civic Duty, and Paideia from Constantius to Theodosius.* Ann Arbor.

Vasunia, P. 2001. *The Gift of the Nile: Hellenizing Egypt from Aeschylus to Alexander.* Berkeley.

Vatin, C. 1971. 'Le tarif des poissons d'Akraiphia.' In F. Salviat and C. Vatin, *Inscriptions de Grèce centrale,* 95–109. Paris.

Veïsse, A.-E. 2004. *Les 'revoltes egyptiennes': Recherches sur les troubles intérieurs en Egypt du règne de Ptolemée III à la conquête romaine.* Leiden.

Vélissaropoulos, J. 1980. *Les nauclères grecs: recherches sur les institutions maritimes en Grèce et dans l'Orient hellénisé.* Paris-Geneva.

Veyne, P. 1990. *Bread and Circuses*. Translated by B. Pearce. London.

Vial, C. 1984. *Délos indépendante (314–167 avant J.-C.). Étude d'une communauté civique et de ses institutions*. BCH Supplement 10. Paris.

– 1988. 'La conservation des contrats à Délos pendant l'Indépendance.' In *Comptes et inventaires dans la cité grecque*, edited by D. Knoepfler, 49–60. Neuchâtel.

– 1997. '*Délos Indépendante* treize ans après,' *RÉA* 99: 337–443.

– 2002. 'Les débiteurs,' in Prêtre et al. 2002: 258–62.

Vincent, J.-C. 2007. 'Le bouclier d'Aristoménès: une arme de proagande politico-religieuse dans la *Périégèse de Pausanias*.' In *Les armes dans l'antiquité*, edited by P. Sauzeau and T. van Compernolle, 231–47. Montpellier.

Virgilio, B. 1982. 'Eumene I e i mercenari di Filetereia e di Attaleia,' *Studi classici e orientali* 32: 97–140.

Visser, E. 1938. *Götter und Kulte in ptolemäischer Alexandrien*. Amsterdam.

Viviers, D., and A. Tsingarida, eds. Forthcoming. *Les marches de la céramique dans le monde grec (VIIIe – Ier s. av. J.-C.)*. Brussels.

Vlassopoulos, K. 2009. 'Beyond and Below the Polis. Networks, Associations, and the Writing of Greek History.' In Malkin, Constantakopoulou, and Panagopoulou 2009: 12–23.

Vogeikoff-Brogan, N., and S. Apostolakou. 2004. 'New Evidence of Wine Production in East Crete in the Hellenistic Period.' In *Transport Amphorae and Trade in the Eastern Mediterranean*, edited by J. Eiring and J. Lund, 417–27. Monographs of the Danish Institute in Athens 5. Aarhus.

von Gerkan, A. 1925. *Milet I, 8. Kalabak tepe, Athena-Tempel und Umgebung*. Berlin.

– 1935. *Milet II, 3. Die Stadtmauern*. Berlin.

von Prittwitz, H. 1998. 'The Divine Circle: the Roundels of Mahdia.' In Palagia and Coulson 1998: 69–73.

von Schoeffer, V. 1901, 'Delos,' *RE* 4, cols. 2459–2502.

Wace, A.J.B. 1902–3. 'Apollo Seated on the Omphalos,' *BSA* 9: 211–42.

– 1903/4. 'Grotesques and the Evil Eye,' *BSA* 10: 103–14.

Walbank, F.W. 1967. *A Historical Commentary on Polybius 2*. Oxford.

– 1979a. *A Historical Commentary on Polybius 3*. Oxford.

– 1979b. 'Egypt in Polybius.' In *Orbis Aegyptiorum Speculum: Glimpses of Ancient Egypt*, edited by J. Ruffle, G. Gaballa, and K. Kitchen, 180–9 (=Walbank 2002: 53–69). Warminster.

– 1988. 'From the Battle of Ipsus to the Death of Antigonus Doson' In Hammond and Walbank 1988: 199–366.

– 1989. 'Antigonus Doson's Attack on Cytinium (*RÉG* 101 [1988], 12–53),' *ZPE* 76: 184–92.

– 1994. 'Supernatural Paraphernalia in Polybius' *Histories*.' In *Ventures into Greek Historiography*, edited by I. Worthington, 28–42. Oxford.

– 2002. *Polybius, Rome and the Hellenistic World: Essays and Reflections.* Cambridge.

Walde, A., and J.B. Hofmann. 1939. *Lateinisches etymologisches Wörterbuch.* Third edition. Heidelberg.

Wallace-Hadrill, A. 1994. *Houses and Society in Pompeii and Herculaneum.* Princeton.

Walsh, J., and T.F. Reese, eds. 1996. *Alexandria and Alexandrianism.* Malibu.

Waltz, K.M. 1959. *Man, the State and War.* New York.

– 1979. *Theory of International Politics.* New York.

– 1988, 'The Origins of War in Neorealist Theory,' *Journal of Interdisciplinary History* 18: 615–28.

– 2000. 'Structural Realism after the Cold War,' *International Security* 25: 5–41.

Ward, G., and C. Eilers. Forthcoming. 'Embedded Fragments in Josephus' Caesarian *acta* (Joseph. *AJ* 14.196–212),' *Phoenix.*

Waszink, J.H. 1972. 'Problems Concerning the Satura of Ennius.' In *Ennius*, edited by O. Skutsch, 97–147. Entretiens sur l'antiquité classique 17. Geneva.

Watts, D.J. 2003. *Six Degrees: The Science of a Connected Age.* New York and London.

Weber, G. 1993. *Dichtung und höfische Gesellschaft.* Stuttgart.

– ed. 2007. *Kulturgeschichte des Hellenismus. Von Alexander dem Grossen bis Kleopatra.* Stuttgart.

Weber-Hiden, I. 2003. 'Keramik aus hellenistischer bis frühbyzantinischer Zeit aus Tavium/Büyük Nefes,' *Anatolia Antiqua* 11: 253–322.

Webster, T.B.L. 1970. *Studies in Later Greek Comedy.* Second edition. Manchester.

– 1974. *An Introduction to Menander.* Manchester.

Weiher, A. 1913. *Philosophen und Philosophenspott in der attischen Komödie.* Diss. Munich.

Weissbach, W. 1910. *Impressionismus: Ein Problem der Malerei in der Antike und der Neuzeit.* Berlin.

Weißhäupl, R. 1889. *Die Grabgedichte der griechischen Anthologie.* Wien.

Weissl, M. 1999. 'Die Befestigung der jüngeren Stadtanlage von Pleuron in Aitolien,' *ÖJh* 68: 105–46.

Welles, C.B. 1962. 'The Discovery of Sarapis and the Foundation of Alexandria,' *Historia* 11: 271–98.

West, M.L. 1974. *Studies in Greek Elegy and Iambus.* Berlin.

– 1982. *Greek Metre.* Oxford.

Westgate, R. 1997–8. 'Greek Mosaics in Their Architectural and Social Context,' *BICS* 42: 93–115.

– 2000a. 'Space and Decoration in Hellenistic Houses,' *BSA* 95: 391–426.

– 2000b. '*Pavimenta atque emblemata vermiculata*: Regional Styles in Hellenistic Mosaic and the First Mosaics at Pompeii,' *AJA* 104: 255–75.

– 2007a. 'Life's Rich Pattern: Decoration as Evidence for Room Function in Hellenistic Houses.' In Westgate, Fisher, and Whitley 2007: 313–21.

– 2007b. 'House and Society in Classical and Hellenistic Crete: A Case Study in Regional Variation,' *AJA* 111: 423–57.

– 2010. 'Interior Decoration in Hellenistic Houses: Context, Function and Meaning.' In *Städtisches Wohnen im östlichen Mittelmeerraum, 4. Jh. v. Chr. – 1. Jh. n. Chr.*, edited by S. Ladstätter and V. Scheibelreiter, 497–528. Archäologische Forschungen 18. Vienna.

– Forthcoming. 'Space and Social Complexity in Greece from the Early Iron Age to the Classical Period.'

Westgate, R., N. Fisher, and J. Whitley, eds. 2007. *Building Communities: House, Settlement and Society in the Aegean and Beyond*. BSA Studies 15. London.

Whitmarsh, T. 1999. 'The Birth of a Prodigy: Heliodorus and the Genealogy of Hellenism.' In *Studies in Heliodorus*, edited by R. Hunter, 93–124. Cambridge Philological Society Supplementary Volume 21. Cambridge UK.

– 2001. ' "Greece is the World": Exile and Identity in the Second Sophistic.' In Goldhill 2001: 269–305.

Wickhoff, F. 1895. *Die Wiener Genesis*. Vienna.

Wifstrand, A. 1926. *Studien zur griechischen Anthologie*. Lund.

Wiles, D. 1991. *The Masks of Menander: Sign and Meaning in Greek and Roman Performance*. Cambridge.

Wilhelm, A. 1939. 'Athen und Kolophon.' In Calder and Keil 1939: 345–68.

Wilkins, J. 2005. 'Fish as a Source of Food in Antiquity.' In *Ancient Fishing and Fish Processing in the Black Sea Region*, edited by T. Bekker-Nielsen, 21–30. Black Sea Studies 2. Aarhus.

Wilkins, J., and S. Hill, S. 1994. *Archestratus, The Life of Luxury: Europe's Oldest Cookery Book*. Totnes.

Will, E. 1979a. 'Le monde hellénistique et nous,' *Ancient Society* 10: 79–95.

– 1979b. *Histoire politique du monde hellénistique (323–30 av. J.-C.) 1*. Second edition. Nancy.

– 1982. *Histoire politique du monde hellénistique (323–30 av. J.-C.) 2*. Second edition. Nancy.

– 1985. 'Pour une anthropologie coloniale du monde hellénistique.' In *The Craft of the Ancient Historian. Essays in Honour of Chester G. Starr*, edited by J. Eadie and J. Ober, 273–301. New York.

– 1988. '*Poleis* hellénistiques : deux notes,' *EchCl* 32: 329–52.

Williams, D. Forthcoming. 'Greek Potters and Painters. Marketing and Moving.' In Viviers and Tsingarida forthcoming.

Williams, F. 2006. 'Cercidas: The Man and the Poet.' In *Beyond the Canon*, edited by A. Harder et al., 345–56. Hellenistica Groningana 11.

Willrich, H. 1924. *Urkundenfälschung in der hellenistisch-jüdischen Literatur.* Forschungen zur Religion und Literatur des Alten und Neuen Testaments 21. Göttingen.

– 1944. *Cicero und Caesar.* Göttingen.

Wilson, P. 2000. *The Athenian Institution of the* Khoregia: *the Chorus, the City, and the Stage.* Cambridge.

Winter, I.J. 1995. 'Homer's Phoenicians: History, Ethnography, or Literary Trope?' In *The Ages of Homer,* edited by J.B. Carter and S.P. Morris, 247–71. Austin.

Wiseman, T.P. 1995. *Remus: A Roman Myth.* Cambridge.

Wolohojian, A.M., trans. 1969. *The Romance of Alexander the Great by Pseudo-Callisthenes.* Translated from the Armenian Version. New York.

Woolf, G. 1994. 'Becoming Roman, Staying Greek: Culture, Identity and the Civilizing Process in the Roman East,' *PCPS* 40: 116–43.

Wörrle, M. 1975. 'Antiochos I., Achaios der Ältere und die Galater. Eine neue Inschrift in Denizli,' *Chiron* 5: 59–87.

– 1988. 'Inschriften von Herakleia am Latmos I: Antiochos III, Zeuxis und Herakleia,' *Chiron* 18: 421–76.

– 2000. 'Pergamon um 133 v. Chr.,' *Chiron* 30: 541–76.

– 2004. 'Der Friede zwischen Milet und Magnesia. Methodische Probleme einer Communis opinion,' *Chiron* 34: 45–57.

Wörrle, M., and P. Zanker, eds. 1995. *Stadtbild und Bürgerbild im Hellenismus.* Munich.

Ypsilanti, M. 2005. 'Literary Loves as Cycles: From Meleager to Ovid,' *AntCl* 74: 83–110.

Zagagi, N. 1995. *The Comedy of Menander: Convention, Variation and Originality.* Bloomington.

Zanker, G. 1987. *Realism in Alexandrian Poetry: A Literature and Its Audience.* London.

Zeitlin, F.R. 2001. 'Visions and Revisions of Homer.' In Goldhill 2001: 195–266.

Ziebarth, E. 1917. 'Delische Stiftungen,' *Hermes* 52: 425–41.

Zimmermann, K. 2002. 'Eratosthenes' Chlamys-Shaped World: a Misunderstood Metaphor.' In Ogden 2002: 23–40.

Zwintscher, A. 1892. *De Galatarum tetrarchis et Amynta rege quaestiones.* Diss. Leipzig.

# CONTRIBUTORS

**Sheila Ager** is Associate Professor and Chair of Classical Studies at the University of Waterloo, Ontario. She researches political history in the Hellenistic period, and especially the relations between city states. She is the author of *Interstate Arbitrations in the Greek World, 337–90 BC* (Berkeley, 1997) and of several articles.

**Patrick Baker** is Professor of Ancient Greek History at Laval University, Quebec. His research focuses on military institutions in the Greek cities of the Hellenistic world, and on Hellenistic and imperial epigraphy. He is author of numerous articles on military history and epigraphy.

**Peter Bing**, Professor of Classics at Emory University, is a specialist in Archaic and Hellenistic Greek poetry, Greek and Roman drama, and Greek myth and religion. He is the author of *The Well-Read Muse* (2nd ed., Ann Arbor, 2008) and *The Scroll and the Marble: Studies in Reading and Reception in Hellenistic Poetry* (Ann Arbor, 2009).

**Glenn Bugh**, Associate Professor of History, Virginia Polytechnic Institute and University, specializes in Athens of the post-classical era and Hellenistic military developments. He has authored several articles, and is the editor of the *Cambridge Companion to the Hellenistic World* (Cambridge, 2006).

**Altay Coşkun** is Associate Professor of Classics at the University of Waterloo. His research interests include Roman foreign policy and ancient Galatia. He has written several articles and books, including *Bürgerrechtsentzug oder Fremdenausweisung? Studien zu den Rechten von Latinern . . .* (Stuttgart, 2009).

**Mary Depew** is Associate Professor of Classics, University of Iowa. She concentrates her research interests in Hellenistic poetry and Greek religion. Professor Depew co-edited (with Dirk Obbink) *Matrices of Genre: Authors, Society, and Canons* (Cambridge, MA), several articles on Kallimachus, and is currently completing *Myth, Mimesis and Innovation in Callimachus' Hymns*.

**Arthur Eckstein** is Professor of History, University of Maryland. He is a specialist in Hellenistic and Roman history and historiography. He has written numerous articles, particularly on Roman expansion in the eastern Mediterranean, and several books, of which the most recent is *Rome Enters the Greek East* (Malden, 2008).

**Claude Eilers** is Associate Professor of Classics, McMaster University, Ontario. His research interests include Roman history, and especially the evolution of Jewish privileges in Roman Asia Minor. He is author of *Roman Patrons of Greek Cities* (Oxford, 2002) and several articles on Roman politics.

**Andrew Erskine** is Professor of Ancient History at the University of Edinburgh. His research concentrates on Hellenistic history and thought, and on the relationship between Romans and Greeks. He is the editor of Blackwell's *A Companion to the Hellenistic World* (Oxford, 2003) and author of *Troy Between Greece and Rome* (Oxford, 2001).

**Riemer Faber** is Associate Professor of Classics at the University of Waterloo, and director of the Waterloo Institute for Hellenistic Studies. His research interests include Hellenistic and Augustan poetry, Greek and Latin philology, and literary descriptions of works of art. He has published several articles on epic poetry and ekphrasis.

**Kathryn Gutzwiller** is Professor of Classics at the University of Cincinnati. She has published widely on Hellenistic poets, and is the author of several books, including *Poetic Garlands: Hellenistic Epigrams in Context* (Berkeley, 1998), and she is editor of Blackwell's *A Guide to Hellenistic Literature* (Oxford, 2007).

**Craig Hardiman** is Associate Professor in Classics at the University of Waterloo. His research focuses on Greek (especially Hellenistic) sculpture, domestic architecture, and Greek and Latin poetry. He has published several articles on Hellenistic art and aesthetics.

**Regina Höschele** is Associate Professor of Classics at the University of Toronto. A specialist in Hellenistic poetry, she is particularly interested in the intersection between the Greek and the Roman world. She is author of *Verrückt nach Frauen: Der Epigrammatiker Rufin* (Tübingen, 2006) and *Die blüten lesende Muse: Poetik und Textualität antiker Epigrammsammlungen* (Tübingen, 2010).

**Ephraim Lytle** is Assistant Professor of Classics at the University of Toronto. He focuses his research on Greek social and economic history (especially Hellenistic), and non-agricultural economies. His published articles treat various Greek documents from Hellenistic Delos, and fishing economies throughout ancient and Hellenistic Greece.

**Léopold Migeotte** is Professor Emeritus in the Department of History at the University of Laval. He specializes in social and political history of Greece, and in particular public finances and epigraphy. His many publications include *The Economy of the Greek Cities: From the Archaic Period to the Early Roman Empire* (tr. Janet Lloyd, Berkeley, 2009).

**Daniel Ogden** is Professor of Ancient History, University of Exeter, and Research Fellow, UNISA. He has published widely on topics ranging from ancient traditional narratives to Greek religion and the Hellenistic dynasties. His books include *Alexander the Great: Myth, Genesis, and Sexuality* (Exeter, 2011) and *Drakōn: Dragon Myth and Serpent Cult in the Greek and Roman Worlds* (Oxford, 2012).

**Gary Reger** is Professor of History at Trinity College, Hartford, Connecticut. His research focuses on Hellenistic economy and epigraphy, especially in Asia Minor. He is author of *Regionalism and Change in the Economy of Independent Delos* (Berkeley, 1994), and co-editor of *Regionalism in Hellenistic and Roman Asia Minor* (Bordeaux, 2007).

**Joseph Scholten** is Associate Professor of Classics, University of Maryland. He is a specialist in state formation in Greece (600 to 300 BC) and early Hellenistic political institutional developments, on which he has contributed several articles. He is author of *The Politics of Plunder: Aitolians and their Koinon in the Early Hellenistic Era, 279–217 B.C.* (Berkeley, 2000).

**Christina Vester** is Assistant Professor of Classics, University of Waterloo. Her research interests include Greek and Roman drama, identity in the ancient world, and Neronian literature. She has written several articles, including '(Mis)Remembering Magnus in Lucan's *de bello civili*,' *Latomus* (2008).

**Ruth Westgate** is Lecturer in Ancient History and Archaeology at Cardiff University. Her research concentrates on domestic architecture and its socio-political contexts in ancient Greece. She is co-editor of *Building Communities: House, Settlement and Society in the Aegean and Beyond* (London, 2007), and has published several articles on mosaics and home decoration.

# INDEX

Achaia, Achaians, 104–5, 138, 141

Achaian War, 114, 118

Acropolis, Athenian, 101, 107, 114, 118, 199

Adonia, 232

Aegean, 48, 84, 138, 148, 293, 295–6, 300, 302, 305; Greeks, 96–7, 102, 106

Agathokles of Istria, 122–3

Agathos Daimon: association with Alexander, 191–2; association with Alexandria, 179–80, 191–2; association with Ptolemies, 192–3; Šaï, counterpart, 192

Aitolia, Aitolians, 71–2, 76, 96–108; attitude towards: Classical, 96–100; – early Hellenistic, 100–3; – Hellenistic, 104–7; personification, 100–2; Social War, 105

Akraiphia, 299–301

Alexander the Great, 20–1, 173, 184; association with Agathos Daimon, 191–2; association with Alexandria, 169–70, 173–80, 191–2; association with Ptolemies, 184–93; association with Seleukids, 193; birth myths, 187, 189–90, 193; cult, 188; symbolism, 187–92, 206; visit to Ammon at Siwah, 173, 176–9

Alexandria: Alexandria-centrism, 325–38; artistic style, 171, 173, 199–211, 215–16; association with Agathos Daimon, 179–80, 191–2; association with Alexander the Great, 169–70, 173–80, 191–2; exemplum of diversity, 170–80, 212, 215, 325–31; foundation, 167–70, 173–80, 191; literary style, 178, 180, 201, 211–16

amicitia populi Romani, 85–7

Ammon, 173, 177–9, 189, 193, 206

anarchy, 132–5, 139, 141

Anatolia, 73–89, 101, 107

ἀνδρόγυνε, 233–4

Andros, 317

Ankyra, 74, 84, 273; metropolis, 87–8

Anthedon, 300, 305

Antigonos I, 319

Antigonos III, 138, 274

Antigonos of Karystos, 34, 39, 41

Antiochos I, 74–5, 82

Antiochos III, 107, 136–9

Antiochos IV, 118, 136

Antiochos VII, 159, 161

Antiochos VIII, 158–9

Antiochos IX, 157–9, 161–2

Antiochos Hierax, 273–4

Antipater of Sidon, 48, 57–9, 64

*aparchai*, 317

Apemantos (son of Leophon), 306

Aphrodite, 51–2, 57, 253

Apollo: birth, 23, 288, 316–24, 335–7; sanctuary at Delos, 316–22; sanctuary at Delphi, 73, 100–1; sanctuary at Thermon, 97–100

Apollonia, 120, 123, 136, 151

Apollonios of Miletos, 277–8

Appian, 114, 159

Areopagos, 115, 119–20

Argead, 185, 193

Argos, Argives, 42, 337–8; Heraion, 42, 332

Aristion of Athens, 114, 119

Aristophanes, 51, 60, 236

Aristotle, 41, 99, 111–12, 119, 212–13, 302

Arkadia, 333–5, 337

Arsinoë (Ptolemy Soter's mother), 185–6

Arsinoë II, 171–2, 188–9, 206, 207, 212

Artemis, 27, 101, 334; temple at Ephesus, 187

Asia Minor, 74–6, 79, 82–6, 89, 113, 125–6, 273–4, 279–80, 285

Askalon, 159

Asteria, 334, 336–7

*asylia*, 130, 136, 147

Athena, 60, 101, 188, 191–2, 320, 334, 337; Parthenos, 121, 192

Athenaios, 21, 33, 38–40, 59–61, 112, 306

Athenion of Athens, 112–14, 119

Athenodoros (Mithridatic commander), 277

Athens, Athenians, 21, 77, 96, 98–102, 104, 107, 138, 144, 150, 170, 175, 192, 279, 283, 293, 305, 316–24; Acropolis, 101, 107, 199; citizenship, 227–41; Anthesteria, 327–8; constitution, 112–15, 119; critical enquiry, 212; decrees, 130, 149, 156–7, 160–2; democracy, 111–21, 124, 126; domestic

decoration, 250; foreign relations, 134, 147, 149, 156–7; Parthenon, 192; power capabilities, 134–5, 293; protector of Delos, 48

Attalids, 74, 118; artistic program, 77, 101, 107, 213–14; *cistophori*, 147

Attalos I, 77, 274

Attalos II, 118; Stoa of, 113

Augustan period, 49, 88

Augustus, 74, 76, 87–9, 179

Balkans, 73, 83

Basileia, 23

*basileus*, 81, 96, 173

Berenike I, 185

Berenike II, 209, 338

Berytos, 149–50

Bias of Priene, 282

Bithynia, 73–4, 84

Black Sea, 72, 85, 111, 120–6

Boiotia, 101, 172, 299

*boule*, 116–17, 121–4

*bouleterion*, 170

Brennos, Gallic chieftain, 73, 78

Byzantion, 34, 73, 125, 169

Cavari, 79

Celts, 71–3, 76–87, 97, 100, 139; attitude towards, 75–8, 80–4, 86–7, 89–90, 96, 101–2

Chaos, 19–20

*charis*, 62

*cheirotonia*, 114

Chersonesos, 121, 282; civic oath, 121–2, 291

*chlamys*, 171, 176

*choliamb*, 17, 33–6, 38–9, 326

*chora*, 121, 123, 161

*choregos*, 231–2, 234–5, 241, 334

Chrysis the Samian, 227–9, 232–41

Cicero, 48, 85–6, 147–8, 152, 190, 255

Cilicia, 86, 273

citizens, citizenship, 268–91, 227–41; double endogamy, 227, 230; ἑταίρα γαμετή, 238, 240; γνήσιος, 235, 241; γυνή, 226–7, 235–9, 241; hetaira, 60, 225–6, 228, 230, 232, 236–41; isopoliteia, 103, 277, 285; κοσμίος, 231–3; nothos, 227, 230, 233, 238; pallake, 223, 227–8, 232, 236–7, 240–1; Periclean law, 227, 230; philotimia, 235; politeia, 81–2, 99, 111–21, 132, 228; πονηρός, 227, 233, 241; Roman, 71, 74, 89; sympoliteia, 130, 147, 277; χρηστός, 226–7, 233, 235

Classical art style, 200, 203, 205

coinage: Aitolian, 99, 101–2, 107; Anatolian, 88; Athenian New Style silver, 116, 118; Attalid cistophori, 147; of Alexander, 187–9, 206; of Hellenistic kings, 76, 210; Ptolemaic, 159, 188–9, 193, 206

comitia centuriata, 138

Compitalia, 251–2

Corinth, 48, 101, 104, 114, 135, 187; sanctuary at, 98

Council of 600, 116–17

Crete, Cretans, 268–91; birthplace of Zeus, 23; domestic architecture and decoration, 223–4, 246, 255–8, 261

cretic-paeonic metre, 33, 35

cultural specificity, 326, 331, 333

Curtius Rufus, Q., 169, 176–8, 185–6, 190

Cyclades, 317, 337

Cyclopes, 72, 98, 126

Cynic, 39, 60–3

Cyprus, Cypriots, 33, 41–2

Cyrene, 17, 151, 170, 187, 325

Danaos, 337; daughters of, 337

Deiotaros Philorhomaios, 74, 80–1, 85–7

Delos, Delians, 24, 77, 149–50, 336–7; Apollo treasury, 293–4, 316–24; as cosmopolitan city, 245–6, 255, 261; as cleruchy, 48, 116; commercial activity, 303–7; domestic architecture and decoration, 223, 245–9, 252–5, 258, 260–1; fish diet, 301–2; fishing industry, 296, 298–301

Delian League, 317

Delphi, Delphians, 37, 76–8, 80, 100, 102, 107, 115; Delphic-Anthelic Amphiktyony, 101–2; sanctuary of Apollo, 73, 98–9, 101, 270

Delphinion (Miletos), 270

Demeas, 227, 230, 232–41

Demeter, 113

Demetrios I, 99, 102, 113, 175, 210

Demetrios II, 102

Demetrios of Phaleron, 240

democracy, 111–12, 228; Athens, 111–20; Black Sea, 121–6

demos, 104, 111–25

dikasteria, 117

Diodoros, 75, 77, 169, 174, 176–7, 178, 190

Diogenes Laertios, 40

Diomedes, 38, 59, 62

Dionysios (Meleager), 53–4, 56–8

Dionysios of Pergamon, 157

Dionysos, 331, 333

Diophantos (Mithridatic commander), 282, 291

Diphilos, 299, 301

dithyrambic chorus, 231

domestic architecture and decoration: amphora, 152, 250, 254; andreion, 256; Archaic, 256, 261; as a tool for inclusion/exclusion, 245–6, 249–56, 258–62; Athenian, 250; Classical, 258, 260; Cretan, 255–8, 261; Delian, 246–9, 252–5, 258, 260–1; fauces, 249; Greek, 249, 252, 261; Hellenistic, 250, 254–5, 258, 260; Jewish, 249; Masonry Style (First Pompeian style), 246–7, 249–50, 253–4; oeci minores, 252; Roman, 249, 251–3, 255; Syrian, 249–50; tablinum, 249; triclinium, 253

Drynemeton, 80, 82

Egypt, Egyptians, 22, 26, 118, 167–8, 170, 184–6, 212, 294, 325–38; foreign relations, 136–8; religion, 177–9, 190–3; style 171–5, 202–3, 205–6, 210–11, 215–16

'Elephant Victory,' 75, 78, 82

*eleutheria*, 99, 102, 114

Eleuthernai, 272, 285

Ennius, 59, 62, 64

Ephesos, 151, 187, 306–7, 326

epigrams: anonymous epigrams, 52–6; *Garland* of Meleager, 19–20, 26–8, 49–51; self-epitaphs of Meleager, 19–29

*erastes*, 51, 57–8

Eratosthenes, 177, 231

*eromenos*, 53, 56

Eros, 26, 39, 50–2, 54–5, 58, 61

Erythrai, 279–83, 289–90

ethnic labels, 78–80, 82–4, 89, 96–7, 103–4

*ethnos*, 96, 98, 103–4

Eubios, 54–5

euergetism, 122–4, 150

Euhemeros of Messene, 326–7

Eukrates, 19, 22, 26–7, 47

Euripides, 20, 61, 98

Eurydike, 185, 189

fish: *pesce fino*, 300; *pesce nobile*, 300; *pesce ordinario*, 300; *pesce populo*, 300

fish markets, 295–6, 300, 303–5; Delian, 301–3, 307

fishermen, 295–6, 301, 304–7

Gadara, 17, 19, 20–2, 24–5, 47, 59, 61, 63, 97

Gaia, 121, 333–4

Galatia, Galatians, 71–90, 81–4, 86–90, 96, 101, 107, 274, 279–80, 282

γαμετή, 238; ἑταίρα, 238, 240

Gaul, Gauls, 77–80, 83–4, 101, 122, 125, 188; spolia of, 100–2

Germany, Germanic, 79, 83–4, 86

Glaukos, 50

Goddess Roma, 87, 150

Gortyn, 270, 272, 284–5

Graces, 20, 22, 26, 156

*grammatikos*, 213, 327, 331

Greece, Greeks, 41–2, 71–6, 78–9, 81, 83, 96–108, 136, 140, 175; claims to heritage of, 325–38; democracy in, 111–26; domestic architecture and decoration, 249, 252, 261; hegemonic war, 133–4, 137–41; literature and language, 58–60, 63–4, 71; *oikoumene*, 17, 20–9, 47–8; power capabilities, 131, 133–5, 137, 139–41, 160, 162; power transition crisis among, 133–5, 137–9

γυνή, 236–8

Hades, 19, 327

Hadrian, 88, 300

Halys, 74, 79, 89

Hasmonean state, Hasmoneans, 48, 130, 155–63

Hegemon (Milesian navarch), 277

Hegesagoras (son of Monimos of Istria), 122–3

Helen, 238–9

Helikon of Priene, 281–2

Helios, 121, 193

Hellas, 20–1, 24, 29, 97, 114; School of, 118

Hellenistic art style, 199–201, 211; Alexandrian style, 201–3, 205–6, 211–12, 214–16; Egyptian style, 171, 173, 202–3, 205–6, 210, 215–16; Greek style, 173, 205–6, 215–16; Italian style, 249, 251–2, 255; Pergamene School (High Baroque, High Pergamene), 199, 203, 214; Praxitelean style, 202–3; Rhodes School, 216

Hellenistic literary style, 211

Hellenocentric cosmopolitanism, 19–29

Hellespont, 21, 73

Herakleia (Latmos), 277–9, 285, 287, 289
Herakleides, 151, 176
Herakleitos, 49, 52
Herakles, 193, 206, 333
Hermeias of Kourion, 17–18, 33–42
Herodas, 34, 48
Herodotos, 125, 135, 185, 335, 338
Hesiod, 37, 187, 328, 333–4
Hieron II of Syracuse, 140
Hipponactean verse, 34–5
Hipponax, 34–8, 326–7
Homer, 17, 20–2, 38, 40, 60, 97, 117, 175–6, 212, 213, 326
Hybandis, 271, 274–5, 286–7
Hyrkanos I, 130, 155–8, 160–2
Hyrkanos II, 156, 158

iambographic tradition, 35–8, 40–1, 326–7
Ikos, Ikians, 327–9, 331
Inachos River, 337–8
Inopos, River, 294, 336–7
international law, 131, 133–4, 136–7
international systems theory, 131–41
Io, 337–8
Ionia, Ionians, 79, 83, 123, 150, 274, 279–80, 286, 337; poetry of, 326
Isis, 174–5, 193, 203, 206, 210, 334, 338
isopoliteia, 103, 277, 285
Isthmia, 331, 338
Istria, 120–3
Italy, Italians, 113, 139, 246, 249, 251–2

Jews, 130, 155–6, 158, 161–2, 167, 172, 246, 249; attitude towards, 157, 162, 179
Jonathon (Jewish high priest), 158, 162
Joppa, 159, 161, 163
Josephus, 155–61, 179
Judaea, Judaeans, 156–7, 159–62, 162
Julius Caesar, 78, 85–7, 155–6
Justin, 77, 83, 176–7, 184

Kallimachos, 23, 34–7, 211–12, 294, 325–38
Kappadokia, 74, 85, 118
Karia, 137, 274, 277
Karystos, 34, 41, 317
Kasian Sea, 332
kathesimon, 116–17
Kavaros, 79
Keltensieg, 76, 78
Keos, 104, 304, 317, 329
Kerkidas of Megalopolis, 34, 38
kindynos, 134–6
Kition, 18, 21, 33, 39–41
kleroteria, 118
Knossos, 270, 272, 284–6
koinon, 96, 103, 149–50, 201, 211, 281
Kos, 17, 22–5, 47–8, 212
Krates, 40, 60–1
Kydonians, 136
kyrios, 233–4, 237, 241
Kyrbissos, 277

Lade, Battle of, 272
Lagos, 184–6, 190
Lato, 255–7
Lebanon, 136
Leonnorios, 73–4, 80–1, 84
Lepsia, 277–8, 287
Leros, 277–8, 287
Leto, 23, 336
Libanios, 145, 193
Libya, 337
Livy, 78, 80, 83, 84, 107, 138, 140
Loutarios, 73–4, 80, 84
Lucilius, 59, 62
Lucullus, 89, 277
Lutatius Catulus, Q., 49, 57, 59
Lysias, 231–2, 236
Lysimachos, 73, 144

Maccabean movement, 160
Macedonia, Macedonians, 20, 96, 99–100, 102–3, 112, 138, 140, 167, 170–1, 173–4, 178, 184–6, 191,

215, 228, 240–1, 294, 337; attitude towards, 191; *chlamys*, 171, 176; military campaign, 103; soldiers, 83, 102, 179; War, Second, 105; War, Third, 107, 112, 116, 139–40

Magnesia, Magnesians (Maiander), 151, 269–91

Mannius (L. Manlius Torquatus), 161–2

Medeios of Athens, 113–15, 120

Mediterranean, 156–7, 162–3

Meleager, 17–29, 47–64; name as metaphor, 27–9

Meleagros, 97–8, 101

Memnon of Herakleia, 80, 83–4, 189

Memphis, 174, 178, 191, 215

Menander, 223, 225–8, 230, 238, 240–1

Menippos, 19, 22, 59, 63; satire of, 21, 26, 61–3

mercenaries, 102, 106, 122, 140, 167, 172, 179, 224, 256, 268–91, 293, 296; Galatian, 75–6, 83

Mesembria, 120–1, 123

Messene, 136

Miletos, Milesians, 79, 112, 151, 224, 269–91

Mithridates I, 84

Mithridates VI, 81, 85, 112–13, 126, 150, 277, 288–9, 291

Mithridatic Wars, 112, 114–15, 118, 120, 158, 277

Mithridatids, 74

Moschion of Priene, 280, 289, 290

Moschion the Athenian, 227, 229–35, 237–8, 240–1

Mouseion, 168, 211–12, 214–15, 326–7

Muses, 17, 19, 22, 26, 29, 37, 57–8, 211, 327–9

Mykale, 277

Mykonos, 305, 317

Mylasa, 151, 277–9, 286

Myous, 269, 271–6, 286–7

Naxos, 317

Nemean games, 331, 338

Nero, 88, 192

Nesiotic League, 318–19

networks: clustering, 143–5, 148; diplomatic friendship, 156–63; economic, 143–53; flow of information, 147–51; geographic regions, 148–9; homophily, 144–5, 148–9, 150, 152; hubs, 144–5, 148, 152; kinship, 157–60; organizational membership, 148–9; quantitative data, 151–2; short-pathedness, 143–5; social identity, 144–5, 179, 150, 172–3, 259–61; technical communities, 148–9, 252, 254, 256

New Comedy, 228, 241

New Institutional Economics, 146–7, 151, 153

Nikeratos, 234–7, 240

Nikokles, 41

Nikokreon, king of Salamis, 42, 46

Nikomedes I, 73–4, 84

Nile River, 137, 167, 171, 210, 294, 332–8

Nymphon of Priene, 282, 290

*oikos*, 223, 225–8, 231–3, 235–6, 238–9, 241

*oikoumene*, 17, 20–1, 24–5, 28–9, 96, 111–12, 158, 176

Okeanos, 334–5, 337

Olbia, 121–2, 125

*olbos*, 330, 335

Olympia, 98, 338

Olympian gods, 23, 121, 326–7, 333

Olympias, 178, 186–7, 189, 190

*opus signinum*, 249, 251

Oscan, 64, 97

Ouranos, 334

Ovid, 125

Pacuvius, 59, 62

Panathenaia, 118, 332

Panathenaic amphora, 248, 250

Parmeniskos, 60–1, 147

Parmenon, 229, 233–4
Paros, 317
Parthia, Parthians, 85–6, 88
Pausanias, 100, 114, 185–6, 189
Pax Romana, 126
Peiraeus, 119, 303
Peisistratids, 118
Peleus, 184, 327
Peloponnesian crisis, 138
Peloponnesian War, 134, 320
pentekoste, 296–8, 303
Perdikkas, 186
Pergamon, Pergamenes, 74, 118, 157–9,
    161–3, 213; foreign relations, 130,
    137–8, 157–61; Library of, 213–14,
    330; propaganda, 77, 101; School of,
    168, 199–200, 214
Persia, Persians, 20, 100
philhellenism, 58–9
Philip II, 173, 178, 184–9, 193, 272,
    285
Philip V, 105–6, 136–9
Philitas, 48, 212
Philokles of Sidon, 318
philologoi, 326–7
philotimia, 235
Phoenicia, Phoenicians, 18, 21, 24–5,
    40–1, 47–8, 57–8, 62–4, 149; goddess
    Tanit, 249; sanctuary of Astarte, 52
Phoenix of Kolophon, 34, 36
phoros, 317
phrouria, phrourarch, 161, 274, 276–9,
    282, 288–90
Phrygia, Phrygians, 74–5, 78, 88, 172
phylarch, 232, 234
Pidasa, 277–9
Plangon, 229, 233–4, 237
Plato, 37, 304
Plutarch, 20, 61, 63, 86, 169, 175–7, 184,
    187, 189, 225–7, 238
polis (poleis), 21, 72, 78, 99, 101, 103–4,
    111–12, 121, 125, 129–30, 156, 161,
    170, 223, 227–9, 231–2, 241, 300, 305,
    307; networking between, 145, 147–9;

polis-centrism, 72, 293–6, 305, 307;
    West Pontic, 123
politeia: Aitolian, 99; Athenian, 111–21,
    228; Galatian/Celtic, 81–2; Roman,
    132
politeumata, 172
Polybios, 71, 77, 104–6, 125, 129,
    131–41, 172, 179
Polykritos of Erythrai, 283
Pompey, 48, 85–6, 89
πονηρός, 227, 233, 241
Pontos (kingdom), 81, 89, 118, 121, 123
Pontos (sea), 334
Poseidon, 210, 301
Poseidoniastai (Delos), 149–50
Poseidonios, 80, 112, 114, 117
power capabilities, 131, 133–5, 137,
    139–41, 160, 162
power transition crisis, 133–5, 137–9
Praxitelean style (Atticizing style), 202–3
Priene, 200, 279–83, 288, 290–1
prodaneistai, 319, 323
Protogenes of Olbia, 122
psephos, 114
Ptolemies, 48, 101, 106–7, 129, 137–9,
    167, 169–73, 175, 177, 180, 184–6,
    188–9, 191–2, 210–11, 215, 294,
    325–8, 330–4, 336–8; artistic style,
    203, 205–6, 208–9, 211, 215; associa-
    tion with Cyprus, 42, 46; association
    with Kos, 48; Library of, 327
Ptolemy I, 42, 58, 167–8, 184–93,
    206–7, 212, 327, 330–1, 335, 337
Ptolemy II, 17, 22–5, 48, 185, 188, 193,
    203–4, 212, 318, 330
Ptolemy III, 192, 203–4
Ptolemy IV, 137, 170, 173–6, 180, 188,
    192, 331
Ptolemy VI, 203–4, 206, 208
Ptolemy VIII, 206, 209
Ptolemy IX, 192
Ptolemy XII, 192
Ptolemy Keraunos, 73, 185, 189
Pythaïs, 115

Realism, 131–5, 139, 141
regionalism, 199–203, 212, 216
*reguli*, 80–1
Rhea, 333–4
Rheneia, 254, 305
Rhodes, 35, 48, 105, 117, 137–8, 147, 168, 171, 200, 252, 330–1; School of, 216
*riges*, 81
Rome, Romans, 129, 132, 169, 170, 322; attitudes towards, 50, 63–4, 113, 140, 158; citizenship, 71, 74, 89; Civil War, 85; cultural metaphors, 49–50, 58–9, 60; domestic architecture and decoration, 249, 251–3, 255; dominance, 18, 47–8, 87–9, 107, 112, 126, 130, 133, 139–40, 160–2, 170–1, 180, 246; foreign relations, 74, 85–9, 107, 114–15, 130, 138–9, 155–63; influence in Greek literature, 48–9, 63–4; literary metaphors, 58, 60; sack of, 78; Social War, 113; war against Mithridates, 277

Samos, Samians, 99, 151, 212, 229–30, 232, 236, 238–9
Sarapis, 326
Scythia, Scythians, 50, 72, 79, 89, 121–3, 125; artistic style, 250
Seleukeia-Tralles, 277–9, 286
Seleukids, 47–8, 74, 78, 101, 106–7, 137, 158–9, 162–3, 203, 273
Seleukos I, 73–4, 175, 189, 193, 210
Seleukos II, 273
*senatus consultum Fannianum*, 161–2
Seriphos, 317
*sfumato*, 203, 205
Sidon, 48, 57–8, 64, 149, 318
Siphnos, 317
Skyros, 116
small-world networks, 144–5, 148, 152
small-world problem, 143–4
social network analysis, 145–53
Sosibios of Alexandria, 331–3
Sotas of Priene, 282–3

Soteria, 102
Sousarion of Megara, 36
Sparta, Spartans, 124, 186, 325; foreign relations, 135–6, 138, 158, 163
stoa: Athens, 107, 113, 118; Delphi, 100; Thermon, 100
Stoics, 21, 33–41, 213–14
Strabo, 80–3, 114, 169–72, 176
Straton (king of Sidon), 149
Sulla, 85, 114, 120
*symploke*, 129, 139
*sympoliteia*, 130, 147, 277
*synergasia*, 120
Syria, Syrians, 17, 19–22, 24–5, 27–8, 47–8, 60–1, 63–4, 118, 159, 246; artistic style, 249–50; foreign relations, 136
Syros, 317

*tabellaria*, 151
Tanit, 248–9
Tavium, 74, 87
Tektosages (Tectosages), 74, 79–80, 83–5, 87–8
Telon, Teloneia (Priene), 281, 290
Tenos, 317
Teos, 277
*Terror Gallicus*, 76–8
Tethys, 334–5
tetrarchy, 81–2
*thalattourgoi*, 305–7
Thebes, 60, 151, 186, 328
Themistios the philosopher, 89–90
Theodosius, 89
Theokritos, 17, 23–4, 48, 170–1, 188, 327, 330
Thermon, 102–3, 105
Theseia, 116–17
Thessaly, 99, 327
Thrace, Thracians, 73, 89, 122–3, 125, 173
Thucydides, 71–2, 98, 103–4, 129, 131–2, 134–6, 141
Timon of Phlios, 36, 40, 61

Timotheos of Miletos, 277–8
Titans, 77, 334
tithes: *enoikion dekate*, 296–8, 303; *hypotropion*, 303; *ichthuon dekate*, 296–9, 301, 303, 306; *pentekoste he astia*, 296–8, 303; *sitou dekate*, 296–8, 303
Tolistobogioi, 74, 77, 79–81, 84–8
Tolosa, 80
Tomis, 120, 124–5
Tower of the Winds, 118
Trajanic period, 88
Trokmoi, 74, 79–81, 84, 87–8
Troy, 97, 239
Trypetos, 255–7
Tyche, 131, 138–9, 207
Tyre, 17–19, 21–2, 24–5, 47–8, 52–3, 57–8, 63–4, 150

Valerius, C. (Roman legate), 277
Varro, 59, 61, 63
Volcae, 79–80, 83–4

war, hegemonic, 133–4, 137–41

*xeinos*, 327, 332–3

Zeno of Kition, 17–18, 21, 33–4, 39–41
Zenodotos (Stoic), 21, 40, 212
*zeugitai*, 115
Zeus, 22–4, 121, 168, 184, 186, 193, 326–7, 333–5, 337; Ammon, 167–8, 189, 206; Basileus, 23; Kasios, 332; Meilichios, 189; Soter, 24; statue of Olympian, 326; temple of Olympian, 98, 118; Zeus-eagle, 168, 187–90
Zoskales (king of Adoulis), 150

# PHOENIX SUPPLEMENTARY VOLUMES

1 *Studies in Honour of Gilbert Norwood* edited by Mary E. White

2 *Arbiter of Elegance: A Study of the Life and Works of C. Petronius* Gilbert Bagnani

3 *Sophocles the Playwright* S.M. Adams

4 *A Greek Critic: Demetrius on Style* G.M.A. Grube

5 *Coastal Demes of Attika: A Study of the Policy of Kleisthenes* C.W.J. Eliot

6 *Eros and Psyche: Studies in Plato, Plotinus, and Origen* John M. Rist

7 *Pythagoras and Early Pythagoreanism* J.A. Philip

8 *Plato's Psychology* T.M. Robinson

9 *Greek Fortifications* F.E. Winter

10 *Comparative Studies in Republican Latin Imagery* Elaine Fantham

11 *The Orators in Cicero's Brutus: Prosopography and Chronology* G.V. Sumner

12 Caput *and Colonate: Towards a History of Late Roman Taxation* Walter Goffart

13 *A Concordance to the Works of Ammianus Marcellinus* Geoffrey Archbold

14 *Fallax opus: Poet and Reader in the Elegies of Propertius* John Warden

15 *Pindar's* Olympian One: *A Commentary* Douglas E. Gerber

16 *Greek and Roman Mechanical Water-Lifting Devices: The History of a Technology* John Peter Oleson

17 *The Manuscript Tradition of Propertius* James L. Butrica

18 Parmenides of Elea *Fragments: A Text and Translation with an Introduction* edited by David Gallop

19 *The Phonological Interpretation of Ancient Greek: A Pandialectal Analysis* Vít Bubeník

20 *Studies in the Textual Tradition of Terence* John N. Grant

21 *The Nature of Early Greek Lyric: Three Preliminary Studies* R.L. Fowler

22 Heraclitus *Fragments: A Text and Translation with a Commentary* edited by T.M. Robinson

23 *The Historical Method of Herodotus* Donald Lateiner

24 *Near Eastern Royalty and Rome, 100–30 BC* Richard D. Sullivan

25 *The Mind of Aristotle: A Study in Philosophical Growth* John M. Rist

26 *Trials in the Late Roman Republic, 149 BC to 50 BC* Michael Alexander

27 *Monumental Tombs of the Hellenistic Age: A Study of Selected Tombs from the Pre-Classical to the Early Imperial Era* Janos Fedak

28 *The Local Magistrates of Roman Spain* Leonard A. Curchin

29 Empedocles *The Poem of Empedocles: A Text and Translation with an Introduction* edited by Brad Inwood

30 Xenophanes of Colophon *Fragments: A Text and Translation with a Commentary* edited by J.H. Lesher

31 *Festivals and Legends: The Formation of Greek Cities in the Light of Public Ritual* Noel Robertson

32 *Reading and Variant in Petronius: Studies in the French Humanists and Their Manuscript Sources* Wade Richardson

33 *The Excavations of San Giovanni di Ruoti, Volume I: The Villas and Their Environment* Alastair Small and Robert J. Buck

34 *Catullus Edited with a Textual and Interpretative Commentary* D.F.S. Thomson

35 *The Excavations of San Giovanni di Ruoti, Volume 2: The Small Finds* C.J. Simpson, with contributions by R. Reece and J.J. Rossiter

36 The Atomists: Leucippus and Democritus *Fragments: A Text and Translation with a Commentary* C.C.W. Taylor

37 *Imagination of a Monarchy: Studies in Ptolemaic Propaganda* R.A. Hazzard

38 *Aristotle's Theory of the Unity of Science* Malcolm Wilson

39 Empedocles *The Poem of Empedocles: A Text and Translation with an Introduction, Revised Edition* edited by Brad Inwood

40 *The Excavations of San Giovanni di Ruoti, Volume 3: The Faunal and Plant Remains* M.R. McKinnon, with contributions by A. Eastham, S.G. Monckton, D.S. Reese, and D.G. Steele

41 *Justin and Pompeius Trogus: A Study of the Language of Justin's* Epitome *of* Trogus J.C. Yardley

42 *Studies in Hellenistic Architecture* F.E. Winter

43 *Mortuary Landscapes of North Africa* edited by David L. Stone and Lea M. Stirling

44 Anaxagoras of Clazomenae *Fragments and Testimonia: A Text and Translation with Notes and Essays* by Patricia Curd

45 *Virginity Revisited: Configurations of the Unpossessed Body* edited by Bonnie MacLachlan and Judith Fletcher

46 *Roman Dress and the Fabrics of Roman Culture* edited by Jonathan Edmondson and Alison Keith

47 *Epigraphy and the Greek Historian* edited by Craig Cooper

48 *In the Image of the Ancestors: Narratives of Kinship in Flavian Epic* Neil W. Bernstein

49 *Perceptions of the Second Sophistic and Its Times – Regards sur la Seconde Sophistique et son époque* edited by Thomas Schmidt and Pascale Fleury

50 *Apuleius and Antonine Rome: Historical Essays* Keith Bradley

51 *Belonging and Isolation in the Hellenistic World* edited by Sheila L. Ager and Riemer A. Faber